D0058370

THE DIVIDER

THE DIVIDER

Trump in the White House, 2017–2021

Peter Baker and Susan Glasser

DOUBLEDAY / NEW YORK

For Theo
and our fathers Ted and Steve

Contents

The Calling Card of a Presidency

When we set out to write *The Divider*, we began with a simple premise, that Donald Trump's refusal to accept defeat in the 2020 election, and the insurrection at the Capitol he summoned to overturn his loss, were no violent outliers but the inexorable culmination of a sustained four-year war on the institutions and traditions of American democracy. As the historian Michael Beschloss observed on the afternoon of January 6, 2021, while the pro-Trump mob surged through the halls of Congress, chanting "Hang Mike Pence! Hang Mike Pence!" and sending the vice president and lawmakers fleeing for their lives, "This day has been foreshadowed by every hour of this presidency."

This is a book about what happened in that presidency, about an unimaginable period in our history when the United States had a leader for the first time who neither knew nor subscribed to many of the fundamental tenets of the Constitution and even actively worked to undermine them. From the day he took office until the day he left, Trump sought to bend if not break many of the rules that constrained presidents in the American system, so that holding on to power despite the will of the voters was only the next logical step. To understand what happened on January 6, 2021, it is necessary to understand what happened on January 20, 2017, and all the days in between.

This is not exclusively a work of history, however. Trump, and Trumpism, have captured the Republican Party and radicalized it. The former president, twice impeached and twice acquitted, is the only chief executive since the founding of the nation to obstruct the peaceful transfer of power and he has spent the time since his exit from the White House seeking to become only the second president ever to return to the office. Tens of millions of his followers believed the big lie that he was not defeated and continue to do so to this day. His party's leadership, rather than repudiate him, still looks to him as its titular head and president-in-waiting. The Trump era is not past; it is America's present and maybe even its future.

We could think of no more urgent project than to record and seek to understand what really happened when Trump was in the White House. It is not yet a matter for the archives; it is a report from an active crime scene, still under investigation by multiple authorities. Someday, whether soon or not, it will no longer be a subject of current events. And then, we hope, this book can play a different role, explaining for future disbelieving generations what it was like when a crude New York real estate mogul with an itchy Twitter finger, an outsize self-regard, and an extreme disdain for all who came before him ended up as the president of the United States.

We chose to call the book *The Divider* because for four years, from the "American Carnage" speech that opened his tenure to the "Rigged Election" charade that cursed its tumultuous ending, Trump pitted Americans against Americans, the United States against its allies, and his own staff and family members against each other. He threw matches on the dry kindling of race relations in the United States and escalated a polarizing culture war over competing visions of national identity. Even when the deadliest plague in a century struck, the nation's forty-fifth president spoke of two countries—his America, Red America, and that of the blue states opposed to him. He soon turned a simple thing like a face mask worn to protect against a public health threat into a wedge issue between warring parties. Trump made divisiveness the calling card of his presidency.

This alone set him apart from all the other American presidents of our lifetime. George H. W. Bush called for a "kinder, gentler" America. Bill Clinton vowed to be a "repairer of the breach." George W. Bush presented himself as a "uniter, not a divider." Barack Obama declared there was not a Blue America and Red America but "the *United* States of America." None of them fully lived up to those ideals, but they at least gave voice to the aspiration that a president should endeavor to bring the country together. Trump never saw it that way. He exploited the fissures in American society to gain, wield, and hold on to power. He did not create those fissures, any more than he created the weaknesses in the people around him that he so effectively used for his own purposes. America on the eve of his ascendance was more fractured than at any other time in generations. But he leveraged America's differences for his own ends and created new ones along the way. He was, is, and always will be a "wrecking ball," as a

Republican senator once put it, the "chaos candidate" who would become a "chaos president," just as one of his 2016 Republican rivals had warned. He sought out enemies and where they did not exist, he invented them. With Trump, there was always an *us* and always a *them*.

For most of his seventy years before arriving at the White House, this was of little consequence outside his family and the business worlds in which he operated. The fact that he lied and cheated and did not pay his bills harmed mostly the creditors affected by his six bankruptcies or those ripped off in his various failed ventures. The producers at NBC profited from his flair for conflict with a hit television show whose signature moment each week was Trump firing a different contestant. The New York City tabloids feasted on his many personal and professional feuds, to his shame-free delight.

But when he improbably won election as president of the United States in 2016, this became America's reality too. Over the next four years, Trump identified the vulnerabilities in Washington, and in those who served there. He weaponized his prolific lies for his political benefit and bullied any who opposed him, setting up his administration as an endless series of loyalty tests. He hijacked a Republican Party that was riven and ailing—a party that has now lost the popular vote in seven of the last eight presidential elections—and turned it into a cult of personality so dedicated to him that instead of producing a policy platform at its last convention it simply issued a resolution saying it was for Trump.

The Divider draws on our four years of covering Trump's presidency for *The New York Times* and *The New Yorker* as well as about three hundred original interviews conducted exclusively for this book. We obtained private diaries, memos, contemporaneous notes, emails, text messages, and other documents that shed new light on Trump's time in office. We spoke with many of those who worked most closely with Trump—his cabinet secretaries and senior White House officials, his political strategists, lawyers, national security advisers, and counselors. Many spoke with us for their first extensive interviews. We also talked with others who struggled with how to respond to Trump's volatile presidency, including members of Congress, generals, business executives, and foreign leaders. And we traveled twice to Mar-a-Lago to interview Trump himself.

What emerged from our reporting were stories we had never heard and fresh understandings of stories we thought we knew. To a remarkable degree, it was a portrait of a rogue president, one whose combative instincts, erratic ways, and tendency to conflate the national interest with his personal interest took the country closer than we realized to outright conflict with Iran and North Korea, and to the brink of blowing up NATO even as Russia prepared to use force to redraw the map of Europe. He vindictively ordered the pullout of thousands of troops from Germany because he was mad at its leader. He tried to buy Greenland after a billionaire friend told him it was a good idea. He secretly sought to abolish a federal appeals court after it ruled against him. He privately expressed admiration for Hitler's generals, while calling his own generals "fucking losers," and subjecting them and others to racist rants that made it clear his infamous Oval Office comment about "shithole countries" was no isolated lapse.

The people who were most fearful of his reign were those in the room with him, the ones he himself appointed, who behind his back compared him to a czar or a mob boss or even, in the case of his first White House counsel, a monster in a horror movie. His handpicked chairman of the Joint Chiefs of Staff grew so outraged at the president's conduct that he secretly drafted a resignation letter accusing Trump of subscribing "to many of the principles that we fought against" in America's wars, only to put it in a drawer and resolve to stay in order to resist a commander in chief he considered a threat to democracy. Another top general warned Trump to his face that he was acting like a dictator. His intelligence chief privately wondered whether the president was a Russian stooge. His chief of staff secretly consulted a book by psychiatrists questioning Trump's mental fitness. His wife thought he was blowing it against the coronavirus and his daughter and son-in-law thought he was wrong about the supposedly stolen election.

Our reporting revealed in a way that was not always evident in the fog of the moment just how much some members of Trump's administration felt compelled to save the country from its own president, as more than one of his top officials put it. The internal resistance to Trump was fiercer than recognized, if not always effective: there were repeated mutual-resignation pacts among cabinet officers and senior officials; advisers who worked around him to secretly organize opposition to his proposals in Congress or even foreign capitals; aides who not only swiped papers off Trump's desk but came up with elaborate rationales to ignore orders unless they were issued three times or more. The story of the demands they disregarded or sidestepped alone could fill many books: Prosecute Joe Biden. Prosecute Hillary Clinton. Prosecute James Comey. Close the border. Withdraw from NAFTA, from NATO, from Afghanistan, from Iraq, from South Korea. Immediately. This was going on long before the tragic excesses of 2020, when Trump wanted active-duty troops mobilized to quash protests inside the United States and sought the outright nullification of an American presidential election.

Trump was often just one yes-man away from doing what he wanted. One attorney general. One military commander. One vice president. Many of those who blocked Trump were complicated figures who had spent years enabling him before finally deciding he had gone too far. Even then they often remained in his orbit or refused to speak out. Mike Pence, Bill Barr, Mike Pompeo, his four chiefs of staff, his lawyers, the Republican leaders on Capitol Hill. For them, every day was a moral challenge, a series of tradeoffs in which they weighed the benefits of accomplishing whatever agenda had brought them into Trump's world in the first place—whether patriotism or personal ambition or policy goals or simply partisanship—against the need to stop the situation from spiraling out of control. There was a not inconsiderable element of hubris to this; they believed they could manage him, and often succeeded for a while in doing so, only to claim they were shocked it had not worked out when it all ended badly, as it inevitably did. This book is their story too, because without them Donald Trump might have been just another angry old man shouting at the television between golf games.

The painful fact is that those who stopped Trump from committing this or that outrage also helped him learn how better to get what he wanted the next time. A senior national security official who regularly observed Trump in the Oval Office compared him to the Velociraptors in the movie *Jurassic Park* that proved capable of learning while hunting their prey, making them infinitely more dangerous. It was a chilling thought: Who can forget the scene where the audience discovers this, when one of the predators chases the film's child protagonists into an industrial kitchen by turning a handle to open a door?

In four years, Trump adapted. He tested limits. He pushed boundaries. He failed. And then he tried again. He had started out in office more ignorant about Washington and the federal government than perhaps any president in history. He did not know what power he had, or how to use it to do what he wanted to do. But he began to figure it out. He purged his staff. He hired more loyalists and fewer independent actors who might defy his orders. He busted norms and made progressively more outrageous demands. He was disgraced by scandal and renounced by his party's last three presidential nominees. Yet his followers kept following. When he told them the election was stolen and the pandemic was a Democratic hoax and the violence on January 6 was just a legitimate protest, they believed him. They still believe him today.

———————

The Divider is our third book together. Our first subject was Vladimir Putin and his successful assault on the fledgling Russian democracy that emerged after the collapse of the Soviet Union. We witnessed Putin's rise in the first assignment of our married life, landing in Moscow on a frigid January day more than twenty years ago. No one, including us, suspected that Putin, an obscure former KGB lieutenant colonel, would go on to become Russia's longest-serving leader since Joseph Stalin. At the time, even our conclusion that Putin was an authoritarian modernizer who believed in the resurrection of a police state was seen as controversial in Washington, where many at the highest levels wanted to believe, against experience and evidence, that the man who called the breakup of the Soviet Union "the greatest geopolitical catastrophe of the century" would somehow turn out to be a Western-oriented reformer.

Never did we imagine that two decades later we would be covering the rise of an American leader who venerated Putin and his strongman tactics, who admired the world's other autocrats in China, Egypt, Turkey, the Philippines, and elsewhere, who "fell in love" with the overseer of North Korea's Gulags, and who attacked basic principles of constitutional democracy at home.

When we arrived in Russia, it was still only a decade after the fall of the Soviet Union. At an event one day in Moscow, the reformist politician Grigory Yavlinsky was asked about the state of its flawed and faltering democracy. He responded with an old Soviet *anekdot* about an ambulance driver who picks up a patient.

"Where are we going?" the patient asks.

"The morgue," replies the driver.

"Why? I'm not dead yet," the patient protests.

"We're not there yet," the driver responds.

Two decades ago, that was a mordant joke about where Russia was headed. Today, Russia under Putin is an outlaw nation, waging a war of conquest against its neighbor with a dictatorship at home as repressive as anything in the latter days of the Soviet era. The driver, tragically, made it to the morgue. The joke could also serve as commentary on the health of American democracy after four years of President Trump: We're not there yet but it does not look good.

I

AMERICAN CARNAGE

"We didn't win an election to bring the country together."

—STEVE BANNON

CHAPTER I

Ready, Set, Tweet

On the afternoon of January 20, 2017, just hours after taking the oath of office, Donald John Trump strode into the Oval Office for the first time as the forty-fifth president of the United States. In that profound moment of transition, he was not moved to comment about the history of the room or the burden he had just assumed. He did not ruminate out loud about the weighty decisions that had been made there nor his ambitions for the next four years.

Instead, the first thing that struck him as he looked around the storied space once occupied by Roosevelt and Kennedy and Reagan was the fantastic illumination.

"How do they get the lighting to do that?" he wondered.

Then he invited his daughter Ivanka Trump and his son-in-law, Jared Kushner, to take pictures with him.

Trump, America's first reality television star turned president, had long fixated on lighting. Wherever he expected to be photographed, he evaluated the angles and shadows and brightness of the sun or artificial bulbs that would frame the shot. As he entered the White House, he did not know much about government or health care policy or foreign affairs. But he knew a lot about lighting.

Trump preferred not to allow artificial illumination when cameras were on him. The harsh light changed the ever-shifting color of his hair and highlighted the caked-on makeup that gave his skin an orange tint. He hated artificial lighting so much that news photographers were reproached for using a flash in his presence. Trump's preference for natural lighting would soon lead him to hold many of his encounters with reporters outside on the White House's South Lawn on the way to his helicopter. Never mind that the roar of the rotor blades made it hard to hear what he was saying—it was the visual that counted. He studied iPad images of himself before television interviews to check the best angle, preferring to be shot from his right side so the part in his hair did not show. And if he did not like a picture on the front page of the newspaper, he sometimes called the photographer to complain. "That made me look horrible," he would grouse.

All presidents are image conscious. But Trump was something different, the first president for whom the shaping of reality to fit his demands became the preoccupation of his presidency. He would spend exhaustive amounts of time each morning combing and twisting the long strands of his awkwardly colored hair into place, a three-step process that "required a flop up of the hair from the back of his head, followed by the flip of the resulting overhang on his face back on his pate, and then the flap of his combover on the right side," as his lawyer Michael Cohen once explained.[1] Trump cemented it with TRESemmé TRES TWO hair spray (extra hold). An aide carried a travel-size can everywhere they went. When the wind was strong, Trump wore one of the red Make America Great Again baseball caps that had become a signature of his improbable candidacy. When his hair was not done, it fell over the right side of his head below the shoulder, making him look "like a balding Allman Brother or strung out old '60s hippie," as Cohen put it.[2] Trump cut it himself with giant scissors, like the kind used at shopping mall ribbon cuttings.

Trump was also sensitive about his weight. He did not like being photographed from below, fearing that would make him look heavier than the 236 pounds he claimed to weigh. Hope Hicks, his communications adviser, had issued an edict during the campaign barring news cameras from the buffer zone in front of the stage beneath Trump; only after vociferous complaints did she finally allow photographers there for just a few minutes. For that matter, Trump did not like being shot from above either. The angle had to be on the same plane as he was, because he felt it looked better on television.

Whatever the circumstances, he almost always appeared in public in a dark suit with a tie knotted all the way to the top and hanging below his belt in a way that he thought was slimming—not for him the casual bomber jacket and blue jeans that George W. Bush and Barack Obama donned for photo ops. Even in Florida, in hundred-degree heat, Trump kept the suit on, usually an off-the-rack Brioni costing several thousand dollars and worn extra-baggy so that the pants flopped around his legs. The only time he did not wear the suit jacket typically was on the golf course, but even then he tried to stymie photographers from recording that image, ordering palm trees planted to block the view on his Florida golf course after television networks managed to shoot too many pictures of him there. Perhaps even more important than the suit was what aides called "the stare." Trump did not smile often for the cameras; he preferred an intense, slightly menacing glare, which he thought made him look more imposing. "How's the look?" he would ask aides.[3]

It was all part of maintaining his own cartoonish mythology. In Trump's telling, the new occupant of the Oval Office was an American superman—physically strong, mentally gifted, healthy as a horse, rich as sin, and a magnet for beautiful women. He worked around the clock and barely slept. He was not fat, his hair was natural, his skin color perfectly normal, his hands were not small and neither was any other part of his anatomy. The fact that he had an uncle who had taught at the Massachusetts Institute of Technology meant that he too must be brilliant. "It's in my blood," Trump once said. "I'm smart."[4] The fact that he went to an Ivy League university attested to his erudition. "I'm very highly educated," he assured supporters. "I know words. I have the best words."[5] During the campaign, he secretly ordered up a much lampooned letter that he got his personal doctor to issue under his own name declaring that Trump's "physical strength and stamina are extraordinary" and predicting he "will be the healthiest individual ever elected to the presidency."[6]

No one was to admit anything to the contrary. In the West Wing, it became clear that aides should never acknowledge any human frailties on the part of the president even to each other, much less to the American public.

"He looks exhausted," a worried Madeleine Westerhout, Trump's executive assistant, told Hope Hicks one day.

Hicks promptly corrected her. "Donald Trump is never tired," she said, "and he is never sick."[7]

From his first day in office, the new president wanted to project himself as the hero America had been waiting for, a strong man for troubled times. Even those working for him were not entirely sure what to make of it. Were these merely the weird quirks of a vain septuagenarian? Or the menacing affectations of an aspiring dictator?

After his upset victory, many in Washington simply refused to believe that Trump could be as self-absorbed, ignorant, untruthful, and dangerous as he had made himself out to be in the 2016 campaign. An American president who admired Vladimir Putin and declared NATO "obsolete"?[8]

A businessman who would flout the rules that applied to the rest of the federal government and take payments from foreign governments and lobbyists while in the White House? It was unthinkable, and therefore easier somehow to deny that it was actually happening. He was an accidental president but, it was assumed, he would learn. And if he did not, well, this was what checks and balances were for. Congress would push back; the courts would push back; the media would push back.

A few days after the inauguration, Trump sat down for the first time with his national security team in the Situation Room, the nerve center in the basement of the White House where the nation's most sensitive decisions are made. The idea was a formal introduction to the problems facing the country around the globe, but Trump had neither the patience nor the preparation. Instead, he took off on tangents that would soon become familiar rants: He complained about NATO. He complained about faithless allies like South Korea, and even about how much they charged his hotels for their televisions. He talked, his aides talked, the meeting degenerated into a free-for-all. When it was finally over, Reince Priebus, the new White House chief of staff Trump had hired from the Republican National Committee, asked several of the participants to follow him upstairs to his corner office to figure out what to do next.

General Joseph Dunford, chairman of the Joint Chiefs of Staff, was the only holdover who had been present for Barack Obama's National Security Council meetings. A brainy, by-the-books Marine in his fifth decade of service to the country, Dunford had observed Bill Clinton, George W. Bush, and Obama at close range. Although stunned by what he had just witnessed, Dunford struck a calming note.

"Listen, I don't think we ought to be too concerned about today's meeting," Dunford told the others in Priebus's office. "Once we understand the Trump Doctrine and the new president's approach to the world, we'll be able to anticipate what he's looking for—and we'll be able to frame these problems in a way that helps him."

Jared Kushner, the ranking relative in a White House that Trump meant to run like his family business, looked at Dunford like he just did not get it.

"Well, that's never going to happen," Kushner said. "That's not the way it works."

And of course he was right. Trump was Trump—only now with the whole world watching. He would not learn. He would not change. There would be no doctrine, no process, no pivot. The general's misreading of the new president showed how much official Washington had yet to absorb the new reality.

If they had heard Barry Sternlicht, they would have understood better. The day before the inauguration, Sternlicht, the billionaire cofounder of the Starwood hotel chain and a longtime golfing buddy of the new president, had explained the essential facts of Trump to an audience of power players at an off-the-record gathering in New York's Metropolitan Club. Trump, he said, had been a friend for decades. "He's the *last* friend who should be president," Sternlicht confided.

Trump's mind was "unusual," Sternlicht said. Something was "wrong" in his head. He could not pay attention, could not do details, was not bothered by inconsistency. "He hasn't read a book in thirty years," Sternlicht said. "He's not encumbered by the truth." To golf with him was to see the real Trump. "Anyone who's ever played with Trump knows the rules are for suckers," he said. Trump would take the regulator off the golf cart so he could go faster. He sometimes raced off even before his partners took their swings. Trump always insisted that he won, whether he did or not. He did not even think of it as cheating.

Trump's New York friends knew what Washington would find out: he planned to live in his own reality in the White House just as he had in Trump Tower. The uncomfortable truth for those encountering him for the first time—including much of his own staff—was that Trump really was what he seemed to be, and he had come to office without a plan for the four-year term that neither he nor his campaign had expected to win. It was an oft-cited fact that Trump was the only president never to have served a single day in either government or military service before being elected. If anything, that understated how unprepared he was for the business of governing. He was probably the least knowledgeable new president in the modern era.

He did not know that Puerto Rico was part of the United States, did not know whether Colombia was in North America or South America, thought Finland was part of Russia, and mixed up the Baltics with the Balkans. He got confused about how World War I started, did not understand the basics of America's vast nuclear arsenal, did not grasp the concept of constitutional separation of powers, did not understand how courts worked. "How do I declare war?" he asked at one point, to the alarm of his staff, who realized he was unaware that the Constitution prescribes that role for Congress.[9] He seemed genuinely surprised to learn that Abraham

Lincoln had been a member of the Republican Party. "He knew nothing about most things," observed one top aide. Advisers soon realized they had to tutor him on the basics of how government worked.

As he settled into the Oval Office, Trump believed he had more power than he did, expecting to rule as he always had in the Trump Organization, a family-owned company with no shareholders where he called all the shots. He never liked the idea of sharing power. "Making choices is a lot easier when you have to answer only to yourself," he once said.[10] To the extent that government would be different than the private sector, he assumed he could run the country like the municipal chieftains he knew who ran New York. He often told the story of a Democratic Party boss in New York who kept a baseball bat under his desk to enforce his decisions. Trump figured he could do the same, laying down the law, dictating deals, and forcing others to bow to his will.

Nor did Trump show much inclination to learn on the job. He famously would not read briefing papers longer than a single page. He unashamedly boasted that he got most of his understanding of the world from television. Asked once where he turned to for military information, he said, "Well, I watch the shows."[11] Where other presidents received an intelligence run-down every workday and often on weekends too, Trump met with his briefers on average two and a half times a week in his first five weeks in office.

Barack Obama reviewed the President's Daily Brief, or PDB, the compendium of information solicited from the nation's spy agencies, each night on a tablet computer. That was too much for Trump, who insisted his PDB be printed out in hard copy, yet still did not look at it in advance. "He doesn't really read anything," recalled Ted Gistaro, his first intelligence briefer.[12] He would "fly off on tangents," said James Clapper Jr., the holdover director of national intelligence who briefed the incoming president during the transition before later becoming a prime target of Trump's ire. "There might be eight or nine minutes of real intelligence in an hour's discussion."[13]

Trump was simply far more interested in what he had to say than in what others did. In fact, Trump fully admitted to being a narcissist who avoided even a hint of self-examination. "Narcissism can be a useful quality if you're trying to start a business," he wrote in *Trump: Think Like a Billionaire*. "A narcissist does not hear the naysayers."[14] Skimming the surface was a survival technique. "You're a very shallow person," Michael Bailkin, an attorney who negotiated a hotel project for Trump, once told him. "Of course," Trump replied, "that's one of my strengths."[15]

Plenty of other presidents had come to office arrogant and unprepared for aspects of the job. Bill Clinton, a brilliant Rhodes Scholar, not only had a famously rocky start to his administration but hardly felt comfortable dealing with foreign affairs until his second term. Obama, a first-term senator with little Washington experience before he became president, dived deep into his briefing books but later said he had been stunned at the constraints of the office.

What Trump had that none of the rest of them did was supreme self-confidence that it did not matter. Having won an election against all odds, he acted as if he did not have to listen to the experts because, after all, he had prevailed when they said he could not. His most fervent allies would cite that victory as proof that even his most inane or uninformed ideas might turn out to be right since he had already disproved conventional wisdom. He was wedded to his successful formula. He did not need a policy process or an organization chart or a rigorous schedule or message discipline in 2016, so why would he need them in 2017?

The worldview that Donald Trump brought to the Oval Office marked a sharp departure from his recent predecessors, Democrat or Republican. It was not so much an ideology as an idée fixe that had not evolved since the 1980s: the conviction that the country had been taken for a ride by foreign allies and adversaries alike. The nation's presidents before him, in Trump's narrative, were chumps who set the country on a path to second-rate status. He admired strongmen like Vladimir Putin or China's Xi Jinping. But while he spoke of making America great again, a campaign slogan he had lifted from Ronald Reagan, he did not have much of a program for how to accomplish it.

Advisers such as Steve Bannon, Trump's self-styled chief ideologist, improbably claimed America's first billionaire president was the political heir of America's first populist president, Andrew Jackson, and urged him to hang a portrait of Old Hickory in the Oval Office and visit his estate in Tennessee. But the comparison was forced—Jackson was a self-made man and had far more experience, as a judge, general, and senator—and, in any case, Trump was no student of populism. When Bannon first tried to educate him, Trump seized on the word without understanding it. "A popular-ist," Trump said, mangling the term. "Yes, that's what I am." Bannon corrected him. "No, you mean *populist*." Trump paid no attention. "Yeah, a popular-ist. I'm a popular-ist."[16] Bannon had also summoned another historical analogy. The first time he saw Trump descending the escalator at Trump Tower to announce his candidacy with perfectly choreographed strongman imagery, he thought, "That's Hitler."[17] He meant it as a compliment.

The truth was that there had never been a president like Trump. There were, of course, many historical antecedents for him, but they tended to be the kind of outsider who cropped up every generation or so to shock the system without actually making it to the White House—fact-free demagogues like Joe McCarthy, race-baiters like George Wallace, eccentric businessmen like Ross Perot. In some ways, the modern presidential contender Trump took after the most was Patrick Buchanan, the pugnacious former Nixon White House aide and conservative commentator who in his own campaigns in 1992, 1996, and 2000 arguably set the stage for the Trump movement. Buchanan had vowed to build a fence along the border with Mexico to keep immigrants out, railed against the "globalist" elite, promised to rip up deals like the North American Free Trade Agreement (NAFTA), and made "America First" his campaign slogan.

As it happened, even Trump thought Buchanan was too far off the deep end to be president. When the two of them briefly ran against each other for the 2000 nomination of Perot's Reform Party, Trump denounced Buchanan as "a Hitler lover," a "racist," and an "anti-Semite" who "doesn't like the Blacks, he doesn't like the gays" and was appealing mainly to the "wacko vote."[18] But by 2016, Trump would find himself adopting Buchanan's playbook.

Unlike Buchanan, Trump was an ideological chameleon, opportunistically embracing and discarding positions depending on the moment. He went from being "very pro-choice" to a hardline opponent of abortion.[19] He spoke out in favor of same-sex marriage before he became the scourge of transgender rights. He favored an assault rifle ban and waiting period to buy other guns only to later cast himself as "a very big Second Amendment person."[20] He proposed raising taxes on the rich when he was a private citizen, then promised to cut taxes on the rich when he was president. He boasted of his opposition to the Iraq War without conceding that he had originally supported it. He switched political parties at least five times, constantly looking for one that would welcome him as the savior that he believed himself to be.

His most powerful skills, in business, media, and now the presidency, were branding and salesmanship. He was, as his niece Mary Trump put it, a "savant of self-promotion."[21] For years, he had slapped his name on anything he could—hotels, golf courses, residential towers, casinos, an airline, even steaks, bottled water, and neckties. He brought that sensibility now to Washington. When he visited Mount Vernon after becoming president, he was baffled that George Washington had not named the estate after himself. "If he was smart, he would've put his name on it," Trump told others touring with him. "You've got to put your name on stuff or no one remembers you."[22]

Trump began his presidency as an ideological work in progress but he had spent decades as a real estate developer and showman thinking about how to control the environments in which he lived and worked. It was not just the lights in the Oval Office, or the vanity of a politician who wanted to make sure the cameras caught his good side. The White House was Trump's new stage set. He wanted to construct the reality of his presidency. Hard as it was to believe in a city where policy fights were the stuff of money, power, and consequence, *this* more than anything was what he cared about.

The first thing he did on Inauguration Day was to get rid of Barack Obama's Oval Office decor, replacing his crimson-colored drapes with gold ones (from Bill Clinton's era). Obama's brown couches were ditched in favor of cream-colored sofas of George H. W. Bush vintage and Obama's rug was warehoused in favor of Ronald Reagan's golden-sunburst carpet. Trump personally picked out the gray damask wallpaper, eventually installed over the summer to replace Obama's cream-striped paper, and brought back a bust of Winston Churchill that Obama had removed.

Trump kept the Resolute Desk, given to Rutherford B. Hayes by Queen Victoria in 1880 and used by modern presidents since Jackie Kennedy rescued it from obscurity. He made it the centerpiece of a daily power play, often requiring officials to stand in front of him or sit in a series of chairs arranged in a half circle as if they were supplicants before a medieval lord. He also installed a twelve-inch wooden box with a red button on his desk and delighted in pressing it in front of visitors and implying that it would launch some sort of military strike when, in fact, it summoned a server to bring a Diet Coke. (He was not the only president who cherished such simple power—Lyndon B. Johnson had a button too, which got him a Fresca.)

In his early days in the White House, Trump became infatuated by the eight flags normally standing in the Roosevelt Room—the American flag, the presidential and vice presidential flags, and the flags of the five military services—so much so that he kept ordering them moved to the Oval Office for his photo ops. When he later found that they had been returned to the Roosevelt Room, he would demand that they be brought back again. This happened frequently enough that aides eventually ordered a second set of flags to be kept in the Oval Office.

Trump loved Air Force One as well. During the campaign, he had traveled around the country on his private jet, a Boeing 757 that he dubbed "Trump Force One," with Rolls-Royce engines, gold-plated fixtures, leather seats, a master bedroom, dining room, large-screen television, and high-end sound system. Yet he marveled over the presidential plane he inherited, which was far less plush but far more sophisticated in its electronics and equipment. "Isn't Air Force One really something?" he gushed during a flight early in his tenure. "I mean, we all have our own private planes and have for years, but this is something else."[23] Eventually, Trump would push the military to purchase a vastly upgraded new plane and backup for nearly $4 billion; it was necessary, he said, because the Saudis and other world leaders had much fancier, more recent Boeing 747-800s at their disposal. "The United States should be properly represented," he would insist.

As much as Trump relished the trappings of power, it soon became apparent that he did not like the office itself. Other presidents had chafed at the constraints of the job. John F. Kennedy repeatedly snuck out to meet girlfriends, aided by friendly Secret Service agents. Richard M. Nixon, a workaholic with no such outside interests, outfitted a hideaway in the ornate Old Executive Office Building across from the White House and spent more time there than in the Oval Office. When Obama briefly escaped the White House for an unplanned walk to Starbucks, he ruefully compared himself to a circus animal. "The bear is loose," he joked.[24]

But even more than other presidents, Trump would become a prisoner of the stage set he constructed for himself. Unwelcome in the Democrat-dominated town—the District of Columbia gave him a mere 4 percent of its vote, the lowest ever for a president in his capital city—Trump virtually barricaded himself in the White House.[25] When he did leave, he generally traveled only four blocks down Pennsylvania Avenue to his Trump-branded hotel in the Old Post Office Building or to his Trump National Golf Club twenty-five miles out of town in Sterling, Virginia. He disdained Camp David (too "rustic"), so he would take weekends and vacations at Trump properties too, wintering at Mar-a-Lago, his Palm Beach estate turned private club, and summering at the Trump National Golf Club in Bedminster, New Jersey.[26] In four years, Trump would never go out to a restaurant in Washington that was not owned by his company. He did not take advantage of the presidential box at the Kennedy Center or appear at the city's many social events. He knew he would be heckled, therefore he almost never ventured out in public. One time that he did, to attend a World Series game hosted by the Washington Nationals, he was greeted by a chorus of boos and jeers.

Trump did not want to roam Washington so much as to shed its rituals, protocols, and obligations. He craved not personal freedom but rather a new definition of the job itself. The modern presidency, with its day segmented into rigid increments of fifteen-minute meetings and highly regimented formal sessions, was not for him. Instead of the Oval Office, Trump gravitated toward the small private dining room next door, where he spent much of his official workday.

While LBJ famously kept a three-screen television setup in the Oval Office to monitor each of the national networks, Trump did him one better, installing a sixty-inch television in that private dining room along with a DirecTV Genie HD DVR, a whole-home system that he called his "Super TiVo" and that let him record multiple shows at once and replay them from the same point on any screen in the building. "This is one of the great inventions of all time—TiVo," he told visitors.[27] It was in effect his own media bunker, from which he often called the hosts of his favorite Fox News programs after their shows to offer his critique or solicit their advice.

The atmosphere in the dining room was redolent of the men's grill at one of Trump's golf clubs, with the television blaring and uniformed Navy stewards bringing in his daily lunch of a cheeseburger (well done). A glass jar on a side table was stocked with Starburst candies, culled of all flavors except his favorite pink and red. Overhead, he hung an opulent crystal chandelier—paid for with his own money, he claimed. But the overall effect was less historic grandeur than Trump Tower kitsch. When a California congressman, Darrell Issa, gave him a copy of *The Republican Club*, a museum-gift-shop-style painting of Republican presidents kibitzing with each other—Trump is featured chuckling over a Diet Coke across the table from Abraham Lincoln—he loved it so much he hung it on the wall, causing a minor sensation when he showed the room off to Lesley Stahl on *60 Minutes*. In the tiny nearby pantry he called the Monica Lewinsky Room in honor of Bill Clinton's reported trysts with the former intern there—another favorite stop on his White House tour—he stored cheap trinkets for visitors stamped with his name and the presidential seal.

When he was in the Oval Office, he used the space differently than its previous occupants. In private too Trump staged a show. The room was constantly crowded with aides and even more loitered just outside, in the outer Oval. Even when Trump was doing mundane work like signing papers in red folders with his favorite black Sharpie pen, the couches were crowded with staff and visitors. Trump loved to impress his billionaire friends with the historic new digs. Ron Lauder, the cosmetics heir and a major art collector, was awed by the famous Rembrandt Peale portrait of George Washington that hung over the fireplace. Trump did not care so much about the painting, but loved to describe how impressed Lauder was. He often invited guests upstairs to the private family quarters—strictly off limits to outsiders for much of Obama's tenure—to point out the Lincoln Bedroom or Lincoln's old desk in the Treaty Room.

But Trump did not take long to discover that everyone wandering in and out of the office got in the way of his television watching. "This is way too much," he told aides who scheduled meetings starting at 9 a.m.[28] So he began lingering in the residence later and later each morning. Eventually, his first meeting in the Oval Office would not start before 11 a.m. and he often did not show up until 11:30. Even then, he hated structured discussions, preferring a spontaneity that no other modern president would indulge. It got to the point that aides would mark as much as 60 percent of his official calendar as "Executive Time," much of which was spent with the screen on.[29] "I do not watch much television," Trump claimed when this astonishing fact was first reported, but exactly no one who knew him believed him.[30]

He was, as one White House official observed, the first president who seemed to interpret the job as an extended tryout for the role of Mike Teavee in *Willy Wonka & the Chocolate Factory*, the television-addicted American kid glued to the box at all hours of the day and night who persuades Wonka to transport him inside a television set. When the Oompa-Loompas sing of his downfall—he was shrunk by one of Wonka's wondrous machines into thousands of tiny pieces and had to be stretched back like a piece of taffy—they chant about how television turns the brain into goop.

Trump woke up around 5:30 a.m. many days and the first thing he did was flip on the tube. The last thing he did many nights was to click it back on. Over the course of a day, he would have it on for six or eight hours, flickering in the background, so he could check out the chyron at the bottom of the screen. Once during a meeting on health care with Paul Ryan, the House speaker, Trump grew so bored he stood up without saying anything, wandered off to his dining room, and turned on the television. Ryan, not knowing what to do, kept talking. Vice President Mike Pence, realizing that Trump was not coming back, slipped out to the dining room and convinced him to return.

Trump tuned in not just to conservative media that slathered him with praise but hate-watched shows he knew would excoriate him. Even as he denied monitoring them, he regularly demonstrated granular knowledge of what Don Lemon was saying late at night on CNN or what Joe Scarborough and Mika Brzezinski were discussing in the early mornings on MSNBC—and then offered scathing public reviews on his Twitter feed of "Psycho Joe" and "Crazy Mika" and Lemon, the "dumbest man on television."[31]

The feedback loop of TV and Twitter consumed Trump to a degree that was simply unprecedented. Modern presidents before him had adapted to the media of the moment, from Franklin D. Roosevelt with his fireside chats over the radio to John Kennedy's live news conferences to Ronald Reagan's artfully stage-managed events for the nightly television news. But Trump, who came to office with 20 million Twitter followers and would quadruple that over his term, saw his incessant tweeting from his off-the-shelf Android smartphone as both an escape from the job and, increasingly, his definition of doing it. Before the inauguration, it was reported, incorrectly, that he had handed the phone in over security concerns; instead, he was soon pulling it out to send tweets from the Oval Office itself. "He needs to tweet like we need to eat," Kellyanne Conway, his campaign manager turned White House counselor, once told *The New York Times*.[32]

For Trump, Twitter was not just a way of controlling the national conversation, but an outlet for outrage, a distraction from unwelcome story lines, a means for self-praise, a forum for test-driving new messages, a megaphone for conspiracy theories, and even a delivery service for you-are-fired pink slips to his most senior officials. It was both cannily strategic and utterly random. In those early days in the White House, he delighted in showing off his ability to command attention. "Watch this," he would tell aides or visitors as he picked up his phone, typed a few words, hit send, and then watched for a minute or two before the television chyron suddenly switched to whatever he had just written.

Most of the time he wrote the tweets himself or dictated them to Dan Scavino, his golf-caddie-turned-social-media-director, or Madeleine Westerhout, his assistant. Sometimes aides proposed tweets or edited his drafts. Scavino would print out his suggestions in extra-large font to show the president, even offering variations labeled "hot," "medium," or "mild."[33] Trump invariably chose "hot." Usually, though, Trump just sent them as he thought of them, often to the surprise of his advisers.

Fact-checking was never part of the process. He now had access to experts on basically every subject known to humanity but would rely instead on something he saw on Fox News or read online without asking if it was true or caring if it was not. Spelling and punctuation were strictly optional. "He often said that he was creating a new language," Westerhout recalled.[34] At the beginning, he tweeted on average nine times a day, and many were so inflammatory that he would generate multiple news stories. When Washington erupted in outrage over some wild tweet, he took it as a victory—"owning the libs," as his people put it. And if something he wrote proved problematic, he simply changed the subject by posting something even more explosive. Stories that would have bedeviled other presidents for days or weeks quickly vanished with the next sensation.

At times, he wielded the phone like a threat. During an argument with aides over a decision in the early days of his presidency, he reached into the drawer of his desk, pulled out his phone, and threw it on the desk. "Do you want me to settle this right now?" he asked.

Not long into his tenure in the White House, Trump brought several journalists from *Time* in for dinner and a tour. Trump's obsession with the media had for decades extended to the magazine, and he viewed being on its cover as the ultimate validation, so much so that his first week in office, at a soon-to-be-legendary appearance at the CIA, he took time out of lying about the crowd size at his inauguration to falsely claim he had "the all-time record in the history of *Time*" for appearing on its cover.[35] He had even hung fake *Time* covers featuring himself in at least five of his clubs. Trump went all-out for this cover story, including a four-course dinner in the Blue Room, at which he explained the animating principle of his still new presidency. A senior White House official had recently offered up a list of Three Rules of Trump: 1. When you're right, fight. 2. Controversy elevates message. 3. Never apologize. Trump amplified those guideposts for his guests. "The only way you survive," he told the journalists, "is to be combative."[36]

Combative was Trump's default setting. During his campaign and early months in office, Trump would attack virtually every major institution in American life—Congress, the courts, Democrats, Republicans, the news media, the Justice Department, Hollywood, the United States military, NATO, intelligence agencies, the cast of *Hamilton*, the cast of *Saturday Night Live*, the pope, and professional sports. He distorted a comment by the Muslim mayor of London to paint him as soft on terrorism. He accused Obama of tapping Trump Tower—a claim his Justice Department debunked—and called his predecessor a "Bad (or sick) guy!" He termed various targets of his ire "crazy," "crooked," "short and fat," "totally inept," "disgusting," "sleazy," "wacky," "totally unhinged," and "dumb as a rock."[37] Among others.

The night he defeated Hillary Clinton against all odds, his first thought when told by an aide that he would become president was how to use the office to take revenge on his enemies. The one who initially came to mind was John Kasich, the governor of Ohio and the last Republican who had stood against him in the primaries. "When I get to Washington," Trump said, according to the aide, "I'm gonna shove it up Kasich's ass!"[38]

Kasich was not his only target; he was just the stand-in for all of them. Trump's election was the ultimate vindication for a man never accepted by the exclusive set whose approval he so craved. He would rail about "the elite." Why were they elite and he was not? "I have a much better apartment than they do," he would say later in his presidency. "I'm smarter than they are. I'm richer than they are. I became president and they didn't."[39]

Washington was no different than New York in that sense. Trump's quest for the White House became a "hostile takeover," in Jared Kushner's words, launched against the nation's ruling class.[40] First, Trump overcame the Republican candidates often described as the best the party had to offer and toppled the Clinton dynasty that had dominated American politics for years. Even then, he knew they did not respect him. He could feel their contempt. "Trump had never been allowed in the room," said Newt Gingrich, the former House speaker who was also a proponent of the combative style in American politics and had become an occasional confidant of the new president. "He was a guy who preferred cheeseburgers to foie gras. In every way you can imagine, the Rockefeller-Bush wing of the party was appalled. It's as if we allowed the Clampetts to come in and take over the party."

This resentment formed the foundation for his political appeal, a sense of grievance that he both shared with his supporters and stoked. While he was surely the richest man ever to claim the presidency—even if, with an estimated $3.7 billion, he was not as rich as he claimed to be—Trump had won office as the tribune of millions of working Americans.[41] The tycoon with the palatial fifty-three-room Manhattan penthouse and gold-plated private plane eagerly refashioned himself as their champion in a war of class and culture with coastal elites constantly whining about discrimination, sexual harassment, and political incorrectness. How dare they call us, as Hillary Clinton had just a few months earlier, the "deplorables"?

From Trump's perspective, he had plenty of reason to complain. The elites he railed against had never taken him seriously. Why would they?

His ambitions for the White House always seemed like a joke—until they were not. Starting in 1987, when he was marketing his first book, *The Art of the Deal*, Trump floated his name as a possible presidential candidate every few years. "Everyone laughed it off," recalled Barbara Res, who managed many of his building projects.[42] When he decided not to jump into the 1988 race, virtually no one noticed; he then sent word to George H. W. Bush offering himself as a vice presidential running mate, a suggestion the Republican nominee found "strange and unbelievable."[43] In 2000, Trump did enter the race briefly, in that abortive contest against Pat Buchanan for the nomination of the Reform Party founded by Ross Perot. He flirted with runs again in 2004, 2008, and 2012 before finally jumping in for real in 2016.

"What's the worst thing that happens?" he asked as he contemplated the campaign. "We lose? So what? This can be the greatest infomercial in the history of politics."[44] As Sam Nunberg, one of his early campaign aides, recalled, it was more of a lark than a carefully considered enterprise. "He would say this will be the greatest branding exercise of all time," Nunberg said. It was not clear what Trump wanted to do with the office he was seeking. "You could never really talk about whether he wanted to *be* president because he would look at you and say, 'I want to *win*,'" Nunberg said.

For Trump, that was what it had always been about. His father, Fred Trump, had taught him to be "a killer," a term of admiration that his son would adopt throughout his career. He learned to seek every advantage and give no concession. Fred Trump even had a special chair with one leg shorter than the rest to keep others off balance, according to Barbara Res, and he advised his son to set up his office so that the sun would shine through the blinds in his adversaries' eyes. That was an approach the president emulated. Life was a zero-sum game; if the other guy was doing well, it meant that Trump was not. "I don't believe in win/win," he once told biographer Michael D'Antonio. "I believe in I win."[45]

And so Trump opened his administration with a howitzer blast at all of those who never gave him his proper due. Forget the traditions of the Inaugural Address, where his predecessors sought to purge the poisons of the campaign season and celebrate American unity. Trump used his Inaugural Address to accuse those who came before of mismanaging and even selling out the country. The nation's leaders, the ones arrayed behind him on the Capitol platform in a cold midday drizzle, had "reaped the rewards of government while the people have borne the cost."[46]

The result, he said, was an America afflicted by "the ravages" of economic dislocation, foreign exploitation, and political corruption, a country where mothers and children were "trapped in poverty in our inner cities," where "rusted-out factories" were "scattered like tombstones across the landscape," and where drugs and crime "have stolen too many lives." It was an us-against-them speech, not only dark but divisive—the people versus the establishment, foreigners versus the native-born, Trump versus his enemies. He made little effort to leaven the dystopian message with the sort of shining-city-on-a-hill optimism that Ronald Reagan and other presidents invoked. "This American carnage stops right here and stops right now," Trump declared in the most memorable line.

Republicans and Democrats alike found the address ominous. George W. Bush, who attended the ceremony along with other former presidents, seemed flabbergasted. "Well, that was some weird shit," he remarked to Hillary Clinton.[47] Like Clinton, many of those at the Capitol that day had come for what they saw as both a bipartisan ritual and a democratic obligation to welcome the new president, no matter how distasteful they might find him. Trump had tried sounding gracious briefly on that stunning night when he had claimed victory a couple months earlier, only to draw protests from his hardline advisers. It was, Steve Bannon said, "just not Trump," as watered down and pointless as a "group hug."[48] The inauguration would be different. This time, Bannon and Stephen Miller, the young Bannon ally and anti-immigration crusader who had become Trump's unlikely warm-up act on the campaign trail, had the pen.

Drafts were closely held and when other aides to the new president asked Miller for copies, he put them off. When one senior official in the incoming administration was finally given a printout of the draft, he was shocked by the harsh and unpresidential language and tried to strike some of it with a red pen only to have his feedback thoroughly ignored. Bannon once recalled for an interviewer the internal pushback he had gotten about the speech. "We should bring the country together," Bannon remembered them telling him. But that was not where he was at. It was not where Trump was at. "We didn't win an election to bring the country together," Bannon remembered saying. "It's not time to bring the country together. It's time to take on the elites in this country. Take the torch to them. Hit them with a blowtorch."[49]

"American carnage" was certainly a blowtorch. Some of those listening to Trump that day at the Capitol, including some members of his new White House team, had fooled themselves into thinking that President Trump would somehow be different than candidate Trump, that once in office the historic weight of the presidency would sober him up. Despite all the evidence, they told themselves that the office would change the man. But it was hard to seriously believe that after his speech, which was not a last gasp of fiery rhetoric from the campaign but a template for how he would govern.

Within days, there were presidential tweetstorms attacking Republican senators—his nemesis John McCain and sidekick Lindsey Graham were "sadly weak on immigration" and "always looking to start World War III"—and early-morning rants about Iran and Mexico and Barack Obama. There was a threat to "send in the Feds" to battle "carnage" in the streets of Chicago. There were the repeated preposterous claims about the crowd size at his inauguration, which he forced his new press secretary, Sean Spicer, to repeat from the White House podium in a fatal blow to his spokesman's credibility.

And then there was Trump's boast that he had won not just the Electoral College but the popular vote too, when in fact he had lost it to Clinton by three million votes. It was completely invented. But that did not stop the new president from insisting on it to the astonishment of congressional leaders he invited to the White House on his first full workday in office. "You know, I won the popular vote," Trump told them. When Nancy Pelosi, the House Democratic leader, challenged him, he simply repeated it. "Five million people voted illegally," he asserted. "Five million immigrants voted illegally." When Pelosi objected again, Trump added, "And I'm not even counting California!"

Trump even appointed a commission to prove this made-up claim, a panel that would quietly close down a year later, having found no evidence whatsoever. It was all unthinkable and, ever since 2:29 a.m. on November 9, when the Associated Press had declared the presidential election of 2016 decided in Donald Trump's favor, inevitable.

CHAPTER 2

Team of Amateurs

The first time Reince Priebus interviewed Rob Porter, the incoming chief of staff confessed that he was already in a brutal knife fight for control of the Trump White House, and Trump had not even taken office yet. The enemies, Priebus made clear, were Steve Bannon on one flank and Jared Kushner on the other.

Trump's unlikely new top aide knew that Porter, the Harvard-educated, Rhodes Scholar scion of a Republican establishment family, was no Trumpist. He had not been part of the campaign and had worked for a series of old-school conservative senators including Rob Portman and Orrin Hatch. But Priebus was not so concerned about Porter's fealty to the president. "I really need somebody who's going to be loyal to me," Priebus said.

Kushner also needed allies in the struggle for control of the White House that was emerging. When Porter went in for an interview with the president's son-in-law, Kushner spent the first hour grilling him as if he were an establishment spy. "How can we trust you?" Kushner demanded. Then he pivoted, spending the second hour of the meeting selling himself, explaining how he thought things would work in the new regime and declaring, in so many words, that Porter would be *his* guy.

In the end, the rivals each agreed to bring Porter on board as the White House staff secretary, an obscure but critical position in any presidency that serves as gatekeeper for all documents and executive orders coming in and out of the Oval Office. By the time Porter arrived in the White House, however, he discovered that the battle lines had already shifted. The chief of staff now told him to forget all that stuff about a knife fight with Bannon and Kushner. In fact, contrary to what Priebus had indicated in their initial interview, they were getting along surprisingly well.

"It's really Kellyanne that nobody likes," Priebus confided.

Every White House has its factions, with officials vying for the best titles, the biggest staffs, the most time with the president, and the most prime real estate in the cramped warrens of the West Wing. But none had ever been torn apart by tribal warfare as intense and toxic as Trump's White House. It was personal, it was political, it was philosophical. And from the very start, it was all-consuming. The polarization that Trump encouraged in the outside world, he fostered inside his own building too.

There was the Republican National Committee crowd led by Priebus and the hard-core *Breitbart News* crew championed by Bannon. There was the family represented by Kushner and Ivanka Trump and the lone rangers like Kellyanne Conway. Fault lines divided the traditionalists and the revolutionaries, the globalists and the protectionists, the New Yorkers and everyone else. There were ideologues and showboaters, enablers and obstructionists, MAGA true believers and even a few "Bushies" who managed to find jobs in a White House where the most recent Republican president was seen as much of an enemy as the Democrat who had just left.

Competing alliances had formed—and re-formed—with remarkable speed, leading to instant chaos. Joe Hagin, a longtime Reagan-Bush White House official being recruited to come back to help run the West Wing, met Chris Liddell at Trump Tower one day and asked what he would do in the new administration. Liddell, a New Zealander in his late fifties who carried himself with a quiet corporate confidence after stints as chief financial officer for Microsoft and vice chairman of General Motors, said he was on tap to run presidential personnel. Five days later, Hagin was at the transition headquarters in Washington when a young man appeared and introduced himself as Johnny DeStefano. A Midwesterner with an easy smile and experience on Capitol Hill working for the former speaker John Boehner, DeStefano told Hagin that he would run presidential personnel. This was more than just confusion; Liddell was seen as Kushner's man while DeStefano was seen as Priebus's. Ultimately, DeStefano would get the title of personnel director while Liddell was made an assistant to the president working for Kushner and later promoted to deputy chief of staff.

Within weeks, it was apparent that the Trump White House was a place where almost no one trusted anyone else—and for good reason. "Everybody lied. All the time. About everything," recalled one aide who was there at the start. "It really started to get ugly," Bannon once told an interviewer, "after about the second week."[1] Many on the staff blamed that ugliness on Bannon himself, but he was not the only one responsible. Leaking about rival factions, secretly taping colleagues, and surreptitious messaging on encrypted apps like Signal and Telegram were soon endemic. As one cabinet secretary put it, "In the Trump administration, if you're not actively throwing other people under the bus, all you do is find yourself squarely under it."

The chaos was no accident. It was how Trump had run his own business for decades and what he had preached on *The Apprentice*. "Life's a vicious place," he said in 2004 while promoting the series. "No different than a jungle."[2] His politics were jungle politics, the war of all against all, and his management style was straight out of the divide-and-conquer playbook. He refused a more conventional organization for his administration and thrived on the internal feuds, which left him the lone authoritative decider. "Trump wasn't trying to lead a unifying team," said one White House official caught up in it. "He wasn't trying to prevent the rivalries and the squabbles and the knife-fighting. It was almost *Apprentice*-esque. He liked competition and infighting among the people below him. It's like a competition for his favor."

The result was an insecure president who fostered perpetual insecurity on his staff. As much as Trump talked about loyalty as a paramount value, what he meant was loyalty *to* him, never *from* him. He was, as another of his newly acquired senior officials put it, like a teenage boy obsessed with a girl until she agreed to go out on a date with him, at which point he would start to focus on all her flaws and wonder how to get out of the relationship. "The president likes two kinds of people," Priebus told colleagues. "The people who *used* to work for him and the people who are *going* to work for him."

Even months into his tenure, Trump did not understand the duties and reporting lines of his own staff. Nor did he care. "Who do you work for?" he asked Rob Porter at one point. "I guess I work for Reince," Porter said. "No, no, no, forget it," Trump said. "You don't work for Reince. You work for me. You don't have to go through him. Just come to me."

Trump made several decisions in the immediate aftermath of his upset election that virtually guaranteed a White House mired in dysfunction. The first was to blow up whatever modest planning had gone on for his transition in advance of the election. During the campaign, Trump had casually assigned his friend, Governor Chris Christie of New Jersey, to prepare for a transition that neither of them thought would be necessary since he would surely lose. But Christie had a fierce enemy inside Trump's family: Jared Kushner. When serving as a federal prosecutor more than a decade earlier, Christie had sent Jared's father, Charles Kushner, to prison after the real estate magnate set up his brother-in-law in a video-taped encounter with a prostitute, then sent the tape to his own sister as revenge for cooperating with authorities. When the transition planning idea came up, Trump overruled Kushner's emotional objection, perhaps reasoning that it did not matter since it was just make-work anyway. But when Trump actually won, Christie was forced out, a decision he blamed on Kushner, who denied it. Either way, Christie's binders full of potential candidates, vetting memos, and ideas for organizing and staffing the new administration were tossed.

On paper, the new transition leader was Mike Pence, but Trump made clear from the start that his incoming vice president's role was purely advisory. The president-elect's first major personnel decision, taken within days of his victory, was naming Priebus his chief of staff. He did so despite his own anger at the party chairman, who had suggested barely a month earlier that he drop out of the race after the emergence of the *Access Hollywood* tape with Trump's crude "grab them by the pussy" discussion of women. Priebus's appointment was a nod to the Trump-skeptical Republican establishment, but that did not mean he would let Priebus or anyone else actually run anything.

A forty-four-year-old lawyer with a nebbishy look and a talent for fundraising, Priebus was a creature of the party, having worked his way up from Wisconsin politics to become national chairman. He had been close friends with House Speaker Paul Ryan since the congressional leader's first run for office in the 1990s and the two shared similar ambivalence toward Trump. After Mitt Romney's defeat in 2012 with Ryan as his vice presidential running mate, Priebus sponsored a review of what went wrong, a one-hundred-page autopsy report that, recognizing the country's growing Hispanic population, urged the party to be more inclusive while supporting comprehensive immigration reform. "A more welcoming form of conservatism," as one of his coauthors explained.[3] In Trump, Priebus found the antithesis of the autopsy's recommendations and assumed he would never win the presidency, "not in a million years," as he told friends.[4] But Priebus also rebuffed aides such as Katie Walsh and Sean Spicer, who urged him to distance the party from the brash billionaire or even ban him from primary debates, reasoning that it made no sense to alienate Trump's supporters or give him an excuse to run as an independent and drain support from the eventual GOP nominee.

Now asked to head up Trump's team, Priebus reached out for advice from James A. Baker III, who served as White House chief of staff to Ronald Reagan and George H. W. Bush. Baker had voted for Trump but was no fan and thought Priebus would be in an untenable position working for such an erratic president.

"Don't take the job," Baker told Priebus, "because if you're not granted full authority, it's going to be a nightmare."

"Yeah," Priebus agreed. "But if I don't take the job, it's going to be Steve Bannon. So I think I better do it."

Thus were big decisions made—blocking rivals mattered as much as anything else. Bannon was quite the rival, a self-styled revolutionary whose stated objective was to blow up the party that Priebus had spent his career building. In fact, Bannon wanted to demolish the whole superstructure of American politics, a project he called "the deconstruction of the administrative state."[5] He had spent years trying to do so from the fringe as a filmmaker, agitator, and eventually head of *Breitbart News.* "If there's an explosion or a fire somewhere," one of his employees at *Breitbart* once said, "Steve is probably nearby with some matches."[6] The product of a blue-collar family in Richmond, Virginia, who served in the Navy and Goldman Sachs before refashioning himself into a right-wing rebel, the sixty-three-year-old Bannon, perpetually disheveled and shaggy-haired, gloried in grievance, rallying the "hobbits" with populist fury against elites like the Clintons.

That Trump, a billionaire who had invited the Clintons to his third wedding, would become Bannon's vehicle for doing so involved no shortage of irony. But Bannon treated Trump as an empty vessel for his ideology and he planned to make the most of the opportunity before the new president flamed out—or he himself did. From the start, Bannon told associates that he did not expect to survive in the White House long. "I won't make it past August," he confided, a prediction that would prove eerily prescient. If in the short time he had, he could push Trump to follow his most nationalist-populist instincts, Bannon thought he could reshape the Republican Party.

But he was not optimistic. Little more than a week before the election, Representative Mark Meadows of North Carolina, a leader of the far-right agitators in the House Freedom Caucus, had approached Bannon and handed him an envelope with a pitch for Trump to endorse his plan to force out Paul Ryan as speaker and take control of the party apparatus on the Hill. But after Trump won, he quickly decided not to embrace Meadows's idea, which was soon abandoned. Instead, the new president chose

not only to work with Ryan but even to tap his close ally Priebus as chief
of staff, what Bannon would later call the "Faustian bargain" that shaped
the Trump White House.[7] "We will rue the day we don't do this," Bannon
later quoted Meadows telling him when they failed to use the moment to
purge the party. "I fully understand," Bannon had replied. "I'm ruing with
you." Inviting the establishment in the form of Priebus into the building,
he concluded, was "an original sin of this administration."[8]

Nonetheless, when Trump offered Bannon the role of chief strategist
and counselor in his White House, he took it. While Priebus was granted
the chief of staff's traditional southwest corner office in the West Wing
with the fireplace and patio that Baker once occupied, it was immediately
evident that Priebus would not have the singular authority that previous
chiefs had had. The very statement announcing his selection twinned his
appointment with Bannon's—and Bannon was listed first. The two would
work "as equal partners to transform the federal government," the statement said.[9] It was almost as if Trump were putting them in a ring together
and telling them to duke it out.

The cage match soon began, with each racing to hire their own aides
onto Trump's White House staff. Priebus brought in some of his lieutenants from the Republican committee, including Katie Walsh as his
deputy and Sean Spicer as the press secretary, and he installed Madeleine
Westerhout as Trump's executive assistant so he would have eyes and ears
just outside the Oval Office. These were not Trump people but Priebus
people—not only did Westerhout not vote for Trump, she had burst into
tears on election night when he won and was so disgusted she intended to
move back to California until a Priebus aide convinced her to join the staff.

Bannon had taken to heart the Bolshevik principle that personnel were
the key to any revolution, but while he sat in on Trump's interviews with
prospective cabinet secretaries at Trump Tower, he soon felt frustrated
that he had not been able to bring into the White House as many of his
ideological fellow travelers as he had hoped. He watched with dismay as
key jobs went to Wall Street types such as Gary Cohn, the national economic adviser, and Steven Mnuchin, the treasury secretary. Basically, Bannon complained to associates, all he got were Michael Flynn, a retired
lieutenant general who had parlayed "lock her up" campaign rally chants
into the national security adviser's job, and Sebastian Gorka, a goatee-
sporting, Muslim-bashing flame-thrower with ties to Hungarian far-right
groups. Bannon would also make common cause with Jeff Sessions, the
Alabama senator who had leveraged his early endorsement of Trump into
a position as his new attorney general, and Stephen Miller, the former

Sessions aide who had been primary author of the "American carnage" Inaugural Address.

Then there was Kellyanne Conway, who had served as the last of Trump's campaign managers but was a lightning rod within the new president's circle—and within his family. A veteran pollster, Conway had worked for such Republicans as Jack Kemp, Newt Gingrich, and Mike Pence while making herself a star of conservative cable television with her pithy, sometimes caustic commentary. While she had the title of campaign manager, her internal critics saw her more as a surrogate on television than the operation's chief executive; Kushner thought that had been *his* role. Along with Kushner, Trump's adult children from his first marriage—Ivanka, Donald Jr., and Eric—all lobbied against Conway being given a position in the White House, arguing that she was out for herself more than Trump. And while Priebus, Bannon, and Kushner disliked each other, the one thing they agreed on was they all loathed Conway. She did not think much of them either, referring to them as "three jealous boys" and the "Three Stooges."[10]

Her future in the new White House remained unsettled for more than six weeks after the election while Priebus, Bannon, and others scooped up top jobs and prime offices. She stewed at the affront, detecting sexism. She was, after all, the first woman ever to manage a successful presidential campaign and considered herself the rescuer of Trump's candidacy. She told anyone who asked that the delay in determining her next step owed to her own hesitation as a mother of four to join the round-the-clock White House staff and her rivals hoped she would instead run a Trump super PAC on the outside. But Trump liked her aggressive defense of him on television and just before Christmas gave her the title of White House counselor. As a condition, she insisted she have the same rank as Kushner, Bannon, and Priebus.

In assembling his White House, Trump essentially sought to replicate the Trump Organization, where he was the sole decision-maker, unaccountable to any board and surrounded by his own children as executives. He invited his daughter and son-in-law to join his official government staff, while maintaining control over his global business empire through his two eldest sons without divesting himself of it or setting up a blind trust, as his predecessors had. For the new president, these were two critical decisions that would shape his entire time in office, setting up an endless series of conflicts of interest—and personality.

In many ways, the fractures among his staff hardly compared to the fractures within his family. Most pronounced was the rivalry between Melania Trump and Ivanka Trump, two sculpted former models who had long vied for Donald's attention and favor, had little love for each other, and immediately began a quiet competition for the role of leading lady in the White House.

Melania, a native of a small town in Slovenia, was the first foreign-born first lady since Louisa Adams, the wife of John Quincy Adams, who was born in Britain, and she planned to play a low-key role. At forty-six, nearly a quarter century younger than her husband, she was sensitive about her accent and said little in public. She had scant interest in policy or personnel, none of Nancy Reagan's fierce devotion to protecting her husband or Hillary Clinton's progressive passion. Melania was so unenthusiastic for her new life that she refused to move to the White House for the first five months of the presidency, remaining in New York with Barron, her ten-year-old son with Trump, until the end of the school year—and, as her biographer Mary Jordan discovered, using the time to negotiate a more favorable prenuptial agreement guaranteeing that Barron's inheritance was more in line with his older siblings.[11]

At the White House, Melania took one look at the family quarters and declared them unacceptable. "I'm not moving to D.C. until the residence has been renovated and redecorated," she told her friend Stephanie Winston Wolkoff, "starting with a new shower and toilet."[12] She would not tolerate a used toilet. She insisted that workmen convert one of the chambers in the historic mansion into a "glam room" for her wardrobe and her personal appearance team, which included a makeup artist and hairdresser. Trump did not make it easy for her. When she ordered some of the old White House furniture moved out and put into storage in favor of more modern replacements, he waited until she headed back to New York and then overruled her. "Can't you let her have this one thing?" an exasperated aide asked him. No, he could not.

But the first lady had no intention of ceding her place to her stepdaughter. Preparing for the inaugural festivities, Melania did not want Ivanka or Trump's other children to accompany her to Arlington National Cemetery for a ceremonial wreath-laying, so she had the event left off their schedule. Melania was also convinced that Ivanka was maneuvering to make sure that she and Jared were positioned on the inaugural stage to be visible in the iconic photograph of the new president taking the oath. So the new first lady and Wolkoff, a former chief planner of New York's Met Gala who was helping organize the celebrations, conspired to keep the first daughter out of camera range. Wolkoff called it "Operation Block Ivanka."[13]

During the first week of the administration, the first lady took offense when Ivanka organized a showing of the movie *Finding Dory* in the White House theater. Melania considered it an intrusion into her domain and decreed that no one, including Jared and Ivanka, would be allowed into the residential sections of the White House without her permission. (It probably did not help that the movie's saccharine pro-immigration plot line seemed a poor fit for the new administration's politics, either.) "Do they come walking into my apartment in New York whenever they want?" she asked a friend. "No."[14]

The tension reflected the complicated family dynamics brought to the White House by the new president, only the second in American history to have been divorced and the first to have two former wives. While he had kept his business in the family, he was hardly much of a family man. Over the years, he had rarely made it home in time for dinner with the kids and kept no pictures of the children in his office at Trump Tower. "Statistically, my children have a very bad shot," he once told an interviewer. "Children of successful people are generally very, very troubled."[15]

The exception, though, seemed to be Ivanka, clearly his favorite child. Now thirty-five, she had spent the previous few years as an executive vice president at the Trump Organization and as a boardroom judge on *The Apprentice* before developing her own brands of clothing, handbags, and jewelry. She had acquired the reputation as the one who could calm her father's rages or steer him in a more constructive direction—sometimes. His admiration for her sometimes took on a creepy tone. More than once in the years before the White House, he had praised her body, most infamously during a 2006 joint appearance on *The View* when he said, "if Ivanka weren't my daughter perhaps I'd be dating her."[16] He thought so much of her that he proposed putting her on his ticket in 2016 as his vice presidential running mate. Campaign aides thought he was kidding at first, but he kept pressing. "She's bright, she's smart, she's beautiful, and the people would love her!" Trump insisted at one meeting.[17] As would happen so many times in the four years to come, his advisers humored him, hoping he would simply forget the idea. But after spending weeks vetting other candidates he did not like, Trump came around to his daughter again. "I think it should be Ivanka," he said.[18] This time the team agreed to test the idea in a poll, figuring the results would make clear how nutty it was. But she tested better than they thought, in low double digits, stronger than some of the real candidates.

The notion of making his daughter vice president was, of course, preposterous. Aside from the fact that she had no qualifications at all, it would
make Trump seem like even more of a clown than he already did to tens
of millions of Americans. It would put every Republican candidate on the
spot, requiring them to embrace or renounce the ludicrous suggestion.
But everything around Trump was so bizarre that some advisers began to
take it half seriously. "As crazy as it sounds and as ridiculous as it might
have been, it wasn't that far off the rocker in the context of everything else
that had happened so far," Rick Gates, the deputy campaign manager, said
later.[19] Finally, Ivanka herself told her father to drop it. "No, Dad. It's not
a good idea," she said after letting it germinate for weeks.[20] But that would
not stop Trump from later imagining her as ambassador to the United
Nations or even president of the World Bank.

When they moved to Washington, Jared and Ivanka chose a presidential enclave, leasing a $5.5 million, seven-thousand-square-foot mansion
for $15,000 a month, with six bedrooms, six and a half baths, and five
fireplaces, in the Kalorama neighborhood two blocks from the Obamas'
equally grand post-presidency home and half a mile from the Clintons'
Washington house.

Ivanka positioned herself as a champion of working mothers and had
already pulled together a book to be published shortly after her father
took office, *Women Who Work: Rewriting the Rules for Success*, that presumed to offer parenting tips for everyday moms from a real estate heiress
who made millions of dollars a year marketing her name for "affordable"
women's office wear, $10,000 fine jewelry bracelets, and an array of made-
in-China shoes at accessible price points. Copies of the thin volume, "a
strawberry milkshake of inspirational quotes," as Jennifer Senior of *The
New York Times* dubbed it, would soon be strewn around the West Wing
for anyone to pick up.[21]

Kushner, Trump's new minister without portfolio, came with his own
share of a family $1.8 billion real estate empire and no shortage of self-
confidence. He was skinny to the point of wraithlike, favoring tailored
suits that hugged his narrow frame, and he flashed the wry grin of a man
who assumed things would always go his way. At age thirty-six, he had
gone to Harvard, managed his family's business while his father was in
prison, purchased a small New York newspaper, and all but ran his father-
in-law's presidential campaign. He had none of the blowhard rough edges
that characterized Don Jr. or Eric Trump, nor the hunger for the public
spotlight that consumed his father-in-law. But he was ambitious, and he
navigated the shadows of the media world better than either of his grown

brothers-in-law. "I don't play the press," Kushner would tell reporters on background even as he was playing them.

While it would take Ivanka a few months to decide to formally join the White House staff, Kushner was all in from the start, carving out a wide portfolio effectively outside of the normal White House structure. He formed an Office of American Innovation as his base of operations, staffing it with some of his friends from the business world to bring what he considered private sector savvy to the government. Like his father-in-law, he and Ivanka would donate their salaries to charity, not a huge sacrifice given the tens of millions they would still earn through their various businesses and investments.

Other White House officials made the mistake of trying to pin down Kushner about how far his scope would reach. When Priebus asked at an early meeting what the innovation office would do, Kushner brushed him back.

"What the fuck do you care, Reince?" he snapped. "We are not even being paid."

"Okay," Priebus replied, backing down. "You do whatever you want."[22]

Raised in an Orthodox Jewish family whose house guests included Prime Minister Benjamin Netanyahu of Israel, Kushner took on the mission of negotiating Middle East peace at his father-in-law's instructions. Trump also told him to deal with China, Mexico, and Saudi Arabia—basically anywhere an early problem emerged. Kushner planned to upgrade technology throughout the federal government. He would take on criminal justice reform. And more generally he would be in on most every meeting and every decision. Foreign ambassadors looking to navigate Trumpworld called him. Henry Kissinger called him. It did not take long for colleagues in the West Wing to refer to him as the Secretary of Everything.

Kushner demonstrated scant humility given his lack of knowledge and, while he was a quick learner, at times he acted as if anybody who had served in government before he arrived was an idiot. During an early meeting with Senator John McCain, White House officials asked about his priorities as chairman of the Senate Armed Services Committee. McCain started talking about reforming the Pentagon acquisition process. Kushner cut him off.

"Senator, we're going to change everything about how the government does business," he said.

"Well," McCain replied, "good luck with that."[23]

The senator did not bother to say another word for the remainder of the meeting but dined out on that anecdote for the rest of his life, regularly offering a devastating impersonation of Kushner for the benefit of friends.

One of those lobbying for a high position in the new administration was Rudy Giuliani, the former New York mayor who had a long-standing relationship with Trump since his real estate days and had even spoken at Fred Trump's funeral. Giuliani had been slow to endorse Trump in the 2016 campaign, but once he did, he became one of his most stalwart allies, most notably volunteering to go on television to defend him after the *Access Hollywood* tape. Trump was not especially impressed by Giuliani's performance, shouting on his campaign plane, "What the fuck is Rudy doing? Get this guy off the television!"[24] But he never forgot that Giuliani had done all five Sunday television talk shows on his behalf that weekend when so many other Republicans refused.

Giuliani now wanted to be secretary of state. Nothing else, he declared, was important enough. But no one around Trump thought that was a good idea. In the decade and a half since leaving Gracie Mansion, Giuliani had built a global consulting business with plenty of ethical questions and shady associations. Trump's advisers conducted their own opposition research on Giuliani, including a thirty-five-page dossier listing the myriad issues his nomination would raise. There were "many conflict of interest allegations" against Giuliani, the dossier warned, and an "extensive array of foreign clients," including governments, major firms, or prominent figures in Russia, Ukraine, Saudi Arabia, Qatar, Mexico, Chile, Brazil, Colombia, Honduras, and elsewhere.[25]

The Trump team warned in its dossier that Giuliani would be suspected of "giving former clients preferential treatment" if he entered government, setting him up for "the same questions of conflict of interest that hounded Hillary Clinton." It also raised questions about his continuing relationship with Bernard Kerik, his former police commissioner who had spent years in prison for tax fraud and other crimes. The dossier highlighted a controversial "failed" Mexico City contract Giuliani had undertaken with much fanfare to help the Mexican capital fight crime. It noted Giuliani's corporate speeches for which he charged between $100,000 and $300,000 and insisted on private jets and posh hotel accommodations. Another problem was the money he took from an Iranian opposition group that had been listed as a terrorist organization by the State Department until 2012.

Even Trump, usually immune to questions of integrity, blanched at the scandals that would erupt. So he brushed off Giuliani and looked for someone else. Newt Gingrich seemed like a possibility, except for the fact that the former House speaker was among the least diplomatic figures of the modern age. There was also John Bolton, a hawkish former United Nations ambassador and favorite of conservatives, although he seemed unlikely to help Trump stop the "endless wars" as he had promised. Another possibility was Bob Corker, a moderate Republican senator from Tennessee who chaired the Senate Foreign Relations Committee. Trump even claimed to be considering Mitt Romney, the 2012 presidential nominee who had pointedly refused to back Trump.

For counsel, Mike Flynn, the incoming national security adviser, called Bob Gates, who served as defense secretary under George W. Bush and Barack Obama and was widely seen as one of Washington's wise men. Gates had written an op-ed in *The Wall Street Journal* calling Trump "unqualified and unfit to be commander-in-chief."[26] But with the election over, Gates felt obliged to help. Flynn arranged a meeting.

Trump wanted Gates's thoughts on secretary of state and went through his list—Romney, Gingrich, Corker, Giuliani.

"The words Giuliani and diplomacy don't seem to me to belong in the same sentence," Gates interjected.

Gates had a different suggestion. "I think you ought to think about Rex Tillerson," Gates said, raising the soon-to-retire chief executive officer of ExxonMobil. "Rex knows the world. Rex has spent decades negotiating with foreign governments." But "he's not a foreign policy establishment figure if you're looking for somebody different."

Gates and Tillerson had gotten to know each other on the board of the Boy Scouts of America, and ExxonMobil had done business with the firm that Gates formed after leaving office along with George W. Bush's secretary of state, Condoleezza Rice, and national security adviser, Stephen Hadley. Rice also put in a good word for Tillerson when Trump called her a few hours after meeting with Gates and she called Mike Pence to recommend him as well.

Tillerson was not looking for the position. Stocky with a stern face and a shock of white hair, he was the picture of a corporate titan, which is what appealed to Trump. But they had little in common. Rex Wayne Tillerson came from modest roots in Texas and Oklahoma and was named for two Hollywood cowboys, Rex Allen and John Wayne. His father worked for the Boy Scouts and Rex, an Eagle Scout, would eventually become president of the Boy Scouts of America. Trump, needless to say, was no Boy Scout. Tillerson spent his life at Exxon, working his way up from a production engineer to chief executive officer over four decades. He was on the verge of retirement, which would bring him a huge $180 million payout, meaning he did not need the work.[27] "I didn't want this job. I didn't seek this job," he said later. "My wife told me I'm supposed to do this."[28] And so he accepted. Trump knew little about Tillerson other than that he was head of the world's fifth-largest company and had negotiated deals with the likes of Vladimir Putin and Arab princes. He loved the idea that such a business giant would be working for *him*.

He also loved the idea that he could get four-star generals to serve him. Shipped off to a military boarding school by his father, Trump had developed a fetish for those with stars on their shoulders even though he never served himself—or perhaps because he never served himself. Having avoided Vietnam through a diagnosis of bone spurs in his foot apparently facilitated by a doctor who owed his father a favor, Trump now set about recruiting his own team of retired officers.

In addition to enlisting Mike Flynn as national security adviser, and John Kelly, a retired Marine general, as secretary of homeland security, Trump set his sights on Jack Keane for defense secretary. Keane, a retired four-star general and vice chief of staff of the Army, was one of Trump's favorite television officers on Fox. But when they met, Keane turned him down. His wife had just died, and he had a pile of medical expenses.

Trump suggested that Ron Perelman, one of his billionaire friends, could take care of Keane's debt—and did not understand when Keane said no, he would pay his own bills. Besides, it would not be legal to have a private businessman pay someone to take a position in government. Trump looked around the room. Was that right? His advisers nodded. For Trump, money was always the answer.

So Trump turned to retired General Jim Mattis for the Pentagon. Mattis would be the most prominent member of his new cabinet, a Marine widely respected in the military for his drive and discipline. Mattis had led forces in Afghanistan, where his pleas to be sent to Tora Bora to capture Osama bin Laden went unheeded, and in Iraq, where he commanded the First Marine Division on the drive to Baghdad. His later stint as head of the United States Central Command, in charge of both wars as well as military operations in the rest of the region, ended badly amid tension with Barack Obama, who pushed Mattis out early in a disagreement about the administration's plans for a nuclear agreement with Iran. When Trump asked him to be defense secretary, Mattis was uncomfortable; even his mother asked him why he would go to work for such a man. But the lifelong Marine felt that if a president called you to serve, you had to do it.

The media had dubbed him "Mad Dog" during the Iraq War, a name that appealed to Trump, who loved the macho tone of it so much that as time wore on he would claim, falsely, that he was the one who gave it to him. But Mattis winced every time Trump called him that. He preferred his call sign, "Chaos."

Trump respected three types of people—those with money, those with Ivy League credentials, and those with stars on their uniform. Rich businessmen and generals were people who, in his view, had accomplished something and were worthy of admiration. Everyone else was a failure, a loser. There was no worse judgment.

Looks mattered as much as anything to Trump, who stocked his administration as if he were casting a new reality show. He had to be able to visualize the person in the role he was giving them. Mike Pence, he declared, was "out of central casting."[29] David Shulkin, his new veterans affairs secretary, was "a good looking guy."[30] After Judge Neil Gorsuch left a secret interview for a Supreme Court nomination at Trump Tower, Trump remarked, "This guy's out of central casting." When Trump first hosted Prime Minister Theresa May of Britain, he told her that her ambassador, Kim Darroch, was "from central casting."[31] On the first day of his presidency, just after he took the oath, he introduced Jim Mattis as, yes, "from central casting."[32]

One result of this hiring process was that nobody had ever staffed a modern White House with so few people who knew how government worked. Rather than seeking out experienced hands, he enlisted a team as unschooled and unprepared as he was. In part, this was out of disdain for expertise and "the Swamp," as he called Washington, but it was also a function of his refusal to hire anyone who had said anything critical of him during the campaign, which ruled out a large swath of Republican professionals.

Among those he did not refuse to consider, an anguished debate raged around Washington about whether to work for a president many Republicans found loathsome. Was it better to stand on principle or was there a duty to try to steer an erratic commander in chief in a responsible direction? It was a decision that tore apart friendships and families. All over town there were spouses threatening to leave if their partners went to work for *that man* while longtime associates stopped speaking to each other when one went into the administration and another refused. Some, like Dan Coats, a former Republican senator from Indiana tapped to serve as director of national intelligence, took on the new mission with the understanding that their job would be to protect their agency from the president who appointed them.

Others decided a White House job would give them a chance to push their own philosophical goals regardless of their antipathy for the president they would serve. Marc Short, a longtime conservative activist who had worked for Mike Pence among others, had served as president of Freedom Partners Chamber of Commerce, the political arm of the conservative billionaires Charles and David Koch. Short was so opposed to Trump during the primaries that he quit when the Kochs would not finance the eight-figure anti-Trump campaign that he had proposed. Now, with his old boss in the vice president's office, Short joined the Trump team as head of White House legislative affairs.

With such a small talent pool available to him, Trump wound up with a building full of amateurs and troublemaking misfits who had no idea how to craft an executive order, arrange a phone call with a foreign leader, or get lunch from the White House Mess. Trump may have believed that Reince Priebus understood how Washington worked and would serve as his ambassador to the city that had recoiled from his candidacy. But in fact, Priebus's only experience in the capital was campaign politics, which gave him an impressive rolodex of wealthy donors and media consultants but little expertise in running a government. Rex Tillerson had traveled the world negotiating deals for ExxonMobil, but that did not necessarily make him an ideal secretary of state. Jim Mattis had served in the military for decades, giving him more exposure to a large public sector bureaucracy than any of his new colleagues. But he did not have extensive experience in Washington, a battlefield quite unlike Afghanistan and Iraq. Steve Bannon, Kellyanne Conway, Jared Kushner, Ivanka Trump—none of them had ever served in government. Neither had Steven Mnuchin, the new treasury secretary, or Wilbur Ross, the new commerce secretary, or Ben Carson, the new secretary of housing and urban development, or Betsy DeVos, the new education secretary, or Peter Navarro, the trade adviser who had been recruited to the campaign after Kushner found his book on China while scrolling Amazon and read it. The twentysomething former model Hope Hicks, who had become close to Trump on the campaign as his spokesperson and now would serve in his White House as an all-purpose adviser, was so new to politics that her disgruntled ex-boyfriend Corey Lewandowski said she had confused the Koch brothers with Coke the soda. Dan Scavino, Trump's social media director and aide de camp, was once his golf caddie. Brad Parscale, his campaign strategist, was originally his website developer.

One of the few exceptions was the vice president. Mike Pence had never been Trump's favorite for running mate. He was, instead, the least common denominator after everyone else was ruled out. Barrel-chested, with perfect white hair and perfect white teeth, Pence fit the central casting requirement. A native of Indiana, he lost two races for Congress before hosting a conservative radio program for most of the 1990s, "Rush Limbaugh on decaf," as he termed it.[33] But he was just as conservative, at one point calling climate change "a myth" and insisting that "smoking doesn't kill."[34] In 2000, he finally won a seat in the House, where he served for twelve years. He liked to say he was "a Christian, a conservative and a Republican in that order" and with the help of the Koch brothers was elected governor in 2012.[35] The most memorable moment of his term came when he was forced to back down on a religious freedom law allowing businesses to refuse to serve gay and lesbian customers after a boycott threat by sports leagues and major corporations.

Trump thought Pence was weak and unimpressive. At one point during the primaries, he heard about a poll showing Pence trailing for re-election in Indiana. "Why would I want a guy like that to be my VP?" Trump asked aides on his campaign plane.[36] But his family and staff rallied behind Pence, seeing him as reassuring to both the Republican establishment and the conservative movement. It was an odd marriage. How could a devoted evangelical Christian serve a foul-mouthed, thrice-married vulgarian who boasted of grabbing women by their pussy? What mix of ambition, duty, and expedience led to this bargain?

When the *Access Hollywood* tape came out, Pence's wife, Karen, was outraged and pushed him to drop off the ticket. But Pence concluded it was too late. His wife did little to hide her disgust. On election night, when the improbable happened, the vice-president-elect approached her backstage to celebrate.

"Do I get a congratulations kiss?" he asked within earshot of others.

"Don't push your luck, Mike," she answered. "You already got what you wanted."[37]

Faced with assembling a White House, Priebus set out looking for experienced staff. Karl Rove, the strategist who helped elect George W. Bush twice, recommended he track down Joe Hagin, who after fourteen years in Republican administrations had spent perhaps as much time in the modern White House as anyone. Hagin, who most recently had served as Bush's deputy chief of staff for operations, was the kind of official who knew how to organize a presidential trip to a war zone, renovate the Situation Room, upgrade the secure communications on Air Force One, or establish a new cabinet department.

Priebus asked Hagin to come back to his old workplace for twelve months or less to help set up Trump's White House. While reluctant, Hagin agreed, reasoning that it would be no good for the country if everyone turned down Trump. But he quickly recognized this would be like no other White House. Sitting in the lobby of the offices in Trump Tower one day, he saw the glass doors suddenly fly open and a glamorous woman in furs sweep in followed by an entourage. Hagin asked the receptionist who that was.

"That's Omarosa," the receptionist said.

"What the hell's an Omarosa?" he asked.

"Don't you watch *The Apprentice*?" she asked.

The opening days of Trump's administration were the most chaotic of any in modern history, which was perhaps no surprise given the team of amateurs Trump had assembled.

Prodded by Steve Bannon, who urged him to "hit, hit, hit" in the administration's opening days, Trump wanted to demonstrate action with a flurry of executive orders that he had promised on the campaign trail.[38] He did not care if neither he nor any of his new advisers knew how to do it. The point was how it looked—how *he* looked—not whether the orders were done right, or even legally.

Trump quickly reversed the government's opposition to the Keystone XL Pipeline and pulled the United States out of the Trans-Pacific Partnership trade deal with Asian allies that Barack Obama had negotiated. He ordered government agencies to delay or waive certain provisions of Obama's Affordable Care Act. He signed a couple orders meant to pave the way for planning his wall along the border. His absurd claim that Mexico would somehow pay for the wall, though, quickly blew up the relationship with America's southern neighbor when Trump insisted on it during an introductory phone call with President Enrique Peña Nieto, who called it "completely unacceptable" and immediately canceled a trip to Washington in response. A lot of this had not been thought through or subjected to the scrutiny of a real process. "Some of the executive orders came in looking like crayon on the back of a napkin," moaned one of the few advisers who had served in government before. "It was that bad."

The most emblematic moment came when Trump tried to translate his campaign vow of "a total and complete shutdown of Muslims entering the United States" into an actual policy that would pass legal muster.[39] On his first Monday in office, stunned career officials obtained and began slipping each other bootleg copies of a draft executive order imposing an indefinite ban on new Syrian refugees, a 120-day ban on new refugees from anywhere else, and a ninety-day ban on all travelers from seven predominantly Muslim nations. The president planned to sign it during a visit to the Pentagon that Friday, leaving no time for a policy review, much less a plan to implement it.

As the lawyers on the White House staff examined the document, they grew alarmed, concluding it was so sloppy that it would not get past a first-year law school seminar. But Bannon and Stephen Miller had their feet on the pedal, revving the engine.

"You can't do this, it's not going to be ready," protested Rob Porter, who was supposed to vet documents before they were signed by the president.

"Do whatever you need to do," Bannon instructed, "but we're going to sign it."

Porter and other lawyers worked through much of the night trying to turn the inchoate draft into something resembling a legal document. No one had time to review all the case law. Porter coordinated with the Justice Department's Office of Legal Counsel, which had the responsibility to sign off on the "form and legality" of such orders before they were signed, but there was no Trump political appointee there yet, only the career staff lawyers, who kept pointing out flaws in the document.

The morning of the planned event, it had still not been approved by the Justice Department. "I don't think we're going to be ready to sign the travel ban," Porter told Bannon and Reince Priebus. "It's not going to be ready."

"Well, it *has* to be ready," Priebus said.

Porter explained that the Justice Department had not signed off yet.

"Is there a law that says we have to do that?" Bannon asked.

Porter was floored. No, he explained, there was no law requiring it, but it had been the standard procedure for years and it would be foolish to suddenly abandon that legal safeguard. But Trump, it turned out, was not the only one willing to bust norms.

With Priebus and Bannon making clear that there would be no delay, Porter got back on the phone with the Justice Department lawyers and scrambled to make whatever edits he could. He printed the latest version and brought it in the motorcade to the Pentagon with Trump. Upon arriving, Trump went on a tour with Priebus, Bannon, and Jim Mattis while Porter and Stephen Miller huddled in a back room, scrambling to finish the incomplete order that was minutes away from being signed. With the Justice Department lawyers on the phone, Porter typed in changes they dictated, then emailed the latest draft to his office back at the White House for an aide to print out on official parchment paper and then rush in a White House car to deliver to the Pentagon.

As Trump returned from the tour, Porter was still on the line with the Justice Department lawyers, who had not given their sign-off. "We're signing this in five minutes," Porter was told. He quickly scrawled in by hand the last edits required by the lawyers just as the president was about to appear on live television. Fortunately, the changes were not on the first page that Trump held up for the cameras.

The handling of the whole thing was so slipshod that few in the administration had even been notified that the order was about to be signed. Mattis, who had publicly criticized Trump's proposed Muslim ban during the campaign, was not told what order the president would be signing and immediately resented being forced into the picture memorializing a policy he found noxious.

John Kelly, who as secretary of homeland security was in charge of putting the policy into place, had known the order was being drafted but not how imminently it was to be unveiled. He was aboard a Coast Guard plane flying from Miami to Washington on a conference call with aides discussing the implications of the order when someone cut in to let him know that CNN was reporting that the president had just signed it.

Stunned, Kelly now had to figure out what to do. The order was going into effect immediately, with no transition time, and no one had been told how it would work. Hundreds of people now officially barred from the United States were already on airplanes heading there. What would happen when they landed? Would they be detained? Sent immediately back? No one could say. None of the nation's airports or border guard posts was prepared. Suddenly, airports became scenes of anarchy. Lawyers raced to the scene to offer help to travelers. Within hours, courts started to weigh in; ultimately, five judges separately ordered a halt to Trump's first major decision.

For Kelly, the week-old Trump administration had already been one shock to the system after another—so much so that he had almost quit before he even took office. A retired four-star Marine general who had served under Mattis, he had agreed to join the cabinet on the same theory that animated many others, that the untested president would need a crew of steady hands. But despite promises that he would have a say in who worked under him, he kept fighting the incoming White House team over new hires made without checking with him. One day, when Trump was scheduled to meet with Kris Kobach, an immigration hardliner serving as secretary of state in Kansas, Reince Priebus implored the president not to offer a job on the spot. Trump, of course, offered him a job on the spot, inviting Kobach to be deputy homeland security secretary. Kelly was incensed when he heard about it and even more when Kobach listed his expectations for the job. He was to have his own Secret Service detail, round-the-clock access to a government plane, a staff of dozens answering directly to him, and a separate office near the border in addition to one in Washington. Moreover, he informed Kelly, it was his understanding that he would be a "co-equal" with the secretary in charge of immigration while Kelly handled other duties. A strict military chain of command guy, Kelly told the White House he would not accept this. Ultimately, Priebus had to retract the job offer.

Kelly was also angered when the White House resisted his decision to elevate Kevin McAleenan, the deputy commissioner of Customs and Border Protection, to head the agency. The week of the inauguration, Kelly grew so exasperated he declared that he was going to resign even though he had not been sworn in yet. Aides had to talk him off the ledge and convince him to stay. He did, and won the round on McAleenan too.

But it would not be the last blowup. Within weeks, Kelly was in another scrap with the White House, this time over his selection of Randolph "Tex" Alles, a retired Marine major general, to lead the Secret Service, a pick that again generated resistance. "Fine, I'll put the choice in your hands," a colleague remembered Kelly telling the White House. "Tex either becomes the head of Secret Service or you get a new secretary of homeland security." Alles got the job and Kelly kept his.

Of all the collaborators Trump would bring with him to the White House, none would cause a bigger furor—or better presage the larger threats to his presidency—than Michael Flynn, the ramrod-straight retired lieutenant general who set up shop in the northwest corner office previously occupied by the likes of Henry Kissinger, Brent Scowcroft, and Colin Powell.

Flynn had been Trump's chief foreign policy adviser in the campaign and, for a time, one of the candidate's favorites. Trim and intense, with a cropped haircut and military bearing after thirty-three years in the Army,

Flynn exuded perpetual energy that he sometimes could not focus, a "rat on acid," as a staffer once put it.[40] He came from a family with a long history in the armed forces; his father fought in the Battle of the Bulge under George Patton and both Mike and his brother would rise through the ranks to become general officers. Flynn served in Afghanistan and Iraq before becoming director of the Defense Intelligence Agency but was forced out in 2014 after being accused of an abusive management style and a loose relationship with the truth. He blamed Barack Obama, insisting the president did not take the threat of Islamic terrorism seriously enough.

The retired general eagerly joined the campaign of the man seeking to undo the Obama presidency, ingratiating himself to Trump during the campaign with his fierce denunciations of Hillary Clinton and so impressing the candidate that he even considered making Flynn his vice presidential running mate. Trump, whose admiration for Vladimir Putin had generated widespread suspicions during a campaign rocked by Russia's release of hacked Democratic emails, was unbothered by Flynn's own curious ties to Moscow. After leaving the military, Flynn had flown to Moscow to give a speech for $45,000 as part of an anniversary celebration for RT, the Russian state's English-language propaganda network, even sitting next to Putin at a gala dinner. Nor did Trump seem to care that while advising his campaign, Flynn was also working on behalf of Turkish interests without registering as a foreign lobbyist. After the election, Trump brushed off warnings from Chris Christie and even Obama to steer clear of Flynn, whom they considered a "dangerously loose cannon," as the New Jersey governor put it.[41]

But if Trump was dismissive, expecting the Russia furor from the campaign to fade once he took office, he was wrong. In the weeks leading up to his inauguration, Trump became increasingly sensitive to intelligence reports that Russia had intervened in the election on his behalf—and to the fact that the FBI was examining his campaign's interactions with Moscow. In early January, Trump grew irate when James Comey, the FBI director, privately informed him about a dossier compiled by Christopher Steele, a former British agent making unverified claims about Trump's ties to Russia, including a sensational but unsubstantiated story involving prostitutes urinating on each other on a hotel bed in Moscow once used by a visiting Obama. He was even madder when, a few days later, the Steele dossier was published by the website *BuzzFeed News*, blaming Comey for giving the media a hook to report the dossier by briefing him about it.[42]

Flynn was making matters worse. On the same day in December that

Obama imposed sanctions on Russia for its pro-Trump election interference, Flynn spoke by phone with Sergey Kislyak, the Russian ambassador, not once or twice but five times, at one point urging Moscow not to escalate in response to the sanctions and suggesting the new administration would reverse Obama's tougher policy.

A week before the inauguration, the *Washington Post* columnist David Ignatius revealed Flynn's contacts with Kislyak.[43] Flynn insisted to Mike Pence, Reince Priebus, and Sean Spicer that he did not discuss sanctions with the ambassador, a reassurance that the vice president and press secretary then repeated publicly. But the Russian ambassador's phone calls were routinely monitored, and FBI agents knew that Flynn's denial was untrue. So just after the inauguration, they met with Flynn at the White House to ask about the conversations with Kislyak only to be surprised when he repeated that sanctions did not come up.

Sally Yates, the deputy attorney general under Obama who was now running the Justice Department until Trump's nomination of Jeff Sessions was confirmed, went to the White House to tell Donald F. McGahn II, the White House counsel, that Flynn had lied, suggesting it made him vulnerable to blackmail. Trump had already begun to sour on Flynn, in part because the retired general had hired his own grown son to work on the transition and the son had promoted a bizarre conspiracy theory on Twitter about a pedophile ring supposedly run by Hillary Clinton out of the basement of a Washington pizza parlor.

The White House took no action against Flynn after Yates's warning. Instead, Trump fired Yates herself four days later, when she refused to defend his hastily drafted travel ban in court. This was the first decapitation by a president who would soon become as famous for dumping government officials as he had been for dismissing reality show contestants. More than a week later, McGahn learned that the *Post* was about to publish a story quoting a spokesman for Flynn acknowledging that he may have discussed sanctions with the ambassador after all.[44] McGahn interrupted Trump and Priebus, who were having dinner in the White House residence, to let them know.

Priebus rushed to the West Wing in a rage and summoned Flynn to the Situation Room, where he grilled the national security adviser.

"Did you or did you not talk about sanctions to the Russian ambassador?" Priebus demanded.

"Well, I don't *think* I did," Flynn answered.

"Are you kidding me?" Priebus erupted.

A White House lawyer mentioned that the FBI had a transcript of the call between Flynn and Kislyak, so Priebus ordered it brought to the White House. As he read it, Pence's face hardened and he shook his head no. "I can't believe this," he said. "It's not what he said to me."[45]

Pence and Priebus called Trump in the White House residence and filled him in. "He's either lying or has got the world's worst memory," Priebus said. Trump took the weekend to think about it but by the following Monday, with the press bearing down, he decided to fire Flynn. Priebus summoned the national security adviser to his office.

"This conversation's not going to end well," Priebus said. "You can either resign or I'm going to fire you. You can take your pick."

Flynn did not object. "Well, I'll resign," he said.

He had lasted twenty-four days.

CHAPTER 3

Never Put Rupert Murdoch on Hold!

I t was only his twenty-eighth day in office, but Trump was already picking his third White House communications director. His first choice had to back out before even starting the job because of a sex scandal. His second choice was only brought on in an acting capacity. And so the matter was of some urgency by the time Mike Dubke came to meet Trump in the Oval Office on the morning of February 16.

Tall and husky with an easy youthful grin, Dubke was a veteran Republican operative who specialized in advertising for candidates and industry groups. When his business partner turned down the White House job and recommended him instead, Dubke decided it was an opportunity that was hard to refuse for someone who had spent a life in politics. Trump could not have cared less about his résumé. He dispensed with the usual job interview questions and went straight to what was on his mind.

"Do you think I should do a press conference?" Trump asked Dubke.

Dubke was not sure if this was a test, but gamely said yes. "Next week would be good," he offered.

Next week? Trump did not want to wait that long. "What if I want to do it sooner?"

"Everyone is working for you," Dubke answered ambiguously.

"I think today is a good day," Trump declared.

By this point, it was clear that he was serious. Typically, a full-scale formal presidential news conference required preparation, briefing, and even rehearsals—especially the first one of a new administration. In the back of the room, Reince Priebus and Sean Spicer sat up and took notice.

"Well, Mr. President, I would not do it in the briefing room. It has to be more presidential than that," Dubke ventured. A statelier setting such as the East Room would be more appropriate. "I don't think you can do it today."

Trump shouted to aides sitting in his outer office. "Will you call the usher and see if we can get the East Room set for a press conference?"

In the Trump White House, it was becoming clear, impulse and instinct ruled. Priebus and Spicer rushed to alert everyone. By just after noon, Trump marched into the East Room for his first presidential news conference.

It was anything but presidential. For an hour and seventeen minutes, Trump held forth with a raw and angry defense of both his administration and his character. At times abrupt, often rambling, characteristically boastful yet seemingly pained at the portrayals of him, he lashed out at the media. "The press, honestly, is out of control," he said. Channeling Steve Bannon, he spoke of the "entrenchment" of a corrupt "power structure." He complained about CNN and the "failing *New York Times*." Again and again, he returned to a favorite new phrase. "It's all fake news," he said. "It's all fake news." Later, he amended himself. It wasn't just "fake news" he was complaining about. It was "very fake news."

Trump in recent weeks had starting using the attack line that, arguably more than any other, would come to be associated with his presidency. "You're fake news!" he had raged in January at CNN's White House correspondent, Jim Acosta—his first spoken utterance of what would become his standard-issue insult.[1] But his embrace of "fake news" was, in fact, an act of shameless linguistic larceny. In the three months since his upset win, the term had initially been popularized to describe the torrent of false information spread online on Trump's behalf. *BuzzFeed News* reporter Craig Silverman had been first to do so, breaking a story a few days before the election about fake news troll farms in Macedonia that had been disseminating lies favoring Trump to American voters via Facebook.[2] In a December speech after Trump won, Hillary Clinton had used the phrase herself, complaining about "the epidemic of malicious fake news and false propaganda that flooded social media over the past year."[3]

Now Trump was appropriating a label favored by his critics and turning it around on them, a bit of political jujitsu that proved to be stunningly successful. "Fake news" stopped being about the avalanche of pro-Trump falsehoods and became instead Trump's weapon in a rapidly expanding war on the media that would become a hallmark of his tenure. "He decided to take it and turn it into his term, and to take ownership of it and use it as a cudgel to beat the media," Silverman reflected later.[4]

The day after his news conference, Trump was fuming about the coverage of it and adopted what would become another signature term. Shortly after landing in Florida for a weekend at his Mar-a-Lago club, he tweeted: "The FAKE NEWS media (failing @nytimes, @CNN, @NBCNews and many more) is not my enemy, it is the enemy of the American people. SICK!" Only a couple weeks into his tenure, Trump had already gone far beyond the rhetorical press-bashing favored by Republicans since Richard Nixon, demonizing the media with terminology more often used by the world's autocrats and dictators. While Nixon told Henry Kissinger behind closed doors that "the press is the enemy" and secretly had an "enemies list" that included journalists as well as Democrats, he understood that it would not be good to advertise it; the list only became public as part of the Watergate investigation and Nixon himself kept his most scathing rants about the press private.

Presidents in Western democracies simply did not employ such language, which evoked tyrannies like Stalin's Soviet Union, where "enemy of the people" was the official designation used to condemn millions to the Gulag. In his 1956 secret speech denouncing Stalin, Nikita Khrushchev perhaps best explained the true horror of the phrase. "Stalin originated the concept 'enemy of the people,'" he said. "This term automatically rendered it unnecessary that the ideological errors of a man or men engaged in a controversy be proven; this term made possible the usage of the most cruel repression, violating all norms of revolutionary legality, against anyone who in any way disagreed with Stalin."[5] Yet even after its historical antecedents were the subject of endless public commentary, Trump had no qualms about repeating it hundreds more times over the course of his presidency.

For a man who needed enemies, the mainstream media proved a convenient foil. "The opposition party," as Steve Bannon described the news industry.[6] It was calculated, purposeful, and as indispensable to Trump's political persona as the endless stream of Twitter insults he deployed to wage the fight. "I have a running war with the media," he told an audience on his first full day in office.[7] The goal was to neutralize one of the major independent power centers in Washington, with Trump in effect telling supporters to trust no one but him and his "alternative facts," in the memorable phrase introduced by Kellyanne Conway on *Meet the Press* two days into Trump's presidency.[8]

It was, though, a love-hate relationship. He loathed the media and craved it in almost equal proportions. His decades coming up as a New York developer and reality show star whose adventurous love life and spectacular bankruptcies had landed him repeatedly on tabloid covers had left him firmly in the all-publicity-is-good-publicity school. He once told his campaign adviser Brad Parscale, "There's no bad press unless you're a pedophile." And it was a mutual dependence. In the 2016 campaign, he had dominated the news in a way that no other untested, unelected candidate ever had, trailed by cameras everywhere he went from the minute he descended that golden escalator at Trump Tower to greet a bought-and-paid-for crowd of sign-wavers earning $50 each. His rallies were aired live from start to finish on cable networks that found the unpredictable rants to be ratings boosters. "It may not be good for America," Les Moonves, the network's chief executive, famously said, "but it's damn good for CBS."[9]

But as the campaign accelerated and Trump moved from curiosity to contender, the mainstream coverage turned tougher and Trump chose a strategy of performative confrontation, banning certain news organizations from even covering his rallies, while at the same time working closely with the pro-Trump amplifiers at Fox News and *Breitbart News*, the alt-right website that Bannon ran until formally joining Trump's campaign. At that opening news conference in the East Room, Trump objected to how he was portrayed. "The tone is such hatred," he complained. "I'm really not a bad person." His preferred model was Fox. "They have the most honest morning show, that's all I can say," he proclaimed. "It's the most honest."[10]

His staff soon got the hint. They spent much of their time making appearances on Fox while battling with the rest of the media. Under pressure from Trump to be combative, Sean Spicer, the new White House press secretary, seemed almost eager to pick fights during his briefings, only to be lampooned by Melissa McCarthy on *Saturday Night Live*, a running gag that cost him with the president, who thought being played by a woman made his spokesman look weak.

Some journalists instinctively resisted Trump's us-against-them framework. "We're not at war," Martin Baron, the executive editor of *The Washington Post*, said a few weeks into the administration. "We're at work."[11] Still, his newspaper's new slogan, "Democracy Dies in Darkness," introduced days after that opening news conference, was hardly subtle and for many in the media, it was indeed a war, an existential moment in the life of the country that required new rules. MSNBC and CNN leaned heavily into critical commentary about the disruptive new presidency, increasingly blurring the traditional lines between reporting and punditry. Producers found fewer Trump surrogates they were willing to put on air to make statements their audiences considered untruthful and offensive, while the president's allies became less willing to appear on networks they deemed overtly hostile.

Trump thought all of it benefited him in the end, and his fake-news, enemy-of-the-people diatribes grew ever more incendiary at the campaign-style rallies he soon began holding again, dispensing with any notion that he should be more "presidential" now that he was in office. As he whipped crowds into a frenzy, red-faced supporters would turn toward the press risers shouting at the assembled reporters and even threatening violence, so much so that the television networks hired security guards to accompany their White House correspondents.

"Why are you doing this?" Lesley Stahl of CBS News asked Trump about the media bashing during an off-camera conversation.

"You know why I do it?" Trump replied. "I do it to discredit you all and demean you all so when you write negative stories about me, no one will believe you."[12]

One day early in his presidency, Trump was in the Oval Office on the telephone with his daughter Ivanka when Madeleine Westerhout, his assistant, stuck her head in the door.

Rupert Murdoch was on the line, she reported. "Would you like me to tell him you will call back?" she asked.

Trump erupted like Mount St. Helens, as Westerhout later recalled. "Never put Rupert Murdoch on hold!" he shouted at her. "Never!"[13]

To Trump, talking with Murdoch was more important than just about anything. No one played a more central role in Trump's media world than the Australian-born impresario of conservative journalism who owned Fox News, Fox Business, *The Wall Street Journal,* the *New York Post,* and other properties. If the mainstream news outlets were the new president's enemies, Murdoch's empire was to be his prime ally, amplifying his messages, taking on his adversaries, shaping the debate, and influencing his thinking. Fox was a source of power and a source of inspiration, an endless feedback loop in which the president took his cues from the network's shows while its anchors delivered his party line.

For decades, Murdoch had coveted a close relationship with an American president but never had that kind of intimacy. At one point during the 2008 campaign, he had even taken an interest in Barack Obama, met with him and flirted with the notion of endorsing the Democrat, which would have been a huge break from his conservative roots. But Roger Ailes, the former Republican operative who created Fox News for Murdoch, got wind of what was happening and threatened to quit. Murdoch backed off.

With 2016 approaching, he finally saw his chance in Trump. Not that he thought much of the reality television star. The two had first met in the 1970s through Roy Cohn, the infamous lawyer-fixer who gained fame hunting communists for Joseph McCarthy and later mentored Trump. Murdoch always saw Trump as something of a poser. "This is a guy who has no regard for Donald Trump. None," said one longtime Murdoch associate. "He thought he was a fraud. It's one billionaire looking at another billionaire saying, 'He's not a billionaire, he's not of my ilk.'" But Murdoch also thought Trump was "the perfect vessel" because "he's not that smart."

Trump had been courting Murdoch's team at Fox for years, particularly the hosts of the morning show *Fox & Friends*. Starting in the spring of 2011, while pushing the lie that Obama was not actually born in the United States, Trump began going on the show once a week, every Monday. Arguably those years of appearances were as important to his rise to the presidency as *The Apprentice*, introducing him to conservative viewers who would become his political base.

Still, even at Fox, Trump was seen by some hosts more as a celebrity curiosity than a serious political force. On the day he announced his candidacy for the White House in June 2015, Dana Perino, a former White House press secretary for George W. Bush who had become a Fox anchor, mocked his promise to force Mexico to pay for his border wall.

"On what planet could that actually happen?" Perino asked on *The Five*.

"Planet Trump," replied Greg Gutfeld, one of her cohosts.[14]

Murdoch was not yet ready to move to Planet Trump. "When is Donald Trump going to stop embarrassing his friends, let alone the whole country?"[15] Murdoch wrote on Twitter a few weeks later after Trump scorned John McCain's war service. There was still an assumption that Trump was a sideshow while one of the other Republican candidates would win the nomination.

But soon after, a clash with one of the network's top female anchors reset the terms of Trump's dealings with Fox—in Trump's favor. His feud with Megyn Kelly had begun a few weeks after Trump's announcement, when she aired a segment about newly reported divorce papers from his first marriage in which Ivana Trump claimed that her husband had once raped her. Kelly had invited on her show a *Daily Beast* reporter who wrote about the matter, then pressed the journalist on whether it was fair to Trump given that his ex-wife had later retracted the claim.

But Trump was in a rage that Kelly had even brought up the rape allegation, and he called Roger Ailes, who then told Kelly to call the upset candidate to smooth it over before a scheduled appearance on her program.

"You had no business putting it on your show!" Trump railed at Kelly over the phone. "Oh, I almost unleashed my beautiful Twitter account against you, and I still may."

"You don't control the editorial content on *The Kelly File*, Mr. Trump," she replied.

"That's it!" he shouted. "You're a disgrace! You should be ashamed of yourself. You should be ashamed of yourself!"[16] He hung up and canceled that night's appearance.

A few days later, Kelly arrived in Cleveland for the first Republican presidential debate. She was to be one of three moderators and she approached Bill Sammon, the Fox News managing editor for Washington, with an extra question she wanted to throw in to confront Trump about his history of misogynistic comments about women.

Then, just hours before the debate was to begin, Sammon's phone rang. It was Trump.

"I heard Megyn has some totally unfair bombshell question she's going to hit me with," Trump said.

Sammon's blood ran cold. *How did he know? Did they have a leak?*

"What do you think this question is?" Sammon asked.

"My divorce papers finally got unsealed and my ex-wife used the word 'rape,'" Trump said.

Sammon breathed a sigh of relief. Kelly had no plans to bring that up during the debate. Trump did not actually have an inside line on what was coming. Sammon told Trump that he was not in the business of telegraphing questions in advance of a debate. "But I can tell you," he added, "if you think we're sitting around here looking through your divorce papers and trying to think of questions based off of allegations from your ex-wife, I mean, that's just not where our head is at."

At the debate, with millions of Americans watching, Kelly did not mention the rape charge, but challenged Trump as he had rarely been taken on before.

"You've called women you don't like 'fat pigs,' 'dogs,' 'slobs' and 'disgusting animals,'" she began.

"Only Rosie O'Donnell," Trump interjected, prompting laughter.

"For the record, it was well beyond Rosie O'Donnell," Kelly corrected.

"Yes," Trump acknowledged, "I'm sure it was."

Kelly went on. "You once told a contestant on *Celebrity Apprentice* it would be a pretty picture to see her on her knees. Does that sound to you like the temperament of a man we should elect as president?"

Trump denounced the question as political correctness run amok, then turned on Kelly. "Honestly, Megyn, if you don't like it, I'm sorry," he said dismissively. "I've been very nice to you, although I could probably maybe not be, based on the way you have treated me."[17]

The debate proved to be must-see television. Altogether, 24 million Americans tuned in, making it the most watched presidential primary debate in history.[18] All anyone could talk about was the confrontation between Trump and Kelly.

Trump called Ailes at home afterward to complain. "I thought you were my friend, Roger," he snapped.[19] His protest worked. When Ailes reached Bill Sammon, instead of crowing about the ratings, he let his bureau chief have it.

"What the hell was that?" Ailes demanded. "Why did she hit him so hard?"

Sammon explained that it was a legitimate question, but Ailes was hardly mollified.

Neither was Trump. The next night he went on CNN and lashed out at Kelly in crudely personal terms that had the effect of validating the premise of her question. "You could see there was blood coming out of her eyes, blood coming out of her—wherever," he told Don Lemon, a remark instantly interpreted as implying she was menstruating.[20] Trump did not drop the matter either. He made good on his threat to turn his "beautiful Twitter" on her and berated the anchor relentlessly for months.

This was the moment, in the view of some network insiders, that Trump effectively cowed Fox News into submission. For years, Republicans had largely deferred to the network. Ailes was the kingmaker and Republicans who wanted to be president genuflected to him. The network's unofficial motto when dealing with pushback from politicians, or anyone else, some Fox veterans joked, was "Fuck me? Fuck you!"

But not with Trump. Ailes was flummoxed by him. "Roger didn't know how to control him," said one senior network official. Where once he would have shut down anyone who attacked one of his stars like Kelly, barring the offender from Fox's air, and effectively sucking the oxygen from a Republican, Ailes responded to Trump's attacks by trying to appease him, calling him almost daily to defuse the rift. A couple times, after a particularly offensive Trump insult aimed at Kelly, the network put out a statement pushing back, only to retreat again when the candidate heaped on more abuse.

What Ailes saw in Trump that he did not see in any other Republican politician of recent years was someone who connected with the Fox audience even more than Fox did. As the next debate approached, Ailes demanded to see the questions in advance. Network executives told Sammon to put him off. For the first time, Ailes's own staff was not sure they could trust him. Was he trying to protect Trump? Sammon could not avoid Ailes forever but was purposely vague when they eventually talked and never gave the specific questions. "We were withholding stuff from the boss because we didn't know if it would be secure," said a Fox journalist aware of the situation.

What lines there used to be between newsmakers and the news organization were increasingly blurred. A Fox producer sent daily emails to a Trump campaign list summarizing the latest news developments while offering suggestions about how, for instance, to reply to a Hillary Clinton speech. When Diana Falzone, a Fox reporter, uncovered allegations that Trump had had an extramarital tryst with a porn star who went by the professional name of Stormy Daniels and negotiated a cash settlement buying her silence, the story was quashed. "Good reporting, kiddo," her boss told her, according to a report by Jane Mayer in *The New Yorker*. "But Rupert wants Donald Trump to win. So just let it go."[21]

Not only was the old Ailes gone, soon enough so was the new one. In July 2016, just as the Republicans were meeting to formally nominate Trump, Ailes was pushed out by Fox over sexual harassment allegations. To many, it seemed like the final transition. Blessed by Murdoch, right-wing TV became Trump TV.

For Ailes, it was a bitter finale to a long career as power broker of the American right. By early 2017, he was living in a sort of exile. Megyn Kelly, his onetime protégée, left the network two weeks before the inauguration. Her coveted 9 p.m. time slot went to Tucker Carlson, a Trump favorite and rising star in the universe of nighttime pot-stirrers. And the "Fair and Balanced" motto that Ailes had crafted for Fox, always ironic in the eyes of its critics, was officially retired.

Ailes had tried to insinuate himself back into Trump's favor after his ouster from Fox, serving as an adviser for the fall debates and calling up Steve Bannon shortly before the election proposing to launch an actual Trump TV network once the candidate lost. Trump's unexpected victory mooted that idea and the president-elect kept Ailes at a distance. Shortly before he died in the spring of 2017, Ailes complained to a former colleague that Murdoch had not only betrayed him but iced him out of the relationship with Trump.

"Rupert talks to him every day," Ailes said bitterly. "I never talk with him."

Whether it was daily or not, Murdoch did enjoy unprecedented access to Trump and his White House. Rick Gates, the Trump campaign aide, said Murdoch was "absolutely one of Trump's top outside advisers," and estimated that Trump or Jared Kushner spoke with Murdoch once a week; some suggested Kushner was on the phone with the media mogul even more often than that.[22] The two families were close enough that Wendi Deng Murdoch brought Jared and Ivanka back together after a break-up, the Murdoch daughters served as flower girls at the resulting wedding, and the young couple vacationed on the Murdoch yacht. Ivanka for years helped oversee a $300 million trust fund for Murdoch's children, a position she gave up only after her father was elected. "Rupert's been a lot better to me than Roger ever was," Trump was overheard saying on a live microphone before an interview with Maria Bartiromo, one of the most supportive of the Fox hosts.[23]

Once he was in the White House, the relationship between Trump and Fox grew closer and the president regularly gave interviews to Carlson, Bartiromo, Sean Hannity, Jeanine Pirro, and his other favorite hosts. In his first two years in office, he would grant forty-nine interviews to Fox, compared with just thirteen for all the other major networks combined.[24] He even rated the Fox personalities, Mayer disclosed, based on their loyalty to him. Bret Baier, anchor of the nightly *Special Report* and one of the leading figures on the news side of the Fox operation, got a six. Hannity, who often heard from Trump immediately after his show was over, was a ten. Steve Doocy, one of the *Fox & Friends* hosts known for his on-air admiration of Trump, got a twelve.

But it was not always clear who was setting the agenda. Was Trump dictating to the network or was he taking his cues from it? One top Fox journalist compared it to a Fred Astaire–Ginger Rogers dance—sometimes Trump "was driving the conversation," sometimes the Fox hosts were.

On the Friday night after Trump's incendiary news conference, Carlson aired a six-minute segment describing a crisis of violence in Sweden ignited by a recent wave of Muslim immigration and covered up by the government. "That is grotesque," Carlson declared.[25] Trump was watching. The next day, he threw a line into a speech suggesting that a terrorist attack had happened "last night in Sweden."[26] Except there had been no terrorist attack. Just like that, the president created a diplomatic dispute with a longtime American ally that resented his false characterization.

Undaunted, Trump would do it again. And again. And again. In just one year of his presidency, he would tweet in response to something he saw on Fox News or Fox Business 657 times, according to a count by Media Matters for America, a liberal monitoring group.[27] It got to the point that White House aides watched *Fox & Friends* or made sure to check out the transcript later to get a sense of how their day might go. Trump loved it when Fox went after his enemies, asserted grand conspiracies that he embraced, and stoked grievances over his treatment by the professional Washington crowd. "Fox was the gas station where Trump stopped to fill up his tank of resentment," Brian Stelter, the CNN media critic, wrote in *Hoax*, his book on the conservative network.[28]

It did not take long for White House aides, cabinet secretaries, and members of Congress to get wise to this unique symbiosis between president and network—and to begin lobbying Trump via Fox. During an early congressional debate on repealing Barack Obama's health care program, Trump saw Representative Jim Jordan, a Republican from Ohio and one of the leading conservative flame-throwers in the House, and mentioned that he had watched the congressman on Fox that morning. Jordan later summoned aides and told them to start booking him on shows if he had a message for the president. "Every time we were on TV, we weren't just talking to people in the television audience; we were talking to POTUS," Jordan observed.[29] Whenever the president's political adviser Brad Parscale needed help getting a point through to Trump, he called Sean Hannity, who could either raise the issue on his show or directly by phone with the president. "The two most effective ways of communicating with Trump are *Fox & Friends* and *Hannity*," Newt Gingrich said early in Trump's tenure.[30] Even Senator Lindsey Graham, a Republican from South Carolina who would become one of the president's chief allies, found that sometimes it was better to go on Hannity's show than to call Trump directly. "He'd listen more on a TV program than if you were with him. A lot," Graham said. "I'd tell Sean, 'You've got to ask me this question.'"

Fox benefited not only by its unprecedented power in the White House; there were also crass commercial gains from being the official network of Trump. By the end of 2017, Fox was attracting 1.5 million daytime viewers and 2.4 million in prime time, way up from the year before and far ahead of MSNBC and CNN; by Trump's last year in office, that would climb to 1.9 million during the day and 3.6 million at night.[31] It was, as Megyn Kelly put it in her memoir, "television crack cocaine" for the network.[32] Soon enough, not only were Democrats increasingly scarce on Fox, so were conservative contributors who did not toe the Trump line such as George Will and Rich Lowry, who lost their contracts. "It's a pure business decision," said one Fox insider.

The Fox personalities were not the only ones in the conservative media world who flip-flopped on Trump. During the Republican primaries, Brent Bozell, president of the Media Research Center and a Ted Cruz supporter, called Trump "the greatest charlatan of them all," lamenting, "God help this country if this man were president."[33] But once Trump secured the nomination, Bozell changed his mind, attacking Trump's critics at the Cleveland convention with signs saying, "DON'T BELIEVE THE LIBERAL MEDIA."[34] Hugh Hewitt, host of a syndicated talk show on the Salem Radio Network, exposed Trump's deep ignorance about national security during the campaign by asking him about topics like the nuclear triad and Iran's Quds Force only to have the candidate fumble through confused or nonsensical answers. "Don't be fucking around with me like that!"[35] Trump screamed at Hewitt over the phone the next day. Hewitt later called on Trump to drop out after the *Access Hollywood* tape was released. But Hewitt would become an important validator for Trump on the right after he took office, at one point urging fellow conservatives to "find the good and praise it."[36]

Still, Fox remained the president's focus, not to mention a feeder source of personnel for the Trump administration. Trump would eventually hire straight off the Fox airwaves a national security adviser, a deputy chief of staff, a press secretary, multiple communications directors, cabinet secretaries, ambassadors, and the top spokespeople for the State and Treasury Departments. At one point, an adviser even tried to sell him on naming the Fox legal commentator Andrew Napolitano, a former local judge in New Jersey, to the Supreme Court; Trump met with Napolitano and invited him to make the case for himself, although he was probably just humoring him.

For Murdoch, the Trump takeover in Washington was not just a political proposition but a business one. In 2014, he had tried to buy Time Warner, only to be rebuffed. So when Time Warner agreed in 2016 to be acquired by AT&T for $85 billion, making it the nation's largest media company and a threat to the 21st Century Fox empire, he felt burned and looked for ways to thwart the merger. Trump was so eager to declare himself publicly on Murdoch's side he did not even wait for the deal to be formally announced. On the same Saturday in October that the AT&T board of directors was making its final decision on the merger, they picked up their phones to discover that Trump had already vowed to block the deal if he were elected president, "because it's too much concentration of power in the hands of too few."[37]

Trump was hardly concerned about the danger of monopolies in a free society. His real problem with the merger was the fact that Time Warner owned CNN. As he saw it, CNN was his personal enemy as well as a competitor to Murdoch's Fox. The network was run by Jeff Zucker, the former NBC executive who first put *The Apprentice* on the air, arguably paving the way for Trump's eventual political career. As Trump began running for president, Zucker put his rallies on CNN from start to finish, savoring the viewership bonanza. But when it became clear that Trump was not the "sideshow" Zucker once thought he was, CNN took a tougher tone and Trump became convinced his former sponsor was a traitor.[38]

After his election, Trump summoned Randall Stephenson, AT&T's chief executive officer, to Trump Tower for a meeting where he erupted about Zucker and CNN. "Jeff Zucker's a bad guy," Trump ranted. "I made that guy. I got that guy his job." It was the most bizarre meeting Stephenson had ever had with a national leader and the moment he realized that the threat to the merger with Time Warner was probably real. AT&T sought to play Trump's game, donating $2 million to his inaugural fund and hiring Michael Cohen, his personal attorney, to advise them on how to navigate the new administration, a move Stephenson later called "a big mistake."[39]

In the following months, Stephenson received two unsolicited calls from Murdoch offering to buy CNN from him. "How's the deal going?" Murdoch asked during the first call in May 2017. "Look, if it would help you get the deal done, I'd be happy to buy CNN from you." Stephenson was shocked. The overture seemed to him so clearly coordinated with Murdoch's friend in the White House. Murdoch was presenting a solution that would satisfy both of them: Murdoch would take over a competitor and Trump would neutralize an independent media voice that he saw as an adversary while also taking revenge against Zucker. "Rupert," Stephenson told Murdoch, "I'm not interested in selling." Murdoch called a second time in August, just a week after attending a private dinner at the White House with Trump, Kushner, and John Kelly, where the prospect of buying CNN came up in conversation. Again, Stephenson said no.

AT&T executives interpreted the calls as an implicit quid pro quo—if AT&T agreed to hand over CNN, Trump would not obstruct the larger acquisition using the Justice Department's antitrust division. The executives viewed it as crude, almost mob-style extortion. "Randall was beyond pissed, totally beyond pissed," recalled a colleague. "He just felt that this was the most outrageous abuse of power that he had ever seen. And I think it's one of the reasons that he fought so hard about it. He wanted to beat them. It wasn't just a deal. It got personal."

With AT&T refusing to play ball, Trump kept badgering aides like Kelly, Gary Cohn, and Rob Porter, separately and together, to call the Justice Department to tell it to stop the merger, a direct presidential intervention that violated every protocol governing such matters. The aides understood how inappropriate that would be and never followed through on Trump's orders. But when the Justice Department went to court to stop the deal anyway in November 2017, Trump assumed that it had been done at his behest and thanked his advisers. Trump saw nothing wrong with using the power of the presidency to pick winners and losers in the marketplace, especially if it benefited himself or his friends.

Makan Delrahim, who worked as Trump's deputy White House counsel before the president sent him to the Justice Department to be his antitrust chief, later insisted that he had acted on the merits of the case. But the Justice Department suit represented a reversal of Delrahim's own view of the AT&T–Time Warner merger from just a year earlier when, as a law professor, he had said, "I don't see this as a major antitrust problem."[40] Stephenson told his board that he had "no doubt, none whatsoever, that this is a lawsuit that is being brought because President Trump does not like the coverage he got from CNN." All twelve board members agreed to fight.

Among those who thought it looked untoward was William Barr, the once-and-future attorney general who sat on the Time Warner board at the time and attended a meeting with Delrahim. The session grew so contentious that Delrahim accused the visiting executives of threatening him, prompting Barr to file an affidavit calling that account "inaccurate and incomplete."[41] The antitrust case that Delrahim filed was thrown out by a federal judge, and in the end the merger went through, Murdoch never did gain control of CNN, and Zucker outlasted the Trump presidency.

Trump, however, continued to publicly support Murdoch's business interests and when Murdoch later decided to sell most of his 21st Century Fox entertainment assets to Walt Disney for $71 billion, Trump had no concern about the "concentration of power in the hands of too few" and instead gave it his immediate blessing. The sale raised far clearer antitrust concerns than the AT&T–Time Warner deal ever did, but Trump called Murdoch to congratulate him and then instructed his press secretary to endorse the deal by saying "this could be a great thing for jobs"—even though in fact the companies envisioned mass layoffs.[42]

CNN was not the only media organization in Trump's sights. From the start of his administration, he wanted to go after Amazon's Jeff Bezos, owner of *The Washington Post*. "He'd do anything to hurt Bezos," one of his senior officials came to believe. When the Pentagon requested bids for a $10 billion cloud computing contract, the military's largest ever, Trump privately sought to block Amazon from getting it. "Don't give it to Bezos because he never supports me," Trump told the senior official. Eventually, the Pentagon in 2019 awarded the contract to Microsoft, prompting a lawsuit from Amazon accusing Trump of exerting improper pressure due to his animus toward Bezos. After Trump lost, the Pentagon rescinded Microsoft's contract and opened it up to bids from multiple companies, including Amazon, but later canceled the contract altogether.

Another weapon Trump thought he had was the United States Postal Service, which delivered many of Amazon's packages. Trump would often complain that Amazon was getting preferential postal rates, when in fact it was the sheer and growing volume of Amazon's business that was keeping the Postal Service afloat. He also got it in his head that Amazon did not pay state sales taxes and should be forced to.

Gary Cohn, Trump's chief economic adviser, was on the receiving end of this particular tantrum repeatedly. "It's total bullshit," Cohn told an associate. "Amazon may actually be saving the Postal Service, not killing it," Cohn explained. Cohn had little doubt about Trump's real motivation. "He's just mad at Bezos for owning *The Washington Post*," he told the associate.

But Cohn could not shake Trump of his Amazon obsession. After leaving the White House, Cohn estimated that he probably had that same conversation with the president maybe thirty times. Cohn eventually had a PowerPoint created showing that Amazon did pay state sales taxes. Trump never actually looked at it, so Cohn just kept bringing it back every time the issue came up.

"Sir, Amazon pays taxes in forty-five states," Cohn told him at one point.

"What about the other five?" Trump demanded.

"They don't have a sales tax," Cohn said.

As with the AT&T–Time Warner dispute, Trump's obsession with Bezos and Amazon went beyond his media fixation and into the realm of Trump's business friendships. Unknown to most, the president had also been prodded to go after Amazon by Nelson Peltz, a billionaire investor who owned an even more palatial estate in Palm Beach not far from Mar-a-Lago and golfed with Trump.

Invited to the Oval Office, Peltz brought Trump a dossier on Amazon and the Postal Service, arguing that the company was receiving preferential rates that amounted to unfair competition. The president summoned an aide to listen to Peltz's complaint. Trump's staff was left trying to figure out what Peltz's interest was in the matter. It turned out that Peltz's Trian Fund Management had recently taken a $3.5 billion stake in Procter & Gamble, the consumer products giant. When Amazon acquired Whole Foods, Procter & Gamble, which sold many of its products in North America directly in Walmart stores, suddenly faced a major threat from the online retailer. Peltz accused Amazon of controlling prices and wanted Trump to take action against it. And Trump was eager to help.

For Trump, the war on the media would dominate much of his presidency. Most of those who sat in the Oval Office in modern times had chafed at their coverage and at times despised reporters, but either grew a thicker skin or tried not to let on how much the reporting bothered them. George W. Bush and Barack Obama made a point of not watching television news.

None of them let it drive their presidency the way that Trump did. He savored the fawning treatment he received most of the time on Fox, citing it to anyone who would listen, while erupting over what he read and saw in the rest of the media. To him, it was transactional: he made news with his outrageous behavior, he drove ratings and clicks, he was probably the most available president to reporters in generations, so why did they not love him?

The New York Times, in particular, seemed to rent penthouse space in his head. Ever combative, Trump called it "failing" and "fake news," but he read it every morning and reacted to its stories like no other newspaper. He gave its reporters interviews one day, then trashed them by name on Twitter the next. The paper would continually disappoint him. The man who once maneuvered the *New York Post* into running a banner cover headline claiming that Marla Maples described her affair with Trump as the "Best Sex I've Ever Had" would never get that kind of gushing treatment from the *Times* or any other mainstream news organization.[43] Once during a meeting in the Oval Office, Trump practically pleaded with A. G. Sulzberger, the publisher of the *Times*, to give him, a fellow New Yorker, even a single flattering headline. "I came from Jamaica, Queens, Jamaica Estates, and I became president of the United States," he complained. "I'm sort of entitled to a great story from my—just one!—from my newspaper."[44]

When he did not get what he wanted, he would lash out. The news conference that day in February 2017 was the perfect introduction of what would come, the attacks and intimidation, the twisting of reality, the up-is-down assertions. *The Washington Post*'s "Fact Checker" column found fifteen "dubious claims" in this one session.[45] But Trump was just getting started.

Nothing stung the new president more than the criticism that his White House, less than a month into his administration, was already a dysfunctional mess. "I turn on the TV, open the newspapers and I see stories of chaos—chaos!" Trump roared during the news conference. "Yet it is the exact opposite. This administration is running like a fine-tuned machine." He called one article about him "disgraceful" and another "nasty." He told a CNN reporter to yield to a Fox reporter because "your ratings aren't as good."

Still, even he seemed to recognize that his bombastic performance might not be received well. At one point, he predicted the next day's head-lines. "Tomorrow, they will say, 'Donald Trump rants and raves,'" he said. "I'm not ranting and raving."[46]

He was right about the next day's headlines, which reported that he ranted and raved. Trump had expected nothing less.

CHAPTER 4

Allies and Adversaries

Have you read Donald Trump's *Playboy* interview?" Angela Merkel, the staid chancellor of Germany, asked Justin Trudeau, Canada's suave young prime minister, a second-generation celebrity politician named one of *Vogue*'s "sexiest men alive."

Trudeau had just flown to Germany for his first visit since meeting the new American president and Merkel, who had not met Trump yet but had spent the months since his election wondering what to do about him, was eager for a debrief over dinner. The idea of a skin magazine as her source of intelligence seemed mind-boggling. "If I could take a picture of this moment and tweet it, it would break the internet," one of those present remembered thinking as the German leader asked her question.

Ever since November, that nearly three-decade-old interview of Donald Trump, stuffed between ads for Trojan condoms and Malibu Ultra Lights in the March 1990 issue of *Playboy*, had become something of a Rosetta Stone, anxiously pored over on both sides of the Atlantic. In it, Trump laid out in striking detail many of the themes that he would emphasize years later upon entering politics: America was being "laughed at" on the world stage. America was being ripped off, "defending wealthy nations for nothing." Japanese and German automakers were killing us. Just as he now praised autocrats Xi Jinping and Vladimir Putin, back then he celebrated Chinese "strength" in cracking down on the Tiananmen Square protests and predicted the collapse of the Soviet Union because it was not ruled by "a firm enough hand." Trump complained that "our 'allies' are making billions screwing us." If he were to become president someday, Trump promised, he "wouldn't trust anyone."[1]

Merkel was the antithesis of Trump, a cautious East German scientist by training who believed in methodical preparation as the foundation of political success. "She is," a close Merkel adviser said, "obsessed with detail." In addition to studying *Playboy*, she had watched episodes of *The Apprentice*. She had read *The Art of the Deal*. And she had paid close attention to Trump's campaign statements that railed against NATO as "obsolete," praised Putin, and personally criticized Merkel for "ruining" Germany by allowing a million refugees from the Syrian civil war into the country.[2] In an emotional three-hour dinner just days after the November election, at the historic Hotel Adlon in the shadow of Berlin's floodlit Brandenburg Gate, Barack Obama had lobbied Merkel to run for a fourth term as chancellor so that she could serve as a counterweight to Trump and the rising forces of right-wing populism in Europe. Merkel reluctantly agreed, announcing her re-election bid two days after Obama left, as a response to "insecure times."[3] Obama's adviser Ben Rhodes had ruefully toasted her as the new "leader of the free world."[4]

Now Merkel wanted to hear in detail about Trudeau's experience with Trump, who had granted the prime minister one of his first in-person meetings with a foreign leader. The Canadians prided themselves on understanding the United States better than anyone, and what choice did they have, with a 5,500-mile border and a new president who campaigned against the North American Free Trade Agreement, or NAFTA, that was the foundation of their economy? "In a way, we were the least surprised government in the world," a senior adviser to Trudeau recalled. Well before he was elected, "we had a plan for Donald Trump," although, to be fair, he added: "Did we think it was going to be implemented? No." Trudeau's center-left government had reached out for advice from a surprising source: former prime minister Brian Mulroney, a conservative whose rivalry with Trudeau's father, Pierre Trudeau, was so bitter that in his memoir he called the elder Trudeau a "coward" who had failed to stand up to Nazism.[5] Mulroney owned a house in Palm Beach not far from Mar-a-Lago and had become friendly with Trump over the years, but now he agreed that the threat to NAFTA and thus to the Canadian economy was almost an existential one, overriding partisan concerns. Mulroney soon became Canada's designated Trump-whisperer, "probably the most useful Canadian who wasn't in the government," as the Trudeau adviser would conclude.

By the time Trudeau was invited to Washington to meet the new president weeks into his tenure, the Canadians understood that Trump was, "charitably, a narcissist," as the Trudeau adviser put it, and that nothing would count for him except the relationship he established directly with Trudeau. After Trump's election victory, Trudeau had called him. The president-elect raved about the time he had met Trudeau's father. A search in the archives turned up a photo of the two, and the Canadians sent it to Trump as a present—because, as the Trudeau adviser said, "what better gift to give Donald Trump than a picture of himself?"

Still, the first meeting, on February 13, had been a shocking introduction to the brutal court politics around Trump. At the formal diplomatic lunch in the White House, Trump was flanked by Reince Priebus and Mike Flynn, but before the meal was over, Steve Bannon looked down at his phone, leaned back, and tapped Priebus on the shoulder. After the two talked, Bannon went over and tapped Flynn to get up, and then all three left the room. Flynn never returned to the lunch, and that evening the reason why became public: this was the moment that he was being forced out as national security adviser.

Bannon met later with Gerald Butts, Trudeau's chief of staff, to discuss NAFTA. Bannon, however, was distracted by the evident turmoil in the White House. Bannon was already worried about his own status. He had been featured on the latest cover of *Time* magazine as Trump's "Great Manipulator," and he was sure the president would be furious at him for taking away some of the spotlight.[6] Eventually, their conversation was interrupted by a man who came into the office and put his hands on Bannon's shoulders. "Buddy, don't worry about this *Time* magazine thing. We've got your back," the man told Bannon. He walked out, and Bannon explained. "Oh, that was the president's lawyer," he told Butts. "That's Michael Cohen."

But the meetings with Trump had gone well. Trudeau, well briefed, had sufficiently flattered Trump, including apparently dazzling his daughter Ivanka, who was captured gazing at the prime minister during a White House photo op—an image that quickly went viral on social media. Trump claimed he had bonded with the Canadian liberal, which was not really true, but at least Trudeau succeeded in creating the illusion of a personal relationship, which was what all the world leaders were striving for now that they had a clear read on Trump's *l'état c'est moi* view of international diplomacy. The Canadians passed lessons of their experience along to other perplexed allies. "After we had that first successful meeting in the White House, all the leaders in the world wanted to talk to Justin about how he did it," the Trudeau adviser recalled. The German chancellor got the message over their dinner, but there was a problem: Angela Merkel, as one of her closest aides said, "doesn't flatter."[7]

Trump's unlikely ascension was a global disruption as well as a domestic one, rewriting an international order that had survived frayed but still largely intact since the end of the Cold War. Trump's "America First" campaign slogan, his decades-old suspicion of allies, his unsettling predilection for adversaries like Putin, and his hiring of rogue ideologues like Bannon all portended an abrupt shift in American foreign policy. Merkel and other leaders remained uncertain what to do about it and received deeply conflicting advice from Washington, where many traditional Republicans had kicked into reassurance mode since the election.

But the red flags were hard to miss. After Trump's "American carnage" Inaugural Address, Peter Wittig, Germany's ambassador to the United States, immediately called Berlin in a panic. "God, what I've just heard is a nightmare," a colleague recalled Wittig saying. "Everybody had thought once he was president, he would be different."

The allies would have been even more nervous if they had been privy to a meeting five days after Trump took office when retired Army Lieutenant General Keith Kellogg, the new chief of staff at the National Security Council, complained so vociferously about NATO in front of Trump at a White House dinner that Joe Dunford, the Joint Chiefs chairman, got into an argument with him. At one point, Kellogg lamented that NATO did not have sufficient tanks to confront a genuine threat, to which an exasperated Dunford responded: "Keith, tanks are not any way to determine whether or not we have the forces we need!" That, the Marine four-star general lectured him, was "yesterday's metric." But Kellogg, no doubt sensing a receptive audience in Trump, had gone on and on about NATO, about how screwed up it was and how the alliance could not get anything right.

Another worrisome private conversation that did go public was the sensational early leak of a transcript of Trump's introductory call with Malcolm Turnbull, the prime minister of Australia. The president lectured Turnbull about letting refugees into his country. Trump's obsession with Germany—and Merkel—came through. "You do not want to destroy your country," Trump told Turnbull. "Germany is a mess because of what happened." He proceeded to rant about a "stupid," "horrible," and "disgusting" deal made with Turnbull by the Obama administration to accept 1,250 refugees. "Putin was a pleasant call," Trump yelled at him. "This is ridiculous," he added, before cutting the conversation short.[8]

Like the Germans, the Japanese knew they had a Trump problem. They too had read the *Playboy* interview, in which Japan's economic strength and military dependence on the United States featured as early Trump obsessions. Japan's 1980s dominance as an economic power had become so ingrained in Trump that even decades later when he was in the White House, he would sometimes stun his advisers by mistakenly referring to Japan when he meant China. Prime Minister Shinzo Abe had bet Japan's strategic future on a strong regional alliance with the United States to counter China. His government was not really prepared for an American president for whom alliances counted little. "Washington, D.C., is now the epicenter of global instability in the world," one of Abe's top advisers told Strobe Talbott, a former deputy secretary of state who headed the Brookings Institution.[9] Breaking protocol, Abe flew to New York to meet the president-elect at Trump Tower before he was inaugurated. Soon after, while hosting a delegation of American experts in Tokyo, the prime minister pulled one of them aside and urged him to join the new Trump White House. When the Republican demurred, joking that his wife would probably divorce him, the Japanese leader shot back: it was worth a broken marriage to save the Japan-America alliance.

Abe was a believer in the emerging conventional wisdom that the best way to manage Trump was personal face time—and, if necessary, egregious flattery. Abe persisted in this even when early returns suggested that Trump prized good personal relations but did not necessarily change his views as a result. Abe's lobbying did nothing to stop Trump from withdrawing the United States from the Trans-Pacific Partnership, the trade deal that Abe and Obama had seen as key to a strategy for countering China.

In early February, Abe was invited for a weekend at Mar-a-Lago, becoming the first foreign leader Trump would receive at the private club he was eager to rebrand as the Winter White House, and it proved to be an unsettling primer on the improvisation of the new Trump team. Just as wedges of iceberg lettuce drenched in blue-cheese dressing were served on the club's outdoor terrace, news of a North Korean ballistic missile test reached Trump and Abe. Mar-a-Lago members, who paid Trump $200,000 to join and thousands of dollars in annual fees for the privilege of eating and schmoozing on his terrace, posted pictures on social media of the two leaders conferring by candlelight. As if to underscore the point that national security was no longer all that secure, one enterprising Trump fan, a retired investor from the Boston area named Richard DeAgazio, even posted to Facebook a photograph of himself posing in the gilded Mar-a-Lago lobby with the presidential military aide carrying the nuclear "football." (Trump was not actually showing Abe secret photos, according to a senior White House official who was seated next to Abe, but an old black-and-white photograph of Abe's grandfather, also the prime minister of Japan, playing golf with Dwight Eisenhower.) After dinner and a short statement to the press with Abe, Trump insisted on dropping by a wedding in the club's main ballroom. "C'mon, Shinzo, let's go over and say hello," Trump recalled saying. "They've been members of this club for a long time. They've paid me a fortune."[10]

Trump was back at Mar-a-Lago the following weekend, urgently summoning candidates to replace Mike Flynn as his national security adviser after his first choice turned him down. Retired Vice Admiral Robert Harward told others the job would be a "shit sandwich" and said no.[11] Two other finalists, Lieutenant General H. R. McMaster and John Bolton, the former United Nations ambassador and regular inflammatory presence on Fox News, flew to Florida for interviews. McMaster—the H.R. was short for Herbert Raymond—was a veteran warfighter serving as head of the Army Capabilities Integration Center. Squat, almost neckless, the burly fifty-four-year-old often looked like he was about to burst out of his uniform. McMaster had graduated from the United States Military Academy at West Point during the twilight of the Cold War. In 1991, during the Gulf War, he had defeated a much larger force of Iraqi tanks in what was considered the last major tank battle of the twentieth century. He himself rode to the Battle of 73 Easting in a tank called Mad Max.

In reality, though, McMaster was no more a Mad Max than Jim Mattis was a Mad Dog, and his peacemaking efforts working with the local population in the northern city of Tal Afar during the Iraq War more than a decade later became a model for the new Army counterinsurgency strategy advocated by General David Petraeus. McMaster was a serious student of presidential leadership in wartime. His doctoral dissertation, a study of how military leaders failed in advising Lyndon Johnson during the Vietnam War, had been published to widespread praise. *Dereliction of Duty* was a cautionary tale of how Johnson, "a profoundly insecure man," with a "real propensity for lying," surrounded himself with sycophantic yes-men and succeeded in politicizing the military so that its leadership went along with his lies about the war rather than confront unpleasant truths.[12]

When McMaster showed up at Mar-a-Lago for his interview, Trump had not been especially taken with him. "He looks like a beer salesman!" the president complained, a comment soon leaked by McMaster's White House rivals.[13] His résumé was impressive, however, and Jared Kushner and others told Trump his appointment might soothe critics. McMaster also had something in common with Trump: he was a harsh judge of the previous administration's foreign policy. McMaster had never spoken out publicly given his active-duty status, but he was privately scathing. "The worst foreign policy administration since Vietnam was the Obama administration," he told associates. "I think they were an utter disaster—on Iran, on the Middle East, the so-called pivot to the Pacific, the unenforced red line in Syria."

McMaster was named national security adviser on February 20, exactly one week after Flynn's firing and Trudeau's visit. In hiring the credentialed McMaster along with impressively silver-haired pillars of the establishment such as Jim Mattis and Rex Tillerson, Trump appeared to have caved quickly to the national security wise men he claimed to disdain. A couple weeks later, Colin Kahl, a former national security adviser to Joe Biden when he was vice president, was trying to make sense of it all. He perceived a glimmer of good news: perhaps McMaster, Mattis, and Tillerson would form a sort of "Axis of Adults," Kahl posited in a Twitter thread early one Saturday morning, to ensure that Trump, no matter how alarming his public statements, would be "constrained from making epically bad decisions."[14] Kahl's nickname for Trump's new foreign policy team stuck.

In March, Angela Merkel flew to Washington for her own first meeting with Trump. She had done all the homework by then. Beyond reading *Playboy*, her staff had consulted Republican elders such as Henry Kissinger and Stephen Hadley. On a visit to Berlin, Hadley counseled "strategic patience," urging the Germans to pay no attention to Trump's intemperate tweets, which was more or less the same thing Rex Tillerson was already saying back in Washington. Kissinger, for his part, suggested meeting with Jared Kushner, but the conversations with the presidential son-in-law had been less than reassuring—in part because of the counsel Kissinger himself had given to Kushner. He told Kushner during the transition that the allies were all nervous about Trump and he should use that—don't reassure them, he advised, keep them on edge. So when Merkel's national security adviser, Christoph Heusgen, met with him in the White House days before the chancellor's visit, Kushner did just that. Heusgen began with an emotional speech about the postwar bonds between the United States and Germany, recounting everything from the Berlin Airlift to America's indispensable role midwifing German reunification at the end of the Cold War. Kushner was unmoved and unsentimental. "You have to understand that Trump is a businessman and businessmen are not going to be wed to old conventions," he said. "Look, Germany and America were old enemies and now we're great allies. But just because we're great allies today doesn't mean we'll be great allies in the future and just because other countries are enemies today doesn't mean they'll be enemies in the future." In other words, Heusgen told worried colleagues: "The past doesn't count." It was hardly an endorsement of the alliance around which Germany's entire foreign policy was built.

Heusgen was even more concerned after an audience with Steve Bannon, who explained that Trump was not interested in confronting Russia, no matter how offensive Vladimir Putin's misdeeds were, and would reorient American policy to focus on a long-term conflict with China. When Heusgen tried to explain the European concern about Putin—his 2014 invasion of eastern Ukraine and illegal annexation of the Crimean Peninsula had led Obama and Merkel to organize international sanctions—Bannon was dismissive.

"What is the GDP of Russia?" Bannon said. The point was that Russia was an economic weakling and thus a geopolitical one. "You shouldn't care about Russia. You should care about China," Trump's strategist lectured the German.

"Maybe in thirty years you are right," Heusgen responded, "but in thirty years Russia can do a lot of nonsense."

Merkel decided she would simply have to convince Trump and his advisers they were wrong. Her first phone call with Trump had been a disaster. "After thirty seconds, the chancellor lost the president," recalled one of those who listened. The word came back to the Germans: Trump hated the conversation and thought he was being lectured by Merkel. For the Washington meeting, Merkel insisted on focusing on Russia, and her aides—having gotten the message that Trump was not engaged by briefing papers or PowerPoint presentations—crafted what they thought was an attention-getting graphic showing Putin's aggressive actions in Eastern Europe imposed on top of a map of the former Soviet Union as it stood in the 1980s.

Trump was not interested. He and Bannon had their own plans for the meeting. He opened their session by presenting a figurative bill. "Angela, you owe me one trillion dollars," the president said shortly after they sat down.[15] This, according to the funny math Bannon had an aide pull together, was the amount that Germany *should* have been spending on defense if it committed the 2 percent of its GDP annually that NATO allies had agreed to. Never mind that 2 percent was just a goal and not due to go into effect until 2024. Even then, the money was meant to go to Germany's own defense budget, not to NATO's coffers and certainly not to the United States. But Bannon and Trump pretended it was money being sucked directly from the United States Treasury, a fiction the president would go on to repeat scores of times.

To Trump, NATO was a sort of protection racket that the United States had been suckered into for decades. Facts were irrelevant. He believed that "literally, Angela Merkel owed him a check," one senior aide said. Trump's more responsible advisers would later claim they tried to tell him over and over that the 2 percent was not owed to America or even owed at all. He did not listen.

Trump's disdain for America's traditional allies came with an equally striking corollary—his desire, even eagerness, to court the world's autocrats. And not just Vladimir Putin. The same week as Merkel's visit, in fact, Trump played host to a figure who would end up having far more influence over American foreign policy in the Trump years than the chancellor of Germany: Prince Mohammed bin Salman of Saudi Arabia, known by his initials MBS.

Although just thirty-one years old and technically still the deputy crown prince, MBS was the ascendant power in Saudi Arabia, a self-styled modernizer and architect of his country's stalemated, American-supported war in neighboring Yemen. The Saudis and their allies in the United Arab Emirates decided early on to forge a close relationship with Trump after years of disappointment with Barack Obama, whom they viewed as too sympathetic to the Muslim Brotherhood opposition movement and too soft on Iran, the mortal enemy of the Gulf Arabs. They got their entrée into Trump's circle through Tom Barrack, a wealthy Lebanese American investor and Trump friend who had managed his inaugural festivities. Barrack recommended they meet Jared Kushner. "You will love him and he agrees with our Agenda!" he wrote in May 2016 to Yousef al-Otaiba, the politically connected ambassador from the United Arab Emirates in Washington.[16] After the election, Rick Gerson, a hedge fund manager also close to Trump, brokered a visit by Prince Mohammed bin Zayed, the de facto ruler of the Emirates, to meet Kushner in New York. "I promise you this will be the start of a special and historic relationship," Gerson texted the prince afterward.[17]

The Emirati leader in turn connected Kushner with MBS in Saudi Arabia. Just four years younger than Kushner, MBS had grand ambitions for transforming Saudi society, lifting some of the most oppressive religious-based rules while drawing international investment, although he had a strong autocratic side that did not brook dissent. Barrack reassured the Arabs not to worry about Trump's anti-Muslim campaign rhetoric. "He's just being hyperbolic," he told Otaiba. A Saudi delegation that met with Kushner after the election came away cautiously optimistic. "The inner circle is predominantly deal makers who lack familiarity with political customs and deep institutions, and they support Jared Kushner," the delegation said in an internal report on its trip.[18]

Having bonded over the phone and in text messages, MBS worked behind the scenes with Kushner on an unlikely idea that no other American president would have even contemplated. They wanted Trump to make his first foreign trip as president to Saudi Arabia. This would be an epic snub of America's democratic neighbors. Every president since Ronald Reagan had made his first official visit to Canada or Mexico. MBS further bypassed diplomatic channels by snagging a last-minute lunch in the State Dining Room with Trump after Merkel's trip to Washington was delayed a few days because of a snowstorm. It was not an auspicious start for the so-called Axis of Adults.

Unorthodox ideas like this seemed to come from nowhere all the time in the new administration. Outside advisers, old friends and business associates, canny lobbyists, random Mar-a-Lago members, and junior senators all had as much chance, if not more, than any member of the cabinet at getting Trump's ear. But it was not always clear whose interests were being served. Tom Barrack would later come under investigation for what prosecutors claimed was an undisclosed foreign-lobbying effort to shape the new administration's policy toward the Middle East—including pushing for close ties between Trump and the young Saudi prince.

Foreign policy was being made in a free-for-all. This dynamic was immediately apparent to Bob Corker, the Tennessee senator who chaired the Senate Foreign Relations Committee and had been considered at one point as Trump's vice presidential running mate. Just after Thanksgiving following the election, Corker had been called to Trump Tower for an interview for secretary of state. Corker showed up early, only to find Trump talking with the Republican megadonor Sheldon Adelson, the casino magnate whose major cause other than the GOP was the state of Israel and its longtime prime minister Benjamin Netanyahu. Adelson had announced a $25 million gift to Trump in September of 2016, as part of a $65 million overall donation to Republican campaigns, making him the largest single Republican donor that year. His investment looked prescient when Trump won, and several weeks later, the president-elect and Bannon listened approvingly in Trump Tower as Adelson demanded action on a pet issue: moving the American embassy in Israel from Tel Aviv to Jerusalem. Such a relocation had been official American policy for years but had been perpetually put off because of the furor everyone was sure would erupt and the expectation that the move should come only along with real progress toward a lasting settlement between Israel and the Palestinians. "Sheldon was saying we need to move the embassy and do it on day one," Corker recalled. Trump was eager to oblige—so eager that Corker later learned he had to be talked out of literally announcing the embassy move in the first hours of his presidency.

Like other senators used to the discipline of past White Houses, Corker found himself both dazzled by the access and disturbed by it. In the early weeks of Trump's tenure, he would go to the White House for a meeting and find himself pulled into the private dining room off the Oval Office to share a cheeseburger with the president. It was quickly apparent to Corker and others that decision making was essentially random, as much about who got to talk to Trump, and when, as anything else. White House staffers were soon calling Corker with strategic advice on how to be the last voice in Trump's ear: "I would get calls at 6:30 in the morning from a staffer asking me to weigh in on a decision that was going to be made at 10," Corker would recall, "and they asked me to call him at 9:45." Over the holidays, Corker had spoken with Trump and asked him to nominate a fellow Tennessean, Bill Hagerty, as ambassador to Japan. Within an hour, Trump had called Hagerty and offered him the job.

Trump, Corker came to realize, was especially drawn to outlandish ideas that might offer the chance to fulfill his campaign promise to blow up the existing international order. The new president was absolutely the "wrecking ball" he had claimed to be, the Senate Foreign Relations chairman said a few weeks into the administration; the only question was whether he could, or would, "evolve."[19]

On April 6, the evolution theory got a surprising boost. Trump, once again visiting Mar-a-Lago for the weekend, this time for a summit with China's Xi Jinping, hastily convened his most senior advisers in a room at his club little bigger than a broom closet and decided to launch a missile strike against the rogue Syrian regime of President Bashar al-Assad in retaliation for a sarin nerve gas attack on civilians.

Photographs of the victims had horrified the normally indifferent president. "Even beautiful babies were cruelly murdered in this very barbaric attack," Trump said in announcing the decision to hit the Syrian airbase from which the chemical weapons had been launched, a sharp change in policy for someone who had never previously expressed concern about the hundreds of thousands of civilians dead in the Syrian civil war, including an estimated 55,000 children.[20] For months, in fact, Trump had made clear his skepticism of even the modest existing level of involvement in Syria; he had gone ahead with plans made by the Obama administration to help Syrian rebels attack the ISIS stronghold of Raqqa but saw the offensive as a get-done-and-get-out kind of antiterrorism mission. He had no interest in overturning the Russian-supported Assad government, although that remained stated American policy inherited from the Obama years.

The military prepared three options for Trump in the days after the gas attack, including an all-out "decapitation strike" on the Assad government's leadership; Trump chose the least aggressive of the three, a barrage of fifty-nine cruise missiles on a single airfield.

The sort of cavalier, anyone-can-come-in nature of the decision appalled Joe Hagin, the White House deputy chief of staff who had served in more serious Republican administrations. So many people squeezed into the cramped room used as an away-from-home Situation Room who had little business being there, like the commerce secretary and economic adviser and speechwriter. In describing it to colleagues later, Hagin called it "the cruise missile cocktail party." To him, he related, "It just summed up the frivolous lack of understanding."

And then Trump turned the whole business into another grand spectacle he had arranged for his important guest. The missiles were due to smash into their targets just before 9 p.m. as he was finishing dinner in the Mar-a-Lago dining room with Xi. Dessert had just been served—"the most beautiful piece of chocolate cake that you have ever seen," Trump later revealed to Maria Bartiromo on Fox Business—when he received a message that the attack was imminent and told Xi about it.[21] Xi, according to Trump, paused for about ten seconds, then asked his interpreter to repeat the information. Wilbur Ross, the commerce secretary, later regaled a California audience with the scene. Trump, he said, had made the strike into "after-dinner entertainment."[22] After dinner, Trump and his team returned to the makeshift secure room for an update on the strike, then many in the party retired to Mar-a-Lago's Library Bar, where they ran up a $1,000 tab that was billed to the government.

Trump's decision to punish Syria for its horrific chemical attack, however, turned out to be just the signal that some anxious foreign policy elites had been looking for, and Trump woke up to unexpectedly glowing reviews. "I think Donald Trump became president of the United States," Fareed Zakaria enthused on CNN.[23] Other national security veterans in both parties greeted the airstrike as if it were a transformative event—and a stark contrast to Obama's much criticized failure to enforce a "red line" he had set when Assad launched chemical attacks against civilians. Trump "finally accepted the role of Leader of the Free World," Elliott Abrams, a hawkish veteran of past Republican administrations who had just been vetoed by Trump to serve as deputy secretary of state because of his past criticism, wrote in *The Weekly Standard*.[24]

In reality, of course, Trump was still Trump. He had not at all changed his mind about Syria, or anything else. It was just another spur-of-the-moment decision, driven by what he had seen on television.

More lasting would be Trump's impression of Xi Jinping, the self-confident autocrat he had been threatening with a nasty trade war. Like Putin, Trump decided, this was a tough guy he could do business with. "I really liked him," Trump told Bartiromo after the Mar-a-Lago weekend. "We had a great chemistry, I think." In a verdict that sounded almost affectionate, he added: "We understand each other."[25]

Soon after the summit with Xi, H. R. McMaster found himself in hostile territory for a general with a tin ear for politics, being yelled at by the president on the telephone as he headed to the Fox News studio on Capitol Hill. Trump had ignited an international freakout that week with comments warning of the possibility of a "major, major conflict with North Korea."[26] But McMaster's problem at that point was not so much Kim Jong-un as it was managing his unmanageable boss. The allies had invested their hopes in McMaster, but failed to anticipate that titles, even one as exalted as national security adviser, did not necessarily confer power in the Trump White House.

The problem that had set Trump off, as far as McMaster could tell, was Reince Priebus. McMaster had ended up on the wrong side of one of the Trump White House's most toxic divides, the running power struggle between the insecure and overwhelmed Priebus and the preternaturally self-assured Jared Kushner. Preparing for the Xi summit, Trump had, uncharacteristically, praised McMaster. Priebus heard it and, according to the account McMaster would later give others, from that day on did everything he could do to cut the national security adviser's legs out from under him. For Trump, it was a zero-sum game.

That Sunday morning, McMaster was convinced, Priebus had given Trump a story in a South Korean newspaper claiming that McMaster had contradicted the president on an issue that had rapidly become an obsession of sorts for Trump: the THAAD missile defense system that the United States had stationed in South Korea. As with the Germans and NATO, Trump thought the South Koreans should be paying more for their own defense and he wanted a billion dollars for the THAAD battery. He appeared neither to know nor care that the United States had just agreed with the South Koreans in 2016 to finance the missile deployment. McMaster had told his South Korean counterpart that of course Washington would still honor the deal, boilerplate assurance that was interpreted as a rebuke of Trump. Angry, Trump called McMaster as he was about to be interviewed by the sharp *Fox News Sunday* host, Chris Wallace, cursing him out and then hanging up.

Rattled, McMaster sat down for the television interview. When the camera came on, McMaster praised Trump to Wallace as a "masterful" diplomat in Asia who had not only developed a strong personal rapport with Xi but had also "reinvigorated and strengthened our alliances with key nations in the region, including South Korea and Japan."[27] McMaster, it seemed, had already learned the clutch move of the Trump White House: sucking up to the Fox audience of one.

The THAAD fight would be one of many recurring internal battles over how and even whether to defend South Korea and other traditional partners of the United States. Trump complained the battery cost too much and wanted to put it in Portland, Oregon, even though the military believed it would be far less effective there at intercepting North Korean missiles. But the argument on THAAD, as with those on NATO, on Syria, and Afghanistan, was never really won. Trump would circle back to make his same points again and again.

Few themes were more persistent than Trump's desire to prove that his predecessors, all of them, had made the worst deals. His plan was to blow them up and make better ones—or at least new versions of the old ones, with full credit to himself.

NAFTA was the first big target and, on April 26, Justin Trudeau's nightmare of Trump torching the world's most successful free trade pact seemed to be coming true. Neither Trudeau's flattery of Trump nor his attention to Ivanka, whom he took to a Broadway showing of *Come from Away*, a musical highlighting Canadian support for Americans after the September 11 attacks, had dissuaded the president from deciding to abruptly withdraw from NAFTA. The 1994 agreement had helped shape the richest trading bloc in the world, but Trump had campaigned against it as the "worst deal ever."[28] That morning, Steve Bannon had walked into the Oval Office with an executive order drafted to exit NAFTA by formally triggering a six-month pullout clock. The plan was for Trump to sign the order and announce it at a prime-time rally in Harrisburg, Pennsylvania, on Saturday night, as the signature event of his hundredth day in office.

Belatedly hearing of the plot, Reince Priebus hit the panic button. Priebus might have made an uneasy truce with Bannon, but there were no truly permanent partnerships inside Trump's Darwinian White House. His years as Republican chairman had made Priebus acutely sensitive to the needs and views of the party's donor class and he knew that immediate withdrawal from NAFTA would create an economic crisis—and a political catastrophe for Trump. Seeing no other way to stop his boss, he called all the cabinet officers he could think of who supported NAFTA, including Rex Tillerson and Wilbur Ross, and urged them to race to the White House to try to stop Trump. Word leaked to Republican allies on Capitol Hill, who also started calling the White House. When the news hit the markets, corn futures dropped precipitously. Business leaders drafted urgent letters. An estimated $1.2 trillion in trade among the countries and 14 million American jobs depended on the free flow of commerce with Canada and Mexico.

Ross called Sonny Perdue, the agriculture secretary, who rushed into the Oval Office, bringing two maps printed out on eight-by-eleven paper, one showing in red and blue the areas where farmers and industries would be harmed by an abrupt withdrawal and another showing in red and blue the counties won by Trump and Hillary Clinton. The overlap was clear. "These are your people," Perdue told Trump. By dinnertime, the president of Mexico, Enrique Peña Nieto, was on the telephone, promising to open negotiations on a new and improved NAFTA if only Trump would not blow it up on the front end. Then Trudeau called Trump. He told reporters after the call that he had urged the president not to cause "a lot of short- and medium-term pain for an awful lot of families" on both sides of the border.[29] Privately, both the Mexicans and Canadians warned Trump that if he took such a dramatic step, they would not be able politically to return to the negotiations.

By 10:30 p.m. the immediate crisis was over and the White House issued a statement saying Trump would not pull out of NAFTA. "For now."[30] Publicly, Priebus claimed that it had all been a brilliant ploy by Trump to begin the negotiations on advantageous terrain. "The president has put himself in a perfect position on NAFTA," the chief of staff told *The Washington Post* the next day. "The leverage is all with the president."[31]

That is not at all what Priebus actually thought. For years afterward, in fact, Priebus would take credit for having "orchestrated"—his word—the successful pushback. That day, Priebus confided to others, had been the closest of close calls, a moment when Trump was truly prepared to upend the global economy for the sake of an applause line at a political rally.

"I was all set to terminate," Trump told the *Post* the day after he had decided not to. "I looked forward to terminating. I was going to do it."[32]

In May, Trump embarked on his first foreign trip, flying to Riyadh, Saudi Arabia, for an Arab summit, in the visit that Jared Kushner and MBS, the two princelings, had orchestrated. The trip was most memorable not for any diplomatic breakthroughs but for its sheer bizarre optics, which included courtly Rex Tillerson awkwardly swaying along to a sword dance with their Saudi hosts—"not my first sword dance," joked Tillerson, who had spent years in the Middle East as ExxonMobil's chief executive.[33]

When Trump and the Saudi king placed their hands on a glowing orb, as the first lady looked on, the eerie photo op spawned endless social media memes. More to the point were Trump's glowing words to his Saudi hosts, promising them that in his presidency they would no longer hear annoying speeches about human rights and pretending as if he had never said all those terrible things about Muslims. "We are not here to lecture," he said, offering instead "partnership based on shared interests and values."[34] Within a few months, MBS would undertake a massive purge of leading Saudis as he consolidated power in the kingdom. He locked up nearly four hundred members of the country's small elite, many of them his fellow royals, in the Ritz-Carlton Riyadh, the same lavish hotel where Trump had stayed during the summit and on whose facade had been projected five-story-high portraits of the president and his Saudi host.

The real confrontation on the trip would come later, not with Arab autocrats or the Israelis and Palestinians he visited next, but with the European allies. In Brussels, NATO was set to have its annual leaders summit and much advance care had gone into Trump's debut, including a decision to build the public portion of the summit around a grand opening of the new, not-actually-quite-finished NATO headquarters building, sure to appeal, it was thought, to the real estate mogul. The ceremonies would also include dedication of a September 11 memorial, whose centerpiece was a large, twisted piece of wreckage from the fallen World Trade Center towers. This too was meant as a teaching moment for Trump; perhaps, it was hoped, he would be reminded that the 2001 attacks on the United States had prompted the only time that NATO had invoked its Article 5 provision of all-for-one, one-for-all mutual defense, the cornerstone of the alliance. It would be the perfect moment for Trump to finally put to rest the speculation about his commitment to NATO that his own comments had caused.

Ever since his campaign, and much to the delight of Vladimir Putin and other adversaries, Trump had put NATO on notice that he was hardly committed to the "obsolete" alliance. For months leading up to the Brussels summit, McMaster, Mattis, and Tillerson, the Axis of Adults, sought to explain away or reframe his criticism, insisting to allies that Trump was merely the latest president to lobby Europeans to spend more on defense—he was just louder about it. At points, they even got Trump to make public statements suggesting that he was supportive of NATO and only trying to make sure other countries paid their fair share.

The reassurance had worked, to a point. "There was still a kind of hopefulness—'oh, that was just his campaign, he doesn't really mean it,'" a senior NATO official recalled of the lead-up to Brussels. "They were used to hearing it from every president from Eisenhower on down the years, and it was kind of 'yeah, yeah, the Americans are asking for more money.'"

Their hopefulness was misplaced. Trump had been briefed early in his tenure about Article 5 and how mutual defense in NATO worked. "You mean, if Russia attacked Lithuania, we would go to war with Russia?" he responded. "That's crazy."[35] After a few more statements like that, his foreign policy team concluded that Trump's animus toward NATO was more than just Twitter bluster. It was so serious that Trump repeatedly threatened to pull out of the alliance altogether. "He hinted many times that he wanted out of NATO," a senior defense official recalled. "He never said, 'Do it.' But he got really close." A senior White House official confirmed: "He wanted to pull out of NATO on a number of occasions. That was actually much more serious than people realized."

Trump's visit to NATO headquarters had been shaping up for months as a major confrontation not only with the allies, but within his administration. In a government where no one was exactly sure what was official policy and what was just the latest thing Trump had blurted, or tweeted, out, sometimes there was just nothing to do but show up and see what happened. That, in essence, was what the Brussels trip came down to. Drafts of Trump's speech ricocheted around the bureaucracy for weeks. In versions approved by the Defense Department and National Security Council, there was a twenty-seven-word statement explicitly affirming Trump's commitment to Article 5. It read in its seemingly noncontroversial entirety: "We face many threats, but I stand before you with a clear message: the U.S. commitment to the NATO alliance and to Article 5 is unwavering."[36]

Reporters were told that the Article 5 language would be in the speech and NATO officials were also shown a copy with the language in it. "Everybody assured us it had been cleared all the way up," recalled a senior NATO official who saw the draft. But in reality, the fight over what Trump would say continued until the very minute when he would say it. Jim Mattis was so nervous about what Trump would do that he had rearranged his schedule to attend the Brussels summit. Rex Tillerson was also present. H. R. McMaster had spent weeks trying to ensure the meeting came off without a disaster, only to find himself in the motorcade on the way to NATO headquarters, screaming at Stephen Miller, the speechwriter, to delete various attacks on allies in the text—"just gratuitous insults," as McMaster would later put it. The fight persisted for so long that McMaster had to call ahead to aides to make sure the excised phrases were taken out of the version of the speech already loaded in the teleprompter.

Trump, meanwhile, had already created the first diplomatic crisis of the day just by walking with his fellow NATO leaders to a photo op. On a tour of the new headquarters building, Trump lashed out, denouncing it to NATO Secretary General Jens Stoltenberg as an expensive monstrosity. Nearing the end of the tour, a glowering Trump shoved aside the prime minister of tiny Montenegro—whose accession to the alliance was being celebrated at the meeting—to secure his place in front for the cameras set up to record them.

Then came the speech.

Standing backstage with Trump were McMaster, Rob Porter, the White House staff secretary, and Gary Cohn, the economic adviser who was filling in for Reince Priebus on the trip. "You have one thing to say, one thing only to say: Article 5," Cohn told the president as he walked onstage. But when it came time to do so, Trump never uttered the promised twenty-seven words.

"Holy shit," the senior NATO official thought as the president spoke. Standing nearby was the rest of Trump's White House staff team, and the official noticed they "were looking at each other with shock in their eyes—except Stephen Miller, he was calm." Backstage, meanwhile, Cohn and the others were stunned.

"What now?" Cohn asked McMaster.

The national security adviser shrugged. There was no training for something like this. "I shoot guns," McMaster joked.

Eventually, the aides wrote up a short statement saying in essence that of course the United States still supported the NATO treaty, and McMaster put it out in his name.

Brussels was a bracing reminder that the Axis of Adults had not managed to tame Trump. McMaster and Cohn, who had become allies in the White House's fierce internal wars after meeting back in February while waiting on a couch in Mar-a-Lago the day of McMaster's job interview, spent the ride back to the United States dealing with the fallout. They settled on a strategy of public denial. "America First does not mean America alone," the pair insisted in a *Wall Street Journal* op-ed they drafted on the plane. In this wishful-thinking version of his inaugural international trip, Trump had not rattled the allies and undercut their mutual defense pact but was "reconfirming America's commitment to NATO and Article 5," while also bolstering "strong alliances."[37]

Of course, they knew that Trump had done no such thing. McMaster had long since concluded that convincing Trump of the value of allies was the biggest challenge he faced on a daily basis. After the disaster in Brussels, he spent weeks begging Trump to fix the problem by making the public statement of support for NATO that he had withheld. But McMaster found that Trump was reflexively contrarian. If he told the president he should do something, he would instead do the opposite.

Trump flew home from Europe late on a Saturday. A few days later, he announced that he was unilaterally pulling the United States out of the Paris climate accord, a decision that McMaster and Cohn, along with Ivanka Trump, the president's other senior foreign policy advisers and the allies with whom he had just met in person for the first time, had spent months resisting.

In Munich, Angela Merkel had her own response to Trump's disruptions. For all her obsession with studying the new American president, she had not really been prepared for "this degree of unpredictability," as a close adviser put it. The *Playboy* interview did not begin to cover it. But the evidence was now clear. After the meetings with Trump, Merkel had reached a conclusion. "The times in which we could completely depend on others are, to a certain extent, over," she announced in a speech that sounded like an obituary for the American-led international system. She added, "We Europeans truly have to take our fate into our own hands."[38]

CHAPTER 5

The Ghost of Roy

Late on the afternoon of May 9, Trump summoned several aides to the Oval Office. Reince Priebus and Stephen Miller were already there. So were Jeff Sessions, the attorney general, and several lawyers for the White House and Justice Department, looking grim. The new arrivals were handed copies of a letter from the president to James Comey, director of the Federal Bureau of Investigation: "You are hereby terminated and removed from office, effective immediately."[1]

Comey terminated? The man leading the investigation into Russian interference in the 2016 election and any secret collusion between Moscow and Trump's campaign? The one investigating Mike Flynn and who knew how many other Trump associates? The aides were stunned.

"Mr. President," Mike Dubke, the communications director, asked in astonishment, "did you just fire the director of the FBI?"

"Yes, I did," Trump said.

It soon became clear that the most consequential decision thus far of the Trump presidency was little more than an amateurish, slapdash affair. It was already 4:30 p.m. by the time Trump told his aides he was ordering them to release the letter at 5 p.m. But there was no plan for how to announce this monumental news, much less how to spin it, no talking points for allies, no notifications for congressional leaders, no schedule for administration officials to go on television shows explaining it. No one had even been told—not even Comey.

"Before you contact members of Congress and before this becomes public, don't you want to confirm that Comey is aware and has received the letter?" ventured Jody Hunt, Sessions's chief of staff.

Trump harrumphed. "I don't care if he knows about it," he said.

Eventually, Priebus tried again. "Shouldn't we make sure Comey gets that letter before it gets out in the media?" he asked.

Trump repeated himself. "I *don't care* if he learns about it in the media," he snapped.

No one had even figured out how to deliver the news. When someone asked whether the FBI director was at his office, the president responded that he was. But, in truth, he had no idea. "Can someone find out if he's in his office?" he shouted to an assistant. Without waiting for an answer, Trump summoned Keith Schiller, his longtime bodyguard now granted the glorified title of director of Oval Office Operations.

"Keith, get in here. Would you like to fire the director of the FBI?"

"Yes, sir," Schiller said. "It would be my pleasure, Mr. President."

But Comey was not, in fact, in his office to receive the letter. He was in Los Angeles, where he would soon find out that he had been fired from the chyron scrolling across a muted television screen.

Trump, who was sucking down Diet Cokes and chomping on a Hershey's chocolate bar, seemed pumped up. "This is historical," he kept saying. Finally, he summoned an official White House photographer to record the moment, then got into a discussion about how he should pose. "I should be reading something," he said. "I can be reading Jeff's letter." Mike Pence arrived. "Mike," Trump said, "this is a historic moment."

Historic, yes; well-planned, no. "How do you think they'll take it?" Trump asked his aides as he prepared to make a round of calls to congressional leaders.

"I think they'll be fine because Schumer has called for Comey to step down multiple times," Dubke said.

But when Trump called Chuck Schumer, the Senate Democratic leader, there was a painfully long pause after he heard the news. Finally, Schumer responded, "I'm going to have to get back to you, Mr. President." And in that moment Dubke realized how bad all the advice to the president had been, his included.

If there was a before and an after in the Trump presidency, the firing of James Comey on a lovely May afternoon was it, a power play gone bad that transformed much of the rest of his tenure into an endless brawl over the investigation that had prompted him to fire the FBI director in the first place. But if Trump hoped that getting rid of Comey would end or allow him to contain the inquiry, he was quickly proved wrong.

What the lawyers who had been called to the Oval Office were slow to grasp was that the poorly planned and politically ill-advised ouster of

Comey was not only a scandal, it would also be seen as an effort by the president to obstruct a federal investigation into his own campaign, one they had failed to stop. They had even helped Trump concoct an implausible cover story claiming that the real reason for Comey's dismissal, six months after the election, was that he had mishandled the FBI inquiry into Hillary Clinton's emails—as if Trump, who had led crowds at his rallies chanting "lock her up" and vowed to throw Clinton in prison if elected, cared whether she had been treated unfairly. Many Democrats loathed Comey for what he had done to Clinton, especially his last-minute decision before the 2016 election to briefly reopen the probe to examine a trove of newly discovered emails, a move that many believed had helped Trump win the presidency. But it was a fatal miscalculation on Trump's part to think that Democrats might welcome Comey's firing at this point rather than see it as an act intended only to protect Trump.

The blowback was immediate. Within minutes of the letter's release, television airwaves were filled with comparisons to the Saturday Night Massacre of 1973, when Richard Nixon ordered the firing of the Watergate prosecutor only to have his attorney general and deputy attorney general refuse to carry out the directive and resign in protest. The Nixon Presidential Library joined the fray with a tweet noting that even though the late president had pushed out the special prosecutor, "President Nixon never fired the Director of the FBI," cheekily adding the hashtag "#notNixonian."[2]

Since Watergate, presidents had largely left FBI directors alone to avoid the appearance of political interference. Bill Clinton despised Louis Freeh, the FBI director whose agents were digging through his finances and sex life for independent counsel Kenneth Starr, but never thought he could get away with firing him. George W. Bush was so afraid of a Saturday Night Massacre repeat that he backed down when his FBI director, Robert S. Mueller III, and deputy attorney general—the same James Comey—threatened to resign rather than reauthorize a terrorist surveillance program they deemed illegal. There was a reason why Congress mandated ten-year terms for FBI directors, to insulate them from politics.

Trump's fundamental misunderstanding of Washington was laid out there for all to see in a series of self-pitying tweets that night and into the next day:

"The Democrats have said some of the worst things about James Comey, including the fact that he should be fired, but now they play so sad!"

"Comey lost the confidence of almost everyone in Washington, Republican and Democrat alike. When things calm down, they will be thanking me!"

"Dems have been complaining for months & months about Dir. Comey. Now that he has been fired they PRETEND to be aggrieved. Phony hypocrites!"

At the heart of the decision to fire Comey was the mystery of Trump's relationship with Vladimir Putin, the master of the Kremlin for whom he had expressed such inexplicable admiration. By the time Trump sent his bodyguard to FBI headquarters with his peremptory dismissal letter, the new president had given the world every reason to wonder what Russia's leader had on him.

Trump's history with Russia went back long before he was in politics. A Putin cheerleader of long standing, he had written him a mash note in 2007 after the Russian was named *Time*'s Person of the Year, an honor Trump himself craved. "You definitely deserve it," Trump gushed, adding, "As you probably have heard, I am a big fan of yours!"[3] For years, Trump had tried to build a tower with his name on it in Moscow potentially worth hundreds of millions of dollars. Ever since American banks stopped doing business with him because he was so unreliable, Trump had been financed by Deutsche Bank, the German institution with close ties to Russia. "Russians make up a pretty disproportionate cross-section of a lot of our assets," Don Jr. said in 2008.[4] Five years later, Eric Trump reportedly said the family did not need American banks because "we have all the funding we need out of Russia."[5]

In 2008, the future president sold a massive Palm Beach beachfront mansion complete with art gallery, ballroom, and forty-eight-car garage that he had bought for $41 million to a Russian oligarch for $95 million, an astonishing profit that drew plenty of suspicion.[6] Even then, he tried to keep the buyer's nationality secret. "Don't say Russian," he asked a reporter at the time.[7] Buyers tied to Russia and other former Soviet republics separately made eighty-six purchases of Trump-branded condominiums in New York and Florida for a total of nearly $109 million—all in cash.[8] In 2013, the future president brought the Miss Universe contest to Moscow and tried unsuccessfully to meet with Putin while in town. "Will he become my new best friend?" Trump asked on Twitter.

During his 2016 campaign, Trump talked admiringly about Putin ("a strong leader") and compared him favorably to Barack Obama ("he is getting an A and our president is not doing so well").[9] "You can get along with those people and get along with them well," he told Bill O'Reilly on Fox News the day he announced his campaign. "You can make deals with those people."[10] He then hosted the Russian ambassador in the front row for his only foreign policy speech of the primaries, at which he promised "improved relations" with Moscow.[11] He even suggested he was perfectly fine if Russia wanted to keep Crimea, the peninsula it seized by force in 2014 from neighboring Ukraine. "The people of Crimea from what I've heard would rather be with Russia than where they were," Trump told George Stephanopoulos of ABC News.[12] He told a German reporter at a news conference that he would consider lifting sanctions on Russia imposed after the Crimea takeover. At the Republican National Convention that summer, Trump campaign advisers stripped language from the party platform calling for "lethal defensive weapons" to be sent to Ukraine in its ongoing efforts to counter Russian-sponsored separatists on its eastern edges, substituting softer wording merely suggesting "appropriate assistance."

After firing his first campaign manager, Trump replaced him with Paul Manafort, a Republican who had built a lucrative lobbying career working for Russians and Ukrainians aligned with Putin. And Trump openly asked Moscow for help winning his campaign, calling on the Kremlin to hack into Hillary Clinton's email ("Russia, if you're listening").[13] When WikiLeaks obtained stolen Clinton campaign emails from Russian agents, Trump's campaign, with the help of his old friend and adviser Roger Stone, appeared to know in advance when they would be released. Indeed, a wave of Clinton campaign emails was posted online hours after the American intelligence community publicly accused Russia of election interference and the *Access Hollywood* tape was disclosed. The timing was so extraordinary that it seemed like a deliberate effort to change the story line away from revelations that could hurt Trump.

What voters did not know at the time was that Trump surrogates had a remarkable amount of contact with Russian figures and intermediaries throughout the campaign. Manafort, who had volunteered to work for Trump for free, secretly slipped internal campaign polling to Konstantin Kilimnik, an old business associate who also happened to be a Russian spy and passed along the data to Russian intelligence. At the same time, Kilimnik was urging Manafort to share with Trump a supposed "peace plan" for Ukraine that would reinstall the country's ousted pro-Russian president, Viktor Yanukovych, a Manafort client and Kremlin ally who had been pushed out in a 2014 revolution and fled to Russia after allegedly misappropriating billions of dollars in stolen Ukrainian funds.

Through all of this, Trump's personal lawyer Michael Cohen was secretly negotiating to build the elusive Trump Tower Moscow even as his boss campaigned for the presidency. By November 2015, Trump had signed a letter of intent with a Russia-based developer. Cohen directly sought help from Putin's office and pursued the deal as late as June 2016, even though Trump repeatedly denied any business interests in Russia. "I have nothing to do with Russia," Trump insisted that July without disclosing the effort to build the tower.[14]

Trump's campaign welcomed help from Moscow while Cohen was still pursuing the real estate deal. In June, a business acquaintance reached out to Don Jr. to set up a meeting at Trump Tower with a "Russian government attorney" who promised to bring dirt on Hillary Clinton as "part of Russia and its government's support for Mr. Trump." Don Jr. replied, "I love it," and invited Manafort and Jared Kushner to join them.[15] In the end, the attorney offered no useful damaging information but pressed them on adoption policy, a thinly veiled reference to American sanctions that had prompted Putin to retaliate by curbing foreign adoptions of Russian children.

Trump stoked suspicions with conflicting accounts of whether he had ever met Putin. "I do have a relationship with him," he told an interviewer in 2013 and told another that he had "met him once."[16] Referring to his Miss Universe contest in Moscow, he said at an appearance at the National Press Club in 2014 that "I spoke indirectly and directly with President Putin, who could not have been nicer."[17] During a primary debate, he implied that they had talked in a television green room.[18] "I got to know him very well because we were both on *60 Minutes;* we were stablemates and we did very well that night," he said.[19] In fact, they never met at *60 Minutes* because they were interviewed separately thousands of miles apart, Trump in New York and Putin in Moscow.

Later, as the issue became more problematic, Trump started denying that he had ever encountered the Russian president. "I never met Putin," he said at a news conference in July 2016. "I don't know who Putin is."[20] But by the time he was elected, Trump was back to defending Putin. In a pre–Super Bowl interview on Fox News, Trump stuck up for the Russian president when Bill O'Reilly called him a killer. "We got a lot of killers," Trump said. "Well, you think our country is so innocent?"[21]

All of it fed theories that Trump and his campaign had been acting in collusion with the Russians. American intelligence agencies had firmly established that Putin not only authorized a covert operation to disrupt American elections but specifically wanted to tilt the outcome in favor of

Trump. When a Trump foreign policy adviser named George Papadopoulos confided to an Australian diplomat over drinks in London in May 2016 that Russia had thousands of Democratic emails that would embarrass Hillary Clinton, Australian officials tipped American intelligence, leading the FBI to open an investigation. Unlike the email probe in which Clinton was eventually cleared, the inquiry into Trump's campaign remained little publicized until after the election. The pre-inaugural phone calls with the Russian ambassador that got Mike Flynn fired only fueled suspicions. And when Trump took office, he prepared to lift some sanctions on Russia until Republican senators led by Mitch McConnell threatened to overrule him with legislation.

Some of those around Trump said the explanation of his fawning approach to Putin was simpler than the fishy facts and unexplained affinity for a Russian dictator made it seem. Instead, they argued, it was more about a lifetime of motivation: money. "By ingratiating himself with Putin and hinting at changes in American sanctions policy against the country under a Trump presidency, the boss was trying to nudge the Moscow Trump Tower project along," Michael Cohen later wrote in a memoir blasting his former boss. "The campaign was far too chaotic and incompetent to actually conspire with the Russian government. The reality was that Trump saw politics as an opportunity to make money and he had no hesitation in bending American foreign policy to his personal financial benefit."[22]

By the time he was inaugurated, the Moscow project was off the table. But Trump saw no reason he should not monetize the presidency in other ways. Unlike presidents for nearly half a century, he refused to extricate himself from his private business or release his tax returns. Starting during the campaign, Trump claimed he would put out his tax returns once an IRS audit was finished. But he never did, and every year of his presidency he would just repeat the same unconvincing excuse.

His Trump International Hotel in Washington, which opened in the city's historic Old Post Office Building on Pennsylvania Avenue near the White House weeks before the 2016 election, became a magnet for money from people and institutions currying favor with the president. The Saudi government spent more than $270,000 at the hotel in just three months after the inauguration. In the years to come, the governments of Turkey, Kuwait, the United Arab Emirates, and the Philippines, among others, would host events at the Trump hotel or one of his other properties.[23] Republican operatives and Washington lobbyists made the Trump hotel a regular venue for receptions. Trump himself often held court in the restaurant on the mezzanine, at Table 72, a round booth with an unmissable view. Servers were instructed to bring him a bottle of hand sanitizer and a Diet Coke immediately upon arrival; his menu of shrimp cocktail, steak, and fries never varied either. Incredible access, in other words, for those who might be looking for it.[24]

It all looked like a violation of the emoluments clause of the Constitution, which forbids public officials from accepting "any present, Emolument, Office or Title, of any kind whatever, from any King, Prince, or foreign State." Critics quickly filed lawsuits, although courts eventually rejected the claims.[25] Trump was more accustomed to lawsuits and investigations than most presidents because he had been sued and investigated so many times for everything from racially discriminatory rental practices to questionable stock dealings to violations of casino regulations. Most of the time, he got off without consequence or perhaps with a fine. When he entered politics, another slew of investigations followed. Just before being sworn in as president, Trump paid $25 million to former students of his defunct Trump University to settle fraud claims. The New York State attorney general later found a "shocking pattern of illegality" at the Trump Foundation, which functioned "as little more than a checkbook to serve Mr. Trump's business and political interests."[26]

So Trump was delighted to now have the Justice Department under his purview and wasted little time moving to protect himself. Within days of his election, he began courting Preet Bharara, the United States attorney for the Southern District of New York, whose jurisdiction included Trump's business and home. Within days, Bharara was invited to Trump Tower to meet with the president-elect. Trump made a point of asking for Bharara's mobile phone number. Less than two weeks later, he used it, calling Bharara for no apparent reason other than to shoot the breeze. He called again right before the inauguration, with no evident purpose.

U.S. attorneys rarely hear from a president and Bharara was mystified. He decided it was all right to return the calls while Trump was still president-elect and not yet technically his boss. But then Trump called again after being sworn in, this time on March 9. Bharara considered secretly taping their conversation or having an aide listen in, but instead told the White House he did not want to take the call. The next day, Trump fired Bharara.

No reason was given and because he was a political appointee from the previous administration none was needed. Bharara concluded that Trump had been trying to woo him in case any prosecutorial issues came up involving him or his business—or in case he had any enemies he wanted investigated. Bharara later decided, "He would have called me up eventually and asked for something—I have zero doubt."

The Bharara episode foreshadowed Trump's ultimately futile efforts to win over James Comey and their resulting conflict. At six-foot-eight, Comey was a giant of a man who stood out in any room. Known for a stubborn streak of either principle or self-righteousness, depending on who was talking, Comey had prosecuted money launderers, mobsters, terrorists, and even Martha Stewart before being appointed deputy attorney general by George W. Bush and FBI director by Barack Obama.

His relationship with the new president got off to an awkward start days before the inauguration with that pull-aside to let Trump know about the Steele dossier, followed by the publication of the document by *BuzzFeed News*. Assuming that the FBI director was trying to undercut him rather than warn him, Trump decided to test Comey's loyalties by inviting him to dinner at the White House on January 27, a week after taking office. "Don't talk about Russia, whatever you do," Reince Priebus urged the president, worrying that it would be seen as improperly influencing an investigation.[27] Trump barely listened. Over shrimp scampi and chicken parmesan, the president demanded a virtual oath from the FBI director. "I need loyalty," Trump said. Trying to duck without a direct confrontation, Comey settled on: "You will always get honesty from me." Trump reinterpreted his answer to be what he wanted to hear. "That's what I want," he replied, "honest loyalty."[28] Comey was troubled. Neither Bush nor Obama had ever demanded such a thing. The whole exchange recalled the mobsters Comey had prosecuted as a younger man, so he made a point of recording every conversation with Trump in a memo immediately afterward to protect himself. "To my mind," he wrote later, "the demand was like Sammy the Bull's Cosa Nostra induction ceremony—with Trump, in the role of the family boss, asking me if I have what it takes to be a 'made man.'"[29]

All of this was so out of the norm, but Trump had no real understanding of the rules and certainly no respect for them. His ignorance of both political reality and what it was like to be in the crosshairs of the FBI was clear when he and Jared Kushner had lunch with Chris Christie on February 14, the day after he dismissed Mike Flynn.

"Now that we fired Flynn, the Russia thing is over," Trump told Christie.

Christie laughed. As a former prosecutor, he knew that was ridiculous. "No way," he said. "This Russia thing is far from over." Indeed, he predicted, "we'll be here on Valentine's Day 2018 talking about this."

Trump seemed shocked. "What do you mean?" he said. "Flynn met with the Russians. That was the problem. I fired Flynn. It's over."

Quite the opposite, Christie said. There was no way to curtail the investigation. And Flynn, he said, would remain a problem for Trump for a long time, "like gum on the bottom of your shoe."

Almost as if to prove the point, Kushner's phone rang during the lunch. It was Flynn, calling to complain about how the White House had characterized his departure. Kushner sought to reassure him. "You know the president respects you," he told the fired adviser. "The president cares about you. I'll get the president to send out a positive tweet about you later." Trump nodded in agreement.

But the president was worried about Comey. Trump asked Christie to call the FBI director to "tell him he's part of the team." Christie thought that was "nonsensical" and had no intention of doing so.[30]

As it happened, Comey was at the White House a few hours later for a homeland security briefing. Trump asked him to stay afterward to talk privately. After shooing away Priebus, who tried to join them, Trump leaned on Comey to drop his investigation of Flynn, in effect trying to determine whether the FBI director really was a made man.

"I hope you can see your way clear to letting this go, to letting Flynn go," Trump told him. "He is a good guy. I hope you can let this go."

As he did at their dinner, Comey again tried to dodge without directly contradicting the president. "I agree he is a good guy," he said noncommittally.[31]

Trump called Comey a few more times in the following weeks, complaining that "the cloud" from the Russia inquiry was complicating his ability to manage foreign policy and asking for a public statement affirming that he was not under investigation. "Because I have been very loyal to you, very loyal, we had that thing, you know," Trump said on April 11, alluding to his Mafia-like loyalty request.[32] That was the last time Comey would speak with Trump.

Trump was frustrated. He had already lost one measure of control over the investigation when Jeff Sessions recused himself in March from overseeing the probe on the grounds that he had been a campaign adviser. "I've got a bunch of lawyers who are not aggressive, who are weak, who don't have my best interests in mind, who aren't loyal," Trump complained one day in the Oval Office.[33] The attorney general, the FBI director—they were supposed to answer him and do his bidding. As he saw it, they were his sword against his enemies and his shield against danger. At one point, while pressuring his White House counsel, Don McGahn, to stop Sessions from recusing himself, Trump had bellowed in frustration, "Where's my Roy Cohn?"

That's what he wanted. Another Roy Cohn.

To understand Trump's view of law and justice, it was necessary to understand his relationship with Roy Cohn, the infamous red-baiter turned brass-knuckled New York fixer. More than three decades after his death, Cohn still wielded enormous influence over Trump, a mentor from the grave whose take-no-prisoners approach to business and politics would define the forty-fifth president. To Trump, every lawyer was measured against his memory of Cohn, judged by their willingness to wage unrelenting war on his behalf. All of them, in one way or another, would be found wanting. "Where's my Roy Cohn?" became a regular mantra.

No other modern president would embrace a figure like Cohn. Lean and eternally tanned, with heavy-lidded, often bloodshot eyes, and a scarred nose, Cohn looked the part of the Mafia lawyer he was—the word "reptilian" was used a lot—and he reveled in his brazen defiance of tax collectors, prosecutors, judges, regulators, and civil libertarians.[34] As a young prosecutor, he helped send Julius and Ethel Rosenberg to the electric chair for espionage, then earned national notoriety as the interrogator at Joseph McCarthy's hearings. After McCarthy was eventually censured, Cohn reinvented himself as a New York lawyer who could get anything done for corrupt politicians, mob bosses, Catholic cardinals, the accused wife killer Claus von Bülow, the New York Yankees owner George Steinbrenner, and a young developer on the make named Donald Trump.

By Trump's account, they met in 1973 shortly after the Justice Department filed a lawsuit against his family company for racial discrimination in renting apartments (applications from Black would-be tenants were secretly marked C for "colored").[35] They were introduced at Le Club on the East Side and in the dark haze of the members-only nightspot that catered to the rich and famous, Trump asked Cohn for advice about the lawsuit. "Tell them to go to hell and fight the thing in court," he remembered Cohn counseling.[36]

Which is exactly what he did, with Cohn as his lawyer. Cohn filed a $100 million countersuit, which a federal judge promptly dismissed for "wasting time and paper."[37] After dragging out the fight, Trump was forced to sign a consent decree agreeing to do more to rent to Black applicants. Trump tried to spin it as a victory, but the Justice Department called the settlement "one of the most far-reaching ever negotiated."[38]

Cohn went on to represent Trump in multiple scrapes. He helped wangle an unprecedented forty-year, $410 million tax abatement for redevelopment of the old Commodore Hotel (conveniently hiring the city official who granted it) and a $22.5 million tax exemption for Trump Tower (smoothing things over with the mob-dominated concrete industry).[39] After Trump bought a United States Football League franchise in New Jersey, Cohn filed an antitrust lawsuit for him against the National Football League, a quixotic battle that ultimately backfired and forced the collapse of the USFL. Cohn was an adviser in all things for Trump, even convincing him to insist on a parsimonious prenuptial agreement before his first marriage, then serving as a virtual emcee at the wedding reception.

Cohn was one of the flashiest, most connected men of the era, splitting time between New York and an estate in Greenwich, spinning around in a Rolls-Royce and sailing on a yacht appropriately named the *Defiance*. He dodged taxes so assiduously that the IRS audited him twenty years in a row and had a $7 million lawsuit pending against him when he died. Cohn was a mass of contradictions, "a Jewish anti-Semite and a homosexual homophobe, vehemently closeted but insatiably promiscuous," as the journalist Michael Kruse described him.[40] He was charged at various points with bribery, conspiracy, and bank fraud, yet acquitted in three trials. Eventually, he would be disbarred for lying and swindling a client. Other clients might have shrunk from such an association. Not Trump.

He regularly called Cohn his "best friend" and "the greatest lawyer in the world."[41] He admired the attorney's underhanded ways. "If you need someone to get vicious toward an opponent, you get Roy," Trump said once.[42] Aside from his father, Fred, Cohn was "the most important influence on his early career," the late investigative journalist Wayne Barrett wrote. "He became Donald's mentor, his constant adviser on every significant aspect of his business and personal life."[43] He also introduced Trump "to the netherworld of sordid quid pro quos that Cohn ruled." According to Mary Trump, his niece, the future president got Cohn to secure a federal judgeship for his sister Maryanne from Ronald Reagan's administration, then held it over her whenever she irked him. Maryanne insisted she had earned the post and told him, "If you say that one more time, I will *level* you."[44]

When Cohn fell ill with AIDS, he denied it and insisted it was liver cancer, but Trump knew because everyone knew and pulled some of his business. "I can't believe he's doing this to me," Cohn complained. "Donald pisses ice water."[45] At the memorial service after Cohn's death in 1986 at age fifty-nine, Trump stood in the back, uninvited to speak. "Roy is a terrible lawyer," Trump once joked to a crowd gathered at a party hosted by Cohn. "But I only need to mention his name and people are too scared to challenge me."[46] By comparison, every other lawyer he ever had was weak, unfaithful, inadequate. "The way he told the Roy Cohn story was they were 12 and 0 and he always won," one aide recalled.

In the White House, Trump once erupted at Don McGahn for scribbling down what they were saying on a notepad. "Why do you take notes?" Trump demanded. "Lawyers don't take notes. I never had a lawyer who took notes."

McGahn said he kept notes because he was a "real lawyer."

"I've had a lot of great lawyers, like Roy Cohn," Trump said. "He did not take notes."[47]

McGahn did not respond. It was not, he later recalled, the first time that "the ghost of Roy had come into the Oval Office."[48]

By May 3, Trump had lost what patience he had with Comey. The FBI director testified on Capitol Hill that day that he felt "mildly nauseous" knowing his last-minute decision to reopen the investigation into Hillary Clinton's emails might have influenced the outcome of the election.[49] He meant that he never wanted the FBI to play any role in politics, but it sounded as if he considered Trump's election stomach-churning.

Meeting with McGahn, Jeff Sessions, and others in the Oval Office that day, Trump asked about the hearing. "How did Comey do?" he asked.

"Not well," McGahn replied. "He had opportunities to make clear that you weren't under investigation but didn't."

At that point, Comey's fate was sealed. If Sessions would not act, then Trump would. By Steve Bannon's count, the president brought up the FBI director at least eight times on May 3 and May 4. "He told me three times I'm not under investigation," Trump complained to his adviser. "He's a showboater. He's a grandstander. I don't know any Russians."

Bannon told him it was too late to fire Comey because it would not stop the investigation. "That ship had sailed," he said.[50]

But holed up that weekend at his golf club in Bedminster, Trump watched replays of Comey's testimony and decided with Jared Kushner and Stephen Miller to fire the FBI director. He returned to the White House on Monday, May 8, with a letter of dismissal drafted by Miller, who was not a lawyer. The rambling four-page letter encapsulated Trump's rants about "the fabricated and politically-motivated allegations of a Trump-Russia relationship with respect to the 2016 Presidential Election."[51]

When Don McGahn read the letter, he saw trouble. He was already scheduled to have lunch with Sessions and summoned Rod Rosenstein, the new deputy attorney general, only a couple weeks into his job, to join them so the three of them could talk it over. Later that afternoon, they met with Trump in the Oval Office.

Trump had copies of the Miller letter handed to Sessions and Rosenstein. The president was talking a mile a minute while Rosenstein tried to concentrate on reading.

"Do you agree with my letter?" Trump asked.

"I don't think it's a good idea to send this letter," Rosenstein answered.

There were so many problematic points in it, Rosenstein thought, but he opted to focus on just one. "Why would you mention Russia?" he asked.

"Well, that's very important," Trump said. "He told me three times I'm not a subject."

"Well, if it doesn't have anything to do with Russia," Rosenstein said of the decision to fire Comey, "you shouldn't mention Russia."

The president's determination to rid himself of Comey put his three top lawyers in a bind. Sessions, Rosenstein, and McGahn were all long-standing Republicans and seasoned Washington figures. The diminutive, silver-haired Sessions had served for years as a backbench senator railing about immigration. In 2016, he was driving in his home state of Alabama when he heard on the radio that Trump was coming for a rally. He turned the car around, finagled his way into the event, and became the first senator to endorse the billionaire for president—and won the Justice Department as his reward. Rosenstein was a longtime prosecutor who was appointed U.S. attorney in Maryland by George W. Bush and kept on by Barack Obama, making him the nation's longest-serving U.S. attorney when he was tapped as Sessions's deputy. And McGahn was a veteran GOP campaign finance lawyer who served on the Federal Election Commission before going to work for Trump's campaign and eventually his White House.

As it happened, all three agreed that Comey should go. Sessions, in fact, had recommended during the transition that the president replace the FBI director. Rosenstein agreed that Comey had overstepped his bounds during the Clinton inquiry by arrogating to himself the power to decide whether to charge a crime, normally the province of prosecutors, and then announcing his decisions publicly. McGahn concurred. But none of them thought Trump should fire Comey to stop the Russia probe and none of them thought the way he was going about it made sense. So it was decided that they would put aside the Miller letter, with its scorching, decidedly unlegalistic language attacking Comey, and instead Rosenstein would draft a memo critiquing Comey's performance in the Clinton case, due the next day. He left the White House around 6 p.m., headed back to the Justice Department and stayed there until around 3 or 4 a.m., before returning around 8 a.m. to finish it. Sessions added a cover memo endorsing the judgment and it was sent to the White House.

"You're going to like this," McGahn told Trump when he handed him Rosenstein's memo.

Trump skimmed through it. "Oh, this is good. I see why you like this better than my letter."

Rosenstein's memo harshly condemned Comey's actions during the Clinton affair. "The way the Director handled the conclusion of the email investigation was wrong," Rosenstein wrote. "As a result, the FBI is unlikely to regain public and congressional trust until it has a Director who understands the gravity of the mistakes and pledges never to repeat them."[52] Rosenstein made no mention of the Russia investigation.

But Rosenstein was fooling himself if he thought that was not the president's real motivation. And Rosenstein failed to understand that the White House planned to set him up as the fall guy for Trump's decision. Within minutes of the announcement of Comey's firing, Sean Spicer went to Pebble Beach, the area outside the White House where television cameras were set up. The decision to fire Comey, he explained, was Rosenstein's doing. "It was all him," Spicer said. "No one from the White House. That was a DOJ decision."[53]

Sarah Huckabee Sanders, then Spicer's deputy, repeated the same fiction at a briefing the next day. Rosenstein, she said, had decided that Comey should be removed and approached the president "on his own" to share his view—neither of which was true. Sanders went on to adopt another Trump fabrication, telling reporters that "we've heard from countless members of the FBI" that they did not support Comey, an assertion she later acknowledged was made up entirely.[54] Mike Pence followed the party line as well, saying the president had decided to "accept the recommendation of the deputy attorney general and the attorney general to remove Director Comey."[55] In past administrations, such falsehoods would have been credibility-destroying career-enders.

As he would so many times, Trump then undercut his own staff by contradicting the cover story and admitting his real purpose to a pair of Russian officials who were visiting him in the Oval Office the day after Comey's ouster—in and of itself a highly unusual audience that Trump had granted at Putin's personal request. "I just fired the head of the FBI," the president exulted to Sergey Lavrov, the Russian foreign minister, and

Sergey Kislyak, the ambassador to Washington, in comments that quickly leaked. "He was crazy, a real nut job. I faced great pressure because of Russia. That's taken off."[56]

Trump further broadcast his real aims when he admitted to Lester Holt of NBC News the next night that he had the Russia investigation in mind when he fired Comey. "When I decided to just do it, I said to myself, I said, 'You know, this Russia thing with Trump and Russia is a made-up story,'" Trump said. Rosenstein's memo, he confirmed, was not the instigation. "Regardless of recommendation, I was going to fire Comey," Trump said.[57] Rosenstein and the other lawyers gasped when they saw the clip. It was practically an admission by the president that he was trying to shut down the Russia investigation, as close to a confession of obstruction of justice as prosecutors ever hear. Instead of removing the "great pressure" on himself, Trump had only increased it.

Comey, meanwhile, was intent on making sure Trump would face accountability. He authorized a friend to leak to Michael Schmidt of *The New York Times* that Trump had pressed the FBI director for "loyalty" before firing him. The resulting story set off Trump, who responded with a bizarre tweet suggesting he might have secretly recorded his interactions with Comey. "Lordy, I hope there are tapes," Comey replied.[58]

Trump was about to find out what it meant to fire the FBI director who was investigating him. At 12:30 p.m. on May 16, Rod Rosenstein and a couple of his aides met with Andrew McCabe, the Comey deputy now serving as acting FBI director, who dropped a bombshell: he had just authorized his agents to expand the investigation of Trump's campaign to look at whether Trump himself had colluded with Russia or obstructed justice, and he planned to tell congressional leaders the next day.

Rosenstein was reeling. The president was under investigation? With Jeff Sessions's recusal, Rosenstein was in charge of the matter and now confronted a scenario that sounded like a Cold War spy novel, the acting FBI director telling the acting attorney general that the commander in chief might be under the influence of a hostile foreign power. But it was no John le Carré plot line. It was real.

Rosenstein and McCabe were barely acquainted, but quickly grew deeply suspicious of each other. While Rosenstein was a Republican political appointee, McCabe was a career FBI agent who had investigated the Russian mob and international terrorists before moving up the ranks to become Comey's top lieutenant. McCabe had already been a target of

Trump, who seized on the fact that his wife had run for the Virginia legislature as a Democrat with nearly $675,000 in donations from the state
party and a political action committee controlled by the governor, Terry
McAuliffe, a close friend of the Clintons. A Republican himself, McCabe
in the week since taking over the bureau had found himself on the receiving end of Trump's loyalty tests as the president, in phone calls and meetings, pressed him to agree that the FBI workforce was happy Comey had
been fired. McCabe knew that was not true but like so many others chose
not to argue with the president.

As Rosenstein absorbed the latest developments, he grew exasperated
by McCabe. He believed the FBI and its new leader were out of control. How could McCabe initiate an investigation of the president of the
United States without consulting the Justice Department? And how could
he schedule a meeting to inform Congress without the acting attorney
general? To McCabe, Rosenstein seemed almost unhinged. He told associates afterward that the deputy attorney general teared up and had to
excuse himself to go to the bathroom to blow his nose and calm down.
Each thought the other had a conflict of interest and should bow out of
the investigation.

At some point, McCabe said later, Rosenstein even suggested that he
could wear a wire to a meeting with Trump to get him to talk about his
real motives for firing Comey. And if they did obtain evidence that Trump
was compromised, according to McCabe, Rosenstein raised the possibility
of invoking the Twenty-fifth Amendment of the Constitution, which per-
mits the vice president and cabinet to remove a president who is "unable
to discharge the powers and duties of his office." In McCabe's recollec-
tion, Rosenstein even mulled which cabinet members might go along—
for starters, there was Sessions and maybe John Kelly.

The discussion was so astonishing that McCabe recorded it in a memo:
"As our conversation continued the DAG proposed that he could potentially wear a recording device into the Oval Office to collect additional
evidence on the President's true intentions," McCabe wrote, using the
initials for deputy attorney general. "He said he thought this might be
possible because he was not searched when he entered the White House.
I told him that I would discuss the opportunity with my investigative team
and get back to him."[59] In the declassified version of McCabe's memo that
was later released, there was no mention of the Twenty-fifth Amendment,
but large sections were redacted. Rosenstein later told associates that he
had asked if *McCabe* was going to wear a wire with the president, not volunteered to do so himself, and he denied having any "serious discussion"

of the Twenty-fifth Amendment, the kind of squirrelly phrasing that did not mean there was no discussion at all.

No one, in the end, wore a wire to tape the president. But McCabe's squeeze play worked. Rosenstein had already been considering appointing a special counsel to take over the Russia investigation to avoid appearances of conflict of interest. Now that he had been told that the president himself was under examination, there was little real choice. A special counsel investigation would have a greater chance of being credible to the public. Moreover, Rosenstein was irritated by McCabe. By installing a special counsel who would report to himself, Rosenstein could take control away from the acting FBI director.

The person Rosenstein had in mind was Robert Mueller, the former FBI director who had served under George W. Bush and Barack Obama and was almost universally respected as a model of probity. Even before the McCabe meeting, Rosenstein had already sounded Mueller out about whether he would serve as special counsel if it came to that. When Rosenstein made clear it would require leaving his law firm, WilmerHale, to commit to the assignment full-time, Mueller declined.

As it happened, on the same day McCabe was forcing Rosenstein's hand on a special counsel, Mueller was at the White House at the president's invitation to discuss Comey's replacement at the FBI. While Trump would later claim Mueller was applying for his old job, Mueller insisted he was only there to offer advice. By day's end, Mueller reached out to Rosenstein to say that he had changed his mind and would leave his firm to accept the special counsel appointment.

The next day, May 17, unaware of Rosenstein's plans, Trump was interviewing another candidate to replace Comey, Frank Keating, a former Oklahoma governor who once served as an FBI agent. Don McGahn was told he had a phone call and slipped out. When he returned, he whispered to Jeff Sessions, "Rod is on the phone and needs to speak with you now." Sessions then left the room, returning only as Keating was leaving. They shut the door.

"Mr. President, I need to tell you I just got a call from Rod Rosenstein and he has appointed a special counsel on the Russia matter and it will be public in half an hour," Sessions said.

Trump slumped in his chair, leaning way back. "Oh my God," he said. "This is terrible. This is the end of my presidency. I'm fucked."

Others in the room thought much the same. Annie Donaldson, McGahn's deputy, scribbled in her notes: "Is this the beginning of the end?"[60]

It would be hard to overstate Trump's agitation as he absorbed the consequences of the new investigation that he had just brought upon himself. The immediate target of his ire was right in front of him and he turned on Sessions ferociously. "How could you let this happen, Jeff?" he demanded. "How could you let it happen? I appointed you attorney general. You recused yourself. Left me on an island by myself."

He went on to attack Rosenstein and Sessions's decision to hire him. "You let me down, Jeff," Trump continued. "Kennedy names his brother AG. Obama names Holder. It's the most important appointment and I appoint you and you have let me down."

Sessions stiffened. "Well, if you feel like I need to step aside and you don't have confidence in me, you can put someone else in as attorney general," he said.

"Everyone tells me if you get one of these independent counsels, it ruins your presidency," Trump moaned. "It takes years and years and I won't be able to do anything. This is the worst thing that's ever happened to me."

Mike Pence tried to console him. "This may not be so bad," he offered. "Nobody here thinks it's the end of your presidency. It could be a good thing in the end."

Trump was not buying it. "It's not," he said. "It's terrible."

He turned back to Sessions. "Jeff, you really let me down. I think you should resign. I think you should submit your resignation."

"Okay," Sessions said. He picked up his papers and shoved them in a folder. "You'll have it." He turned to go and then paused to say that he still supported Trump and his agenda. He stuck out his hand. "It has been an honor to serve as attorney general."

Pence tried to intervene. "Could the three of us just have a moment?"

The others stepped out, but the president would not be talked out of his rage. Don McGahn rushed to find Reince Priebus.

"We've got a problem," McGahn said, red-faced and out of breath.

"What?" the chief of staff asked.

"Well, we just got a special counsel and Sessions just resigned."

"What the hell are you talking about?" Priebus exclaimed. "That can't happen."

But it could and it had. Priebus bolted down the back stairway of the West Wing, out the door, and into the parking lot to find Sessions in a black sedan with the engine running about to leave. Priebus banged on the car door, then jumped inside.

Sessions told him he was resigning.

"You cannot resign. It's not possible," Priebus insisted. "We are going to talk about this right now."[61]

Priebus dragged Sessions out of the car and back into the White House to his office. Pence and Steve Bannon joined them, pressing Sessions not to step down.

Trump's eruption would open a remarkable standoff between the president and the attorney general that would drag on for a year and a half, leaving a broken relationship at the heart of the administration that would drive decisions by a weakened, insecure Justice Department chief and prove a source of never-ending rage for Trump as he tried to figure out how to stop this new special counsel that he saw as an existential threat.

Back in the Oval Office, Trump was interviewing the next candidate for the FBI, former senator Joseph Lieberman of Connecticut, who had been recommended by Trump's longtime lawyer Marc Kasowitz. Lieberman, who worked part-time at Kasowitz's law firm, had been a Washington iconoclast, the Democratic vice presidential candidate in 2000 who was effectively run out of his party because of his support for the Iraq War and later endorsed his Republican friend John McCain for president in 2008. Now Lieberman found himself in the Oval Office with a steaming mad Trump.

"Did you hear the shocking news?" Trump asked him. The president then told Lieberman that a special counsel had just been named. "The guy they just appointed was sitting in the same chair you are!" Trump exclaimed. He was furious at his attorney general. "I can't believe Jeff Sessions allowed it to happen."

For the next hour and fifteen minutes, Lieberman got a taste of how Trump's White House operated. The Oval Office was like a train station as advisers filed in and out—McGahn, Kushner, Bannon, Priebus. Trump alternated between pitching Lieberman on the FBI post and railing about Mueller's appointment. Trump dictated a blistering statement to Hope Hicks attacking Sessions. Lieberman was taken aback at how harsh it was. Hicks left to type it up and came back about twenty minutes later for Trump to approve it. She had taken out a lot of the vitriol. "Okay, okay, fine, put it out," Trump said grudgingly.

Lieberman could hardly sleep that night. Did he have a responsibility to take the job? In the end, he was saved from having to decide because Trump in the meantime had asked Kasowitz to represent him in the investigation, making it a conflict of interest for Lieberman to take over the

FBI. Lieberman was relieved. "I felt like I had been saved by some sort of divine intervention," he said later.

To take over the FBI, Trump eventually went with a recommendation from Chris Christie, who suggested his personal attorney, Christopher Wray, a by-the-book former assistant attorney general who had defended the New Jersey governor in the Bridgegate scandal after Christie's aides were caught closing the George Washington Bridge in an effort to punish a political adversary. Wray, who had prosecuted the lobbyist Jack Abramoff as well as corrupt congressmen of both parties when he served in the Bush Justice Department, would go on to assure the Senate that he would not be a Trump stooge—"I am not faint of heart," he promised—and be confirmed 92 to 5.[62]

Sessions, in the meantime, had returned to the Justice Department thoroughly deflated. He sat in his office stewing, uncertain what to do. It was almost 10 p.m. "You have to give him a letter because you told him you would," Jody Hunt, his chief of staff, told him. "But what you should do is write down in the letter that he *asked* you for your resignation and make it say, 'if you accept it,' so it's his choice. Otherwise, it will be that you abandoned him."

Sessions agreed and started to write the letter, then gave up. "Let's do it in the morning," he said.

By 8:15 the next morning, though, he had already been summoned to a 9 a.m. meeting at the White House. "You have to have that letter," Hunt told him.

"Go write it," Sessions said.

After a scramble, they got a few sentences on paper, making clear it was written "at your request," and rushed out the door, arriving at the White House five minutes late. Sessions was escorted into the residence, where he put the letter on a coffee table. Trump asked Sessions if he still wanted to serve as attorney general and Sessions said yes. Trump agreed to let him stay, but stood, picked up the letter, and put it in his pocket.

When Priebus, Bannon, and McGahn learned later that Trump kept the letter, they were stunned. They worried that Trump could use it to improperly influence Sessions, holding it over his head to get him to do whatever the president wanted. Priebus told the group that it amounted to a "shock collar" keeping the attorney general on a leash, an extraordinary comment for a White House chief of staff to make about his boss.[63]

A few days later, during his first overseas trip, Trump took the letter from his pocket while on Air Force One flying from Saudi Arabia to Israel and showed it off to Hope Hicks and other aides. But later on the trip, when Priebus tried to retrieve the letter from him, Trump claimed he did not have it, saying it was back at the White House. Priebus insisted he could not keep it.

Three days after returning to Washington, Trump gave in. Jody Hunt was summoned to the White House to take the letter back. Trump was on the phone with Wilbur Ross, the commerce secretary, when Hunt was escorted into the Oval Office, but motioned him to open the envelope. On it, Trump had written, "Jeff, not accepted. Make America great again. Donald Trump."

Trump was not the only one naive about the ways of the nation's capital. Jared Kushner reacted to the Mueller appointment as if it had solved their political problems, at least in the short term, by forcing Congress to back off the various investigations it too had launched into Russian interference in the election.

"This is great, this is great," he told Mike Dubke. "Now we won't have to answer all these questions from these senators."

"What do you mean?" Dubke asked.

"Now there's a prosecutor so it'll go into the courts and we won't have to answer these senators."

Dubke was flabbergasted. "You really don't understand how Washington works, do you?" he said. A special counsel inquiry would be the most intense investigation Trump or Kushner had ever endured. "I hope you have a good proctologist, because you're going to bend over, my friend," Dubke told Kushner.

That was something Dubke had no interest in himself. He had promised his wife when he took the White House job that he would quit if it ever became necessary to hire a lawyer. He was not going to bankrupt his family to defend Trump. And so, nine days after Mueller was appointed, Dubke turned in his resignation.

Trump turned to another Washington veteran for advice on how to handle the special counsel probe. George Conway, the husband of Kellyanne Conway, had agreed to head the Justice Department's civil division, when his wife asked him to write a memo for the president on the Mueller inquiry. This was a sideline expertise of Conway's. A graduate of Harvard and Yale Law School who went on to become a partner at Wachtell, Lipton, Rosen & Katz, he had been one of the so-called Elves, a loose group of conservative lawyers who secretly provided information and legal advice to Bill Clinton's antagonists during the investigation that led to the impeachment of 1998. In his memo for Trump, Conway contrasted Trump's "fake news" scandal with Clinton's "real scandal"—but then advised him to handle it just as Clinton had. Play "rope-a-dope." Just be president. Let your lawyers take care of the investigation. "Everything you say or tweet becomes the story of the day because you're the president and you have the bully pulpit," Conway wrote. "The people of the country want to see a president being president, not being his own defense lawyer."

Trump called a couple days later. He was not, of course, going to follow Conway's advice, at least not the part urging him to shut up about the investigation, but he wanted to know who should represent him. He coveted famous attorneys like Brendan Sullivan of Iran-contra fame or Theodore Olson, the Republican lawyer who had won *Bush v. Gore*, but the city's most celebrated lawyers wanted nothing to do with him. And as more information came out, Conway increasingly came to understand why. Over the course of the next few weeks, he grew uncomfortable with Trump too, and pulled his name from consideration for the Justice Department job.

The next time he saw Trump was at Steven Mnuchin's black-tie wedding three weeks later at Washington's Andrew W. Mellon Auditorium. Mike Pence officiated as the fifty-four-year-old treasury secretary married Louise Linton, a thirty-six-year-old actress who had recently appeared in a remake of the horror movie *Cabin Fever*. It was his third marriage and her second. They had already moved into a $12.6 million house off Massachusetts Avenue, although she split her time between Washington and Los Angeles, posting red-carpet appearances on her Instagram account in between animal rights advocacy.

Some of Mnuchin's relatives despised the president, seeing him as a vulgar narcissist, and were unhappy to be in his presence. Mnuchin's mother went so far as to feign a broken arm, wrapping it in a sling, to avoid having to shake hands with Trump. Mnuchin's father later complained to friends that the affair was tacky and expressed astonishment that the president did not even offer a toast. Gary Cohn, a Mnuchin rival since their days at Goldman Sachs, skipped altogether. Asked why, he told an associate, "Well, I've been to a couple of his weddings. Neither of them worked out."

At the cocktail reception, the president ran into the Conways. As they talked, it became clear that Trump mistakenly believed that George had turned down the Justice job because Jeff Sessions was "weak," then began ranting about the attorney general. George and Kellyanne later escaped to the bar and laughed at how bizarre it was to have a president act that way.

By the next morning, though, George had a change of heart. "Yeah, but it's the president of the United States," he remembered telling his wife. "It's not funny."

She did not see it that way. "What are you talking about?" she asked. "He's hilarious."

The Mnuchins were not the only family being torn apart by Trump.

Whatever the president hoped to gain by firing James Comey, it soon became clear that the investigation Comey started and parallel inquiries by the House and Senate intelligence committees were only becoming more threatening.

The next big blow came within weeks of Comey's firing and Mueller's appointment, when a search of Trump campaign emails in response to investigators' requests turned up the message traffic that had led to the June 2016 meeting at Trump Tower that Don Jr., Jared Kushner, and Paul Manafort held with the visiting Russians promising dirt on Hillary Clinton. Soon enough, *The New York Times* let the White House know that it had learned about the meeting and was about to publish a story. Aboard Air Force One flying home from a trip to Germany, Trump dictated a deceptive statement to be released in his son's name. "We primarily discussed a program about the adoption of Russian children," the statement said.[64] Only after Don Jr. realized that the *Times* had copies of the emails did he post the entire exchange to get ahead of the reporters, but the message chain exposed how misleading the presidentially dictated statement was.

Trump was livid. "He's such a fuckup," he railed about his son. "He screwed up again, but this time, he's screwing us all, big time!"[65] In fact, while the original meeting was a huge mistake, it was the president who had screwed up now by drafting a statement that would quickly be exposed as disingenuous.

In the Trump family, father and son had long had a fraught relationship. From the start, Trump doubted that Don Jr. was worthy of the family mantle. When Ivana gave birth, he objected to sharing his name with his newborn son. "What if he's a loser?" he asked.[66] Ivana prevailed, but Don Jr.'s upbringing was tumultuous. At age twelve, he grew estranged from his father during the divorce from his mother. "You don't love us!" he reportedly yelled at Trump. "You don't even love yourself. You just love your money!"[67] Don Jr. did not speak with Trump for a year, hanging up on him whenever he called.

Reconciliation did not fully close the rift. Don Jr. eventually went to work for the family business, but Trump regularly berated him, grousing about the latest "shit deal" his son brought him. It often seemed like Don Jr. could do no right. When he once asked his father if he was nervous as he was about to participate in a staged televised wrestling match, Trump snapped at him for putting such a thought in his head right before going onstage. "What kind of stupid fucking question is that?" he roared. "Get out of here." Then, as if his son were not still in the room, Trump exclaimed, "The kid has the worst fucking judgment of anyone I have ever met." When Michael Cohen, the Trump lawyer, later asked if he was okay, Don Jr. brushed it off. "We have a torturous relationship," he said. "It's not the first time he said that and it won't be the last."[68]

Nonetheless, Trump had invited his son to join the campaign and Don Jr. eventually became a leading surrogate for his father. More than anyone else in the family, he channeled the culture war grievances that animated his father's campaign crowds. In his warm-up speeches, Don Jr. acerbically defied political correctness and suggested the media would be "warming up the gas chamber" if Republicans acted like Democrats.[69] He even compared Syrian refugees to a bowl of Skittles with one poisoned candy among the sweets, only to generate a furor. "Look what he did now," Trump growled. "He screwed up again. What a fuckup."[70]

When Trump moved into the White House, Don Jr. remained in New York but continued his new sideline in politics, firing away at Democrats, journalists, and other perceived enemies as he sought his father's approval. During James Comey's testimony before Congress a month after his dismissal, Don Jr. posted more than eighty tweets attacking the former FBI director. "Basically, Trump Jr. is the voice of undiluted Trumpism," observed Roger Stone, the president's longtime friend.[71]

Publication in July of the emails regarding Don Jr.'s Russia meeting sparked the predictable firestorm and made Trump furious all over again at Jeff Sessions. Just days after the revelations, Trump unexpectedly unloaded on his attorney general during an interview with the *Times*. "Sessions should have never recused himself," Trump declared. "And if he was going to recuse himself, he should have told me before he took the job, and I would have picked somebody else." He complained that the recusal was "very unfair to the president." As a result, the responsibility fell to Rod Rosenstein, who Trump pointed out was from Baltimore. "There are very few Republicans in Baltimore, if any," he complained.[72]

Actually, Rosenstein was a longtime Republican who lived in the Washington suburbs, not Baltimore. But that was not Trump's point.

The point was he was no Roy Cohn.

CHAPTER 6

My Generals

On June 12, Trump convened his first full cabinet meeting. By way of opening, he offered one of his trademark fantastical claims. "Never has there been a president who has passed more legislation and who has done more things than what we've done," Trump said, offering a possible grudging exception for Franklin Roosevelt at the height of the Great Depression. What came next was unlike any other presidency as well, not so much a cabinet meeting as a televised Trump testimonial.

Mike Pence set the tone. "It is the greatest privilege of my life," he said, "to serve as vice president to a president who is keeping his word to the American people."

Jeff Sessions seconded the sentiment. "It's an honor to serve you," the attorney general said.

"I want to thank you for getting this country moving again," Transportation Secretary Elaine Chao said.

"I just got back from Mississippi, they love you there," Agriculture Secretary Sonny Perdue said.

Reince Priebus thanked Trump "on behalf of the entire senior staff around you, Mr. President, for the opportunity and the blessing that you have given us to serve your agenda."

Midway through this extraordinary display of personal fealty reminiscent of North Korea–style prostrations to an autocratic leader came Jim Mattis, sitting next to Trump on his left, austere in a gray suit and red tie, the bags under his eyes sagging even more than usual. "Mr. President," the defense secretary said simply, skipping the paeans and lavish praise of his colleagues, "it's an honor to represent the men and women of the Department of Defense."[1]

This was no minor departure in tone. A few weeks earlier, Mattis had given a commencement address at the United States Military Academy at West Point in which he praised the standard of "apolitical" service by "defenders who look past the hot political rhetoric of our day." He exhorted the graduating cadets to live by that creed. "Hold the line," he told them.[2] It may have been a pep talk, but it sounded a lot like a personal mission statement too. Days before the cabinet meeting, Mattis had refused to publicly endorse Trump's withdrawal from the Paris climate accord, another stark contrast with the rest of the cabinet, whose statements of support were released in a coordinated wave by the White House. Instead, Mattis told an audience the next day at an annual defense conference in Singapore: "Bear with us." Alluding to the famous quote often attributed to Winston Churchill, he added, "Once we have exhausted all possible alternatives, the Americans will do the right thing."[3]

Not even six months into Trump's presidency, the accumulating pile of evidence made publicly apparent what had been privately obvious for some time: the country had, for the first time since Richard Nixon's final days, a defense secretary who saw his job as constraining the president of the United States rather than empowering him. And it was not going well.

Trump's profound misunderstanding of Mattis and the rest of the military hierarchy had been evident from his first hour in office. "See my generals, those generals are going to keep us so safe," the new president said at his inaugural luncheon in the Capitol, gesturing toward Mattis and John Kelly. "If I'm doing a movie, I'd pick you."[4] To Trump, the movie was and always would be *Patton*, the George C. Scott paean to the kind of general who shot first and asked questions later.

He had no idea that his own generals considered Patton a model of how *not* to be a leader. The present-day generals Trump admired were ones he saw on Fox News, like Mike Flynn and his chief of staff, Keith Kellogg, a retired lieutenant general described by a colleague as "more Trump than Trump" in his America First views. In the reviewing stands in front of the White House as the inaugural parade rolled by, Trump approached Mattis and Joe Dunford, the chairman of the Joint Chiefs of Staff. "Get out of Afghanistan," Trump told them. They would long remember the moment. Was that what their new commander in chief regarded as presidential decision making?

"His entire context for the military at this point was watching the movie *Patton*," said a retired general who served with Mattis, Dunford, and John Kelly. "The guy had no idea what a general did. He respected their power and status and he wanted to have them around him because he felt that having generals around him—'my generals'—would make him appear even more powerful. What he hadn't bargained for was the fact that his generals were going to oppose him on moral grounds on many things. He just thought they were all about power, and the wielding of power and destruction."

Knowing little about his appointees as he hastily selected them, Trump had not realized that his national security policy would now be in the hands of three of the most influential Marines in a generation, all tied together by bonds of war and friendship. Both Dunford and Kelly had served under Mattis in Iraq as colonels commanding battalions on the famous First Marine Division's blitz toward Baghdad, the longest ground march in Marine history. All three would go on to become four-star generals together. In 2010, Kelly's son, First Lieutenant Robert Kelly, stepped on a landmine in Afghanistan and died. "When Kelly opened the door to go to work that morning, it was Joe Dunford standing in the rain on the porch to tell him," as the retired general recalled. Dunford had been quietly waiting there since 4:30 a.m. "So you can't articulate in words the depths of the relationship and I also don't think you can put into words the value of those relationships to the country at that particular moment."

Mattis, no longer in uniform and officially a civilian political appointee, had the most public and thus most challenging job of dealing with the president. By the time of the cabinet meeting, it had already become clear that Mattis was more of a "warrior monk," as the glowing profiles of him often put it, than the Rambo-style killer Trump presumed. The coverage invariably mentioned the library of thousands of books Mattis brought with him from posting to posting, his ascetic personal habits, modest beginnings in the Pacific Northwest, and the macho aphorisms for which he was known. Mattis had fought George W. Bush's "global war on terror" initially in Afghanistan, where his Marines seized an airstrip outside Kandahar for the first American forward operating base in the country, and then in Iraq, where he oversaw the brutal Marine battle in Fallujah. Eventually, under Barack Obama, he became head of the United States Central Command, responsible for all American troops in the Middle East.

Mattis took from those assignments an abiding hatred of Iran, which he blamed for a devastating campaign of roadside bombs that had killed or injured thousands of his men in Iraq. When Obama asked him his priorities in the new role, Mattis famously replied: "I have three: Iran, Iran, and Iran."[5] The Obama team, convinced that Mattis was not on board with the president's plan to negotiate a nuclear deal with the Iranian regime, eventually forced him out and effectively ended his storied military career. "In combat, he was the ultimate paragon of courage and nobility; nothing ever worried him," a former official close to Mattis said. That is, until the day "he'd been fired by the Obama administration. That was the only time I ever saw him really emotional."

Knowing of the bad break with Obama, Trump and those around him embraced Mattis but failed to understand that he was not driven by animus toward Trump's predecessor. Nor did he have the blood lust that Trump seemed to imagine lurking in all the uniformed brass. Mattis reveled in Marine tough talk—"Be polite, be professional, but have a plan to kill everybody you meet," he was famous for saying—but he also styled himself as a thinking man's general.[6] "The most important six inches on the battlefield is between your ears" was another, less cited, of his sayings.[7]

At his confirmation hearing, he openly acknowledged that he envisioned his role as a check on some of Trump's impulses, most notably the president's penchant for undermining alliances. "History is clear," Mattis told the Senate Armed Services Committee. "Nations with strong allies thrive, and those without them wither."[8] From the start, he was repeatedly asked what circumstances would prompt him to quit. "If I ever thought it was something immoral, I'd be back fishing on the Columbia River tomorrow," he would say.[9] Once confirmed, he pushed back on Trump so often that another cabinet officer joked that every comment the defense secretary made began, "Again, Mr. President, I have the misfortune of disagreeing with you."

Mattis's partner in all this was Joe Dunford. Known as "Fightin' Joe" as he led the Fifth Marine Regiment into Iraq in 2003, Dunford was the thoughtful son of a Boston cop, with master's degrees from Georgetown and Tufts. After serving under Mattis in Iraq, Dunford went on to command American forces in Afghanistan as Obama reduced the military presence there. Named chairman of the Joint Chiefs by Obama in 2015 after a brief stint as Marine Corps commandant, Dunford was reappointed by Trump in May and worked hard to present a united front with Mattis, often playing the role of the silent Marine in uniform at the secretary's side, determined not to be drawn into the president's hyper-politicized world. "I'm part of the furniture," he told Trump, a professional who came with the Situation Room, in effect. "I'm here to provide advice when needed, and that's it." While sitting there biting his tongue, he would often recall the example of George Marshall, the legendary Army chief of staff during World War II. After Franklin Roosevelt once called him "George," Marshall famously made clear that he preferred not to be on a first-name basis. Dunford would tell associates he now understood the story. It was dangerous for military officers to allow a civilian commander in chief to think they were friends. "Still waters run deep in him," Mattis would say of Dunford. "You simply can't shake his faith in his fundamental values."[10]

At the Pentagon, both men told colleagues they were shocked by Trump's conduct in those early months. Dunford informed his staff that the president was so voluble and undisciplined in meetings on crucial national security matters that he had to prepare an "elevator speech" before going to the White House, memorizing whatever points he believed were most important to get across and then waiting for a pause in Trump's endless monologues to jump in and offer them, regardless of what the president was pontificating about at the time.

If the military was not the monolithic killing machine that Trump imagined, filled with made-for-television tough guys who simply saluted at his orders, neither was it united in the effort to constrain him. It had not yet become public, but Mattis feuded from the start with the other senior officer to hold a senior post in Trump's orbit, H. R. McMaster, who remained on active duty as a three-star Army general while national security adviser and was thus technically under Mattis's command. When McMaster took the job, Mattis told him he should retire from the military rather than remain on active duty and was angry that he did not do so.

Another early warning sign came when McMaster planned a fact-finding trip to Afghanistan and the region in the spring of 2017. Afghanistan was the issue that McMaster felt most passionately about. He believed Obama had mishandled the war there—McMaster served in Afghanistan during Obama's presidency as head of the international forces' anticorruption task force—and wanted, as one colleague said, "a do-over."[11] Obama had initially expanded forces in Afghanistan to 100,000 troops in hopes of establishing a secure state and finishing off the Taliban. But Obama's reinforcements came with a two-year expiration date, a crucial mistake, McMaster and other generals believed, that allowed the Taliban to wait out the surge. When Obama left office, just under 10,000 troops remained with an uncertain mission. As Trump indicated on Inauguration Day, he wanted even those withdrawn. McMaster sought to convince him otherwise and spent his first months in office on a drawn-out policy review to provide options other than an abrupt end to an American war that had dragged on for nearly sixteen years already. As a close adviser said, "He believed his job was to prevent the debacle of leaving."

McMaster's self-appointed mission put him on an almost immediate collision course with his commander in chief. And also, as it turned out, with Mattis and the secretary's increasingly close ally, Rex Tillerson. Mattis and Tillerson had not known each other before both becoming unlikely recruits in Trump's cabinet but quickly bonded; they met weekly and often talked daily, even multiple times a day as needed. ("Saint Rex," Mattis nicknamed Tillerson.) As far as policy went, they were not in substantive disagreement with McMaster about Afghanistan or most other matters. Where Trump wanted to blow up international accords like Paris and freely disparaged allies, they were all conservatives in a more old-fashioned sense, seeing themselves as stewards, not disruptors, of a world shaped and guided by American power. Despite the president's militaristic bluster, Trump's "America First" agenda of walking away from contested zones such as Afghanistan and Syria, they believed, would embolden great power rivals Russia and China while making America less secure at home.

That did not mean they agreed with each other, however, about how to stop him. In public, Mattis, Tillerson, and McMaster were portrayed as fellow members of the Axis of Adults. In private, there was pettiness that at times suggested a middle school cafeteria. When McMaster tried to organize weekly breakfasts with just the three of them, as Brent Scowcroft had done during the George H. W. Bush administration, Mattis and Tillerson would not come. McMaster bitterly called them the "G-2" and eventually told colleagues that he had confronted them directly, saying, "Whenever you want to turn the club of two into a club of three, I'm embarrassingly free." On Afghanistan and other issues on which they disagreed with Trump, McMaster believed that Mattis and Tillerson had a strategy of withholding information and options from the president, which in his view was not the way to win the argument.

The schism was compounded by military hierarchy and service rivalries. McMaster was not a Marine but an Army man through and through since his West Point days. Just as importantly, he had not made it into the exclusive club of four-star generals. From the start, Mattis seemed to treat McMaster as a subordinate, not a peer. "Oh, that's how a *three*-star would think," a senior White House official once heard Mattis say dismissively in McMaster's presence.

The issue with McMaster and Tillerson was also hierarchy, but of a different sort. Tillerson, a newcomer to government used to running one of the world's most powerful corporations, had no real understanding of the role of the National Security Council and thought, in effect, that when the topic was foreign policy, the interagency process should be run by him rather than the national security adviser. When that did not happen, Tillerson grew angry with McMaster and withdrew the State Department officials who were, as a matter of routine, detailed to staff the National Security Council. Tillerson's mistake was a simple one, as a senior official who worked with him said: "He didn't understand that if you're not the president, you're staff."

In the case of the early trip to Afghanistan, Mattis and Tillerson not only tried to block McMaster from going, but even took the matter directly to Trump, according to an account that McMaster later gave. He would eventually cite the incident as the beginning of the troubles on Team Adult. Mattis and Tillerson were "slow-rolling" Trump on Afghanistan, McMaster would later reflect. "This was part of the strategy of keeping information from him." McMaster argued, on this fight as on the many that would follow, that he had not succumbed to Trump's agenda so much as that he believed outright obstruction was improper and ultimately counterproductive. "I thought it was my job to give him all the options," McMaster would tell people in justifying his approach to Trump. "I was working for the guy who got elected; so were they." Later, McMaster told others that dealing with Tillerson and Mattis was worse than dealing with the president. It was, he said, "really fucking toxic." He especially resented Mattis, lamenting to one interlocutor that the secretary of defense treated "me like shit the whole time." He also called Mattis "a complete prick" and Tillerson "an insufferable fucking prick." This was hardly standard-level White House infighting.

Mattis and Tillerson were more circumspect, even in their private comments, but they considered McMaster to be inept in his handling of the president to the point of being dangerous, an enabler rather than a guardian of responsible policy. In May, before Trump's trip to the NATO summit, McMaster had tried to present an Afghanistan plan that involved sending in thousands more troops and a four-year time commitment. "I'm not selling this to the president," Tillerson flatly told McMaster.[12] The secretary of state and others were incredulous that McMaster thought this would go over with Trump, believing it showed a willful misunderstanding of the president. More generally, Tillerson and Mattis worried McMaster did not get that presenting Trump an array of options meant he might pick the most reckless. "They were of the view that I'm not going to hand a sharp knife to a child just because he asked me to," said a Republican on Capitol Hill who dealt with them.

Process-obsessed, even didactic at times, McMaster never really connected with the president, producing an instant personality clash in Trump's almost cartoonishly chaotic White House. McMaster had a near-photographic recall of names and dates and often barraged Trump with details that the president neither wanted nor remembered. He frustrated other White House officials by sending over thick briefing books for the indifferent president. At times, Trump would mock McMaster in front of other advisers even as he demanded that the national security adviser show up in full dress uniform to go on television to defend him. What were his generals for, after all, if not for television?

But McMaster was not a pundit. He did not have a feel for politics and had already made several missteps in trying to stay on Trump's good side, straying over the line into audience-of-one sycophancy that Mattis had so notably avoided. One example was the "America First doesn't mean America alone" op-ed in *The Wall Street Journal* that he wrote on the plane home from Europe with Gary Cohn, his friend and ally in the White House's internecine feuds.[13] Another was his ill-fated appearance on Fox praising Trump's "masterful" diplomacy in Asia while privately lamenting it. Mattis, by contrast, had refused altogether to go on television to defend or promote Trump's policies, aside from a single Sunday appearance on CBS in May. After one too many entreaties from Sean Spicer, who served in the Navy Reserve, Mattis reportedly told him, "Sean, I've killed people for a living. If you call me again, I'm going to fucking send you to Afghanistan. Are we clear?"[14]

From the start, McMaster had found himself fighting enemies "inside the wire," as he put it—that is, within the National Security Council itself and on the White House staff. It felt like a three- or four-way fight, with Mattis and Tillerson making life difficult from outside the building and then what he called "the alt-right lunatics" who were planted inside his own team to advance a radical, disruptive agenda. Chief among them was Steve Bannon, the Trump ideologue who had been granted an unusual seat on the NSC. In April, McMaster managed to get Bannon kicked out, but not without an internal fight that included a confrontation in the Oval Office. When Bannon later spotted Rob Porter in the hall heading back to the Oval Office taking the resulting order removing him from the NSC to the president for his approval, Bannon shouted, "Don't fucking get that signed!" But it was already a fait accompli.

The disputes were not only over personnel and power. McMaster believed Bannon and others fed the president a warped view of history that played into Trump's own idea of a world order closer to the brute realism of the late nineteenth century when great powers dominated lesser nations, exploited their resources, and competed for spheres of influence. Afghanistan was to be their defining White House fight. Bannon would claim the first proposal he heard from McMaster was to send fifty thousand troops back to Afghanistan. McMaster and his allies denied it. "I think Bannon made that up as part of his campaign to take down H.R.," one of them said. The actual number was around twelve thousand, although even that was too much for Trump.

Bannon had set his sights on McMaster after coming to an uneasy rapprochement with Reince Priebus. For all their differences, they decided they had enough common enemies that it was worth working together. Even though he had an office of his own nearby, Bannon made a point of planting himself in Priebus's office for hours every day, sitting at the chief of staff's conference table staring at his phone, an omnipresent force. In his scheming, he set himself up as a rogue alternate policy shop to the National Security Council. He grabbed Trump's attention with a proposal from the security contractor Erik Prince, the Blackwater founder and brother of Education Secretary Betsy DeVos, that would, in effect, privatize the war in Afghanistan by sending in 5,500 of Prince's mercenaries to fight alongside the Afghan military and appointing an American "viceroy" to oversee the war. Prince had, with Bannon's connivance, designed a proposal so shamelessly aimed at Trump that the PowerPoint presentation he prepared for it compared his war plan to Trump's turnaround of the Wollman ice-skating rink project in New York's Central Park and likened the recommended imperial "viceroy" to a "bankruptcy trustee," a description that Trump, after six bankruptcy proceedings, found all too familiar.[15]

McMaster had not been in the job long before the Bannon wing orchestrated attacks to undermine him with Trump. The campaign, using the full ecosystem of the alt-right media led by Bannon's old team at *Breitbart News*, portrayed McMaster and others on his staff, such as the Russia expert Fiona Hill, as shadowy "globalists" with a subversive anti-Trump agenda, often invoking the anti-Semitic trope that they were pawns of the wealthy Jewish financier and philanthropist George Soros.[16] In late May, the conspiracy website Infowars "unmasked" Hill as a "mole" from Soros who was, as she later summed it up, "in cahoots with General McMaster in a plot against the president."[17] Hill believed the smear had come from Connie Mack, a Republican lobbyist for Viktor Orbán, the authoritarian leader of Hungary, who saw her as an obstacle to him meeting with Trump. On a radio show with Alex Jones, the conspiracy theorist who headed Infowars, Roger Stone later bragged that the Infowars hit piece had been the first to identify Hill as "the globalist leftist Soros insider who had infiltrated McMaster's staff," with Jones adding that the evidence was "hand-delivered" to Trump at Mar-a-Lago that summer.[18]

Some of Trump's conservative Jewish allies were also part of the McMaster pile-on, including Sheldon Adelson, the casino magnate and donor who had pushed to move the American embassy to Jerusalem. Privately, both Prime Minister Benjamin Netanyahu and Avigdor Lieberman, Israel's defense minister, called McMaster offering to help defend him, but the narrative was set and the campaign against him would continue as long as he stayed in the White House.

McMaster had a hard time purging some of the more extreme types who had been brought in by Bannon and Flynn—the "Flynnstones," as they were called. Hiring loyalists of his own was no easier. Establishment Republicans were still wary of working for Trump—the feeling being, of course, entirely mutual—and when McMaster had initially tried to recruit as deputy national security adviser two former Bush-era officials, Stephen Biegun and Juan Zarate, each had rejected him, even after McMaster sent flowers to their wives.

By the summer of 2017, the national security adviser was embroiled in conflicts with several aides he would eventually fire with great effort. Rich Higgins, a former Pentagon official and Bannon ally serving as the National Security Council's director for strategic planning, was finally canned in July after writing a seven-page memo arguing that Trump was being undermined by subversive forces inside the government, a "hostile complete state" within the state somehow aligning "globalists," Islamists, and cultural Marxists, in a "Maoist"-inspired campaign.[19] But McMaster was severely constrained in his ability to take on even lower-level subordinates, as he found in trying to fire Ezra Cohen, the senior director for intelligence who had worked under Flynn at the Defense Intelligence Agency. McMaster blamed Cohen for feeding sensitive information that spring to Devin Nunes, the chairman of the House Intelligence Committee who then falsely claimed that Trump associates had been unlawfully "unmasked" in intelligence intercepts by the Obama administration. "He was running a collection operation inside of our organization and then leaking whatever he thought would be damaging," McMaster would later say. He first tried to fire Cohen in the spring but had been blocked by the unusual combination of Bannon and Jared Kushner, who hated each other but supported Cohen. It would take months to overcome the resistance.

The biggest rogue actor McMaster faced, however, was Trump himself. The president was repeatedly warned by advisers that Russia, China, and other countries were eavesdropping on his cell phone calls. He made them anyway and continued to crowdsource advice on even the most sensitive national security subjects. "He's just talking to the fucking lunatics all weekend, with the Chinese and Russians and everybody listening," a national security official said. Did they know for sure? "Fuck yeah," the official said. The intelligence was clear-cut. One Republican senator recalled Trump calling to ask him about proposed military strikes in Syria. The senator begged Trump not to talk on the unsecured line and simply to listen. "He just can't help himself," the national security official said.

Mattis for once wanted to be that voice in the president's ear. He wanted the adults, perpetually drowned out by the Fox News conspiracies and telephone gossip that filled Trump's days, to have their say. Coming back from the contentious first foreign trip, with Trump having alienated allies and exited the Paris climate accord, the defense secretary invited Gary Cohn to his office at the Pentagon for lunch and the two of them came up with a plan to hold a tutorial for Trump with the explicit hope of getting him to stop dumping on the international system that had been built and maintained by the United States to its own great benefit.

Mattis suggested they hold the meeting in the Joint Chiefs' hallowed conference room known as the Tank. Improbably, they seemed to hope that a setting evoking the grand traditions of the American military would impress Trump. "This was me and Mattis trying to get the president to understand what allies are," Cohn would later explain to an associate. "We did Allies 101."

Beforehand, Mattis met with Bannon to coordinate. McMaster, awkwardly, happened by on his way back from the Oval Office and saw Mattis sitting in Bannon's office. How was it, he raged to others, that the secretary of defense would not give him the time of day but had plenty to spare for Bannon, the architect of Trump's mayhem? Bannon, however, was also making his own plans separately with Trump. The result was mutual incomprehension and disdain, which was evident from the opening minutes of the meeting at the Pentagon on a roasting hot July morning. Mattis began the session with a slide announcing to Trump that "the greatest gift of the Greatest Generation is the postwar rules-based international order."[20] Bannon considered "this fetish of the liberal international order" around which the meeting was organized to be "totally meaningless," a point he made to anyone who asked and some who had not.

Bannon had primed Trump to be ready to attack. Rather than accept Mattis's lecture, the president repeated his greatest-hits gripes about NATO and the allies, eventually falling into a diatribe about all the "losing" the American military had done since World War II up to the present day in Afghanistan. "You're all losers," Trump lectured his military hosts. "You don't know how to win anymore." The meeting was not supposed to be about Afghanistan, but the timing made it inevitable that Trump's complaints about the war would be aired as well. Just that week he had rejected McMaster's latest plan after a contentious meeting at the White House.

Joe Dunford, generally reticent, had until then mostly deferred to Mattis when Trump would go off, reasoning that, as a political appointee, it was more appropriate for the defense secretary to argue with the commander in chief than the uniformed chairman of the Joint Chiefs. During the Tank meeting, however, Trump enraged Dunford with his attacks on the integrity of the generals and their failure in Afghanistan, including a pointed critique of the current commanding general there, General John "Mick" Nicholson, who was not present. So when the president yelled at the chairman and started to accuse the military of undermining him by talking to the press, Dunford responded in kind.

"You guys are fucking leakers," Trump said.

"We're not fucking leakers," Dunford fired back.

Then Trump started in again on them as losers, "dopes and babies." Dunford pushed back on that too. To the generals, Trump was the third straight president who seemed to want to leave the military on the hook for failing to win an Afghan war that the politicians never really committed to. "Mr. President, you can tell me to take all forces out of Afghanistan and I'll do it. It's a physics problem," he said. "But here's what you need to know: If there's an attack on the Mall of America twenty-four months from now, no one sitting around this table is going to be able to say, 'We didn't see that happening.'" Dunford added, in what would become a refrain whenever the subject of Afghanistan came up with Trump, as it often would: "This is not us telling you what you should do. This is us offering a plan to mitigate the risk associated with extremism in South Asia. If you politically want to accept that risk, then you need to just tell us that." Trump did not, but neither did he appreciate his bluff being called in a roomful of his generals.

The tutorial in the Tank was destined to become an iconic Trump moment; fragmentary accounts began leaking out within days and continued to emerge, a few crazy details at a time, for the next several years as different participants offered their versions. The bottom line was that it was a debacle for those who had organized it. "The low point," Cohn would later call it. The attention that the meeting in the Tank drew was understandable. Here was the draft-avoiding president attacking all that his top military advisers held dear in a place they revered. Yet when a senior national security official who was present was asked years later if this was the worst meeting with Trump, he replied immediately: No. "That was the worst first," he said, or rather, "the first worst." Another senior national security official agreed: "The meetings went from worst to worst. There was never bad. The first meeting was horrible, and they just got worse from there."

Each of the adults in the room had his own break point with Trump. For Rex Tillerson, anger at Trump's willful ignorance about the world, about "what the president knew and didn't know," had been building up for weeks, as a senior State Department official who worked closely with him recalled. The secretary of state was offended by Trump's behavior and outraged at his reckless disregard. Unlike Mattis, he was not good at keeping his indignation to himself.

An engineer by training, Tillerson had been the opposite of a glad-hander at ExxonMobil, rising to the top in a rigid, hierarchical system. At the State Department, officials adopted the same name for Tillerson's small inner circle on the department's seventh floor as colleagues at Exxon had: the God Pod. It included his chief of staff, Margaret Peterlin, and head of policy planning, Brian Hook, who showed up at almost every White House meeting. Part of it was Tillerson's insularity; part of it, others belatedly realized, was his Boy Scout's distaste for the disorganization, chaos, profanity, and lack of professionalism he saw in Trump and his White House. The senior State official recalled once begging Peterlin to send more State experts to important White House meetings. "I understand that," she told the official, "but we don't want people to see what's happening in those meetings." He concluded that Tillerson "was horrified by what he saw."

By the end of the Tank meeting, Tillerson had seen enough. Trump had kept interrupting him, once when he tried to explain what the Iran nuclear deal actually did and again when Tillerson objected to Trump likening American soldiers to mercenaries. Tillerson did not like being interrupted and turned silent and visibly annoyed. After Reince Priebus finally cut the meeting off, Gary Cohn went up to Tillerson.

"Are you okay?" Cohn asked.

"Fucking moron," Tillerson responded, referring to the president.

Bannon was delighted. "That was probably the nastiest, meanest meeting of the whole Trump administration," he once said, and he did not mean it as a criticism. He had primed the president for the clash and relished it when it happened, all the more so because it was on the generals' turf. In the fight over Afghanistan, Bannon was not hesitant to draw their fire. He wanted Trump to understand that "the apparatus has a mind of its own." When the famous Tank meeting came up, he would brag, "I called those fuckers out."

McMaster, who had gone out west for his daughter's wedding, was not surprised when he heard the shocked readouts from the meeting. "I knew it was going to be a disaster," he told associates later. "I could see it. I felt like Buford at Gettysburg rolling up on Seminary Ridge. I can see what's going to happen. And I was like, 'Okay, have fun, man, because I'll be on vacation. It's going to be a friggin' disaster.'"

In the days after the Pentagon confrontation, Trump managed to alienate Mattis even further when he tweeted, seemingly out of nowhere, that he was reinstating the military's ban on transgender troops that Barack Obama had lifted. The president even lied about doing so "after consultation with my Generals and military experts." There had been no such consultation.

In the meantime, the tenuous status quo of Trump's White House under Reince Priebus had shattered and the staff infighting had gone public in the form of a foul-mouthed new White House communications director, Anthony Scaramucci, who had been hired by the president over vehement objections by Priebus and Sean Spicer. So offended was Spicer, who had already lost Trump's faith, that he immediately handed in his resignation.

Days into this mess, Scaramucci called Ryan Lizza, a *New Yorker* writer, and unloaded on Priebus and Bannon. "Reince is a fucking paranoid schizophrenic," he said, accusing Priebus of having "cock-blocked" his hiring for months before Trump finally overruled him. And that was polite compared with what he had to say about Bannon. "I'm not Steve Bannon. I'm not trying to suck my own cock," he said. Scaramucci told Lizza his goal was to "fucking kill all the leakers" and "get the president's agenda on track."[21] Unsurprisingly, the X-rated phone call from a Wall Street finance guy turned self-styled PR guru who called himself the Mooch was not seen as a sign of a White House getting its agenda on track.

The day the interview was published, Priebus vented his frustration with Trump and offered to step down. "Look, I don't think you're happy. I'm not happy. Why don't we just make a move now?" Priebus later told people that he said to the president. The next day, Trump flew to Long Island for a speech to law enforcement officers. Trump's aides knew he was in a rage about reports of chaos inside his White House, as well as furious at all of them after Senator John McCain sank his plans to repeal Obama's health care program in a dramatic late-night vote that week. Priebus confided in a colleague that he thought his time might be up and scrambled to get his name added at the last minute to the manifest of the flight to Long Island. "It's going to be uncomfortable," his colleague warned him.

While on Air Force One heading back to Washington after the speech, with Priebus on board, Trump placed a phone call to John Kelly. The president reminded him about a conversation they had after James Comey's firing when Kelly had commented on how his White House was so messed up and how ill-served he had been. "You're right," Trump told him, "the staff is terrible." On and on the president went: His aides were "not good for me." They were not loyal. They were all fucked up. "You need to come here and be chief of staff," Trump told him. Kelly demurred. "John, I really need you to do this," Trump said. After Kelly hesitated some more, Trump concluded, "Okay, how about this: Come in and see me on Monday and we'll talk about it." Kelly agreed. Minutes later, Air Force One landed at Joint Base Andrews and the president's staff, including Priebus, disembarked into a miserable rain that seemed to symbolize the dark moment.

At 4:49 p.m., Trump, while still on board, sent out a series of tweets. "I am pleased to inform you that I have just named General/Secretary John F Kelly as White House Chief of Staff," the president wrote. "He has been a true star of my Administration." Trump had not only publicly announced Kelly was taking a job he had not accepted, the president had not bothered to inform Priebus either. Sitting in a White House car on the tarmac waiting for the motorcade ride back to the office, Priebus looked down at his phone to discover that he had just been kicked to the curb. Soon after, Trump exited the plane and his motorcade pulled out.

Despite his complaints about all the "loser" generals, Trump had put his presidency in the hands of another Marine. Tall and angular, Kelly had come to the service, like Dunford, from a working-class background in Boston. Both were from Irish Catholic families and even shared the same middle name, Francis. After signing up in 1970, Kelly spent virtually his entire adult life in the military. In 2003, while fighting in Iraq with the First Marine Division, Kelly was promoted to brigadier general by Mattis, who personally "frocked" him—that is, pinned the star on his uniform—in the first combat-zone promotion of a Marine general since the Korean War. Mattis later selected Kelly as his deputy when he ran Central Command. Once in the White House, Kelly would come to be regarded as a political naïf, but he spent a significant part of his career in the Pentagon and Congress, serving as the Marines' congressional liaison and eventually as senior military assistant to defense secretaries Bob Gates and Leon Panetta.

Kelly's final assignment in the military before retirement had been as head of the United States Southern Command, the combatant command for Latin America, where he acquired a jaundiced view about the porous southern border and the need to do something more to stop the human traffickers and drug cartels that flowed through it.[22] Like Mattis and McMaster, he had emerged from the previous administration a critic of Obama on issues such as allowing women into combat and closing the prison at Guantánamo Bay. Despite that, his only contribution to the 2016 campaign was an interview with *Foreign Policy* magazine in which he criticized fellow former generals such as Mike Flynn who entered what he called the "cesspool of domestic politics." The danger of activist generals, he warned, was that they might cause a president "to ever think for a second that he's getting anything but the absolute best military advice, completely devoid of politics."[23] A few months later, Kelly joined Trump's cabinet as a political appointee.

As homeland security secretary, he was immediately drawn into publicly backing many of Trump's most controversial policies. In that interview with *Foreign Policy*, Kelly had criticized Trump's signature proposal, saying "no wall will work by itself." By the next April, he was telling reporters that "a border wall is essential."[24] A senior Obama official who had dealt with him daily at the Pentagon marveled at his transition from "apolitical, capable military officer" to Trump factotum. "Is that really what he thinks," Kelly's former colleague wondered, "or is that what he thinks being a good political appointee sounds like?"

All of which may be why Trump decided to offer Kelly another battlefield promotion, on that rainy July afternoon when his administration, at war with itself and facing a growing list of existential threats from the outside, was desperate for new leadership. "No WH chaos!" Trump tweeted amid the shakeup. Despite his braggadocious claim at the cabinet meeting, Trump had not managed to pass any of his legislative agenda. His Obamacare repeal was dead, thanks to McCain. His tax reform proposal did not yet exist. His promised "infrastructure week" had not only never materialized but was on its way to becoming a Washington joke. His major accomplishments so far consisted of blowing up international agreements negotiated by his predecessor and reinventing the American presidency as a round-the-clock Twitter and television show. Trump fashioned himself a dealmaker, but so far had only tanked deals, not made any.

Kelly's first act on showing up at the White House a few days later was to fire Scaramucci, who had lasted little more than a week in the job. A "Scaramucci" would soon become a Trump-era unit of measurement, a sort of Washington shorthand for how long an official could make it in Trump's turnover-ridden administration, although, tellingly, there remained a heated debate over whether his tenure was in fact ten or eleven days.

In the Oval Office, the new chief of staff sought assurances from Trump that he would be fully empowered to run the place, with no more free-floating sessions in the Oval, aides coming and going as they pleased, and little discernible decision-making process. Trump agreed that Steve Bannon as well as Jared Kushner and Ivanka Trump would be subject to the new discipline. Kelly's point to Ivanka was straightforward: "If you're a staff person, you work for me. If you're his daughter, see him on week-ends." All paths to Trump would, in theory, run through Kelly.

At first, August seemed to offer a respite. Trump left Washington once again for his club in Bedminster and planned to spend much of the month on a "working vacation" in New Jersey. On August 8, however, he showed that the much touted new discipline of the Kelly era was not yet in evidence.

Hijacking a photo op that was supposed to be about the growing epidemic of opioid abuse, Trump began talking about North Korea, whose nuclear weapons program had become a source of escalating concern in recent months. Intelligence reports indicated that new ballistic missiles being test-fired might soon be capable of reaching the continental United States. The United Nations Security Council, prodded by the United States, had just imposed tough new sanctions. "North Korea best not make any more threats to the United States. They will be met with fire and fury like the world has never seen," Trump said, glowering as he showily consulted a piece of paper that was actually an opioid fact sheet. Melania Trump looked on in puzzlement, sitting next to him dressed as if for a summer garden party. To underscore the point that this was no ordinary threat, but a potential nuclear holocaust, Trump added, "They will be met with fire, fury and, frankly, power the likes of which this world has never seen before."[25]

Up until then, the North Korea portfolio had been primarily handled by Rex Tillerson, who had been traveling around Asia coordinating with allies. The intelligence community had told Trump's top officials in February that North Korea would never give up nuclear weapons because its dictator Kim Jong-un believed they were inextricably linked to his regime's survival. But China, despite its ongoing support for Kim, might nonetheless cooperate with the United States in seeking to rein in Pyongyang's continued development of destabilizing long-range missiles, according to the intelligence assessment. Tillerson had responded crisply to the conclusions. "We're going to test both," he had said. The military agreed, and Tillerson designed an aggressive, though conventional, diplomatic and economic campaign to pressure Kim. There was no talk of courting Armageddon.

The problem was Trump. He was not on board with Tillerson's initiative, Joe Dunford later told colleagues, "because it wasn't his. He never respected it. It begins with him being dismissive of anything else the government was doing that didn't involve him." When the generals heard Trump's "fire and fury" remarks, they were stunned but not surprised. The extraordinary threat had not been planned. "It was a stray ray," Dunford would conclude, reflecting not so much Trump's desire to start a nuclear war as his ability to blunder into an unintended one.

The next day, Tillerson tried to contain the damage. "I think Americans should sleep well at night, have no concerns about this particular rhetoric of the last few days," he told reporters, which was consistent with his private counsel to allies as well.[26]

Trump's Twitter barrage on North Korea over the following weeks would make clear how out of step the secretary of state was with the president. "Military solutions are now fully in place, locked and loaded, should North Korea act unwisely," Trump tweeted a few days later. In private, he had in fact demanded that H. R. McMaster draw up military options, which was exactly the scenario that Tillerson, Jim Mattis, and the generals had been trying to avoid. Little noticed amid the alarm over Trump's North Korea remarks had been another threat in that same photo op, suggesting that the president was also considering a "military option" aimed at Venezuela and the leftist regime of Nicolás Maduro.[27] Advisers like Tillerson continued to insist publicly that Trump's words were just that, but on Venezuela, as with other policy standoffs, Trump was now accompanying inflammatory rhetoric with closed-door demands for action. Trump ordered McMaster to produce a plan for a military strike against Venezuela too. Kelly, channeling Mattis, told him not to do any such thing.

By the end of the month, Trump was explicitly rebutting his national security team's approach. If his generals would not provide the saber-rattling bluster that Trump craved, then he would provide it himself. "The

U.S. has been talking to North Korea, and paying them extortion money, for 25 years," the president tweeted. "Talking is not the answer!"

Four days after "fire and fury," a white supremacist march in Charlottesville, Virginia, that turned deadly temporarily knocked the controversy over Trump's threat of nuclear war off the front pages. Trump stepped in the middle of that fight too, declaring that there were "very fine people on both sides," as if there was an equivalence between the torch-bearing white racists marching through the streets defending Confederate statues and the peaceful counter-protesters who came out to reject them. His comments shocked a country that thought it was inured to Trump's most shocking pronouncements.[28]

In Washington, Paul Ryan, the House speaker, told a CNN town hall that Trump had "messed up" with his "moral equivocation."[29] After watching Ryan, the remote control "in his left hand, like a pistol," as an aide who witnessed it later wrote, Trump immediately called Ryan and lit into him. "Paul, do you know why Democrats have been kicking your ass for decades?" Trump said, and, without waiting, answered his own question. "Because they know a little word called 'loyalty.'"[30] The criticism nonetheless kept coming. The White House was forced to disband three advisory committees of business leaders rather than prolong the embarrassing process of having its members announce they were quitting one by one in protest. Even inside the White House, aides debated whether this time Trump had gone too far. Gary Cohn had stood uncomfortably beside Trump at the photo op where the president made his "very fine people" comments; a few days later, invoking his Jewish roots, Cohn gave an on-the-record interview to the *Financial Times* saying the White House "can and must do better" in condemning hate groups and let it be known that he was considering resigning.[31] But Cohn did not quit, nor did any other top aides, although he would later claim that he had told Trump he would leave as soon as they secured passage of the tax cut legislation. Cohn told himself he could be more effective inside the White House than outside, neither the first nor the last Trump adviser to rely on such a rationale.

Steve Bannon, on the other hand, reassured Trump that the flap would ultimately help with his base. Even if the neo-Nazi thugs now cheering him were an embarrassment, Bannon told the president, embracing their cause of refusing to tear down Confederate monuments was a compelling grievance to energize his largely white, male, and Southern super-fans.

"Our heritage, our statues—I told the president to stand up for who we are. *They* want to take it all away," Bannon told another administration official. "We've got to take control of the narrative. This is a winner."[32]

But Bannon was in the midst of too many fights with too many powerful constituencies. In addition to his campaign against H. R. McMaster, he had also alienated Ivanka Trump and Jared Kushner—Bannon referred to them scornfully as "Javanka"—and told others their recommendations were politically disastrous for the president. He would later call the firing of James Comey that Kushner advocated the biggest mistake "in modern political history."[33] He had even gotten into a shouting match with Ivanka in front of Trump. "You and Jared spend all day long leaking on people," he yelled at her. "You're a fucking liar," she fired back. "Everything that comes out of your mouth is a fucking lie." Bannon retorted, "Go fuck yourself," adding, "You are nothing."[34]

As soon as he was named Trump's chief of staff, Kelly discussed with Bannon the need to plan an exit; they settled on mid-August for a departure date. There was no way this general was going to let Bannon remain in the White House, forever sniping at his leadership. But when the Charlottesville crisis came, Bannon was still around. He quickly clashed with Kelly in front of colleagues over whether Trump should try to clean up his "both sides" remarks about Charlottesville. Bannon said not to bother, because who would believe Trump anyway—which was more or less what happened after Kelly persuaded Trump to give what turned out to be a transparently insincere walk-back.

With Trump faltering, Bannon's became the obvious head to roll. That outcome proved inevitable once Bannon gave a bizarre interview to the editor of a small liberal journal, *The American Prospect*, amid the Charlottesville controversy. Headlined "Steve Bannon, Unrepentant," the interview depicted Bannon as a White House infighter, bragging about the imminent firing of a State Department official with whom he disagreed on China and undercutting Trump's newly aggressive North Korea policy. Despite Trump's bellicose words about "fire and fury," Bannon said, "There's no military solution, forget it."[35]

From the administration's early weeks, Bannon had predicted that he would be gone by August, which is exactly what happened. In the end, his firing on August 18 came on the same day that Trump, Kelly, McMaster, Mattis, and the other generals helicoptered up to Camp David for a war council on Afghanistan. Kelly had already made it clear that Bannon was not welcome. "There will be no children in the room," the chief of staff had decreed.

In preparation, McMaster had secretly arranged an extensive briefing for Trump in Bedminster before the Camp David summit with a new
ally, CIA director Mike Pompeo, who had cultivated Trump's approval by
appearing regularly in the Oval Office to personally attend the president's
intelligence briefing. It was not that Pompeo had radically different views
on Afghanistan, McMaster later acknowledged, but just that "he was not
Mattis or Tillerson." The final proposal presented to the president emphasized how, by getting Afghanistan right, the president had an opportunity
to show up Obama, an argument designed to appeal to Trump. In reality,
though, the option that everyone in the room supported was essentially
status-quo-plus: a few thousand more troops, more training and equipment for the Afghan military, more stern words, and an aid suspension for
the Taliban's tacit supporters in Pakistan.

This time, for once, the outcome was precooked in McMaster's favor.
After threatening nuclear war with North Korea and appearing to endorse
white supremacists at home, Trump was in no position to defy the entire
national security establishment on Afghanistan as well. The balance of
power in Trump's administration had shifted, at least temporarily. At
7:33 a.m. the day after the Camp David summit, the president sent out a
curt message bidding Bannon farewell. "I want to thank Steve Bannon for
his service," he tweeted. Fourteen minutes later, he wrote that he had an
"Important day spent at Camp David with our very talented Generals and
military leaders." He added that "many decisions" had been made, including on Afghanistan.

Three days later, in an uncharacteristically restrained speech at Fort
Myer, across the Potomac from the White House, Trump announced that
he had overcome his skepticism about Afghanistan and would give the
Pentagon more time. "My original instinct was to pull out, and historically I like following my instincts," he acknowledged, but he claimed to
have been persuaded that an immediate withdrawal would be a disaster
that could lead to a renewed terrorism threat from al Qaeda and ISIS.
Trump being Trump, he could not resist adding a rhetorical flourish that
his generals knew they could not deliver on, given the modest additional
commitment of troops and resources that he had grudgingly accepted. "In
the end, we will win," he promised.[36]

Joe Dunford had called his bluff back in the Tank. Trump wanted to
leave Afghanistan but would not risk owning the political consequences.
By the end of August, his approval ratings from the public, already meager
by historical standards, had sunk to the lowest point of his presidency so
far, with barely a third of the country endorsing his performance.

The generals were under no illusion that they had tamed Trump, on Afghanistan or anything else. They had been watching closely and what they had learned was that Trump's fixations were Trump's fixations. They might disappear as suddenly as they appeared, but they would never really go away.

One abiding fixation was with the military itself, which Trump saw as an irresistibly theatrical backdrop for his presidency. After his election, Trump had not only stocked his government with generals but had also tried to order up an explicitly militarized inauguration until aides talked him out of it. "I don't want floats," Trump had said at one planning session, according to Stephanie Winston Wolkoff, the New York society friend of the first lady who had been hired to help produce the event. "I want *tanks* and *choppers*. Make it look like North Korea."[37] Trump never seemed to understand or care that his generals might recoil at such a display, or why his strongman style might be incompatible with the world's oldest democracy.

In the summer, taking a brief break from the Russia controversy and the internal White House intrigue, Trump had flown to Paris for Bastille Day celebrations thrown by Emmanuel Macron, the new French president. Macron, who had taken up from Canada's Justin Trudeau the task of serving as designated Trump-pleaser among the Western allies, staged a hardware-filled display of military might to commemorate the hundredth anniversary of the American entrance into World War I, including vintage tanks rolling down the Champs-Élysées and fighter jets roaring overhead, all calculated to appeal to Trump. "You are going to be doing this next year," the French general in charge had predicted to an American counterpart as they watched Trump's delight.

Sure enough, Trump returned home determined to have the Pentagon throw him the biggest, grandest military parade for the Fourth of July ever. "I'd rather swallow acid," Mattis said, when the idea came up in one of many Pentagon meetings meant to find a way out of having to give in to the president.[38] Eventually, military officials would point out that the parade would cost millions of dollars and the heavy equipment would ruin Washington's city streets.

But the gulf between Trump and his generals was not really about money or practicalities, just as the endless policy battles were not only about clashing views of Afghanistan or North Korea or Syria. Their divide was wider than that—it was about what the generals believed in and what the president believed in. That was never clearer than when Trump told John Kelly about his vision for the parade. "Look, I don't want any wounded guys in the parade. This doesn't look good for me," Trump said, explaining that in the Bastille Day parade in Paris there had been several formations of injured veterans, including wheelchair-bound soldiers who had lost legs and arms. Kelly, still early in his tenure, could not believe what he was hearing.

"Those are the heroes," Kelly told him. "In our society, there's only one group of people that are more heroic than they are and they are buried over in Arlington." Including, he did not add, his own son.

Trump was not buying it. "Yeah, but I don't want them," the president replied. "It doesn't look good for me."

Not long after Kelly became chief of staff, he was in the Oval Office for a briefing with Paul Selva, an Air Force general and vice chairman of the Joint Chiefs. At the end, Kelly joked in his deadpan way about the parade, already a sore spot with Trump. "Well, you know, General Selva is going to be in charge of organizing the Fourth of July parade," Kelly told the president. Trump did not get the joke. "So, what do you think of the parade?" he asked the general. No matter how many times he had been told that the military did not want his parade, he refused to believe it.

Selva, however, had one of those moments that were all too rare in the Trump presidency: instead of saying what Trump wanted to hear, Selva said what he thought. "I didn't grow up in the United States, I actually grew up in Portugal," he told the president, according to an account he later gave colleagues. "Portugal was a dictatorship—and parades were about showing the people who had the guns. And in this country, we don't do that." He added: "It's not who we are."

Even after this impassioned speech, Trump still did not get it. "So, you don't like the idea?" the president asked, incredulous.

"No," Selva responded, in as blunt an answer as Trump would ever get. "It's what dictators do."

But it did not matter. Trump would not give up his military parade just because some general had lectured him. Trump continued to bring it up, "dozens and dozens of times" afterward, Joe Dunford would later tell others. Not even being called out in the Oval Office itself as a wannabe dictator by one of the generals he claimed to revere was enough to stop him.

CHAPTER 7

The Adhocracy

The old Marine got up at four each morning to get ready for the day. He put on a dark suit, still adjusting to a coat and tie after a lifetime in green and khaki uniforms. During the ride to the White House, he leafed through *The New York Times, Washington Post,* the websites of CNN and Fox News, and, just to know what missiles were coming his way, *Breitbart News.* He had aides watch Fox, MSNBC, and CNN starting at 7 a.m. so that when the president called to ask, "Did you just see that?" he could get a quick download about whatever cable news segment had caught Trump's interest.

The White House that John Kelly had taken over remained far from a tightly disciplined Marine unit. Chaos was still the order of the day, encouraged by a commander in chief who liked to stir the pot while pitting members of his own team against each other. It was a place with a *"Hunger Games* vibe," in the words of Stephanie Grisham, then communications director for the first lady.[1] Cliff Sims, a media aide, thought it was more like *"Game of Thrones,* but with the characters from *Veep,"* as he put it in a later book aptly named *Team of Vipers.*[2] The departure of Reince Priebus, Steve Bannon, and others had upended and reordered the factions but did not eliminate them. Ideologues such as Stephen Miller and Peter Navarro, the trade adviser, all but ran their own separate shadow White House, bypassing the process to slip paper onto the Resolute Desk for a Trump signature. Their establishment rivals, such as the unlikely duo of Gary Cohn and H. R. McMaster, tried to keep the most far-fetched ideas away from the president lest he pull out his Sharpie pen and abruptly approve something crazy without discussion. Kellyanne Conway and Hope Hicks, wary allies, had Trump's ear and access to the Oval Office. Jared Kushner and Ivanka Trump, having soured on Priebus and helped push him out, remained a power center unto themselves. Mike Pence floated above it all, rarely saying much of anything that anyone could remember.

As they settled into their offices in the fall of 2017, Kelly and his deputy, Kirstjen Nielsen, were stunned to find presidential aides still fighting over the spoils of victory months into the administration, demanding fancy titles and fancy offices they swore they had been promised and unfairly denied. Some believed they should have private government airplanes anytime they traveled; others openly ignored security rules and carried cell phones with them even into meetings with the president. After the first lady complained to him, Kelly even found himself telling the White House staff that they could no longer use the White House pool or tennis courts because she considered them family space. Kelly was determined to stop the Grand Central Terminal–style crowds in the Oval Office. He decreed that access to the Oval would be limited and phone calls to the president monitored and logged. And Kelly tried to cut out the freelancing, at one point confronting Miller, the young immigration hawk and speechwriter: "You have no authority. You're not Senate confirmed. You have no authority to direct operations."

Six-foot-two and two hundred pounds, Kelly remained a formidable figure at age sixty-seven. In age, height, and bearing, he was more of a match for Trump than Priebus and not easily intimidated. White House officials who thought nothing of calling Priebus by his first name addressed his successor as "General Kelly." Even Trump seemed a little daunted by the Marine at first, which is the only reason Kelly would have some early success imposing order.

Kelly had quickly realized through the shocks of August that he would never transform Trump into a normal president nor stop him from tweeting. But he told himself that if he could control the information that got to Trump, if he could keep some of the nuttier figures in the president's orbit off the phone and out of the Oval Office, if he could stop some of the wackier *Breitbart* clips from being slipped to him by the hardliners in the building, then there was a chance of keeping him focused on reality. If Kelly could make sure the input was better, then maybe the output would be too.

To that end, he decided to empower Rob Porter, the White House staff secretary, whom he had gotten to know in Bedminster during the hectic early days of his tenure while Trump was promising "fire and fury" for North Korea in between golf rounds at his New Jersey club. Porter, a forty-year-old Harvard Law School graduate who exuded calm professional competence and would have been at home in any normal Republican White House, was eager to help right the ship. He considered Trump's White House thus far nightmarish, a living manifestation of an *adhocracy*, a term his father, Roger Porter, a Harvard Kennedy School professor and chief domestic policy adviser to George H. W. Bush, had famously coined.

The senior Porter had realized that many presidents were attracted to the sort of improvisation that had taken hold in Trump's White House. Franklin Roosevelt used to hand out assignments almost willy-nilly to favored aides with no mechanism for follow-up; John Kennedy often acted as his own chief of staff, presiding over a team of generalists who worked through issues with him. They both met the definition for adhocracy that Porter came up with in 1980, a White House that "minimizes regularized and systematic patterns of providing advice and instead relies heavily on the President distributing assignments and selecting whom he listens to and when."[3] But no one had taken it to the chaotic extremes that Trump had, the point of which, as Porter had foreseen, was to show the American people a president who was personally in command.

Among those who had taken Porter's class at Harvard was a young Jared Kushner, who was living in the most radical version of adhocracy. Now Porter's son set out to do something about it. He drafted two memos for Kelly to issue to top officials. They codified in writing what Kelly had been telling the staff: even Trump's White House needed at least a basic form of regular order. Specifically, the first memo said, all paper, including news articles like those that various internal intriguers snuck onto Trump's desk when no one else was looking, had to first go through the staff secretary's office and be "approved by the Chief of Staff" before being presented to the president. Any event with the president had to include talking points and a list of attendees in the formal Event Memorandum. *"People not listed on the EM may be excluded from the event,"* the memo said, in italics for emphasis.[4] Any remarks to be delivered by the president should be submitted by the speechwriter to Porter at least three days in advance. Any executive orders would require sign-off from the White House counsel and the Justice Department's Office of Legal Counsel.

The second memo confronted perhaps the most challenging issue raised by Trump's unique approach to the presidency: just what constituted a presidential decision. With Trump tweeting pronouncements early in the morning and late at night, and prone to dictate abrupt shifts in policy in the midst of Oval Office soliloquies, what were advisers supposed to make of his decrees? Less than a month earlier, Trump had infuriated Jim Mattis and the military leadership by ordering the Pentagon to ban transgender soldiers in a three-part barrage of tweets. Was it legal? Did the Pentagon have to obey? Joe Dunford quickly sent an internal memo to the Joint Chiefs indicating that the military would make "no modifi-cations" to current policy unless a proper policy was developed through channels.[5] Porter, and Kelly, now adopted that position as theirs too.

"Decisions are not final—and therefore may not be implemented—until the Staff Secretary secures a cleared DM that has been signed by the President," the memo said.[6] Trump could tweet all he wanted but without a Decision Memorandum prepared by the staff secretary and signed by the president, it was not legal. The sentence was underlined to make the point clear.

Nothing in either memo would have been especially surprising in any other White House—that was how most of them worked. Only in Trump's was it out of the ordinary. Aides who had grown accustomed to the way Trump operated and had figured out how to manipulate the system to advance their own goals bristled at the new strictures. But no one was about to challenge Kelly. Not at first. Rob Porter now ended each day by giving the president a thick briefing book full of schedules, informational documents, press clippings, screenshots of television chyrons that might interest him, and duly vetted Decision Memoranda to be signed with his black Sharpie, along with a separate manila folder with a few one-page summaries of the most important issues on the assumption that the presi-dent would never read the longer documents. "The fact it was Kelly, that he empowered it, everybody else at least for a time kind of saluted, which was just a huge difference," recalled one White House official.

Even as Kelly strived to calm the West Wing, Trump was still using Twit-ter to wreak havoc outside the building against targets that included his own party's leaders. He was particularly irritated by Mitch McConnell, the Senate Republican leader, blaming him for John McCain's late-night vote killing legislation to repeal and replace the Affordable Care Act. McConnell, for his part, did not think much of Trump's handling of the issue either and their disagreement went public during the August recess at the same time Kelly was trying to plant his feet.

While traveling in Kentucky, McConnell told a local Rotary Club that Trump's inexperience was responsible for the failure of the legislation. "He had excessive expectations about how quickly things happen in the democratic process," the senator said.[7] Trump was angry when he saw the comments. He was not the one who had been promising for so long to overturn the Obama program. He called McConnell to ream him out, then went public on Twitter. "After 7 years of hearing Repeal & Replace, why not done?" he tweeted at the senator. "Can you believe that Mitch McConnell, who has screamed Repeal & Replace for 7 years, couldn't get it done," he added the next day. "Mitch, get back to work," he went on.[8] When a reporter asked if McConnell should step down, Trump said, "If he doesn't get repeal and replace done and if he doesn't get taxes done, meaning cuts and reform, and if he doesn't get a very easy one to get done, infrastructure—if he doesn't get them done, then you can ask me that question."[9]

Indeed, Trump seemed to relish throwing his own side off balance. Perhaps because of his new feud with McConnell, he decided after Labor Day to throw a wrench into negotiations over a spending measure that would also raise the debt ceiling. Democrats led by Nancy Pelosi in the House and Chuck Schumer in the Senate wanted a bill that would keep the government open and extend the deadline for the debt ceiling by three months, a relatively short period to give them leverage in coming negotiations. Republicans wanted a longer-term bill to avoid a politically damaging collision. Speaker Paul Ryan called the Democratic proposal "ridiculous and disgraceful," then headed to the White House to meet with the president and other congressional leaders only to be under-cut when Trump agreed to the very Democratic plan that Ryan had just deemed unacceptable.[10]

Ryan and McConnell left the meeting stewing. Even Steven Mnuchin was caught off guard and upset at the surprise deal across party lines. It was the first genuinely bipartisan moment of Trump's presidency. Trump delighted in the positive reaction and called Pelosi and Schumer separately to revel in it. "The press has been incredible!" he gushed to Pelosi.[11]

But rather than opening a new era of cooperation, it was a short demonstration of what could have been. Trump more than any president in generations had come to the White House without strong party affiliation or philosophical moorings and in theory might have bridged the capital's divides had he chosen to. Trump won the presidency in spite of his party's establishment rather than because of it, having challenged traditional Republican orthodoxy on foundational issues like trade, war, and Russia.[12] He was openly scornful of the party's last three presidential nominees, all of whom had refused to vote for him. And once in office, Trump seemed just as comfortable blasting fellow Republicans as he did Democrats. In the days following his deal with Pelosi and Schumer, Trump dismissed dis-content within his party, posting a tweet that began, "Republicans, sorry," as if he were not one of them, and criticizing their leaders for having a "death wish."[13]

All of which left McConnell in a bind. After thirty-two years in the Senate, McConnell, famous for his owlish face, round glasses, and maximalist use of Senate procedure in service of his goals, was no mushy moderate but no Trump-style Republican either. He had arguably played a decisive role in electing Trump by refusing to consider any nominee from Barack Obama in 2016 to replace the late Justice Antonin Scalia, leaving the open seat to be filled by whoever won the November election and providing extra incentive to conservative voters to turn out. McConnell considered the early confirmation of Neil Gorsuch to the Supreme Court after Trump took office as validation of his strategy. His wife, Elaine Chao, even served in Trump's cabinet, as transportation secretary—a post Trump would later claim he had offered her only because McConnell "begged" him to do so, an assertion the senator dismissed as laughable. But McConnell found Trump vulgar, unserious, and difficult to work with.

It did not help that Steve Bannon, the self-styled keeper of the "America First" flame, was targeting McConnell's fellow Republicans for defeat. While no longer in the White House, Bannon was acting as if he were Trump's outside field marshal purging the party of those deemed insufficiently loyal to the president. At the end of September, Bannon helped beat McConnell's candidate in a Republican primary for Jeff Sessions's old Senate seat, sending to the general election a deeply flawed nominee in the form of Roy Moore, a flamboyant far-right former chief justice of the Alabama Supreme Court who had been twice removed from his post after defying federal rulings barring display of the Ten Commandments on government property and requiring the issuance of marriage licenses to same-sex couples. Bannon then openly attacked McConnell, going on Sean Hannity's Fox News show to threaten a series of primary challenges to incumbent GOP senators. "Right now, it's a season of war against a GOP establishment," Bannon reaffirmed at a Values Voter Summit in mid-October. Addressing McConnell directly, he added, "Up on Capitol Hill, it's like the Ides of March. They're just looking to find out who is going to be Brutus to your Julius Caesar. We've cut your oxygen off, Mitch."[14]

John Kelly had no experience in politics and little feel for it, but he knew a thing or two about war and he understood that having one between a president and Senate majority leader of his own party was a losing proposition. He reached out to McConnell and invited him to meet with Trump in the Oval Office to smooth over their dispute. Two days after Bannon's fiery appearance at the Values Voter Summit, McConnell arrived in the Oval Office. Encouraged by Kelly, Trump was ready to patch things up.

As for McConnell, he had confided to advisers that having such a volatile president as Trump meant "we were all in real danger, not just Republicans, but the country," as one adviser to the senator put it. He concluded that the best way to avoid disaster was to stay close to the Oval Office. But he was not going to prostrate himself to Trump as some of the president's other supplicants had.

Rob Porter, who had spent years working on Capitol Hill for several Senate Republicans, tried to explain McConnell to the president beforehand. "What animates him, first and foremost, is being Senate majority leader," Porter told Trump. "What he cares most about is making sure that Republicans continue in the majority, that they have at least fifty-one Republican senators." Bannon's "war," and Trump's attacks on McConnell, were threatening that. Porter also tried to tell the president that he should stop bitching about McConnell never defending him on television. "He's never going to be your outside champion," Porter explained. "He's just not that guy." McConnell, unlike Trump, did not care about appearing on Fox or the Sunday shows. His memoir was titled *The Long Game* for a reason. In June, he had become the longest-serving Republican leader in the Senate ever. "It's nothing against you," Porter had insisted to Trump. "That's just who he is."

In their Oval Office session, McConnell had come prepared with a plan to align his interests with the president's. He pitched Trump on a bold idea: if they focused on it, McConnell said, they could transform the federal judiciary. He ran through all the progress that he and Don McGahn, Trump's White House counsel, had been making already on this by pushing federal judicial nominations through with factory-like efficiency. If Trump made this a priority, he could make history, McConnell suggested, and lock down his conservative base as well.

In the midst of McConnell's explanation, Sarah Huckabee Sanders, who had replaced Sean Spicer as White House press secretary, popped into the Oval Office and asked if they would like to do a news conference together. McConnell, surprised, soon found himself in the Rose Garden standing next to Trump declaring their mutual admiration in front of cameras.

"We have been friends for a long time," Trump said of the man he had been trashing on social media days earlier. "We are probably now, I think, at least as far as I'm concerned, closer than ever before."[15]

"We've been friends and acquaintances for some time," McConnell offered. "Contrary to what some of you may have reported, we are together totally on this agenda to move America forward."[16]

Disingenuous as it may have been, that moment in the Rose Garden sealed a truce that would last three years. From that day on, the two would refrain from attacking one another and focus on shared goals. Trump would green-light McConnell's judges plan, then happily stand back and take credit for it. As for the president's flirtation with the Democrats, it did not last. Washington's gridlocked politics simply would not allow it. Nor would Trump's personality. He needed enemies too much to be a bridge-builder. And with Robert Mueller's investigation bearing down, he needed Republicans to defend him. Trump and McConnell did not like each other on the evening of October 16 any more than they had when they woke up that morning, but by the time they went to sleep that night they realized they were in bed together, whether they liked it or not.

John Kelly's biggest mistake in his crusade to impose order on the White House was the same one that had tripped up Reince Priebus and Steve Bannon: taking on Jared Kushner and Ivanka Trump. As part of his agreement with the president, Kelly wanted "the kids," as he called them, to report to him.

It did not take long for Jared and Ivanka to grow resentful of Kelly's strictures and conclude that he was a wrong fit for the office. Kelly, in Kushner's view, was a black-and-white guy, but with Trump you had to be able to focus on a thousand shades of gray. While Kelly presented himself as a process man, Kushner thought he tried to bias the decision every time, giving the impression that he as a retired four-star general thought he knew better than a rookie president. Kelly kept trying to trap Trump into positions, a strategy that Kushner considered counterproductive. Trump would go along with it for a while, but was like a caged beast eventually seeking to escape.

At least that was the indictment that Kushner shared with others. The part he did not mention as much was what really rankled: Kelly's efforts to control the family. Suddenly they were not invited to every meeting and their counsel was no longer decisive. Jared and Ivanka believed they were the only ones who truly understood Trump and had his best interests at heart. For Kelly, an outsider, to try to control them was an affront. To save face, Kushner told associates that he was actually glad to have his wings clipped because it meant he did not have to juggle so many issues all at once and could focus on the causes that mattered most to him, like Middle East peace. In fact, he felt humiliated and aggrieved.

The tension between Kelly and Kushner was so palpable that it was evident even to outsiders. One day when the chief of staff was hosting Kim Darroch, the British ambassador, for a ham and cheese omelet in the White House Mess, Kushner happened to walk in with some guests of his own. Darroch could hardly help noticing that when Kelly and Kushner saw each other, "the temperature in the room dropped instantly by about ten degrees."[17]

Kelly was smart enough not to confront Ivanka directly, always taking care to praise the president's daughter to her face, smiling and hugging her and calling her an "American patriot." But he groused behind her back and had no compunction about railing at her aides. He once yelled at her chief of staff, Julie Radford, for twenty minutes after the president called Ivanka without going through him. "With all due respect, sir, her dad called her," Radford replied. "Are we supposed to come down and ask permission for a daughter to talk with her dad?"

In his own way, though, Kelly thought he was reflecting the president's wishes. Trump was torn about having Jared and Ivanka in the White House. Whenever he would see the latest cable television reports involving one or both of them, he would grouse that it was not a smart idea for them to have joined his White House staff. "We'd be better off if Jared and Ivanka weren't here," he told aides. "They're not doing us any good." The president repeated to Kelly, Hope Hicks, and Rob Porter more than once that he wanted the kids to go back to New York. Sometimes Trump would frame his complaint as if it were fatherly concern for how tough Washington could be. Kushner, after all, had already been summoned to Capitol Hill to testify in the Russia investigation, contrary to his naive prediction after Robert Mueller was appointed.

The ongoing saga of the couple's financial disclosure forms, meanwhile, had become a running embarrassment for the White House, as the two were repeatedly fined and forced to amend their filings after failing to reveal dozens of assets, including Kushner's stake in a real estate finance start-up he owned with his brother and the couple's art collection valued between $5 million and $25 million. Who forgets a multimillion-dollar art collection? And their economic entanglements raised all sorts of questions. Ivanka's firm received provisional trademark approvals from China on the day Xi Jinping was at Mar-a-Lago with her father, while a Chinese insurer negotiated to buy the massive 666 Fifth Avenue office building in New York from Jared's family company for $2.86 billion before the deal fell through.

But the kids' well-being was not always the thrust of the president's remarks, and many aides were certain that he was more concerned about their impact on him rather than the other way around. While he doted on Ivanka and regularly handed Jared important assignments he did not entrust to outsiders, Trump did not shy away from undercutting Kushner in meetings when he was not there. "Jared, all he cares about is his New York liberal crowd," Trump harrumphed. "These are not my people." Kelly seemed to interpret Trump's remarks as tacit instruction to find a way to pressure the children to leave.

Jared and Ivanka were polarizing figures in the West Wing. Some aides viewed them as calming influences and appealed to them to stop reckless decisions or nudge the president in a more responsible direction. They were seen as the more rational members of the family, not hotheaded screw-ups like Don Jr., and willing to listen in a way that the president did not. But others came to resent the pair, seeing them as entitled, pampered, arrogant, and self-aggrandizing. They always seemed to be trying to get into the photograph at major events. They were widely accused of leaking flattering stories about themselves and scathing stories about their rivals. And their preternatural confidence in their own judgment rankled many. Although in their late thirties, both Jared and Ivanka had spent most of their working lives at their own family businesses. Some in the White House began referring to them as "The Interns"; John Kelly called them "the Royal Couple" and eventually adopted Melania's nickname for Ivanka, "Princess."

The family dynamics at court were not Kelly's only challenge. Every day seemed to bring some new conflict for a president who gravitated toward it. In late September, the president went to the United Nations General Assembly, where he vowed to "totally destroy" North Korea if it threatened America and mocked Kim Jong-un as "Rocket Man" in a speech that not all his national security team had even seen in advance.[18] So much for Rob Porter's memos. Then Trump picked a racially charged fight with the National Football League at a rally in Alabama when he attacked players who took a knee during the National Anthem to protest police brutality against Black Americans. (His pollster had tested the issue and found his position popular with the base.) Trump forced out Tom Price, his health and human services secretary, over costly charter flights. And he got into a running feud with the mayor of San Juan, who criticized the federal response when back-to-back storms, Hurricanes Irma and Maria, ravaged Puerto Rico.

The dispute over Puerto Rico once again demonstrated the limits of Trump's understanding of the country he governed. When he asked his staff why he should spend so much money on disaster relief there, they had to explain that Puerto Rico was part of the United States.

"They're American citizens," Kelly told him.

"They're not Americans," Trump insisted.

"Yes, they are," Kelly replied.

Trump toyed with ways to make that not the case, even asking in one meeting whether they could sell the island or "divest" themselves of Puerto Rico.[19] The idea, like so many, went no further. But Trump's grudging, belated visit to Puerto Rico for a photo op backfired anyway, when he cavalierly tossed rolls of paper towels to people desperate for more serious help. (They were "beautiful, soft towels," he explained later.)[20]

Kelly was also left trying to manage the rapidly deteriorating relationship between the president and his secretary of state. While Trump had not heard Rex Tillerson's "fucking moron" comment after the disastrous meeting in the Pentagon Tank, neither man did much to hide growing contempt for the other. By fall, they were barely on speaking terms. While Trump was threatening North Korea's "Rocket Man," Tillerson was trying to talk with Kim Jong-un. He had been working back channels to set up a meeting and was already on the way there when, during a stop in China, his legs were cut out from under him via Twitter. "I told Rex Tillerson, our wonderful Secretary of State, that he is wasting his time trying to negotiate with Little Rocket Man," Trump wrote. "Save your energy Rex," he added, "we'll do what has to be done!"[21] As soon as the tweet appeared, North Korea canceled the meeting. Tillerson was beside himself. Rarely if ever had a commander in chief so undermined his secretary of state on a diplomatic mission.

Days later, NBC News reported Tillerson's "moron" quote—and *The New Yorker* later correctly added the expletive.[22] Trump fired back publicly, suggesting that Tillerson was the moron. "I guess we'll have to compare IQ tests," Trump said. "And I can tell you who is going to win."[23] Not even a year into his tenure, this was what it had come to: an insecure president challenging his secretary of state to an intelligence test to prove that he was not an idiot.

While Kelly was cast as a calming force instilling order on a fractious White House, the chief of staff had a temper of his own and strong feelings on issues like immigration that coincided with Trump's. As homeland security secretary, he had rebuked members of Congress who complained about what they saw as overly aggressive immigration enforcement. "If lawmakers do not like the laws they've passed and we are charged to enforce, then they should have the courage and skill to change the laws," he snapped. "Otherwise, they should shut up and support the men and women on the front lines." One of the Democratic congressmen, Henry Cuellar of Texas, had pushed back. "I don't think it's correct for you to tell members of Congress to shut up," Cuellar told him.[24]

Later that fall, Kelly got into a racially charged fracas with another member of Congress stemming from a consolation call gone awry. When Trump telephoned the widow of a soldier killed in action in Niger, he offended her by saying that her husband—whose name he seemingly could not remember—"knew what he signed up for."[25] Trump was echoing a comment that Kelly had made to him before the call, that troops who die in combat, like his own son, understood the risks they were taking on. But in Trump's telling it came across as callous. A Democratic congresswoman, Frederica Wilson, who happened to be with the widow at the time of the call, publicly accused Trump of insensitivity.

Kelly was incensed and marched to the White House briefing room to give an impassioned defense of the president, reflecting his own experience as the father of a slain Marine and bringing tears to the eyes of White House aides who were listening. But in doing so, he accused the congresswoman of being an "empty barrel" and told an unflattering story about her making self-aggrandizing comments at a public ceremony—an account that turned out not to be true once a video of the event surfaced. Wilson, who is Black, complained that the White House was "full of white supremacists."[26] Kelly did not help matters when a few days later he told Fox News that "Robert E. Lee was an honorable man" and that "the lack of an ability to compromise led to the Civil War," as if there were an acceptable compromise version of slavery.[27] It was a reminder that, as one presidential adviser put it, "there are no heroes" in Trump's White House.

With the effort to repeal Barack Obama's health care plan effectively dead on Capitol Hill, Trump and Republican congressional leaders turned to their other major priority—a sweeping set of tax cuts that they argued would turbocharge the economy. In the end, it would be Trump's most important legislative achievement, but one he had very little to do with. Which may be why it passed in the first place.

Trump knew he wanted to cut taxes but had little interest in the details.

He issued a one-page "plan" in April that was so unsophisticated and vague that his own top tax policy appointee was horrified. The only specific point that seemed to matter to Trump was lowering the corporate tax rate from 35 percent to 15 percent, a headline-friendly cut that by itself would drain the Treasury of $2 trillion, which even advocates of lower taxes deemed excessive. Otherwise, the plan was left to Republican congressional leaders to figure out. "This was done on the Hill," said Dana Trier, Trump's deputy assistant treasury secretary for tax policy, who oversaw the initiative. "Donald Trump certainly had no clue."

John Kelly had no experience in tax legislation, so the two key figures in the administration were Steven Mnuchin and Gary Cohn. They were not friends. "There were blood battles between them," recalled a member of the economic team. The old Goldman Sachs rivals had carried their feud to the Trump administration, acquiring new grievances along the way. Mnuchin viewed Cohn as a showboat who was trying to insert himself in a matter more logically left to a treasury secretary. The national economic adviser believed that Mnuchin was mainly interested in recognition. "He'll take credit for everything," Cohn complained to an associate. "I think he takes credit for the sun rising in the east and setting in the west." During one meeting over the spending and debt legislation, Cohn related, Mnuchin practically tanked the bill before it got anywhere by treating the lawmakers as hired help. In Cohn's telling, "Mnuchin basically got up and said, 'Look, I don't give a fuck. We can't shut the government down. We can't not extend the debt ceiling. You have to vote for this.' Mnuchin basically told Congress how to vote." In response, one lawmaker lectured Mnuchin right back: "You know, Secretary, the last time someone told me what to do, I was nineteen and it was my dad—and I never talked to him again."

Mnuchin's camp considered that a distorted picture. The onetime Wall Street financier and Hollywood producer was generally seen as unflappable, rarely reacting to Trump's broadsides or Cohn's barely veiled attacks. When a negative story appeared in the newspapers that Mnuchin's team attributed to Cohn leaking, aides would urge the secretary to push back. "He said, 'Nah,'" one adviser recalled. "He just glided over it. He never let himself get drawn in." Mnuchin realized that the key to survival in Trump's administration was staying on the president's good side and, with some notable exceptions, he was more successful than almost any other major figure. When Trump did lash out, Mnuchin remained calm. "The goal is to get the president tired of fighting with you, so he'll move on to somebody else," the adviser explained.

While Mnuchin and Cohn worked the Hill, Trump remained aloof. All he really seemed to care about was what to call the bill—branding was his specialty, after all. He hated the term "tax reform." "No one knows what tax reform is," he complained to aides. "No one knows whether their taxes are going to go up or down during tax reform." As far as he was concerned, it was a tax *cut*. He told Republican congressional leaders he wanted to name the bill the "Cut Cut Cut Act," which even allies considered too cartoonish.[28] "He's like a carnival guy," said Trier, who served in the Treasury Department under Ronald Reagan and George H. W. Bush before returning as Trump's top tax policy official. "He wanted to say this is the biggest tax cut in history." It did not matter how many times his own advisers told him that was not actually true.

As everyone else focused on the bill, Trump headed off on a trip to Asia. Two aides, Tony Sayegh and Cliff Sims, worried that the president's absence would sap momentum for the tax legislation, went to Kelly and proposed asking Ivanka Trump to highlight the issue in her father's absence. Kelly approved it but his dismissive reaction hinted at his tensions with the first daughter.

"Make sure she knows this isn't one of her pet projects," Kelly huffed. "I don't want her just talking about the child-care tax credit."[29]

Sayegh and Sims were taken aback. Kelly's tone was so scornful that it "made it seem like there was a dead skunk somewhere in the room," as Sims later put it.[30] If Kelly was that openly disdainful of Ivanka with them, they thought, imagine what he said to his true confidants.

Ivanka soon heard about the remark. Like her husband, she had grown disenchanted with Kelly, whom she considered a sexist bully who limited the president's access to information to secure the decisions that the chief of staff favored. The child tax credit was a high priority for her even if Kelly belittled it and she pushed against the Republican grain to include it in the legislation, enlisting allies such as Senators Marco Rubio of Florida and Mike Lee of Utah. The provision doubled the maximum credit from $1,000 to $2,000 per child under age seventeen, although for lower-income households, the benefit was more marginal, as low as $75.[31]

Ivanka served as an important lobbyist for the overall bill, one of the few times she invested herself publicly in one of her father's high-profile priorities. During a trip to Maine to lobby Senator Susan Collins, Ivanka joined the moderate Republican in the car on the way in from the airport. "Maybe we'll call my father," Ivanka suggested with practiced nonchalance. She reached the president in Asia and handed the phone to Collins seated next to her—a way of flattering the senator while demonstrating her own clout.

With no chance of meaningful Democratic support, Republican lawmakers negotiated the substance of the bill among themselves. The version they developed bore only passing resemblance to what Trump promised on the campaign trail. "There was very little participation in the drafting," Trier said. "I guarantee you the Trump administration had nothing to do with that." But Republican lawmakers did finally score a victory against Obamacare by inserting a provision repealing the so-called individual mandate at the heart of the health care law, the requirement that Americans obtain insurance or pay a penalty. Even though they had lost the war to kill the program, this would hollow out a critical element.

In the end, the one Republican to take a stand on the deficit, Senator Bob Corker, forced the sponsors to cap the total net cost of the tax cuts at $1.5 trillion over ten years. To keep under that limit, negotiators went after Democrats' core constituencies by capping deductions for charitable contributions and state and local taxes that hit high-tax states on the East and West Coasts the hardest. They also slapped a new tax on private university endowments and even stripped tax breaks for bicycle commuters that predominantly affected urban areas. The measures seemed like punitive retribution against Blue America. The rest of the cost would supposedly be offset by smoke-and-mirrors accounting changes and revenue growth, but in fact the bulk of it would be added to the already considerable national debt.

Republican campaign donors considered the bill an important part of their reward for sticking with a president they had only reluctantly supported. On December 2, Trump attended a $100,000-a-plate fundraiser at a sprawling Park Avenue apartment once owned by John D. Rockefeller that now belonged to Stephen Schwarzman, the chief executive officer of Blackstone, where the president was hit by complaints that the top income tax rate was too high; soon after, it was reduced from 39.6 percent to 37 percent in the bill. By the end of the process, one Republican congressman revealed the pressure the caucus felt. "My donors are basically saying, 'Get it done or don't ever call me again,'" said Representative Chris Collins of New York.[32]

In Trump's absence, the final version of the bill did not even deliver his most specific promise. It slashed the corporate tax rate to 21 percent rather than the 15 percent he demanded, while bringing down individual income rates and nearly doubling the standard deduction and child tax credit. The changes for corporations were permanent but the cuts for individual tax-payers would expire in 2025 unless renewed by Congress first. The Senate passed the final plan 51 to 48 followed by the House, which voted 224 to 201.[33] Even Corker went along with it on final passage after being lobbied relentlessly by Ivanka Trump. "Thank YOU for delivering Corker vote!" Marc Short, the legislative affairs director, emailed Ivanka. "I didn't think that was possible."

Trump, having played little role in the bill's passage, nonetheless soaked up the adulation. Speaker Paul Ryan praised his "exquisite presidential leadership," which may have been an ironic way of thanking him for staying out of it.[34] Trump even bungled the signing of the bill. Angry at television reports questioning whether he would enact it by Christmas, he abruptly summoned photographers to the Oval Office on December 22 and signed it right there, thus forgoing an extravagant televised ceremony that would have generated more political bounce.

Still, he took credit with those who mattered to him. That night, after flying to Florida for the holidays, he told wealthy guests over dinner at Mar-a-Lago, "You all just got a lot richer."[35]

Even in what should have been Trump's moment of triumph, he could not escape the whiff of scandal. While negotiators fashioned the tax bill, Robert Mueller issued his first indictments, sending a chill through the White House. On the morning of October 30, prosecutors unveiled a variety of tax and financial charges against Paul Manafort, Trump's former campaign chairman, accusing him of laundering more than $18 million through overseas shell companies while working for a pro-Russia political party in Ukraine, money used to buy luxury cars, real estate, antique rugs, and fancy clothes. His deputy, Rick Gates, was charged too. It was the first time since Watergate that a president's top campaign official had been charged with a crime, but Trump at first was modestly relieved because the counts were about Manafort's private activities, not his work for the campaign. He quickly tweeted that the case had nothing to do with him and insisted, "There is NO COLLUSION!"

But an hour later, prosecutors surprised the Trump team with another indictment, this one against George Papadopoulos, a campaign foreign policy adviser who pleaded guilty to lying to the FBI about attempts to arrange a meeting between Trump and Vladimir Putin while obtaining information that Russia had "dirt" on Hillary Clinton. Shocked Trump advisers discovered that Papadopoulos had been secretly arrested three months earlier and was now cooperating with prosecutors.

Papadopoulos was a small fish, a volunteer the Trump team could dismiss as unimportant. But just a month later, a much bigger fish, Mike Flynn, pleaded guilty to lying to the FBI about his conversations with Russia's ambassador. Trump's efforts to protect Flynn by pressuring James Comey to drop the case had failed. None of the charges so far had alleged a conspiracy with Russia to manipulate the election, but Mueller seemed to be bearing down and had some cooperating witnesses. Now the White House had to worry about what Flynn might have to tell prosecutors as part of his plea deal.

Trump soon faced exposure on another front. Michael Rothfeld and Joe Palazzolo of *The Wall Street Journal*, pursuing the story that Fox News killed during the 2016 campaign, reported on January 12, 2018, that Michael Cohen, the president's personal attorney, had sealed a deal just eleven days before the election to pay $130,000 in hush money to the porn star Stormy Daniels for silence about an extramarital sexual romp with Trump in 2006.[36]

Trump and his team responded, as they often did, with deception. Cohen, who months earlier boasted that he would "take a bullet for the president," told reporters that he paid the money himself, as if Trump had nothing to do with it.[37] When reporters asked the president on Air Force One about the secret payments, he said, "You'll have to ask Michael Cohen. Michael's my attorney." A reporter asked if he had known about the payments. "No," Trump said. Did he know where the money came from? "No, I don't know."[38] In fact, Trump knew perfectly well, since he had reimbursed Cohen for the payments, personally signing six out of eleven checks from his own bank account or trust.

The affair with Daniels, known for adult movies like *Good Will Humping* and *Porking with Pride 2*, reminded the public of Trump's sordid past with women at the very moment the #MeToo movement seeking to hold prominent men to account for sexual misbehavior was getting under way—a reaction, many believed, to Trump's own history of getting away with such acts. The president who had boasted on the infamous *Access Hollywood* tape that he could grab women by their private parts had been accused over the years by more than two dozen women of sexual harassment or assault—ogling women backstage at his beauty pageants, groping a woman on an airplane flight, kissing another outside her office at Trump Tower, reaching under other women's dresses. Several of the women had gone public all over again in the weeks following revelations about other powerful men like the Hollywood mogul Harvey Weinstein. Trump, ever defiant, not only rejected all allegations against him, he rejected them against anyone else who was accused, at least if they were on his side of the political aisle. Most notably that fall, he stuck with Roy Moore, the controversial Senate candidate in Alabama, even after he was accused of molesting a fourteen-year-old girl and pursuing other teenage girls— allegations that cost Republicans the seat in a special election in a deep-red state where the party had not lost a Senate race in thirty years.

As for allegations against him, Trump rarely claimed to be an innocent who was incapable of that sort of thing. Instead, he typically scoffed that he would not do that sort of thing with *her*, whoever she was at the moment. "She has a horse face," he told aides about Stormy Daniels over and over. "I wouldn't touch that."[39] At one point, he even ordered a press aide to go over to reporters waiting on the South Lawn to tell them that Daniels had a horse face. The aide wisely avoided that assignment, but eventually the president went public himself by using the phrase in a tweet.

The unenviable task of informing the first lady about the Stormy Daniels revelations fell to Stephanie Grisham, her communications director. Grisham tried to be matter-of-fact. "Ma'am," she said when she reached Melania by phone, "I got a call from a reporter that the *Wall Street Journal* is going to do a story on payments supposedly made to a woman named Stormy Daniels to keep quiet about some alleged affair with the president." The first lady offered no real reaction, no anger, no hurt— and no surprise. Did she want to comment? "No replay," she said in her Slovenian-accented version of "no reply."[40]

Melania had been a largely invisible figure in Trump's White House. More than any first lady in modern times, she had eschewed much of a public role, mostly keeping to herself. She almost never showed up at the East Wing office that Laura Bush, Michelle Obama, and other first ladies used, preferring to deal with her staff by telephone and text or, if need be, meeting in the Map Room on the ground floor of the White House. She spent most of her time with her son, Barron, and her parents, and her main occupation seemed to be photo albums that she curated meticulously. If her staff could get her to do a single event a week, they considered it a victory. Secret Service agents who thought of her as a beauty locked away in a tower privately nicknamed her "Rapunzel."[41] She was so absent that journalists spent enormous energy investigating rumors that she secretly lived in a suburban Maryland house near her son's private school but could never prove it. Her few public appearances tended to generate more questions about the state of the marriage.

It had not gone unnoticed that Trump on Inauguration Day had forgotten to wait for Melania as he exited the limousine to enter the White House for coffee with the Obamas. Nor did anyone miss it when Trump walked ahead of his wife on the tarmac in Tel Aviv, seemingly oblivious until he reached back for her hand, which she then swatted away with evident annoyance. When reporters drinking with a White House official on a rooftop bar in Jerusalem that night asked about the episode, the official explained that Melania simply did not want to embarrass Benjamin Netanyahu and his wife, Sara, since they were not holding hands; when a reporter pulled up video showing that the Netanyahus were, in fact, holding hands, the official shrugged and said resignedly, "I've got nothing." It was not easy to lie for Trump.

Many Trump critics assumed the first lady despised her husband as much as they did and was all but held hostage by him, coining the online hashtag #FreeMelania. Theirs, after all, often seemed to be a transactional partnership. Asked once if she would be with Trump if he were not rich, she retorted, "If I weren't beautiful, do you think he'd be with me?"[42] But while her relationship with her husband was complicated and not always loving, she was not some closet liberal who disagreed with him on issues. She tried to temper his Twitter habit from time to time, but she shared his hostile view of the news media and his political opponents.

Melania could hardly have been surprised by stories of her husband's crude and lascivious ways. Days after the *Access Hollywood* tape emerged during the campaign, she had lunch with her friend Stephanie Winston Wolkoff and seemed unbothered. "Aren't you angry?" Wolkoff recalled asking. "Nope!" Melania responded. "He is who he is." Likewise, she expressed none of the fury that one might expect after the Stormy Daniels story broke. "It's just politics," she told Wolkoff.[43]

But that did not mean she was not upset. In the days that followed, she made her displeasure known in her own way. On the one-year anniversary of the inauguration, which came a few days after the Daniels story, she edited the tweet that her staff had written for her to delete any mention of her husband and tweeted a photo of herself on the arm of a good-looking young military aide. She also skipped Trump's trip to the World Economic Forum in Davos, Switzerland.

Grisham lobbied her for days to put out a statement just to deflect media inquiries, something simple saying she was focused on family. When Grisham wrote the phrase "wife, mother and First Lady," Melania took out the word "wife" before agreeing to issue it. The next time they were to fly to Florida for the weekend, she made clear she wanted to be driven to Air Force One ahead of her husband and acknowledged that the sex scandal was the reason. "I do not want to be like Hillary Clinton, do you understand what I mean?" she told Grisham, referring to the public spectacle after Bill Clinton's trysts with Monica Lewinsky were revealed. "She walked to Marine One holding the hands with her husband after Monica news and it did not look good." She scoffed when Michael Cohen tried to protect Trump by telling her that Daniels's allegations were false and that he had only paid hush money to make them go away. "Oh, please, are you kidding me?" she told Grisham later. "I don't believe any of that bullshit."[44]

Trump, for his part, seemed less concerned that he would be seen as a cheat than a not-particularly-well-endowed cheat. A few months later, when Stormy Daniels published a book in which she said he had a small and oddly shaped penis, the president called Grisham from Air Force One to deny it.

"Did you see what she said about me?" Trump said. "All lies. All lies."

Grisham was not sure how to respond. "Yes, sir," she said simply.

"Everything down there is fine," he insisted.

"Okay," she replied, hoping the call would somehow be disconnected.[45]

For John Kelly, dealing with Trump's history of sexual misconduct allegations was one more distasteful duty. By that winter, the old Marine had grown increasingly sour and made little effort to hide it. He told colleagues that this was "the worst fucking job" he had ever had and when leaving for home at the end of the day often grumbled that he was not sure whether he would be back the next morning. He began discouraging people from joining the White House staff, warning that they would have "the stink" on them for the rest of their career if they came to work for Trump.

At the heart of his discontent was Trump himself. "He fundamentally did not like the president," said a fellow official. To a man who had devoted his life to his country and even sacrificed a son defending it, Trump was a loathsome narcissist with no calling larger than himself. Kelly considered Trump a pathological liar, not just someone disconnected from reality but someone who did not even seem to understand that there was a reality other than what he decided it was.

The president would sit with Kelly and Sarah Huckabee Sanders to go over what to tell the news media about one issue or another, and Trump would try out lines without any regard for whether they were accurate or not. He would tell Sanders to say something he just made up and Kelly would reply, "but that's not true," and Trump would say, "but it sounds good." Many times in this period, Kelly defined a good day at the office as stopping Trump from making yet another reckless tweet or demanding another impulsive firing. He told associates that if he were to write a book on his time as chief of staff, he would title it *Tweets Not Sent, Decisions Not Made.*[46]

Rob Porter, Kelly's wing man, often felt the same way. It sometimes seemed like his job was to throw sand in the gears to head off disasters promoted by some of the in-house renegades taking advantage of a president willing to believe whatever he was told.

Among those Kelly was most anxious to keep away from Trump were Peter Navarro, the trade adviser, and Wilbur Ross, the commerce secretary. Navarro was the Harvard-educated, flame-throwing protectionist whose book with Greg Autry, *Death by China: Confronting the Dragon—A Global Call to Action,* condemned American business for acting as "soldiers in the pro-China lobby."[47] Ross was a seventy-nine-year-old billionaire investor who made a fortune off trade deals with China and Mexico. His Manhattan apartment was festooned with Chinese art and artifacts. Senator Elizabeth Warren, the liberal Democrat from Massachusetts, had dubbed him "a cartoon stereotype of a Wall Street fat cat."[48] But now Ross was positioning himself as an ally of the trade hawks like Navarro.

Although he had never served in the federal government—and lost five campaigns for elected office—Navarro proved a tenacious political intriguer in Trump's White House, demonstrating a talent for getting around gatekeepers and prodding the president to take action when no one else was around to argue the other side. He showed up on weekends when he knew Trump would sometimes come down to the Oval Office without the usual coterie of aides to guard the door. One time he did that, he used the opportunity to trash Gary Cohn's deputy, Kenneth Juster, a veteran of both Bush administrations who was known as pro-trade and wanted to take on issues with China without blowing up all existing trade agreements. To Navarro, that meant he was a "globalist," one of those words that had become radioactive with Trump. By the next day, Cohn was told that Juster would have to go. He was soon shipped off to India as ambassador.

Kelly considered both Navarro and Ross dangerous influences who promoted half-baked ideas that got into the president's head and were hard to dislodge. At one point, Kelly implored Rob Porter to block their access to the president. "Look, just for a little while, you've got to keep Peter Navarro and Wilbur Ross out of the Oval Office and off the phone," Kelly pleaded. Porter tried. He succeeded for maybe three weeks. But Trump would not be cut off from his more radical advisers for long. The adhocracy lived, and Kelly and Porter knew it.

With Trump, there was never a single meeting that ended a debate or put a stake in the heart of a bad idea permanently. Pulling out of NATO, terminating NAFTA, withdrawing troops from South Korea, privatizing the Postal Service, eliminating birthright citizenship for children of foreigners born on American soil—no matter how many times advisers thought they had talked Trump out of such notions, he would bring them up again a day or two or several weeks later. Kelly tried to head off the more half-baked schemes by creating a process to examine them; whenever the president ordered something off-the-wall, Kelly would say okay, let's bring some folks over, draft some options, and have a meeting. Not saying no, exactly, just trying to slow things down.

Sometimes that worked. But Trump often would not let go. He was so determined, for instance, to punish Obama-era national security officials who criticized him on television, like John Brennan, the former CIA director, and James Clapper, the former director of national intelligence, that he insisted their security clearances be revoked for disloyalty. Trump demanded again and again that it be done—anywhere between fifty and seventy-five times, Kelly estimated to associates—only to grudgingly back off each time when told it would blow up in his face. For Kelly and other advisers, deflecting the constant stream of wild demands was exhausting. Gary Cohn would stop by Porter's office at the end of the afternoon after the latest Groundhog Day debate, collapse on the couch, and exclaim, "I thought we did this two weeks ago!"

Kelly could not get rid of Navarro or Ross, but he did try to weed out some of those in the White House he considered problems, among them Omarosa Manigault Newman, the former *Apprentice* star who was one of the only Black members of the White House staff but was seen as a disagreeable colleague just as she was on the reality show. Kelly fired her after she was accused of misusing the White House car service. "This has to do with some pretty serious integrity violations," he told her in the Situation Room in a conversation that, in classic Trumpworld fashion, she secretly taped. "Everyone on the staff works for me, not the president," he told her curtly before having her marched out of the building.[49]

Other troublemakers were not even on staff. When Kelly took over, he discovered that political advisers including Corey Lewandowski, Trump's famously pugnacious first campaign manager, were on a list admitting them to the White House anytime they wanted. Kelly, convinced that the hangers-on were marketing their access to high-paying clients, rescinded that practice, forcing them to be cleared in for any specific meeting. That did not end the problem. One day Kelly heard that Lewandowski was not only in the building but in the Oval Office. He stormed down the hall and found Lewandowski with the president as well as Kellyanne Conway and Bill Stepien, the White House political director. Lewandowski was trashing Trump's aides, pressing him to fire people.

Kelly erupted. "Enough of this, everyone out," he barked.

"Well, I haven't finished talking with them," Trump protested.

"No, everyone out," Kelly insisted.

Lewandowski followed Kelly to the outer Oval Office and loudly assailed Kelly, seemingly eager for a confrontation. Kelly, thinking the younger man would get physical, warned him, "Don't be stupid, Corey, because you'll wake up tomorrow with a broken jaw." As Kelly later recounted to associates, Lewandowski started to approach him, so the retired Marine grabbed him by the lapels and shoved him against the wall. Lewandowski later asserted that the incident took place not after that meeting but on another occasion when he was visiting Trump and Kelly began accusing him of profiteering off his relationship with the president. When Kelly threw him against the wall, Lewandowski said he dared him to "go outside and finish it out there."[50] Either way, further blows were avoided.

No matter how much Kelly tried to impose a process, though, the president wriggled out of it. Trump would simply call aides and ask them to do things outside their portfolio, which would sometimes leave Kelly sputtering mad at the wrong people. When Trump assigned Hope Hicks to take care of something for him one day, she called Kelly to let him know. "Would you like to do this or would you like me to do it?" she asked deferentially. "Why don't you just be the goddamn chief of staff!" Kelly snapped and then hung up the phone. On another occasion at a staff meeting, Kelly threw up his hands at the latest Trump tweet that he knew would disrupt all the plans they had made for the day. "We might as well go home," Kelly groused. "The president tweeted this and the whole day's gone to shit."

Trump finally tried to get around Kelly's restrictions on who he could talk with by secretly sending Dan Scavino, his social media director, to a store to get a new mobile phone for him that Kelly would not know about.

They did not have Apple Stores back when Roger Porter had first studied the adhocracy.

The tabloid story that blew up whatever tentative stability Kelly had imposed on the White House had nothing to do with Trump himself. On February 1, the *Daily Mail* of London published paparazzi photos of two White House staffers canoodling in the back of a cab.[51] One was Hope Hicks, the statuesque former model and Trump favorite, and the other was Rob Porter, Kelly's closest White House aide.

Since the fall, the two had secretly been dating, which Porter's previous girlfriend, still living with him at the time, discovered to her rage when she stumbled on a series of suggestive texts from Hicks. But the story turned out to be about more than a clandestine workplace romance. A few days later, the tabloid followed up with a shocking report that Porter had been accused by two former wives of abusing them.[52] The next day, the newspaper revealed that the woman with whom Porter had been living when he started dating Hicks had also accused him of violence in messages with his ex-wives, telling them, "He can go from being the sweetest, kindest person to a complete abusive monster in minutes."[53]

Hicks, twenty-nine, was devastated by the allegations. Porter, eleven years older, had seemed to her a mature and gentle man. But now she read that his first wife, Colbie Holderness, had accused him of kicking her during an argument on their honeymoon in 2003 and punching her during a vacation two years later. Holderness gave a photo of herself with a black eye to *The Intercept*.[54] A year after their divorce in 2008, Porter married Jennifer Willoughby, who accused him of frequently becoming angry, yelling expletives at her, and physically dragging her naked out of a shower. In 2010, after they separated, she filed a protective order against him when he came to their apartment and punched the glass in the door. They divorced in 2013.

Porter adamantly denied the allegations but believed nothing he could say would convince anyone in the heat of the #MeToo moment and decided to resign even though Trump urged him to stay, depriving Kelly of the aide he relied on the most. The revelations provoked days of damaging news stories about Porter's FBI background check and who knew what when. Worse for Kelly, his own credibility was badly marred, both inside the building and out. Just hours before Porter stepped down, Kelly had put out a statement saying he had "full confidence" in the staff secretary.[55] By the end of the same day, after Porter left the White House,

Kelly released another statement saying he had not known about the allegations. Making matters worse, he told a staff meeting the next day that he had only learned the details of Porter's situation forty minutes before he threw him out—a comment believed by few. Kelly told colleagues that Porter had not been straight with him, but many in the White House had already lost faith in the chief of staff, believing that Kelly had not been straight with them either. He would never fully recover.

Hope Hicks soon departed too. For a year, she had felt whipsawed by all the infighting in the White House, isolated, overwhelmed, and sometimes betrayed, never really knowing whom to trust. Then the man she had fallen for turned out to be someone different than she had thought. She left for a high-paying executive position at Fox Corporation, the parent company of Fox News. Her exit removed one of the few people who could get through to Trump and, sometimes, curb his worst instincts.

Porter's departure had a broader ripple effect on the building as well. He had been a steady hand, competent and levelheaded at least at work, someone who had smoothed out a tumultuous operation and stopped some of Trump's more extreme ideas from getting too far. He insisted that "these outrageous allegations are simply false" and the result of "a coordinated smear campaign," without going into further detail.[56] But it said something about the Trump White House that the resignation of an accused domestic abuser would cost it perhaps its most effective and professional staff member.

As for Trump, he left it to his communications staff to clean up the mess. Raj Shah, a deputy press secretary, was scheduled to brief reporters the day after Porter resigned, one of his first times at the podium. He went to the president to ask questions about the flap.

"Here are some things I need to know from you," Shah started.

Trump seemed thoroughly disinterested, as if all he wanted was for Shah to make it go away. "We did everything fine," the president insisted. Tell them that.

Shah knew that was not true. It was a hot flaming dumpster fire mishandled from start to finish. "I'm going to get killed if I say that," he pleaded with the president.

"Well, say what you think is right," Trump allowed. "But everything was fine."

Shah headed to the briefing room. "I think it's fair to say that we all could have done better over the last few hours, or the last few days, in dealing with this situation," he told reporters.[57]

Afterward, Shah was summoned to the Oval Office and found the president in his private dining room with the giant television on. "I didn't see the briefing," Trump said. "How did it go?"

Out of the corner of his eye, Shah could see on the television screen an image of himself walking out of the briefing room—meaning that Trump had in fact just finished watching a replay of the briefing. Trump lied to his aides about even the smallest of details. Shah gamely suggested that he thought it had gone all right.

Then Trump lit into him, all pretense that he had not seen the briefing now gone. He hated the admission that everything was not in fact handled perfectly. "Terrible job on that answer!" the president barked. "Never admit we got something wrong!"

II

YOU'RE FIRED

"The insanity has been loosed."

—KIRSTJEN NIELSEN

CHAPTER 8

I Like Conflict

On March 22, 2018, with Washington digging out of a surprise spring snowstorm, Trump was scheduled to have yet another phone call with President Recep Tayyip Erdoğan of Turkey. The increasingly autocratic leader was one of Trump's favorite international interlocutors—and one of the most vexing problems of his administration. At the National Security Council, aides often spent as much time worrying about Trump caving into the latest outrageous demand from Erdoğan as they did about Trump's mystifying desire to please Vladimir Putin. Trump called Erdoğan "the Sultan" and bantered with him in phone calls and meetings about the Turkish leader's "seemingly boundless ability to get his own way at home," as Fiona Hill, the senior National Security Council official responsible for Europe and Russia, put it.[1] "People think he loves Putin," his banished chief strategist Steve Bannon recalled. "Erdoğan is the one he loves."

Turkey had wired the Trump-era capital, spending millions to hire figures close to the White House like Mike Flynn, whose firm was paid $500,000 by the Turks in the fall of 2016 even as he served as Trump's foreign policy adviser, and Brian Ballard, dubbed by *Politico Magazine* "the most powerful lobbyist in Trump's Washington."[2] H. R. McMaster told others he was so concerned about Trump's friend Rudy Giuliani acting as an "influence agent" on behalf of Turkish or other interests that he had a policy of making sure he was in the Oval Office whenever the former New York mayor visited. In advance of this call, Trump's advisers had once again tried to prep the president to take a harder line as Erdoğan demanded that the United States abandon its Kurdish allies in Syria and extradite one of his chief critics, the cleric Fethullah Gülen, from the farm in Pennsylvania where he was living in exile. McMaster and John Kelly warned Trump that the Turkish leader was trying to put one over on the United States, flattering Trump while playing a double game with the Iranians and the Russians. "Especially the Russians," McMaster would tell him. They appealed to the president's vanity by saying that Erdoğan thought he was tougher than Trump. "He's going to try to push you around," McMaster told Trump. "He's going to try to bully you like he bullies other people."

But when Trump got on the phone with Erdoğan, he made only a halfhearted effort to follow the plan, then reverted to his default setting. He would rather schmooze Erdoğan than confront him. After the call, Trump was furious—not at the Turkish leader but at his own staff. He was done being managed by his national security adviser. He started to poke at McMaster on one of his perennial grievances, the war in Afghanistan. Harkening back to McMaster's first months in office, Trump complained about General "Mick" Nicholson, the American commander in Afghanistan, and brought up the scheme by Blackwater's Erik Prince to privatize the war—a plan that had been leaked, disavowed, and widely mocked by this point, but had never left Trump's mind.

McMaster, finally, erupted. It had been a horrible week, a horrible month, a horrible year. Trump never listened, no matter what his national security adviser told him. Two days earlier, Trump had called Putin after the Russian leader won a new presidential term, his fourth, in a transparently rigged election. "DO NOT CONGRATULATE," Trump had been warned in all capital letters in the briefing that came over from the National Security Council.[3] Trump had, of course, congratulated Putin anyway, yet the scandal inside the White House was not that the president had done so, but that the guidance urging him not to then leaked to *The Washington Post*. On the call, Trump had even invited Putin to Washington for a summit, an astonishing fact that his aides withheld from the official readout and only confirmed after the Russians made the offer public. And now this Erdoğan call had gone as badly as McMaster had feared. He was in no mood to revisit Afghanistan too.

"Have you ever talked to Mick Nicholson?" McMaster said, raising his voice in the Oval Office. "Have you ever even talked to him? Let's get him on the phone right now." Then he stomped out the door. Kelly followed him and McMaster acknowledged he had probably crossed some line that, even with Trump, remained uncrossable. "Just give me a fucking date," McMaster told the chief of staff. A date when he could step down.

What McMaster did not know was that date was already at hand. Trump had secretly been talking with John Bolton, the Fox News commentator and former Bush administration official who had lost out to McMaster the year before. That same day, around 4 p.m., Bolton came striding up the icy White House driveway in full view of reporters. Once he was inside, Trump offered Bolton the job and he accepted. McMaster was in a meeting with the Indian national security adviser when Trump called to give him the news. Soon after, Trump tweeted it out. "I am pleased to announce," the president wrote, "@AmbJohnBolton will be my new National Security Advisor."

McMaster had been warning his staff for months this would happen. "Guys, you should be careful, you could end up with somebody a lot worse, like John Bolton," he would say. Now it actually *had* happened and he had somehow not been entirely prepared. In just a few short weeks in March, Trump had moved to personally seize back control over his foreign policy from Bannon's hated "globalists." First, Gary Cohn had quit as the president's economic adviser days after Trump announced steel and aluminum tariffs on American allies that Cohn and others had been resisting for months. A week after that, Trump had finally fired Rex Tillerson. And now, just a week after that, he was getting rid of McMaster as well.

Trump was on such poor terms with his White House chief of staff that few doubted John Kelly would soon follow. Not even eight months into his tenure, Kelly was so demoralized, especially after the Rob Porter scandal, that he often threatened to quit. With Porter's departure what process had been established began to break down again and the adhocracy was reasserting itself. Kelly's former deputy Kirstjen Nielsen, who had succeeded him at the Department of Homeland Security, would enlist sympathetic cabinet officials such as Jim Mattis and Dan Coats to call the White House chief of staff and implore him not to leave, a mission that had become such a frequent occurrence that she joked she had them "on speed dial." Trump, meanwhile, was often heard openly musing about getting rid of Kelly. Their relationship was so bad that Jared Kushner, who had his own reasons for hating Kelly, would tell others that Trump had not even bothered to inform his White House chief of staff in advance that he was firing his national security adviser.

Once McMaster and Gary Cohn were gone, they noticed that the situation grew crazier and their replacements had different agendas. For more than a year, each of them as they saw it had thrown themselves on the grenades. Now there were fewer people left to jump on the grenades.

Throughout the Trump presidency, there were mass firings, aides were exiled and rehabilitated, courtiers appeared and disappeared and appeared again. In the opaque court politics of Trumpworld, advisers were often reported to be on the verge of quitting or being cashiered or both. Trump was always asking outsiders—golfing partners, Fox News hosts, dinner guests at Mar-a-Lago—how his staff was doing and who he should get rid of next.

But rarely had there been as tumultuous a month in the modern White House as March of 2018, when Trump decided to purge America's national security leadership.

Turnover in the upper levels of the administration was already unprecedented in modern times. "We have vacancies on top of vacancies," said Kathryn Dunn Tenpas, a Brookings Institution scholar who tracked such things, and that was before March began.[4] On the eve of his most consequential White House shuffle yet, Trump was already burning through his staff at a rate three times that of Barack Obama's first year and twice that of Ronald Reagan's. By the end of the month, Tenpas had recorded more than 40 percent turnover in the White House, even as the disorganization and feuding and Trump's aversion to congressional oversight left a record number of lower-level political posts vacant. "I'm the only one that matters," Trump had said the previous fall, when asked about all the many unfilled positions.[5] And now he seemed determined to prove it.

Even after all the mayhem, there was something remarkable in this latest shakeup. It was not Trump on some spur-of-the-moment rampage, discarding advisers on a whim. It was Trump declaring independence. He was sick of being managed. Sick of the establishment types who loved the power and access while assuring friends they were appalled by Trump's antics. After the 2016 election, he had believed he needed figures like Tillerson and Cohn, had been even a bit awed that big-time business leaders from ExxonMobil and Goldman Sachs would be working for him. By his second year, he did not think he needed them anymore. And in forcing them out, Trump was getting rid not just of troublesome aides, but also of troublesome policies with which he disagreed. The days of rationalizing Trump as all Twitter and no action were over.

Trump had been planning to fire Tillerson for months. Once Tillerson's "fucking moron" quote had been reported by the media, it was a foregone conclusion. "He was very deliberate about waiting," a senior White House official who discussed it with Trump said. "If he fired him after that comment, it would be a tacit admission that it was true." But advisers understood that Trump intended to push Tillerson out and there would be no face-saving exit. "He wanted to have someone lined up, so it was clear he was firing him and not that he was resigning," the senior official recalled.

The one person who did not seem to get the message was Tillerson himself. Until the end, he and Mattis remained a team. They talked daily, sometimes more than that. They often discussed leaving. "They would talk each other down from the ledge. 'You can't go,' 'If you go, I'll go, so you have to stay' sort of a thing," a Republican in close contact with Tillerson recalled. But even with the writing on the wall, he refused to quit. "The president may fire me tomorrow," Tillerson told one caller that winter, "but I'm not a quitter."[6] One senior State Department official who worked closely with Tillerson believed he had taken the wrong lesson from Trump's public abuse of Jeff Sessions while never actually firing the attorney general. Others who spoke with him believed that Tillerson just decided it was better to stay and push back against Trump from the inside.

Tillerson, an introvert, rarely confided in other officials aside from Mattis, but toward the end of his tenure, he told one colleague that when he was first asked by Trump to be secretary of state, "he thought he understood what God's plan for him was—it was all about accomplishing things." Eventually, though, Tillerson said he had realized that was not the mission at all. "His job wasn't to get things done but to stop certain things from happening, to prevent disaster. And over time I think he came to emanate that—and emanate that in a way that the president found demeaning."

Jared Kushner had come to loathe Tillerson too, seeing him as an outright obstacle to his plans for Mideast peacemaking. "I feel like I have four secretaries of state," Tillerson once made the mistake of complaining to him. Kushner responded sharply: "Well, if you were doing the policies that the president actually wanted, then there would be only one secretary of state and we'd all be working for you. The problem is that you're doing shit that's against what the president wants."

At a dinner party at the lavish home of Yousef al-Otaiba, the plugged-in ambassador of the United Arab Emirates, a guest referenced Tillerson's troubles with Trump. "The problem will be solved very quickly if I have my way," Kushner responded. When another guest suggested the job should go to Mike Pompeo, the CIA director sitting at the table, Kushner replied, "Of course."

In fact, Jared and Ivanka had initially pushed not for Pompeo to replace Tillerson but for Nikki Haley, the U.N. ambassador. Trump, however, balked. Some in the White House thought it was because Haley was too tough on Vladimir Putin, but the president, who made no secret of judging even the most senior female officials on their looks, told John Kelly the real reason was the blotch marks on her cheeks, which were neither particularly visible nor in any way a reason not to pick someone for secretary of state. "She's not good for me. She's got that complexion problem," he told Kelly. "She'll be here all the time. It doesn't look good."

By March, the "Rexit," as Washington wags were calling it, was inevitable and Kushner had become a Pompeo convert. Pompeo understood the president and was clear he was aligned with the president's policies, whereas Tillerson was not, Kushner would tell others. A former Republican congressman from Kansas, Pompeo had reinterpreted the job of CIA director to be a personal briefer of the president. While Pompeo presided over thousands of employees, he had taken to haunting the White House on most days, hanging around in the area outside the Oval Office like just another West Wing staffer. Steve Bannon and others viewed Pompeo as the administration's best Trump-whisperer.

The one question left to resolve was Pompeo's successor at the CIA. Pompeo was pushing his deputy, a career officer named Gina Haspel who would be the first woman head of the agency and a rare female presence in Trump's male-dominated cabinet. Gary Cohn, in the midst of losing his long battle over tariffs, made a late play to stop the Pompeo ascension by becoming secretary of state himself. Cohn argued to Trump that, by picking him, the president would only have to get one new cabinet officer through the Senate rather than two if he selected Pompeo. Cohn, still nominally a Democrat, would get a lot more votes from the other side of the aisle than the sharply partisan Pompeo, best known on Capitol Hill for his relentless pursuit of Hillary Clinton over the attack that killed four American personnel in Benghazi, Libya.

But in truth, Trump and Cohn were done with each other too, a topic they had been dancing around since January, when Cohn came back from the holidays and told the president over lunch in the White House that, with tax reform done, he wanted to leave "in the very near future" and hoped to do so "amicably." Trump kept trying to postpone the date and at one point that winter had even dangled the possibility of Cohn replacing John Kelly as chief of staff, an idea that quickly leaked. But it was never clear Trump was serious, and in any case Cohn told others that he was not willing to abase himself for Trump as Pompeo was. "He sort of wants you to get down on your hands and knees and beg for stuff and that's not my personality," Cohn told an associate later that spring. "My personality is that I'll tell you what I think I'm good at. I'll tell you what I think I can do. I'll tell you how I can be helpful. I'll offer to help. And if you want me, great. But I'm not going to go in there. You know, like, a couple of people are saying like, 'Get him on the phone. Get him on the phone. Beg. Beg him.' No. No. I'm not going to do it."

On March 6, the dance was over. Trump's plan to hit steel imports with a 25 percent tariff and aluminum imports with a 10 percent tariff disregarded what Cohn considered sound economic advice. Trump even planned to invoke a rarely used national security provision of American law to justify the action against American friends such as Canada. The allies were apoplectic. Cohn and others thought it was crazy: How could Canadian steel be a national security threat to the United States? Cohn had told Kelly the previous week that he would quit this time for sure if Trump went through with it. But it was hardly a surprise. In White House discussions, even on unrelated subjects, Trump had long referred to himself as "Tariff Man," and, as Fiona Hill later wrote, "he often commented in meetings on how long he had been waiting to do this."[7]

Although he was prepared for Cohn to quit and had even already interviewed candidates to replace him, Trump was still enraged when the news went public, especially when the stock market tanked out of fear that it presaged a global trade war. Trump privately derided Cohn as a "globalist" and ranted about his disloyalty. Always eager to control the narrative, the president tweeted that reports of "CHAOS in the White House" were "Fake News" while strongly hinting that the turmoil in his administration was not yet over and more personnel shuffles were soon to follow. "I still have some people that I want to change," he wrote, adding the coy parenthetical: "(always seeking perfection)."

Two days later, time would finally be up for the secretary of state as well.

The meeting that ended Rex Tillerson's short career in public service was not even on the president's schedule for March 8. Nor, for that matter, did Tillerson attend it. He was thousands of miles away on an apology tour of Africa, saying he was sorry in stop after stop because Trump during a meeting with a bipartisan group of senators that winter had referred to their homelands as "shithole countries."

For months, Trump had been undermining Tillerson's diplomacy on North Korea, at times in embarrassingly public fashion. The president had followed up his inflammatory rhetoric about "fire and fury" with repeated demands for specific war plans from the Pentagon and had privately charged Mike Pompeo with responding to the various secret feelers from the North Koreans that were starting to come in with increasing frequency. The recent Olympics in South Korea had provided an opening for direct engagement between top South Korean officials and Kim Jong-un's powerful sister, sent to represent her country at the Games. Now, after a flurry of cross-border talks, the South Koreans had a message they wanted to convey to the White House.

Their envoy, Chung Eui-yong, the national security adviser, flew to Washington and was meeting with McMaster, Kelly, Mattis, and others when Trump got word and summoned the group to the Oval Office for an impromptu session. Once there, Chung got to the point: Kim Jong-un, the "Little Rocket Man," wanted to meet Trump in person for a summit and South Korea's new pro-peace government under President Moon Jae-in thought he should accept. To the dismay of his national security team arrayed around him, the president immediately said yes. Trump's advisers feared it was a carefully choreographed plan between the two Koreas to "try to box in the president," as Matthew Pottinger, the National Security Council's senior Asia director, later put it. But that's not how Trump saw it. To him, the summit was the big opening for a deal he had been coveting.

Trump's advisers often fell silent or worked around him at moments like this. But this time, the stakes were too high simply to fight a rear-guard action later to get Trump to reverse course. With Pottinger visibly grimacing in the background, McMaster spoke up, explaining the bedrock assumption of American officials for more than two decades that granting an in-person presidential summit to a North Korean leader would be a mistake without major concessions by Pyongyang. Why would the world's most powerful man trade away a summit with Kim for nothing? North Korea had just begun to feel the pressure, Kim's invitation was proof of it, their strategy needed more time. But McMaster understood Trump well enough by then to get that he was not going to convince the president. "I know you're going to do it anyway," McMaster said, resignedly. He began talking about how to "manage the downside to ensure that we do not make any concessions just for the privilege of talking." But of course that was precisely what Trump's yes already was.

The president was so enthusiastic that he immediately began throwing out dates and locations for the summit. Why not hold it next month? Eventually, the group got him to agree to a more realistic target of May. And let's announce it right away, Trump demanded. He urged Chung to go to the White House briefing room to tell the media. After forty-five minutes the meeting broke up and stunned aides left to figure out what to do. McMaster holed up in his office with the South Korean envoy and helped write the statement that Chung would deliver. Elsewhere in the White House, aides determined that using the White House briefing room podium for an announcement by a foreign official would be inappropriate and settled on an outdoor news conference in the White House driveway instead. McMaster decided not even to stick around for it. He headed home. He was having a farewell dinner party for Gary Cohn to celebrate his departure. They had been foxhole buddies if unlikely ones, the Wall Street millionaire and the wonky general.

Flying around Africa, meanwhile, Tillerson had received an alarmed message asking him to urgently call the president to convince him to back off the summit. The resulting call to Trump proved "the final blow," as one official put it. "The president had made a decision and here was the secretary of state telling him not to do it." The bottom line was that Trump did not want to do it with Tillerson at his side. Trump had already given the North Korea portfolio to Pompeo, and he was sure that the CIA director would know better than to step in his limelight. "The president thought, 'If we're going to do this, I'm going to do this,'" a senior State Department official said. "'The secretary's not going to get the Nobel Peace Prize, I am.'"

Over the weekend following the South Korea meeting, Trump told John Kelly that it was time to fire Tillerson. Kelly was resigned to it. "That's what chiefs of staff do," he had taken to saying. "They clean up messes." On Sunday, he called Tillerson in Africa and told him to get back to Washington right away because Trump was about to get rid of him. Kelly later claimed to an off-the-record gathering of journalists that he had informed Tillerson he was to be fired while the secretary was on the toilet with a bout of diarrhea, a version the secretary's camp disputed. Tillerson landed back at Joint Base Andrews at 4:30 that Tuesday morning and was apparently asleep when Trump's tweet dumping him hit. "Thank you to Rex Tillerson for his service!" the president wrote, announcing Pompeo as his successor and Gina Haspel for the CIA post. "Congratulations to all!"

At Tillerson's direction, his spokesman Steve Goldstein put out a statement contradicting the no-big-deal gloss that White House officials were putting on the morning's events. Tillerson "had every intention of staying," the statement said, and had never even heard directly from the president. "The secretary did not speak to the president and is unaware of the reason," Goldstein added.[8] When Trump saw that statement reported on television, he ordered Goldstein fired too.

Tillerson had never understood Trump. He had never wanted to and by the end he had no constituency other than the secretary of defense. A key mistake was alienating his own building. The professional diplomats at Foggy Bottom had initially welcomed Tillerson, seeing a voice of gravitas who might talk reason into the unsettling new president. But Tillerson embraced Trump's draconian budget cuts for the department and spent much of his year in office on an ill-conceived and unpopular reorganization plan dreamed up by outside consultants. Morale was so terrible that ultimately more than one hundred out of nine hundred senior Foreign Service officers, including many of the most prominent Black, Hispanic, and female diplomats, were fired, pushed out, or chose to leave during the administration's first year. Tillerson's imperious management style and extreme isolation from virtually the entire staff bred resentment as well. His chief of staff, Margaret Peterlin, who had sent out a memo warning even senior officials not to trouble the secretary, was widely blamed for cutting him off. But the small handful who worked closely with the secretary knew the fault was Tillerson's. "He set it up that way," one said. "Anybody who ran Exxon—I don't think he missed too much in terms of how he ran his operation." Tillerson had also made a mess of the public duties that came with the job. He mostly refused to talk to the media, did not trust his department spokeswoman, former *Fox & Friends* anchor Heather Nauert, enough to let her travel with him—he saw her as a White House plant—and evinced little concern when many of the Foreign Service's most experienced ambassadors quit rather than serve under him and Trump.

By that March, several of Tillerson's subordinates were in open rebellion: Nikki Haley technically reported to him but, citing her seat in the cabinet, refused to do so in practice. David Friedman, the Trump bankruptcy lawyer now serving as ambassador to Israel, worked closely with Jared Kushner to engineer a cutoff of aid to the Palestinian Authority and move the embassy to Jerusalem over Tillerson's objections.

The turf battles with Kushner and others infuriated the secretary right up until his last day in office. "Tillerson came in and saw an eight-lane highway and thought he had all eight lanes," noted a senior State Department official who worked closely with him. But that was not how government works. "Some days you have four lanes, some days you have five, but you never have eight."

McMaster and Tillerson, meanwhile, were barely speaking by the end. McMaster told other White House officials that Tillerson was "the least collaborative person in the world," and said foreign ministers were calling him to complain they could not get in touch with the secretary. For his part, Tillerson told aides he believed that McMaster and Haley had teamed up to hasten his end in an Oval Office meeting with Trump on the Friday before the fateful tweet.

None of it might have mattered had Tillerson agreed more with the president or at least made a show of it. But it was often said of Tillerson that he did not suffer fools gladly. Or in this case "fucking morons." By March, the list of issues on which he disagreed with Trump was long. It was not just North Korea. It was the Paris climate accord and the Trans-Pacific Partnership, the steel and aluminum tariffs, the attacks on NATO, the embassy move to Jerusalem. More fights loomed. Trump was threatening to exit the Iran nuclear deal negotiated by Barack Obama. Tillerson was against that too. He had not gotten to be the chief executive of ExxonMobil by being a yes-man. And a yes-man is what Trump wanted. "We disagreed on things," Trump told reporters at the White House after his Twitter announcement. "It was a different mindset."[9]

McMaster's victory over his internal rival was short-lived. Trump already intended to get rid of him too. Despite months of advice from colleagues more skilled in the courtier-like treatment the president preferred, McMaster had continued to alienate Trump. "McMaster never learned the trick of agreeing with the president for the first five minutes and then saying, 'but . . . ,'" noted one keen observer on the White House staff. "He went straight to the 'but.'" McMaster kept lecturing Trump long after the president stopped listening.

This charge infuriated McMaster, who believed that he had gone out of his way to accommodate Trump by dumbing down complicated national security issues, using charts, maps, photos, and other illustrations. We may think it's a great idea to write long papers and give them to the president to read at night, but that's not how he receives information, he would tell his staff. Which was, of course, revealing about the state of their relationship. Regardless, it did not go over well. "McMaster is a quintessential Army general—he's always on transmit and is very rarely on receive," a national security official recalled. "He just talks and talks and talks." This invariably angered the president, whose attitude was described as, "What the fuck are you talking about? What planet are you from?" There was only one person in Trump's orbit allowed to be in constant transmit mode: Trump himself.

McMaster's determination to talk the president out of withdrawing from Afghanistan was perhaps his biggest misreading of Trump, who had been calling on the United States to get out since at least 2012. "H.R.

really wanted to make the president a convert on Afghanistan," a senior State Department official recalled. "He would wake up, go into the Oval, right into the buzz saw, right into the wood chipper. And, God bless him, he'd get up the next day and walk into the wood chipper again."

Like others in Trump's troubled White House, McMaster spent much of his tenure in an internal dialogue with himself over how long he could stay. He had first threatened to quit the previous fall after a particularly off-the-rails Trump phone call in which he disparaged President Emmanuel Macron of France on November 27. McMaster was so offended that he muttered something intemperate, as one of those present recalled, and walked out of the Oval Office. He agreed to remain only after John Kelly followed him back to his office and brandished a copy of McMaster's book, *Dereliction of Duty*, about the Vietnam-era generals who had failed to offer the honest counsel that might have prevented a debacle. "You wrote the book!" Kelly exclaimed. The point, not lost on either modern-day general, was that Trump was their LBJ and his administration was their Vietnam; they had an obligation to stay and head off disaster. "We've got to hang with this guy," Kelly pleaded with him. "Otherwise, God knows who he'll bring in."

McMaster had first discussed leaving with Trump in December, he later told others, and he knew in a broad sense that he was on his way out. This was publicly obvious to the rest of the world by February, when McMaster had appeared at the annual Munich Security Conference and spoken about Vladimir Putin and the 2016 election, saying evidence of Russian interference was "incontrovertible."[10] To everyone except Trump, this was merely a restatement of known facts. To Trump, it was a disloyal breach and he soon sent out pointed tweets rapping "General McMaster" for what he "forgot to say" about the Russia "hoax" and the "crooked" Democrats out to get him.

From then on, as was his disconcerting habit, Trump often asked McMaster about possible successors, including John Bolton, who had been openly campaigning on the president's favorite television channel for the job since losing out to McMaster a year earlier. The campaign was as lucrative as it was ultimately successful; Bolton's financial disclosure form showed he was paid $600,000 by Fox News in 2017.[11] Bolton had a well-deserved reputation for wanting to bomb America's way out of almost any foreign policy problem, an aversion to international agreements, and a brash personal style as undiplomatic in its own way as Trump's—all the makings, it seemed, of the kind of national security adviser who could easily goad the uninformed president into a war.

Bolton was also a famous bureaucratic knife-fighter; when nominated by George W. Bush as ambassador to the United Nations, his nomination was sunk by Senate Republicans after scorching testimony from an assistant secretary of state, who called him a "serial abuser" of lower-level staff and a "kiss-up, kick-down sort of a guy."[12] Bush gave him a recess appointment anyway, a move the former president regretted when Bolton criticized the administration after leaving government. "I don't consider Bolton credible," Bush snapped to a group of conservative writers at the end of his tenure.[13] Bolton would later acknowledge that he had been lobbying Trump hard for the national security adviser job; it was difficult to imagine any president other than Trump even considering him.

For Trump's part, Bolton's trademark walrus mustache seemed to bother him more than the militant views that conflicted with his own. At one point, he asked Raj Shah, his deputy press secretary, to weigh in on Bolton. Not sure where Trump was going with it, Shah replied, "He's a communicator, but I don't think he thinks anything that you think about these issues." Trump brushed that off. "Yeah, yeah, they say he's a warmonger," he said. "I got it."

John Kelly, Jim Mattis, Rex Tillerson, and even Mike Pompeo had scrambled for months for an alternative to Bolton. In the winter, they had approached Stephen Biegun, another veteran of the Bush administration they regarded as a much more palatable choice and who had the added benefit of not having publicly joined the #NeverTrump opposition because of his job as a top lobbyist at Ford Motor. A Mattis aide told Biegun that the group had come to him after creating a Venn diagram of possible candidates who were politically acceptable to Trump, competent, and willing. That left a small universe. At first, Biegun was hesitant, saying he refused to be used in a plot to oust McMaster and would only be considered if he was assured the lieutenant general would be given a fourth star and an appropriate military assignment. But the group told Biegun that, with or without him, McMaster was going. Mattis personally told Biegun that the president had already decided to fire McMaster. When word got out, Biegun called McMaster to say he wanted no part of forcing him out, but the general told him not to worry and that he would be a worthy successor.

Mattis's role, though, infuriated McMaster. Tensions between the two had been rising for months, largely over McMaster's increasingly insistent pressure on the Pentagon to follow up Trump's rhetoric with war plans for North Korea. McMaster believed he was carrying out the president's wishes and that it was the only way to force North Korea into meaningful concessions, but Kelly and the others feared that McMaster was aiding Trump in a reckless march to war. Publicly McMaster adopted Trump's bluster too, even bragging in an interview with George Stephanopoulos of ABC News that the United States was "locked and loaded" to hit North Korea.[14] Word leaked that among the military options McMaster had advanced was a "bloody nose" scenario: a preemptive conventional attack on North Korea to convince the regime to give up its nuclear weapons. Mattis was on record calling that a disastrous idea, which would result in "probably the worst kind of fighting in most people's lifetime."[15]

That winter, Victor Cha, a widely respected Korea expert, was informed he would be nominated as ambassador to South Korea. His nomination was cleared with the South Koreans and publicly announced. In the meantime, Cha attended briefings at the Pentagon and elsewhere, where he learned that this idea of a "bloody nose" strike was not just speculation but that Trump was seriously contemplating a major escalation. In January, Cha wrote a memo to McMaster and Matt Pottinger saying he could not go along with such a plan and warning that casualties in the wake of a strike would be so high it would be equivalent to losing an American city like Pittsburgh. After this, his contacts with the administration ceased. Eventually, Cha was told by the White House personnel office that "we're going in a different direction" and his nomination would not proceed. When he went public with qualms about the Trump strategy, White House officials put out untrue stories about why he had not been chosen.

Cha's information had been correct. Trump not only was considering escalation, he had actually demanded an evacuation of Americans from the Korean Peninsula, a move that Cha and other experts considered an "insane" ratcheting up of tensions that would cause panic and signal to North Korea that the United States was on the brink of war. Trump had ordered the move in January, after watching Jack Keane on Fox News. Keane, the retired general who had turned down Trump's invitation to serve as defense secretary, had said that if the United States was really serious about its military options, it would "stop sending military families to South Korea."[16] Trump interpreted this as a sign that his "fire and fury" campaign was being undercut by the military. In response, he insisted on a pullout of American citizens to show how serious he was. "Go do it!" Trump ordered.[17] Although it never became public, McMaster followed through. Mark Esper, the secretary of the Army, heard about Trump's demand for an evacuation when he was pulled out of a meeting in late January for an urgent phone call and told "the president was ordering a withdrawal of all U.S. military dependents from South Korea and he was going to announce it that afternoon."[18] It was tabled only after vehement resistance from Mattis, who rushed to the White House to stop it. "If we pull the dependents out," he explained to Trump, "it's like clearing the decks for action and once you do it, you don't have a dramatic statement left to make."

McMaster was frustrated that Mattis and Tillerson refused to act. "They basically said, 'Fuck you, we're not going to do it,'" a national security official recalled. Trump repeatedly demanded to know why it had not happened and became convinced that McMaster, not Mattis and Tillerson, was slow-rolling him. "That contributed to the end of the downward spiral for McMaster and the president," the official concluded.

In February, Mattis and McMaster finally had it out after a particularly tense meeting in the Situation Room over North Korea. Mattis had been offended by the suggestion that the military's refusal to intercept North Korean freighters carrying illicit cargo was somehow evidence that he was not fully on board with the administration's campaign of "maximum pressure" on Pyongyang. After the meeting, Mattis followed McMaster back to his office, and, according to an account McMaster later gave associates, challenged the national security adviser.

"Is there a problem between us?" Mattis asked.

"Fuck yes, there's a problem between us," McMaster shot back.

Aides in the room hastened to leave, closed the door, and turned up the volume on the television to drown out the sound of Mattis and McMaster shouting at each other. McMaster went through a long list of accumulated slights from a year's worth of frustration.

"I hope you fucking get John Bolton," McMaster told Mattis. "Because you fucking deserve John Bolton."

"You just crossed a line, Lieutenant General," Mattis replied. "You can't talk to me that way."

The reference to rank—that old three-star versus four-star dynamic—infuriated McMaster. He told Mattis that in the White House, he was the national security adviser. But both of them knew the truth, which was that he would not be for long.

McMaster's problem was not just with the remnants of the Axis of Adults. Steve Bannon had been fired but continued to push the McMaster-as-evil-globalist narrative from the outside. Scurrilous rumors about McMaster's personal life were spread and made their way back into the White House, where even the president repeated them. McMaster had managed to purge a number of the Bannonites on the staff, eventually firing Ezra Cohen and several others. But there were still enemies "inside the wire," as McMaster put it. "Lunatics," he called them.

McMaster was certain that the leak of the "DO NOT CONGRATU-LATE" guidance about Vladimir Putin had come from one of them. In a screaming phone call, Trump had blamed the embarrassing disclosure on two aides to McMaster, who denied it. Joe Wang, a State Department career officer detailed to the National Security Council to serve as the director for Russia, felt particularly responsible, as he had included the talking point from the State Department in the briefing package that was prepared for Trump and sent to the president's executive secretariat. He suggested to Fiona Hill that they should offer to resign, but when she raised that with McMaster he dismissed it out of hand, reminding his aides that he had personally decided to keep the language after objections were raised. And besides, he told them, it was just an excuse, another stupid and ultimately meaningless controversy in a White House full of them. Whether or not Trump read the guidance—and he probably did not, his aides believed, since he rarely did—McMaster had repeatedly briefed Trump not to accept the results of Putin's "rigged" election. Trump did so anyway.

The "DO NOT CONGRATULATE" leak had happened late on a Tuesday evening. Trump fired McMaster on Thursday. That Friday, before his departure took effect, McMaster had to deal with one last Putin crisis—trying to get Trump to approve retaliatory measures against Moscow for the attempted assassination of Sergey Skripal, a former Russian agent who was poisoned with a military-grade nerve agent by Russian operatives on British soil. The idea was to send a strong coordinated message by having the United States and European allies expel large numbers of Russian diplomats simultaneously.

At an Oval Office meeting that Friday afternoon, Trump's top remaining advisers sat on couches, including McMaster's nemesis Mattis. McMaster stood and made his pitch. He told Trump that he could not let Putin normalize the use of chemical weapons a hundred years after the horrors of World War I led to their prohibition. He told Trump, for the umpteenth time, that it was important to impose higher costs on the Kremlin. But McMaster knew that high-minded appeals to alliance solidarity and the norms of history were not likely to persuade Trump. The argument that worked was pure self-interest: he emphasized that Putin already had undercover agents in the United States to find defectors like Skripal and take them out. In short, he said, this was a message to America, too. If they did not do anything, they might kill people in the United States, too. After Trump reluctantly agreed with the expulsion plan his advisers proposed, McMaster would later tell others that he believed he had been more persuasive with Trump than usual "because he had fired me the day before."

But in a fitting coda to his work in an administration where Trump was never definitively persuaded of anything, McMaster and others then spent the weekend fending off outraged calls from the president. Holed up at Mar-a-Lago, Trump became convinced that he was getting screwed and that the Europeans were not in fact doing their part against the Russians, thus setting him up to be the bad guy with Putin. Gérard Araud, the French ambassador in Washington, received four phone calls from a State Department official over those two days, pleading for more expulsions. Prime Minister Theresa May of Britain was enlisted to call Trump and explain that, taken together, the Europeans' total would match that of the Americans. But then, when the news was announced the following week, Trump exploded in the Oval Office anyway, since the numbers for France and Germany individually were far lower than the sixty diplomats the United States was expelling. "There were curse words," an official present told *The Washington Post*, "a lot of curse words."[19]

On March 28, Trump had one more change to make. At 5:30 that afternoon, he tweeted that he was firing the secretary of veterans affairs, David Shulkin, a doctor who had served in the Obama administration. Within hours, Shulkin would go public with the accusation that Trump political appointees in his department who were trying to privatize the VA had forced him out by successfully hyping a controversy over an expensive taxpayer-funded trip he took to Europe.

A chief proponent of the privatization plan was Ike Perlmutter, the reclusive billionaire chairman of Marvel Entertainment, a major Trump campaign donor and buddy from Mar-a-Lago. In what would have been an extraordinary scandal for any other presidency but barely registered for this one, Shulkin eventually revealed that Perlmutter and two fellow Palm Beach magnates had so much power over the VA under Trump that the president would routinely dial the billionaire into meetings and ask if the secretary was keeping him informed and happy. VA officials would telephone and email the trio they called "the Mar-a-Lago Crowd" to consult on department decisions, even flying to Trump's club in Florida at taxpayer expense to solicit their input.

"Everything needs to be run by them," one of Shulkin's senior officials said later. Perlmutter's interest in the VA was never fully explained. He had never visited a VA hospital until Shulkin took him to one nor served in the American military. But he would call the secretary sometimes multiple times a day. Even so, Shulkin said he was often reproved by White House aides such as Stephen Miller for not keeping in close enough contact with Perlmutter. "There probably weren't too many times I met with the president when he didn't say, 'What's happening with Ike?'" Shulkin would recall.[20]

When Perlmutter soured on Shulkin, so did Trump. A critical report from the VA inspector general about Shulkin's Europe trip—he eventually repaid the department for tickets to Wimbledon and other costs—provided the ammunition his critics needed. Shulkin phoned John Kelly in a panic, saying he had heard a rumor that he was to be fired that day. The White House chief of staff called back and said it was not true. "The president has confidence in you," Shulkin remembered Kelly saying. In a while, Trump himself called and, according to Shulkin, complained about the bad press from the Europe trip, then invited him over to the Oval Office the next day.

But Shulkin's original tip had been correct. By late afternoon, Kelly called back. He told Shulkin that not only was he going to be fired, but that Trump was planning to name his White House physician, Dr. Ronny Jackson, to replace him. "David, I have no idea," Kelly told Shulkin. "He did the same thing with Rex. I just don't know what to say." It was, Kelly added, "one of the worst decisions I could imagine."

Jackson, a Navy doctor, had little managerial experience beyond the White House Medical Unit, where he had a propensity for heavy drinking and freely dispensing prescription drugs to White House aides. But he had forever endeared himself to Trump by holding a news conference after the president's annual physical exam that January, at which he claimed the obese septuagenarian president was in "excellent" health, enthused about Trump's "incredible genes," failed to mention his cardiac disease, and said that "absolutely he is fit for duty."[21] Once again, Kelly had not been consulted on a decision that would soon blow up on the White House.

A few minutes after the embarrassing call from Kelly to Shulkin, Trump tweeted Jackson's nomination and thanked Shulkin for his service to "our GREAT VETERANS!" The White House then claimed that Shulkin had not been fired but had resigned—"a pure lie," Shulkin said. This seemed to be not so much a face-saving statement as a legal maneuver around the Vacancies Act to install Perlmutter's favored candidate as acting secretary rather than the VA's Senate-confirmed deputy, as the law required in the case of a firing. But someone at the VA had been told in advance even if the White House chief of staff had not. Shulkin's government email and phone were turned off "almost instantaneously" after the president's tweet.[22]

At the White House, the chief of staff was so angry that he again threatened to quit. "I'm out of here, guys," Kelly said, as he left the White House early, one of those times his advisers were not entirely sure whether he meant he was leaving for good.[23] Kirstjen Nielsen called Jim Mattis, and then both of them called Kelly, not for the first time and not for the last, beseeching him to stay.

H. R. McMaster left the White House for good on April 6, having had the rare-for-the-Trump-White-House privilege of not having his phone unplugged or being escorted from the premises immediately after his ouster. Neither a promotion to four-star general nor a prestigious new Army posting were offered, a final act of revenge by Mattis, McMaster's allies believed, although he insisted he always intended to retire after the White House.

For years afterward, in fact, McMaster's partisans blamed the abrupt end of his tenure on the other so-called adults—Kelly, Mattis, and Tillerson—as much as on Trump himself. In their view, McMaster was the victim of a rogue group of senior officials who had turned on McMaster because he would not go along with them in constraining the president. "There was the cabal of three that said, 'This man is crazy. We've got to run the country,'" a senior adviser to McMaster said. "The three poisoned the well and pushed him out." Another senior adviser to McMaster added, "They were deliberately trying to undermine H.R. He was the only one who really wanted to get the president what he wanted."

But Trump *had* gotten what he wanted. Tillerson and McMaster were gone, and Mattis and Kelly were on notice. And they themselves, with their backstabbing and their intrigues, had inadvertently helped make it happen. "I like conflict," Trump had said at the beginning of the month, standing in a photo op alongside the somewhat bewildered prime minister of Sweden on the day that Gary Cohn quit. "I like having two people with different points of view. And I certainly have that. And then I make a decision. But I like watching it. I like seeing it. And I think it's the best way to go."[24] He knew something that the rest of them either had not known or had chosen to ignore: it only enhanced his power.

CHAPTER 9

Heat-Seeking Missile

On April 11, Speaker Paul Ryan announced that he was, at the age of forty-eight, quitting at the end of the year to spend more time with his wife and three teenage children in Wisconsin. This did not fool anyone in Washington, where his decision was immediately understood as a signal moment in the fight for control of the Republican Party. The war was effectively over, at least in the House. The establishment had capitulated. Trump had won. Inside his administration, the president was purging those like Rex Tillerson and H. R. McMaster who had dissenting views. But Trump had not gotten Ryan fired; the speaker had taken himself out of the fight. The president welcomed the news, but was confused. Why, he asked, would Ryan quit now and make himself a lame duck for so many months? "Foxhole Paul," Trump started calling him—as in, why would anyone want to be in a foxhole with someone who would cut and run like that?[1]

Ryan, once the party's heir apparent after running as Mitt Romney's vice presidential ticket mate in 2012, was everything Trump was not: polite, smart, a policy wonk who touted the optimistic, opportunity-focused conservatism of his first congressional boss, Jack Kemp. Ryan had worked hard to stop Trump from winning the Republican nomination in 2016, reluctantly endorsed Trump when he became the nominee, then denounced him three weeks before the election when the *Access Hollywood* tape came out on the eve of a Trump visit to Ryan's congressional district. Ryan swiftly canceled their joint appearance. "I am not going to defend Donald Trump—not now, not in the future," Ryan had said then.[2]

After Trump won, however, Ryan had done so, repeatedly. Trump's cabinet was "pretty darn good."[3] The firing of James Comey was legitimate. Even Trump's Charlottesville response had not deterred Ryan from claiming that the president's "heart's in the right place."[4] And then there was his over-the-top celebration of Trump's "exquisite presidential leadership" on tax reform.[5] But his praise was never enough for Trump, and his criticism was never enough for those who loathed the president and believed that Ryan, the very picture of ambivalence, must surely share their views.

"After the election there was clearly a 'we're just going to let bygones be bygones' vibe about it," recalled Brendan Buck, who served as Ryan's counselor. "Everybody sort of let it slide." Trump still called Ryan nasty names—"Boy Scout" was one, which Ryan did not realize was meant as a dig until Trump told him so.[6] Ryan, for his part, said almost nothing about the daily parade of crazy Trump tweets and bizarro news cycles. A not insignificant number of his friends called it "Paul's deal with the devil."[7]

If Mitch McConnell's price in the bargain with Trump was an almost free hand to transform the federal judiciary, Ryan's was the tax cut package. "Once that effort was done, there was no next. There's nothing next on the list," said Michael Steel, a political strategist for House Republicans who had worked closely with Ryan's predecessor as speaker, John Boehner. The bargain was simply less attractive for Ryan—and for Trump. Each had gotten what he could out of the other.

For months, in fact, Ryan had been secretly and methodically discussing an exit with his closest advisers. It made a certain amount of sense. Ryan was likely to lose his speakership anyway, as both history and the polls suggested there was a strong chance that Republicans would not keep control of the House in that fall's midterm elections.

But the real issue was Trump. In March, the president had threatened to veto a painstakingly negotiated funding bill to keep the government open because it had no money for his border wall and only backed down reluctantly, while vowing never to sign such a measure again. This was the endless cycle that Ryan faced if he stayed. In announcing his retirement, he never referenced Trump by name, but his statements that day were clear enough and his interviews over the subsequent years even clearer. "I'm an old Jack Kemp guy that believes strongly in inclusive, aspirational politics that are based on bringing people together and not exploiting divisions," Ryan told reporters in his office that afternoon.[8] Eventually, he would acknowledge that, like Rex Tillerson and Jim Mattis and all the other so-called grown-ups in the room, he had seen his role as staving off Trumpian disaster. "I can look myself in the mirror at the end of the day and say I avoided *that* tragedy, I avoided *that* tragedy, I avoided *that* tragedy," Ryan told Mark Leibovich of *The New York Times Magazine*. "I advanced *this* goal, I advanced *this* goal, I advanced *this* goal."[9]

The lure of an all-Republican-controlled House, Senate, and White House after 2016 had been powerful for someone in politics to get things done. Yet he had swallowed his misgivings along the way and what, in the end, had he really gotten done? Ryan tried to split the difference and made everyone angry. George Will, the conservative columnist who considered Trump a malignant buffoon, wrote a savage epitaph for Ryan, calling him just another one of the "abject careerists" who had become "the president's poodles." In Will's judgment, "Ryan traded his political soul for a tax cut."[10]

His exit was not just a personal failure; it was the marker of an inexorable political shift. A shrewd enough politician even without Trump's killer instinct, Ryan understood that his problem was not just the president, but also his own Republican conference, and the increasingly fanatical support Trump inspired among its members. There was simply no room for a non-Trumpian Republican speaker anymore and while Ryan was not yet facing an explicit revolt, he knew that sooner or later he would. The vast majority of Ryan's 237 members had only one leader they would follow now. Brendan Buck would always remember a Republican coming up to Ryan on the House floor during a vote in the first year of Trump's presidency. "The guy was like, 'You know, I'm with you, I understand, I agree with you. This should be good. But I can't get there until I know the president's for it. Because my people, my people just want to know: Is Trump for it? And until I can say that, I can't be there.'" Ryan was a committed conservative, a policy wonk. But Trump's Washington was a "totally post-policy world," Buck observed. "Policy doesn't matter. Principles don't matter. It's totally cult of personality and he can do no wrong and he can't make a mistake, so like what are you supposed to do?"

The Republican House had been on a sharp descent into performative anarchy ever since the Tea Party election of 2010 swept the party back to power two years into the Obama presidency. Legislating was rarely the goal of this new breed of legislators and indeed the volume of bills passed fell significantly. Rebellion was an end in itself. Ryan had become speaker because of it in 2015, when a few dozen upstarts in the House Freedom Caucus, led by future Trump favorites Mark Meadows and Jim Jordan, threatened to topple Boehner by invoking a rarely used maneuver called a motion to vacate the chair that essentially gave this handful of Republicans veto power over their speaker. Boehner, disgusted by what he considered "legislative terrorists" and fed up with a job he compared to being "mayor of Crazytown," quit instead.[11] Ryan emerged as a reluctant consensus replacement, a national political star who shared some of the libertarian-right views of the House Freedom Caucus but tempered them with the pleasant demeanor and negotiating skills favored by the party's remaining moderates.

But the Freedom Caucus had inevitably soured on Ryan once he was in power. While the group's scheme that Meadows shared with Steve Bannon to force Ryan out after the 2016 election fell apart when Trump refused to go along, Ryan knew he was just one fight with the president away from triggering a Freedom Caucus revolt like the one that unseated Boehner.

The Freedom Caucus candidate to replace Ryan as speaker in that abortive coup plot, incidentally, had been a then-obscure Kansas congressman who did not belong to the caucus but was every bit as much a partisan flame-thrower: Mike Pompeo, Trump's new secretary of state.

The ascendance of Pompeo at just the moment of Ryan's reckoning made perfect sense in a political world reordered by Trump. Republicans were now defined by their choices about whether and how to accommodate their leader and his strongman style; most of them did so, but few with more skill and ardor than Pompeo. On paper, Ryan and Pompeo had not started out all that differently in 2016. Both were hawkish Republicans who claimed to love Ayn Rand and loathe a lot of what Trump stood for. But where Trump had proved to be the death of Ryan's political ambition, he was the catalyst for Pompeo's—another figure who, like John Bolton, the polarizing new national security adviser, likely never would have been chosen for high office by any president other than Trump.

A husky, evangelical Christian from Wichita, Kansas, with a hair-trigger temper who had started out life as an establishment conservative from Southern California, Pompeo was little known in Washington or anywhere else before Trump came to power. In his first venture in politics, barely a decade earlier, he finished third in a three-way race for chair of the Kansas Republican Party. A Harvard Law School graduate, he had practiced for less than two years at a blue-chip law firm in Washington before abruptly leaving for his late mother's home state of Kansas. His national security experience, aside from a couple terms on the House Intelligence Committee, consisted of serving as an Army captain in the waning days of the Cold War. The "small business" experience he bragged about as a politician turned out to have been a struggling venture, Thayer Aerospace, that sucked up nearly $100 million in investments, including from the conservative Wichita-based Koch brothers, before Pompeo was forced out as chief executive. The Kochs financed his political career too, making him the single largest recipient of their congressional giving in the 2010, 2012, 2014, and 2016 election cycles. In his six years in Congress, he had never chaired so much as a subcommittee or passed any significant legislation. The major cause with which he was associated was castigating Hillary Clinton for not doing enough to prevent the Benghazi attack. Clinton's alleged cover-up, he averred at one point on NBC's *Meet the Press*, was even "worse, in some ways, than Watergate."[12]

None of it would seem to have made him an ideal candidate, or even a realistic one, for secretary of state, especially because, like many Republican members of Congress, Pompeo had come out hard against Trump during the campaign. But Trump, it turned out, had come along at just the right time for Pompeo. In the fall of 2016, Pompeo had been in the midst of a career crisis of sorts. Restless, eager to climb, and not sure where to do it, he had publicly flirted with and then abandoned a primary challenge against Kansas's Senator Jerry Moran earlier that year. Pompeo had long been interested in national security and an executive branch appointment was a logical next step. But he had bet on the wrong Republican presidential candidate in the primaries, Marco Rubio.

Like his allies in the Freedom Caucus, Pompeo had been a scathing critic of Trump. In fact, only a single member of the group that was now the president's main congressional support base had endorsed Trump in the primaries, Scott DesJarlais, a doctor who had had sex with patients and pressured a mistress and an ex-wife to have abortions. Meadows, the Freedom Caucus chair, had openly debated not going to the Republican convention in Cleveland that year so he would not have to be present for Trump's coronation. Another future Trump cabinet official and Freedom Caucus founding member, Mick Mulvaney, had endorsed Senator Rand Paul of Kentucky, suggested that a President Trump might shred the Constitution, and promised to fight him if he did.[13] Then he endorsed Trump anyway and, like Pompeo, expressed no qualms about going into his administration after the election, in his case as director of the Office of Management and Budget.

Pompeo made his own dramatic pivot. When Trump was already well on his way to securing the nomination, Pompeo convinced Rubio's campaign to make a late stand in Kansas and appeared in a Wichita arena on the day of the caucuses to pitch the Florida senator while Trump stood backstage and listened in mounting rage. In his speech, Pompeo cited Trump's boast that if he ordered a soldier to commit a war crime the soldier would just "go do it." As the audience booed, Pompeo warned that Trump would be "an authoritarian president who ignored our Constitution." American soldiers "don't swear an allegiance to President Trump or any other president," Pompeo declared. "They take an oath to defend our Constitution, as Kansans, as conservatives, as Republicans, as Americans. Marco Rubio will never demean our soldiers by saying that he will order them to do things that are inconsistent with our Constitution." A few minutes later, Pompeo concluded, "It's time to turn down the lights on the circus."[14]

After Rubio lost Kansas and dropped out, Pompeo reluctantly endorsed Trump but continued to criticize him. Trump, Pompeo said, was simply "not a conservative believer."[15] Pompeo's patrons, the Koch brothers, were hardly enthusiastic about Trump either, although they had refused to make the eight-figure media buy attacking him advocated by Marc Short, the head of their political arm, Freedom Partners, and a friend of Pompeo's. Short quit to work for Rubio, but after Rubio lost ended up working for Mike Pence, another longtime Koch beneficiary, when Trump selected him as his running mate. Short then brought in Pompeo to advise Pence on debate preparations that September. The Koch network had found its way into the Trump camp after all.

After Trump's victory, Pompeo immediately began lobbying for an appointment, hoping for either secretary of the Army or director of the CIA. One of his calls was to a West Point classmate and Washington friend, a lobbyist named Dave Urban who had run Trump's winning campaign in Pennsylvania. Urban also heard from Steve Bannon, who urged him to call "the old man" and recommend Pompeo to be CIA director. Urban did. So did Pence and Marc Short, soon to become head of legislative affairs for the White House. In late November, after Pompeo's obligatory interview in Trump Tower (they agreed to disagree about Vladimir Putin, Pompeo would later tell others), Trump selected him for the CIA post so quickly that Devin Nunes, the House Intelligence Committee chairman and a member of the Trump transition team, said later that he did not think Pompeo had even filled out the vetting questionnaire.

Trump knew so little about Pompeo, in fact, that he seemed to have forgotten the nasty speech Pompeo gave back in Wichita. At the time, Trump had been standing near Ted Cruz's campaign manager, Jeff Roe, and demanded to know in a rage who was the congressman attacking him. When Roe heard of Pompeo's appointment, he called Jared Kushner to remind him of the incident and Kushner put Roe on speakerphone so Trump could hear. According to the journalist Tim Alberta, Trump bellowed: "No! That was him? We've got to take it back," adding, "This is what I get for letting Pence pick everyone."[16]

But the appointment stood and two weeks later Pompeo was hanging out in Urban's box at the Army-Navy football game with the president-elect. His stated rationale for joining the administration was similar to that of many Republicans: Trump had won, and besides, the Democrats were the real enemy. "He just made his political peace with reality—this is our president," one of his friends said.[17] A few months earlier, he had warned that Trump would be an "authoritarian president"; now he told colleagues that he would quit Congress in order to "right the wrongs" of the Obama years.[18] He also deleted his entire congressional Twitter feed, with its occasional biting criticism of Trump, and was confirmed by the Senate, 66 to 32, supported by fourteen Democrats, including Chuck Schumer.[19] "Pompeo's singular ability is in navigating power," reflected Raj Goyle, the Democrat he defeated in a nasty congressional campaign in 2010. "On that I give him massive respect: the way he mapped Wichita power, the way he mapped D.C. power, the way he mapped Trump."[20]

When Pompeo arrived at the CIA, he faced a political furor generated by the new president. Days before his swearing-in, Trump had compared the U.S. intelligence community to Nazi Germany for its handling of the Steele dossier and then, at a welcoming ceremony in the lobby of CIA headquarters, made a sharply political speech in what was supposed to be an apolitical setting. Still, Pompeo managed to soothe the CIA bureaucracy. He promised members of the Directorate of Operations that they would no longer be micromanaged, as they were under Obama. He vowed "to serve as an important bridge, if not a heat shield, not just from the White House but from any sort of political attacks," according to Juan Zarate, a former George W. Bush administration official tapped by Pompeo to manage his transition.[21]

Most importantly, Pompeo personally delivered the President's Daily Brief to Trump, giving the CIA valuable access to a skeptical president. "Mike got them in the room every day and that is the most important thing the agency expects to have with its director," a former senior intelligence official said.[22] Pompeo used the sessions to establish a jocular rapport with the president, a contrast to Trump's friction-filled dealings with other top national security officials. "He clicked with Mike early on and Mike has had the benefit of that. Mike gets the president," said Christopher Ruddy, a close friend of Trump's.[23] The president, who still bragged about having attended the University of Pennsylvania, also valued Pompeo's establishment credentials and often told Oval Office visitors that Pompeo had been first in his class at West Point and a graduate of Harvard Law School.

After a year at the CIA, Pompeo's campaign to replace Rex Tillerson was an open secret at the White House. "Pompeo was working it hard. He saw and heard from the president how much he was souring on Tillerson," recalled a senior White House official. "He was making the case to Trump: You've got a whole lot of people around you who don't agree with you. I'm your guy."[24] At a time when Tillerson and Jim Mattis were resisting Trump's calls to withdraw from the Iran nuclear deal, Pompeo, a vocal Iran hawk, twice recommended in the Situation Room that Trump renounce the agreement, despite the unwritten rule that CIA directors should stick to analysis, not policymaking.

All of which underscored the remarkable fact that by this point in the administration, Pompeo had managed the dual feat of spending more face time with Trump than almost any other cabinet member while also never getting in an argument with him. The senior White House official who watched Pompeo with Trump found him to be, aside from Mike Pence, perhaps "the most sycophantic and obsequious" of Trump's advisers.[25] He was, according to an American ambassador who worked with Pompeo during this period, "like a heat-seeking missile for Trump's ass."[26]

Trump noticed. On the day he anointed Pompeo to be his new secretary of state, Trump highlighted the CIA director's remarkable turnabout from critic to agreeable sidekick. A relationship born in derision had been remade in flattery. "We're always on the same wavelength," Trump told reporters when they asked why he had selected Pompeo. "The relationship has been very good and that's what I need."[27] By later in the year, he was even more definitive. "I argue with everyone," the president told Olivia Nuzzi, a *New York* magazine writer. "Except Pompeo."[28]

On his first day as secretary of state, Pompeo invoked the bluster of George Patton, a favorite of his as well as Trump's, vowing that the United States would "get its swagger back."[29] Pompeo followed up with a social media campaign featuring photographs of himself and Patton, along with a State Department logo with an unofficial new motto: the "Department of Swagger." Diplomats quickly surmised, as a senior department official who worked closely with him put it, that Pompeo's opening pitch was to a "constituency of one."[30]

While appealing to the man in the White House, Pompeo and his advisers also sought to persuade the foreign policy establishment that he was no Bannonite bomb-thrower, but a responsible figure who might be as close as the post-purge Trump presidency would get to a grown-up in the room. Pompeo had made a point of consulting all the living former secretaries of state, including Hillary Clinton, who took his call even though he had savaged her for years over Benghazi. (The call to Clinton was leaked to the press days before his confirmation hearing, which was of course surely the purpose of it.) Pompeo also promised to lift Tillerson's hiring freeze, promoted David Hale, a career Foreign Service official, to serve as the department's number three official, and reached out to some of the veteran diplomats who had quit in the Tillerson era. One of the former State Department officials Pompeo contacted said he gave the impression that he was doing the best he could with Trump, that he would truly be a secretary with "his finger in the dike."[31]

Managing Trump, however, would prove harder than he anticipated. As CIA director, Pompeo spent many hours with the president and could punt difficult questions by saying that it was not his role to offer policy advice, even though he sometimes did. In his new job, he would often be away traveling, while John Bolton, a veteran bureaucratic infighter, had daily Trump time. Bolton had immediately cleaned house at the National Security Council, pushing out Tom Bossert, the homeland security adviser, both deputy national security advisers, the media spokesman, and assorted other aides. Among the changes he made was to eliminate a pandemic preparedness directorate created during the Obama years and fold it into a broader biodefense office. He also made clear that he had no interest in McMaster's focus on deliberative process, which, if hardly endorsed by Trump, had at least enabled a certain transparency across the embattled bureaucracy. H. R. McMaster, for example, had conducted biweekly classified phone calls with the national security cabinet. Not a single one happened under the new regime. "Bolton never had a process," a senior defense official said. "Bolton had a process of one."

Trump had blown up one dysfunctional national security team by getting rid of Tillerson and McMaster, but the new team would have tensions that soon became as bad, or worse. One thing Pompeo and Bolton had in common, however, was a generally hardline approach to the use of American power in the Middle East and a focus on, even obsession with, Iran. In Washington, many Democrats and foreign policy hands greeted their dual appointments as proof that Trump was headed in a militaristic direction, that this was, finally, the "War Cabinet" they had always worried about. And a war quickly presented itself.

On April 13, exactly a month to the day after Trump fired Tillerson, Trump convened his new national security team to discuss more airstrikes in Syria. For days, Trump had been vowing a harsh response to "Animal

Assad" in the wake of the Bashar al-Assad regime's latest chemical weapons attack on the rebel-held enclave of Douma, horrific photos of which had made their way onto Trump's Fox News screen. Bolton, who had only officially started work that week, pressed for punishing strikes, as did outside advisers. "We should bomb the shit out of them, Mr. President," a Republican senator said when Trump called for advice.

When Trump authorized the strike, however, he listened, reluctantly, to the more cautious counsel of Jim Mattis, opting for a single predawn volley against three Syrian government chemical weapons sites, carefully chosen to avoid hitting known Russian or Iranian bases, which could have escalated a war Trump was trying to exit. "He was inclined to a farther-reaching strike," the senator said, "but he deferred to Secretary Mattis."[32] A former government official close to Mattis joked that the fearsome retired Marine was now the lone "peacenik" in Trump's inner councils.[33]

They had lost a round on Syria, but the new team of Bolton and Pompeo was far likelier to prevail over Mattis on Iran, as Trump faced a self-imposed deadline in early May to decide whether to finally follow through on his threats to pull out of the nuclear deal. Mattis had opposed the deal in the first place but did not want to go back on America's word now that it had been made, especially when Iran appeared to be honoring its terms. Mattis had recently made those views public, testifying before Congress that it was not in the national interest to exit the deal. He and Tillerson had been united in pushing back on the president whenever this came up, which it often did, because of a congressional requirement that Iran's compliance be recertified every ninety days—a measure that infuriated Trump, because it meant that every three months of his presidency thus far he had effectively been endorsing an agreement he considered to be "the worst deal ever."[34]

For months, Brian Hook, Tillerson's policy planning director and confidant, had been negotiating with the three European allies—Britain, France, and Germany—that had signed the original pact along with China and Russia. The hope was to get them to agree to tougher conditions to present to Iran to salvage the deal. Mattis and Tillerson had used the prospect of a breakthrough with the allies to buy time with Trump, and the Europeans were hopeful, if uncertain, that Hook was negotiating in good faith. "They believed that it is for real," a senior German official recalled. "They didn't know that it is for real—until it isn't."

Even if Hook was on the level, Trump was not. Months earlier, when the two of them met privately in the Oval Office, Bob Corker, the Senate Foreign Relations Committee chairman, had asked Trump about the

Iran talks with the Europeans. "I just said, 'Mr. President, let me ask you something: Do you want to be successful?'" Corker recalled. "He said, 'Nobody's ever asked me that.'" Trump did not really reply, however, so at the end of the meeting, Corker asked Trump again. "Answer the question," he prodded the president. "No," Trump replied. In other words, the talks were just for show, Corker realized, "strictly politics that made him look like he was working on an Iran deal." The truth was that "he didn't really want it to be successful. And it wasn't."

With Tillerson gone and Mattis increasingly marginalized, the last-ditch case for preserving the deal would be made by the European leaders who cared the most about it, France's Emmanuel Macron and Germany's Angela Merkel. Macron, still a Trump favorite after the grand Bastille Day parade he had thrown for Trump the previous year, had been accorded the honor of the first official state visit to Washington under Trump, an occasion that would include public hugging, kissing, and hand-holding with Trump, a helicopter ride to a double-date dinner with the president and first lady at Mount Vernon, and an address to Congress in which Macron managed both to praise Trump and damn Trumpism. In private, he and Trump had a blunt conversation about the Iran deal he had come to save. But it did not take a private session to see where it was headed, given that Trump told journalists during a photo op at the start of their meeting that the deal was "insane" and "ridiculous."[35]

By the time Merkel arrived in Washington days later, Trump had already privately told his national security team that "I can't stay in" and ordered them to make sure they had "the heaviest possible sanctions" ready to impose on Iran as soon as he gave the order.[36] The Merkel meeting, a mere "working visit" in contrast to the pomp-filled reception Macron had merited, featured all the familiar Trump complaints about Germany—it was not contributing enough to NATO, it was screwing the United States on trade, and so on. Iran, Bolton later said, hardly came up. Merkel's staff was "shocked by the tone" the president took with the chancellor. Never again would she return to Washington for an official visit during Trump's presidency.[37]

Mattis, meanwhile, continued to resist a withdrawal from the Iran agreement, even sending Bolton a classified memo registering his objections in writing. But Trump was finally resolved. The only remaining questions were when and how to reimpose sanctions. Bolton and Pompeo teamed up to insist, over the Treasury Department's objections, that it be done right away. On May 7, Bolton was on the phone with the French national security adviser, Philippe Étienne, when Étienne exclaimed that

Trump had tweeted: "I will be announcing my decision on the Iran Deal tomorrow from the White House at 2:00 p.m."

Bolton, as was now standard practice in an administration where the president felt no obligation to coordinate major international statements with his national security adviser, had not known about the tweet. But Bolton saw it as vindication. "It had taken one month to shred the Iran nuclear deal," he would later write, "showing how easy it was to do once somebody took events in hand."[38]

The Europeans, in the end, were not surprised either. They finally understood what had just happened in Washington. Trump was done with being managed. He had wanted to blow up the Iran deal and now he was going to do it. "With friends like that who needs enemies?" Donald Tusk, president of the European Council, tweeted. "But frankly EU should be grateful. Thanks to him we got rid of all illusions. We realize if you need a helping hand, you will find one at the end of your arm."[39] More such course corrections would inevitably follow. "He has decided enough is enough. He is taking the power," Gérard Araud, the French ambassador, explained in cables to Paris after the previous month's purges. "The new team, their mission is to do what he tells them to do."

That was not always easy. On Iran, at least, Bolton and Pompeo not only agreed with Trump, they had publicly rooted for an end to the deal for years. The bigger challenge for Pompeo was Trump's first assignment for him—the upcoming summit with North Korea's Kim Jong-un. Pompeo had not been there for the meeting where Trump had decided to go for it, but was "very skeptical," as one State Department official put it, that talking with Kim would produce a breakthrough on denuclearization.[40] Bolton, for his part, was even more dubious. A veteran of the George W. Bush administration's fierce internal debates on North Korea who had been called "human scum" by the regime back in 2003 for his hardline views, Bolton was of the over-my-dead-body school of negotiating with Pyongyang.[41] As far as he was concerned, the Trump administration should have a regime-change strategy for both Iran and North Korea.

On the morning of May 10, Ashok Mirpuri, the ambassador from Singapore, happened to be at the White House for meetings. Singapore was a close partner in Asia and Mirpuri one of Washington's most experienced diplomats. At 10:37 a.m. Trump tweeted: "The highly anticipated meeting between Kim Jong Un and myself will take place in Singapore on June 12th. We will both try to make it a very special moment for World Peace!"

But no one had officially informed Singapore that the two leaders and the entire international press corps would be descending on the city-state in barely a month. Soon after the tweet, Bolton's staff called the ambassador to ask him to come by the national security adviser's office. When the ambassador arrived, Bolton apologized for not letting him know in advance and revealed that even he had not known for sure the location of the summit until Trump tweeted it out.

The Jared Kushner factor may have once again been at play. As Bolton and Pompeo would see firsthand, Kushner had a disconcerting habit of floating in and out of high-level diplomatic engagements. In the first year of Trump's presidency, that had led to open warfare with Rex Tillerson. Pompeo was more solicitous of Kushner, who had helped him get the job, and had been dealing with his freelancing on North Korea since the days at the CIA, when the presidential son-in-law sent Pompeo what Kushner regarded as a particularly promising feeler. The "reach-out," as Kushner later recounted, came via a young Singapore-based financier named Gabriel Schulze, whose family had made billions in mining and ran a company dedicated to investments in "frontier economies" such as North Korea.[42] Schulze's contacts sought the meeting with Kushner because, they said, of the role he had played in helping to broker Trump's first meeting with Xi Jinping and because North Korea, with its third-generation ruler, was also a family business. Kushner would later claim it was one reason Pyongyang had invited Pompeo for an initial trip that winter.

Normally, a summit like that now proposed between Trump and Kim would take place after months or even years of negotiations, with deliverable outcomes carefully agreed in advance, allies painstakingly consulted, and the two leaders only brought in to ratify the deal and announce it publicly. In fact, every White House since Bill Clinton had debated, and rejected, a presidential summit with the North Koreans. This, needless to say, was not how Trump rolled. Bolton thought the whole thing, as he later wrote, was a "diplomatic fandango," cooked up by South Korea's new government, and every time there was a snag in the logistical preparations, he silently cheered. "My hope: maybe the whole thing would collapse!"[43]

Pompeo, despite resolving never to be caught publicly disagreeing with Trump, was also uncertain, and he and Bolton feared the influence of President Moon Jae-in of South Korea, who was now personally negotiating with Kim and relaying what he said were North Korea's commitments to full denuclearization. Moon also advocated for Trump to broker an official end to the Korean War, which had never been formally concluded with a peace treaty. Trump loved the idea of playing peacemaker and would repeatedly return to it, although his advisers considered it a concession that would be given away for nothing.

Bolton messaged Pompeo that one call with Moon had been "a near-death experience."

Pompeo, who had been listening in from the road in the Middle East, wrote back: "Having cardiac arrest in Saudi Arabia."[44]

The new national security adviser's disdain for the whole affair was soon publicly evident when he went on two Sunday television shows that Trump watched and spoke about the North Korea summit as an opportunity to replicate the "Libya model" for nuclear disarmament. He was referring to Libyan dictator Muammar al-Qaddafi's agreement with the Bush administration in 2003 to voluntarily relinquish his rudimentary nuclear weapons program. But given that Qaddafi ended up dead after being pulled from a ditch amid a U.S.-supported revolution eight years later, this sounded not at all appealing to the North Koreans. Bolton knew what he was doing; he had even tried out the line in advance, leading an aide to warn him how it would be interpreted. The North Koreans responded to Bolton with a statement that said, "We do not hide our feelings of repugnance toward him."[45]

The Japanese were particularly worried about the summit, preferring "maximum pressure" to premature talks. "They were concerned about concessions that would let North Korea off the hook politically as well as economically," recalled Matt Pottinger, the aide who dealt most closely with them. "It was a real nail-biter for the Japanese." Prime Minister Shinzo Abe had cultivated perhaps the best relationship with Trump of all the democratic leaders, and in a sign of the seriousness with which Japan viewed the summit, he scheduled two in-person sessions with Trump before Singapore, one at Mar-a-Lago and one in Washington.

A meticulous leader who reportedly rehearsed before each meeting with the president, Abe pressed Trump to ensure the talks covered North Korean missiles that could hit Japan, not just its long-range missiles capable of reaching the United States. But their sessions did not go well. In fact, Trump immediately rebuffed Abe's suggestion that they coordinate in advance with their teams and practice what he planned to say to Kim. Trump's reply, according to an account the Japanese national security adviser later gave, went something like this: "No, I never prepare for a big deal. I go in and I look the other guy in the eye and I make the big play and that's how I built my business empire—and that's why I am the greatest negotiator in the history of the presidency."

At the last minute, the summit almost did not happen. Barely two weeks out, North Korea threatened to cancel, and Trump told Bolton he wanted to preempt that. "I want to get out before they do," the president said.[46] He explained to Bolton that this had also been his preferred model in dealing with women he was dating—break up first before they could beat him to it. But Trump did not really want to cancel and, barely twelve hours after saying the summit was off, seized on another, slightly less antagonistic North Korean statement to declare the meeting back on. "Trump was desperate to have the meeting at any price," Bolton concluded. When Bolton pushed to postpone a few more weeks, Trump resisted, saying he did not want to "risk the momentum." Although nothing had been decided yet, Trump told Bolton, "This is a big win here. If we make a deal, it will be one of the greatest deals in history. I want to make him and North Korea very successful."[47]

Reports of the internal discord over how or whether to proceed surfaced in *The New York Times*, prompting Trump to tweet that there was "ZERO disagreement within the Trump Administration as to how to deal with North Korea." With a flourish that seemed to invoke the dictatorial powers of the leader with whom he would soon meet, he added: "And if there was, it wouldn't matter." When a North Korean envoy personally delivered a letter from Kim to Trump before the summit, Trump overruled his advisers again to host the visitor in the Oval Office. The letter said nothing—it was "pure puffery," Bolton judged—but Trump loved it. In hindsight, Bolton wrote, "This was the beginning of the Trump-Kim bromance."[48]

Trump's new national security team was just as worried about how to manage him as his old national security team had been. Going into the meeting, Pompeo suggested that he, Bolton, and John Kelly agree to always have at least one of them present whenever Trump interacted with Kim: Who knew what Trump might promise?

First, however, Trump had another summit to attend, this one with America's closest friends. For Trump, autocrats, not allies, held the most allure, and he was dreading the Group of Seven, or G7, meeting in Charlevoix, Canada, hosted by Justin Trudeau and featuring all the European leaders he had so recently blown off on Iran and slapped with punitive steel and aluminum tariffs on national security grounds. "Look, he personally decided he wanted to be fighting with everybody," a senior adviser to Trudeau said hours before the summit. "Maybe he thinks it's in his best interests to be combative and fighting."[49]

Once he arrived, Trump was in a mood to poke his hosts and did so immediately, threatening them with more tariffs, questioning the purpose of NATO, and even demanding that Russia be invited to rejoin the G7, four years after it was expelled in response to its illegal annexation of Crimea. "It would be an asset to have Russia back in," Trump said during an impromptu news conference. "It would be good for the world."[50] The other G7 members objected loudly. Readmitting Russia, Trudeau said, was not something "we are even remotely looking at."[51] In private with the allies, Trump was even more insistent, telling them that Crimea was by rights Russian and that Ukraine was a corrupt state not worth defending. Once again, it was not his enemies but Trump himself putting the Russia issue front and center. Just why was he so insistent on doing a favor for Vladimir Putin?

The debacle for which the Canada G7 became famous unfolded at the end of the conference when Trump insisted on personally sitting down with his fellow leaders to resolve stalled negotiations over the wording of the group's final communiqué. The talks hit a logjam after Larry Kudlow, the cable news Wall Street pundit Trump had just hired to replace Gary Cohn as his national economic adviser, pushed for a Trump-friendly communiqué and objected to previously uncontroversial positions on matters such as climate change and Iran's compliance with the nuclear deal. Kudlow, in his first major test as a White House official, had pulled multiple all-nighters, and would suffer a small heart attack when the summit ended. As the leaders haggled, Trump at one point threw two Starburst candies—red ones—down on the table and gestured to Angela Merkel. "Here, Angela, don't say I never gave you anything," he told her.[52] Eventually, the communiqué was agreed to and Trump left the summit a few hours earlier than scheduled on Air Force One, bound for Singapore and his date with the dictator.

From his plane, however, Trump became enraged watching coverage of Trudeau's closing news conference when the Canadian leader blandly stated the obvious, that his country would respond to Trump's tariffs with measures of its own. The president demanded that aides wake Mike Pompeo, sleeping in preparation for Singapore, and bring the secretary of state to his office on the 747. A series of angry tweets followed as Trump accused Trudeau of being "so meek and mild" in person, only to criticize Trump's tariffs once he was in the air, which, Trump said, was both "dishonest & weak." The president repudiated the very communiqué he had just approved.

From then on, Trudeau was almost persona non grata with Trump. The young Canadian had started out willing to play along with Trump's photo ops but had ended up a target just like all those who challenged Trump publicly. While en route to Asia, Trump dispatched advisers to attack the Canadian prime minister in television interviews. Peter Navarro would prove to be especially zealous, claiming in one appearance "there's a special place in hell" reserved for Trudeau.[53] For years afterward, Trump would randomly disparage Trudeau during unrelated conversations. Once, flying on Air Force One, he turned to Stephanie Grisham, then his White House press secretary. "Trudeau's mom," he said out of the blue. "She fucked all of the Rolling Stones."[54]

Back on the ground in Quebec, meanwhile, the Germans exacted a bit of revenge for all those Trump Twitter blasts, releasing on Instagram a soon-to-be-iconic photograph of a scowling Trump, sitting with his arms crossed, as he was confronted by Merkel, who stood over him surrounded by the world's other democratic leaders. She seemed the very picture of determination in a pale-blue silk jacket, intently trying to talk some sense into the petulant president.

Thus did Trump land in steamy Singapore on his way to meet with a thirty-four-year-old nuclear-armed tyrant who ran the world's biggest modern-day Gulag.

It did not matter that Mike Pompeo, John Bolton, and John Kelly never let Trump out of their sight in Singapore. In the end, he did what he came to do while they were sitting right next to him and none of them could stop him. Soon after landing, in fact, when Pompeo briefed the president on the pre-summit negotiations and acknowledged they were at an "impasse," Trump revealed his plan.[55] He would declare a great diplomatic coup regardless of what actually happened. "This is an exercise in publicity," Trump told his team, vowing that Singapore would "be a success no matter what."[56]

The next day, June 12, Trump went early to the five-star Capella hotel, where the reclusive Kim, who had rarely left his homeland and needed to borrow a modern jet to get to Singapore, was staying in an $8,000-a-night suite, billed to Singapore's government.[57] According to the detailed in-the-room account Bolton later offered, Trump bonded with Kim through translators about everything from the "tremendous dishonesty" of the press (Trump's words) to the lameness of Barack Obama and George W. Bush to Kim's admirable personal qualities (which Trump listed as smarts, sincerity, and a great personality).[58] At one point, when Trump observed that he planned to seek Senate approval of any nuclear agreement he reached with Kim, drawing a pointed contrast with Obama and his nuclear deal with Iran, the posturing was too much even for Pompeo. The secretary of state scribbled down a note to Bolton: "He is so full of shit."[59]

Kim spun a big story about his willingness to abandon nuclear weapons, claiming to be committed to full denuclearization of the Korean Peninsula, without Trump fully grasping that meant something very different to each of them. To Kim, it meant all American troops out of South Korea and a series of steps—"action for action," in the catchphrase of the negotiators that Kim used at the end of the summit, to Bolton's horror—that each would take along the way. To Trump's hardline national security team, "action for action" was unacceptable. They were looking for Kim to unilaterally give up his weapons first; only then would sanctions relief and other measures follow.

The trouble began when Kim pleaded for a gesture to help him with his own hardliners: Couldn't Trump offer something, say, by canceling or cutting back the military exercises conducted jointly by the United States and South Korea that were a regular source of friction? Trump, who had repeatedly pressed Jim Mattis to halt them as a waste of time and money, agreed on the spur of the moment without consulting his national security team or the Pentagon. He even adopted Kim's language, calling them "war games" instead of exercises, and thanked Kim for saving the United States a lot of money. That was exactly the concession that Vladimir Putin would want to see, an America pulling back. Matt Pottinger, the senior Asia adviser who had been in the meeting, told others bluntly that it was "a complete giveaway with nothing in return."

Back at the Pentagon, the nation's military leadership found out by watching cable news. "Let's take a deep breath," Chairman Joe Dunford told the emergency meeting that gathered in his office to figure out what to do. The major twice-a-year exercises were a key part of the deterrence strategy against North Korea and were held so frequently because of the annual rotations of American personnel on and off the peninsula; many smaller ones also took place. The White House did not formally notify the Pentagon of Trump's decision until days later. The order was to "just cancel all exercises," a senior defense official recalled. "We said that's not doable. You actually have to have exercises." Eventually, a complicated matrix was produced; exercises over a certain size would require White House approval, while smaller ones or those that were virtual could be held without permission.

When it was all over, what had happened in the room with Kim

Jong-un was almost irrelevant to how Trump described the summit, which he termed the most successful in the history of the world. Trump's favorite part was the cheesy video he had ordered made for Kim, with the president himself cast as a hero "in a meeting to remake history"—a real estate pitchman's version of all the great things that awaited North Korea should it open up. "The past doesn't have to be the future," a narrator informed Kim in melodramatic tones. "Out of the darkness can come the light."[60] Trump liked the video so much he even played it at the news conference afterward. His tweet on arriving back in Washington was nothing short of grandiose. "Everybody can now feel much safer than the day I took office," he wrote. "There is no longer a Nuclear Threat from North Korea."

This was not even close to true. But his advisers, who had seen their skepticism borne out, joined the public puffery. Pompeo bragged to reporters that the vague statement signed by the two leaders would lead to "major denuclearization" by the end of Trump's first term in office. Reminded that just a day before the summit he had insisted on "complete and verifiable and irreversible denuclearization" as "the only outcome the United States will accept," Pompeo showed reporters his explosive temper for the first time as secretary of state. It was "ludicrous" and insulting to point that out, Pompeo told them. Asked how the agreement Trump was touting would be verified, he snapped, "Don't say silly things," adding, "It's not productive."[61]

Throughout his tenure, there was nothing that made Pompeo angrier in public than being caught disagreeing with Trump. But no amount of sophistry could confuse the basic point that Trump had settled on a predetermined outcome and was now asking his advisers to reverse-engineer public statements to somehow make it a reality. In late July, back in Washington, when Bolton convened cabinet-level officials in the Situation Room to analyze what had come out of Singapore, the unanimous conclusion was "nothing much," he later wrote. Pompeo, too, was just as clear. The secretary of state was adamant in the Situation Room that not only had North Korea made no significant steps toward denuclearization, but that, looking forward, there was "zero probability of success."[62]

If Trump failed to bring peace in our time to Korea with his Singapore summit, he never stopped talking about it as his greatest diplomatic moment. Left unanswered was the question that shadowed many of Trump's more transparently false claims: Did he really believe an incredible, world-transforming deal had been reached merely because he said that it had? For years afterward, he would boast in numerous tweets and rally speeches to his MAGA faithful that he had even been nominated for a Nobel Peace Prize by the prime minister of Japan because of Singapore. Shinzo Abe had written the Nobel Committee "the most beautiful five-page letter," Trump once explained at a White House news conference, and given him a copy of it.[63]

What Trump never mentioned was how the Abe nomination had come about. The truth, as often was the case with Trump, turned out to be obvious: Trump personally requested Abe to do it, during a private two-and-a-half-hour dinner in Trump Tower on Sunday, September 23, while both were in New York for the United Nations General Assembly. "The president asked Abe over dinner to nominate him," a senior Trump national security official confirmed, while hastening to add that the National Security Council and the rest of the United States government had not been involved. "That was a Trump-to-Abe one," the official added.[64] Aides were chagrined but not surprised given Trump's frequent resentful mentions of the Nobel Peace Prize that Obama had won, and they kept Trump's embarrassing secret for years. When the winner was announced by the Nobel committee in Oslo, Trump, needless to say, was not it.

CHAPTER 10

Russia, Russia, Russia

Helsinki was beautiful that July day in the summer of 2018. The sun glinted off the Gulf of Finland and onto the yellow neoclassical Presidential Palace where Trump met with Vladimir Putin. More than five hours after Trump arrived, forty minutes into the news conference that assured that Helsinki would become indelibly associated with his presidency, Trump was asked a question, *the* question, about his 2016 election and Russia.

> JONATHAN LEMIRE, ASSOCIATED PRESS: President Trump, you first. Just now President Putin denied having anything to do with the election interference in 2016. Every U.S. intelligence agency has concluded that Russia did. My first question for you, sir, is who do you believe? My second question is would you now, with the whole world watching, tell President Putin—would you denounce what happened in 2016 and would you warn him to never do it again?

> TRUMP: So let me just say that we have two thoughts. You have groups that are wondering why the FBI never took the server. Why haven't they taken the server? Why was the FBI told to leave the office of the Democratic National Committee? I've been wondering that. I've been asking that for months and months and I've been tweeting it out and calling it out on social media. Where is the server? I want to know, where is the server and what is the server saying? With that being said, all I can do is ask the question. My people came to me, Dan Coats came to me and some others and said they think it's Russia. I have President Putin. He just said it's not Russia. I will say this. I don't see any reason why it would be, but I really do want to see the server. But I have confidence in both

parties. I really believe that this will probably go on for a while, but I don't think it can go on without finding out what happened to the server. What happened to the servers of the Pakistani gentleman that worked on the DNC? Where are those servers? They're missing. Where are they? What happened to Hillary Clinton's emails? Thirty-three thousand emails gone—just gone. I think in Russia they wouldn't be gone so easily. I think it's a disgrace that we can't get Hillary Clinton's 33,000 emails. So I have great confidence in my intelligence people, but I will tell you that President Putin was extremely strong and powerful in his denial today. And what he did is an incredible offer. He offered to have the people working on the case come and work with their investigators, with respect to the twelve people. I think that's an incredible offer. Okay, thank you.[1]

Trump, it turned out, still had the power to shock. In one long, confusing answer mixing conspiracy theory, misdirection, and outright fiction, Trump acknowledged that he would accept the word of Putin over that of his own intelligence agencies. After years of controversy and while he was the subject of a special counsel investigation on this very subject, he praised the "extremely strong and powerful" denial of the Russian president about the 2016 election interference. And he welcomed Putin's vague but "incredible offer" to supposedly cooperate with American investigators, an offer that his own aides on the sidelines of that disastrous news conference were frantically warning him was a trap.

Worse, if that was possible, Trump sounded flat-out unbalanced. The DNC server? Hillary Clinton's emails? The "Pakistani gentleman"? What the hell was he talking about? Through it all, as Trump spoke, there was Putin standing to the side, smirking. When the Russian president left the hall, he turned to his press secretary, Dmitri Peskov, and shook his head. The news conference was "bullshit," he said in Russian loudly enough to be overheard.[2] The debacle immediately raised more disturbing questions— never really answered—about what had gone on in the private two-hour session between the two leaders.

Back in the United States, dying of cancer, Senator John McCain, Trump's fierce Republican critic, put out a statement that spoke for many in both parties. It was, he said, "one of the most disgraceful performances by an American president in memory."[3]

What do you do when you are a White House adviser and the president of the United States has the whole world wondering whether he is in the pocket of the former KGB spy leading Russia? The first thing Trump's national security aides traveling with him in Helsinki did was to question the interpreter, a State Department professional named Marina Gross, who had probably been in the room with Putin over the years more than any other American official. Fiona Hill, the National Security Council senior director for Russia and Europe, Michael Ellis, an NSC lawyer who had worked for the Republicans on the House Intelligence Committee, and Joe Wang, the Russia director, debriefed Gross during the short break between the long one-on-one Trump-Putin meeting and an expanded luncheon that would include other officials. Gross's job had not been to take notes, but because Trump insisted on flouting standard protocol by meeting with Putin without a notetaker, hers would be the only independent account of what happened in the room.

In a telephone call soon afterward, John Bolton admitted to a senior Republican senator what he and his staff had learned from Gross about the private part of the meeting: Trump had been played. First, Bolton told Senator Roy Blunt of Missouri that, no matter what Trump might say, Putin was still the same thuggish adversary he always had been. "Putin has not changed a bit," Bolton said. Then he quoted Hamlet: "A man may smile and still be a villain."

The Russian leader, Bolton told Blunt, had privately deflected questions about the election interference by suggesting they invoke the Mutual Legal Assistance Treaty between the two countries. Trump somehow thought Putin was offering to extradite twelve Russian intelligence agents just indicted by Robert Mueller in connection with the campaign meddling—hence, the "incredible offer" he mentioned to reporters. In reality, Bolton acknowledged to Blunt, it was a ploy to get the United States to hand over Americans Putin considered foes, such as Michael McFaul, the former ambassador to Russia and a vocal Putin critic. "Russians tried to use" the treaty "to get Ambassador McFaul," Bolton told the senator.

Still, things were not as disastrous as they could have been or as they seemed from Trump's public meltdown at the news conference, Bolton promised Blunt, a confidant of Mitch McConnell. The interpreter had told Bolton's staff that Putin talked for "90 percent of the time" and Trump really "didn't agree to anything except continuing talks." Trump had offered Putin another meeting that fall but, Bolton pointed out, "fall means September 21 to December 21," and he would do what he could to make sure that happened "after the election." Bolton knew that Republicans were already worried about going into the midterm congressional contests that November with a deeply unpopular president widely seen as Putin's lapdog. The last thing Blunt's Senate colleagues wanted was yet another embarrassing summit meeting. But there was only so much damage control Bolton could, or would, do. He was pretty scathing about what had happened. "Deterrence doesn't mean anything if the enemy doesn't think there will be a cost," Bolton observed.

Blunt listened and took it all in. But Senate Republicans were angry, he said. Trump could now forget about being cleared before the midterms by the Senate Intelligence Committee's Russia investigation, the senator warned. The committee, led by Senator Richard Burr, a Republican from North Carolina, had been conducting a rare bipartisan effort in the increasingly divided capital and Blunt told Bolton that Trump's disastrous performance meant the investigation would have to continue until after the election. Helsinki had "just pumped a bunch of oxygen into the room," as the senator would later put it. Maybe there really was something more to the Trump-Putin thing after all.

That was the question haunting Dan Coats, the director of national intelligence. Coats had been in his office outside Washington when his staff rushed in during the Helsinki news conference to tell him what just happened. Coats was flabbergasted. So much effort had gone into a massive intelligence operation to prove Russian culpability in the 2016 election interference and Trump had just attacked the American government's findings while onstage with Putin himself. It was a gut punch, he told others, "to see the president of the United States say, 'well, you know my intelligence director Dan Coats tells me one thing and Vladimir Putin tells me another. Why would I have any reason to not agree with Vladimir?' I just, I was in shock."

A former Indiana senator who had been George W. Bush's ambassador to Germany, Coats had been persuaded to serve as intelligence director by his fellow Hoosier Mike Pence, but the soft-spoken conservative had been visibly uncomfortable from the start with Trump's style of politics. He did not publicly flatter Trump at the famous cabinet meeting, instead praising his own vast intelligence workforce. Now Coats had a premonition that this was, for his tenure in Trump's government, "the beginning of the end."

Coats reached John Bolton as soon as Air Force One lifted off from

Finland and said he was putting out a statement defending his intelligence community's work. Bolton asked for a couple minutes to consult with John Kelly. But when the White House chief of staff tried to get Coats to change the statement to include the questionable claim that the Trump team had done more than the Obama administration to combat Russian interference, Coats refused. He read the statement line by line to Bolton, then pressed send. Bolton, relieved that at least Coats was not quitting on the spot, did not object. Three days after Helsinki, appearing live at the Aspen Security Forum with Andrea Mitchell of NBC News, Coats gasped out loud when she told him the breaking news that Trump had invited Putin to continue the conversation with a meeting in Washington. "Okaaay, that's going to be special," he said sarcastically.[4] Trump was livid when he heard about that and so, instead of quitting over the president's dramatic show of no confidence, Coats apologized to Trump for the comment.

But Coats would tell others that Helsinki had been such an extraordinary event it had forever changed his view of the allegations about Trump and Russia. The summit had been so clearly without a point, and politically detrimental, that no rational leader would have insisted upon it. "I never could fully understand the why. The history we've been through, our adversarial relationship with Russia, the Skripal killing, all the things that they've done and that we know that they've done—I couldn't see how it benefited him politically," Coats reflected to associates later. "I never could come to a conclusion. It raised the question in everybody's mind: What does Putin have on him that causes him to do something that undermines his credibility?" *What does Putin have on him?* Remarkably, the head of the intelligence community, even after sixteen months in office and access to the nation's most sensitive secrets, could not answer that question.

Robert Mueller was watching the news conference, too, along with his team. The special counsel was more than a year into his investigation and fresh off the indictments of the Russian intelligence officers. Yet to Mueller as well, Trump's dealings with Putin still seemed inexplicable. At the daily 5 p.m. meeting of his staff that day, the special counsel was exasperated when the subject of the bizarre Trump appearance with Putin came up. Well, Mueller told the lawyers, if the president was in fact in the tank for Russia, "it would be about money."[5]

In effect, the Helsinki summit had put the Russia part back into the Russia scandal, which Trump had, largely successfully, turned into a daily narrative of persecution and grievance all but divorced from the strange realities of his pro-Putin policy. Ever since Mueller's appointment, the president had been in attack mode, complaining endlessly that he was being tormented by Mueller's staff of "13 Angry Democrats," by rogue FBI agents, by James Comey, by Andrew McCabe. He often ranted about his faithless attorney general, Jeff Sessions, whose recusal had led to Mueller's appointment in the first place.

On the road in Brussels before flying to Finland to meet Putin, Trump had been watching Fox News coverage of the latest subplot, the disclosure of anti-Trump text messages by Peter Strzok, the lead FBI agent on the Russia investigation, and Lisa Page, an FBI attorney with whom Strzok was having an extramarital affair. By the time of Helsinki, Trump had tweeted a total of eighty-five times since the investigation began about the "Witch Hunt," forty-nine times asserting "No Collusion," nineteen times about Mueller, and a dozen times about the "Russia Hoax." His obsession with the probe and its metastasizing array of side issues and fantastical characters *(The DNC server! The Pakistani gentleman!)* was succeeding in one respect. Trump so dominated the news cycle with his Mueller fog machine that it obscured the question of what to make of the president's many compromising dealings with Russia.

In private too, Trump was consumed by the investigation and by extension with the belief that any mention of Russia's 2016 election interference was tantamount to questioning the legitimacy of his victory over Hillary Clinton. One result was that discussing actual policy toward Russia had become a huge problem for his advisers, who considered the subject a red line they would just as soon not cross with Trump. His own staff had no idea what to make of Trump's flirtation with Putin. The first time Fiona Hill was introduced to Trump, his only question to her was this: "So, what do you think, is he a nice man, Putin? Am I going to like him?"[6] Then he did not stick around for the answer.

The bottom line was that the Trump administration had one Russia policy while Trump had another Russia policy and the two were in stark conflict with each other. "I've seen Washington where State and Defense were at odds. I've seen Washington where State and NSC were at odds. I've never seen Washington where State, NSC, and Defense were all in one place, with a couple of exceptions, and the president was in another place," recalled Daniel Fried, a career diplomat who served forty years in the State Department and had been in charge of sanctions policy toward Russia until quitting a few weeks into Trump's presidency.

In the opening days of the Trump administration, when Mike Flynn was still his national security adviser and Steve Bannon was still in the

White House promoting the plan to make nice with Russia in order to take on China, the president had seriously considered lifting sanctions on Russia imposed after the takeover of Crimea until Mitch McConnell, John McCain, and others threatened to stop him legislatively. "Trump was checked in his ability to do what he was tempted to do in the early weeks of the administration, which was to cut a deal and simply give them Ukraine," Fried recalled. "They were blocked by Congress." In July of 2017, Congress passed a version of the measure that McConnell had threatened, the Countering America's Adversaries Through Sanctions Act, broadened to include Iran and North Korea as well as Russia. Faced with a certain bipartisan veto override, Trump reluctantly signed it "for the sake of national unity," he said in a statement nonetheless complaining that the measure was "significantly flawed."[7] It was a rare example of the Republican-controlled Congress passing legislation over Trump's objections.

But it did nothing to diminish Trump's disconcerting affection for Putin. He seemed to take anything the master of the Kremlin told him at face value. The same month that Congress was passing its sanctions bill, Trump was relying on Putin's word over that of his own intelligence agencies, just as he would in Helsinki with the whole world watching. At a meeting to discuss whether to renew Barack Obama's decision to close Russian diplomatic dachas in the United States in retaliation for Moscow's election interference, Trump brushed aside concerns raised by his FBI briefer about their utility in conducting espionage in the United States. Instead, according to an account the astonished briefer later gave to Andrew McCabe, then the acting FBI director, Trump spent nearly the entire meeting talking about reports of a North Korean test of an intercontinental ballistic missile capable of striking the United States. Trump insisted that the test had not happened—it was a hoax. Why did he think that? Because that was what Putin had told him, Trump explained. Told that was not consistent with any intelligence held by the United States, Trump shrugged it off. He believed Putin.[8]

If members of Congress knew that at the time, they would have been alarmed. As it was, lawmakers in both parties were still trying to stiffen Trump's spine in dealing with Russia by pushing him to support military assistance, including lethal weapons, for Ukraine in its long-running war with Russian-backed separatists in the country's eastern regions. Obama had authorized millions of dollars in aid, but balked at sending lethal weapons, despite the urging of advisers. Trump's senior officials, including Jim Mattis and Rex Tillerson, lobbied him to green-light the sale of Javelin antitank missiles to Ukraine, pointing out that if he did so he could credibly claim to be "tougher" on Russia than Obama had been. But Trump was hardly sympathetic to Ukraine. In June of 2017, Trump even told the president, Petro Poroshenko, to his face in an Oval Office meeting that he considered Ukraine a corrupt country—"because a Ukrainian friend at Mar-a-Lago had told him," as the American ambassador, Marie Yovanovitch, who sat listening in stunned silence, later recounted—and also that Crimea was really Russian anyway, because the locals spoke the Russian language.[9] Given such views, aides held back asking Trump for a formal decision on military assistance for months. Eventually, Trump signed off on the sale of $47 million in weaponry, including 210 Javelins and thirty-seven launchers.

It was confusing and inconsistent, to say the least, when Trump, weeks later, extended his offer to Putin for what became the disastrous Helsinki summit. "There's no stopping him," a senior Trump official confided that spring. "He wants to have a meeting with Putin, so he's going to have a meeting with Putin."[10]

As with the Singapore summit with Kim, Trump had no use for organized preparation or briefings. Although he wanted to meet Putin, no one could say why, or what the goal was beyond Trump finally getting some alone time with the Russian president. The pre-summit negotiations with Russia consisted of a single John Bolton visit to Moscow, from which he came away with none of the "deliverables" that would commonly be agreed to in advance of such a summit so that the two leaders could then unveil them. "The meeting is the deliverable," Bolton was told by the Russians.[11] There was no structured agenda either. The centerpiece would be the private session between Trump and Putin, after Bolton rejected Fiona Hill's suggestion that he propose a two-plus-two format instead, with at least Mike Pompeo in the room alongside the president. "A president should be able to have a one-on-one," Bolton told her, nodding to Trump's wishes.

The president's view of the world in general, and Russia in particular, had been formed in his younger days, when Trump had been fascinated by nuclear weapons and the definition of international statesmanship was a big arms control deal between the United States and the Soviet Union. Trump had even volunteered himself at one point to be Ronald Reagan's arms control negotiator. "His view on arms control, which he was a strong advocate of, was shaped by the 1980s, when important people got big treaties, and that was an attribute of an important person," Hill would say later.

Putin had rattled and angered Trump in March by showing a video to the Russian parliament before his re-election that featured an "invincible" new hypersonic missile targeting Trump's adopted home state of Florida.[12] White House aides and cabinet secretaries were not the only ones who had become adept at playing to the Trump audience of one. Now, to the extent that he had a substantive agenda with Putin, Trump seemed to harbor a fantasy of a sweeping arms control agreement, although his advisers disagreed over the one arms control item that was actually pressing, the New START agreement made by Obama that was set to expire in 2021. Trump supported an extension; Bolton had called it an "execrable deal."[13]

When Jon Huntsman, the ambassador to Russia, came to Washington before the summit, Trump's national security team was delighted, hoping this would give them an opportunity to discuss Putin with someone Trump might listen to. But when Trump saw Huntsman, the former governor of Utah, it reminded him of another Huntsman he often watched on television, the ambassador's thirty-two-year-old daughter, Abby Huntsman, cohost of *Fox & Friends Weekend.* Instead of planning for Helsinki, Trump demanded that they call her, right away, from the Oval Office. Her father could hardly say no. "We never got the meeting back on track," Hill said later.[14]

As with Singapore, Trump planned a stop with Western allies before heading to Helsinki—in this case, a NATO summit in Brussels and a quick visit to Britain. His tea at Windsor Castle with Queen Elizabeth II was perhaps the perk of office most anticipated by Trump, whose mother was a diehard royalist born in the United Kingdom. But the date with the queen was only a sideshow. Once again, as before Singapore, the main event was a brutal Trump attack on the allies, specifically the NATO alliance that Putin considered his main enemy.

Headed to Brussels, Trump was still furious with Angela Merkel about the release of the photograph of her staring him down at the G7 summit in Canada. The photo had given rise to innumerable snide memes about Trump, including this caption from a former prime minister of Belgium: "Just tell us what Vladimir has on you. Maybe we can help."[15] Trump's combative new ambassador to Germany, Richard Grenell—previously best known as a right-wing Twitter troll who had been Bolton's spokesman at the United Nations during the Bush administration—told a senior German official that the photograph was an outrageous personal "affront" to the president. To the Germans, it seemed as if Grenell's appointment was an affront to Merkel. "He loves the fight like Trump, Trump welcomes that, and it is what Germans hate the most," a senior Trump administration official said soon after Grenell took up his post.[16]

By now, Merkel's effort to "detox the relationship," as the senior German official put it, had clearly failed. And worse, Trump had clearly developed a deep personal animus toward the chancellor. No one was quite sure why. Was it because she was a strong woman? Because his own father had been of German heritage yet denied it for years after World War II? Trump had gone along with his father's lies, even falsely claiming in *The Art of the Deal* that the family was Swedish. Everyone had a theory, but whatever the reason, there was little doubt about the result. "There's a single-mindedness to it and almost an obsession, it seems, and this is something we are hearing from colleagues in the administration too: an obsession with Germany," another senior German official said.

Going into the NATO meeting, Grenell and others had been urging Trump to focus on Germany's deal with the Russian state energy firm Gazprom to build the Nord Stream 2 natural gas pipeline. The Trump administration, like the Obama administration before it, strongly opposed the pipeline both because it would hurt Ukraine, which would lose the money it made as the conduit for Russia's gas to Western Europe, and because it would give Russia additional political leverage over the Germans. Trump readily seized on the Nord Stream issue and would make it a theme of his Germany-bashing for the rest of his presidency.

At a televised pre-summit breakfast with Jens Stoltenberg, the NATO secretary general, Trump opened his attack. "Germany is totally controlled by Russia," he announced. "Germany is a captive of Russia."[17] As he said it, John Kelly, sitting two places down from Trump, was caught on camera grimacing. The resulting furor over the video gave rise to one of the great attempted spins of the Trump era, when Sarah Huckabee Sanders, the White House press secretary, told reporters that Kelly had looked so "displeased because he was expecting a full breakfast and there were only pastries and cheese."[18] (Asked about this later, Kelly told others that what he was actually thinking was: "I'm so incredibly embarrassed.") Merkel, who had grown up in East Germany and remembered adults bursting into tears when the Berlin Wall was built, issued a withering statement in response, noting that she had personally witnessed what actual Russian control of Germany was like.

Trump followed up with a tweet that made clear his target was not just Germany but NATO itself. He had been banging on the allies for failing to spend the full 2 percent of their GDP on defense. Now he issued an ultimatum: pay up or else. "What good is NATO if Germany is paying Russia billions of dollars for gas and energy?" he tweeted. "The U.S. is paying for Europe's protection, then loses billions on Trade. Must pay 2% of GDP IMMEDIATELY, not by 2025."[19]

Behind the scenes, Bolton and other advisers had been frantically trying for weeks to stop this showdown. In late June, Trump had called Stoltenberg and told him that he was sick and tired of the United States paying "80 to 90 percent" of NATO's budget—which was not true—and that he was going to lower the American "contribution" to NATO to what Germany paid.[20] It did not actually make sense. Was Trump planning to reduce American defense spending from more than 3 percent of its GDP to Germany's level of under 2 percent, a cut of hundreds of billions of dollars? Of course not. The United States spent so much more because it flexed its military muscle all around the globe, not just in Europe. But Trump went on and on in the call with Stoltenberg to register his complaint.

Bolton, listening in, sensed disaster coming, and summoned Mike Pompeo and others to help dissuade Trump before the Brussels meeting. They decided that the best argument was a practical one. They would tell the president that picking such a momentous fight over NATO would be a political distraction from Trump's top domestic priority at the moment, which was confirming his nominee Brett Kavanaugh to the Supreme Court. Bolton also sought to head off a debacle like the one that had just happened at the G7 summit in Canada, working around the president with Kay Bailey Hutchison, the ambassador to NATO, to convince the allies that they should approve the NATO end-of-summit communiqué before the summit even started so Trump could not swoop in and blow it up.

Trump had claimed to agree when Bolton and Pompeo warned him about Republicans not being up for a big, distracting fight over NATO. But he had not really been convinced. Bolton and Pompeo believed the president was secretly being egged on by Keith Kellogg, the retired lieutenant general and ally of Mike Flynn who had since been shuffled out of the National Security Council and made Mike Pence's national security adviser. Despite the transfer, Kellogg maintained a pipeline to Trump and was well known for his frequent anti-NATO diatribes. Trump seemed to confirm his aides' suspicions in Brussels by bringing up Kellogg's name unprompted. "Keith Kellogg knows all about NATO," Trump told Bolton and Pompeo.[21] And by the way, Trump added pointedly, looking right at

Bolton, he had actually wanted to hire Kellogg in March as his national security adviser instead of him.

Trump made that comment before the second morning of the summit in a meeting where the president informed his new national security adviser and secretary of state, both only a few months into their jobs, that he was going to withdraw entirely from NATO. "Do you want to do something historic?" Trump asked them. Then he repeated his complaint about Germany and the Russians. "We're out. We're not going to fight someone they're paying." He added, "I want to say we're leaving because we're very unhappy."[22] The two advisers made a final pitch to Trump not to blow up the entire Western alliance. But neither knew where the day would end.

In a panic, Bolton summoned reinforcements. "Hey, get over here, we're about to pull out of NATO," Bolton said when he reached John Kelly, who was busy elsewhere working on preparations for the Putin meeting in Helsinki.

Arriving late for what would be perhaps the most contentious NATO summit in its seven-decade history, Trump took his seat during a session with the leaders of Ukraine and Georgia to discuss their aspirations to join NATO. "Are we going to do it?" he asked Bolton after summoning his national security adviser to his side. "I had my heart in my throat," Bolton would recall. "I didn't know what the president would do."[23] A few minutes later, without giving Bolton an answer, Trump began his speech, disregarding Ukraine and Georgia and launching into his complaint about the free riders on American power who made up the alliance. Calling across the room, Trump addressed Merkel by name. "You, Angela," he said as he demanded that Germany pay up.[24] Now. In fact, he said, concluding his harangue, if *all* the other nations did not pay up by January 1, the United States was "just going to do its own thing," as Bolton later wrote.[25] Was the president threatening to leave NATO? To the shocked leaders, it certainly sounded like an explicit vow to torch their alliance. Realizing that the meeting was out of hand, Merkel called for an emergency session—the emergency being Trump.

Once the Georgians and Ukrainians were ushered out of the room so the allies could have their family spat in private, Trump resumed his attack on Merkel as the rest of the hall listened in stunned silence. Finally, it fell to another woman, Dalia Grybauskaitė, the president of Lithuania, to defend Merkel. Germany had sent troops to protect Lithuania from Russia, Grybauskaitė pointed out, and Merkel was committed to spending more on NATO common defense. In a corner of the room, Merkel strategized with a huddle of other Europeans clustered around her about how to handle Trump. Eventually, Mark Rutte, the prime minister of the Netherlands, offered the president what he appeared to want most, a way to claim victory. Rutte noted that, since Trump took office and began his pressure campaign, NATO allies had collectively raised their defense budgets by some $70 billion. Take the win, he urged the president. Trump did just that.

Yet when he emerged from the meeting and spoke with reporters, Trump lied, claiming not only that the allies had capitulated to him but also that they would consider his demand to raise their annual military spending to 4 percent of GDP, doubling the current goal, an assertion so politically impossible that Emmanuel Macron immediately issued a public rebuttal. Trump, unbothered at being called out, pretended as if nothing out of the ordinary had just occurred. As he left the summit en route to his meeting with the queen and then on to Helsinki, he interrupted the chancellor while Merkel was addressing their fellow NATO leaders and kissed her on the cheek. "I love this woman," he said. "Isn't she great?" A senior German official who recounted that particular Trumpian flourish resisted any attempt at full understanding. "It's up to psychologists and historians what to make of that," he said.[26]

In fact, Trump's anger toward Merkel and attack on NATO were dead serious. It never became public, but officials later confirmed that the White House had secretly ordered the Pentagon that June to produce an official report on what it would take to remove all American military forces from Germany or even all of Europe—a move that would have tilted the balance of power in Europe radically in Putin's direction if Trump had gone through with it.

Trump's antipathy for America's friends would forever vex his own advisers who saw it as undermining national security. Jim Mattis tried to explain to Trump why Merkel could not simply snap her fingers to do what he wanted since she led a coalition government in a parliamentary system very different from the form of government in Washington.

"It's as if Nancy Pelosi was your secretary of defense and Rand Paul was your secretary of state and both of them could run against you in the next election but you need them to hold your government afloat," Mattis said.

Trump did not seem to get the point. But he was struck by Mattis's analogy. "Nancy Pelosi as *my* secretary of defense?" he exclaimed. "Ha!"

No one felt the indignity of that Helsinki summit more than John Bolton. But three months into the job he had avidly pursued, Bolton did not quit in protest. Despite the hue and cry, no one did. Not at the White House, not at the State Department or in the intelligence agencies. The Republicans who controlled the House and Senate imposed no discernible cost on Trump, beyond, as Roy Blunt had anticipated, keeping the Senate Intelligence Committee investigation going. Trump's defenders in the House Freedom Caucus had no problem defending the president on this one too. "In order for something to be treasonous, it has to undermine who we are as a nation," Mark Meadows opined at a forum the day after the summit. "I've never seen a press conference have that effect."[27]

The question remained, however, what to do about a reckless president who had just come close to singlehandedly destroying the foundation of America's international security and making destabilizing concessions to Russia's leader. After the Singapore and Helsinki summits, Bolton came to an understanding. Unlike H. R. McMaster, he would aggressively go around Trump, seeking out like-minded allies and partners on Capitol Hill and in foreign capitals to manage and constrain him. Bolton was a much more experienced, networked, and savvy Washington player than McMaster. He would now go much further, and authorize his staff to go much further, than McMaster ever had in seeking to obstruct the president he ostensibly served.

He would also keep his distance, unlike previous national security advisers who tended to be constant shadows of their presidents. "He really didn't even make the kind of effort to staff the president the way that you would have assumed any national security adviser would try to," a senior official on Bolton's staff recalled. "He would stay *away* from the Oval Office. He almost never traveled with the president." Even when Bolton did go, he would often take a separate plane. Bolton was not in every meeting and on every call. That left plenty of time for Trump to spend with Keith Kellogg, Rudy Giuliani, and his Fox News friends.

Still, even the biggest screwup is an opportunity for someone in Washington. Trump had undermined his administration's Russia policy with his words and in the process given his advisers the political cover they needed to force him to approve tough-on-Russia measures he had resisted. Soon enough, Bolton and Pompeo used the blowback over the summit to get Trump to sign off on a formal declaration that the United States would never recognize the legality of Putin's annexation of Crimea. Long in the works, the declaration became a "useful thing," another senior official said, to counter the impression of Trump's pro-Putin tilt in Helsinki. They also got him to agree to a new initiative across the federal government to combat Russian intervention in the upcoming midterm elections. Just as importantly, from his advisers' perspective, the Helsinki debacle had made the politics of another summit with Putin on American soil toxic for Trump; no matter how much the president wanted it, that would never happen.

But even the political backlash only caused a temporary retreat. Trump remained a skeptic of his government's support for Ukraine and when Russian warships opened fire and seized three Ukrainian navy boats in the Black Sea off Crimea a few months later, Trump personally blocked his administration from issuing a statement condemning it and canceled a United States ship visit to Ukraine meant to show support. He was talked into scrapping a formal meeting with Putin on the sidelines of a G20 summit in protest of the ship seizure, but then defied his advisers by pulling the Russian leader aside to talk anyway.

By the fall, Bolton was explicitly reaching out to senators to manage Trump, just as he had reached out to the allies to get them to stop the president from blowing up the NATO communiqué. In an early September call with Senator Cory Gardner, a Republican from Colorado, he gave a blunt readout of the Singapore summit and subsequent talks with North Korea, one that was starkly at odds with Trump's public hyperbole. "We don't think they are serious about giving up nuclear weapons," Bolton told Gardner. He explained that North Korea "wants a declaration of the end of the Korean War," and why, in his view, it would be a bad idea for Trump to grant it. The "Japanese would go through the roof," Bolton said. It would undercut the sanctions regime and it would make "it harder to justify keeping troops" in South Korea. Most importantly, he had a request for Gardner: Could he please send a message to the president? Bolton, who in theory could walk into the Oval Office anytime and deliver this message himself, wanted the senator to tell Trump: "You've been effective on Iran, that should be your instinct on" North Korea as well. They both knew that with Trump flattery worked.

Bolton's staff was already coordinating closely with another Republican, Senator Dan Sullivan of Alaska, to try to contain Trump more explicitly on North Korea. Even before Singapore, Matt Pottinger, the senior Asia director, had been so concerned that he reached out to Sullivan to encourage the senator's ongoing effort to insert a provision in upcoming defense legislation blocking Trump from withdrawing troops from the Korean Peninsula without explicit congressional authorization. Sullivan did insert the provision, although in the end it was watered down into a nonbinding resolution. At an October 2 meeting with Senate Republicans on North Korea, Bolton heard a roomful of concerns about what Trump was doing. Sullivan said he worried about Trump making a "nukes for troops trade." Was there anything more they could do to head that off?

Later in October, Bolton spoke with Paul Ryan, the departing speaker of the House. They were both concerned about Trump's desire for a peace agreement with the Taliban in Afghanistan and wanted to stop it. Together, they discussed how to "keep the president from making a rash decision," as notes of the call put it. They tested out lines for Ryan to use on Trump: "You have a good plan, it is just getting started." "Don't pull the plug in the second quarter of a four quarter game." And: "Your strategy is correct, you have to give it time to see if it will work." In the end, they decided to emphasize that a takeover by the Taliban or other radical group would mean that neighboring Pakistan and its "nuclear weapons are in danger."

It had long been a time-honored Washington ploy for executive branch officials to work contacts on Capitol Hill for air cover during internal administration battles. Many an aide had leaked something to a friendly senator in hopes of blocking a bad White House decision, foiling a rival agency, or furthering a pet cause. But a national security adviser sitting in an office just down the hall from the president plotting with members of Congress to organize opposition to his boss? There was little precedent in the historical record for the kind of purposeful strategy that Bolton adopted after Trump's summer of international summitry. And purposeful it was. A White House official familiar with the calls likened Bolton's plan to bowling: he was just hoping to keep the ball from falling into the gutter.

CHAPTER 11

The Eighty-five Percenter

In the cavernous Washington National Cathedral, nearly all of official Washington gathered on the first day of September to pay final respects to John McCain, the Vietnam war hero turned iconoclastic senator, two-time presidential candidate, and, in his last years, voice of Republican resistance to what he considered the dangerous charlatan in the White House. Most of the Senate was there, Democrats as well as Republicans, and McCain was eulogized by both George W. Bush and Barack Obama, the two men who had defeated him for the presidency.

But there was no major role for Lindsey Graham, McCain's best friend in politics, a man so close to him that he referred to their relationship as a "political marriage," a man who spent holidays with the McCain family in Arizona and traveled everywhere from Afghanistan to Ukraine with the late senator. Technically, Graham did speak, reading out a couple lines of Scripture carefully chosen to make a point—"no greater love than this, to lay down one's life for one's friends." But that was it.

The slight was not accidental. In the final months of McCain's life before he succumbed to brain cancer at eighty-one, the two men had grown increasingly estranged over Graham's growing friendship with Trump. McCain thought Trump was an unbalanced buffoon and a danger to America. So did Graham, until suddenly he did not. At the start of Trump's presidency, Graham like McCain had been a determined opponent of a man he had famously called "crazy" and a "kook," a "race-baiting bigot" who was "unfit for office."[1] After Trump overwhelmed a field of sixteen other candidates including Graham to win the Republican nomination, Graham declared that his party had gone "batshit crazy" by anointing "the most flawed nominee in the history of the Republican Party." He refused to vote for Trump that November against Hillary Clinton, casting his ballot for an independent candidate, Evan McMullin, whose name he later could not remember.[2] "You know how to make America great again?" Graham once tweeted. "Tell @realDonaldTrump to go to hell."[3] As he later admitted, "I thought he was a complete asshole."

But as the ailing McCain faded from the scene, Graham had improbably turned his affections to the president he had once excoriated. By the late summer of 2018 when McCain died, Graham was a regular golf partner of Trump's at Bedminster, Mar-a-Lago, and Trump National Golf Club in Virginia outside Washington. Graham flew on Air Force One with the president and was such a frequent presence at Trump's summer retreat in New Jersey that some White House aides began referring to him as "Senator Freeloader." Graham seemed intoxicated. "He let me into his world," he enthused. The access and constant consultations thrilled him. "I have never been called by a president this much in my life," he said. His fealty flipped, he now expressed outrage that anyone would have the effrontery to denigrate Trump, even going on CNN to berate the media for labeling the president "some kind of kook not fit to be president"—the same words Graham himself had once used.[4]

McCain was disgusted and let Graham know it. The two argued about it and at one point all but stopped speaking. Graham's bromance with Trump angered McCain enough that he chose not to have his friend speak for him at the main nationally televised farewell, relegating him instead to a speech the next day at a private burial in Annapolis without cameras or a large audience. The Senate had brought the two together, but Trump had driven them apart.

When the end did come, Graham's main contribution to the day of mourning was to invite Jared Kushner and Ivanka Trump, who were not on the original invitation list and whose presence outraged McCain's grieving daughter Meghan. No one had told her that the president's daughter and son-in-law would be there, and she was livid when she noticed them in the cathedral. "Funeral crashers," she later called them. "When I saw them, I thought, 'I hope this is the most uncomfortable moment of your entire life.'"[5]

During her own turn at the lectern, Meghan used her eulogy to deliver a defiant rallying cry against the Oval Office interloper who had denigrated her father and all that he stood for. "We gather here to mourn the passing of American greatness," Meghan said as Graham sat stone-faced in the audience, "the real thing, not cheap rhetoric from men who will never come near the sacrifice he gave so willingly, nor the opportunistic appropriation of those who lived lives of comfort and privilege while he suffered and served." No one doubted whom she had in mind. Mocking Trump's campaign slogan, she declared: "The America of John McCain has no need to be made great again because America was always great."[6] The audience burst into applause, a rare occurrence during the traditionally solemn services held at the cathedral. Her tribute, delivered through heaving sobs, seemed to channel how much of establishment Washington felt.

Graham said nothing as the daughter of his old friend eviscerated his new friend. In a CNN appearance that week, he was asked about his jarring change in loyalties. Graham made no effort to disguise his motivation. Power had shifted in Washington, and Graham would shift with it. "If you knew anything about me," he told host Dana Bash, "I want to be relevant."[7]

Funny, astute, and disarmingly charming, Graham learned his politics in a bar. He grew up in the small town of Central, South Carolina (population: approximately five thousand), where his parents owned a pool hall called the Sanitary Cafe and the family lived in an apartment in the back. After school, he played pinball standing on a Coca-Cola crate, served Pabst Blue Ribbon to the mill workers, and snuck his fair share of beers and cigarettes, earning the nickname "Stinkball." He spent hours honing the skills of a good bartender, learning how to listen, to tell a good joke, to keep on everyone's good side. "I was expected to entertain folks," he later wrote. "And I knew the more audacious I was the more entertaining I would be."[8] He also mastered the art of defusing tense moments. "Lindsey is a peacemaker," noted Senator Richard Burr, a Republican from next-door North Carolina.

Graham became the first in his family to go to college when he enrolled at the University of South Carolina, but life took a tragic turn when his mother died of lymphoma and his father succumbed a year later to a heart attack. Where John McCain was defined by the burden of living up to the legacy of the father and grandfather before him who had served as admirals, Graham would spend the rest of his life missing the family he had lost early. Left to take care of his sister, Darline, nine years younger, he eventually adopted her and went on to law school before enlisting in the Air Force, where he became a lawyer in the Judge Advocate General's Corps. Graham never married and the military essentially became the family he no longer had; he would remain in the reserves through most of his time in Congress.

As a young congressman, Graham was something of a maverick, origi-nally part of Newt Gingrich's team of Republican rebels yet willing to help lead a failed coup against the speaker when he grew too erratic. Gra-ham came to national fame during Bill Clinton's impeachment in 1998 and subsequent Senate trial in 1999. At first, he broke with his hardline colleagues by seeking a compromise with the White House, but when that went nowhere, he served as one of the most effective and captivat-ing of the House managers, prosecuting the president with an aw-shucks Southern style. ("Where I come from, you call somebody at 2:30 in the morning, you're up to no good," he said of the president carrying on an affair with a former White House intern.)[9] While Clinton was acquitted, Graham's stock rose, and he moved up to the Senate three years later.

He quickly found a mentor in McCain, the Navy pilot shot down over North Vietnam who endured more than five years as a prisoner of war and eventually ended up as one of Washington's most admired mavericks. During McCain's ill-fated campaign for the Republican nomination in 2000, he courted Graham, inviting him to his Arizona ranch, where they palled around with the likes of Warren Beatty and Annette Bening. Gra-ham became a sidekick, joining McCain in supporting militant policies after the terrorist attacks of September 11, 2001, including George W. Bush's invasion of Iraq. The two traveled together to war zones and other foreign destinations dozens of times and teamed up in ultimately unsuc-cessful efforts to negotiate bipartisan deals on issues such as immigration and climate change. Joined by Senator Joseph Lieberman, the defense-minded Democrat, the trio became known as the Three Amigos. Gra-ham was at McCain's side for his second run at the White House in 2008 and McCain returned the favor when Graham launched his own quixotic presidential campaign in 2016.

Little did either recognize that year the threat posed by Trump. They considered him a joke and had no doubt that his boorish appeal would fade quickly. McCain had a little history with Trump. At a 1993 congres-sional hearing, Trump tried to buttonhole McCain as part of an effort to block casinos on American Indian reservations that would compete with his gambling houses in Atlantic City. McCain brushed past him with-out pausing. "I gave money to your campaign," Trump called after him. McCain looked back over his shoulder. "Oh yeah? See what that will get you."[10]

Twenty-two years later, when Trump presented himself as a would-be president, McCain publicly dismissed him again. This time, Trump fired back. "He's not a war hero," declared the tycoon, who had avoided the draft in Vietnam with the questionable bone spurs claim. "He's a war hero because he was captured. I like people who weren't captured."[11] McCain's many fans were outraged, including Graham, but the senator himself just rolled his eyes and told aides not to get worked up.

"All he did was get people to talk about what a hero I am all weekend," McCain observed. "That's not my problem, it's his."[12]

As a rival candidate, Graham proved to be not even a road bump on Trump's path to the Republican nomination. His only memorable moment came when Graham called Trump "the world's biggest jackass."[13] Trump retaliated by dismissing the senator as a "lightweight" and "idiot," then gave out Graham's personal cell phone number on camera, prompting a flood of unwanted calls.[14] Graham responded with characteristic humor, releasing a campaign ad showing him smashing his phone with an axe, burning it in a toaster, and destroying it in a blender. "Or if all else fails you can always give your number to The Donald," the candidate said into the camera.[15]

McCain grudgingly endorsed Trump after he won the nomination, but then withdrew it when the *Access Hollywood* tape was released, saying he was considering a write-in vote for his "old, good friend" Graham instead.[16] Less than two weeks after Trump won, McCain attended an international security forum in Halifax where he was approached by a British friend who told him that a former intelligence officer had collected damning evidence of Trump's ties to Russia. McCain was seized by the tip and instructed an adviser, David Kramer, to fly to London to check it out. "Time is of the essence," McCain said. Mulling it over, McCain said, "You know what this means if it's true? It means Mike Pence becomes president." Kramer flew to Britain and met with the former spy, Christopher Steele, who had assembled what would become the infamous dossier on Trump, working first for Republican opponents and later for Clinton's campaign. Kramer brought it back and gave it to McCain, who consulted his old friend. Graham was intrigued and urged him to turn it over to the FBI, which he did. Behind the scenes, Graham also passed along tips to colleagues on the Senate Intelligence Committee, pressing them to investigate Trump. "Go get him," he told them.

After Trump took office, the two senators were still at odds with the newly inaugurated president. They were among those who responded sharply to his travel ban, issuing a joint statement calling it "a self-inflicted wound in the fight against terrorism," and worked to block Trump from lifting sanctions on Russia.[17] But while McCain remained leery of the newly elected president, Graham quickly accepted an invitation to the White House. Sitting in the Oval Office, Trump opened by apologizing for giving out the senator's phone number.

"I'm sorry, I shouldn't have done that," Trump said.

"Mr. President, that was the highlight of my campaign," Graham laughed.

Trump courted Graham for months. That fall, the president invited Graham to golf with him on Columbus Day at Trump National Golf Club. Graham afterward gushed about the match to a White House aide who reached out to be sure the president had not committed to anything without telling his own staff. Trump was so good, Graham told the aide, he could play on the senior tour. "It was awesome," the senator exulted. He raved about Trump publicly, too, tweeting that the president had shot an excellent round of two strokes over par "in windy and wet conditions!"— a claim so improbable it set off disbelieving commentary among professional golfers.[18] Graham seemed starstruck. "It's something, to play a golf course with the president of the United States on a course he owns," he told golf.com. "He's got that big giant flag there—it's pretty stunning."[19]

The next Saturday, Trump invited Graham to play golf again and accompany him on Air Force One down to South Carolina to campaign for Governor Henry McMaster. On the return flight to Washington, the president's military aide told Graham that Trump wanted to have dinner with him in his cabin. Graham was engaged in a policy discussion with White House officials in the conference room, so a couple minutes after takeoff, Trump appeared in the door with his meal tray. "Lindsey, I have yet since I've been in this job had anyone turn me down for dinner," he chided before sitting down and joining the discussion. When they landed at Joint Base Andrews outside Washington, Trump asked, "Lindsey, have you been on Marine One?" He had not. So Trump invited him to ride on the helicopter back to the White House, plying him with candy and commentary throughout the short trip. "Okay, this is the best part coming up," Trump said as they approached the Washington Monument. Graham posed for a picture with a wide grin and a thumbs-up gesture.

McCain was not so easily won over. Trump called him shortly after taking office too, but began by airing grievances, complaining about McCain's decision to withdraw his endorsement. McCain told Trump how offended he had been by his campaign season attack on the parents of a Muslim American soldier killed in Iraq just because they had endorsed Clinton.

"No," Trump said, "you unendorsed me over the *Access Hollywood* thing."

"Well, that's the *real* reason I unendorsed you," McCain shot back.[20]

Trump tried to bury the hatchet by offering his mobile number so the senator could call anytime but when an aide asked about it later, McCain said he had lost it.

That spring, Graham arranged a peacemaking dinner at the White House between Trump and McCain with their wives and came along as well. Sitting at a table in the Blue Room, Trump was on good behavior and offered to make Cindy McCain, a well-known activist against human trafficking, his ambassador to combat it, pulling out a letter detailing the idea and reading it aloud. But the job never materialized and neither McCain was charmed.

By summer, the senator made that abundantly clear when the fate of a bill to repeal Barack Obama's Affordable Care Act came down to McCain's vote, just a week after his cancer was diagnosed. He was acutely aware how it would look for a wealthy eighty-year-old with access to the best health care possible to vote to repeal a program that provided care for millions of less well-off Americans. Just as importantly, he was offended by what he considered a slapdash version of the bill. As he headed to the floor to vote well past midnight, another senator asked how he was holding up. "Doing well for now," McCain said, the scar from his brain surgery still fresh above his eye. "About to get a lot worse."

After rebuffing last-minute lobbying from Lindsey Graham and Mike Pence, who handed him a phone to speak with Trump, McCain strode to the middle of the chamber and held out his arm, waiting to get the clerk's attention. Once he got it, he turned his thumb down, delivering the death knell to a top priority of the president. Gasps could be heard in the chamber. Mitch McConnell stood a few feet away, glowering, his arms crossed in consternation. The moment of truth in the dead of night was operatic, and McCain, never averse to winning a round, knew it.

Trump would never forgive McCain and never missed an opportunity to denigrate him for years to come. His antipathy for the senator was so unrelenting that when he traveled to Japan and visited a naval base, the White House even asked the Navy to move or hide the destroyer USS *John S. McCain* so Trump would not notice it. "A highly overrated man," he huffed even after leaving office.[21]

But McCain's feud with Trump had little impact on Graham. The senator began spending more weekends sharing a golf cart with the president and did not hesitate to phone him at all hours. It got to the point that when Graham could not get Mike Pompeo to return a phone call, he called the president instead and Trump had the White House operator patch through the call to the secretary of state right there and then.

There was, however, a certain cynicism to it all. "I will play to his vanity, he'll play to mine," Graham said of Trump. Unlike many of Trump's White House advisers who later broke with him and portrayed him as a dangerously ignorant man guided by impulse, Graham went all in on the president he had formerly considered an uninformed idiot. Now, he insisted that Trump was "really smart" and calculating. "There's a method to the madness," he claimed one night over Thai food after congressional votes. In fact, he was sure that Trump's volatile behavior was simply a shtick. "He consciously plays the erratic card," he insisted.

From time to time, Graham still felt it necessary to publicly break with Trump over one crazy tweet or another. Most notably, he warned Trump against firing Robert Mueller and, to drive home the point, even sponsored legislation barring the president from doing so. It was more of a performative statement since he knew it would never become law, but it infuriated Trump. "He went apeshit," Graham recalled. The senator replied, "I wanted to let you know that if you did fire him, that would be the end of your presidency." Graham also publicly warned against firing Jeff Sessions, declaring that "there will be holy hell to pay" if he did.[22]

Trump did not take such messages well and as a result never completely bought into Graham. To his face, Trump nicknamed him "The Broker," flattering Graham as his intermediary with other Senate Republicans. Behind his back, Trump called Graham "Eighty-five Percenter," meaning he thought the senator backed him most of the time but not always. An aide once asked him why he trusted Graham, Ted Cruz, and some of the other Republicans who had criticized him so sharply in 2016 and now positioned themselves as friends. Trump replied with a what-can-you-do shrug. "He didn't really trust them, but he just figured there was nothing else to do," the aide recalled. Reflecting on this after leaving office, Trump claimed to have had few illusions about the opportunistic attitude of many Republicans in the Senate. "The problem is, I'll get this guy elected, then he will be there for six years and he'll probably try and screw me as soon as he gets into office," he said. "So I know that. So what's my choice? Him or a Democrat. Now, you know where the Democrat stands—I mean there's going to be 100 percent no vote."

Some aides thought Graham took advantage of the president's time, calling too often and inviting himself to golf. Once during a visit to Bedminster, he was sitting at a table by the pool, enjoying the free food. "Isn't this great?" he said when he saw Stephanie Grisham, who would serve as Trump's third White House press secretary. "Man, this is the life."[23]

After his thumbs-down repudiation of Trump, John McCain's health slowly deteriorated and he spent more time at his ranch near Sedona, Arizona. Friends and colleagues made the trek there to pay their respects and, without quite acknowledging it out loud, to say farewell.

Among those who visited regularly was Graham, but, while they denied it, his newly close ties with the president whom McCain despised were breaking the Three Amigos apart. How was it even possible that Graham could be hanging out with the man McCain considered a threat to American democracy? And while McCain was dying? "It bothered John and John spoke to Lindsey about it and it affected their relationship for a while," Joe Lieberman acknowledged. For many in their circle, Graham's friendship with Trump was just an out-and-out "betrayal," as another person close to McCain put it.

McCain's attitude was, "You're going to suck up to this fucker over a golf game?" according to his close adviser Mark Salter. Graham's attitude, Salter said, was, "I'm doing the best I can to make him 10 percent less nuts"—although Salter, like McCain, thought he was "doing a piss-poor job of it."

McCain might have been able to understand, or at least tolerate, working with Trump in hopes of keeping an unschooled, unwise commander in chief from making grievous mistakes. But the weekend outings seemed so personal.

"Do you have to play golf with him so much?" McCain asked at one point.

He was especially offended when Graham boasted about Trump's skill on the links, seeing it as unconscionable sucking up.

"Bullshit!" McCain said when Graham reported that Trump had scored well in a recent game. "Oh, come on, Lindsey!"

Graham tried to explain but never convinced McCain. "John, you don't understand Trump," Graham recalled telling him. "He asked me to help him. I'm going to help him whether you like it or not." He appealed to McCain's own unpredictable streak. "Listen, John, I've seen you do shit. You know, you forgive the Vietnamese." He went on: "The only way you can convince this guy to listen to you is if he believes you have his best interest at heart. And on foreign policy, he's more like us than I thought. He wants to be strong."

With McCain receding from the stage, Trump increasingly became Graham's focal point. "You get a lot of amateur psychiatrists who will tell you Lindsey got closer to Trump because McCain was leaving earth and I had left the Senate," Lieberman later reflected. "It's possible it had something to do with it. But I think this was Lindsey trying to find a place where he could be the most productive."

In the months before his death, McCain had time to consider his funeral, and decided he wanted it to make a statement, extolling the American ethos of public service at a time when the United States had a president who seemed driven only by self-interest. "He never said, 'Let's arrange my service as a counterpoint to Trump,'" Salter said, "but it wasn't that we were unmindful that's what we were doing." Looking to make a point about American democracy and national unity, McCain asked Obama, the Democrat who beat him in 2008, and Bush, the Republican who beat him in 2000, to deliver eulogies. Both men readily agreed. As for Trump, McCain never directly said that he did not want to invite the sitting president, but when aides raised the question, he said, "I'm sure he would rather play golf." They took that as a no.

When McCain died on August 25, Trump affirmed the senator's instinct. "We're not going to support that loser's funeral," the president huffed to his advisers. After John Kelly took it upon himself to order flags lowered to half-staff in keeping with custom for someone of McCain's national stature, Trump erupted. "What the fuck are we doing that for? Guy was a fucking loser."[24] The flag over the White House was raised again—a decision that was instantly noticed and taken as the sign of disrespect that Trump meant it to be. A Trump aide even tracked down Miles Taylor, an official at the Department of Homeland Security, on a work trip to Australia, to demand the department reverse its instruction to other federal agencies to lower the flag. "Would you guys be able to rescind the directive?" he was asked.[25] The president's chief of staff could not believe it. "Kelly was beyond furious," recalled a close colleague. He pressed Trump to reverse himself.

"If you don't support John McCain's funeral, when you die, the public will come to your grave and piss on it," an angry Kelly told the president. "This guy's a hero, regardless of what you think about it."

Trump finally gave in, unhappily. "I don't know why you think all these people who get shot down are heroes," the president insisted, "but do what you want to do."

Even in death, though, McCain had the last word. He left a farewell letter to "my fellow Americans" to be read by Rick Davis, his former campaign manager. It was his final rebuke to Trump and all that he represented. "We weaken our greatness when we confuse our patriotism with tribal rivalries that have sown resentment and hatred and violence in all the corners of the globe. We weaken it when we hide behind walls, rather than tear them down, when we doubt the power of our ideals, rather than trust them to be the great force for change they have always been."[26]

The flag flap had infuriated McCain's family and friends. McCain's son-in-law, Ben Domenech, the publisher of the conservative website *The Federalist* who had married Meghan McCain the year before, was dispatched to meet with Jared Kushner and Ivanka Trump to inform them that the family did not want the president at the funeral. "They were a little surprised by that," Domenech recalled, "which surprised me a little." Meghan rewrote her eulogy into a scathing rebuke. On the plane to Washington for her father's service, she read it to Salter and Davis. "Go get him," Salter said. She did.

And then there was Trump. As McCain had predicted, he went golfing.

The public debut of the fully Trumpified Lindsey Graham would come barely two weeks later, when Judge Brett Kavanaugh, who sat on the federal appeals court in Washington and had been tapped to move up to the high court by Trump, was accused of sexually assaulting a fellow teenager as a high school student in the 1980s.

Trump had little margin for error in a Senate controlled by Republicans 51 to 49, and much at stake. In replacing the retiring Justice Anthony Kennedy, for years the Supreme Court's swing vote on issues such as abortion, affirmative action, and gay rights, the conservative Kavanaugh would surely move the high court to the right. A backlash among Democratic voters in the midterm elections just around the corner, however, could move Congress to the left. And Trump's ability to legislate in the last two years of his term would depend on the outcome.

Into the fray leapt Graham, long a key voice on Supreme Court appointments from his perch on the Senate Judiciary Committee. Unlike some of his fellow Republicans, Graham believed that presidents deserved the benefit of the doubt on their choices for the bench no matter what party they belonged to. In that vein, he had voted for Barack Obama's nominations of Sonia Sotomayor and Elena Kagan, despite expressing disagreement with their legal philosophies, generating a conservative backlash against him in South Carolina, where he had to face down six

Republican primary challengers in 2014 to secure another term. Watching Democrats assail Kavanaugh infuriated Graham, who resented what he saw as an unfair pile-on while also identifying the controversy as an opportunity to come to Trump's aid.

The irony is that Trump was never all that hot on Kavanaugh to begin with, seeing him as the sort of establishment Republican that he detested. Kavanaugh was really the choice of Don McGahn, the White House counsel who pushed the president to nominate him for Kennedy's seat. At fifty-three, Kavanaugh had been a sort of Zelig of Republican politics, repeatedly showing up at major moments of drama. He had worked for Ken Starr, the independent counsel, and was a primary author of the report that triggered Bill Clinton's impeachment. Kavanaugh later showed up in Florida in 2000 working for the Republicans during the election recount battle that sealed George W. Bush's victory, then going on to work for him as a White House lawyer and later staff secretary. Kavanaugh was so close to Bush that he married the president's longtime personal assistant, with the first couple attending the wedding. Bush later appointed him to the federal appeals court in Washington, traditionally a stepping-stone to the Supreme Court.

As he considered Kavanaugh for Kennedy's seat, Trump had wavered back and forth. He even called Bush directly to ask about Kavanaugh, one of the only times they spoke during his presidency. He found the former president on the golf course and Bush gave his onetime aide an enthusiastic endorsement. So did Bush's longtime strategist, Karl Rove, when Trump reached him on casino magnate Steve Wynn's yacht off the French Riviera around 1:30 in the morning local time.

Trump also called Leonard Leo, executive vice president of the influential Federalist Society, which put together lists of pre-vetted conservative judges for Trump to appoint. Leo, little known publicly, was perhaps the party's most influential backstage voice reshaping the federal judiciary and a longtime Kavanaugh admirer.

When Trump reached him on the way to the airport, Leo knew that the president was in Bedminster that weekend where his ear would be filled by people like Sean Hannity, former congressman Mike Ferguson, and others who were known to be pushing for Judge Amy Coney Barrett, a hero of anti-abortion conservatives.

"Who do you think I should pick?" Trump asked.

Leo hedged. "You've got to pick whoever you're most comfortable with."

"You think it ought to be Kavanaugh, right?"

"I think it should be whoever you're most comfortable with," Leo repeated.

Trump finally revealed his hand. "I'm going to save Barrett for Ginsburg," he said—meaning that at some point in the future he could put forth a conservative woman to replace Justice Ruth Bader Ginsburg if she retired or died.

Still chewing it over, Trump called Leo another time from Air Force One. With the weekend coming, Leo worried about who would be at Bedminster with Trump, knowing that the last person to talk with the president often ended up swaying the decision. So Leo called Derek Lyons, the White House staff secretary, to ask who would be golfing with Trump over the weekend.

"I don't really know," Lyons said.

"Don't give me this bullshit, Derek," Leo snapped. "Give me the names." He did not want anyone trashing any of the candidates. "We can't have a circular firing squad here."

Lyons finally admitted that Ferguson would be in Trump's golf cart on Saturday and Hannity on Sunday. Leo called each of them and pleaded—if they wanted to advocate for Barrett, fine. But don't trash anyone else.

The conservative activists were not the only ones wary of Kavanaugh. Mitch McConnell warned Trump against him as well, on the assumption that his service in Bush's White House meant that Democrats would ask to examine all the documents that had crossed his desk, a monumental undertaking that would delay the proceedings and potentially provide ammunition for opponents.

But Trump rarely made decisions based on tactical calculations. It was a gut check. He viewed judges as political actors who were either loyal to him or not. To reassure himself that Kavanaugh would be his man, Trump invited the nominee to come back to the White House for a second conversation, this time over dinner in the residence on a Sunday night. Kavanaugh was surprised to find Melania Trump there as well. Whatever Trump's hesitation going in, soon after the meal he resolved to go with Kavanaugh.

The confirmation battle was heated even before Christine Blasey Ford entered the picture. With so much on the line, Democrats opened fire on Kavanaugh, asserting that he could be the decisive vote to overturn *Roe v. Wade* and accusing him of lying to the Senate during his previous confirmation about an episode involving stolen Democratic emails. As McConnell had warned, Kavanaugh's papers became a major point of dispute. Bush quietly interceded by volunteering to personally pay for an expedited review of the documents.

None of which would have stopped Kavanaugh's confirmation had his conduct as a teenager not emerged as a major flashpoint late in the process. In a letter to Senator Dianne Feinstein of California, the top Democrat on the Senate Judiciary Committee, Christine Ford alleged that during a small high school party in Maryland just outside Washington, a drunken Kavanaugh had pinned her to a bed, groped her, tried to remove her clothes, and covered her mouth when she tried to scream, while a friend of his watched. She said she managed to extricate herself and lock herself in a bathroom until they stumbled off. In the letter, she asked Feinstein to protect her anonymity, but she also called a *Washington Post* tip line and told others her story. When it began leaking out, she decided to go on the record with Emma Brown, a *Post* reporter.[27]

Just like that, the Senate faced a repeat of the Clarence Thomas case more than a quarter century earlier, with a conservative Supreme Court candidate again accused of sexual misconduct in a highly charged environment. Kavanaugh decided to do what no nominee had done before and speak out for himself, granting an interview to Martha MacCallum of Fox News. Appearing beside his grim-faced wife, Ashley, the embattled nominee adamantly denied the allegations against him, but stuck to his talking points so robotically that he repeated that he had always treated women "with dignity and respect" four times and that he was seeking a "fair process" seventeen times.[28] Among those upset at his flat performance was Trump, who was especially flabbergasted that Kavanaugh claimed to have still been a virgin when he went to college. *Who's still a virgin in college?* Trump asked. *And who would admit it?*

Trump called Kavanaugh to offer support in more encouraging terms than the nominee expected. But at the same time, Trump was testing his resolve.

Was he prepared to fight, Trump wanted to know.

Absolutely, Kavanaugh said.

Never in love with Kavanaugh in the first place, Trump was perfectly willing to throw him overboard if necessary and took the temperature of aides and senators. At one point, he asked McConnell if Senate Republicans were really committed to seeing the nomination through.

McConnell recognized that Trump was wavering and sought to stiffen his spine. "I'm stronger than mule piss," McConnell declared.

———

On September 27, barely a month before the midterms, the accuser and the accused took turns in the hearing chair before the senators. Christine Ford went first, presenting herself as a kind of Everywoman—an Everywoman with a PhD—at once guileless about politics yet schooled in the science of memory and psychology, "terrified," as she put it, to be at the center of the vortex. "I believed he was going to rape me," she said, adding, "It was hard for me to breathe, and I thought that Brett was going to accidentally kill me." What remained searing in her mind, all these decades later, she said, was "the uproarious laughter between the two" at her expense.[29]

Her story brought women to tears and left even Republicans impressed. By the end of her testimony, Senator Charles Grassley of Iowa, the GOP committee chairman, thanked her "for your bravery coming out."[30] Around town, Republicans inside the White House and the Capitol panicked, certain that she had doomed the nominee. "Disaster," one wrote in a text message.[31] They began contemplating what they presumed would be a failed nomination. Even Trump found Ford a "very credible witness" and called McConnell.[32] "We're only at halftime," McConnell said.[33]

In the anteroom of Room 216 of the Hart Senate Office Building, Kavanaugh prepared to go next. Don McGahn cleared the room of everyone except Kavanaugh and his wife. The only way to save your nomination, McGahn told him, was to show the senators how you really feel, to channel your outrage and indignation. You need to remember every time you stayed up late to earn a good grade, McGahn continued, every job you worked overtime to excel at, every extra effort you ever made to get here. "They're about to take it all away from you," he said. "You've got to go in there and put it on the table." In effect, he said, "You need to reboot the room."[34]

Kavanaugh needed no encouragement for that. By the time he sat down in the hearing room, he was brimming with resentment. "I am innocent of this charge!" he said, choking back tears. Practically shouting at the senators, he denounced the "grotesque and coordinated character assassination," accusing Democratic senators of plotting against him and even asserting that it was being done to avenge the Clintons, who had a grudge against him from his days working for Ken Starr. "This confirmation process has become a national disgrace," Kavanaugh declared. "The Constitution gives the Senate an important role in the confirmation process, but you have replaced 'advice and consent' with 'search and destroy.'"

More than perhaps any nominee in a generation, he crossed well beyond the line of impertinence, interrupting senators and haranguing them. After admitting that "I like beer, I like beer," he brazenly challenged Senator Amy Klobuchar, a well-regarded Democrat from Minnesota whose father was an alcoholic, about her own drinking habits, a moment that would be parodied to devastating effect by Matt Damon on *Saturday Night Live*. Even McGahn thought that went too far and slipped Kavanaugh a note. Kavanaugh read it, collected himself, and apologized. "Sorry I did that. This is a tough process. I'm sorry about that."[35]

But Kavanaugh's raw outrage and Trumpian-style fury turned the political dynamics in the room. Stories had been circulating online immediately after Ford's testimony that the White House was thinking about pulling the nomination. McGahn sought to reassure Kavanaugh during a break when an aide called saying the president was looking for him. "Tell him I don't talk to quitters," McGahn said loudly enough for Kavanaugh to hear, hoping to demonstrate resolve to the nominee.[36] And in fact, hours after being written off as lost, Kavanaugh had salvaged his chances.

Sarah Huckabee Sanders, the White House press secretary, called Trump. "Kavanaugh just saved himself," she said.[37]

Among those rallied by the performance was Lindsey Graham, who sat in his seat in the hearing room seething. Afraid of a repeat of the backlash from their party's questioning of Anita Hill during the Clarence Thomas hearings, the committee's Republicans had decided to turn over their share of the hearing to a female sex crimes prosecutor from Arizona, avoiding the spectacle of a bunch of white men grilling a woman victim. But the prosecutor's muted inquiries of Ford, broken into five-minute chunks as the microphone switched between the Democratic and Republican sides, proved ineffectual and when Graham's turn arrived to question Kavanaugh, rather than turn his time over to her, he launched into a tirade.

Shifting angrily in his chair, wagging his finger at his Democratic colleagues, Graham practically spit righteous indignation. "What you want to do is destroy this guy's life, hold this seat open and hope you win in 2020," he roared. "You've said that, not me!"

He turned to Kavanaugh. "You've got nothing to apologize for," Graham said. "When you see Sotomayor and Kagan, tell them that Lindsey said hello because I voted for them," he added. "I would never do to them what you've done to this guy. This is the most unethical sham since I've been in politics."

By this point, Graham's face was contorted in rage and covered with sweat. "Boy, you all want power," he snapped at the Democrats. "God, I hope you never get it. I hope the American people can see through this sham."[38]

Democrats and Republicans alike were stunned, as if an unexpected tornado had suddenly swept through the room. "Shall we let things settle a little bit after that?" asked Senator Sheldon Whitehouse, a Democrat from Rhode Island, whose turn followed.[39] Months later, Whitehouse would tell the journalist Jackie Calmes that Graham's harangue was "probably the single most effective piece of political theater I have ever seen in my life" and may have "single-handedly" saved Kavanaugh's nomination.[40]

Graham emboldened Republicans who had been on the defensive for days, turning Kavanaugh, for them at least, from an accused sex offender to a victim of a partisan smear. It was also a seminal moment for Graham, completing his transformation into one of Trump's most important advocates and thrilling the Trump base. Conservatives who had long been suspicious of Graham suddenly celebrated him. Newt Gingrich, once the target of that coup attempt led by Graham, said his speech on behalf of Kavanaugh "justified Lindsey Graham's entire career."[41] A Tea Party activist in Graham's home state of South Carolina declared that he had "gone a long way in rehabilitating his reputation."[42]

The day had reinforced Washington's deep partisan divide. There was no political fight anymore that was possible in which the two sides could even agree on a shared interpretation of the facts. Ford had come across as highly credible. Clearly uncomfortable in the capital spotlight, she had no evident reason to lie—she had received so many death threats since coming forward that she had fled her home and had to be guarded by private security. While a registered Democrat, she had not been involved in politics to any significant extent. Why would she make this up and put herself through the public ordeal if it were not true? There was also the case of another woman, Deborah Ramirez, who told Ronan Farrow and Jane Mayer of *The New Yorker* about a drunken party at Yale University when Kavanaugh had allegedly exposed his penis in her face.[43]

But Kavanaugh's angry denial and Graham's indignant defense rallied Republicans. As believable as Ford came across, she could not remember some details of that thirty-six-year-old encounter and had no witnesses to corroborate it, although her husband and friends confirmed she had confided in them about it over the years. The emergence of a third accuser also worked against Ford when a woman represented by Michael Avenatti, a slick, publicity-hungry California lawyer for Stormy Daniels who had been careening from one Trump administration scandal to another, claimed that Kavanaugh had attended parties where she and other women had been gang-raped, although she did not accuse him of participating. The allegation was so over-the-top and Avenatti's reputation so poor that it became easier for Republicans to dismiss the whole episode as a partisan setup.

Still, Senator Jeff Flake, an Arizona Republican who had broken with Trump as he headed toward retirement, found Ford's testimony deeply troubling. He reluctantly decided to vote to advance Kavanaugh's nomination out of committee, but as he stepped into an elevator in the Capitol, two angry women describing themselves as survivors of sexual assault confronted him. "You're telling all women that they don't matter, that they should just stay quiet," one of them said through tears. "You're telling them that my assault didn't matter."[44] Flake looked stricken, unsure what to say. By the time he returned to the committee, he huddled with Senator Chris Coons, a Democrat from Delaware, and agreed to force a one-week delay in the confirmation to give the FBI time to investigate.

With Anita Hill and the entire #MeToo movement in mind, most Republicans refrained from attacking Ford directly, preferring to suggest it was simply a case of mistaken identity. Uncharacteristically, Trump held back at first too. But eventually he could not resist and began mocking Ford ruthlessly. His voice dripping with derision, the president who had himself been accused repeatedly of sexual assault and harassment and defended others similarly accused like Bill O'Reilly, Roger Ailes, and Roy Moore, went after Ford at a political rally in Mississippi, imitating her at the hearing. "*How did you get home?* I don't remember. *How'd you get there?* I don't remember. *Where is the place?* I don't remember. *How many years ago was it?* I don't know. I don't know. I don't know. I don't know."[45]

Trump's White House made sure that what ensued after Flake's intervention was not a real investigation. While the FBI received 4,500 tips about the nominee, agents on instruction from the White House interviewed only ten people—and neither Kavanaugh nor Ford.[46] In the meantime, Graham took Flake to dinner at Cafe Berlin, joined by two other wavering senators, Susan Collins and Lisa Murkowski, and talked about whether a limited inquiry would satisfy them.

After the FBI reported back inconclusively, McConnell pushed for a vote, but he was so estranged from Collins that he called Ivanka Trump to ask her to check in with the Maine senator. Ivanka reached Collins, who told her that she had forged a pact with Murkowski and Nebraska's Ben Sasse, another occasional Trump critic among the Republicans, to stick together on the vote. The next day, Collins called back to say she would vote yes but to warn that Murkowski had gone missing and was not returning calls. Sasse had not heard from her either.

Ultimately, Murkowski came out against Kavanaugh, while Flake and Sasse stood by him. When Collins announced during a forty-five-minute speech on the Senate floor that she would vote for Kavanaugh, Trump was in the private dining room off the Oval Office with Senators John Thune and Ron Johnson. The room erupted in cheers. Trump shook hands. Phones started ringing. He had won one of the biggest battles of his presidency. When the vote was counted, Kavanaugh was at home with the television off, only learning that he had been confirmed when Chief Justice John Roberts called to congratulate him.

The battle was huge as well for Graham. His approval rating among Republicans in South Carolina shot up from 51 percent in April to 72 percent in October.[47] Soon enough, a conservative businessman and favorite of the right in South Carolina dropped plans to challenge Graham in the 2020 Republican primary. Graham would later say that the two moments in his political career that made him into a hero for conservatives were prosecuting Bill Clinton and defending Brett Kavanaugh.

The moment also lashed him even closer to Trump, who admired Graham's attack on the Democrats. More than ever, Graham was associated with a president he had once considered a "complete asshole" and from that point on he was, like Kavanaugh, all in. John McCain was gone. Donald Trump was still there. Graham was at the center of power. And he did not care if anyone objected. As he put it one day, "If you don't like me working with President Trump to make the world a better place, I don't give a shit."[48]

CHAPTER 12

Shut It Down

Kirstjen Nielsen, the embattled secretary of homeland security, did not think she could take it anymore, and she was not the only one. Just days after winning the Brett Kavanaugh confirmation battle, Trump in the fall of 2018 was on the verge of a mutiny inside his own cabinet.

With the midterm elections weeks away, the president had been, once again, on the warpath, worried about losing control of Congress and eager to appeal to his anti-immigrant base. Fox News was stirring up anger over a caravan of Central American migrants moving north through Mexico, characterizing it as a potential "invasion" of the United States. Trump in turn was publicly threatening to cut off all aid to Honduras, "effective immediately!," if it did not shut down the caravan, while browbeating Nielsen to harden the border even to the point of pushing her to take action she had no authority to take.

Close the border, just shut it down completely, he told her.

I can't do that, she replied, *and won't do that.*

She was not the only cabinet secretary worried that Trump was off the rails. On October 18, in a text message over the encrypted app Signal, Nielsen delivered a top aide stunning news. She listed five of the most senior officials in the Trump administration: John Kelly, Jim Mattis, Joe Dunford, Betsy DeVos, and Ryan Zinke, the interior secretary. "All," she wrote, were on the verge of quitting en masse, "wanting to go now with Kelly."

"Alas," replied Miles Taylor, her chief of staff, "then we have some planning to do."

"Yeah," she replied. "Ok for the first time I am actually scared for the country. The insanity has been loosed."

Nielsen had already become the face of a wildly controversial Trump administration practice of separating children from their parents at the border, making her in the public mind the heartless executor of Trump's hardline immigration agenda. Now he was pummeling her every day for not being hardline enough and demanding that she not only enact his brutal policies but cross the line into outright illegal ones. Yet quitting never seemed clear-cut. Nielsen was traumatized working for a president who appeared to be unraveling and at the same time convinced that, if she left, Trump would simply appoint a more pliant successor who would carry out his increasingly extreme demands. "How far would I go to save the republic?" Nielsen messaged her aide.

Trump was not making it any easier on her. Two days after that text message, she was on the telephone with the president when he blew up at her again about migrants at the border. "Don't let a single fucking one into the country!" he screamed at her. In the background, Nielsen could hear the television blaring the latest reports about the "invasion."

Disenchanted with Nielsen, Trump had aides working around her looking for other tactics to stop immigrants from crossing the border. Two days after Trump shouted at Nielsen not to let in "a single fucking one," Customs and Border Protection officials reported at a meeting that they had been approached by White House aides asking if it was possible to repel the migrants using millimeter wave devices, a microwave weapon designed by the military to emit invisible beams that make a target's skin feel as if it was burning. "This is out of fucking control," Taylor told Nielsen. "There are people talking about using heat rays on innocent women and children."[1]

The insanity loosed that fall, as Nielsen put it, encapsulated the Trump presidency—the fixation on immigration as a singular threat to the nation, the use of fear as a campaign tactic, and the internal struggles of officials who had to decide what if anything to do about it. Anxious about the upcoming midterms that Republicans were predicted to lose, Trump was lashing out not just at Nielsen but at a wide array of senior officials, seemingly out of control even for a president never known for self-discipline. He believed that immigration had been the reason he won in 2016 and now feared that his failure to deliver tough policies would cost him Congress.

Famous for saying the inappropriate out loud, Trump articulated his plan in a tweet that week, calling the caravan a "Great Midterm issue for Republicans!" Always obsessed with whatever obsessed the conservative media echo chamber, Trump now reacted to the Fox News "invasion" by demanding a militarized response, leaving advisers to wrestle with the moral dilemma of if, when, and how to make a stand against presidential actions they considered both wrong and dangerous. "He went indiscriminately crazy because he was so freaked out about that and that bled into everything else he was doing," said one administration official. "I think he was just flipping out so hard." That was why so many senior officials were quietly talking about whether to leave together.

Trump's administration was already facing an exodus. (Again.) Don McGahn, having gotten Kavanaugh confirmed, was about to leave. Nikki Haley, the wildly ambitious, occasionally Trump-ambivalent United Nations ambassador, had declared that she would step down by the end of the year. John Kelly was clearly on the verge of resigning or being fired. In offices throughout the West Wing and at cabinet departments across Washington, others were contemplating the same. Even Betsy DeVos, the Amway heiress whose family had bankrolled Republicans to the tune of $14 million in the 2016 cycle, was increasingly estranged from Trump, who called her "Ditzy DeVos" behind her back and once grew mad at her because he did not like how her hair looked during a *60 Minutes* interview.[2] And Trump was clearly just waiting out the midterms before firing Jeff Sessions, the attorney general he kept savaging for recusing himself from the Russia investigation. "The Democrats, none of whom voted for Jeff Sessions, must love him now," the president tweeted bitterly in September. Sessions was determined to suck it up for as long as the president would let him stay, but other officials such as Nielsen were struggling that fall to decide where the lines were—how far they would be willing to go, how much they would be willing to take from Trump before finally quitting.

The idea of an internal "Resistance" had captured the public imagination that September with the publication of an anonymous op-ed article in *The New York Times* by an unnamed "senior official in the Trump administration" describing a cabal "working diligently from within to frustrate parts of Trump's agenda and his worst inclinations."[3] That suggested something far more organized than was in fact the case, while also playing into Trump's rhetoric about a sinister Deep State arrayed against him. Still, it was a sign of how many people were said to be disgruntled with the president that everyone from Mike Pence and John Kelly to nearly every member of the cabinet and even Ivanka Trump and Jared Kushner were suspected of being "Anonymous." Peter Navarro, the president's eccentric and combative trade adviser, took it upon himself to investigate and produced a fifteen-page memo that confidently asserted the author had to be a woman and was probably a National Security Council aide named Victoria Coates. He turned out to be wrong on both counts. The secret writer was actually Miles Taylor, the aide Nielsen had been texting with. Even she did not know until he revealed himself publicly two years later.

The public furor over the article and the inevitable guessing game about its author masked a real though unreported drama secretly unfolding that fall as Nielsen discussed with Taylor and senior aides to other cabinet secretaries the idea of a mass resignation. This would have dealt a sensational political blow to Trump had the officials gone through with it. Although several later denied it, at least some of those on Nielsen's list were in fact debating an exit in advance of the midterms. But the group could never find its way to a public revolt against the president.

Dan Coats, the director of national intelligence, for one, remained deeply unsettled by the president's interactions with Russia, even more so since the Helsinki summit, and Trump's refusal to listen to his government's secret briefings. Why was Trump so dismissive of anything negative he was told about Russia? Why had he brushed off the poisoning of a former Russian spy on British soil? Why would he suggest inviting Putin to Camp David? Like Mattis and Nielsen, Coats also had concerns about the politicization of the migrant caravan and his name had come up amid the discussion of mass resignation. Still, he thought such talk was not in the end all that serious and, as far as he was concerned, would not serve the country. If they all left on principle, they almost certainly would be replaced with others who had none. Coats pulled out of the discussions—others involved suspected the former senator was wary of dealing a blow to Republicans before the midterms—and told his team to keep going as best they could.

Ultimately, Nielsen and the rest of the disaffected officials came to the same decision: much as they might be tempted to quit, they would stick it out. Was it partisanship? Personal ambition? Fear of Trump? A sense of duty? Throughout the Trump presidency, far more senior officials had desperately hung on until they were fired than resigned in protest, and even in the midst of the president's pre-election meltdown, that is what happened once again. "It just sort of fell apart," one official involved in the discussions said later. "Something like that, you've got to strike and implement yesterday or just inertia's going to pull it apart." Besides, the official said, "The fact remains that the entire cabinet could resign and it's not going to change the policy probably. If the goal is, would you change the president's mind, the entire cabinet resigning en masse wasn't going to change that."

Kirstjen Nielsen was an accidental cabinet member, who like others had dreaded the idea of working for Trump yet became convinced, or convinced herself, that it would be worse if she did not. As John Kelly's top aide at the Department of Homeland Security, she had come with him to the White House when he took over as chief of staff and helped with the search process to replace him as secretary. The personnel team came up with a list of twenty-five candidates with relevant experience, but all said no, were ruled out because they had once worked for George W. Bush, or were vetoed by Jared Kushner, Steve Bannon, or Stephen Miller. Nielsen personally called Governor Asa Hutchinson of Arkansas, who had served as undersecretary of homeland security for Bush, but he wanted nothing to do with it. Admiral James Loy, a former Coast Guard commandant and deputy homeland security secretary, also declined. So did several police chiefs.

Finally, attention turned to Nielsen herself. The daughter of two former Army doctors, Nielsen grew up in Tampa, Florida, before going on to Georgetown University and the University of Virginia School of Law. She helped set up the Transportation Security Administration after the September 11 terrorist attacks, then served as a homeland security aide in the Bush White House. Smart and driven, Nielsen at forty-five had earned her reputation as one of the competent, efficient staffers that Washington attracts in droves, although her no-nonsense manner alienated some colleagues, who nicknamed her "Nurse Ratched."[4] To Trump, she was always a "Bushie," and thus always suspect. At five-foot-six, she was dwarfed by Trump, who towered over her and condescended to her the way he did to so many women. "Oh honey, you look so tired," he would say if she appeared anything other than camera-ready in the heavily made-up style favored by his wife and daughter.

Nielsen was reluctant to take the job, but kept hearing other, more extreme names being bandied about. Among them were Kris Kobach, the secretary of state in Kansas who had overseen Trump's spurious effort to unearth nonexistent vote fraud in the 2016 election, and Joe Arpaio, a county sheriff in Arizona who received Trump's first presidential pardon in 2017, which spared him from jail time for defying a federal judge's order to stop racial-profiling suspected illegal migrants. Both were favorites of Trump and the hard-right anti-immigration crowd. Nielsen struggled with the decision for weeks before eventually saying yes, telling friends that Trump was going to be president for four years one way or the other, so the question was whether to bail on the country or suck it up. What she did not anticipate was how toxic her relationship with Trump would become.

The troubles did not really start until 2018. Border crossings, which under Barack Obama had already fallen to about 25 percent of their historic peak, fell even further during Trump's first year, to their lowest level since 1971.[5] But by his second year in office, they shot up again and as the numbers rose, so did Trump's ire. He had failed so far to secure money to build his promised wall—Mexico, of course, was never going to pay for it no matter how many times he said it on the campaign trail, and even a Republican Congress was not leaping to allocate the $18 billion Trump had asked for it.

Trump harangued Nielsen. Why couldn't she just put out a contract and build the wall? He did not seem to understand that, even if he managed to get the money, it was the Army Corps of Engineers, not the Department of Homeland Security, that actually handled construction projects. "If I lose re-election," Trump railed at Nielsen, "it's your fucking fault."

Stymied, Trump turned to another strategy—deterring families from trying to cross the border by taking away their children. This was an idea that Trump and hardline aides like Stephen Miller had been pushing since the beginning, only to be blocked repeatedly. As early as March 2017, John Kelly while still secretary of homeland security acknowledged on CNN that he was considering family separations as a deterrent. Behind the scenes, however, Kelly was one of those trying to thwart the idea. He stormed into one meeting with his staff furious because the White House was pressing him to take kids at the border. "No way in hell," he said. He banged his fist on a table and told aides not to respond to any such request from the White House. "If you hear anyone asking for that, you tell them to come to me," he said. "We're never going to do that. That's sick." Beyond moral qualms, he told the White House that it would take at least six months to enact such a policy and $10 billion from Congress to pay for personnel, training, and facilities to house the detainees who otherwise would be released with their children to wait for court hearings. That stopped the plan for a time.

But by the spring of 2018, the hardliners tried again. While the government would not automatically separate children from parents coming across the border, the Justice Department decided to criminally charge any adults who made it into the country except through official ports of entry. Rather than release them pending hearings, as was traditionally done, they would be detained, and since children could not be held in criminal detention facilities, they would be separated from their parents. Jeff Sessions would call that a "zero tolerance" policy but the goal was the same as it had been from the beginning. "We need to take away children," Sessions told five United States attorneys from the border region on a conference call in May.[6] His deputy, Rod Rosenstein, told prosecutors a week later that it did not matter how young the children were.

Nielsen, now in Kelly's old job, had like him resisted for months, arguing that the government had not allocated sufficient resources to cope with the consequences. Under existing law, unaccompanied children could not be held in immigration detention facilities for more than seventy-two hours, at which point they were supposed to be taken by Health and Human Services authorities. Neither department was prepared to carry this out on the scale now envisioned. There were not enough immigration judges to process that many prosecutions nor enough facilities to hold that many adults and their separated children. But Nielsen lost that fight and was pressured into signing a memo facilitating the zero-tolerance policy that Sessions would announce in April.

Even so, it did not assuage Trump. The president's exasperation came to a head at a cabinet meeting on May 9, when he unloaded on Nielsen in front of her colleagues. In a lengthy tirade behind closed doors, he erupted about her failure to build the wall and control the border, making clear that he viewed her as an impediment to the harsher policies he wanted to enact. He screamed that she was incompetent and insisted that all she needed to do was close the border.

"Shut it down immediately," he yelled. "Just shut it down."

It did not help that Sessions, for once happy not to be the target of Trump's rage, threw Nielsen under the bus. "Well, Mr. President, I just think we need to be tougher on the border," Sessions said. Nielsen, he added, could stop migrants from coming across the border if she wanted to.

Kelly, furious, called Sessions out. "Mr. Attorney General, where are we on getting the judges?" he asked. Without more judges, it would be impossible to process all the detainees Sessions and the hardliners wanted to hold.

"We don't need more judges," Sessions said dismissively. Referring to Nielsen, he said, "She just needs to not let them in."

That set Trump off. "Kirstjen, why are you letting them in?" he demanded. "Why don't you not let them in?"

Nielsen, flustered, tried to correct the record. "Respectfully to the attorney general, that's not how the law works," she said. "As soon as they touch U.S. territory, they are guaranteed due process under the law. You can't push them back across the imaginary border or across the line."

Trump refused to accept that. "You're making me look bad," he shouted. "What is the matter with you? Why can't you get on the program? Why won't you do this?"

Trump pounded Nielsen so hard that other cabinet members were shocked and assumed he was on the verge of firing her. "The rest of us just wanted to crawl under the table," another cabinet secretary recalled. Some of the others in the room, including Kelly and Jared Kushner, were shaking their heads, trying to signal Nielsen to stop talking and digging herself in deeper. Finally, she did and just let Trump rant.

When it was over, Nielsen left the meeting bruised and dispirited. "Fine, I guess I'm not doing my job," she told others who had been in the room. "I can just quit." She canceled most of the rest of her meetings for the day and headed over to a nearby federal building where her department had offices to collect herself. By the time she got there, the story of her dressing-down had already leaked, and the media was even reporting that she was going to resign. Maybe, she thought, she should. Not because the president yelled at her, she reasoned, but because if he thought Sessions was right and they could just stop anyone from coming over the border without due process, that was a problem she did not know how to overcome. She sat down at a computer and began drafting a letter of resignation. "Dear Mr. President," she wrote. That was as far as she got before her staff came in and asked what she was doing. They urged her not to step down, seeing her as a guardrail against the radicals at the White House.

Unsure what to do, Nielsen got back in her car and returned to the West Wing to find Mike Pence. Not for the first time, it fell to the vice president to calm the waters after a presidential storm.

"Should I resign?" Nielsen asked him.

"No," he replied. "I think he just had a bad day. It'll be fine. I don't want you to resign."

She also went to see Kelly, who was more equivocal. "I don't want you to resign," he said, "but you need to do what you need to do." Still, he then headed over to the White House residence to confront Trump about the blowup and defend his protégée.

Nielsen swallowed the humiliation and stayed on. But within weeks, the impact of the new zero-tolerance policy became clear when it was reported in June that as many as two thousand children had been taken away from their parents. It all blew up on Trump—and on Nielsen. Soon,

Donald Trump opened his presidency with an inaugural blast against "American carnage" (above) but his White House from the start had what one aide called a *"Hunger Games* vibe," divided between rivals like Stephen Bannon, H. R. McMaster, and Reince Priebus (right). *Jabin Botsford/ The Washington Post*

Republicans found that going on Sean Hannity's Fox News show was one of the "most effective ways of communicating with Trump," as one ally put it, better even than calling.

Vice President Mike Pence (above) hung out so often in the Oval Office that aides connived a way to get him out by passing him messages supposedly from his wife. Senator Lindsey Graham (right) said Trump was a "kook" in 2016 but became a close ally. "He's a lying motherfucker," he told the authors, but also "a lot of fun to hang out with." While at his Mar-a-Lago estate in Florida, Trump ordered an early strike on Syria, gathering so many aides in a secure room that one aide called it "the cruise missile cocktail party" (below).

"Mr. President, did you just fire the director of the FBI?" More than one aide was stunned by Trump's decision to dismiss James Comey, a power play gone bad that set in motion the Robert Mueller investigation, which hung over much of the rest of his tenure. *Andrew Harrer/Bloomberg/Getty Images*

Trump regularly turned to Governor Chris Christie of New Jersey (center) for advice and assignments but he was often boxed out by Jared Kushner (left), who blamed Christie for prosecuting his father. *Shawn Thew/Getty Images*

Trump gave Prime Minister Benjamin Netanyahu of Israel one victory after another but came to resent him by the end. "The president doesn't really like you these days," a White House aide told Netanyahu.

Trump posing with this glowing orb was the unforgettable image of his first overseas trip as president, a tradition-defying visit hosted by Saudi Arabia's autocratic King Salman (center). *Saudi Press Agency*

Trump boasted that Prime Minister Shinzo Abe of Japan, the premier Trump-whisperer among world leaders, nominated him for the Nobel Peace Prize. What he did not mention is that he asked Abe to do so.

John Kelly, Trump's second White House chief of staff, came to despise the president and even secretly consulted a book about Trump's mental health. The problem with Trump, Kelly told associates, was that "he always does the wrong thing."
Susan Walsh/Associated Press

Trump left his tax-cutting package, his most significant domestic legislative achievement, to Republican leaders like Senator Mitch McConnell (left), and Speaker Paul Ryan (second from left). "Donald Trump certainly had no clue," said his own chief tax policy adviser.

Trump was obsessed with his planned border wall, even demanding pikes on top and black paint to make it hotter to the touch (above). He regularly berated Kirstjen Nielsen, his homeland security secretary, who at one point messaged an aide, "The insanity has been loosed" (left, *Mandel Ngan/ AFP/Getty Images*). Amid a furor over family separations at the border, Melania Trump wore a jacket saying "I REALLY DON'T CARE. DO U?"(below, *Mandel Ngan/ AFP/Getty Images*).

No world leader infuriated the president more than Angela Merkel, the German chancellor, who studied an old *Playboy* interview with Trump to try to understand him, then faced off against him at a G7 summit meeting in Canada. *Courtesy of the German government.*

Trump publicly boasted that he "fell in love" with North Korea's Kim Jong-un but privately told an ambassador "that fucker would knife you in the stomach if he had the opportunity." The two met at the Korean Demilitarized Zone.

Trump's chummy meeting with President Vladimir Putin of Russia in Helsinki alarmed Republicans as well as Democrats and made the president's own intelligence chief wonder, "What does Putin have on him?"

After Brett Kavanaugh was accused of sexual misconduct as a teenager, Trump was uncertain whether to yank his Supreme Court nomination. At one point, Don McGahn, his White House counsel, refused to get on the phone with the president, telling an aide, "Tell him I don't talk to quitters." *Michael Reynolds/AFP/ Getty Images*

Trump was enamored at first with "my generals," like Jim Mattis, his first defense secretary (left), and Joe Dunford, his first chairman of the Joint Chiefs (right, *Manuel Balce Ceneta/Associated Press*), but soon grew disenchanted, asking "why can't you be like the German generals" under Adolf Hitler. Snubbing Mattis, Trump picked Mark Milley (below, left) to follow Dunford, only to have Milley and Mattis's successor, Mark Esper (below, right), later privately vow to resist an erratic president.

images of children in chain-link cages provoked a bipartisan uproar, led by former first ladies Laura Bush, Hillary Clinton, Rosalynn Carter, and Michelle Obama. Melania Trump declined to join them, instead issuing a statement saying she "hates to see children separated from their families and hopes both sides of the aisle can finally come together." But that only spurred more outrage as the first lady disingenuously blamed "both sides," as if the horrific pictures were not a consequence of action taken by her husband's administration.[7]

Suddenly, Trump officials who had pushed to take away children were denying that was their intent. Sessions, who had privately told the prosecutors weeks earlier that "we need to take away children" in comments that were only discovered by investigators long afterward, now told the public the opposite, saying "we do not want to separate parents from their children."[8]

Nielsen was apoplectic. "This is exactly what I fucking said would happen," she told colleagues. "Someone needs to get Jeff Sessions on the fucking phone and tell him to halt."

Yet amid the furor, Nielsen blundered her way into becoming the public face of a practice she had tried to prevent. Flying back to Washington on June 18 from a speech in New Orleans, she received a call on the plane from Sarah Huckabee Sanders asking her to come straight to the White House after landing. Arriving in the West Wing, Nielsen found the press secretary, who told her she did not know how to answer questions from reporters and could not have Sessions do it "because he sounds like a fucking idiot." Sanders urged Nielsen to go out into the briefing room right away. John Kelly strongly warned her not to. So did Chad Wolf, her chief of staff, who reminded her that this was not her policy and she had tried to stop it. But Sanders and Stephen Miller pressed her to go out and Nielsen agreed. Upset, Wolf went to a bathroom in the West Wing and threw up.

Standing at the lectern, wholly unprepared, Nielsen sounded technocratic, legalistic, and defensive as she tried to shift blame to Congress for not passing changes to immigration law. She got hung up on the point that it was not the *policy* to separate families per se, but of course that was the inevitable outcome based on the zero-tolerance practice set by Sessions's Justice Department. The reporters were skeptical.

"You have seen the photos of children in cages?" one asked. "Have you heard the audio clip of these children wailing that just came out today?"

Nielsen was caught off guard. "I have not seen something that came out today," she said, blandly referring her questioner to her department's standards for care.

"But is that the image of this country that you want out there? Children in cages?"

"The image I want of this country is an immigration system that secures our borders and upholds our humanitarian ideals," she said. "Congress needs to fix it."[9]

The session was a disaster and Nielsen knew it. A Georgetown classmate of hers later called it her "Cruella de Vil press conference."[10] Mike Pence found Nielsen afterward and tried to buck her up, telling her she had done a good job, but most people in the White House did not know what to say because it had gone so badly. Nielsen was furious. "This is even worse than we realized," she told other officials. "We have to shut it down. I need to talk to the president."

From that point on, Nielsen's place in history as the defender of family separation was set. She would later protest to associates that she had tried to fight Trump's demand for such a cruel policy, but in the end she had gone along with it and not resigned. In bland bureaucratic language, she had publicly defended ripping children from their parents and done nothing to distance herself from an approach that most Americans found abhorrent. Nor would she successfully reunite the children with their families. Of some four thousand children ultimately removed from their parents and detained in separate facilities, hundreds were still not brought back together by the time Trump left office.[11]

Trump, for once, praised Nielsen for doing "a fabulous job" in the briefing room, but she privately went to him afterward to press him to cancel the policy, warning that it would cost him the midterm elections. Just two days after the disastrous Nielsen briefing, Trump caved to the public pressure and signed an executive order purportedly reversing the policy. Ivanka Trump's allies put out word that she had convinced her father to back down, although some of those intimately involved in the issue said they saw no sign of the first daughter's involvement. It was a rare surrender by Trump, but it hardly meant he was going soft on immigration. Soon, he began quietly agitating with his staff to resume family separations.

The next day, Melania Trump sent a message of defiance when she flew to Texas to visit a detention facility wearing a $39 Zara jacket emblazoned, graffiti-like, with the words "I REALLY DON'T CARE, DO U?"[12] on the back. The cryptic jacket precipitated a debate about what exactly the first lady did not care about; whatever it meant, it hardly projected empathy for the children she was visiting. Even her husband recognized it was a public relations disaster. When the first lady arrived back at the White House, Trump summoned her to his private dining room. "What the hell were you thinking?" he demanded. She had no real answer, so he came up with one for her. "You just tell them you were talking to the fucking press," he said, then dictated a tweet to that effect. "I just saved your ass," he told her proudly.[13]

To one friend, though, the slogan really did reflect the first lady's view of the family separation issue. After returning from Texas, Melania had dismissed the whole contretemps in a conversation with her friend Stephanie Winston Wolkoff. "They're not with their parents, and it's sad," she told her. "But the patrols told me the kids say, 'Wow, I get a bed? I will have a cabinet for my clothes?' It's more than they have in their own country where they sleep on the floor. They are taking care nicely there."[14]

On the same day in October that Kirstjen Nielsen fretted about the insanity loosed, Trump appeared at a campaign rally in Missoula, Montana. It was less than three weeks until the midterms. "This will be an election of Kavanaugh, the caravan, law and order and common sense," he declared to cheers.[15] In other words, he would rally his base with grievance over the treatment of Brett Kavanaugh, never mind that he had been confirmed and now sat on the Supreme Court, and the threatening migrant horde from Latin America, never mind that the caravan was a crowd of impoverished men, women, and children still some two thousand miles away from the border and traveling on foot. There was little talk of accomplishments like tax cuts. Instead, it was the all-purpose Trump formula: anger, fear, and resentment.

The caravan that had seized Trump's attention started out as a collection of perhaps two hundred migrants heading north from Honduras into Guatemala toward Mexico and eventually the southwestern United States border. Such processions were not unheard of but rarely resulted in a mass crossing of the border—and had never received nonstop day-to-day television coverage as if they represented a genuine crisis. But rather than discouraging the would-be immigrants, the attention from Trump and Fox drew even more in, with crowds swelling into the thousands.

Many in Washington saw Trump's rhetoric as nothing more than a brazen political strategy to galvanize his conservative base. Some of the president's advisers, however, concluded that it was the other way around—that Fox was really ginning up the story and Trump was reacting to the network's reports. "He was petrified that the caravan was going to make him lose the election, it was going to be promises unkept," said one of Trump's top officials.

Either way, it became a self-perpetuating cycle. In the last two weeks of the campaign, Fox and Fox Business mentioned the caravan nearly eight times an hour, according to a count by the Internet Archive.[16] And Trump made it his primary talking point—an enemy for him to focus on right when he needed one. In private, he pounded on Kirstjen Nielsen and other advisers to do something to stop the migrants and paid no attention when told that he could not do everything he wanted. Nielsen explained to him that neither he nor she had the power to simply "close the border," as he kept demanding, because laws permitted those who made it to designated border crossings to claim asylum. Trump seemed indifferent not only to the law but to the simple economic reality that $500 billion in goods passed across the border each year.[17]

Days after Nielsen told him he could not close the border, Trump tweeted that Mexico must "stop this onslaught" and "if unable to do so I will call up the U.S. Military and CLOSE OUR SOUTHERN BORDER!" He then tweeted out a video supposedly showing someone affiliated with George Soros giving cash to the migrants, the latest in a long string of bizarre and untrue anti-Semitic attacks invoking the Jewish American billionaire circulated by Trump and his followers. "I wouldn't be surprised" if Soros was funding the caravan, Trump told reporters at the White House one morning, days before the election. "A lot of people say yes."[18] Trump also raised the specter of terrorism, tweeting that "Criminals and unknown Middle Easterners are mixed in" with economic migrants.[19] He had apparently picked that up from a comment by Pete Hegseth on *Fox & Friends*, even though Hegseth admitted when pressed by a cohost that "it hasn't been verified."[20] Trump was now blithely spreading conspiracy theories from the Oval Office, and who, after all, was there to stop him? By this point in his presidency, no one even tried.

As Trump ratcheted up the rhetoric, at least a couple Americans listening went even further. In Florida, a Trump supporter named Cesar Altieri Sayoc Jr. went after the president's perceived adversaries, mailing pipe bombs to at least a dozen Democrats and other high-profile figures. Among the targets were Soros as well as Barack Obama, Hillary Clinton, Joe Biden, and several lawmakers. Undisclosed at the time was that Sayoc had researched more potential victims online, including reporters covering Trump. None of the bombs went off and Sayoc was ultimately arrested. He evidently had been living in a white van plastered with pro-

Trump stickers, including an image of the president standing heroically in front of an American flag, a picture of Hillary Clinton in the crosshairs of a rifle, and a slogan that said, "CNN Sucks."

The day after Sayoc was taken into custody, a man yelling anti-Semitic slurs and armed with an AR-15-style assault rifle and several handguns opened fire inside a Pittsburgh synagogue, killing eleven worshippers and injuring several others, including police officers responding to the scene. "I just want to kill Jews," the gunman, Robert Bowers, called out before being captured.[21] For weeks, he had complained on social media that the president was surrounded by too many Jewish people and blamed Jews for helping the migrant caravan that Trump was warning about. Trump decried the violence and insisted on visiting the synagogue, disregarding Pittsburgh's mayor and many community leaders who said he was not welcome.

The pipe bombs and the slaughter at the Tree of Life Congregation called attention to the president's incendiary rhetoric and underscored how polarizing politics had become. While violent extremists existed across the political spectrum—an anti-Trump supporter of Senator Bernie Sanders had opened fire at a group of House Republicans at a baseball practice several months after Trump took office, injuring a congressman and four others—Trump had long inflamed his followers and personalized his conflicts with his critics. To the president, those opposing him were not just political adversaries, they were "evil" and "treasonous." In the wake of the back-to-back events that fall, Trump denounced the culprits but offered no concern about the tenor of the political dialogue and quickly began assailing Democrats again, including some of the bomber's targets.

Two days after the synagogue massacre, Trump doubled down on his crackdown on immigration, ordering 5,200 troops to the border—real troops to combat a fake invasion. This had been a point of contention for weeks, with Jim Mattis, John Kelly, and Kirstjen Nielsen resisting the deployment of the active-duty military. But Trump kept pushing, so Nielsen finally reached out to Mattis and told him that she had consulted with Border Patrol officials, who said they could use some help with support tasks. She said the troops could take over functions such as building barriers and transporting agents, freeing up the Border Patrol to deal with the migrants. Mattis was queasy but recalled that other presidents had sent troops to the border in similar secondary roles.

By the time Trump announced that he was sending in the military, the caravan had shrunk in half to around four thousand people and was still weeks away from the border. But coming barely a week before the election, the troop deployment allowed Trump to look like he was taking muscular action to defend America against brown-skinned "invaders" from the south.

Mattis insisted to reporters that in the military "we don't do stunts," but his speechwriter later admitted that "I knew that's *exactly* what he thought the situation was—a political stunt."[22] Many of Mattis's admirers were stunned that he had gone along with this overt politicization of the troops. Joe Dunford went along with it too, with both defense chiefs reasoning that the limits they put in place made the deployment acceptable.

Trump, however, was not satisfied. He wanted the troops to open fire. "They want to throw rocks at our military, our military fights back," he told reporters who asked about the rules of engagement. "I told them, 'Consider it a rifle.'"[23] Nielsen and the military leaders were alarmed. Kelly explained to the president that it was illegal and officers would refuse to obey an illegal order. "No, no," Trump told him, "they'll do anything I want." The rules of engagement, however, clearly stipulated that deadly force could be used only when facing "imminent danger of serious physical injury or death."[24] Eventually, the officials got Trump to walk it back. But a few days later he brought it up again.

They can't shoot to kill, he said, *but what about just to injure? Can't the troops just shoot them in the legs?*

No, Nielsen and the others said. They could not do that either.[25]

Shoot to kill, shoot in the leg—Trump had long entertained the harshest methods to stop immigrants, no matter how extreme, medieval, or even comical. This was the administration that was considering heat rays to burn border crossers. At one point, Trump suggested digging a moat along the border and even populating it with alligators. It became such a joke that one homeland security official noted wryly in a meeting that "it's not a greatest hits until he brings up sharks and alligators."

Trump's bravado aside, the political context of the military deployment was hard to miss, even at Fox News. "Tomorrow is one week before the election, which is what this is all about," Shepard Smith, one of the daytime news anchors who tried to avoid ideological punditry, told his audience. "There is no invasion. No one is coming to get you. There is nothing at all to worry about."[26]

Smith, though, was the exception at a network where the nighttime hosts with their opinion shows held the president's ear to a remarkable degree. Trump that fall had even taken to incorporating the Fox lineup into his official campaign rallies in a merger of politician and network that had no precedent.

It started in Council Bluffs, Iowa, a few days after Brett Kavanaugh was confirmed, when Trump referred to Democrats as "the Dims," a favorite term on Fox airwaves. That, of course, got him thinking, about all the conservative talkers whose rants filled his nights. He then ran through the entire Fox evening lineup, name by name, lavishing praise on each. "Who says that?" he asked. "Lou Dobbs, the great Lou Dobbs. He says that, right? Sean Hannity says that. The Dims. Sean Hannity."[27]

The crowd cheered.

"Judge Jeanine says that, doesn't she?" he went on.

The crowd cheered again.

"Laura—how good has Laura been, right?" he continued, referring to Laura Ingraham.

The crowd cheered some more.

"We got a lot of good people," he added. "Do we like Tucker?" he asked, referring to Tucker Carlson. "I like Tucker."

The crowd liked Tucker too.

He was not finished. "How about Steve Doocy?" he asked. "How about Ainsley, Brian?" That would be Ainsley Earhardt and Brian Kilmeade, hosts along with Doocy of his favorite morning show, *Fox & Friends.*

The crowd applauded its agreement.

"We got a lot of great friends," Trump concluded.

By the time he flew to Cape Girardeau, Missouri, the hometown of Rush Limbaugh, for a rally three weeks later, Trump took the act even further and invited a couple Fox hosts onstage with him along with Limbaugh. It was the Monday night before Election Day and Trump had just given Hannity an interview backstage featuring such hard questions as "You're not even tired, are you?" and "What do you want to say to Americans?" Hannity was afterward spotted high-fiving with Bill Shine, a long-time friend who had been forced out as co-president of Fox News in 2017 over his handling of sexual harassment scandals only to land at the White House as Trump's sixth and counting communications director.

Speaking in front of the crowd a few minutes later, Trump summoned the Fox host to join him onstage. "Do we love Sean?" he asked.

Hannity took the microphone. He began echoing Trump's favorite lines and even went after the journalists in the back of the arena, who happened to include a Fox crew. "All those people in the back are fake news," Hannity declared, not bothering to spare his own colleagues.

The crowd booed.

Hannity, who had said before the event that he "will not be onstage campaigning with the president," expressed surprise at being onstage campaigning with the president. "I had no idea you were going to invite me up here," he said to Trump, before going on to repeat the president's campaign slogan. "And the one thing that has defined your presidency more than anything else—promises made, promises kept."

After Hannity was done, the president introduced Jeanine Pirro, who, he said, "treats us very, very well." He invited her onstage too.

Pirro was just as enthusiastic as Hannity. "Do you like the fact that this man is the tip of the spear who goes out there every day and fights for us?" she asked the crowd.

Trump thanked her. "Jeanine has been a great, great friend to all of us."[28]

Back at Fox News headquarters in New York and at its bureau in Washington, some of its best-known figures in the news division bristled at being conflated with Trump's opinion show cheerleaders such as Hannity and Dobbs. To have the Fox hosts onstage with the president made it that much harder for the network to claim any independence. Roger Ailes would never have put up with it. Rupert Murdoch, in the old days, would not have either. When Hannity planned to attend a Tea Party rally in 2010, Murdoch pulled the plug, saying, "I don't think we should be supporting the Tea Party or any other party."[29]

At lunch in the Fox executive dining room on Election Day, several leading news operation figures—Chris Wallace, Bret Baier, Brit Hume, and Martha MacCallum—raised hell about the rally with Suzanne Scott, the chief executive of Fox News, and Jay Wallace, the network president. It was true that the lines were sometimes blurry, the anchors conceded. Baier, for one, had golfed with Trump, although he often complained to colleagues that he did not have the access or get the interviews with the president that the prime-time bunch did. Still, they insisted that this time Hannity and Pirro had gone too far; the lines were not just crossed but completely obliterated. Scott said it had been dealt with, which as far as the news anchors could tell meant absolutely nothing.

Scott released a statement calling the Hannity and Pirro appearances an "unfortunate distraction" and insisting that "Fox News does not condone any talent participating in campaign events."[30] But Hannity resented even this mild rebuke and did not show up to join the coverage of the midterm elections later that evening as scheduled.

The news side of Fox struck back in its own way that same night. As the early election returns began coming in, most of the other networks and news organizations were reporting that the Democrats looked to be falling short of their sky-high expectations. But the news team at Fox knew better. In the two years since everyone got the 2016 election so wrong, Fox had thrown out its old system for calling races and developed a new methodology with the Associated Press. As a result, on the night of November 6, 2018, the Fox analysts saw the true picture faster than their competitors and at 9:33 p.m., nearly fifty minutes before any of the other networks, Baier declared that the Democrats would win control of the House.

"A lot of listeners out there, their heads are exploding," Chris Wallace said on air. "But this is going to be a very different Washington."[31] He had that right too. While the Republicans held on to the Senate and even picked up a couple seats, they surrendered forty seats in the House. The lost majority would hang over the rest of Trump's presidency.

The thrashing of the Republicans represented a repudiation of Trump by an electorate that never favored him to begin with. For all of his blustering, chest-thumping rallies, Trump had never won the support of a majority of Americans, not at the ballot box in 2016 when he lost the popular tally by three million votes and not in any mainstream poll since then, all of which had shown his approval rating consistently in the 35 percent to 45 percent range and never once, not for a single day, above 50 percent.

Leading Democrats in the House back to a majority for the first time since 2010, Nancy Pelosi had made a point of focusing her candidates on bread-and-butter issues such as health care, and voters in key districts responded negatively to Trump's efforts to repeal the Affordable Care Act. Eighty percent of voters told Gallup that health care was extremely or very important in determining their choice and Democrats flooded the airwaves with ads on the topic.[32] In October, 57 percent of pro-Democratic television commercials focused on health care, according to the Wesleyan Media Project.[33] The Niskanen Center calculated that the vote to repeal the Obama program—although it ultimately failed due to John McCain's dramatic thumbs-down vote in the Senate—cost Republicans roughly 5 percentage points in their districts, enough to make the difference for many.[34] Trump's efforts to change the subject to immigration and Brett Kavanaugh did not prevent the "blue wave" in the House.

But Trump had benefited in one important respect. While there would be fewer Republicans in Congress, many of those who lost or left office were Trump skeptics, like Paul Ryan. In their place came a new generation pledging personal fealty to the president. In Missouri, Trump held three rallies in the final stretch—including his special appearance with his Fox friends—to help elect Josh Hawley, a fresh-faced Republican still in his thirties who campaigned for Senate with populist fervor as a Trump acolyte, railing against "the D.C. cartel" while downplaying his Stanford-and-Yale-Law-School pedigree. In Georgia, Brian Kemp, the state's secretary of state, won the governorship by declaring that "I strongly support President Trump, our troops and ironclad borders."[35] In Florida, the new governor, Ron DeSantis, distinguished himself with the year's most memorable pro-Trump ad. In the commercial, DeSantis was shown playing "build the wall" with his toddler daughter and reading *The Art of the Deal* to his infant son. The ad closed with an image of the baby squirming in his crib in a red "Make America Great Again" onesie.[36]

The ideological purging of the party had made it almost impossible for the anti-Trump voices that remained, a political reality underscored soon after the midterms when the owner of *The Weekly Standard,* a conservative journal founded decades earlier and run by Bill Kristol, now a leading Never Trumper, shut it down rather than let it keep criticizing the president, even refusing a buyout offer from James Murdoch, the estranged, anti-Trump son of the Fox tycoon.[37]

A major exception to the MAGAfication of the party came in Utah, where Mitt Romney easily won an open Senate seat. Trump had spent years dumping on the 2012 Republican presidential nominee and the animosity was mutual. In his campaign, Romney pledged to speak out if Trump did anything that was "divisive, racist, sexist, anti-immigrant, dishonest or destructive to democratic institutions."[38] Romney now looked to inherit from McCain the title of Trump's chief Republican antagonist.

Still, at a contentious hour-and-a-half news conference the day after the vote, Trump claimed a "great victory" because of the two-seat pickup in the Senate, while playing down the bigger political earthquake of losing the House.[39] It was true that the party of a newly elected president tended to lose House seats in the midterms, but the final tally of losses for Trump's Republicans was twice the historical average going back to the 1930s.[40]

Unlike Bill Clinton, George W. Bush, or Barack Obama, each of whom lost houses of Congress to the opposition in their first midterms, Trump displayed no humility over the defeat and insisted that "people like the job I'm doing, frankly." He warned the newly ascendant Democrats that he would adopt a "warlike posture" if they used their power to investigate him.

And he scorned the defeated Republicans, asserting that they lost because they did not embrace him, not because he weighed them down. "Mia Love gave me no love," he said of a defeated Republican congresswoman from Utah, his voice dripping with disdain. "And she lost. Too bad. Sorry about that, Mia."

Trump was in a cranky mood and lashed out at reporters. He told a Black journalist who asked if he had emboldened white supremacists by adopting the label "nationalist" that it was "such a racist question." He barked at another reporter, "Sit down. I didn't call on you."[41]

He did call on Jim Acosta from CNN, one of his favorite sparring partners, as if he were looking for a confrontation to distract from the election defeat. Acosta pressed him on the migrants. "As you know, Mr. President, the caravan is not an invasion," the reporter began, asking Trump if he had demonized immigrants. The two went back and forth before Trump finally cut him off and a White House intern tried to take the microphone away.

Acosta held on to the microphone and tried to ask another question, only to have Trump berate him. "You're a very rude person," the president scolded.

When NBC's Peter Alexander stuck up for Acosta, Trump said, "Well, I'm not a big fan of yours either."[42]

Hours later, in a brazen act of retribution unlike any taken by a modern White House, Trump's team suspended Acosta's press pass, which would eventually be returned only after a federal judge overruled the decision.

But Acosta was on point. With the election over, Trump abruptly stopped talking and tweeting about the menacing caravan. So did Fox News. Within weeks, the troops sent to guard the border started coming home. When some migrants eventually tried to cross into the United States, American border forces used tear gas to disperse the group. There never was an invasion.

CHAPTER 13

The Adults Have Left the Building

The morning after the congressional election, John Kelly called Jeff Sessions at the Justice Department. *I think it's coming,* Kelly warned him, "it" being the moment Trump would finally fire his estranged attorney general. Sessions turned on the television in his office to watch the news conference where Trump jousted with Jim Acosta and heard the president duck a question about his own fate. "I'd rather answer that at a little bit different time," Trump told reporters.[1]

As soon as the session with the media was over, Kelly called Sessions again. *It's done. I don't know where you are but get someplace where there aren't cameras on you because it's coming.* Sessions wanted to know if he could serve out the rest of the week. Kelly said no. Sessions hung up the phone and reported to his advisers: "It's happening. I'm going to get the tweet." Everyone understood instantly what The Tweet meant.

Sure enough, at 2:44 p.m., just eighty minutes after the news conference, Trump took to Twitter to announce that Sessions was out. Sarah Isgur, the attorney general's spokesperson, showed it to him on her phone. "We thank Attorney General Jeff Sessions for his service, and wish him well!" the president wrote, temporarily putting aside the vitriol of the past eighteen months.[2] The president never called Sessions nor gave any notice, a remarkable way of governing that had become so commonplace in Trump's high-turnover cabinet that it was no longer even remarked on. Sessions then sent an undated resignation letter he had already drafted over to the White House and left for home.

The defeat in the midterm campaign was, paradoxically, a moment of liberation for Trump, a chance to do what he had long wanted without the constraint of worrying about immediate electoral consequences. Rather than chastened by the voter rebuke, he felt free to move ahead as he saw fit. And that meant getting rid of more faithless officials. Trump was in a constant search for a staff that would do what he wanted, when he wanted it—impediments, legal and otherwise, be damned. To that end, firing Sessions would be the start of a year-end purge to match the previous spring's bloodletting, one in which he would also dump his White House chief of staff and anger his defense secretary so much that he would become the first Pentagon chief to quit in protest since the job was created. And once again, their replacements would be weaker, or at least more pliable, than those who had come before. Where other presidents pummeled by midterm setbacks pivoted to the center to make bipartisan deals and brought in staff who could help toward that end, Trump took the opposite lesson. He wanted more power over his White House and more confrontation with his enemies. The Divider became more firmly convinced that divisiveness was the way to go.

The end for Sessions came after months of battering by the president he served. Behind closed doors, Trump had nicknamed Sessions "Mr. Magoo" and derided him as a "dumb Southerner" and "mentally retarded."[3] In public, he had denigrated Sessions as "beleaguered" and "VERY weak," termed his handling of the Justice Department "DISGRACEFUL," and even questioned his masculinity. "What kind of man is this?" he asked on Fox News.[4] Sessions took the beatings without responding and never stopped looking for ways to please the president. He made the mistake of thinking that policy mattered to Trump and figured he would eventually smooth things over since they were in sync on every issue other than his recusal from the Russia investigation. Sessions brushed off friends like Ed Rogers, one of the city's biggest lobbyists, who recommended that he resign. "You see what I just did on sanctuary cities?" Sessions would respond. "We're making progress. You'd be surprised—Trump still needs me over here." He was encouraged to tough it out by allies in the White House. Whenever Trump volleyed another shot at him, Kelly or Don McGahn called to urge him to proceed as if nothing were amiss. Again and again, the president's aides told a cabinet secretary to ignore what the president was saying.

When Trump in the summer of 2017 instructed Corey Lewandowski to go to the attorney general personally and tell him to reassert control over the Russia investigation or be fired, Rogers got word to Sessions, who then ducked the unofficial envoy for days. Lewandowski tried to pawn off the assignment on another adviser and never ended up seeing the attorney general. Rarely did Sessions push back, and even then, only gently. After the president said during an interview in the summer of 2018 that the attorney general had failed to take control of the Justice Department, Sessions issued a statement saying that in fact he "took control of the Department of Justice the day I was sworn in" and would not bend to partisan demands. "While I am Attorney General, the actions of the Department of Justice will not be improperly influenced by political considerations."[5]

But Sessions was not long for the job by that point. Lindsey Graham, who had once drawn a red line around Sessions and warned that there would be "holy hell to pay" if Trump fired the attorney general, reversed course and essentially gave the president permission. "The president's entitled to an attorney general he has faith in, somebody that's qualified for the job," Graham told reporters that August, "and I think there will come a time, sooner rather than later, where it will be time to have a new face and a fresh voice at the Department of Justice. Clearly, Attorney General Sessions doesn't have the confidence of the president."[6] So much for holy hell.

Even before finally pulling the trigger on Sessions, Trump had been going after the attorney general's staff. Three times, Sarah Isgur, the Justice Department spokesperson, was targeted for dismissal by the White House because of her public comments defending her boss. The last time came after the skirmish over Trump's assertion that Sessions was not really in control of his department. Summoned to the White House to answer for Isgur, Rod Rosenstein, the deputy attorney general, explained that he did not have the authority to fire her and that the president's staff would have to take that up with Sessions, who had made clear he would resign first. Isgur opted against stepping down on her own. "They were going after me to get to him," she said. "So I felt I had to stay on." Finally, White House officials figured a way around the problem. They simply *told* the president that Isgur had been fired, even though she had not. To sell the ruse, Isgur was instructed by Rosenstein not to put her name on further media statements so as not to draw Trump's attention. In a plot line right out of a Washington satire, the president's team concluded that lying to him was the only way to placate him.

But Trump was soon angry with Sessions again. A few weeks later, he publicly chastised Sessions because the Justice Department had filed corruption charges against two Republican congressmen, Chris Collins of New York and Duncan Hunter of California. Collins, accused of securities fraud, and Hunter, accused of misusing campaign funds to buy everything from family vacations in Italy to plane flights for the family's pet bunny rabbit, had been among the earliest members of Congress to endorse Trump. Trump saw the indictments entirely through the lens of the upcoming elections. "Two easy wins now in doubt," Trump tweeted. "Good job Jeff."

Sessions stood firm on the charges. But with the midterms around the corner, he came to the realization that his time was short and began working on a plan to exit on his own terms. The idea that he and his advisers came up with was to give Mike Pence a resignation letter and let the vice president decide when to submit it to Trump. Sessions had a good relationship with Pence and like others in the cabinet relied on the vice president to help navigate Trump's moods. But in the days leading up to the midterms, Sessions did not connect with Pence, who was traveling, and never got to execute his plan.

When Trump finally did fire Sessions, neither Lindsey Graham nor any of the other Republicans who once said that would be unacceptable offered any meaningful protest. As acting attorney general, Trump installed Matthew Whitaker, who had been serving as Sessions's chief of staff but was seen by the Sessions team as an ear-to-the-door White House spy. Whitaker, a former college football tight end who had served as United States attorney in Iowa and later lost a race for Senate, had drawn public attention before joining the administration mainly by questioning the scope of Mueller's investigation. As soon as he took over from Sessions, the first thing Whitaker did was vow not to repeat his predecessor's mistake—he would not recuse himself from the Russia inquiry as Sessions had.

But Trump had someone else in mind to take the position permanently. On Election Day, even before Sessions had been tweeted out of the job, Emmet Flood, one of Trump's White House lawyers, showed up at the office of former attorney general William Barr. On behalf of the president, he had a question to ask.

A couple days later, Trump boarded Air Force One to fly to Paris for ceremonies marking the hundredth anniversary of the end of World War I. Other presidents relished the opportunity to get out of the country after a bad midterm not only to escape domestic troubles but to assert themselves on the international stage. Bill Clinton, George W. Bush, and Barack Obama had each jetted off to Asia following elections that turned over one or both houses to the opposition.

Not Trump. He was never all that enthusiastic about foreign travel and had to be talked into making the trip to France by John Kelly. The White House chief of staff had an ulterior motive that had nothing to do with the midterm elections, or even international diplomacy, but said much about the challenge of managing Trump: he secretly regarded the trip as the perfect excuse to avoid having to finally stage that military parade in the streets of Washington that Trump kept badgering him and the generals about. France's World War I commemoration would coincide with Veterans Day in the United States, the date Trump had most recently demanded for his parade. Kelly realized the invitation to Paris for the holiday was the way to subvert the president's plan. "You have to go to France," Kelly told Trump. "You will be a rock star. The whole world will worship you if you go."

No one loved being worshipped more than Trump. He said yes. But when the moment came, he was in a foul mood because of the election results. He became more irritable during the flight over the Atlantic. Just three minutes after touching down at Orly Airport, he tweeted that his host, Emmanuel Macron, had been "very insulting" in a recent interview by talking about the need for a European army to make the allies less reliant on the United States. Trump grew even grouchier when he saw that he was scheduled to visit not one but two cemeteries where American soldiers killed in World War I had been buried.

"Why do I have to go to two?" Trump asked.

"Because that's what you're here for," Kelly answered.

"I don't want to go to two," Trump said.

"The press is going to kill you if you don't go," Kelly said.

"I don't care," the president responded.

As Kelly later related the story to colleagues, Trump seized on a convenient excuse to cancel going to the first one, the Aisne-Marne American Cemetery at the foot of the hill where the Battle of Belleau Wood was fought. A rain shower made flying by helicopter problematic and traveling by car would take two hours and snarl Parisian traffic.

As predicted, Trump's cancellation generated a huge uproar while other leaders, including Macron, Angela Merkel, and Justin Trudeau, ignored the drizzle to attend their own commemorative events around Paris. Kelly and Joe Dunford went to Belleau Wood without Trump, breaking away from the official event to scatter ashes from the place in Afghanistan where Kelly's son had been killed in the war. Trump did visit another cemetery the next day, but it was too late. The damage was done, and he raged that no one had told him he should go, which infuriated Kelly even more because of course he had.

As for Macron, who had tried so hard to charm Trump in their early encounters, he had by now given up. The two leaders shook hands politely and patted each other on the arm stiffly. Their tight-lipped smiles were strained. When it came time for the big ceremony, dozens of leaders walked together in solemn solidarity down the Champs-Élysées to the Arc de Triomphe, while Trump arrived separately by car, isolating himself from his peers and snubbing his host. The America First president, who had called himself a "nationalist" during the midterm campaign at home, then sat and stewed as Macron pointedly reproached him in a speech marking the anniversary. "Patriotism is the exact opposite of nationalism," Macron declared without naming Trump. "Nationalism is a betrayal of patriotism by saying: 'Our interest first. Who cares about the others?'"[7]

The trip proved a breaking point not just with Macron, whom Trump predictably assailed in response to the speech, but also with Kelly. The chief of staff was appalled by Trump's behavior. The president had long scorned soldiers in private, much as he had expressed disdain for John McCain's combat service. "Anyone who went to that war was a sucker," Trump had once said about Vietnam, as Kelly recounted it to colleagues. "I don't know why you guys think these guys who get killed or wounded are heroes. They're losers." When Trump at one point accompanied Kelly to visit his son's grave in Arlington Memorial Cemetery, the president said he could not understand why anyone would give up his life in a war. Kelly told colleagues that Trump seemed genuinely perplexed at the notion of sacrifice for something greater than oneself.

Kelly later asserted that the real reason that Trump did not want to go to the Paris cemetery was that the president did not want his hair mussed by the rain and he claimed that the president called the Marines buried there "suckers" for getting killed.[8] Trump denied saying that when Jeffrey Goldberg later reported it in *The Atlantic* and several aides with the president at the time said they never heard him say it. But other associates acknowledged that he had referred to slain soldiers using similar terms in other settings.

In any case, the relationship between Trump and Kelly was broken. The president had long been preparing to push out his chief of staff and had waited, as with Sessions, until after the election to do it. He spent part of the France trip quizzing associates about who should take Kelly's place.

It all came to a head on December 7, when Trump, over the course of just a few hours, made what were arguably three of the most consequential decisions of his presidency. He resolved, at last, to fire the White House chief of staff and to make sure he did not get another one who would try to restrain him. He named a new attorney general he expected to serve, finally, as his Roy Cohn, protecting him from federal investigators and going after his political enemies. And he selected a new commander of the American military he hoped would end the resistance at the Pentagon and put the armed forces more securely under his control. None of the decisions would work out quite as he planned.

Trump announced the nomination of Bill Barr for attorney general as he headed to his helicopter that morning for a quick trip to Kansas City, praising him as "a terrific person, a brilliant man."[9] At the same time, Trump announced that he would nominate Heather Nauert, a former Fox News anchor serving as the chief State Department spokesperson, for the United Nations position being vacated by Nikki Haley, although her appointment would ultimately fall through. Neither of the nominees was by the president's side as would have been customary in other administrations. It was just Trump, as usual, keeping himself at the center of the action.

Barr was an intriguing choice. Stout and jowly with graying hair and a low-key, unflappable manner, Barr at sixty-eight was a member of the Republican establishment that Trump disdained. A New Yorker by birth and education who used to play the bagpipes and started his career as a CIA analyst, Barr later served as a lawyer in Ronald Reagan's White House and in a series of positions in George H. W. Bush's Justice Department before becoming his last attorney general. After leaving office, Barr worked as a corporate lawyer making millions at GTE and later Verizon. His calm demeanor left many who did not know him with the impression that he was a moderate like Bush, but in fact Barr was a staunch conservative who believed in a strong "unitary" executive branch unfettered by Congress or the courts.

Trump was not exactly Barr's kind of Republican. "He has a long history of acting like an asshole," Barr once observed in characteristic deadpan style. While he had lived in a Verizon-owned apartment in one of Trump's buildings in New York for four years, Barr had never met the president until 2017, when David Friedman, Trump's former bankruptcy lawyer now serving as ambassador to Israel, introduced them in an apparent bid to get the former attorney general to represent the president in the special counsel investigation. Barr was shocked at that get-acquainted meeting to hear Trump openly trash-talk nearly everyone on his staff and did not join the legal team.

But Barr had been impressed with the way Trump rolled over the competition in 2016 and sympathized with his grievances about the Russia investigation. "I smelled a rat with the Russia-gate stuff," Barr later said. He thought James Comey "had an agenda" and he "suspected some foul play was at work" in the decision to investigate the Trump campaign. In the spring of 2018, Barr took it upon himself to draft an unsolicited nineteen-page memo criticizing Robert Mueller's "grossly irresponsible" investigation. "I am writing as a former official deeply concerned with the institutions of the Presidency and the Department of Justice," Barr wrote in the memo, which he sent on June 8 to Rod Rosenstein and Assistant Attorney General Steve Engel. Barr argued vigorously that the special counsel had no business investigating Trump for obstruction of justice in connection with the Comey firing because the president had been acting within his constitutional authority. "It is time to travel well-worn paths; not to veer into novel, unsettled or contested areas of the law; and not to indulge the fancies by overly-zealous prosecutors," Barr wrote. Even if Trump had cashiered Comey to protect himself from investigators, Barr added, "there is no *legal* prohibition—as opposed to a political constraint—against the President's acting on a matter in which he has a political stake."[10]

Trump later gave typically conflicting answers as to whether he examined the memo himself. "I read it afterwards," he told *The New York Times*, only to contradict himself moments later by saying, "I didn't see the memo. I never read the memo."[11] Either way, it was enough to make Barr Trump's first choice to replace Sessions.

When Emmet Flood, the White House lawyer, showed up at Barr's office on Election Day to ask if he would take his old job, Barr initially said no. But friends urged him to reconsider, including Abbe Lowell, the Democratic lawyer representing Jared Kushner, who thought Barr would bring needed credibility and gravitas to the post. As he mulled it over, Barr became convinced that Trump needed his help, that the department had been buffeted by politics from both sides of the aisle, and that he could help stabilize it. So he changed his mind and told the White House he would accept the nomination if offered. Two days before it was announced, he tested his decision at George H. W. Bush's funeral with old colleagues like Bob Gates and Brent Scowcroft, who encouraged him to take the job to safeguard the Justice Department.

As Trump was hiring a general for the Justice Department, he was replacing one at the Pentagon. For months, he had been contemplating a successor to Joe Dunford, the Joint Chiefs chairman who had quietly resisted some of the president's more outlandish ideas, and now was settling on a four-star Army officer named Mark Milley. Never mind that Dunford still had most of a year to go in his term. Dunford would now share the distinction of being effectively dumped by Trump on the same day as his friend John Kelly.

Trump's love affair with "my generals" was long over. He was sick and tired of all the "yes, sirs" that never seemed to get him what he wanted. He would yell at Kelly about it often. "You fucking generals, why can't you be like the German generals?" he once demanded of his White House chief of staff, who relayed the story to associates.

"Which generals?" an incredulous Kelly had asked.

"The German generals in World War II," Trump responded.

"You do know that they tried to kill Hitler three times and almost pulled it off?" Kelly said.

But, of course, Trump did not. "No, no, no, they were totally loyal to him," the president replied. In his mind, the generals had been completely subservient to the Nazi dictator—and this was the model he wanted for his own military. Kelly told Trump there were no such generals in America, but the president was determined to test the proposition.

For months, Dave Urban, the lobbyist and Trump campaign adviser, had been urging the president and his inner circle to replace Dunford with a more like-minded chairman less aligned with Mattis. Urban, a former football player who served in the 101st Airborne Division during the Gulf War, was still an Army man at heart and had grown close to Mike Pompeo, the West Point classmate he had recommended to Trump for the CIA at the start of the administration.

Jim Mattis's candidate to succeed Dunford was an Air Force general named David Goldfein, a former F-16 fighter pilot who had once been shot down in the Balkans and successfully evaded capture. He trusted Goldfein, and they had worked closely together when Mattis ran Central Command. No one could remember a president selecting a chairman over the objections of his defense secretary, but it fell to John Bolton, already barely on speaking terms with Mattis, to relay the word back to the Pentagon that there was no way Trump would accept just a single recommendation. Two obvious contenders from the Army, however, declined to be considered: General Curtis Scaparrotti, the supreme allied commander in Europe, told fellow officers there was "no gas left in my tank" to deal with being Trump's chairman, while General Joseph Votel, the Central Command chief, begged off as well, telling a colleague he was not a good fit to work that closely with Mattis.

Urban's candidate, Milley, currently the chief of staff of the Army, was a bulldog of an Army general, a plainspoken sixty-year-old history buff and son of a Navy corpsman who served with the Fourth Marine Division in Iwo Jima. After growing up north of Boston, he and his brother both went on to play Ivy League hockey—Milley at Princeton, his brother at Harvard. Like his father, Milley then joined the military, where he eventually commanded troops in Afghanistan and Iraq, led the Tenth Mountain Division, and oversaw the Army Forces Command.

Urban had nothing against the reserved Dunford and considered him an honorable officer, but told the president he would connect better with Milley, who was loquacious, blunt to the point of being rude, and pedigreed in the way that always impressed Trump. Milley had already demonstrated that in meetings with Trump while Army chief. "Milley would go right at why it's important for the president to know this about the Army and why the Army is the service that wins all the nation's wars—he had all those sort of elevator-speech punchlines," a senior defense official recalled. "He would have that big bellowing voice and be right in his face with all the one-liners, and then he would take a breath and he would say, 'Mr. President, our Army is here to serve you. Because you're the commander in chief.' It was a very different approach and Trump liked that." Like Trump, Milley was also not a subscriber to the legend of Mattis, whom he considered a "complete control freak."

At the Pentagon, Mattis believed Milley was improperly campaigning for the job and confronted him at a reception that fall.

"Hey, you shouldn't run for office," Mattis told him. "You shouldn't run to be the chairman."

As Milley later told the story to colleagues, he replied: "I'm not lobbying for any fucking thing. I don't do that. That's not me."

Mattis was not convinced. Eventually, Milley raised the issue with Dunford. "Hey, Mattis has got this in his head," Milley told him. "I'm telling you it ain't me." Milley even claimed he had begged Urban to knock it off.

But if Dunford was inclined to give Milley the benefit of the doubt, others were not. In November, the day before Milley's interview with Trump at the White House, he and Mattis had another unpleasant encounter at the Pentagon. As Milley recounted the episode later to others, Mattis urged Milley to tell Trump that he wanted to be the next NATO supreme allied commander in Europe, rather than Joint Chiefs chairman. Milley said he would not do that but would wait to hear what the president wanted him to do instead. This was the end of whatever relationship they had.

When Milley got to the White House the next day, no one knew that John Kelly's tenure was about to end, but the chief of staff seemed particularly distraught when they met before heading into the Oval Office with Trump.

"Jim wants you to go to Europe," Kelly told Milley, "and the president wants you to be his chairman."

Milley asked Kelly what he thought.

"You should go to Europe and just get the fuck out of D.C.," Kelly replied bitterly. It was a cesspool and Trump was very, very hard to work for. "Just get as far away as you can."

In the Oval Office, only the three of them were present, just Trump, Kelly, and Milley. To Trump, here was a guy straight out of central casting and he said right from the start that he was considering Milley for chairman. This time, there was no talk of getting the fuck out of D.C. and Milley did not resist. When Trump then offered him the job, Milley replied, "Mr. President, I'll do whatever you ask me to do."

For the next hour, they talked about the state of the world. Trump might have been surprised that his new chief military adviser was not entirely in agreement with him. On Afghanistan, Milley believed that pulling out all troops, as Trump still wanted to do, would cause a whole new set of problems. On Trump's insistence on banning transgender troops, Milley had already spoken out publicly against it.

"Mattis tells me you are weak on transgender," Trump said.

"No, I am not weak on transgender," Milley replied. "I just don't care who sleeps with who."

There were other differences as well. But in the end, Milley assured him, "Mr. President, you're going to be making the decisions. All I can guarantee from me is I'm going to give you an honest answer and I'm not going to talk about it on the front page of *The Washington Post*. I'll give you an honest answer on everything I can. And you're going to make the decisions and as long as they're legal I'll support it."

As long as they're legal. It was not clear how much that caveat even registered with Trump. He did not seem too concerned about Milley. The decision was a rare chance, as Trump saw it, to get back at Mattis. Trump would confirm this years later, after falling out with both, saying in a statement that he had picked Milley only because Mattis "could not stand him, had no respect for him, and would not recommend him."[12]

Late the evening of December 7, Trump announced he would reveal a big personnel decision having to do with the Joint Chiefs the next day at the 119th annual Army-Navy Game. This was all the notice that Dunford had that he was about to be publicly humiliated. He had served more than forty years in uniform and he spent the night considering not showing up at the game.

In the end, Dunford decided to attend and even go out of his way to stand alongside Milley to be photographed together and to "make clear that there was no daylight between us," as he told colleagues, regardless of Trump's divide-and-conquer aims.

The next morning, while waiting for the president to arrive at the game, Dunford was standing with Milley when Dave Urban, the lobbyist who set it all in motion, showed up. Urban hugged Milley as Dunford watched. "We did it!" Urban exulted. "We did it!"

But it was not even the day's biggest news. As Trump headed to Marine One to fly to Philadelphia for the game, he dropped another surprise. "John Kelly will be leaving toward the end of the year," Trump told reporters.[13] Kelly had lasted seventeen months in what he would always call "the worst fucking job in the world." But at least now the drama of the president and the chief of staff who hated each other was over.

Finding someone to take over the White House staff, however, proved more of a challenge than the president anticipated. The next week would become an embarrassing public demonstration of just how hard it had become for him to recruit top-flight talent, especially in a role that seemed predestined for failure.

Long before pushing Kelly out, Trump had been plotting behind his back to replace him with Nick Ayers, the vice president's chief of staff. A native Georgian with a slow Southern accent and a quick political mind, Ayers at thirty-six was half Kelly's age. When Trump first broached the idea of replacing Kelly, Ayers was wary but open to it and sat down to map out what he would do with the job. Jared Kushner and Ivanka Trump, sworn enemies of Kelly by that point, were supportive too.

Ayers had worked his way up through Georgia politics, helping various Republicans get elected and then running the Republican Governors Association before joining Mike Pence's re-election campaign for governor in Indiana. Accompanying Pence to the White House, he had guided the new vice president through the first couple years of his relationship with Trump and come to admire the president's determination and break-the-crystal approach to politics. He claimed to believe that Trump was perhaps the most effective conservative president ever and would one day win the Nobel Peace Prize. But he had also watched two chiefs of staff fail and planned to learn from their mistakes. Reince Priebus, in his mind, should never have been chosen. Priebus wanted everyone to like him, or at least say good things about him; a good chief of staff needed to be respected, not liked, and had to be tough enough to piss people off. Kelly had no problem pissing people off but seemed to go out of his way to make one of them the president. As Ayers saw it, Kelly had gone to war with Trump and tried to turn the staff against the president as well. Nor was Kelly able to execute, in Ayers's opinion.

As he contemplated taking over for Kelly, Ayers drafted a seven-page plan to get the White House on track. Because of the train wreck of a transition nearly two years earlier, the staff was filled with a lot of people that the president did not know or did not trust or who were not aligned with him on policy. It was also deeply divided into at least six or seven warring factions. The core of Ayers's plan was to systematically get rid of problem actors and create a team of loyalists.

"Wow, you want to make a lot of changes," Trump said when Ayers showed him the plan.

Ayers said there was no choice. There were too many people leaking and looking out for themselves. "It's not that they're bad people," Ayers said. "But they're not going to be here."

Over the course of several months, Trump talked with Ayers about the job perhaps ten or fifteen times and each time the president agreed to go along with his plan but then would back off and urge Ayers to take the job without major changes.

"Let's not actually do that plan," Trump would say.

"What do you mean?" Ayers would respond. "I've laid out a whole team for your success."

"Fuck, Nick, you are so fucking stubborn. Let's talk about it tomorrow."

This went on throughout the fall. Trump would agree but then Ayers would not hear anything for two or three weeks. Finally, the second weekend of December, after Kelly's dismissal had been made public, the deal was done. Sarah Huckabee Sanders had drafted a news release announcing Ayers's appointment and called on Saturday night to say the president was ready to put it out. But the next morning, Trump asked to see Ayers.

Kelly, he told Ayers, wanted a transition where the two would work side by side for a while. Ayers rejected that. It was untenable. Finally, Ayers gave up. He had laid out what he would need for the job. He was not negotiating anymore. If Trump did not want him to do it that way, then the president should have someone who saw things the same way. Ayers told Trump that he would not take the job after all—and not only that, he would leave the White House altogether. After leaving the Oval Office, Ayers stopped by Kelly's office to let him know. To Kelly, Ayers looked white as a ghost, as if he had been shocked by something that had convinced him he needed to get away as fast as he could.

For Trump, it was an embarrassing setback, so he turned to an ally he could count on: Chris Christie, who had completed his tenure as New Jersey governor earlier in the year. This time, Trump secured Jared Kushner's agreement, however grudging, to accept Christie if he became chief of staff. Trump called and asked Christie to come to Washington right away.

Guessing what Trump had in mind, Christie first called James Baker, the former two-time chief of staff, for advice, much as Reince Priebus once had. Baker understood that no one could succeed as this president's chief of staff, so he advised Christie to make a list of conditions. "What you need to do is put it in writing," Baker said.

Christie did just that. On a white sheet of lined paper, he took dictation as Baker rattled off nine demands. Among them were having the authority to attend any meeting, to decide who was on the staff, to determine who was allowed into the Oval Office, and to have a personal representative at the campaign—the kinds of stipulations that Baker or any other chief of staff might require. Several of his recommended conditions, though, were particular to Trump's dysfunctional White House:

* I GET TO MANAGE THE STAFF, WITH THE EXCEPTION OF JARED AND IVANKA. ON JARED AND IVANKA, POTUS DETERMINES ROLE; COS NEEDS TO BE FULLY INFORMED ON THEIR ACTIVITIES.
* COS CONTROLS HIS PUBLIC APPEARANCES WITH ASSUMPTION BEING COS IS BEHIND THE SCENES PLAYER NOT A TV STAR.
* ALL DISPUTES/DISAGREEMENT BETWEEN COS & POTUS TO BE SETTLED IN PRIVATE; NO PUBLIC STATEMENTS OF DISSATISFACTION OR CRITICISM.
* ATTORNEY PAID FOR BY RNC TO ADVISE ON VARIOUS ISSUES.

"If you get all those things, you start to think hard about whether you're willing to do this or not," Baker advised. "If you do, let me say one thing for you, son. I salute you because you're a fucking patriot, because this is the worst job in Washington."

On the train ride down to Washington that Thursday, Christie kept going back and forth in his mind. He knew the risks, he knew Trump's erratic behavior as well as anyone, yet he told himself the same things that Priebus and Kelly and Mattis and H. R. McMaster and Rex Tillerson had told themselves. Later, he admitted, he too was subject to "that disease that can afflict everyone who gets close to him, which is 'I can make the difference.'"

When he arrived in Washington, Christie was escorted into the Yellow Oval Room upstairs in the family quarters to meet with the president and first lady.

"I should have done this from the beginning," Trump said, flattering Christie. "I should never have had Reince or Kelly. You were the right guy from the beginning." But, he acknowledged, Kushner's objection and the lingering fallout from the Bridgegate scandal kept him from doing it.

Christie handed Trump the piece of paper with Baker's conditions. Of the nine points, Trump objected to only one—the notion that the chief of staff would not be on television much. To Trump, that was a dealbreaker. The whole point of having a staff was to have people on television defending him and attacking his critics.

"Whenever I want you on TV, you have to go on," Trump insisted.

"I'm not saying I'll never go on when we really, really need it," Christie said. "But if I'm to be effective, I have to be more staff and less chief."

"Nah, I can't do that one," Trump said.

Melania had just one question for Christie. "How do you intend to handle Jared and Ivanka?" she asked.

"I don't," Christie said.

But before he could go further, Trump scolded the first lady. "What do you ask him that stuff for?" he asked. "I told you that I spoke to Jared and Ivanka. They're both fine."

"Excuse me, Donald," Melania shot back. "I didn't ask you. I asked the governor."

"I wouldn't deal with them at all," Christie said. He had always thought it was a bad idea to have family members on the staff because a president could not fire them. "It was your decision not anybody else's, so they're your responsibility. All I want to know is what they're doing, once a week. I don't even need to meet with them. They can send me an email once a week."

Trump said that was fine. "Are you in?"

Christie said he had to talk with his wife first.

Trump paid that no mind and acted as if it were a done deal. "This is going to be great," he said, putting his arm around Christie's shoulders. "You and I back together as a team. The country doesn't know what they're getting in for now, with me and you. The two toughest guys in politics."

Trump headed down to a Christmas party while Melania walked Christie out.

"You know I love you?" she said.

"I do, Melania."

"Think hard," she said. "Just because I asked my question for a reason."

Back in New Jersey the next morning, Christie got a text message from Kushner, who had told Trump he would be willing to work with the former governor and was reaching out to let him know that. But not long after, Christie's phone rang. It was Don McGahn calling with a warning. "I just want to tell you, as crazy as you think it is, multiply it times one hundred," he said. "And that's the way it is, every day, every day."

From Christie's point of view, the whole thing felt off. And on top of that, word was leaking out; the reporter Jonathan Swan published an item in *Axios* about it. How did that happen when the only three people in the room were the president, first lady, and Christie?

Christie decided to say no. But then the question arose—how do you say no to Trump without letting him trash you? Once he turned the president down, there could easily be a tweet twisting the whole thing. So Christie came up with a contingency plan. He drafted a tweet of his own saying he had taken himself out of consideration and called Maggie Haberman at *The New York Times* to tell her what was happening. He would send her the draft tweet so she could put out the news the minute he posted it. Then he called Trump and told him his decision. It was midday on December 14.

"You know what this means?" Trump said unhappily. "I'm going to have to give it to Mulvaney."

Unlike Christie or Nick Ayers, Mick Mulvaney, the budget director, had made no secret that he badly wanted the job. But Trump told Christie that he would make Mulvaney the *acting* chief for only three months, at which point Christie could still come in.

Christie said he would always be willing to listen. But then he wanted to clear up one other matter. That *Axios* report? "I didn't talk to anybody," Christie said.

"Oh no, I know you didn't," Trump replied.

"How do you know I didn't?"

"Because I did it," Trump said. "I called Jonathan myself."

The president himself was the leak? Don McGahn had been right. It was crazier than anyone realized.

For Trump, the decision was a turning point. Instead of another strong-willed chief of staff who might have told him no, the president gravitated toward one who would basically say only yes. Already on his way out, Kelly made a last-ditch effort to persuade Trump not to go with Mulvaney.

"You don't want to hire someone who's going to be a yes-man," Kelly told the president.

"I don't give a shit anymore," Trump replied. "I want a yes-man!"

By day's end, Mulvaney, Trump's last choice, would indeed only be given the title with an *acting* in front of it, taken almost universally as a signal that the president did not really want him and was still hoping to find someone else. Mulvaney swallowed the indignity, insisting it did not matter because in Trump's administration everyone served at the pleasure of the president and essentially was only acting.

A zealous budget-cutting former congressman from South Carolina who had helped found the renegade House Freedom Caucus, Mulvaney like other Republicans originally saw Trump as a danger to the Constitution and one of the most flawed people ever to run for the White House. Trump, he had said in 2016, was "a terrible human being" with a record of saying "disgusting and indefensible" things about women.[14] Yet when the chance to join Trump's White House as budget director arose, Mulvaney eagerly sought it out, developing a case of selective amnesia and proving surprisingly willing to sacrifice past positions as the budget deficit swelled from $665 billion to $984 billion in Trump's first two years in office.[15]

But he was a product of neither the Republican establishment like Reince Priebus nor the military hierarchy like John Kelly and he set out to do his new job differently than either of them. Rather than try to manage the president and curb his excesses, Mulvaney resolved to let Trump be Trump.

A week before Christmas, Trump announced that he was pulling all American troops out of northern Syria, where they had been fighting the Islamic State alongside Kurdish allies. The withdrawal was a favor to Turkey's Recep Tayyip Erdoğan, who wanted a clear path to go after the Kurds, the cross-border allies of the separatists within Turkey that Erdoğan was determined to eliminate. The abrupt decision after yet another phone call with Erdoğan caused an uproar across Washington, especially at the Pentagon, where Jim Mattis was outraged. He had just returned from a trip where he had reassured American allies that the United States was committed to keeping troops in Syria. Now he felt completely undercut.

Since summer, Mattis had been quietly talking about leaving by the end of the year. For months, his long-term schedule included no events after December and he was wearing down the pages of his copy of Marcus Aurelius's book on meditations trying to deal with the stress. But the betrayal of the Kurds was the tipping point. He printed out the ready-to-go letter of resignation that he, like so many in Trump's administration, had spent hours writing and rewriting just in case, and brought it with him to the White House, where he made one last effort to convince Trump to change his mind. After failing to do so, Mattis handed him the letter. Like Chris Christie, he feared how Trump would spin the decision, so Mattis promptly returned to the Pentagon and instructed aides to print out fifty copies of the resignation letter and spread it far and wide.

The decision was the first time a major cabinet secretary had resigned in protest over a national security dispute with the president in nearly four decades, since Secretary of State Cyrus Vance quit in 1980 over Jimmy Carter's decision to authorize an ill-fated military operation to rescue hostages held in Iran. In his letter, Mattis avoided saying outright that he was leaving because of objections to Trump while making perfectly clear that was exactly what he was doing. "We must do everything possible to advance an international order that is most conducive to our security, prosperity and values, and we are strengthened in this effort by the solidarity of our alliances," Mattis wrote. "Because you have the right to have a Secretary of Defense whose views are better aligned with yours on these and other subjects, I believe it's right for me to step down from my position."[16]

Trump had not bothered to read the letter and missed the jab until he saw media coverage pointing it out. Realizing that he had been dissed, Trump abruptly announced that he would install Patrick Shanahan, the deputy defense secretary, as acting secretary as of January 1 rather than wait until the February 28 departure date Mattis had set, effectively pushing him out the door two months early. Only Trump would fire someone who had already quit.

Pointed as Mattis's letter was, it did not catalogue the many ways he had grown frustrated with the president. He had resisted Trump's efforts to withdraw from Afghanistan, abandon the Iran nuclear agreement, ban transgender troops from the military, cancel military exercises with South Korea and pull out troops or dependents, undercut or even leave NATO, and conduct a military parade down the streets of Washington. More broadly, Mattis thought Trump was wildly reckless, oddly blind to the threat posed by Russia, and irresponsibly cavalier about America's international commitments. The two had grown so estranged that Trump publicly branded the grizzled Marine "sort of a Democrat," which was akin to an accusation of treason in his administration.[17] When a congressman that fall asked how things were going, Mattis had replied, "Well, every morning I get up and I go up to my driver and I say, 'Did they fire me?' And if he says no, I get in the car and I go to work." Everyone including Mattis knew his time was coming to an end, the only question had been when.

A few weeks after his resignation, Mattis met in his transition office with Bill Kristol, one of the most prominent of Trump's remaining Republican critics. "Keep up the pressure, Bill," Mattis told him. "It's worse than you think."

The Axis of Adults was over. There was no mass resignation in the end, but one by one they slipped out the door or Trump shoved them. Not all of them had the same goals or viewpoints; some of them were more supportive of Trump, others outright opposed. None had done as much as the president's critics on the outside thought they should have. But all of them had served as guardrails in one way or another. John Kelly, Jim Mattis, Jeff Sessions, Gary Cohn, H. R. McMaster, Rex Tillerson, Don McGahn, and Joe Dunford were all out or on their way out. And Kirstjen Nielsen was hanging by a thread. Trump hoped to replace them with more malleable figures, ones with less independence, ones who would not tell him no quite so often. Mattis had a line to explain what was happening: Trump was so out of his depth that he had decided to drain the pool. Once it got shallow enough, he must have figured, he would not be underwater anymore.

On January 2, 2019, Kelly sent a farewell email to the White House staff. He said these were the people he would miss: "The selfless ones, who work for the American people so hard and never lowered themselves to wrestle in the mud with the pigs. The ones who stayed above the drama, put personal ambition and politics aside, and simply worked for our great country. The ones who were ethical, moral and always told their boss what he or she NEEDED to hear, as opposed to what they might have wanted to hear."

That same morning, Mick Mulvaney showed up at the White House for his first official day as acting chief of staff. He called an all-hands meeting and made an announcement. Okay, we're now going to do things differently, he told the staff. John Kelly took it upon himself to try to stop the president from doing what he wanted, but we're going to let Trump be Trump. "We're not here to protect the country against the president," he said.

III

CATCH ME IF YOU CAN

"They're trying to take you out with bullshit. Okay?
With bullshit."

—DONALD TRUMP

CHAPTER 14

Going Full Napoleon

They interrupted each other, they talked over each other, they insulted each other. And that was before the cameras were even turned off. The new reality for Trump arrived in the Oval Office a little more than a month after the midterm elections when he sat down on December 11, 2018, to meet with Nancy Pelosi, slated to become the new House speaker, accompanied by Chuck Schumer, the Senate Democratic leader.

The two sides were at loggerheads over a spending bill necessary to keep the government open. Trump had gotten rid of his previous set of advisers and was ready for a fight. Mick Mulvaney was too; sabotaging spending bills was how he had cut his teeth as an obstructionist backbencher in the House. The president's favorite prime-time hosts on Fox News were urging him to make a stand, as was Stephen Miller, now in ascendance at the White House with the departure of John Kelly and the others. So Trump threatened to throw out a spending deal his Republican allies had cut on Capitol Hill and veto the financing measure unless Congress added $5.7 billion as a down payment for his promised border wall. For ten extraordinary minutes in front of news cameras, Trump and his guests squabbled like children on a playground.

"Nancy, Nancy," the president said, jabbing with his hands and leaning so far forward on his seat it looked as if he could fall off. "We need border security, it's very simple."

Trump tried to undercut Pelosi by referencing the fact that a handful of Democrats were balking at voting for her for speaker. "Nancy's in a situation where it's not easy for her to talk right now and I understand, I fully understand that," he said patronizingly.

"Mr. President," she shot back, "please don't characterize the strength that I bring to this meeting as the leader of the House Democrats, who just won a big victory."

Schumer tried to turn the discussion around, putting pressure on Trump. "One thing I think we can agree on is we shouldn't shut down the government over a dispute," he said. "And you want to shut it down. You keep talking about it."

Nettled by Schumer's persistent jabs, Trump suddenly fell into the senator's trap. "You know what I'll say?" the president volunteered. "Yes. If we don't get what we want one way or the other, whether it's through you, through a military—through anything you want to call, I will shut down the government, absolutely."

"Okay, fair enough," Schumer said. "We disagree. We disagree."

Then Trump buried himself deeper. "I'll tell you what, I am proud to shut down the government for border security, Chuck," he said, "because the people of this country don't want criminals and people that have lots of problems and drugs pouring into our country. So I will take the mantle. I will be the one to shut it down. I'm not going to blame you for it."[1]

Schumer could hardly suppress his smile. Trump had just set himself up for a showdown he very likely could not win. And he even volunteered to take the fall.

One person not all that bothered was standing off to the side of the Oval Office—Stephen Miller. If it took closing the government to shut down the border, that was fine with him.

Five days later, Miller took to the Sunday talk show circuit to make that point as explicitly as possible. Appearing on *Face the Nation* on CBS, he said the border wall was more important than keeping the government open.

"We're going to do whatever is necessary to build the border wall," he declared.

"And that means a shutdown?" asked Margaret Brennan, the host.

"If it comes to it," he said, "absolutely."[2]

With the purge of John Kelly and others, Miller and his allies had a clear path to the Oval Office, plotting a post-midterm relaunch of Trump's presidency that would stoke the president's more confrontational side. While Trump had gone along with Paul Ryan the previous spring when the speaker urged him to sign a spending bill without money for the border wall, promising they would get it later, Miller and others now urged Trump to go to war as the new Democratic Congress was coming to power.

The showdown between Trump and Pelosi was a classic Washington power struggle that transcended the specific points of dispute, testing the new limits of a capital reordered by the election results. It was also a reminder of the gaping political divide over the role of immigrants in American society that Trump had made a defining theme of his America First, close-the-borders presidency. With Miller providing the rhetorical heat, Trump had aligned himself with the segment of the country that saw people moving into the United States from abroad not as a source of strength but as an economic, national security, and cultural threat.

Immigration had almost always been politically divisive in the United States, somewhat paradoxically for a nation of immigrants. Since Lyndon Johnson signed the Immigration and Nationality Act of 1965, eliminating national origin quotas that favored white people from Northern Europe, 59 million immigrants had moved to the United States, and the share of foreign-born Americans more than doubled to nearly 14 percent. The newcomers no longer arrived mainly from Europe but increasingly from Latin America and Asia. A country that was 84 percent white when the law passed was 62 percent white fifty years later.[3]

The population changes transformed the Republican Party too. George W. Bush, who said that immigration "is not a problem to be solved" but "a sign of a confident and successful nation," aggressively pushed for a pathway to legal status for millions already in the country without documents, only to be rejected by fellow Republicans.[4] John McCain, the party's next presidential nominee, also favored allowing many to stay. The Republican autopsy prepared by Reince Priebus after Mitt Romney lost the Hispanic vote by 44 percentage points to Barack Obama urged Republicans to support a humane immigration overhaul to reach out beyond the party base.[5]

Trump not only rejected liberalization but embraced deliberately inflammatory rhetoric and nativist policies. Obama was really born in Kenya, Mexicans coming over the border were "rapists," and all Muslims should be banned from entering the country. The United States should admit more people from predominantly white countries like Norway, not "shithole countries" in Africa. During a meeting with advisers in the summer of his first year in office, he ranted about granting visas to people from Haiti. They "all have AIDS," he complained. Letting people visit from Nigeria was a mistake, he added, because once they saw America they would never "go back to their huts."[6] He regularly told aides he wanted to withdraw American diplomats from Africa altogether. "Shut down the embassies in Africa and bring our people home," he said more than once.[7]

For Trump, the son and grandson of immigrants who grew up in

diverse New York, married not one but two women born in other countries, and employed undocumented immigrants at his properties, the harsh
stance could hardly be more opportunistic. His "build the wall" mantra
had started out as a memory trick in Trump's 2016 campaign by aides who
wanted him to talk about immigration on the trail more generally. But the
simple three-word slogan soon became a staple chant at his rallies, and
a symbol of his election for the crowd and the candidate alike. As president he obsessed over the wall's details and look: Should it be concrete or
steel? Should there be slats? How tall should it be? Could they electrify
it? Trump even demanded pikes on the top in case anyone tried to scale
it. And black paint to absorb the sunshine and make it hotter to the touch.

What he had not been able to do yet was actually build it. Without
admitting it, he had long since abandoned the fanciful promise to make
Mexico pay for the wall, but Trump understood that not putting it up at
all could be a fatal blow with his base and believed he could not head into
his 2020 re-election campaign without something solid standing along the
nation's southwestern edge.

His chief consigliere in this fight was Miller, an unlikely power in a
White House brimming with outsized personalities. Rail thin, with an
angular face, and still only thirty-three years old, he had a way of staying
in the shadows while turning the gears of government in the direction he
favored. To his critics, and there were many, he looked the part of a sinister
movie villain. *Vanity Fair* decided that he was a shoo-in if there were ever
a race for "World's Biggest Bastard," and an unsympathetic biographer
titled her book on him *Hatemonger*.[8]

Miller seemed unbothered by his bad-guy image, even embracing it
as a sign of his success in triggering outraged liberals. When he took his
girlfriend, Katie Waldman, a spokesperson at the Department of Homeland Security, out to dinner on New Year's Eve, two women at the next
table harangued her while he was in the bathroom, asking how she could
possibly go out with such a monster. The women later posted about the
encounter on social media, expressing hope that they had disrupted the
evening enough that it had kept Miller from "getting laid." Waldman,
however, later married Miller.

Many of Miller's other colleagues both despised and feared him. Rick
Gates, the deputy campaign manager in 2016, called Miller the "Silent
Assassin," portraying him as a Machiavellian manipulator who outmaneu-
vered rivals at the cost of abandoning mentors and allies who lost their
usefulness.[9] Another colleague compared him to Jonah, the universally

despised fictional White House aide from *Veep*, a toxic combination of unctuous and obnoxious.

Much journalistic effort was invested in trying to understand how a young man from a well-off Jewish family in tony, liberal, and diverse Santa Monica, California, became so fixated on immigrants as the source of all evil. Although his great-grandfather had arrived in the United States fleeing pogroms in Belarus, Miller had little sympathy for modern refugees. The son of Democratic parents who managed a real estate investment company, Miller rebelled early on against the progressive multiculturalism of Santa Monica High School.[10] "He looked people in the eye and said, 'I don't think you should be in this country,'" a fellow student recalled.[11]

After the September 11 attacks, Miller browbeat the school administration into reinstituting the Pledge of Allegiance. "Osama bin Laden would feel very welcome at Santa Monica High School," he wrote.[12] As part of his campaign, Miller sent a letter to Larry Elder, a conservative California radio show host, who invited him on his program. He did so well that Elder had him back repeatedly, putting him on air by Miller's count a total of sixty-nine times. At Duke University, Miller organized "Islamo-Fascism Awareness Week" and took up the defense of white lacrosse players wrongfully accused of raping a Black stripper, which won him appearances on Bill O'Reilly's show on Fox News.[13] After graduation, David Horowitz, another conservative mentor, helped him get jobs on Capitol Hill, first with Representative Michele Bachmann, a Tea Party Republican from Minnesota, and eventually with Jeff Sessions, the most outspoken immigration opponent in the Senate.

During the presidential race, Miller fell hard for Trump, declaring that it was "as though everything that I felt at the deepest levels of my heart were now being expressed by a candidate for our nation's highest office."[14] He joined the campaign to write speeches and soon found himself the flame-throwing warm-up act introducing Trump at rallies. Trump recognized Miller could be off-putting. "He's very intense, as you've seen, and I think probably the intensity gets him into a little problem," Trump told Julie Hirschfeld Davis and Michael Shear for their book, *Border Wars*. "But he's intense in his love for the country."[15] After winning the election, Trump granted Miller a West Wing office with a wide-open portfolio as senior adviser and speechwriter.

Like his boss, Miller relished mixing it up with reporters. Weeks into Trump's tenure, he drew fire for an appearance on CBS defending the president's right to defy a federal judge who had just blocked his Muslim ban. "Our opponents, the media and the whole world will soon see as we begin to take further actions that the powers of the president to protect our country are very substantial and will not be questioned," Miller said. The idea that a president's decisions "will not be questioned" in a democratic society struck an authoritarian chord that would become a theme of the Trump presidency.[16]

Six months later, Miller had a testy seven-minute shouting match with CNN's Jim Acosta in the White House briefing room. When Acosta, the son of a Cuban immigrant, asked if requiring applicants for employment-based green cards to demonstrate English proficiency meant that the United States would just "bring in people from Great Britain and Australia," Miller pounced. "I am shocked at your statement that you think that only people from Great Britain and Australia would know English," Miller said. "It reveals your cosmopolitan bias to a shocking degree."[17] For the American right, "cosmopolitan" was a favorite insult, notwithstanding its ugly history as code for Jews targeted by Nazi Germany and the Soviet Union, and all the more remarkable coming from Miller given his own Jewish roots.

In the two years before joining the White House, he exchanged hundreds of emails with a self-professed white nationalist at *Breitbart News*, in which he passed along links to extremist websites such as VDARE, which inveighed against immigration and warned about "white genocide," and Infowars, which trafficked in conspiracy theories suggesting, among other things, that the massacre of schoolchildren at Sandy Hook Elementary School in 2012 was a hoax.[18] A touchstone for Miller as well as Steve Bannon was *The Camp of the Saints*, a dystopian 1973 French novel popular on the alt-right that described hordes of dark-skinned refugees swamping Europe. The book's original cover described it as "A Chilling Novel About the End of the White World."[19]

From his White House perch, Miller authored Trump's most truculent speeches, starting with "American carnage." He could channel the president's views and provide words that captured his sometimes inchoate thoughts. "The joke was if Karl Rove was Bush's brain, Stephen was literally Trump's voice," observed a senior administration official.

Inside the building, Miller assigned himself to be enforcer of the most radical version of Trumpism. When top presidential advisers met after the blowup over the original travel ban, it was Miller who badgered them to stay with the program. "This is the new world order," he would say. "You need to get on board."[20]

He set about using every tool of government to stop immigrants from coming to the country and penalizing those already in the United States. In addition to the family separations, he would push to expedite deportations, crack down on asylum claims, penalize so-called sanctuary cities that resisted assisting immigration authorities, and enact a "public charge" regulation barring legal immigrants from obtaining green cards if they received government benefits or might in the future. He pressed the administration to force hundreds of thousands of people from crisis-torn countries like El Salvador, Honduras, and Haiti granted theoretically temporary residency in a special program to be sent back home even if they had been in the United States for decades and established productive lives while their home countries remained dangerous. He advocated rescinding Barack Obama's Deferred Action for Childhood Arrivals, or DACA, program allowing 800,000 younger immigrants brought to the country illegally as children to stay. And he led a drive to dramatically slash the quota for refugees from 110,000 a year at the end of Obama's term to as low as 15,000. "I would be happy if not a single refugee foot ever again touched American soil," Miller told fellow aide Cliff Sims.[21]

Miller made little distinction between legal and illegal immigration—he wanted to curb both. He helped convince Trump to endorse legislation to forge a "merit-based" immigration system favoring those with skills and education over family members of people already in the country. In doing so, the measure would cut the total number of legal immigrants each year by half.

Miller emerged not only as one of Trump's ideologues but also one of his backstabbing White House's most adept survivors. Although ideologically aligned with Jeff Sessions and Steve Bannon, Miller displayed no qualms about distancing himself from both once they fell out of favor with Trump. As the president railed at the attorney general, colleagues did not recall Miller offering a word in defense of his former boss. And he plunged the knife in Bannon's back, according to Sims, who recalled walking back along the Colonnade to the West Wing during the early days of the administration with Trump and Miller.

"Your polling numbers are actually very strong considering Steve won't stop leaking to the press and trying to undermine Jared," Miller told Trump.

"So you think that's really hurting me, huh?" Trump asked.

"It's getting nonstop coverage," Miller replied. "If Steve wasn't doing that, I bet you'd be ten points higher."[22]

For someone with no experience in the executive branch, Miller proved a natural at engineering the White House to advance his cause. Without any authority, he convened what became called "pop-up PCs," referring to principals' committee meetings, summoning senior representatives from various departments to direct them to pursue policies he favored. Even senior officials were forced to work around him; Kirstjen Nielsen would use her time alone with Trump on helicopter tours of disaster zones to change his mind about some Miller policy. When he found out, he would lobby Trump to reverse his reversals. Trump, for example, spent much of his first two years wavering on what to do with Obama's DACA program, ordering it ended but then trying to negotiate a way to save it with Democrats. To thwart a deal, Miller called in allies to nudge Trump, including red-state governors and attorneys general as well as congressional negotiators. "As long as Stephen Miller is in charge of negotiating immigration, we are going nowhere," Lindsey Graham, who favored an agreement, lamented in January 2018.[23]

Miller proved adept at circumventing Nielsen and other cabinet officers by contacting their underlings and issuing orders in the name of the president. Nielsen even discovered that he was calling officials down at the southwestern border to weigh in. Nielsen was constantly playing catch up ("Ma'am, we just found out that Stephen called so-and-so") but her subordinates read the newspapers, knew the president was unhappy with her, and could not be sure how long she would be around whereas Miller was clearly staying.

At one point during the summer of 2018, Miller took it upon himself to call Betsy DeVos, the secretary of education. DeVos was overseas for meetings at the ambassador's residence at The Hague in the Netherlands when the White House called and said Miller had to talk with the secretary right away.

DeVos took the call only to find it was no emergency. Miller told DeVos that the White House wanted her to stop federal Title I funding for schools that allowed undocumented students to enroll. There were perhaps 750,000 children without immigration papers in kindergarten through twelfth grade. Miller said he wanted a memo within a week. It was an extraordinary request—not to mention an extraordinary breach of government protocol.

DeVos, exasperated at his nerve, answered carefully. She was about to go into a dinner with the ambassador, she replied. She would have her team look into the issue and get back to Miller. After she hung up, her chief of staff, Josh Venable, called the department's top lawyer in Washington to ask for a one-page memo on the issue. That was an easy one. The Supreme Court had already ruled on that very question, deciding in *Plyler v. Doe* in 1982 that no child could be denied a public education based on their immigration status. What Miller wanted to do was patently illegal. Not to mention objectionable, as far as DeVos and her team were concerned.

Even after DeVos returned to Washington, however, Miller did not let the issue go. He pushed the Education Department to take other measures, such as revoking eligibility for Title IV funds for colleges and universities that granted lower in-state tuition rates for undocumented students, another nonstarter. He was full of ideas. DeVos and her staff wondered who was giving the orders. Was it really the president? Or was it Stephen Miller, assuming the power of the president?

As Miller pressed Trump to shut down the government to win money for the border wall, the president failed, and not for the first time, to take the measure of the person he was picking a fight with. Returning to the speakership eight years after losing it to Republicans, Nancy Pelosi had just become the most powerful Democrat in the country. She would prove to be a most formidable opponent for the president.

Unlike Trump, Pelosi at age seventy-eight was a lifelong practitioner of power in Washington, raised in a family steeped in politics as the daughter and sister of mayors of Baltimore. Since first winning a special election in 1987 to the House from California, where she moved after marriage, Pelosi had spent thirty years accumulating allies and learning the ways of the Capitol. After leading Democrats to victory in the 2006 midterms, she became the first woman ever to serve as speaker. A tough partisan whose frequent references to her five children and nine grandchildren fooled men of Trump's generation into underestimating her, Pelosi was known for steamrolling rivals and paying obsessive attention to the needs of her caucus. This time, her mandate was explicit: to take on the president.

Trump had once been a Pelosi financial patron. The first time they met was during that 2006 campaign when she and Charles Rangel, a New York congressman, came to Trump Tower hustling for dollars. She left saying that Trump "was a gentleman, and lovely."[24] He donated $20,000 and sent a note of congratulations after her victory that November.[25] "I think that I'm going to be able to get along with Pelosi," he said during the 2016 campaign.[26] Pelosi had no such illusions. She now considered him "the most dangerous person in the history of our country."[27]

The most important advice she ever received about how Trump operated came in 2016, when she attended a ceremony honoring Geraldine Ferraro, the late congresswoman from Queens who had been the first woman nominated by a major party for vice president. Several attendees with firsthand experience dealing with Trump in New York came up to warn her how he did business: "First he'll flatter, then he'll bully, then he'll sue."

If Trump thought he could flatter or bully Pelosi, he had not been paying much attention. He had only the most superficial understanding of her. Behind her back, he trashed her looks. He told visitors to the Oval Office that Pelosi was an example of why women ought to be cautious about plastic surgery. For her part, she considered Trump a "snake oil salesman" and a mentally unstable budding "autocrat." He was maddeningly unreliable, making it impossible to forge bipartisan deals. "One day I said to him, 'Who's in charge here? Is there somebody else we should be talking to? Because you agree to these things and nothing happens,'" she recalled. By the time she returned to the speakership, she had concluded that "this is not a well person."

With Trump triggering a government shutdown as the opening act of the new post-midterm era, Pelosi prepared for battle. Although many Democrats had supported fencing or other barriers at the southwestern border in the past, Trump had turned the border wall into a signature issue in a presidency rife with demonization of migrants. There was no way Democrats could support that, and she now declared the wall "immoral."[28] Once something is immoral, then compromise is not simply splitting the difference between the $5.7 billion Trump demanded and the zero dollars she was offering.

At midnight on December 22, 2018, much of the federal government formally shut down, leaving 800,000 workers either on furlough at home or required to work without pay as "essential workers" heading into the holidays. Pelosi knew what Trump evidently did not, which was that historically the public blamed Republicans for government shutdowns since they were the party most hostile to the public sector. Trump thought he could force Pelosi to cave. She was not about to fail her first test back in the speaker's office.

———

With Christmas at hand, aides convinced Trump that he could not go to Florida to celebrate at Mar-a-Lago while the government was shut down, so Melania and Barron got on the plane without him. "I am all alone (poor me) in the White House waiting for the Democrats to come back and make a deal on desperately needed Border Security," he wrote on Twitter on Christmas Eve.

The day after Pelosi and the new Congress were sworn in on January 3, 2019, Trump invited her and Chuck Schumer back to the White House to discuss a deal, but the meeting went nowhere. Trump threatened to keep the government closed for "months or even years" if he had to.[29] Although he had agreed not to blame Democrats for a shutdown, of course he did anyway, but polls showed 55 percent of Americans blamed Trump or congressional Republicans while just 32 percent faulted congressional Democrats.[30]

Trump assigned Jared Kushner to broker a solution. His son-in-law had just proven his congressional deal-making skills by delivering Trump a win on a significant criminal justice reform bill reducing sentences for non-violent drug offenses and improving prison conditions, the only major bipartisan legislation of Trump's tenure so far. Kushner had learned a lot from the exercise, not just about how to force action on Capitol Hill but how to manage his mercurial father-in-law. The young man's interest in overhauling criminal justice, of course, was as personal as it was political given his father's time in a federal prison in Alabama. But Kushner knew he had to sell Trump on the idea, which he did by mobilizing celebrities like Kim Kardashian West and allies like Rupert Murdoch and Sean Hannity.

Looking to assuage Trump's fears of a conservative backlash, Kushner had brought four Republican senators to the Oval Office one day to convince him. They walked Trump through the main elements of the legislation, and he seemed on board. "That all sounds very fair," Trump said. "I'll go ahead and do it."

As the group walked out of the Oval Office, Senator Mike Lee of Utah gave Kushner a hug. "So we got it!" he said, excited.

Kushner knew better. "No, no, no," he said. "That's a soft yes."

"What do you mean?"

"So right now, what I have to do is bring in people who hate the policy that we're trying to do," Kushner explained. "Because if we think it's a yes, he'll change his mind when Tom Cotton's on Tucker Carlson basically explaining how we're letting rapists and murderers out."

Kushner's approach worked and Trump became a firmer yes. But then he needed to persuade Mitch McConnell, who agreed to schedule a vote only if Kushner and his allies came up with sixty votes beforehand to ensure there would be no filibuster, then raised his demand to eighty votes. Working with liberals like Van Jones, the activist and CNN pundit, Kushner and Mike Pence managed to secure the requisite votes on both sides of the aisle. Even at that point, it took a threatening tweet from Trump to prod McConnell to bring it to the floor. Ultimately, the First Step Act passed both houses with wide margins and was signed by Trump on December 21, right as his budget negotiations with the Democrats broke down and the shutdown loomed.

Kushner was less than sure how to proceed on his father-in-law's latest fight with Congress, however. In fact, he increasingly harbored doubts that the border wall fight was worth it at all. A few days after Pelosi took office, he convened a meeting and asked a hypothetical question: Which would be more effective, a fully funded border wall or getting Congress to close every loophole it wanted eliminated from immigration law?

Kevin McAleenan, the Customs and Border Protection commissioner, said a complete wall would cut illegal immigration by 20 or maybe 25 percent. Closing the loopholes, he said, would decrease it by 75 percent to 80 percent.

"Okay," Kushner said with resignation. "So we've wasted the last two years."[31]

At Kushner's urging, Trump delivered his first formal Oval Office address to the nation on January 8 to offer his case for the border wall, a speech bearing all the hallmarks of a Stephen Miller text, denouncing "vicious coyotes and ruthless gangs" and citing the case of a veteran "beaten to death with a hammer by an illegal alien."[32] It made little difference.

Trump met the next day with congressional leaders.

"Why are you hurting people with this shutdown?" Pelosi asked.

"I don't want to hurt anybody," Trump said. He said he would reopen the government if Pelosi committed to paying for the wall. "If we open the government today, in thirty days, will you also fund border security, including the wall?" he asked.

"No," Pelosi said. That was a bottom line for the Democrats—no money for the wall.

"Okay, then this is a waste of time," a frustrated Trump declared, abruptly standing up. "Bye bye," he said and stormed out of the room.[33]

Trump and his team exhibited tone-deaf indifference to the burden imposed on the 800,000 unpaid government employees, many struggling to make the rent or pay utility bills. Wilbur Ross, the billionaire commerce secretary, expressed bafflement at why the sidelined workers did not simply borrow from a bank since they would eventually get back pay once the crisis was over.[34] Kevin Hassett, a top economic adviser to the president, said the workers were basically getting a free vacation.[35] Trump himself insisted that workers had told him they were happy to forgo paychecks so that he could promote border security.[36]

Stephen Miller was not the only one encouraging Trump's defiance. In Mick Mulvaney, Trump finally had a chief of staff who would not try to tame him. Having watched Reince Priebus and John Kelly get singed, Mulvaney would just let the fire burn. If anything, he fanned the flames. His let-Trump-be-Trump approach made him the president's chief enabler, encouraging his more confrontational instincts.

Mulvaney knew how to push Trump's buttons when he needed to. Like his predecessors, he considered Peter Navarro a loose cannon. Mulvaney brought Trump charts showing how stock markets would fall when Navarro went on television, which was enough to convince the president to pull the opinionated aide off air for months. But otherwise, Mulvaney's West Wing was geared to serve the president's daily impulses, not restrain them. When criticized, Mulvaney would shoot back: John Kelly might have had "a well-functioning policy process" but he had failed at the real job, "getting the president the type of things that he wanted," as a close ally put it.

As the government shutdown dragged on, Trump knew what he wanted but he had no plan for forcing Democrats to back down. The drawn-out battle turned increasingly petty. On January 16, Pelosi told Trump that she thought he should postpone his State of the Union address to Congress since security officers who would normally guard the Capitol had been furloughed. Angry at being denied his biggest audience of the year, Trump retaliated the next day by canceling Pelosi's military plane for an overseas trip she was scheduled to take. A week later, Pelosi formally disinvited Trump from the Capitol for his State of the Union until the government reopened.

For Trump, the end of what had become the longest government shutdown in American history came ignominiously. Mitch McConnell, who knew all along what a wasted effort it was, finally came off the sidelines a month into the stalemate, convinced that it had gone on long enough for Trump to grasp that he could not win. The Senate leader scheduled votes on two plans to end the impasse, one on Trump's terms and another Democratic version, mainly to show the president that he did not have enough support to prevail. After both failed to muster the sixty votes required to overcome a filibuster, McConnell called the president. With televisions in the White House showing air traffic slowing in the Northeast because of the shutdown, Trump knew it was over. He was already threatening to use his executive power to declare a national emergency to divert funds without congressional permission. McConnell urged him to sign the spending bill without the full wall funding.

"I don't know, Mitch, some of my people are telling me this legislation ties my hands," Trump said. "If I can't do a national emergency and build the wall, I can't sign this legislation."

"Sure, you can," McConnell said. "My lawyers say you can."

"So, you'll support the national emergency?"

"If you sign the legislation, yes," McConnell said.

McConnell wanted to lock it in before Trump could change his mind. "I'm going to the floor to announce your support now," he said. "Do I have your permission to do so?"[37]

The president said yes. McConnell wasted no time heading to the cameras. But it was a surrender by the Senate majority leader too. He had finally ended the spending crisis but just agreed to let a president dilute the most fundamental authority of Congress, the power of the purse.

Trump strode out to the Rose Garden to declare "that we have reached a deal to end the shutdown."[38] In fact, there was no deal. There was defeat. The bill he now accepted was the same as the one that he had refused to sign five weeks earlier. For a president who believed in zero-sum politics and considered compromise a sign of weakness, it was a bruising setback that underscored the limits of his ability to bull his way through the opposition in a new era of divided government. He had lost the thirty-five-day shutdown with nothing to show for it.

But barely thirteen hours after Congress passed a final spending measure without the money he had demanded, Trump took the money anyway by declaring a national emergency at the border. With Jim Mattis gone and a more compliant acting defense secretary in Patrick Shanahan now in place, Trump unilaterally siphoned off $6.7 billion from military housing projects as well as counter-narcotics programs and other funds, daring Congress or the courts to stop what even some Republicans called a blatant abuse of power. Mulvaney claimed this as his first big victory for the president. "He had been asking for many months: Can I use military funding to build a wall?" the Mulvaney ally recalled. "We were stymied because John Kelly didn't want to do that." His new chief would get Trump what he wanted.

In the Senate, Lindsey Graham took it upon himself to bring around conservatives outraged by the move. One night he called Trump's executive assistant, Madeleine Westerhout, announcing that he was in a car with Ted Cruz and Ben Sasse heading to the White House and needed to see the president urgently. Trump was having dinner with Melania and Barron at the time. "I haven't had dinner with my wife in six months," Trump groused. But he let Graham and the others come anyway and ordered appetizers for the unwelcome guests. "He was pissed," Graham remembered. "You could fry an egg on his head."

Nonetheless, Trump summoned White House lawyers and they went at it with Cruz, arguing over the legality of the plan. Trump took it all in as if he were at a tennis match.

"This is pretty good, isn't it?" he whispered to Graham. "Who do you think's winning?"

"It's too early to tell," Graham said.

In the end, Trump was the winner, with his party at least. Only a dozen Republican senators ended up joining Democrats in passing legislation meant to bar Trump from seizing the money without congressional authorization, the last group of institutionalist holdouts, including Mitt Romney, Susan Collins, Marco Rubio, Roy Blunt, and Lamar Alexander of Tennessee. But Trump and Graham succeeded in keeping Cruz and Sasse on board. The president used his veto power for the first time to reject the measure and enough House Republicans stuck by him to sustain his action. But Trump had gotten what he wanted despite the shutdown, not because of it.

By the time the government reopened, Kirstjen Nielsen's relationship with Trump had been deteriorating for months. The homeland security secretary he blamed for his immigration woes was one of the few cabinet officers who often pushed back, which did not endear her to him. She tried to offer alternatives that were legal or doable but rarely as dramatic as the flamboyantly harsh policies he pushed on her. He would call her at 11 or 11:30 at night at home to demand she take some action on immigration, then call again the next morning at 6:30 to ask if it had been done. "People were sleeping," she would try to explain, an excuse that rarely satisfied. On one conference call with her staff, Trump ranted about some wild idea he had. "Yes, sir," she said into the phone. Then she muted the line. "We're not going to fucking do that," she told her aides. At meeting after meeting, the president would demand action only to have her explain why it could not be done practically or legally. "Honey, just do it," he would say. Nielsen told aides that if she ever wrote a memoir, it would be titled *Honey, Just Do It.*

Trump even kept raising the idea of restarting family separations, the practice that had proved so politically disastrous the previous summer. From the minute he signed the executive order reversing course on family separations amid a national uproar, Trump basically regretted it and routinely threatened to consider "turning it back on."

Nielsen talked about it with Alex Azar, who as secretary of health and human services was charged with finding places to hold the children after the first seventy-two hours. The two of them had forged a bond of sorts, both Bush administration veterans still traumatized from the last time they had waged the family separation fight with Trump. As the president privately agitated to resume the practice, they agreed that they would not go along again and formed a mutual suicide pact: if Trump did turn it back on, they would resign together. Both knew a fight was coming. Stephen Miller would make sure of it.

On March 12, it happened. During a meeting at the White House, Trump melted down again about the high numbers of migrants crossing the border and how he was losing repeatedly in the courts. Trump then declared that Miller was now officially in charge of border security and immigration issues. He had already been acting as if he were for quite some time, but now had the imprimatur of the president.

Nielsen called her aide Miles Taylor, now serving as her chief of staff, to let him know. "It looks like Stephen is going to be the border czar," she said. "This is fucked. We need to get ready."

Taylor then called Miller and found the White House aide exceedingly excited to "put on the crown," as he put it. Miller said he was going to go "full Napoleon" once in charge. "I want to make sure you recognize that this moment was my coronation," Miller said. "And things are going to be changing around here."

Miller wasted little time pulling out his political guillotine for his internal enemies—and even for internal allies he perceived to be moving too slowly or letting legal niceties get in the way. The first to go was Ronald Vitiello, acting director of Immigration and Customs Enforcement, or ICE, the agency that deported people. After three decades as a Border

Patrol agent, Vitiello was hardly a liberal functionary of the anti-Trump Deep State; he had once referred to the Democratic Party as the "liber-alcratic party or NeoKlanist Party."[39] But he was not tough enough for Miller. One day when Vitiello was set to join Trump for a trip to California to inspect the border, he got word that the president was pulling his nomination and was left behind. In his place, Miller helped install Matthew Albence, the agency's acting deputy director, who had publicly dismissed concerns over the family separation policy by comparing detention facilities for children to "summer camp."[40]

No one had been harder on Nielsen than Lou Dobbs, the jowly anti-immigration crusader who hosted a show on Fox Business. Nielsen did not watch it, but she knew every time he took a shot at her on air because Trump would call her the next day in a fit. She made a point of trying to ignore it and had never engaged directly with Dobbs. But finally one day that spring, she decided to call him up because she considered what he was telling his viewers to be so inaccurate.

Dobbs named three actions he thought she should take. "Lou, two of them we're doing and one of them is illegal," she told him.

She did not mention to the president that she had made the call, but the next day, he knew about it. "I'm glad you talked with Lou," he told her.

Still, it did not win over the cantankerous host. On March 27, Dobbs railed about her again. "The Department of Homeland Security looks like a joke," he said on air. "They're acting as a joke. Kirstjen Nielsen—in my opinion, she is utterly unqualified for the job."[41]

Nielsen was not the only source of Trump's frustration. It seemed like every time he turned around, some federal court was blocking one of his immigration crackdown policies. The day after the latest Dobbs broadside against Nielsen, Trump railed about the judicial system in a meeting with aides in the Oval Office. The Ninth Circuit Court of Appeals in California, probably the most liberal bench in the country, particularly angered him. In a recent decision blocking him, the Ninth Circuit had barred immigration authorities from immediately deporting asylum seekers who failed an initial screening, ruling that they had to be allowed to stay and have another chance in court. To Trump, who was convinced that migrants were exploiting the system, it was just one more example of a court run amok.

A few days later, he called Nielsen and told her to get rid of the Ninth Circuit altogether. "Let's just cancel it," he said, as if it were a campaign event, not a court established by law. If it required legislation, he said, then draft a bill to "get rid of the fucking judges" and have it sent to Congress as soon as possible.

Nielsen was hardly surprised by anything by that point, but even for Trump it seemed a step beyond, to demand elimination of a court just because it ruled against him. FDR had generated a debilitating political scandal by proposing to pack a hostile Supreme Court with friendlier justices, but she could not remember any president trying to flatly wipe out a court altogether. Nielsen did not bother arguing with him. She just did what she and so many other administration officials did when Trump issued nonsensical demands—ignored it and hoped it would go away.

By then, it was only a matter of time for Nielsen anyway. She flew to London for the start of a week of meetings with European counterparts that had little to do with immigration—she had always resented that Trump treated the Department of Homeland Security as if its only duty was immigration when in fact her responsibilities covered everything from terrorism to cybersecurity to aviation safety. Trump could not have cared less about any of that. Prodded by Miller, he was back at the White House complaining that with crossings on the rise Nielsen should be at the border, as if she were an agent charged with personally arresting migrants coming into the country. Trump decided that he would head to the border himself. Nielsen was on the ground in London for maybe five hours on April 1 when the phone rang.

"I don't know why you're out of the country," Trump snapped at her. "You need to get your ass back here."

Nielsen flew back to the United States, racing to catch up with Trump at Calexico, a border town in California. While she was still en route, the president confronted some of her department officials in the conference room on Air Force One during the flight down, badgering them to close the border entirely to migrants. "Just send them back, we shouldn't let them in," he instructed. Kevin McAleenan, the director of Customs and Border Protection, explained, just as Nielsen had again and again, that by law they could not do that. "If you get in trouble for it, I'll pardon you," Trump told him. McAleenan was chagrined at the inappropriate comment but chose to believe the president was not really seriously instructing him to violate the law.

When Nielsen arrived, both Miller and Jared Kushner gave her hugs, a sure indication, she thought, that she was finished. Trump said nothing about her future during the visit to the border, but when she later called him on Air Force One as she headed back to Washington separately on a Coast Guard plane, he invited her to come see him at the White House that Sunday night, April 7.

Nielsen arrived with a list of six ideas that she had sketched out by hand on notebook paper during her flight, hoping they might satisfy the president's desire to crack down at the border. But as they sat in the family quarters of the mansion, Trump made clear that he was done with her. After a half hour, she left and submitted her formal letter of resignation the next morning. Just as he had when Nielsen was forced to publicly defend the family separation policy, her top adviser Chad Wolf threw up in his office trash can after learning she was being pushed out.

With the exception of Jeff Sessions, no other cabinet secretary had endured as much abuse from the president as Nielsen had for sixteen painful months. To him, she was an obstacle. To his critics, she was the face of cruelty. She had sought a balance she could not find. For the rest of Trump's term, he would not even bother to replace her with a Senate-confirmed secretary of homeland security who might defy him once again, merely cycling through a series of acting officials who had neither the president's mandate nor the Senate's approval to wield the department's vast powers. Napoleon reigned unchallenged.

Nielsen was not the only one on Miller's target list. So were Nielsen's acting deputy, Claire Grady, and the director of the Secret Service, Randolph "Tex" Alles, both of whom were forced out. And then there was Francis Cissna, the director of the United States Citizenship and Immigration Services, the agency that determined who got visas, granted asylum and refugee status, and approved citizenship applications. Cissna, a public proponent of more stringent enforcement of immigration laws, appeared to be ideologically in agreement with Miller. He had even edited his agency's mission statement to delete the phrase "nation of immigrants."[42]

But he considered himself a "rule of law" guy and found himself repeatedly telling Miller that the government still had a legal obligation to consider asylum claims and had to go through a process to enact the "public charge" policy he wanted. During one heated conference call involving dozens of officials, Cissna snapped at Miller to stand down.

"I won't stand down," Miller yelled. "I won't stand down. I won't stand down."[43]

The month after Nielsen was ousted, Cissna was forced out of his job too. Stephen Miller was not going to stand down.

CHAPTER 15

Split Screen in Hanoi

Michael Cohen had once been so close to Trump that he vowed to "take a bullet" for him.[1] A rough-and-tumble New York lawyer who sometimes wore a pistol in an ankle holster, Cohen fashioned himself as Trump's fixer, the man who bullied reporters, paid off accusers, and did whatever else was necessary to protect his boss. When Trump needed to cover up an affair with a porn star, Cohen sent the hush money. When Trump told him to lie about it to the first lady for him, Cohen did that too. After Trump himself lied on the campaign trail in 2016 about having no business dealings in Russia, Cohen repeated the lie in sworn testimony to the House and Senate. "I will do anything to protect Mr. Trump," he told Fox News in 2017.[2]

But that was before FBI agents busted down his door, before Trump pretended Cohen had been little more than an office boy of no consequence, before he finally turned against the president. By the end of 2018, Cohen confessed that "blind loyalty" to Trump had led him to a career of covering up the president's "dirty deeds" and made a deal with federal prosecutors.[3] He pleaded guilty to an array of charges and was sentenced to three years in prison, becoming the first presidential fixer since Herbert Kalmbach, Richard Nixon's personal lawyer and Watergate bag man, to be locked up for crimes committed on a president's behalf.

In late February 2019, before reporting to serve his time, Cohen made an unusual appearance on Capitol Hill to testify before the House Oversight and Reform Committee, now controlled by Democrats who were eager to begin using their new majority to investigate the president. Over the course of more than seven hours, Cohen testified that the president had reimbursed him for the hush money to cover up his tryst with Stormy Daniels and produced signed checks to prove it; that Trump had known in advance about the WikiLeaks dump of hacked Democratic emails during the 2016 campaign; that he had engaged in a wide array of questionable and possibly illegal business practices; and that he had lied to the public about doing business in Russia throughout his race for the presidency. While under oath, Cohen also accused Trump of being a "racist," a "con man," and a "cheat," and, in a comment that did not draw as much attention as it should have, predicted that if Trump lost the 2020 election, "there will never be a peaceful transition of power."[4]

In effect, Cohen offered Republicans a cautionary tale warning them not to be seduced, as he had been, into doing Trump's suspect errands. Finally, Jim Cooper, a veteran Democratic congressman from Tennessee, asked Cohen a key question, arguably *the* key question. He had continued to work for Trump for so long, even after all that. "What," Cooper said, "was the breaking point?"

In his response, Cohen addressed Trump's political allies and advisers and apologists directly. "I did the same thing that you're doing now for ten years. I protected Mr. Trump for ten years," Cohen said. "I can only warn people: the more people that follow Mr. Trump, as I did blindly, are going to suffer the same consequences that I'm suffering."

After more than a decade in Trump's service, Cohen had come to understand something that the most senior officials of the administration were learning as well. "Everybody's job at the Trump Organization is to protect Mr. Trump,"[5] Cohen said. And as far as the president was concerned, the entire United States government was now the Trump Organization.

Amid Cohen's many sensational claims, his allegation that Trump was both a Vietnam draft dodger and an inveterate liar about it was almost a throwaway. The president, Cohen said in his opening statement, had admitted to him during the 2016 campaign that his decades-old story about why he did not serve in the Vietnam War was false: he had never even had bone spur surgery to receive a medical deferment. "You think I'm stupid?" Cohen recalled Trump telling him. "I wasn't going to Vietnam."

Cohen disclosed this on a day when Trump was actually in Vietnam, having traveled there to broker a breakthrough deal on nuclear disarmament with North Korea's Kim Jong-un nine months after their first summit in Singapore. "I find it ironic," Cohen said in his testimony, addressing his estranged boss, "that you are in Vietnam right now."[6] But Trump had long been an irony-free zone. Earlier that morning, sitting in his Hanoi hotel suite at the JW Marriott before going to one of the most important negotiating sessions of his presidency, Trump took the time to preempt Cohen's Vietnam-draft-dodger allegation with an attack of his own,

Twitter-taunting Senator Richard Blumenthal ("Da Nang Dick," he called him) as a "total fraud," because the Connecticut Democrat had misrepresented his Vietnam-era service record. "I have now spent more time in Vietnam," Trump tweeted.

By the next morning, however, no amount of deflection or bluster by the president could obscure the fact that he had finally gone to Vietnam and lost the battle, if not the war. In Hanoi, the deal that Trump had hoped to cut with Kim failed to materialize. Even the flattery that Trump had lavished on the young dictator was insufficient to sway Kim, who insisted on maintaining North Korea's nuclear arsenal while demanding immediate sanctions relief. "The only two leaders who can do it are you and me," Trump had written Kim in a gushing letter just a couple months earlier.[7] But now Trump had no choice except to leave Hanoi empty-handed. Trump had been a casino owner for years in Atlantic City until his operations there went bust. He knew well what happened when you made a bad bet. "Sometimes you have to walk," Trump said, visibly unhappy as he announced the collapse of the talks.[8]

His national security team was relieved. For them, this counted as a victory in the fight to manage the president, a job that had only gotten harder since Jim Mattis had quit. John Bolton and Mike Pompeo now had essentially the same problems—with Trump and with each other—that Mattis, H. R. McMaster, and Rex Tillerson had faced. If anything, shedding his first team of advisers had emboldened the president. Trump's peremptory order to withdraw all forces from Syria had left them scrambling to head off what they feared could be a massacre of America's Kurdish allies, not to mention an embarrassing blow to American prestige and power in the Middle East.

"I feel like a funeral director," Bolton had told an aide soon after Mattis left while working the phones to Republicans on Capitol Hill who might help convince Trump to revisit his Syria decision. Bolton and Pompeo and the rest wanted to prove they could succeed where Trump's previous set of national security officials had stumbled, but once again they often defined success as stopping Trump from doing what he demanded, or at least convincing him, however temporarily, to pursue another course.

While Mattis had created an uproar by refusing to stay at the Pentagon after the president insisted on a complete exit, Bolton and Pompeo tried a less direct approach to change Trump's mind on Syria. They used a presidential trip to Iraq over the holidays to spotlight the importance of an American presence in the region and enlisted allies such as Lindsey Graham and Benjamin Netanyahu to lobby Trump about the necessity of keeping at least a small contingent of Americans inside Syria to counter Iran. Graham was particularly blunt about the stakes. In a private meeting on the sidelines of the Munich Security Conference that winter with General Curtis Scaparrotti, the top American commander in Europe, Graham asked the general, "Is it fair to say if this is carried out to the end, we will not have any allies? Would it be fair to say it would lead to a disaster?" The answer was as straightforward as the question: "Yes, sir."[9]

Trump's newer advisers, however, were more circumspect about airing their disagreements with him publicly. Pompeo was not one for testifying to Congress that he was at odds with the president, as Mattis and Tillerson had. Pompeo even pretended that Trump had not ordered them to do what he had in fact ordered them to do. "Fake news," the secretary told reporters at one point while on a weeklong Middle East tour designed to reassure allies who were unsettled by Mattis's departure and the uncertainty about American strategy in the region. "There's no contradiction whatsoever."[10]

Even when Trump embarrassed Bolton and Pompeo with his handling of a scandal that fall over the killing of a Saudi dissident columnist for *The Washington Post* named Jamal Khashoggi by Saudi agents working for the crown prince, they had stuck by him publicly. Mohammed bin Salman had remained a key contact and confidant of Jared Kushner, and Trump refused to condemn him even after it was revealed that Khashoggi, who had once worked as an adviser to the Saudi royal family before going into self-imposed exile in 2017 in the United States, was murdered by a hit squad inside the Saudi embassy in Turkey. Turkish surveillance tapes had even recorded the grisly sounds of a bone saw being used to cut up the body.

Trump personally dictated to Pompeo a statement supporting MBS without consulting Bolton or any of his other advisers, choosing to believe the crown prince's denials of responsibility over his own nation's spy services. (It was clear the statement came directly from Trump given the number of exclamation points.) Bolton managed a few wording changes but failed to stop it from going out. While the murder was "an unacceptable and horrible crime," Trump brushed off suspicions that MBS knew about it in advance. "Maybe he did and maybe he didn't!" Trump wrote. But he vowed to "remain a steadfast partner of Saudi Arabia." Pompeo then flew to Saudi Arabia in January and met with MBS, a prominent display of support for him despite the outcry back in Washington.

Sticking with Trump in public, though, did not guarantee an easier time managing him in private. At the Pentagon, Joe Dunford, serving out the last lame-duck months of his tenure, played a more direct role dealing directly with Trump than when Mattis was still around and strongly warned against a pullout. "Look, Mr. President, if you want out of Syria, we'll give you a plan to get out of Syria," he said at a White House meeting. "What I recommend is, we'll give you an opportunity to transition out of Syria, not have a precipitous withdrawal, and look to see if we can't get some of our allies to pick up some of the burden." Trump agreed to give him time to develop a plan, so Dunford and Pompeo spent weeks intensively talking with European counterparts about a way forward in Syria.

Still, the president insisted that he was being slow-rolled. One day in the Oval Office that winter, Dunford confronted Trump about it. "Mr. President, please don't say that, please don't say that. It's not true," Dunford insisted. "If you tell me what to do, I'm going to do it. The whole machine will focus on you. All I'm trying to do is listen to you and offer you military options that are consistent with where you want to be, but perhaps give you options that maybe have less risk than the one that you're suggesting."

Nothing irritated Dunford more than Trump's view that the Pentagon was actively resisting his orders. In Situation Room meetings, it had become routine for Trump to demand an exit from Syria or some other war zone, only to have Dunford push back, presenting the downsides and complications the demand presented. "My job is not to blindly do what he says," the chairman would tell others. "My job is to make sure he makes a fully informed decision and I provide him the best advice I can, benchmarked against what he has said, in writing, are our national interests." The Pentagon's top brass had long since concluded that Trump was indecisive, forcing his officials to argue with him over the same demands again and again. More than one called it a game of "whack a mole."

Whatever they called it, the campaign by his national security officials to get Trump to reconsider exiting Syria worked, sort of, and later that winter Trump reluctantly agreed to leave a few hundred troops in Syria after the April pullout to secure a buffer zone for America's Kurdish allies along the border with Turkey. In truth, it was never entirely clear how many American troops actually were left in Syria, although it was almost certainly closer to a thousand—a conscious strategy of "shell games," Jim Jeffrey, the administration's Syria envoy, would later say, to avoid inflaming Trump further.[11]

On North Korea, Trump had placed his team in a different sort of a bind. He had declared a historic victory in his Singapore summit without having, in fact, achieved the nuclear deal with Kim he touted, forcing American negotiators to scramble afterward to secure concessions he had already claimed. In the months after Singapore, Trump's advisers delayed and equivocated and did everything possible to avoid the president's wish for another summit with Kim, but they knew it was inevitable. Trump often pulled out the "love letters" as he called the correspondence he had received from the North Korean leader, and showed them to random Oval Office visitors, not seeming to recognize that they were just typical diplomatic pabulum mixed with saccharine flattery.

John Bolton was clear on his goal for the Kim meeting: "to prevent a debacle."[12] This time there would be no Jim Mattis or John Kelly to join him in pushing back on the president. In fact, there was neither a permanent defense secretary nor a permanent White House chief of staff. Both Patrick Shanahan at the Pentagon and Mick Mulvaney at the White House remained "acting," a bizarre state of affairs without precedent. Bolton was already actively feuding with both. At State, Pompeo was still the official North Korea lead. He and Bolton both remained skeptics of Trump's talks with Kim, but their inevitable personal and institutional rivalry was escalating. By summer, they would barely be on speaking terms. When it came to this summit that neither was enthusiastic about, each pursued his own plan for dealing with the North Koreans—and the president.

Bolton organized elaborate preparation, including three formal practice sessions for the president before leaving for Vietnam. Trump "was much more prepared for the Hanoi summit than he was for Singapore," said Matt Pottinger, the Asia adviser. "Singapore was completely seat-of-the-pants." Bolton's goal for the president was "to train him to smell a rat," as an outside expert briefed by Trump's advisers put it, and they drilled into him what Kim was likely to say and what it would really mean. "They made the case to the president, if Kim Jong-un asks for A, B, C, it's an ambush, he's tricking you."

This was not summit prep as it would have been conducted with any other president. For Singapore, the National Security Council had made a propaganda film to show to Kim. For Hanoi, it would make a video for Trump. The short film Bolton showed the president began with clips of Trump's predecessors bragging about deals with North Korea that later turned bad and ended with a clip of Ronald Reagan explaining why he had left his Reykjavik summit with Mikhail Gorbachev in 1986 without a deal. At the end of the session, Bolton felt his approach was working when Trump told him his takeaways:

"I've got the leverage."

"I don't need to be rushed."

"I could walk away."[13]

The next session also featured a video, in this case an actual North Korean propaganda film, showing they were still conducting "war games," even though Trump had ordered the American military to cease its own exercises in a surprise concession to Kim in Singapore. After that summit, it had become clear to advisers that part of the problem had been Trump's willingness to accept Kim's use of the term "denuclearization" without clarifying what it meant, because if he had clarified, it would have been obvious that the North Korean and American definitions were radically different.

As the Hanoi summit approached, Bolton pushed through the bureaucracy a set of four bullet points describing the American position. "Bolton obviously understood you've got to have bullets for the president because he's not going to read fifty-five-page documents," a national security official recalled. The third and final prep session included "wild cards" that were given to Trump to ready him with preplanned rebuttals to possible gambits that Kim might introduce at the summit.

Bolton was not just worried about Trump but was outright warring with the State Department. He believed the negotiating team led by Stephen Biegun, a fellow veteran of the George W. Bush administration, was reenacting the failed Bush-era nuclear talks that Bolton had tried to sabotage from inside that administration. The national security adviser would later write that the American diplomats were "uncooperative," "uncommunicative," and "overcome by zeal for the deal," and also that they were "out of control," "dangerous," "and "intoxicated by the publicity."[14] Both sides in the internal American feud, meanwhile, were suspicious of America's ally South Korea, fearing that the government of President Moon Jae-in had staked its political future on a deal and was actually working in concert with the North Koreans to box in Trump.

Negotiators arrived in Hanoi five days before the leaders. Day one consisted of the North Koreans threatening the Americans: lift all sanctions or else Kim would not show up. Biegun called Pompeo that night and told him of the demand. Pompeo called Trump and they decided no way. That one, at least, was easy. The next day, the North Koreans agreed to drop their opening ultimatum, "and then we got to work," as Biegun would later put it. Plans were under way for the declaration ending the Korean

War that Trump wanted and the beginning of a formal peace treaty. There was discussion of economic cooperation and how investment and trade might begin to flow. "But on denuclearization, they simply refused to talk about it," Biegun later informed associates. The North Koreans told their American counterparts that only Kim could deal on that point, and even then, only if the United States would agree to lift all sanctions up front. If it did so, the Americans were told, Kim "would bring a proposal that would be a big present for the president."

The State Department team had come up with a new catchphrase to describe its approach to the talks, offering Kim a package of "simultaneous and parallel" moves, on the way to full denuclearization. But this was diplomatic-speak for a set of proposals that did not differ all that much from the Bush-style "action for action" framework that Bolton had feared from the beginning. "He hated it," a senior American negotiator recalled. But as far as the American diplomats were concerned, Bolton was unreasonable. "What he wanted was simply: 'Give us all your weapons and then we'll figure everything else out,'" the negotiator said. The Bolton approach, in other words, was a nonstarter.

In the days before the summit, Bolton worked to make sure Trump did not go for the North Koreans' deal—or the State Department's. Rather than join Trump on Air Force One to Hanoi, Bolton flew separately, stopping in Tokyo to meet first with Prime Minister Shinzo Abe, the premier Trump-whisperer among world leaders. Bolton knew that he had an ally who was deeply uncomfortable with negotiations with the North Koreans. "I think he conspired with the Japanese to try to kill it," a fellow senior official recalled. Abe called Trump before the Hanoi meeting, as he had before the previous summit, to run through his list of concerns coordinated beforehand with Bolton and Matt Pottinger. The priority list included not promising to pull troops off the Korean Peninsula, not signing a peace declaration before a real nuclear deal was in place, and not allowing Kim to keep missiles that could hit Japan. And Abe urged Trump to get any deal in writing.

When Biegun circulated a final proposal to the North Koreans, it infuriated Bolton, who said the plan had not been pre-cleared with the rest of the American side and would require the United States to make disastrous concessions if the North Koreans accepted it. Already en route to Japan, Bolton called Mike Pence to complain and mobilized his deputy, Charles Kupperman, flying on Air Force One in his place, to brief Trump on the plan in the least favorable terms possible. "Kupperman's job is to stick the knife in this proposal," one of the State Department negotiators said, and someone—Biegun was sure it was Bolton himself—told John Roberts of Fox News that Biegun was "getting too far over his skis" in the negotiations.[15]

When the sharply divided American team finally assembled in Vietnam, Trump met Kim for dinner at the historic French colonial Metropole Hotel. The president was accompanied only by Pompeo and Mick Mulvaney, as the North Koreans had insisted on leaving out Bolton, a condition that suited the national security adviser's internal rivals just fine. Sitting down to shrimp cocktail, steak, and chocolate lava cakes, Kim offered his first and what would be his only proposal of the summit. He would close North Korea's Yongbyon nuclear reactor and in exchange the United States would lift all sanctions. This was one of the scenarios the advisers had prepped Trump for, explaining to him in advance that Yongbyon was not the only part of the North Korean nuclear complex and that its weapons program could continue without it.

Another problem was that Michael Cohen's testimony back in Washington began that night Hanoi time and Trump stayed up so late watching it after the dinner that he insisted on canceling the remaining briefings the next morning before the formal summit with Kim began. His advisers were worried. Hate-tweeting at his former fixer was not the best frame of mind for a president to conduct delicate negotiations over nuclear weapons. On a break after his first one-on-one meeting with Kim, Trump strode into the holding room with his advisers at the Metropole and turned on the television so he could watch the latest coverage of the Cohen hearing.

In the meeting room itself, Kim never wavered from his initial demand for immediate sanctions relief and offered no more than the closure of Yongbyon in exchange. Despite their internal divisions, both Bolton and the State team of Pompeo and Biegun agreed "there was not a deal that any of us would recommend," as one of them later put it.

But right up until the summit collapsed, they feared that Trump might agree to Kim's proposal anyway. "Please don't take it, please don't take it," Biegun whispered to himself as Trump was speaking. He believed that "not only was it a bad deal, but as a practical matter, it was impossible to sell—it was so bad." In the end, though, the gap between what Kim proposed and what Trump knew he could accept was just too big. Despite their feuding, "I give Bolton credit for the president understanding the gap," Biegun would tell others.

Going into Hanoi, the American delegation had prepared a one-page document for Kim outlining the American definition of "denuclearization" and another one, which they nicknamed the "bright future" paper, about all the great things awaiting North Korea if it gave up its weapons. After Trump handed the papers to Kim, he glanced at them, but one of the Americans noticed that when Kim got up to leave, he left the documents on his chair, not bothering to take them with him—an accurate foreshadowing, as it turned out, of what would happen after the summit.

Still, it was a close call. To some advisers, Trump appeared to be looking for a deal and trying to give Kim maneuvering room rather than rejecting his offer out of hand. During the break, a White House official recalled speaking with Trump. "Keep it up, hold the line," the official told the president. But Trump, he thought, seemed less than resolute, as if "he just did not want to make Kim look bad."

To him and others in the delegation, it appeared that Kim had misread Trump by not responding to their overeager president's cues. "He could move an inch and change history. Trump might have taken it," Biegun told associates. Kim "could have fooled us on a bad deal."

Kim and the other North Koreans seemed surprised at the collapse of the talks. They appeared to have had the same view as Trump's staff, that he was so eager for a deal he might agree to anything. Kim's sister and increasingly public adviser, Kim Yo-jong, looked angry. She had "smoke coming out of her ears," one of the Americans recalled.

Biegun and Bolton, despite their differences, believed the South Koreans had promised North Korea that they could deliver Trump for whatever Kim Jong-un offered. But Kim was not prepared to take steps toward actually getting rid of his nuclear weapons, the whole point of the talks in the first place—and exactly what the American intelligence agencies had warned Trump and his top advisers about in the winter of 2017 at the first high-level meeting on North Korea of his administration. Kim, as with his father and grandfather before him, viewed nuclear weapons as essential to his regime's survival and had no intention of giving them up.

The failure of the summit marked the end of meaningful diplomacy with North Korea for the duration of the Trump presidency. Both leaders would continue to invoke what the North Korean vice foreign minister, Choe Son-hui, called the "mysteriously wonderful" chemistry between them.[16] But Trump may have understood Kim's game better than he publicly let on. An American ambassador once asked Trump about Kim and was surprised at the response. "That fucker would knife you in the stomach if he had the opportunity," Trump told the ambassador, who concluded that all the talk about love letters was a show designed at least in part to enrage and confound the media. "Because it just drives you all crazy. He just revels in that," the ambassador said.

Either way, there never was a deal, let alone the deal of the century. By the end of the Trump administration, North Korea had continued to grow its nuclear arsenal by an estimated fifteen more warheads since the two leaders first met, while improving its long-range missile capability, expanding its nuclear complex, and hardening it against attack.[17]

The sense of relief had been palpable and largely bipartisan when Washington absorbed the news from Hanoi. "No deal is better than a bad deal," said Senator Marco Rubio, which was nearly identical, for once, to what Nancy Pelosi said.[18] This was also the view in Tokyo, where, a senior American official was told, a bottle of champagne was opened that night for a toast among the prime minister's top advisers. They drank to the failure of the summit.

Trump, for his part, remained furious that Democrats had sought to embarrass him with the Michael Cohen testimony even as he was meeting with Kim. When he returned to Washington after the long flight across the Pacific, Trump sent out a single tweet about the Hanoi summit ("Relationship very good," he reported, "let's see what happens!") and a dozen over the next few days about Cohen. "For the Democrats to interview in open hearings a convicted liar & fraudster, at the same time as the very important Nuclear Summit with North Korea, is perhaps a new low in politics and may have contributed to the 'walk,'" he tweeted a few days after returning to the White House. "Never done when a president is overseas. Shame!"

CHAPTER 16

King Kong Always Wins

Not long after he got back from Vietnam, Trump traveled to Maryland just outside of the capital to appear before the annual gathering of the Conservative Political Action Conference, a collection of some of the loudest and fringiest voices from the hard right. Once a powerful forum for rebels against the Republican establishment, the group had become a Trump adoration society, so much so that Kellyanne Conway joked that CPAC should really be called TPAC. The convention center was filled with Trump shirts, Trump hats, Trump socks, Trump paintings. When Trump took the stage on March 2, the audience roared its approval, especially when he approached an American flag and wrapped his arms around it. Flag hugging was not just a metaphor for Trump.

For the next two hours, he held forth—"totally off script!"—to boast, attack, spin, joke, complain, ramble, dissemble, improvise, extemporize, and otherwise give voice to whatever happened to be on his mind. Mostly, what was on his mind, because it was always on his mind, was the special counsel investigation into Russian election interference. He celebrated his decision to take out the "bad cop" James Comey, the action that triggered Robert Mueller's appointment in the first place, and asserted that the prosecutors were "angry Democrats" out to get him, "all killers" putting him in the crosshairs. "They're trying to take you out with bullshit. Okay? With bullshit," he said. "So now we're waiting for a report," Trump added, "and we'll find out whether or not, and who we're dealing with."

Nearly two years after Mueller's appointment, Trump was nearing the end of the investigation that had hung over his presidency and nervously anticipating the results. He had fired Jeff Sessions and replaced him as attorney general with Bill Barr with the explicit mission of protecting him from Mueller. The probe weighed on him constantly. He would tweet about it at six in the morning and still be complaining about it at mid-night. There were entire days when Trump would just hide out in his din-ing room next to the Oval Office, staring at cable news about the Russia probe. If aides needed documents signed, they tried to slip in and out as quickly as possible lest they be subjected to one of his self-pitying mono-logues that could last thirty minutes, an hour, even an hour and a half. "What the fuck are they talking about?" Trump would rail. "No one did anything wrong! I didn't do anything wrong! I'm not involved with any-thing! This is crazy!" He repeated his denials to anyone who would listen. "I've gotten away with more stuff than you'll ever know. I've done a lot of bad things in my life," Trump claimed over dinner one night with Lindsey Graham. "But I didn't do this."

In policy meetings, maybe thirty seconds or two minutes in, the dis-cussion would be derailed because Trump would ask about the latest news of the investigation. "There were moments where you just almost had to give up," one senior official recalled. Trump was so far gone that at times it seemed they ought to find someone to actually perform the duties of the president while the real one was busy nursing his grievances in the other room. "It was almost like we needed to give somebody a proxy," the official added, "so that if we needed a presidential decision on something, we can still move forward."

The investigation had transformed Trump's presidency in profound ways. For a president who thrived on conflict, it was the ultimate show-down, pitting him against all those out to get him, an ever-evolving cast of characters who fit into his conspiratorial views of the Deep State enemy— the Democrats, the FBI, the intelligence agencies, the news media, the State Department, the Pentagon, the career civil service, the establish-ment writ large, fellow Republicans who had never fully accepted him. In other words, Washington. In keeping with his approach to the presi-dency overall, Trump treated the investigation as a daily battle to be won or lost on television and Twitter. He made the probe the subject of a thousand rants at his campaign-style rallies, elevating his resentment to the level of political theology for his followers. It was, increasingly as the months went on, a consuming private obsession of Trump's as well.

After Gary Cohn left the White House in the spring of 2018, an old associate from Wall Street asked if Trump obsessed about the investiga-tion. "Twenty-two-point-nine hours a day," Cohn deadpanned. Some advisers slyly used this to their own benefit. Barr and Mike Pompeo, the secretary of state widely viewed as a master Trump-whisperer, had a "run-ning joke," as Barr called it, with each other. When Trump would appear on the verge of screaming at them over something, Pompeo would quickly raise the matter of the FBI agents investigating the president and say he hoped that one day they would be held accountable. This would invariably send Trump off into long tangents of grievance. "By the time the president was done," Barr would recall, "he had forgotten any gripe he had with Pompeo."[1]

The investigation fed not only Trump's sense of victimhood but his manifest insecurity. In the view of some advisers, he had arrived in office with a bad case of impostor syndrome. So sensitive was Trump to the notion that he might not have won properly that in his private dining room he kept a stack of color-coded maps that he gave out to visitors showing how the United States voted in 2016, broken down by county so that the red swaths of Trump voters in sparse rural America misleadingly dominated the smaller blue splotches of Clinton voters in denser, more populous urban areas. The Russia inquiry exacerbated his self-doubt by seeming to question his very legitimacy as president. The result was that, while national security officials wanted him to confront the reality of Russia's attack as a national security threat to the United States, Trump viewed it only as a threat to himself. He was determined to fight back. He was not going to let that righteous Bob Mueller bring him down.

Donald Trump and Robert Swan Mueller III were both born to wealthy families in New York City just twenty-two months and ten miles apart, but they could hardly have turned out more differently. While Trump's supposed bone spur troubles saved him from the draft in the 1960s and he once said that "my personal Vietnam" was avoiding venereal disease on the dating circuit, Mueller was taking fire with his fellow Marines at places like Mutter's Ridge in Vietnam and later earning the Bronze Star.[2] While Trump amassed a real estate fortune by day and went clubbing with platinum blond supermodels at night, Mueller married his high school sweetheart and settled for government wages as a prosecutor, taking down crime bosses such as John Gotti. While Trump chased celebrity with a television show featuring manufactured conflict, Mueller chased bomb-wielding international terrorists as the FBI director who took over just a week before the September 11 attacks.

Mueller was one of the few figures in Trump's Washington who commanded respect across the aisle, the only FBI director to have had his tour extended beyond the statutory ten-year limit adopted after J. Edgar Hoover died. Tall, with chiseled features, tightly combed gray hair, and an unfailingly pressed white shirt and dark suit, Mueller had the bearing and demeanor of a man comfortable being in charge and the reputation of someone who never colored outside the lines. An old-school Episcopalian of the sort that once dominated the capital, he was nicknamed Bobby Three Sticks, after the III at the end of his name. When his family talked him into hosting a holiday party for top FBI staff at his house, he tolerated the soirée for exactly two hours before flicking the lights on and off to indicate that it was time to go home. Most Friday nights, he dined with the same friends at the same Washington restaurant, tucking into a plate of scallops accompanied by a glass of white wine, then headed each Sunday to one of the Episcopal parishes he frequented, including St. John's Church across Lafayette Square from the White House. But he had a dry sense of humor and a keen understanding of how Washington worked. "If you are going to insist on being logical," he once told Andrew Weissmann, one of his prosecutors, "you have no future in this town."[3]

To investigate the president, Mueller had recruited a platoon of experienced investigators and prosecutors such as Weissmann, many of whom he had worked with before. They set up shop in an office building aptly called Patriots Plaza on the waterfront not far from Nationals Park. The staff was divided into three groups: Team R was to pick up the FBI's investigation of ties between Russia's 2016 election interference and the Trump campaign. Team M was to look at Paul Manafort, the president's one-time campaign chairman, and his various financial entanglements. And Team 600, named after a relevant section of the Justice Department regulations covering special counsels, was to look at Trump's possible obstruction of justice.

The center of the action was the Russia investigation. Led by Jeannie Rhee, a veteran prosecutor and partner of Mueller's at the white-shoe Washington law firm of WilmerHale, Team R set up two large whiteboards to map out Russia's election operation. One in Rhee's office was filled over time with a cascade of Russian names, essentially a schematic of who was who in Putin's effort to tilt the election to Trump. The other, even larger, was set up in the open-floor-plan common area anchoring the end of a long conference table where investigators gathered every day. On this one, multiple empty boxes with no lines were drawn at first; eventually, over time, each of the boxes was filled in and linked to others.

Mueller was especially interested in following the trails to Moscow. He would emerge from his office and plunk down in a chair at the large table for Team R's late-morning meetings, sitting expectantly, almost as if to say, what did you learn today? For some of the younger agents and analysts, his regular presence was unintentionally intimidating, rendering some of them tongue-tied. Mueller was not particularly fond of throat clearing. He wanted his investigators to get to the point. "Stop playing with your food," he would say.

Team M was led by Weissmann, a relentless investigator who had prosecuted everyone from mobsters to the corporate executives in the Enron scandal before becoming Mueller's special counsel at the FBI. His part of the investigation was broken off from the rest of the Russia probe because Manafort was seen as a complicated scandal in his own right. He had already been under investigation for a wide array of financial crimes for years before joining Trump's operation and his extensive ties with Russian figures made his sudden appearance in a presidential campaign particularly suspect. Team 600, led by James Quarles, another WilmerHale partner and a former Watergate prosecutor, was aimed directly at the president and therefore even more politically fraught. More than the other two, this team found over the course of the inquiry that it was investigating possible crimes as they were being committed in real time.

To defend himself, Trump wanted big names from the past, names he recognized from his heyday in the 1980s. But after the likes of Brendan Sullivan, Ted Olson, and Abbe Lowell all said no, he was left with his longtime New York attorney Marc Kasowitz, a combative lawyer who had seen Trump through divorces and bankruptcies but was unschooled in the ways of Washington. Trump had to quickly shift course when Kasowitz responded to a critic calling on him to resign with a profanity-laden string of late-night emails: "You are fucking with me now. Let's see who you are. Watch your back, bitch," adding, "I already know where you live."[4] Trump then settled on a couple of longtime Washington attorneys well past their professional prime. Ty Cobb, a former prosecutor whose handlebar mustache, beard, and bow tie gave him the appearance of an amiable grandfather, joined the White House staff as special counsel; John Dowd, a gravelly-voiced retired Marine with a short temper, represented Trump from the outside along with Jay Sekulow, one of the legal leaders of the Christian conservative movement.

Like others, they quickly discovered the ongoing tribal warfare within Trump's White House. Cobb later told people that his first three meetings at the White House were all about enlisting him in what he called the "We Hate Jared and Ivanka Club." Trying to duck that, Cobb spent two weeks studying the case before concluding that Trump really was not guilty of anything and so advised him to cooperate fully with investigators, including providing documents and allowing testimony by advisers without asserting privileges. In exchange, Trump's new lawyers told him, the inquiry would be over by Thanksgiving. When that did not happen, they told him it would surely be wrapped up by Christmas, and when that did not happen, the spring, and so on. Cobb's theory was that if investigators could get all the evidence they needed from other sources, they would have a harder time demonstrating to a court that they needed to force the president to testify. But that strategy flabbergasted Don McGahn, the White House counsel who thought it was crazy to so readily abandon Trump's claims to executive and attorney-client privileges. Cobb, for his part, thought McGahn was jealous of turf and trying to get rid of him from the day he arrived in the White House.

The friction spilled into public view when Cobb and Dowd made the curious choice one day to have lunch outdoors at BLT Steak, which happened to be next door to the *New York Times*'s Washington bureau. Predictably enough, Ken Vogel, a *Times* reporter, was sitting at the next table as the two attorneys groused about the internal dispute. Cobb could be heard talking about an unnamed White House lawyer he deemed "a McGahn spy" and complaining that McGahn had "a couple documents locked in a safe" outside his access. He blamed a colleague for "some of these earlier leaks" and for trying "to push Jared out."[5] When the newspaper printed a story on the overheard conversation, McGahn blew up at Cobb while John Kelly, still White House chief of staff at the time, reprimanded him for indiscretion.

Trump, impatient and fuming, would put up with only so much of this. He was still looking for his Roy Cohn.

For investigators trying to unlock the secrets of Trump's aberrant relationship with Russia, Paul Manafort seemed like an obvious target. With broad shoulders, a helmet of hair dyed jet black, and a taste for extravagantly expensive clothes, Manafort had once been a respected operative for Republicans like Gerald Ford, Ronald Reagan, and Bob Dole. But over time he drifted away from American campaigns, drawn by the lure of huge payoffs and rules-free politics in the frontier of the former Soviet Union.

By the time he showed up on Trump's doorstep offering to work for free as a convention strategist and later campaign manager, Manafort was generally shunned in Washington as an overseas political profiteer with shadowy ties to Russia and Ukraine. He had worked for Oleg Deripaska, a Russian billionaire aluminum magnate who was close to Vladimir Putin and had been banned from the United States, and he helped the

Moscow-aligned Party of Regions take back power in Ukraine after the 2004 Orange Revolution, when peaceful protesters successfully blocked the party from stealing an election won by the opposition. Over the following years, Manafort transformed Viktor Yanukovych, Putin's favorite, from a thuggish party leader into a more polished figure with a better wardrobe, hairstyle, and elocution who captured the Ukrainian presidency in a 2010 election. Later, as Yanukovych jailed his leading opponent and presided over a corrupt state, Manafort helped whitewash his reputation. "Manafort was said to be running a shadow government in Ukraine, operating out of a luxury suite at a top hotel, as well as offices in downtown Kiev," Andrew Weissmann wrote later.[6]

Yanukovych was ultimately ousted in Ukraine's 2014 pro-Western revolution and fled to Russia after his forces opened fire and killed more than a hundred protesters. But not before Manafort had pocketed millions of dollars using offshore accounts. Manafort's daughter suggested in text messages that were hacked that her father had culpability in the deaths of the demonstrators. "That money we have is blood money," she wrote to her sister.[7] Yanukovych's fall led Putin to invade and annex Crimea and sponsor a pro-Russia separatist uprising in eastern Ukraine.

Trump either did not know that or did not care. What he knew was that Manafort was a name brand from the 1980s, Trump's perennial frame of reference, and that he was willing to work without pay.

Manafort was no philanthropist; deep in debt, he figured out how to cash in on his work for Trump through what investigators eventually determined was a kickback scheme from a Trump-supporting PAC. More important, Manafort seemed intent on parlaying his high-visibility role in Trump's campaign to revive his business with Russian and pro-Russian Ukrainian figures. "I assume you have shown our friends my media coverage, right?" Manafort wrote Konstantin Kilimnik, who helped run his operations in Ukraine for a decade, in an email a couple weeks after joining the campaign. "Absolutely," Kilimnik replied from Kyiv. "Every article."[8]

Weissmann's investigators soon discovered that Manafort effectively opened a pipeline to Moscow from Trump Tower. His campaign deputy Rick Gates told investigators that at Manafort's direction he slipped Trump's internal polling data to Kilimnik, who simultaneously worked for Russian intelligence, according to the American government, and who, it was later discovered, passed the confidential research along to a spy agency in Moscow. "I assume it was to help Paul financially," Gates told investigators. At the same time, Kilimnik was pushing a "peace plan" for

Ukraine on Manafort that would effectively reverse the 2014 revolution in Russia's favor and reinstall Yanukovych, Putin's ally, as president.[9]

With income hidden from tax authorities, Manafort had financed a grotesquely lavish lifestyle, covering his tracks with false invoices, sham companies, and mysterious wire transfers from Cyprus. He owned extravagant homes in Florida, New York, and Virginia, including an estate in the Hamptons with a pool house, putting green, home theater, tennis court, and a $100,000 annual gardening bill. He spent millions of dollars on clothes, carpets, cars, and antiques. Among his purchases: a $32,800 "blue lizard" jacket, an $18,000 suede coat with leather detailing and houndstooth lining, and a pair of $12,000 suits with pink and green pinstripes.[10]

Mueller and Weissmann moved against Manafort methodically, raiding his Virginia home in the summer of 2017, indicting him in the fall, flipping Gates into a witness against him in early 2018, and then jailing Manafort without bail in the summer after discovering that he was tampering with witnesses. But as powerful as the case against Manafort was, Trump did what he could to keep his former campaign manager from turning against him. Over and over again, Trump took to Twitter to assail the prosecution against Manafort and hint that a pardon was coming if he remained loyal—an extraordinary breach of presidential protocol in the midst of an ongoing case involving serious corruption. Manafort was being "treated worse" than "Alfonse Capone, legendary mob boss," Trump tweeted, in one of those unintentionally revealing Trump Twitter moments. Locking him up for witness tampering was "very unfair!"

Manafort went to trial in Virginia in August 2018 and was convicted of eight counts of fraud. Trump made a point of immediately signaling Manafort to resist pressure from prosecutors. "Unlike Michael Cohen, he refused to 'break'—make up stories in order to get a 'deal,'" Trump wrote on Twitter, comparing Manafort favorably to his former fixer. Trump sounded more like the leader of a crime family pleading with his consigliere not to turn state's evidence than the nation's chief executive. Facing a second trial in Washington, Manafort finally did agree to plead guilty and was sentenced to a cumulative seven and a half years in prison. But he never provided the evidence that Mueller's prosecutors wanted, either because it did not exist, as Trump's allies argued, or because he could reasonably anticipate a pardon, as prosecutors suspected.

Jeannie Rhee's team had been filling in the boxes on her whiteboards, painstakingly assembling a granular portrait of Russia's expansive operation to influence the 2016 election and how Trump's team took advantage of it. There were so many contacts between the Trump campaign and Moscow that it was hard not to wonder what it all added up to. There was the Trump Tower meeting hosted by Don Jr. There were the ancillary campaign advisers such as George Papadopoulos and Carter Page, who had sought to act as intermediaries with Moscow. There was Roger Stone, the Trump political adviser and former Manafort partner, who was suspected of being in touch with WikiLeaks as the group went public with troves of hacked Democratic emails stolen by Russian agents. And there was the Moscow tower project that Trump pursued through Michael Cohen, even as he ran for president and falsely claimed to the public that he had no dealings with Russia.

Working with U.S. intelligence agencies, Rhee's investigators confirmed that Russian agents had mounted an elaborate shadow campaign to damage Hillary Clinton and elect Trump, concluding it was a revenge plot that Putin ordered up against the former secretary of state he blamed for encouraging street protests against him in 2011 and the Democratic administration he blamed for the sanctions imposed on Russia after the 2014 invasion of Ukraine. A troll factory using the bland name of the Internet Research Agency, set up in St. Petersburg and financed by Yevgeny Prigozhin, an oligarch so close to the Kremlin that he was called "Putin's chef" because his restaurants and catering business provided meals for the Russian leader, flooded social media sites with false messaging. "Main idea: Use any opportunity to criticize Hillary and the rest (except for Sanders and Trump—we support them)," read one internal email obtained by Rhee's team.[11]

The Russians set up fake accounts masquerading as American anti-immigration groups, Tea Party activists, Black Lives Matter protesters, LGBTQ organizations, and religious associations, among others. They created Facebook groups called "Being Patriotic," "Stop All Invaders," and "Secured Borders."[12] Trying to suppress voting by people of color, a fake group calling itself Woke Blacks declared on Instagram that "hatred for Trump is misleading the people and forcing Blacks to vote Killary. We cannot resort to the lesser of two devils. Then we'd surely be better off without voting AT ALL."[13] Altogether, Twitter identified 50,258 automated accounts tied to the Russian government.[14] Among those who retweeted or otherwise responded to these posts were Donald Trump Jr., Eric Trump, Kellyanne Conway, Brad Parscale, Roger Stone, Sean Hannity, and Mike Flynn.

As Rhee sorted through the intelligence, a holy-shit moment came when she realized that Russia had sent scouts to the United States to take what amounted to a driving tour of swing states to be able to speak in an authentic voice when they were trying to disguise themselves as American patriots. Two female Russian operatives, armed with cameras, SIM cards, and disposable cell phones, conducted a three-week reconnaissance trip in 2014 to nine states, including battlegrounds like Michigan and Colorado. Another operative was sent to Georgia. The notion of undercover Russians conducting field research in the American heartland looking for ways to undermine faith in democracy seemed to Rhee especially disturbing. Investigators were also stunned to discover that on the same day that Trump publicly called on "Russia, if you're listening," to hack Hillary Clinton's computer, Russian agents tried to do exactly that, almost as if taking direction.

In the end, Rhee's team was able to identify and indict twenty-five Russians and three affiliated companies for their roles in the operation, knowing that they would never be extradited from Russia. But the question remained: What Americans, if any, had played an active role in this unprecedented Russian attack on an American election?

For the president's lawyers, managing the prosecutors was one thing. Managing their client was another. From the start, they urged him not to publicly attack the special counsel and he had largely restrained himself at first. He lashed out angrily about the "witch hunt" but did not mention Robert Mueller by name on Twitter until nearly seven months after his appointment.

But every time Trump came back from Mar-a-Lago, he would be wound up by friends like Rudy Giuliani or Alan Dershowitz, the famed Harvard Law School professor and celebrity attorney, leaving him ready to go to war with Mueller until his lawyers talked him down again. Giuliani kept second-guessing the legal team. At one point, he told John Dowd that he did not know what he was doing. That seemed pretty rich to Dowd, who thought but did not say out loud that at least he did not get drunk and go on television. Eventually, Trump could contain himself no longer and began waging a ferocious assault on Mueller and his team, a campaign designed to convince his supporters, at least, not to trust anything investigators came up with.

Mueller was a hard figure to demonize. A lifelong Republican, he could not be tarred as a leftist so Trump focused on Mueller's staff, the prosecutors like Andrew Weissmann, Jeannie Rhee, and Jim Quarles, all of whom had donated to Hillary Clinton. Trump labeled them "13 Angry Democrats" and later "17 Angry Democrats." It was true that most of Mueller's prosecutors were registered Democrats in part because a Justice Department policy barred him from asking job applicants their party affiliation. It was hardly surprising that Democrats would volunteer more readily to investigate Trump; Ken Starr's office had similarly been filled with Republicans during his investigation of Bill Clinton.

The president's attacks gained momentum in late 2017, with the discovery of the anti-Trump text messages between Peter Strzok and Lisa Page, the FBI officials having an extramarital affair. Here, Trump insisted, was proof that he was being unfairly persecuted. Mueller removed Strzok from his team. But Strzok and Page became a peculiar obsession of Trump's, who would mimic "the lovers," as he called them, during campaign rallies. Once, onstage in front of thousands of supporters, the president even simulated Strzok having an orgasm as he mockingly reenacted their text messages.

Some of the attacks on Mueller's team were farcical. Trump maintained that Mueller was too compromised to serve as special counsel because he had once been refused a refund of golf fees from a Trump club. Paul Manafort's team accused Weissmann of bias because he had dropped by Clinton's election night party in New York in 2016 without mentioning that he had gone with a group that included a lawyer now representing Manafort. The attacks were so intense that Rhee's husband eventually sought to ease the tension by making two customized baseball caps, one for Weissman emblazoned "Angry Democrat #1" and one for his wife, "Angry Democrat #2." Rhee fretted not just about being fired but about congressional Republicans using their oversight power to go after the prosecutors. "If they retain the House, we all need to retain criminal lawyers," Rhee said before the midterm elections. "That's how batshit crazy they are now. I am not joking."[15]

Uniquely skilled at finding an adversary's weak point, Trump seized on the Christopher Steele dossier to present himself as a victim. Because it turned out that the dossier had been financed by Clinton's allies and many of its most sensational claims were unproven, it became a useful tool for Trump to undermine all allegations against him. But, contrary to Trump's claims, the bureau's inquiry was not triggered by the dossier, nor were its contents the basis of much other than a secret warrant against Carter Page, a Trump campaign foreign policy adviser. An inspector general later faulted the FBI for relying on the dossier as part of its request to surveil Page and for not being more forthcoming about the document's partisan origins with the judge who issued the warrant. But that had little to do with the other evidence gathered by investigators.

Even when Trump made over-the-top allegations, Mueller never hit back, and would not allow his team to privately share damaging information about Trump with the media. He ran what may have been the least leaky office in Washington in modern times. Having experienced real war, Mueller was unruffled by the political kind. "What's the worst thing that's going to happen?" he asked members of his team. "They're going to send me to Vietnam?"

But Trump wanted vengeance that extended well beyond mean tweets and nasty nicknames. He repeatedly and publicly pressured Jeff Sessions and later Bill Barr to bring criminal charges against his adversaries, including Clinton and James Comey. At one point in the spring of 2018, Trump instructed Don McGahn to direct Sessions to prosecute Clinton and Comey and, if the attorney general refused, said he would do it himself as president. McGahn had to explain that the president had no such power. "You can't prosecute anybody," he said. Then he set about compiling an extraordinary memo explaining to Trump how inappropriate it was to use the criminal justice system as a political weapon, as if the United States was a dictatorship. "Congress could seek to *'impeach and remove'* the president if it concluded that he abused the power of intervening in a criminal matter," McGahn wrote, using boldface and italics to emphasize his point.[16]

Trump also wanted the Justice Department to indict Andrew McCabe, the acting FBI director who formally opened the criminal and counterintelligence investigations into the president, after an inspector general found that McCabe had displayed a "lack of candor" with internal investigators looking into disclosures to the media related to the Hillary Clinton investigation.[17] With no charges forthcoming, Trump pressured Sessions to at least fire McCabe before he could qualify for his pension. Sessions complied, dismissing McCabe in March of 2018 twenty-six hours before his planned retirement. Much like Comey, McCabe learned that he had been dismissed via television. Trump taunted him on Twitter: "Andrew McCabe FIRED, a great day for the hard working men and women of the FBI."

The Trump team's war against Mueller was coordinated closely with allies at Fox News, who eagerly amplified the president's assaults and initiated their own. Sean Hannity exchanged hundreds of texts with Paul Manafort collaborating on the best way to undercut the special counsel; investigators eventually obtained the texts and released them nine months after Manafort's sentencing. Hannity made no pretense of journalistic detachment. "I'm in campaign war mode every day," he wrote Manafort in one text. "We are all on the same team," he added in another.

Manafort suggested points to hit the Mueller team on and Hannity would echo them on his radio and television shows, and sometimes vice versa. "Your monologue tonight was the best summary ever of the case against Mueller and his team," Manafort wrote late one night.

At another point, Manafort admitted to Hannity the pressure he was under from prosecutors to disclose what he knew about the president in exchange for a lesser sentence. "They would want me to give up Dt or family, esp JK," he wrote, referring to Donald Trump and Jared Kushner. "I would never do that."

It fell to Hannity to remind Manafort that their official line was that Trump was innocent—although he was not so willing to exonerate Kushner. "There is nothing to give up on DT," he wrote Manafort back. "What did JK do?"

Manafort promptly jumped back onto script. "Nothing, just like I did nothing," he wrote.[18]

Manafort never did flip. But Mueller had a secret weapon in his quest to uncover the truth about Trump and his circle, a source inside the White House informing prosecutors about what was happening: Don McGahn.

Even as he was serving as White House counsel, McGahn was practically the chief witness for the prosecution, passing along inside information to Mueller's team almost in real time. Trump had only himself to blame, having authorized McGahn to talk with Mueller's team in keeping with the strategy set by Ty Cobb and John Dowd. McGahn had objected—the very idea of a lawyer providing information to prosecutors about his client was anathema. But once he was told to cooperate, McGahn did so fully and comprehensively in keeping with what he took to be his legal obligation to tell the truth if not barred by a privilege claim.

McGahn was an unusual character even in a White House full of them; a staunch libertarian with a passion for rock music, he boasted a collection of more than thirty guitars and played as many as a hundred shows a year with a cover group called Scott's New Band before joining the White House staff. He grew up in Atlantic City as Trump casinos began dominating the oceanfront, then studied at Notre Dame and earned a law degree at Widener University. Specializing in election law, McGahn served as general counsel at the National Republican Congressional Committee before George W. Bush appointed him to the Federal Election Commission, where he led a bloc of Republican members that sought to ease the regulation of campaign money. He signed on as general counsel of Trump's campaign when other lawyers stayed away and was rewarded with the storied second-floor corner office in the West Wing occupied by previous presidential lawyers.

While other officials agreed to work for Trump perhaps not knowing what he was really like, or at least fooling themselves, McGahn had no such excuse. His uncle, Paddy McGahn, a legendary power broker and attorney in Atlantic City, helped Trump expand his casino empire and at one point was so close to the developer that a bar in the Trump Taj Mahal, Paddy's Saloon, was named after him. But as with many who worked for Trump, the two fell out over legal bills and sued each other. At the time of his death in 2000, Paddy claimed Trump still owed him $1 million. The president's new counsel decided not to mention to Trump that he was Paddy's nephew, but their relationship would turn out to be just as fraught.

McGahn grew so frustrated with Trump's management by tantrum that behind his back he called the president "King Kong" and "fucking Kong."[19] He rationalized staying in his post as John Kelly and H. R. McMaster had, telling others the situation would get much worse with another lawyer who would not stand up to Trump. It was not purely a matter of self-sacrifice, though. McGahn used his power in the Trump White House to fulfill a longtime goal of transforming the federal courts with conservative appointees. Working with Mitch McConnell, McGahn had managed to confirm Neil Gorsuch to the Supreme Court and scores of other judges to appeals and district courts. As he contemplated resigning at one point, he talked himself into staying by accurately predicting that Justice Anthony Kennedy would retire and succeeded in persuading Trump to tap Brett Kavanaugh to replace him. But otherwise he avoided Trump. A good day, he told colleagues, was a day he did not even see the president, who got the message. "I don't know what he does other than judges," Trump told aides.

All the while, McGahn was talking with Mueller's team, spending more than thirty hours answering their questions. Trump knew his counsel was cooperating, but had no idea just how extensively. With McGahn's help, Jim Quarles's team documented Trump's determined campaign to impede the investigation—the James Comey firing, the efforts to pressure Jeff Sessions to rein in the special counsel, all of it. Quarles was stunned at the brazenness. When he got hold of the original draft letter that Trump had Stephen Miller write firing Comey, Quarles was blown away by the conspiratorial tone. "It's tinfoil helmet material," he told Andrew Weissmann. At one point, McGahn told the prosecutors, Trump called him at home and instructed him to tell Rod Rosenstein, the deputy attorney general, that "Mueller has to go," an order that McGahn chose to ignore and almost resigned over.[20] When that episode was later reported by *The New York Times*, Trump blamed the leak on that "lying bastard" McGahn and insisted that he had not said what his counsel had clearly heard him say.[21] Trump even demanded that McGahn write a false memo denying the *Times* story, itself an attempted cover-up that the lawyer refused to go along with.

But Trump's efforts went even beyond what Mueller's team would eventually report. On at least two occasions that never became public, Trump secretly tried to enlist members of his cabinet to help him force Sessions out as attorney general in order to assert control over the Mueller investigation and end the threat to his presidency. During a trip on Air Force One in late 2017, Trump summoned Alex Acosta, his labor secretary, to the front cabin. Rob Porter, the staff secretary still working in the White House at that time, fetched Acosta for Trump and hurriedly warned him as they headed forward to Trump's quarters that the president was likely to sound him out on helping oust Sessions and becoming attorney general himself. The expectation was clear that Acosta would do what Sessions would not with the Mueller inquiry. Acosta, a former assistant attorney general under George W. Bush, recognized the danger of being drawn into a possible obstruction of justice and rebuffed Trump's entreaty.

After being refused by Acosta, Trump then asked Porter to telephone Scott Pruitt, his administrator of the Environmental Protection Agency, to take his temperature about replacing Sessions. Pruitt, who had served as attorney general of Oklahoma, was more nakedly ambitious than Acosta; he thought he should be the next secretary of state and even entertained dreams of running for president. But Porter worried that it could be interpreted as part of an illegal scheme to interfere in the Mueller investigation and, like Lewandowski and McGahn before him, did not follow through. After some time passed, Trump asked again and Porter still ignored the order. Finally, Trump talked with Pruitt by phone himself and said that Porter would be in touch, then lashed out at Porter for not obeying his instruction. At that point, Porter felt he had no choice.

Much like H. R. Haldeman did with Richard Nixon, some Trump aides loosely observed what they called the Third Time Rule, meaning they would disregard erratic or potentially improper orders from Trump once or twice in hopes that he would forget or move on. But if he returned to a command a third time, they had to find a way to comply or talk him out of it. Trump had now reached the third time with Pruitt, so Porter reluctantly picked up the phone. When Porter called, Pruitt was in fact more amenable than Acosta, raising no concerns about participating in a plot to get rid of an attorney general and seize hold himself of the politically fraught investigation of the president. The only reason Trump did not follow through on the plan was that he deferred to advisers who warned him that it would make matters worse. The idea to elevate Acosta or Pruitt would have been politically disastrous, as it happened, even if Mueller had gone untouched. Both men were ultimately forced out of Trump's cabinet by scandals that would have been debilitating had either of them become attorney general. Once again, his advisers had saved Trump from himself. Because if they did not, no one else would.

But Trump's efforts to undermine the investigation were, in a sense, working. No other target of a federal investigation had the power to fire his investigators or dangle pardons for witnesses against him to encourage their silence. Mueller complained to Trump's lawyers that his tweets were discouraging witnesses from cooperating, but that would not stop the president. At one point, gallows humor took over on the Mueller team. Quarles took to strolling through the office calling out "Pardon me! Pardon me!"[22]

Eventually, several senior members of Mueller's team concluded that Trump's pressure campaign had gotten the special counsel's office to pull its punches. Mueller, an inherently cautious man, was reluctant to pursue a more aggressive approach to the investigation and Aaron Zebley, his chief of staff, regularly shot down more assertive tactics for fear of angering the White House so much that the special counsel would be fired and the entire investigation shut down. From the start, Zebley took other prosecutors aside and told them "we may not be long for this earth."

Frustrated, Andrew Weissmann came to refer to the schism in Civil War terms, likening Zebley to the early Union general who was reluctant to engage the enemy while comparing himself and Jeannie Rhee to two later generals who attacked ferociously. "He was a timorous McClellan to my and Jeannie's Sheridan and Grant," Weissmann later wrote in a memoir.[23]

The Mueller team never investigated Trump's possible financial ties to Russia, with Mueller reasoning that there was no need to look for evidence of motive if they could not establish an underlying conspiracy to begin with. Nor did prosecutors call Ivanka Trump to testify, fearing that it would make them look like bullies and enrage the president. They never forced Don Jr. to testify either, allowing him to invoke the Fifth Amendment without immunizing him to compel him to talk. Zebley would not even let Rhee subpoena Trump Organization emails to get more information about the Trump Tower meeting with Russians because he believed it would hurt negotiations for an interview with the president. "From the outset, the specter of our being shut down exerted a kind of destabilizing pull on our decision-making process," Weissmann wrote.[24]

Perhaps the most significant concession by Mueller was his decision not to try to force the president to testify. Trump claimed publicly that he would be happy to talk and John Dowd was initially supportive of that. At one point, they even agreed on a date for an interview at Camp David and began organizing logistics. But Dowd changed his mind, concluding that Mueller was laying a perjury trap for a president incapable of telling the truth. Camp David was canceled. But Trump continued to flirt with an interview, perpetually confident that he could talk his way out of anything.

The issue came to a head on March 5, 2018, when Mueller met with Dowd and other Trump lawyers. "You know, John," Mueller said, "I could issue a subpoena."

Dowd erupted and slapped his hand down on the table. "Go get it," he dared Mueller. "I can't wait to get in front of a federal judge."

Dowd could be combustible and had a habit of swearing at prosecutors, fellow lawyers, White House staff, and even the president. But his bluster obscured the fact that he was having trouble convincing his client not to testify. "That's exactly what Mueller wants to do, which is to trap you," he told Trump.

Finally, a couple weeks after the meeting with Mueller, Dowd gave up. He called Trump one morning to resign since the president would not commit to not testifying. "I'm just telling you, you're not going to remember what happened on these matters," Dowd argued.

By that point, Trump had tired of Dowd anyway. To replace him, the president brought in his old friend Rudy Giuliani and gave him free rein to lead the combative defense against the prosecutors that he had wanted to unleash all along. Not everyone was happy about the former New York mayor gaining such regular access to the president, much less speaking for him on television. Giuliani had become such an eccentric, conspiracy-minded figure that White House aides tried to keep him away from Trump, lest he fill the president's ears with all sorts of nonsense. But Giuliani told Trump what he wanted to hear. Within a few weeks, Cobb was out too, replaced by Emmet Flood, a former impeachment lawyer for Bill Clinton. A few months after that, Trump would push out Don McGahn as well, announcing on Twitter that the White House counsel would leave after Brett Kavanaugh's confirmation. McGahn only learned of his departure when John Kelly burst into his office asking why he had not been told first.

With all the turnover, Jay Sekulow picked up negotiations with Mueller and he too resisted making the president available for questioning. "If you were me," he asked Mueller, "would you do it?"

Mueller hesitated for a moment. "For the good of the country," he answered.

That was no incentive for Trump, and ultimately he opted against testifying. Mueller did not seek the subpoena. He could have. There was precedent. Ken Starr had subpoenaed Bill Clinton, who agreed to a voluntary interview in exchange for prosecutors withdrawing a court order requiring him to talk. But Mueller did not want to push it.

Weissmann protested. "Without his testimony our report is like *Hamlet* without Hamlet," he complained at a meeting with Mueller and other prosecutors. "The character at the very center of the drama would never come onstage." He argued that they should not let the threat of being terminated stop them from acting. "If taking our shot with a subpoena leads to our getting fired, so be it," he said.[25] Mueller said nothing in response. The decision had been made.

In the end, Trump agreed only to provide written answers to written questions—and even then only about his 2016 campaign, not about actions he had taken in office that might have constituted obstruction. Trump's lawyers camped out in the Cabinet Room around Thanksgiving, grabbing the president for a few minutes here or there between meetings as they drafted his responses. The answers they ultimately submitted were next to useless. Trump, who had boasted of having "one of the greatest memories of all time" and had mercilessly mocked Christine Blasey Ford for not remembering tangential details of her encounter with Brett Kavanaugh three dozen years earlier, told the prosecutors "I do not recall" or some variation thirty-six times.[26]

The decision about Russia, in the end, was not a hard one for the Mueller team. They had conclusive intelligence proving that Moscow conducted a wide-ranging operation to interfere in the 2016 election with the goal of electing Trump. They also had plenty of evidence that the Trump campaign had extensive contacts with various Russians and intermediaries, welcomed Moscow's help, and profited from it.

What they did not have, the prosecutors agreed, was enough evidence to prove in a court of law beyond a reasonable doubt that there was a criminal conspiracy on the part of the president or members of his staff. As an intellectual matter, they thought they could string together the disparate episodes and connections to make a technical case as if it were a law school exercise. There were an awful lot of "coincidences" there. But it would be a tendentious argument, they believed, not one an experienced prosecutor would take to a real court with a real jury. The only meaningful debate was about the Trump Tower meeting—some prosecutors thought they did not need to make a big deal out of it since it turned out to be so inconsequential, while others argued that even if not criminal it was still a deeply troubling episode that belonged in their final report.

The case against Trump for trying to hinder the investigation was far different. The prosecutors thought they had rock-solid evidence of obstruction of justice. There was no question in their minds that the president sought to thwart investigators and if anything was saved only by advisers like Don McGahn who refused to go along. But the Justice Department's long-standing policy, formulated under one president facing impeachment (Richard Nixon) and reaffirmed under another (Bill Clinton), held that a sitting president could not be indicted for a crime while in office. Although that opinion was hotly debated and had never been tested in court, Mueller under special counsel regulations was bound by it. But Mueller took it one step further: if he could not indict Trump, he told his staff, then he should not even state in his report that the president had violated the law because Trump would have no opportunity to defend himself in court. That, in Mueller's mind, deprived him of basic due process. And so even though Mueller's team identified ten potential counts of obstruction, the special counsel ordered his staff not to make a straightforward declaration that those acts constituted crimes. This logic once again drew protests from Andrew Weissmann and other prosecutors, who thought that let the president off the hook.

Another internal battle took place over the writing of their final report, which Weissmann and other prosecutors believed was edited by Aaron Zebley to take out anything he considered needlessly inflammatory. For instance, the investigators had obtained an email from a Russian working at the Internet Research Agency describing the celebration at their headquarters when Trump was elected. "We uncorked a tiny bottle of champagne, took one gulp each and looked into each other's eyes," the Russian wrote. "We uttered almost in unison: 'We made America great.'"[27] Zeb-ley kept that out of the report. Similarly, Konstantin Kilimnik, the Paul Manafort associate, was described as having "ties to Russian intelligence" rather than being an intelligence officer himself.[28] A later bipartisan report from the Senate Intelligence Committee was not so reticent.

Finally, on Friday, March 22, 2019, Mueller sent the 448-page report to Bill Barr. The prosecutors knew Barr would not simply release it sight unseen to safeguard confidential grand jury information so they had pre-pared summaries that could be quickly made public without a long review process. But Barr opted instead to write his own summary. Working late and into the weekend with Rod Rosenstein, the deputy attorney general who had participated in the firing of Comey that set the special counsel investigation in motion in the first place, Barr drafted a four-page letter to Congress interpreting the Mueller report in the best possible light for Trump.

Barr's letter selectively characterized the report in several important respects. He wrote that Mueller did not find that the Trump campaign "conspired or coordinated with Russia" but did not mention that the spe-cial counsel report nonetheless documented extensive links between the two and noted that the Trump team knowingly benefited from Moscow's help in the election. As for obstruction of justice, the attorney general quoted Mueller saying that "while this report does not conclude that the President committed a crime, it also does not exonerate him"— entirely leaving out that Mueller identified ten episodes that were poten-tially obstruction. Barr left the impression that Mueller "did not draw a conclusion—one way or the other" even though the clear message of the special counsel's report was that Mueller did consider them potentially obstruction but felt he could not say so because of the Justice Department policy barring indictment of a sitting president.[29]

Trump knew what was coming. His lawyers had been kept up to date by the Justice Department. On that Sunday, March 24, around 3 p.m., Barr's chief of staff called Emmet Flood, who was down at Mar-a-Lago with the president, to read him the letter the attorney would soon send Congress. Flood and Pat Cipollone, who had replaced Don McGahn as White House counsel, then made their way to the president's private quarters to fill him in.

An hour later, Trump arrived at the West Palm Beach airport to head back to Washington and paused for a few minutes on the tarmac to crow about it. "There was no collusion with Russia," he told reporters. "There was no obstruction—and none whatsoever. And it was a complete and total exoneration."[30]

When he arrived back at the White House, Trump found his lawyers waiting for him. "What's the overall thought?" he asked.

"The overall thought," Jay Sekulow replied, "is we won."

Trump may have won, but it was hardly a complete and total exoneration. Even Barr's letter, favorable as it was, made evident that Mueller was not clearing Trump on obstruction. Mueller's team was furious at Barr for giving the president cover to claim that. Andrew Weissmann, who heard a radio report on the attorney general's letter while driving on the New Jersey Turnpike down to Washington, was outraged at what he deemed "unbridled lies."[31] So were others in the office.

Mueller was genuinely upset at Barr; the two were longtime friends and their wives were close. "The summary letter the Department sent to Congress and released to the public late in the afternoon of March 24 did not fully capture the context, nature, and substance of this Office's work and conclusions," he wrote Barr. As a result, Mueller added, "There is now public confusion about critical aspects of the results of our investigation."[32] In Mueller-speak that was the equivalent of bristling indignation. He urged Barr to release the two summaries Mueller's office had produced right away. For his part, the attorney general was miffed at the letter, which he considered "a bit snitty."[33] Barr concluded that Mueller's staff was angry and had put him up to it.

More than three weeks passed during which Barr's misleading summary hardened in the public mind. When the attorney general finally released the full report with some redactions on April 18, Barr once again framed it in terms beneficial to Trump. At a news conference right before the report's release, Barr declared four times that Mueller had found "no collusion," asserted that "the White House fully cooperated with the special counsel's investigation," and claimed that "the president took no act that in fact deprived the special counsel of the documents and witnesses necessary to complete his investigation." Barr even seemed to suggest that Trump was justified in seeking to hinder the inquiry because "the president was frustrated and angered by a sincere belief that the investigation was undermining his presidency, propelled by his political opponents and fueled by illegal leaks."[34]

In fact, Mueller made no determination about "collusion," which is not a legal term. What he concluded was there was not enough evidence to prove a criminal conspiracy. At the same time, his report pointed out that Trump willingly and knowingly accepted help from Russia for the purpose of winning an election, certainly scandalous and unprecedented in American history even if not illegal. As for fully cooperating, the president had deprived Mueller of the most important witness—Trump himself. And Trump tried repeatedly to have Mueller restrained or fired even while hinting at pardons for witnesses who might testify against him.

But as damning as the report's findings were, its language was maddeningly passive and Mueller himself said nothing at all in defense of it. For some time, there had been whispers in Washington that the aging Mueller was not as sharp as he had once been, but House Democrats ignored the warning signs and pressed him to testify about the report against his wishes. Democrats argued that seeing Mueller on television would transform his dry report into a dramatic visual indictment of a corrupt president. While Americans might not read the script, the argument went, they would watch the movie.

But if so, the movie that played on July 24 was hardly the blockbuster Democrats had sought, nor was Mueller the action star they had cast. For two years, Trump's critics had built up Mueller into some sort of superhero, investing in him their hopes for taking down the president. NPR even did a report on Americans in their nineties hanging on to life until Mueller's report came out, so certain were they it would lead to Trump's comeuppance.[35]

But that is not how it turned out. Dignified but shaky in the hearing room, at times struggling to keep up, Mueller largely limited his answers to "yes" and "no" and "refer you to the report," steadfastly refusing even to articulate his conclusions. He offered none of the moral dudgeon Democrats were seeking. Adam Schiff, the House Intelligence Committee chairman who led the hearing, and other Democrats stiffened when they saw how monosyllabic Mueller was. "Had I known how much he had changed, I would not have pursued his testimony with such vigor—in fact, I would not have pursued it at all," Schiff wrote later.[36] Schiff quickly told colleagues to change their approach mid-hearing—no open-ended questions, no questions calling for narrative, just simple straightforward inquiries.

By the time Mueller finished after nearly seven hours, Democrats had not gotten the made-for-television accusatory moment they wanted and the prospects of an impeachment based on the special counsel's investigation had essentially evaporated. "Far from breathing life into his damning report," Laurence Tribe, the Harvard law professor who favored impeachment, wrote on Twitter, "the tired Robert Mueller sucked the life out of it."[37] Trump could barely contain his glee. He pumped out taunting tweets and then stopped to talk with reporters on the South Lawn to gloat. "Robert Mueller did a horrible job both today and with respect to the investigation," he said.

Trump was not exonerated but he had won. He had cowed the investigators. He never had to answer for his actions in person under oath. And with the help of an attorney general chosen specifically for this moment, he had distorted and publicly reframed the findings of the investigation to his own advantage. Over the course of his time in the White House, starting one day after Mueller was appointed, Trump would use the term "hoax" on 789 occasions and "witch hunt" on 715 occasions to refer to the Mueller investigation.[38] No wonder many Americans assumed the probe was a hoax and a witch hunt.

CHAPTER 17

John Bolton's War

For months, John Bolton and Mike Pompeo had feuded with each other, while each claimed to have discovered the secret to dealing with the president that had eluded their predecessors. To Pompeo, that meant unwavering fealty to Trump—at least in public—no matter how much Trump's demands contradicted his own instincts and ideology. "A secretary of state has to know what a president wants," Pompeo said during an appearance that spring. "To the extent you get out of sync with that leader, then you're just out shooting the breeze." He understood well that loyalty was the major and perhaps only attribute Trump valued in his subordinates. Asked in March how long he would serve as secretary, Pompeo had joked, to knowing laughs, "I'm going to be there until he tweets me out of office."[1]

At the State Department, Pompeo had initially been greeted as a relief from the insular, out-of-the-loop Rex Tillerson and he quickly moved to show that his slavish public tributes to Trump gave him more private running room—enabling him, for example, to hire even a few Trump election-year critics such as Jim Jeffrey, the Syria envoy who had signed an anti-Trump letter, and Elliott Abrams, the veteran Republican foreign policy official previously vetoed by Trump for a senior post but now made special envoy for Venezuela. Pompeo had assured Trump that figures such as Abrams would take jobs that did not require Senate confirmation and thus embarrassing public airing of their views on Trump. It was not lost on Pompeo that their hiring helped burnish his own credentials with the Trump-skeptical Washington foreign policy establishment, which increasingly saw him as what remained of grown-up supervision. "He's not an enabler of Trump," one of his Republican advisers insisted around this time. "He does a lot to try to manage him."[2]

By the spring of 2019, however, Pompeo had started making clear to the professional diplomats that there was a cost for this modest amount of freedom. The former congressman had brought to the State Department two of his best friends from West Point, both of them former business partners in Wichita. Ulrich Brechbuhl became Pompeo's counselor and designated troubleshooter and the secretary put him in charge of a pet project, designing a new mission statement for the department. The resulting "professional ethos" was unveiled at an unusual all-hands pep rally in the grand foyer of the department's Foggy Bottom headquarters, held to coincide with the first anniversary of Pompeo's tenure. Many in the Foreign Service greeted the ethos as a loyalty oath aimed at potential leakers, and a veteran diplomat who had been consulted said it was both "incredibly condescending" and something right out of Orwell's *1984*.[3]

Pompeo also unveiled a new department motto—"One team, one mission"—that seemed aimed at reassuring the president rather than the other way around. The word "mission" was the tell. Pompeo in public often referred to the "mission set" he had been assigned by Trump, presenting himself as a mere executor of the president's commands. "He's very focused on whatever the mission is. He's a West Point guy. 'Trump wants a deal, so I'll get a deal,'" a former senior official said. In contrast to the commanding habits of generals like Jim Mattis and John Kelly who had so alienated Trump, Pompeo used the language of "an Army captain, a guy who went to West Point and got out before he became a general."[4] In his pep rally that April, Pompeo redefined the mission of the State Department, America's oldest cabinet department, in strikingly personal terms, as "the premier agency delivering on behalf of the president of the United States."[5] The message to the diplomats was explicit: their client was no longer a country, but a man.

Bolton was not one for such maneuvers. He had flattered Trump when seeking the job of national security adviser, but once in the White House he had increasingly distanced himself from the president. "You need to talk to Trump," his aides would tell him whenever yet another crisis erupted. "It's pointless," he would reply. Instead, Bolton often spent his time working around Trump or avoiding him altogether as he pursued his own foreign policy agenda. In February, the administration announced that it was officially withdrawing from the Intermediate-Range Nuclear Forces Treaty, or INF, the last major relic of the Cold War arms control agreements and a longtime target of Bolton's. He was laying the groundwork to pull out of the Open Skies Treaty of 1992 as well, and successfully pushed the administration to quit the U.N. Human Rights Council.

Another Bolton pet cause was regime change in Venezuela, where the late leftist dictator Hugo Chávez had been succeeded by his lieutenant, Nicolás Maduro, and the country, once one of Latin America's wealthiest and most advanced, had devolved into political and economic chaos. Trump was also interested in Venezuela, mainly because he saw taking a tough line on Maduro as a political opportunity to secure votes from the large and growing exile community in Florida. In Trump's first year in office, Marco Rubio had become a key adviser on Venezuela to the president, a virtual secretary of state for Latin America. It had not gotten much attention at the time, but Trump even professed to be considering a "military option" for Venezuela in the same August 2017 appearance where he threatened to rain down "fire and fury" on North Korea.[6] In January 2019, Rubio, Bolton, and other hardline Republicans had seized on a popular uprising in Caracas, and backed Juan Guaidó, the thirty-five-year-old activist who headed the opposition-controlled National Assembly, as the legitimate interim head of the country. They argued that Maduro was illegally holding on to power after staging an unfree presidential election in 2018, the results of which the National Assembly had refused to accept. After a major diplomatic push by the State Department, more than a dozen other nations, including Argentina, Brazil, and Canada, signed on to the Trump administration's endorsement of Guaidó.

But a new impasse had emerged. Guaidó did not have the military backing to seize power and Maduro did not have the popular legitimacy to stop the protests. Bolton and his staff pushed the Pentagon hard to come up with maneuvers to pressure Maduro. In April, Paul Selva, the generally soft-spoken vice chairman of the Joint Chiefs, had a table-pounding screaming match during a meeting at the White House when the Bolton team proposed what seemed to him like a legally questionable modern-day version of the Bay of Pigs. The Bolton aides wanted to recruit defecting Venezuelan troops coming over the border into Colombia, keep them together as units, house them and train them in case an opportunity arose to send them back into Venezuela to fight. Selva pointed out there was a law called the Leahy Amendment, named for Senator Patrick Leahy, requiring American-trained foreign military to be vetted first for possible human rights violations. "Well, you don't have to do that," Mauricio Claver-Carone, the National Security Council's senior director for Western Hemisphere affairs, insisted, interrupting Selva mid-sentence. "You don't understand the law." The law that mattered, he said, was the National Security Act, which made the National Security Council the coordinator of policy, not the Defense Department. Earl Matthews, the National Security Council's senior director for defense, backed him up, complaining that the Pentagon never wanted to provide options even when directed.

This infuriated Selva, who had been resisting White House pressure for months to use Pentagon assets as leverage in a political campaign that was not working. He believed the idea for the exile army was over-the-top, inappropriate, and possibly even illegal. "I'm tired of your shit. I'm tired of the shit you produce as work and we collectively are tired of wading around in all that shit," Selva yelled at them. "So do your job and give us a set of carefully reasoned options, not a political statement on how you want to support the Venezuelan people, because you're not helping." With that, Selva slammed his hand down so hard on the table that he made a dent in it.

As the rest of the room looked on stunned, one of the other deputies reproved Matthews: "Earl, you're actually wrong, he's actually right, and he's been right all along, so don't ever interrupt him again." Bolton's deputy Charles Kupperman, running the meeting, then closed his briefing book and abruptly adjourned the session. Several officials who attended, including Sue Gordon, deputy director of national intelligence, and Vaughn Bishop, the deputy CIA director, huddled afterward. "If there was a secret ballot, every single person in that room would have voted that Earl was completely out of line," a White House official who had also been in the meeting told them.

Days after Selva's fight with the Bolton team, Guaidó escalated the crisis, calling for an all-out mobilization to topple Maduro and publicly appealing to top officials in the government to change sides. Guaidó appeared to be doing this with the active connivance of top American officials as Bolton and Pompeo each suggested publicly that the United States might intervene militarily on Guaidó's behalf, no matter how improbable that seemed. "Military action is possible," Pompeo told Fox Business. "If that's what's required, that's what the United States will do."[7] Bolton told MSNBC that Trump "has been clear and concise on this point: All options are open."[8] In a series of tweets, Bolton personally taunted Maduro, urging him to seek "long, quiet retirement" on a "nice beach somewhere far from Venezuela."[9] But the threats were not enough and Trump remained notably quiet. In a few short days in April, Guaidó's uprising sputtered, and Maduro stayed in power.

The blustery war talk about Venezuela from Pompeo and Bolton seemed to prove the assumptions many had when they were appointed that they represented the advent of a new "War Cabinet." But Trump was wary of war and had been all along. That spring, the president had taken to joking that if Bolton had his way, he would be in four wars all at once. When Guaidó's effort to topple Maduro failed, Trump blamed Bolton to other White House aides, saying the national security adviser had underestimated Venezuela's "tough cookie" of a leader.[10] This time, when he said that Bolton was trying to get him into a war, it did not sound like a joke. Pompeo, more skilled or simply more willing to offer Trump the flattery he craved, endorsed the same policies as Bolton, but avoided the presidential blowback.

Asked by reporters about his national security adviser after the collapse of the Venezuela plot, Trump made his qualms explicit. "John is a—he has strong views on things," the president said, "but that's okay. I actually temper John, which is pretty amazing, isn't it? Nobody thought that was going to—I'm the one that tempers him. But that's okay. I have different sides. I mean, I have John Bolton, and I have other people that are a little more dovish than him. And ultimately I make the decision."[11] Once again, Trump embraced the internal conflict that was endemic in his White House. This was not a failure of his administration, as he saw it, but a guarantee that he was the only one who mattered.

John Bolton's failed revolution in Venezuela, however, was a sideshow. For Trump's national security team, Iran remained the main event. Bolton had been preaching regime change in Tehran for years, deeming it the only real way to prevent Iran from acquiring nuclear weapons. He regarded Trump's decision to pull out of the hated Iran nuclear deal within weeks of his becoming national security adviser as an early triumph and had even hung a framed copy of Trump's order doing so in his office. In February, Bolton had released a video of himself threatening the regime on the occasion of the fortieth anniversary of the Iranian revolution. "So, Ayatollah Khamenei," Bolton said, addressing the supreme leader directly, "I don't think you'll have many more anniversaries to enjoy."[12]

After the administration exited the nuclear deal, Pompeo had designed a "maximum pressure" campaign of economic sanctions on Iran, but it had become clear that Trump's advisers had different goals on Iran than Trump. While they sought to topple the ayatollahs, the president was running his North Korea play again, hoping to turn the pressure campaign into leverage for negotiations. He wanted more summits, more glory, more shots at a Nobel Peace Prize.

By the spring of 2019, however, Iran had begun to respond to the pressure in ways that threatened to call Trump's bluff. Despite entreaties from the Europeans who had helped negotiate the nuclear deal, Iran had announced a series of steps withdrawing from its conditions, saying it would no longer observe limits on stockpiles of low-enriched uranium and heavy water. It had also increased military pressure on American interests in the region, including harassment of oil tankers in the Persian Gulf.

Bolton and Pompeo clamored for Trump to respond, and Bolton took the unusual step of personally announcing the deployment of an aircraft carrier battle group to the region, which he did the same weekend that the Venezuela plot to oust Maduro fell apart. Bolton remained bitter at the Pentagon for its resistance to his Venezuela campaign and clashed with Paul Selva again in early June when an American drone was shot down in Yemen, with the Iranian-backed Houthis claiming credit. Selva, according to Bolton, was responsible for the United States doing nothing in response, because he "acted like a prosecutor demanding that we show guilt beyond a reasonable doubt" rather than acknowledging a "messy real world" where only Iran and its surrogates could possibly be to blame. The generals, Bolton would say later, were once more acting as outright "obstructionists."[13]

This time, Trump welcomed the skeptical note interjected by Joe Dunford when the lame-duck chairman of the Joint Chiefs warned about the costs of military action against Iran. Trump was still holding out hope for negotiations with the Iranians and had even prodded Japan's Shinzo Abe that June into taking a trip to Tehran in hopes of serving as a secret door-opener, so he saw the generals' pushback for once as helpful. "I just want to know that you guys know that what we're doing is very unlikely to effect a change in Iran's policy and it has a high probability of a conflict," Dunford said in one of the numerous meetings on Iran that spring in the Situation Room. "Do you understand that?"

The chairman was mild-mannered, but clearly fed up with the blustery messaging coming from Pompeo and Bolton. "You can't be BS'ing people and saying that we have a diplomatic and economic pressure campaign designed to have a better" nuclear deal. "That's not actually what you think is happening here, so please be honest about it. My military advice has to be in the context of what you really believe is going on here."

Trump's unwillingness to be managed by Bolton on Iran came to a head over twenty-four hours in June. It began late on the evening of the 19th with confirmation that another RQ-4A Global Hawk drone had been shot down by the Iranians over the Strait of Hormuz, the second one in less than two weeks. The next morning, Bolton and other advisers

met over breakfast and agreed to recommend that Trump retaliate, with
the national security adviser and Pompeo pushing for strong action and
Dunford emphasizing the response should be "proportional" and "nones-
calatory." Later that morning, the group's proposal to hit three sites along
Iran's coast was presented to Trump, who kept saying, "We need to hit
them hard. We need to make them pay."[14] Dunford told Trump the strike
would take place that evening Washington time and that casualties would
be limited because it would be the dead of night in Iran.

Trump that afternoon continued his tough talk in a meeting with congressional leaders. "I think you're going to like what you see," Trump told
Representative Michael McCaul of Texas, the ranking Republican on the
House Foreign Affairs Committee.[15] At one point, he told the visiting
members that he was considering "a hit, but not a hit that's going to be so
devastating." Later, he added, "Doing nothing is the biggest risk."[16]

Around 5:30 p.m., Bolton went home to change clothes and prepare
for what he expected to be a long night ahead. He spoke with Trump by
phone and told him plans were on track for the attack. "Okay," the president told him, "let's go."

But shortly before 7:30 p.m., Trump called back to say he was scrapping the attack. It was not "proportionate," Trump said. He told Bolton
and Pompeo in a conference call that he had subsequently been told as
many as 150 Iranians could die, "too many body bags" for an unmanned
drone. Pompeo argued, but to no avail.[17] Bolton was furious.

Mystified at the abrupt about-face, Bolton soon discovered that John
Eisenberg, a White House lawyer tasked with national security matters,
had gone back to Trump and cited the theoretical figure of 150 casualties to him, a number Eisenberg had apparently gotten from someone in
the Pentagon. Trump had then called Dunford, who denied that was the
official estimate but told him, "Look, if you're not comfortable with that
decision, then we shouldn't do it." Trump later acknowledged in a series of
tweets confirming the bizarre incident that he had been "cocked & loaded"
and ready to go, but then "10 minutes before the strike I stopped it."

The matter was almost certainly not that simple. For days, Trump had
been hearing from political allies who were concerned about a reckless
spiral of retaliatory attacks, the last thing Trump needed headed into a
2020 presidential campaign where he would promise again to end America's "endless wars." Tucker Carlson, the Fox News host and occasional
Trump confidant, had even called Trump that week and told him he could
forget about re-election if he got into a war with Iran.

Minutes after pulling the plug on the strike, Trump turned on his television to catch the opening monologue of Carlson's 8 p.m. show on Fox. Carlson praised Trump for resisting military intervention. "The same people who lured us into the Iraq quagmire sixteen years ago are demanding a new war, this one with Iran," Carlson said. "The president, to his great credit, appears to be skeptical of this—very skeptical."[18]

Bolton would later write that "in my government experience, this was the most irrational thing I ever witnessed any president do."[19] He said that he and Pompeo, both Iran hawks far longer than they had been Trump supporters, spent the next few days in a series of flabbergasted phone calls with each other discussing whether to resign, their fantasy of successfully managing Trump having been long since discarded. But, once again, neither did.

At the start of that week, Trump had flown to Orlando, Florida, for one of his signature political rallies, the sixtieth of his presidency, where he planned to officially kick off his 2020 campaign a year and a half before the vote. As he headed to Air Force One, he stopped to tweet a personnel bulletin. Acting Defense Secretary Patrick Shanahan, who had proven a reliable enough yes-man that Trump had nominated him for a permanent seat in his cabinet, was out, undone by allegations of family domestic violence, including a horrific incident in 2011 in which his son attacked his ex-wife with a baseball bat. In his place, Trump tweeted, he would nominate Mark Esper, the secretary of the Army. Esper, a West Point classmate of Pompeo's and former lobbyist for Raytheon, would become Trump's third nominee in three years for the post.

This was not the first time Esper had been an accidental Trump appointee and unintended beneficiary of the White House's haphazard selection process and lack of rigorous vetting. In 2017, Esper had been Trump's third choice for Army secretary. The first, Vincent Viola, the billionaire owner of the Florida Panthers hockey team, stepped aside after saying he could not leave his business. The second, a state senator from Tennessee, Mark Green, flamed out after it was revealed that he had denounced transgender people as having a "disease," called evolution a "bad argument," and objected to students being taught about Islam.[20]

Esper, who had served in the Gulf War and risen to Army lieutenant colonel before leaving to get a doctorate at George Washington University, had worked for centrist Republicans in the Senate and the George W. Bush Pentagon. Dave Urban, the lobbyist who had pushed Trump to make Mark Milley chairman of the Joint Chiefs, was friends with Esper from their first days at West Point, a fellow Pennsylvanian who went to Operation Desert Storm together with him. Urban introduced Esper to his future wife and was godfather to their child, and he vouched for him to the president. "He'll be a slam dunk," Urban told a White House official.

But Esper was no Trumpist, and the true Trumpists in the administration knew it. His induction to the dysfunctional Trump cabinet had been sitting in on meetings over the Iran strike that wasn't. Esper now called John Kelly seeking counsel on how to navigate the unpredictable president. "How do I survive?" Esper asked.

"You survive if you completely compromise your standards and your integrity and you become a yes-man and a lackey," Kelly later recounted telling him.

"I can't do that," Esper replied.

"I know," Kelly responded. "That's why you're going to get fired."

In Florida, Trump made no mention of the turmoil on his national security team. In his seventy-six-minute speech before twenty thousand fans, he blasted the "permanent political class" and the media, the "great and illegal witch hunt" against him, and his "Radical Democrat opponents." He led the audience in a chant of "lock her up" about his 2016 opponent Hillary Clinton and talked about dangerous illegal immigrants and the terrific economy and the even more terrific trade deal he would soon negotiate with China. His campaign theme, he said, was "Keep America Great," or maybe he would just stick with "Make America Great Again," but either way he was running, and no one except George Washington maybe had been as great a president.

The same day, the Pentagon put out one of those news releases that get little attention beyond those paid to observe the incremental steps in the policy process. In it, the military announced plans to disburse $250 million in security assistance to Ukraine, part of a larger $391 million package that had been approved by Congress and the president the previous year. But at the White House, Mick Mulvaney, the acting chief of staff, noticed and informed his deputy, Robert Blair, that Trump had a problem with sending the promised weapons to Ukraine. Mulvaney did not think much of the president's interest in the issue at the time. Trump was famously allergic to the very concept of foreign aid and had sought to cut assistance to other countries before, although there were limits on his discretion when it had been enacted into law by legislators.

The next day, Blair called Russell Vought, the acting head of the Office of Management and Budget. "We need to hold it up," Blair told him.[21]

When John Bolton dialed into a secure teleconference in the White House Situation Room from Jerusalem a few days later, he was surprised to hear Trump banging on about the money for Ukraine, which had been making its way through the Pentagon bureaucracy without controversy for more than nine months. Ukraine was not the ostensible subject of the meeting, and it was the first Bolton had heard of the mysterious aid freeze.

"Did you approve it, John?" the president demanded to know. "How stupid is this?" Trump then started in on a familiar refrain of Germany-bashing. Ukraine was Germany's neighbor, why couldn't they pitch in, and so on. "John, do you agree on Ukraine?" Trump asked again.[22] Bolton did not answer directly, instead trying to deflect the president. Let Esper, your new defense secretary, handle it, he suggested. But listening to Trump go off about it, Bolton's antennae flared.

He and Pompeo both knew—had known for months, actually—that Trump had a Ukraine fixation fed by Rudy Giuliani and others that portended no good. They had often heard Trump repeat Russian disinformation about Ukraine and 2016, suggesting that the hacking of Hillary Clinton's emails was some sort of false-flag Ukrainian operation—and despite having been told this was a Russian lie, Trump publicly promoted it, just as Vladimir Putin had. Bolton and Pompeo also knew that Giuliani had some new scheme afoot with Ukraine to dig up dirt on former Vice President Joe Biden, the frontrunner for the Democratic nomination to challenge the president the next year, and his son Hunter. "Keep your eye on Ukraine," Giuliani had said on *Fox & Friends* that spring.[23]

In fact, Bolton had personally transmitted Trump's order several times to Pompeo and his aides to fire the ambassador to Ukraine, a well-respected career diplomat named Marie Yovanovitch. On March 25, Trump had called Bolton into his private dining room, where he was meeting with Giuliani and Jay Sekulow, one of his other lawyers. It was then that Bolton learned that Giuliani was the one targeting Yovanovitch, part of an orchestrated campaign that included smear columns in *The Hill* newspaper by conservative columnist John Solomon, a tweet from Don Jr. calling for "jokers" like her to be removed, and segments on Fox News with Trump favorites Sean Hannity and Laura Ingraham.[24] Pompeo himself spoke with Giuliani about Yovanovitch at least twice in late March and Giuliani had a dossier attacking her delivered to the secretary in a White House envelope. On whose behalf Giuliani was acting, it was not entirely clear.

On April 23, after another eruption by Trump during an Oval Office phone call with Giuliani, Bolton called Pompeo again and told him that the president wanted Yovanovitch fired immediately, "no ifs, ands, or buts."[25] Pompeo did so the next day.

There had been further warning signs about Trump and Ukraine for months. Back in February, both Bolton and his deputy, Charles Kupperman, had almost quit over Trump's insistence that they hire Kash Patel, a former staffer on the House Intelligence Committee and protégé of Devin Nunes who had been one of the chief promoters of Russian-circulated conspiracy theories that it was Ukraine, not Russia, that had interfered in the 2016 election. "I will put my badge on the desk and I will leave," Kupperman raged to a colleague, soon after returning from a fight that he, Bolton, and Mulvaney had over Patel. Eventually, they bowed to the order when they were told Patel was a "must-hire, directed by the president" but insisted on putting him in the most obscure post they could find, in the National Security Council's international organizations directorate, practically the definition of Siberia, given Bolton's well-known animus toward all things multilateral. "We tried to mitigate the risk by putting him in a directorate that was not going to cause more trouble than we could handle," Kupperman later told associates.

But by May, as Giuliani's pressure campaign took out Yovanovitch, Patel was already using his new position in the White House to become involved in Ukraine matters. Bolton's team discovered that only inadvertently when Derek Lyons, the White House staff secretary, referred to Patel as "your Ukraine director" in a conversation with Fiona Hill, the National Security Council senior director for the region, and asked to include him in a meeting because Trump had been asking about the "packages" he had received from Patel on the subject.

Yovanovitch's official exit from Kyiv that spring came on the same day as the inauguration of the newly elected Ukrainian president, Volodymyr Zelensky, a television comedian turned politician who promised "zero tolerance" for corruption. Trump had promised Zelensky in a congratulatory phone call to send a high-level delegation headed by Mike Pence to his inauguration and invited the Ukrainian leader to visit Washington as well. But after hanging up, Trump personally ordered Pence not to go, sending a lower-ranking delegation instead, and refused to follow up with an actual White House invitation to Zelensky. When Hill tried to figure out why, Derek Lyons told her explicitly it had to do with Giuliani. "You need to be aware of Giuliani," Lyons explained. "He's in the mix here; he's constantly calling." On May 8, according to Bolton, the president directly ordered him to call Zelensky on Giuliani's behalf and demand that the Ukrainian president meet with Trump's personal lawyer, although Bolton later said that he did not make the call.

On returning from Zelensky's inauguration, the American delegation, which included Energy Secretary Rick Perry; Gordon Sondland, the ambassador to the European Union; and Kurt Volker, the State Department special envoy to Ukraine, reported to Trump in the Oval Office on May 23.

What they heard stunned them. Trump actively opposed the American policy of supporting Ukraine in its long-running fight with Russian-backed separatists, had a "deeply rooted negative view" of Ukraine grounded in Giuliani's conspiracy theories, and had no intention of meeting with Zelensky.[26] He even demanded that they work through Giuliani from then on regarding the Zelensky meeting.

"They're terrible people," Trump said of Ukrainians. "They're all corrupt and they tried to take me down."

Alarmed, Senator Ron Johnson of Wisconsin, who had been part of the delegation and had sat in on the Oval Office meeting with Trump, went to John Bolton to brief him afterward. "We have a problem," he told Bolton. "It did not go well."

Bolton responded that Giuliani was the source of the trouble. "It's like Rudy has a sixth sense" for Trump and Ukraine, he said. Later, Bolton told his aide Fiona Hill that "Rudy Giuliani is a hand grenade that is going to blow everybody up."[27]

But skeptical as he was, Bolton had gone along, however reluctantly, with Trump's dismissal of Marie Yovanovitch, and he did not try to stop Trump or Giuliani now either. Neither did Pompeo. His State Department had reached out to Bill Taylor, a former American ambassador to Ukraine appointed by George W. Bush, hoping to send him temporarily back to Kyiv in Yovanovitch's place, but Taylor sought assurances that Washington would have his back. He was skeptical and soon heard from George Kent, the deputy assistant secretary of state for the region, that Trump and Giuliani were up to something, even if the details were unclear.

"George described two snake pits, one in Kyiv and one in Washington," Taylor wrote in a text to Kurt Volker. "He described much more than I knew. Very ugly."

A few days after the Oval Office meeting, Taylor texted Volker again. "I am still struggling with the decision whether to go. Can anyone hope to succeed with the Guliani-Biden issue swirling for the next 18 months?

Can S offer any reassurance on this issue?" Taylor asked, using the initial referring to the secretary of state and misspelling the former mayor's name.[28]

Heeding advice he got from Stephen Hadley, the former Bush national security adviser, Taylor insisted on an unusual in-person meeting with Pompeo before agreeing to accept the assignment. In the session a few days later, with Volker and Ulrich Brechbuhl, Pompeo's old friend now serving as his counselor, also present, the secretary of state acknowledged they had a Trump problem.

"Mr. Secretary," Taylor said, "the reason I'm not planning to do this is that I don't think your boss likes Ukraine."

"Bill, you're right, he doesn't," Pompeo responded, "and my job is to turn him around." For emphasis, Pompeo turned his hand in the air.

The secretary of state promised that he would shift Trump's thinking. "He even had this mathematical formula," Taylor recalled. "He said, 'Force is pressure over time: Pressure times time.'" Taylor told Pompeo that he had heard that Trump was so adamant about Ukraine that he had even torn into pieces the standard congratulations letter to Zelensky that his staff had pressed him to sign. Pompeo said he had not heard that. "Find out about the letter," Pompeo told Brechbuhl.

Soon after, the letter was signed and Taylor said yes to the assignment, although he, like Bolton and his staff in the White House, quickly realized that Giuliani and a rump group of administration officials were not only pushing Zelensky to open investigations of Biden and the Democrats, but even withholding a White House meeting until the Ukrainian agreed. No one told Taylor about Trump's decision in June to hold up the hundreds of millions in security assistance for Ukraine as well.

But the intrigue continued. In early July, Gordon Sondland, the European Union ambassador, joined a visiting Ukrainian delegation in a meeting at the White House and was so explicit about the linkage between an Oval Office invitation to Zelensky and the investigations Trump was seeking that Bolton ordered Fiona Hill to report it to the National Security Council lawyers. Her deputy, Lieutenant Colonel Alexander Vindman, also reported the meeting to the attorneys.

After arriving in Ukraine, Taylor dialed into a secure videoconference at the White House in mid-July and learned for the first time about the aid holdup. "I and others on the call sat in astonishment," Taylor later testified.[29]

John Bolton was under no illusions about Trump. By the spring of 2019, he already believed that Trump engaged in "obstruction of justice as a way of life," as he later would write, a remarkable statement by a national security adviser about the president.[30] On April 23, the same day that a Trump Oval Office rant had caused Bolton to tell Pompeo he had to fire Marie Yovanovitch and just a week after the release of Robert Mueller's report outlining Trump's obstruction in the investigation, Bolton had confided his concerns to the attorney general over a lunch of sandwiches and chips in Bill Barr's private conference room.

Bolton, who had known Barr for decades, had scheduled the lunch in part to "brief him on Trump's penchant to, in effect, give personal favors to dictators he liked," he later wrote, including the president's willingness to improperly intervene in investigations into companies like Turkey's Halkbank to curry favor with Recep Tayyip Erdoğan and China's ZTE to ingratiate himself with Xi Jinping.[31] Bolton also noted a recent decision to ease sanctions against the Kremlin-connected oligarch Oleg Deripaska.

Bolton did not report whether he brought up Ukraine and Giuliani as well, although it was already top of mind that day. After being yelled at by Trump in the Oval Office, Bolton had asked Pat Cipollone and another lawyer from the White House counsel's office whether Giuliani "had ethical problems" for apparently leveraging his attorney-client relationship with the president for what looked to be some other client's interests.

But that, it appears, is as far as Bolton took the matter. Barr thought Trump assigned too much importance to his relationship with the Turkish leader but did not see illegality. Bolton admitted he was wary of doing more about his suspicions regarding Giuliani because he was afraid it might further jeopardize the security assistance for Ukraine that he wanted Trump to release.

None of these alarming developments was enough to get Bolton to resign. Nor were his months of disagreements with Trump over Iran, Syria, and North Korea.

Many days, Bolton's war was not with the president at all, but with his bureaucratic rivals at the State Department or the Pentagon or in the White House itself. Many of his colleagues did not just dislike Bolton, they loathed him. In June, just a couple weeks before Mick Mulvaney first held up the Ukraine aid, he and Bolton had gotten into an expletive-filled screaming match during Trump's state visit to London, after Bolton, traveling solo in his own motorcade, had blown by the rest of Trump's senior advisers stuck by the side of the road in a bus. "Let's face it, John,"

Mulvaney told Bolton afterward. "You're a fucking self-righteous, self-centered son of a bitch!"[32]

It was hard, in that environment, to decide the difference between a criminal conspiracy and "just another day at the office," as Bolton would write.[33] But he was a graduate of Yale Law School. Pompeo was a graduate of Harvard Law School. They presumably understood that threatening not to disburse hundreds of millions of dollars in congressionally appropriated aid to a country fighting Russia in order to make a foreign leader investigate political rivals was not how the United States government was supposed to work.

CHAPTER 18

The Summer of Crazy

In late June, Trump traveled to the G20 summit in Osaka, Japan, eagerly anticipating a meeting with Vladimir Putin. It would be the first time they had met since the release of the Mueller report. As they posed for media pictures before their meeting began, Trump joked with the Russian leader about his problems with the "fake news." When reporters asked if he would warn against any further interference in American democracy, Trump fake-scolded Putin for the cameras. "Don't meddle in the election," Trump said, half laughing and comically pointing his finger as if it were all a joke. More seriously, he promised that "a lot of very positive things" would come of their relationship.[1]

After the reporters were escorted out, the private meeting offered a spectacle that, had it become public, would have inflamed the media even more than the jocular teasing. One American official described what followed as a "macho chest-thumping" contest over a brewing arms race to acquire hypersonic missiles.

"Well, you know, Donald, we have these hypersonic missiles," Putin told Trump.

Russia may have gotten them first, Trump countered, but "we'll get them too."

"Well, yes, you'll get them *eventually*," Putin responded, "but we've got them first."

Putin's menace was unmistakable to the American officials who heard him, but it was unclear whether Trump picked up on it.

As they continued their discussion, Trump bragged to Putin about his popularity in other countries, telling him that Poland planned to name one of its military bases "Fort Trump" and Israel announced just a week earlier that it would name a new settlement "Trump Heights" in gratitude for his decision to recognize Israel's decades-old occupation of the Golan Heights.

But Putin, unimpressed, had the insecure president's number. "Maybe they should just name Israel after you, Donald," he deadpanned.

For all of Trump's schoolboy crush on Putin, aides could not help noticing that it did not appear reciprocated. Where other autocrats like Xi Jinping, Recep Tayyip Erdoğan, and Kim Jong-un figured out how to stroke Trump's ego during their meetings, Putin never bothered to try. He gave the impression to American aides watching their interactions that he couldn't care less about winning Trump over. It was all a one-way street. Trump, they thought, seemed so inexplicably anxious for the Russian leader's approval, yet never got it.

If taunted by Putin, Trump relished his meetings with other autocrats over the course of the summit, even as he once again attacked America's closest allies. After publicly dumping on the decades-old mutual defense treaty with Japan, he sat with China's Xi on the opening night of the summit and discussed the imprisonment of up to a million ethnic Uighurs in camps by the Chinese. Not only did he express no concern about such a massive human rights atrocity, Trump even agreed that Xi should continue building the camps, according to the account of Trump's interpreter later made public by John Bolton.

In a telephone call the next day with Speaker Nancy Pelosi, who had urged Trump to raise the plight of the Uighurs, Trump told her that Xi had explained that they "like being in those camps." Just a few weeks earlier, Pelosi had publicly questioned Trump's fitness for office and urged his family or his advisers to conduct an "intervention" with the erratic president. She thought there was nothing more Trump could say that would astound her. But she was astounded nonetheless. *They like being in those camps.* Really? "Mr. President," she eventually responded, "that's what an authoritarian would say, but they most certainly do not like being separated from their families."

The weekend after the summit, Trump decided to make a surprise visit to the Korean Demilitarized Zone to meet with Kim Jong-un, where, notwithstanding the collapse of meaningful nuclear talks, they continued to pal around. When Kim suggested Trump step over the border and become the first president ever to enter North Korea, he did so happily. Bolton was so disgusted that he refused to accompany Trump, opting instead to make a previously scheduled trip to Mongolia. Mick Mulvaney thought that was insubordinate and urged Trump to fire Bolton, but for once the president demurred.

Back in Washington, the president was taking an increasingly expansive view of his own powers. That July, he told a conference of pro-Trump teenagers that Article II of the Constitution gave him "the right to do whatever I want as president," which was both flagrantly incorrect and also consistent with Trump's oft-stated view that he had the "absolute right" to do whatever he wanted at whatever moment he wanted to do it—a list that had grown by that point to include everything from pardoning himself and declaring a national emergency to build a border wall to revealing classified information.[2] He not only admired autocrats like Putin and Xi, he appeared determined to sound like one. And the presidential ego, never slight, seemed ever more boundless by the middle of 2019 as he often referred to himself as a "genius" and one of "the smartest people anywhere in the world."

His estimation of his abilities was both vast and highly specific. The list of things Trump publicly claimed to "know more about than anybody" had grown to include borders, campaign finance, courts, construction, drones, debt, Democrats, the economy, infrastructure, the Islamic State, lawsuits, money, nuclear weapons, politicians, polls, renewable energy, social media, steelworkers, taxes, technology, "things" generally, trade, the United States government, and the visa system. He even said he knew more about New Jersey Democratic senator Cory Booker than Booker knew about himself. The president often explained publicly that windmills caused cancer, climate change was a hoax, and American toilets did not work properly anymore because of federal regulations.

If Trump increasingly projected the eccentric grandiosity of a wannabe monarch, he also appeared to be an increasingly paranoid leader obsessed with enemies seeking to destroy his presidency. They were, Trump liked to say, "wacko," "lunatic," or just plain "nuts." When he and Pelosi met in May at the White House to discuss Trump's long-delayed plans to introduce a major infrastructure bill, the session lasted all of three minutes before Trump walked out of his own Cabinet Room. After Pelosi, in response, questioned his fitness for office, Trump called her "Crazy Nancy" and demanded aides appear with him at a news conference to vouch for his behavior.[3] In fact, "crazy" was one of his favorite insults, a label he also bestowed on "Crazy Jim Acosta" of CNN, "Crazy Maxine Waters," a Democratic congresswoman from California, "Crazy Mika" Brzezinski (and "Psycho Joe" Scarborough) of MSNBC, the "Crazy Mueller Report," "crazy trade with China," and "Crazy Bernie Sanders," the Vermont socialist running once again for president.[4]

No one worried the president more, however, than the Democrat he had started to call "Sleepy Joe" Biden. Trump had rolled out the nickname and an ongoing Twitter barrage against Biden in the spring, when the former vice president announced he was running to take on Trump, calling him a "threat to this nation" unlike "any I had ever seen in my lifetime."[5] Trump, who said publicly that he considered Biden his likeliest 2020 opponent and toughest rival among the Democrats, made a particular point of criticizing Biden's age, IQ, and competence—exactly the traits that many critics questioned about Trump himself. "Does anybody really believe he is mentally fit to be President?" Trump tweeted of Biden that summer.

Even many Republicans were amazed: Was that a debate that Trump really wanted to have?

Throughout his presidency, the psychological state of the world's most powerful man was a source of never-ending speculation, commentary, and concern in a way that simply had no parallel in American history. Other presidents had been afflicted with mental illness. Abraham Lincoln suffered from what doctors would later call clinical depression. Lyndon Johnson alternated between bouts of mania and depression. Richard Nixon popped pills and had legendary alcohol-fueled rages as the Watergate scandal closed in around him. But the debate about Trump went to even more fundamental questions about his fitness for office, a controversy that began during the 2016 primary campaign, when several of his Republican rivals criticized Trump as dangerously unsuited to the presidency. Lindsey Graham was not the only one to call him a "kook." Ted Cruz had called him a "pathological liar."[6] Rand Paul called him "a delusional narcissist."[7] Once he was elected, Trump's mental health became a source of private consternation inside his own administration: Was he actually crazy, as many wondered, including some of Trump's most senior appointees, or crazy like a fox, as other Trump advisers often claimed?

Most of the public diagnoses posited that Trump had an extreme case of narcissistic personality disorder along with other problems that likely included a childhood learning disability, which would explain his lifelong aversion to books and written briefings—all compounded by what appeared to be significant age-related decline in his cognitive faculties. But although it was an inescapable part of the conversation surrounding the volatile president, such armchair psychoanalysis also violated longstanding taboos for both the mental health profession and the media, which had been wary of judging a would-be president's sanity since 1964, when thousands of psychiatrists signed a letter asserting that Republican presidential candidate Barry Goldwater was unfit for office.

In *The Dangerous Case of Donald Trump*, a bestselling book that came out in 2017, twenty-seven mental health professionals, led by Dr. Bandy Lee, a Yale professor of forensic psychiatry, explicitly defied the decades-old "Goldwater Rule" banning psychiatrists from offering diagnoses of patients they had not seen. Lee's group considered Trump a public health threat and believed they had a "duty to warn" that overrode their obligation to avoid practicing psychiatry from afar. "It's not all in our heads," they concluded. "It's in his."[8]

Among those who secretly bought a copy of the psychiatrists' book was none other than John Kelly, who sought help to understand the president's particular psychoses and consulted it while he was running the White House, which he was known to refer to as "Crazytown." Kelly told others that the book was a helpful guide to a president he came to consider a pathological liar whose inflated ego was in fact the sign of a deeply insecure person. Kelly often regaled others with stories of Trump's ignorance about basic historical facts and inability to absorb correct information once it was presented to him. A particular low point was Trump's April 2018 meeting with the leaders of the three Baltic countries, which Trump confused for the Balkans. "We don't want to have another war start in the Baltics," Trump told them, to much confusion. When Kelly sought to clarify, Trump explained he meant "World War I, or one of those wars," when "they shot a king," an apparent reference to the assassination of the Archduke Franz Ferdinand in Sarajevo some eight hundred miles to the south of the Baltics that had set off the First World War.[9] But it was Trump's flawed judgment that most rattled Kelly, and he concluded that the problem was not that Trump did not know right from wrong, but that "he always does the wrong thing."

Like Kelly, other top officials who served during the Trump administration came to believe that Trump was mentally ill, unable or unwilling to process basic information necessary to do his job, and dangerously uninformed. "I think there's something wrong with him," one of these senior officials said. "He doesn't listen to anybody, and he feels like he shouldn't. He just doesn't care what other people say and think. I've never seen anything like it." In the cabinet, Trump's behavior led to a running debate among several of his secretaries. Was Trump "crazy-crazy," as one of them put it, or merely someone who promoted "crazy ideas" because they suited him? As for the president's many lies, opinions were divided sharply between officials like Kelly who thought Trump believed at least some of the bizarre and often palpably untrue things he said and those who thought it was all a cynical form of performance art.

The first tentative cabinet discussions about how and whether to invoke the Twenty-fifth Amendment to temporarily remove an incapacitated president from power occurred within months of Trump taking office. But the amendment, passed in the wake of John Kennedy's assassination, was written with short-term physical disability in mind, not a president with a chronic mental condition that made him unsuited to lead. In the wake of Ronald Reagan's post-presidency diagnosis of Alzheimer's disease, Jimmy Carter had been so worried about this scenario that he urged Congress to fix "the great weakness" of the amendment and figure out a way to determine disability in the case of a president unwilling or unable to admit it.[10] But as matters stood in the Trump era, the constitutional process was so cumbersome it was all but insurmountable. Under the amendment, a president who disagreed that he was incapacitated, as Trump surely would, could challenge the decision of his vice president and cabinet by going to Congress, where it would require a two-thirds vote by both the House and Senate to uphold his removal. Even House impeachment and conviction in a Senate trial did not require that level of consensus.

Still, Trump's personality flaws were so manifest that the debate among top Washington officials about Trump's mental state was jarringly public. "I think he's crazy," Senator Jack Reed, a Rhode Island Democrat, told Senator Susan Collins, the Republican centrist from Maine, in an exchange during Trump's first summer in office inadvertently caught on a microphone. "I'm worried," Collins replied.[11] Senator Bob Corker, once considered by Trump a possible vice president or secretary of state, compared the White House to "an adult day care center" and warned in 2017 that Trump "has not yet been able to demonstrate the stability nor some of the competence" to succeed as president.[12]

White House officials, speaking to reporters under cover of anonymity, referred to the president so often as if he were a petulant child that Daniel Drezner, a Tufts University political scientist, started a years-long Twitter thread codifying all the examples of what he called "the toddler in chief." It had hit eight hundred citations by June 29, 2019, when Drezner highlighted a *Politico* item about a presidential temper tantrum over Mick Mulvaney coughing in front of him.[13] "You can't, you just can't cough," Trump insisted.[14] Indeed, Trump's staff sometimes turned to a tried-and-true lullaby strategy to calm the toddler in chief. When he seemed to be heading into a rage, advisers were known to summon one of his favorite aides, a young advance staffer named Max Miller, to soothe the angry Trump by playing show tunes and kibitzing with him over the playlist for his rallies. "Memories" from the Broadway musical *Cats* was a particular favorite. Colleagues nicknamed Miller "the Music Man."[15]

In private, some Republicans strategized about the best response. Paul Ryan, the Republican speaker of the House who eventually quit Congress while despairing of the Trump-era turn in his party, secretly researched how to deal with Trump's obvious mental problems. A New York doctor who was a significant Republican backer emailed Ryan with his views of Trump's psychiatric state and provided recommended reading for how to deal with a person with anti-social personality disorder. Ryan pored through the material looking for insights. That would have been politically explosive had it been known at the time, but it stayed secret until revealed by the authors Bob Woodward and Robert Costa months after Trump left office.

In the spring of 2019, the economist Larry Lindsey, summoned by House Minority Leader Kevin McCarthy to conduct closed-door briefings for Republican leaders about Trump's escalating trade war with China, surprised lawmakers by offering a presentation not on the state of Trump's economy but on the state of his mind. A few days earlier, Trump had finally made his long-delayed, long-threatened announcement that he was imposing tariffs on $200 billion in Chinese goods. Global markets were nervous and Trump's public vacillation between praising Xi Jinping and threatening him had left Washington uncertain, once again, just what the president intended.

A former Harvard professor and governor of the Federal Reserve who had served as George W. Bush's national economic adviser, Lindsey told the Republicans, most of whom had spent the last two and a half years publicly defending the president's questionable behavior even if they privately lamented it, that he had asked two experts to assess both Trump and Xi. The experts, psychologists in Virginia who often testified in court cases, evaluated the two leaders, looking at their photographs over time, to see where they fit on the "Dark Triad," the three personality attributes associated with history's worst dictators.

Trump, not surprisingly, scored off the charts on the first part of the triad: narcissism. In fact, Lindsey said, the president was a "ten out of ten narcissist," which he blamed on Trump's mother, a withholding Scottish immigrant who had not, in his view, given Trump sufficient attention early in life. Lindsey, however, said that Trump did not rate on the two other personality disorders in the triad: Machiavellianism and sociopathy.

"He's not Machiavellian," Lindsey said. "How many steps ahead does he think? Let's just be honest with ourselves." He compared Trump's long-term planning ability to that of an "empty chair." While conceding that Trump said racist, offensive, and untrue things and sought to pit Americans against each other, Lindsey argued that the president's overwhelming desire to be the center of attention was Trump's dominant trait. "What he really wants for you is for you to like him," Lindsey said.

Xi, by contrast, checked all three boxes. He was, Lindsey would say later, "one dangerous puppy." Nonetheless, Lindsey told the Republicans, Trump's erratic behavior, indiscipline, and excessive self-regard had made him a challenging adversary for the Chinese. He was, in effect, a modern-day manifestation of the "madman theory" that Henry Kissinger had employed while working for Richard Nixon, warning foreign interlocutors that the president was so unpredictable that they ought to accept whatever deal he was offering. Trump's craziness was an advantage in threatening a trade war with China, Lindsey posited, given that he might actually go through with it. "One of his assets was it reduced the willingness to take risks by foreign adversaries and it did in Xi's case by a lot," Lindsey would say later.

Lindsey gave the presentation twice—once to about a dozen members of the GOP leadership and again to ranking Republican members of relevant committees. No one in either session spoke up to dispute it when one of the Republican Party's leading thinkers offered the view that theirs was a president with a deeply damaged psyche. The postscript to the briefing was as revealing in its own way as the fact of it. When Lindsey called his contacts in the White House, somewhat sheepishly, after his comments about the president's narcissism leaked out, he got no pushback. "It didn't bother him one bit," Lindsey was told.[16]

In fact, Trump was well aware of his unhinged reputation and at times sought to exploit it. "Tell them you just talked to the president," he once advised Nikki Haley, his United Nations ambassador, when dealing with the North Koreans. "Make them think I'm crazy."[17] When meeting with Bill Barr and other lawyers on another occasion, Trump looked up from his phone. "Do you know what the secret is of a really good tweet?" he asked them. "Just the right amount of crazy."[18] In January of 2018, the publication of Michael Wolff's book, *Fire and Fury*, drawn from inside access to Trump's dysfunctional White House and relying heavily on the account of Steve Bannon, portrayed such a capricious president that Trump responded with one of the most memorable comments of his tenure, proclaiming himself "a very stable genius," which then became the title of yet another shocking insider book about his presidency by the *Washington Post*'s Philip Rucker and Carol Leonnig. Trump liked the phrase so much he used it about himself repeatedly. In May of 2019, the same week as Lindsey's briefing to the House Republican leaders and Trump's latest fight with Nancy Pelosi, the president once again told reporters at the White House, "I am an extremely stable genius."[19]

Eventually, there would be piles of articles and commentary on Trump's mental state, many of them dwelling on the extensive public evidence of Trump's dishonesty, personal attacks on others, highly transactional relationships, over-the-top bragging, and absence of discernible conscience or empathy for others.

George Conway, the conservative lawyer whose growing alarm over Trump had deeply strained his marriage to Kellyanne Conway, was at work on one of them. Ever since googling his way to a 2017 *Rolling Stone* article, "Is Pathological Narcissism the Key to Trump's Behavior?" Conway had been convinced his wife was working for a mentally ill and unbalanced president.[20] For months, he had been compiling a stack of index cards on which he recorded examples of what he considered Trump's crazier actions, and by the spring of 2019 he responded to various Trump tweetstorms by demanding "serious inquiry" into his "mental condition and psychological state."[21] To underscore his point, he tweeted out links to the official criteria for narcissistic personality disorder set out in the *Diagnostic and Statistical Manual of Mental Disorders*, the official diagnostic bible of the psychiatric profession. The criteria seemed to describe Trump with unnerving precision:

1. Has a grandiose sense of self-importance (e.g., exaggerates achievements and talents, expects to be recognized as superior without commensurate achievements).
2. Is preoccupied with fantasies of unlimited success, power, brilliance, beauty, or ideal love.
3. Believes that he or she is "special" and unique, and can only be understood by, or associate with, other special or high-status people (or institutions).
4. Requires excessive admiration.
5. Has a sense of entitlement (i.e., unreasonable expectations of especially favorable treatment or automatic compliance with his or her expectations).
6. Is interpersonally exploitative (i.e., takes advantage of others to achieve his or her own ends).

7. Lacks empathy: is unwilling to recognize or identify with the feelings or needs of others.

8. Is often envious of others or believes that others are envious of him or her.

9. Shows arrogant, haughty behaviors or attitudes.[22]

The tweets, not surprisingly, infuriated Trump, who responded by calling Conway a "husband from hell!" and a "whack job" who was "doing a tremendous disservice to his wonderful wife." But Conway continued to raise the issue of Trump's mental state. In reply, he tweeted, "You. Are. Nuts." The next day, he added, "Congratulations, you just guaranteed that millions more people are going to learn about narcissistic personality disorder and malignant narcissism! Great job!"

With so much material, the draft of the article Conway eventually submitted to *The Atlantic* came in at more than fifteen thousand words; in it, he argued that regardless of the technical medical diagnosis, Trump was unfit for office according to the standards of the Constitution. "You don't need to be a weatherman to know which way the wind blows, and you don't need to be a mental-health professional to see that something's very seriously off with Trump—particularly after nearly three years of watching his erratic and abnormal behavior in the White House," Conway wrote.[23]

The longer Trump served, the more worrisome his actions appeared to some of the actual mental health professionals who had been speaking out about him. "What we're concerned about is the increasing pressure of the presidency causing greater symptoms," Bandy Lee, editor of the psychiatrists' book, said in early 2018, amid the Is-Trump-Crazy clamor sparked by Wolff's book. "We have seen some signs of unraveling." In psychiatric terms, Lee warned that Trump could find himself "decompensating," meaning that his coping skills would no longer be adequate to deal with the stresses of the office. She ticked off possible consequences: losing touch with reality, growing more impulsive and volatile, becoming more prone to conspiracy theories and violence. More filled with rage. More untruthful. The fear, she said, was that Trump would "get worse and uncontainable because of the stresses of the presidency."

By the middle of 2019, Trump's bizarre and unpresidential behavior had in fact grown more extreme. The two most obvious markers of Trump's difference from previous presidents were his excessive lying and use of social media as a platform for bullying personal attacks. And Trump was engaging in both more than ever.

The further into the presidency he got, the more combative Trump had become. In August 2017, the month of "fire and fury" and good people "on both sides" of the Charlottesville white supremacist march, Trump had tweeted and retweeted 287 times. That number jumped to 680 times by August 2019, and he had turned up the volume along with the frequency.[24] As for lying, *The Washington Post*'s "Fact Checker" column found that he had exceeded twelve thousand false claims, exaggerations, and outright falsehoods by that third summer of his presidency and that he had dramatically stepped up the pace, from an average of thirteen a day to twenty a day. Trump repeated some of his false claims so frequently that the *Post* created a new category, "the bottomless Pinocchio," to reflect these and found three hundred times that he had repeated some variation of the same false claim at least three times.[25]

The increasing tempo of falsehoods and flame-throwing may have owed in part to an outrage cycle that required ever more fuel than it did at the start of his term, when the wacky pronouncements and shrill insults emanating directly from the Oval Office were still seen as a stunning novelty. It also reflected Trump's own view of what worked for him politically. Trump believed that his divisive commentary and attacks on enemies were important to rally his base, which was in turn the secret of his power over an otherwise skeptical Washington establishment. He believed this although polls throughout his presidency showed that his lies and Twitter attacks were a consistent turnoff even to Republicans who otherwise supported his agenda. He had also learned by this point that there was essentially no way for him to go too far, that his own party leaders and advisers would excuse and rationalize just about anything he did or said, even if they had previously proclaimed those words or actions to be unacceptable.

The result of all this was that by the summer of 2019 there were few things too shocking to have plausibly come from the mouth, or the Twitter feed, of the forty-fifth president. In August, Trump called himself the "Chosen One" to take on China, grinned and flashed a thumbs-up during a photo op with the family of mass-shooting victims, jeered at the robbery of a Democratic congressman's home, and labeled various critics "nasty and wrong," "pathetic," and "highly unstable," among other insults. The daily stream of invective was dizzying to track, and so voluminous that no one could.

Two years earlier, Trump had used his feed to criticize, belittle, or

humiliate specific targets fourteen times in the month of August. Many
of those he trained his fire on were Republican senators who were still
offering him resistance, including "publicity-seeking Lindsey Graham."
By August of 2019, the number had shot up, and the president made or
shared fifty-two direct insults on his Twitter feed. The now deferential
Republican senators were spared. Instead, most of his personal attacks
were aimed at individual members of the media, from "Crazy Lawrence
O'Donnell" of MSNBC, to "Lunatic" Chris Cuomo of CNN, to "pathetic"
Juan Williams of Fox News. Other targets who were singled out included
"the Three Stooges running against me" in the Republican primary; "car
company executives"; Beto O'Rourke; "the true racists" in liberal Hollywood; the "anti-Semite" Representative Rashida Tlaib; and the "nut job"
Anthony Scaramucci, his former White House communications director
who had finally turned on Trump.

Trump's biggest enemy and most frequent target remained what he
called the "Corrupt and Fake News" at 5:46 p.m. on August 27, and the
"Fake & Corrupt News," three minutes later. All told, "#crookedjournal-
ism," as he now put it, was the subject of twenty-six complaining tweets in
August 2017 versus eighty in August 2019. As with many of Trump's Twitter attacks, this escalation seemed by design rather than the result of passing fits of anger, at least in the sense that, as Trump said in a tweet over the
summer, he hoped his criticism of the media would be one of the lasting
accomplishments of his tenure. "When the 'Age of Trump' is looked back
on many years from now," he said, immodestly naming an era of history
after himself, "I only hope that a big part of my legacy will be the exposing
of massive dishonesty in the Fake News!"

The apparent naïveté behind his many accolades for the world's dictators was sometimes as alarming as the vitriol he aimed at his domestic political rivals. On August 10, Trump revealed a new letter from Kim
Jong-un in which the North Korean dictator "very nicely" asked for a
meeting while offering a "small apology" for his latest missile tests and
claiming that the tests would end when the United States–South Korean
military exercises did. (They did not.) On August 15, amid rising concern
of a Chinese crackdown on protesters in Hong Kong, Trump tweeted, "If
President Xi would meet directly and personally with the protesters, there
would be a happy and enlightened ending to the Hong Kong problem. I
have no doubt!" (The protests ended instead with Xi locking up the protest leaders and eliminating democratic guarantees that had been promised to Hong Kong residents.) On August 26, while in Biarritz, France,
for a G7 meeting, Trump stunned advisers from both countries when he

greeted Egypt's brutal military leader, Abdel Fattah el-Sisi, by calling out, "Where's my favorite dictator?"[26] (A dubious prize.)

A day later, Trump used his Twitter feed to praise his favorite world leader—himself. Citing a favorable new poll from a pro-Trump pollster, Trump congratulated Trump: "Great job Mr. President!"

No matter how reactive and unhinged his rants appeared, behind many of Trump's angriest tweets lay obsessions he had harbored for months or years, often grudges against his own appointees. One of his most frequent targets was the Federal Reserve and its chairman, Jerome "Jay" Powell. As Trump's fears mounted about a slowing economy and the intensifying trade war with China, he posted thirty tweets in August criticizing Powell or the Fed, in which he variously referred to "clueless Jay Powell," complained about Powell's "horrendous lack of vision," and, most strikingly, on August 23, blamed the Fed for China's alleged currency manipulation. "My only question," Trump tweeted, "is who is our bigger enemy, Jay Powel or Chairman Xi?" Not only did he call the chairman of the Fed an enemy of the United States, he even spelled his name wrong.

Like many of those he eventually turned on, Trump had personally installed Powell in the job. In fact, Powell told others he knew there was no way he would have been chairman under any other president. A lawyer by training and not an economist like previous chairs, Powell had made a fortune in banking before turning to public service. In the aftermath of the 2008 financial crisis, he had been Barack Obama's token Republican appointee to the Federal Reserve Board. Once there, he emerged as a solid ally of Obama's chair, Janet Yellen. In his first year in office, Trump had the option of reappointing Yellen, whose liberal fiscal policies and preference for low interest rates matched the perennially indebted former real estate developer's desire to keep it easy to borrow money. But Yellen had been chosen by Obama so Trump wanted his own pick.

The personal feuds and ideological conflicts among his advisers made that complicated. More orthodox Republicans preferred a tighter monetary supply. Their candidate, pushed by Mike Pence, among others, was Stanford economist John Taylor, an undersecretary of the treasury in the George W. Bush administration who in recent years had advanced a debunked theory that the Fed itself had caused the 2008 crash. Gary Cohn wanted the job too, but when candidates were interviewed in the fall of 2017, he had fallen out with Trump over the president's Charlottesville remarks. Cohn's internal rival, Steven Mnuchin, embraced Powell, selling him to Trump as "Janet Yellen, but a Republican," as Powell would later joke. It did not hurt that the tall, wealthy, silver-haired banker looked to Trump like he could play the role on television better than a rumpled female academic who stood barely five-foot-three. Powell was reluctant to work for Trump, but told others that Taylor, the only other serious candidate, would be a "disaster." In their interview, Trump said the right things about the Fed's independence and Powell took the job, becoming what *New York* magazine would call "an accidental Fed chair."[27]

Trump was soon angered at the Fed for failing, in his view, to pump enough cheap money into the economy by cutting interest rates—the key, Trump believed, to his re-election. Previous presidents had disagreed with Fed policy or tried to influence the board's chairman, but generally had kept their lobbying private. It was only when the White House tapes came out years later, for example, that Lyndon Johnson was revealed to have shouted at Fed chairman Bill Martin, "My boys are dying in Vietnam, and you won't print the money I need."[28] James Baker, as Ronald Reagan's treasury secretary, bluntly told Paul Volcker that the president was ordering him not to raise rates before the 1984 election. But since Bill Clinton, a strict tradition had taken hold that presidents should avoid even commenting on Fed actions. That tradition ended on September 11, 2018, while Powell was in Buenos Aires for a G20 meeting, when Trump unleashed a Twitter rant on Powell and his Fed colleagues, calling them "boneheads" for refusing to slash interest rates below zero, as some other nations were doing. It was a shocking moment, but then the tweets kept coming. Eventually, the president would label his Fed appointee a "terrible communicator" and even likened him to "a golfer who can't putt."

In private, Trump seemed obsessed with Powell. He was "a dirty bastard, that motherfucker," Trump told Stephanie Grisham, his press secretary, at one point.[29] The president also cursed his treasury secretary for foisting Powell on him. "POTUS never stopped blaming Mnuchin for Powell. I've never seen anything like it," a senior official recalled. Sometimes, Trump was egged on by Mnuchin's internal rivals, including Peter Navarro, the China hawk who was always looking for a way to gain an advantage over the treasury secretary. "Every time Jay Powell's name would come up, Navarro would say, 'And Mr. President, who was it who recommended Jay Powell to you?'" another senior official recalled.

In late 2018, when the Fed decided to raise interest rates, the stock market began a precipitous slide after comments by Powell that he later walked back. Trump then escalated his campaign against the chairman, insisting he could fire him, an untested proposition that the Fed's legal experts told Powell would not hold up in court. But they also told Powell that because of the way the law governing the agency's structure was written, he would have to personally contest the president if it came to a legal fight. Powell vowed to "spend my last nickel fighting" Trump to retain the Fed's independence. (He had a lot of them; his financial disclosure form indicated that Powell was worth as much as $76 million in 2019.) "It would be institutional vandalism for the United States not to have an independent central bank," Powell would say, and he was not going to let Trump do it on his watch. One senior Fed official later said he woke up every morning for months worried that would be the day when Trump fired Powell, provoking a constitutional crisis that would end at the Supreme Court.

Things got so bad that Mnuchin sought to broker a truce, or at least to, as he told others, "lower the temperature." He persuaded Trump to invite him, Powell, and the Fed's vice chair, Richard Clarida, for dinner in February at the White House. The president gave Powell a tour of the Lincoln Bedroom, chatted about the Super Bowl the night before, and served his favorite ribeye steak in the dining room. It was Powell's sixty-sixth birthday, but Trump had either not been briefed by his staff or did not care since he never mentioned it. The dinner turned out to be pointless anyway. The president, as usual, did most of the talking, boasting that his campaign rallies kept him in touch with the state of the economy much better than their wonky models. The Fed chairman concluded that nothing he said made any real impression on Trump. "He's not on receive; he's on transmit," Powell told those who asked about the president. One particular frustration was Trump's conviction that Powell should not only cut interest rates, but even take them below zero. Trump could not be disabused of it, no matter how many times advisers told him that negative interest rates were a sign of an economy in big trouble—hardly the image the United States, or Trump himself, would want to project.

All of which is to say that there were many months of frustration on Trump's mind by the morning of August 23 when Powell was in Jackson Hole, Wyoming, at the annual gathering of the nation's central bankers. Powell had just given his speech, the centerpiece of the conference, warning of a "deteriorating" global economic outlook but promising only to "act as appropriate" to sustain the economic expansion and blaming, obliquely, Trump's escalating trade war with China. "Trade policy uncertainty seems to be playing a role in the global slowdown," Powell said.[30] That, along with China's imposition of a new round of $75 billion in tariffs on American goods that morning, had set Trump off. Powell was still sitting in the audience after his speech when Trump's tweet calling him an enemy on a par with Xi landed. He thought he had gotten used to it—the cartoonish insults, the manufactured outrage, the people stopping him in airports to commiserate or cheer him on in standing up to Trump. Powell rationalized that the president's public rants about him had become like the weather, something volatile and potentially dangerous that just could not be controlled. He got calls from Republican friends on Capitol Hill begging him not to respond and he invariably agreed. But this was a new low. It was also not accidental.

Trump's tweets were often dismissed as childish displays of temper that would pass as quickly as the latest made-for-Fox-News controversy. Trump's attacks on Powell and the Fed, however, were purposeful, carried out over many months, and had specific goals, including the erosion of an independent institution over which Trump had few explicit levers of influence beyond appointing its members. And the Fed did in fact do at least some of what Trump was demanding—even if Trump was not satisfied with how much or how fast it did so—by repeatedly cutting interest rates, starting that summer with its first rate cut in more than a decade. Economists called the policy shift "the Powell pivot," and credited him with keeping unemployment low and the stock market booming while offsetting many of the effects of Trump's trade war in China.[31] Trump, however, did not tweet about that.

On the final day of August, Trump bragged about low Labor Day gas prices, although they were actually lower on the Labor Day before he became president; congratulated his friend Sean Hannity for the ratings on his Fox News "shoe"; and attacked the "Disgusting and foul mouthed Omarosa" Manigault Newman, his former adviser, whom he was suing after she released a tell-all book about her short time working in the White House. Omarosa, as she was universally known, à la Madonna, had parlayed her time on *The Apprentice* into a job that made her the only high-profile woman of color in Trump's White House until her dismissal by John Kelly. Her book, *Unhinged: An Insider's Account of the Trump White House*, claimed that Trump had declined dramatically since she had appeared on television with him, that his "blade had been dulled," and that she became so concerned about Trump's mental state she consulted Trump's daughter-in-law, Lara Trump, and other senior aides about it.[32] "I seriously began to suspect that the president was delusional or had a mental condition that made him forget from one day to the next," she wrote.[33] Trump, as was his habit with the slew of negative books, then helped to elevate her allegations by hate-tweeting about her and directing his campaign to sue her for violating one of the broad and legally unenforceable nondisclosure agreements he forced senior officials to sign, a lawsuit he would eventually lose years later. "I gave her every break, despite the fact that she was despised by everyone," Trump complained in his tweet.

The president, in other words, was ending the summer of 2019 as he began it, with a blast of ad hominem insults and bizarre fulminations that had become so standard they increasingly did not register. He even tweeted what appeared to be a classified image from his intelligence briefing of "a catastrophic accident" at an Iranian missile launch site, a leak of secret information on social media that would have been unthinkable in any other presidency.

Trump was at home tweeting when he was supposed to be in Poland, for a commemoration of the eightieth anniversary of the beginning of World War II. He had canceled the trip, citing the need to monitor the progress of Hurricane Dorian, which was threatening Florida. Hurricanes were another longtime preoccupation of Trump's and the news organization *Axios* reported that week that Trump had, numerous times during his presidency going back to 2017, asked aides whether the United States could foil the storms by bombing them with nuclear weapons—a story that, a senior administration official told *Axios* in a moment of candor, was inevitably going to "feed into 'the president is crazy' narrative."[34] Which, of course, it did.

Trump's plan to deal with Hurricane Dorian thankfully did not involve atomic warfare. In fact, his monitoring of the storm looked a lot like any other weekend of his presidency in that it included hours spent watching Fox News, tweeting and retweeting nearly sixty times before noon on the last Saturday of the month, and then motorcading to a Trump-branded golf course for his 226th day on the links at one of his own properties since becoming president. That Sunday, Trump erroneously claimed in a tweet that the storm was on track to hit Alabama. Rather than acknowledge the mistake, he then spent the rest of the week feuding with the media about whether he had taken one of his trademark pens and altered a National Weather Service map to prove his point. The resulting "Sharpiegate" lasted for days, unlike the storm, which hit neither Florida nor Alabama in force.

The Poland trip, incidentally, was not even the first foreign visit that Trump had canceled that month. He was also supposed to have gone to Denmark but had pulled out of that trip in a fit of pique earlier in August after the Danish government mocked his efforts to buy Greenland, one more Oval Office scandal that, had it occurred a few years earlier, no one would have believed.

The Greenland affair reflected a Trump fixation that his aides had managed to avoid disclosing for years. A vast, mineral-rich, and sparsely populated territory in the Arctic that Denmark spent hundreds of millions of dollars annually to subsidize, Greenland had grabbed his attention as "essentially, a big real estate deal" that might give him a place in American history like William Seward's purchase of Alaska from Russia. After an early Oval Office meeting where Trump expounded on buying Greenland, one mystified cabinet member was struck by the delusional nature of the president's speech on the matter. "You'd just sit there and be like, 'Well, this isn't real,'" the secretary recalled. "But then you're like, 'Oh, well, maybe this is real in his mind.'"

Trump would later claim a Greenland purchase was his personal inspiration. "I said, 'Why don't we have that?' You take a look at a map. I'm a real estate developer, I look at a corner, I say, 'I've got to get that store for the building that I'm building,' etc. It's not that different," he said one day in his office after leaving the White House. "I love maps. And I always said, 'Look at the size of this. It's massive. That should be part of the United States.'"

But in reality, the idea had been planted with Trump by one of his New York billionaire friends, Ron Lauder, who had been discussing it with him since the early days of his presidency. An active philanthropist who headed the World Jewish Congress, Lauder had known Trump for decades since they attended the University of Pennsylvania together. During the 2016 campaign, Lauder publicly supported Trump and in August 2019 he donated $100,000 to the Trump Victory joint fundraising committee. In early 2018, when the publication of Michael Wolff's book set off public debate over Trump's sanity, Lauder contacted reporters with an unsolicited statement of support that praised the president's "incredible insight and intelligence," dismissed concerns about Trump's behavior as mere quibbles over his refusal to speak in "stale political platitudes," and, as a cryptic aside, spoke of unspecified "diplomatic challenges" that he was working on with Trump.[35]

One of them turned out to be Greenland, as John Bolton learned several months later when he became national security adviser. "A friend of mine, a really, really experienced businessman, thinks we can get Greenland," Trump told Bolton. "What do you think?" Lauder then came to see Bolton, revealing that he had been discussing Greenland with the presi-

dent and had offered himself up as "the back channel to the Danish government to negotiate Greenland," as Bolton would later recount to others.
Worried about increasing Chinese influence in the Arctic and exploitation
of the strategic minerals in which Greenland abounds, Bolton actually
thought this was not a terrible idea. He liked to point out that the capital
of Greenland, Nuuk, is closer to Washington than to Copenhagen. "It's
part of the North American landmass," he would say.

But Bolton also understood that buying Greenland outright was hardly
an option, as Harry Truman found out in 1946, when he offered $100 mil-
lion in gold for it but was turned down by the insulted Danes. (Truman
ultimately settled for a 1951 defense treaty allowing the United States to
build Thule Air Force Base there to monitor the Soviets.) "The Danes
go apoplectic when you so much as say the word 'Greenland,'" Bolton
warned Trump, and he thought Lauder as an envoy was a terrible idea.

As often with Trump ideas he considered wacky, unsuitable, or dangerous, Bolton tried alternately ignoring this one, shutting down discussion
about it, and slow-walking the problem. In late 2018, he pulled aside his
aide Fiona Hill. "We have a situation," Bolton told her. "We mustn't have
too many people talking about this. Pick a small team and head it off."
Hill and three other officials, including Michael Ellis, a National Security
Council lawyer, set about brainstorming how to address Trump's Greenland fixation while hopefully also avoiding a major diplomatic incident.

Throughout February and March, Hill and the other aides engaged in
secret talks with Denmark's ambassador to the United States about Greenland and by summer they produced a memo that laid out various options:
Should they offer to buy Greenland as Trump wanted? Lease it? What
about concepts like "shared sovereignty" or "pooled sovereignty"? The
team knew that outright purchase was a nonstarter and settled instead on
what they thought of as a "totally sensible" plan to "upgrade and renew"
Truman's 1951 security treaty for the modern era. But Bolton told them,
"Stop everything, just stop."

Trump kept demanding action, however. At various points, the president even suggested taking federal money from Puerto Rico, toward which
he had a long-standing animus going back to the criticism of his handling
of the deadly 2017 hurricane, and putting the funds toward buying Greenland. According to Miles Taylor, the former Department of Homeland
Security chief of staff who later publicly turned on Trump, the president
asked aides in August of 2018, before a disaster-recovery trip to Puerto
Rico, whether they could just trade the American commonwealth outright
for Greenland. Trump told them he wanted to do so "because Puerto Rico

was dirty and the people were poor."[36] Bolton also heard something similar from Trump in an Oval Office meeting. "How much hurricane disaster relief are we giving to Puerto Rico?" Trump asked. "Can we just take that and use it for Greenland?" That August, between his feuds with the Federal Reserve and various high-profile media figures, Trump renewed his public attacks on the American commonwealth. "Puerto Rico is one of the most corrupt places on earth," he tweeted. "And by the way I am the best thing that's ever happened to Puerto Rico!"

Bolton had planned to fly to Copenhagen in August in advance of the G7 summit in Biarritz, to meet alone with the Danish prime minister, Mette Frederiksen, to raise the delicate subject of Greenland. A few days before he was scheduled to leave, however, *The Wall Street Journal* broke the story of Trump's interest in a purchase, portraying it as more of a passing fancy than a years-long fascination he had ordered his government to pursue. Even so, it drew a predictably furious reaction. "We're open for business, not for sale," Greenland's Ministry of Foreign Affairs responded. "If he is truly contemplating this, then this is the final proof that he has gone mad," a spokesman for the Danish People's Party opined.[37]

Over the weekend, Trump confirmed his interest in the idea. "Bolton was worrying the whole time that he would just blurt this out about buying Greenland," Hill recalled, "and he did." Trump tweaked the Danes further with a tweet that Monday. It showed a picture of an enormous, gilded Trump Tower photoshopped onto an image of a bucolic seaside village. "I promise not to do this to Greenland!" the president said in his caption.

Amid the days-long furor he himself had generated, Trump then called Bolton to the Oval Office and told him he thought the national security adviser should not go to Denmark after all. Bolton argued that this was a mistake that would only fuel the controversy, but Trump ordered him to cancel the visit. A few days later, Trump canceled his own trip to Denmark as well, because after all, what was the point?

"When it became public, they lost their political courage," Trump said after leaving office, as if the Danes had ever been serious about selling Greenland. Bolton and his staff had believed there was a real chance not of a sale but of an enhanced security arrangement that would be genuinely beneficial in an age of increased competition with China in the Arctic and that might have even led eventually to Greenland becoming more explicitly connected to the United States. "If Trump had just kept his mouth shut," Bolton concluded, "we could have found out. But it was just gone, just completely gone."

Was it crazy for Trump to pursue buying Greenland or merely crazy that he had tanked his own government's efforts to follow up on his whim while taunting a close NATO ally with his tweets? Either way, the embarrassing spectacle was far from the wildest thing that Trump had said and done that August.

If anything, Trump's increasingly bizarre public antics obscured more serious concerns raised by his actions. While he was hate-tweeting Omarosa that month, Trump was also about to close a peace deal with the Taliban that excluded the Afghan government alongside which the American military had been fighting for nearly two decades. While he was lashing out at "enemies of the people," Trump was also pushing out the director of national intelligence, Dan Coats, and seeking to replace him with a more malleable Texas congressman. And while he was musing to aides about nuking hurricanes, Trump was also feuding with his secretary of state, defense secretary, and national security adviser over the secret hold he had placed on the aid to Ukraine.

Bolton's time in Crazytown, at least, soon came to an end. On September 10, he finally resigned after a series of disagreements with Trump, including over the president's insistence on hosting representatives of the Taliban at Camp David on the anniversary of September 11, when he hoped to announce his Afghan peace deal—an idea that "mortified" Joe Dunford, the outgoing Joint Chiefs chairman, and plenty of others.

The acrimonious parting played out, fittingly, on Twitter, where Trump and Bolton argued over whether he had quit or been fired. Trump was first to tweet the news of Bolton's exit that morning, claiming that he had "informed John Bolton last night that his services are no longer needed," and adding, "I disagreed strongly with many of his suggestions." But Bolton had anticipated this and, as proof that he had quit, had printed out copies of his resignation letter even before giving it to the president and had them placed on the desks of senior White House staff so that Trump could not lie and say he had been fired. He also authorized an aide to call reporters immediately after his departure to make clear who had called the relationship off.

Soon after the story broke, Bolton's rivals Mike Pompeo and Steven Mnuchin showed up at a White House news conference that Bolton had been scheduled to attend. Both grinned broadly as they gloated over Bolton's departure. The president "should have people that he trusts and values and whose efforts and judgments benefit him in delivering American foreign policy," Pompeo said pointedly. Asked if he had been blind-sided by Bolton's exit, Pompeo replied, "I'm never surprised." When the two cabinet secretaries, still beaming, left the room, one of the reporters summed up the day's events, in a remark caught on the networks' still-rolling tape: "God almighty. That's a shit show."[38]

A week later, Trump selected the State Department's little-known hostage negotiator, a California lawyer named Robert O'Brien, to be his fourth national security adviser, the most any president had ever had in a single term. O'Brien had less relevant experience than perhaps anyone who had held the post. O'Brien's only foreign policy work included a short assignment on Bolton's staff at the United Nations during the George W. Bush administration, appointments to two obscure government commissions, and stints as an unpaid adviser to several Republican presidential campaigns, including Trump's rivals Scott Walker and Ted Cruz in 2016. He had never worked in the White House or at the National Security Council, and had little firsthand knowledge of the complex interagency process that managed America's massive national security bureaucracy and none at all leading it. He was a perfect fit, in other words, for a president who not only devalued expertise but had come to see it as a threat to his ability to do as he wished. "We got a compliant individual," a senior national security official said at the time. "That's what the president wanted."

O'Brien had sealed his unlikely ascendance in August, during yet another improbable international incident generated by Trump, this one involving a jailed American rapper named A$AP Rocky. The president, apparently responding to a social media campaign on Rocky's behalf by Kim Kardashian and other celebrities, not only called the Swedish prime minister, Stefan Löfven, urging the rapper's release but also demanded that O'Brien fly there to attend his trial, although Rocky, who was accused of criminal assault after a street brawl, was hardly a political prisoner or hostage. At Trump's behest, O'Brien even wrote a threatening letter to the Swedish authorities, warning of "potentially negative consequences" to the Swedish-American relationship, which earned him a rebuke from Sweden's prosecutor general, who defended the independence of Sweden's judiciary.[39] Rocky was released but ultimately convicted and fined $1,300, not exactly the normal concern of heads of state. Nonetheless, O'Brien told reporters, "The president sent me here, so it's totally appropriate."[40]

After two years of feuding with H. R. McMaster and John Bolton over their failed efforts to rein him in, this attitude was just what Trump was looking for in a national security adviser. Speaking to the media on Air Force One a day before he announced his choice, Trump revealed that

O'Brien was one of five finalists, then quoted O'Brien as having told him, "Trump is the greatest hostage negotiator that I know of in the history of the United States."

"He happens to be right," Trump immodestly added.[41]

The next morning, O'Brien got the job.

CHAPTER 19

Fucking Ukraine

Shortly after 9 p.m. one night that September, Lindsey Graham emerged from The Palm, a legendary see-and-be-seen steakhouse in downtown Washington whose walls were festooned with caricatures of its famous political clientele. He had just gotten off the telephone with Trump, who had interrupted his dinner to seek Graham's advice on the biggest threat yet to his presidency.

Less than forty-eight hours earlier, Nancy Pelosi had launched the full-scale impeachment investigation that Trump had avoided for two and a half years. The move was triggered not by Robert Mueller's report on Russia, but by revelations about Trump's secret pressure campaign on Ukraine's new president to investigate Joe Biden even as Trump was holding up the $391 million in congressional-approved security assistance for Ukraine. John Bolton had kept his qualms about Trump's machinations with Ukraine to himself but the Rudy Giuliani grenade that he warned about had finally blown up in public. Just that morning, congressional investigators had released an explosive CIA whistleblower complaint with more startling information that the Trump administration had been withholding from Congress for weeks.

Yet Graham affected a sort of devil-may-care nonchalance when he stopped to talk outside the steakhouse. He boasted about his access to the president and dropped insider details like the phone call Trump told him he had received earlier in the day from six evangelical pastors promising to pray for him. ("Those fucking Christians love me," the president had crowed.) The president's friend seemed oddly sanguine, even giddy, about this new fight that now promised to consume Trump's administration.

The senator had already come out publicly and said it would be "insane" to impeach the president because of the Ukraine matter. But on the sidewalk that evening he wanted two Washington reporters who had known him for more than two decades to understand that he was no mere toady. "He's a lying motherfucker," Graham said of Trump with a what-can-you-do shrug, but also "a lot of fun to hang out with." Still, Graham made no apologies. Like other Senate Republicans who would ultimately have to decide Trump's fate in any trial that resulted from this impeachment mess, Graham had followed Trump through innumerable outrages by this point. They could and would justify just about anything when it came to Trump. "He could kill fifty people on our side, and it wouldn't matter," Graham said. Their reasoning was simple: he was the president from their party.

Graham's advice to Trump was simple too, born out of his experience as one of the House managers who unsuccessfully prosecuted Bill Clinton during the last impeachment trial. Trump, he counseled, should follow Clinton's winning playbook: deny, delay, and attack. "You know what to do," Graham told him. He seemed confident it would work.

For months, Democrats had been fighting among themselves over what to do about Trump. They had taken back power in the House and vowed to investigate a full array of presidential abuses only to find themselves subject to the most successful information blockade ever waged by one branch of government against another. Whether it was subpoenas for documents or testimony or Trump's still hidden tax returns, the Trump White House and its new counsel, Pat Cipollone, had decided on a strategy of total confrontation with the Democratic House. As far as Trump and his allies were concerned, Mueller's report had put an end to the debilitating Russia scandal that had overshadowed so much of Trump's presidency. Impeachment seemed dead. It was time to move on.

But in truth, neither Trump nor his Democratic opponents were prepared to do so. Trump, consumed by grievance, wanted not only vindication but vengeance, pinning his hopes on an inquiry ordered by Bill Barr to be conducted by the prosecutor John Durham into whether the FBI had acted improperly in undertaking its investigation of Trump's Russia ties in the first place. Democrats, for their part, heatedly debated how to respond to the extensive evidence of Trump's obstruction of justice that Mueller had set out in the report. Over the summer, an increasing number of House Democrats argued for impeachment, including, privately, Representative Jerry Nadler, the New York Democrat and chairman of the House Judiciary Committee. By early September, about one hundred

House Democrats supported impeachment. Nadler's team, led by Norman Eisen, a former Obama White House ethics lawyer brought in as counsel by the House Judiciary Committee, privately drafted ten articles of impeachment covering everything from the Mueller obstruction and the dangling of pardons to silence witnesses, to the Stormy Daniels hush money and the usurpation of congressional spending power; the tenth draft article was a placeholder titled "The Next High Crime" on the assumption that there would be one.[1]

But impeachment faced an immovable obstacle in the form of Pelosi, who had categorically ruled it out unless there was a bipartisan consensus. In March, even before the Mueller report was submitted, she had said: "Impeachment is so divisive to the country that unless there's something so compelling and overwhelming and bipartisan, I don't think we should go down that path, because it divides the country. And he's just not worth it."[2] The Nancy Pelosi of March did not find her criteria met in September. There was no bipartisan consensus about Trump's latest outrage. But as the details came spilling out about Trump's pressure campaign on Ukraine and apparent misuse of urgently needed military aid to fight off Russia as leverage for his own personal political purposes, they had their Next High Crime. Pelosi anticipated where her caucus was going, and, typically, got there first.

The exact moment that Trump's impeachment began was arguably on Saturday morning, September 21, when Adam Schiff, the House Intelligence Committee chairman, pulled into an empty parking lot on the way home from Los Angeles International Airport to take a call from Pelosi.

"Are you ready to do this?" she had asked.

"I am," he replied.

Schiff was set to go on the Sunday shows the next day and would strongly preview which way the speaker was headed, suggesting the party might finally be ready to "cross the Rubicon" and begin formal proceedings against Trump.

"All right," Pelosi replied. "Good."[3]

The politics still did not look great, but by the next evening momentum for an investigation had the backing even of reluctant moderates who won election in 2018 in previously Republican districts, the "majority-makers," as Democrats called them, or in the case of five women who had served in national security or intelligence posts before entering politics, the Bad-Ass Caucus. They sought out Schiff and Pelosi directly and, after the speaker gave permission for the public stampede to begin, published an op-ed in *The Washington Post* on September 23 declaring that Trump's "flagrant disregard for the law cannot stand."[4]

The new conventional wisdom that had rapidly replaced the old conventional wisdom was that Trump's Ukraine "quid pro quo" of military aid in exchange for investigations was a slam dunk—a straightforward abuse of power that was so brazen that it would be irresponsible not to respond. The fact that Trump had hijacked security assistance to a country at war with Vladimir Putin's Russia—military aid that was supported by the vast majority of both Democrats and Republicans in the otherwise divided capital—made it seem all the more pressing. "He forced us into it," Pelosi would say when her about-face was questioned. "He gave us no choice."

Pelosi gave Trump a heads-up in a brief phone call the next day.

"How can you do that to me?" Trump insisted. "I have to speak at the General Assembly of the United Nations today."

Pelosi's reply could be more or less summed up as: So what? "Perhaps he mistook me for somebody who gave a damn about his schedule," she would say later.

By 5 p.m., Pelosi publicly announced that the House would officially begin impeachment proceedings. Nodding to the complicated internal politics, she assigned Schiff's Intelligence Committee to lead the investigation and Nadler's Judiciary Committee to handle any resulting articles of impeachment. The idea was to get it done quickly, by the end of the year, to avoid acting in an election year. "The president must be held accountable," Pelosi said in announcing her decision. "No one is above the law."[5]

As the drumbeat for his impeachment built on Capitol Hill, Trump broke off official meetings in New York and ordered his motorcade to make an unscheduled stop at Trump Tower. Soon after, he sent out a quick blast of tweets attacking the "breaking news Witch Hunt garbage." He added: "PRESIDENTIAL HARASSMENT!" And also: "Can you believe this?"

The president, however, had one play left. The next morning, he released the full White House account of a July 25 phone call he had with President Volodymyr Zelensky of Ukraine, a call that was at the center of the CIA whistleblower's complaint. Despite strong pushback from Mike Pompeo and press secretary Stephanie Grisham, Trump had become convinced it was a masterstroke that would undercut the impeachment inquiry before it even started. On Fox News, reporter Ed Henry quoted a Trump source who warned Democrats: "There's no 'there' there."[6] Trump himself got into the pre-spin game. "Will the Democrats apologize after seeing what was said on the call with the Ukrainian President?" he tweeted at 9:17 a.m. that Wednesday. "They should, a perfect call—got them by surprise!"

Then, at 10 a.m., the White House released its call summary. It did not say what Trump had suggested it would say. Not at all. Usually in American politics, the goal in the expectations game is to tamp them down; in this case, Trump had succeeded at the opposite, promoting the notion that his phone call with Zelensky would prove innocuous. Instead, he added new information to the scandal. Trump on the call had not only requested an investigation of Biden and his son Hunter, who had served as a board member of a Ukrainian energy company called Burisma, but had specifically asked Zelensky to cooperate with Rudy Giuliani and Bill Barr on it. He also wanted Zelensky to look into the preposterous Russian-originated myth that the previous government of Ukraine, not Moscow, was responsible for the 2016 hacking of Democrats' emails.

The president's language was hardly subtle. Trump mentioned the attorney general four times. "The United States has been very, very good to Ukraine," Trump said before quickly adding, "I wouldn't say that it's reciprocal necessarily." After Zelensky responded by requesting approval to buy more American antitank Javelin missiles to aid Ukraine's defense against Russia, Trump replied by explaining the reciprocity he really wanted: the investigations.

"I would like you to do us a favor, though," the president said in a line that immediately seemed destined to land in the history books.[7]

Reading the transcript in the secure basement office of the House Intelligence Committee, Schiff was amazed. "Holy shit, holy shit, holy shit," he muttered out loud to his staff. "I can't believe they would release this."[8] It was not the exculpatory moment that Trump had claimed it would be. Impeachment may have been an uncertain outcome before the call's release. Afterward, it was a near-certainty.

For months, bits and pieces of the scandal had been hiding in plain sight. Rudy Giuliani had long promoted the conspiracy theory generated by Russian intelligence agencies suggesting that Ukraine was the actual source of the hacking in the 2016 election. Trump began publicly floating this as far back as the spring of 2017 when he insisted that Democrats had put their email server in the hands of a "very rich Ukrainian" and it had then been attacked. He alluded to it again at the infamous Helsinki news conference with Vladimir Putin in the summer of 2018.

By the spring of 2019, the campaign led by Giuliani was targeting Biden and his son Hunter as well. As vice president, Biden had pushed

Ukraine's leadership to fire a prosecutor, Viktor Shokin, in keeping with the policy taken by the United States, the European Union, and international organizations that all considered him an obstacle to reform. But Giuliani and his allies now claimed that Biden pushed for the prosecutor's ouster in order to shut down an investigation of the energy firm on whose board Hunter sat, even though Shokin was actually described as hindering that inquiry.

Behind the scenes, Trump advisers, cabinet members, and professional Russia-watchers had known for months that there was a Ukraine problem. Some, like John Bolton, had struggled to stop it. Others, like Mick Mulvaney, had abetted it. Many, like the National Security Council aides Fiona Hill and her deputy, Alexander Vindman, knew at least some of the details.

By the time of the soon-to-be-famous telephone call between Trump and Zelensky on July 25, Hill had left her job in the White House but Vindman, listening in, reported the call to the lawyers. "If what I just heard becomes public," he told his twin brother, Eugene, who happened to be the senior ethics lawyer for the National Security Council, "the president will be impeached."[9] That same day, the Office of Management and Budget had put out a formal notice of the Ukraine aid suspension, meaning that even more officials in the vast national security bureaucracy were made aware of the hold, although it included a warning from the Trump political appointee overseeing the process, Michael Duffey, to limit knowledge of the aid freeze to a "need to know" basis.[10] But a CIA official who heard about it connected many of the dots and wrote them up in the whistleblower complaint filed on August 12.

For much of his final six weeks as national security adviser, Bolton tried to quietly get Trump to reverse course on Ukraine. Pompeo, while openly feuding with Bolton, also sought to persuade Trump to release the security assistance. The two, along with Mark Esper, Trump's new defense secretary, and Gina Haspel, the CIA director, confronted Trump several times about the aid. "All of us felt that we needed to bolster Ukraine's security and were appalled at what Trump was doing," Bolton would later say.[11] But Trump rebuffed them when it came up on August 16, during a meeting at Trump's Bedminster club to discuss Afghanistan, and again on August 30. "Clear direction from POTUS to hold," Duffey, the budget official, wrote to the Pentagon afterward.[12]

The Ukrainians learned about the aid freeze when the news broke in *Politico* over Labor Day weekend and freaked out about it.[13] So did the Pentagon and members of Congress in both parties. Mike Pence was in Warsaw, meeting with Zelensky on the sidelines of a summit with Poland's leaders because Trump had refused to make the trip and was instead holed up back in Washington, trash-talking Omarosa on Twitter and tracking Hurricane Dorian with his Sharpie.

At the same time, word of the whistleblower complaint was beginning to leak out. Bill Barr's Justice Department had determined it did not contain pressing evidence of an intelligence matter and therefore did not need to be sent to Congress. But Michael Atkinson, the inspector general for the intelligence community, notified congressional committees of the complaint the same day Schiff and two other committee chairmen announced an investigation into Giuliani and the Ukraine matter. Three days later, under pressure from Republican senators who said Congress would force his hand if he did not relent, Trump abruptly reversed himself and released the frozen aid. But it was too late. The investigation was on.

Even by late September, much of this was still not public. It would be up to Adam Schiff to put it all together. A mild-mannered vegan from Los Angeles, Schiff had started out the Trump years as nobody's idea of a partisan flame-thrower. In fact, he had first won his House seat nearly two decades earlier by attacking the Republican incumbent, James Rogan, for serving as one of Lindsey Graham's fellow House managers in the Clinton impeachment trial. Several of Clinton's wealthy Hollywood friends had recruited Schiff to make the race, which became the most expensive in the nation that year, and he effectively bashed Rogan for ignoring the district in favor of "national partisan ideological crusades."[14]

The lesson Schiff took from that race was to keep his head down and stick to the center, and for eight terms he more or less did. A Harvard-trained lawyer who entered politics after making his career prosecuting an FBI agent who had been caught in a sex-for-secrets trap by Russia, Schiff was invariably described as a "moderate's moderate" before Trump arrived on the scene. He even managed to preserve this reputation through the House Intelligence Committee's years-long Benghazi investigation of Hillary Clinton, when the panel put out a bipartisan report rejecting the elaborate conspiracy theories promoted by the Fox News echo chamber and House Republicans like Mike Pompeo.

But from the earliest days of Trump's presidency, Schiff turned his perch as the top Democrat on the Intelligence Committee into a platform for demanding answers about Trump's Russia ties. He channeled outrage over Trump's fawning statements about Putin and warned Trump not to shut down the Mueller investigation. He became a regular on MSNBC's

Rachel Maddow program and the Sunday talk shows. His relationship with Devin Nunes, the Republican committee chairman, previously cordial enough that they exchanged texts while cheering for the Oakland Raiders, broke down. His Twitter feed, once home to polite policy wonkery, morphed into a rapid-reaction anti-Trump war room.

A close ally and confidant of Pelosi, Schiff became chairman of the Intelligence Committee after Democrats won back the House and reopened the panel's Russia investigation, which Nunes had closed abruptly and inconclusively in 2018. Like Pelosi, however, Schiff had been skeptical of impeachment proceedings over the Mueller report. And like Pelosi, he had become one of Trump's favorite targets. The president nicknamed him "'Liddle' Adam Schiff," and repeatedly called him "one of the biggest liars and leakers in Washington." Schiff chose to take it as a badge of honor, or at least a testament to his effectiveness on television, the medium Trump cared most about. Jared Kushner told him as much during a conversation when he was called to testify about Russia in the summer of 2017.

"You know, you do a really good job on TV," Kushner had told Schiff before the deposition began.

"I don't think your father-in-law would agree," Schiff responded.

"Oh yes, he does, and that's why," Kushner replied.[15]

In March 2019, taking a victory lap after the Mueller report came out, Trump spent several minutes at a Michigan rally going after Schiff, whom he renamed "Little Pencil-Neck Adam Schiff," and Trump's campaign soon began selling $28 "Pencil-Neck Adam Schiff" T-shirts.[16]

After the Mueller furor faded with no impeachment, there had been a short truce. Trump made no public mention of Schiff at all from May to September of 2019. Within minutes of the Democrats announcing the impeachment probe, though, Trump's barrage against him began again with even greater intensity. The president's strategy was to make Schiff the hopelessly partisan face of a hopelessly partisan investigation. Schiff was not just "Liddle" anymore. He was "Shifty," "lying," "disgraced," "corrupt," "a lowlife," and "a lying disaster for our Country." Eventually, Trump would call him "a deranged human being," "a maniac," and "a very sick man."[17] Schiff was soon the only member of the House outside of its leadership to require a twenty-four-hour Capitol Police security detail.

At the Intelligence Committee's first hearing after the start of the impeachment proceedings, the day after Trump had released his White House transcript of the "perfect" phone call, Schiff mocked Trump's explanation for it, saying the transcript read "like a classic organized crime shakedown."[18] He went on to sarcastically deliver his version of what it must have sounded like to Ukraine's leader to have the president of the United States lean on him like that.

Trump quickly pounced, claiming Schiff had "illegally made up" things and "fraudulently read to Congress" quotes from Trump that did not exist. "Congressman Adam Schiff should resign for the Crime of, after reading a transcript of my conversation with the President of Ukraine (it was perfect), fraudulently fabricating a statement of the President of the United States and reading it to Congress, as though mine! He is sick!" Trump tweeted. For months afterward, Trump was still tweeting about Schiff's speech on the opening day of the investigation, Schiff's offense growing with each retelling.

All told, the president attacked Schiff by name in his Twitter feed more than three hundred times during his tenure, all but a couple dozen of those coming after the impeachment proceedings began. House Republicans, taking their cue from Trump, launched a series of procedural resolutions and motions to discredit Schiff, accusing him of secretly conspiring with the CIA whistleblower, although Schiff claimed not even to know the whistleblower's identity. There were motions to censure Schiff and congressional speeches comparing him to Inspector Javert, the persecutor of *Les Misérables.* On Facebook, a false claim went viral asserting that Schiff's sister was married to George Soros's son, pulling the congressman into the elaborate anti-Semitic conspiracy theories invoking the Hungarian-born financier.

Schiff's biggest challenge at the start of the investigation, however, was neither Trump's name-calling nor the Republicans on his panel; it was figuring out how to investigate a complicated international scandal without the resources, personnel, or enforcement powers he had as a federal prosecutor. And he had to do it all with a strict Christmas deadline. When he took over the panel, Schiff had hired Daniel Goldman as chief investigative counsel, having met him in the MSNBC green room—a Republican conspiracy theorist's dream. Goldman, a polished veteran of the Southern District of New York, was an experienced mob prosecutor, and now the two, operating on just a few hours of sleep a night, scoured the whistleblower complaint for leads. Within days, the committee sent out a blitz of subpoenas requesting documents and other materials from Mike Pompeo, Rudy Giuliani, Mick Mulvaney, and others. Closed-door depositions in the committee's secure bunker, three floors below ground, began the following week.

But the obstacles were daunting. The two previous impeachment inquiries of the modern era had been driven by special prosecutors backed by the resources of the Justice Department and FBI. This time, Congress would have to handle the probe on its own and even the courts would be of no practical help given the months and sometimes years it took to resolve disputes between the branches. Schiff could blanket Trump administration officials with subpoenas, but he had no realistic way to enforce them. Stonewalling, always Trump's default, would prove an effective response for a White House that knew Schiff was facing an immovable deadline just a couple months away.

Pat Cipollone, the White House counsel, spelled out the White House strategy in scorching terms in an eight-page letter to Democratic leaders the first week of October. The impeachment investigation, the letter said, was "highly partisan," "unconstitutional," "baseless," and "invalid."[19] His specific claim was that the impeachment proceedings were not legal because the full House had not taken a vote to authorize them yet. (Democrats disagreed with his argument but went ahead and held such a vote on October 31 anyway.) In practical terms, the letter meant a "full halt" to any cooperation with the probe: no documents, no emails, no testimony. Neither Richard Nixon nor Bill Clinton had gone that far.

But the White House quickly turned out to have a problem: the relatively large number of current and former Trump appointees who decided to testify anyway. The first victory for Schiff came days into the investigation, when Kurt Volker, who had quit as special envoy when news of the scandal and his role in it broke, agreed not only to testify but to hand over text messages. The texts offered firsthand confirmation of some of the allegations in the whistleblower letter, documenting Giuliani's role and revealing that some officials had objected bluntly to what was going on. On the morning of Trump's "perfect" phone call, Volker had even made explicit in a text with Zelensky's top adviser, Andriy Yermak, the quid pro quo that was required for Trump to agree to a White House meeting: "Heard from White House," Volker texted that morning, "assuming President Z convinces trump he will investigate / 'get to the bottom of what happened in 2016,' we will nail down date for visit to Washington." In early September, with the aid still held up, Bill Taylor, the acting ambassador, had texted Volker and Gordon Sondland in no uncertain terms: "I think it's crazy to withhold security assistance for help with a political campaign."[20]

Cipollone's stonewall was breached. Over the next couple weeks, an array of current and former Trump officials disregarded the White House's order and appeared under subpoena in closed-door depositions before Schiff and his committee, including Taylor, Volker, and Sondland

as well as Marie Yovanovitch, the fired ambassador; Fiona Hill, the president's former Russia adviser; and George Kent, the deputy assistant secretary of state. It was quickly apparent that the Ukraine scandal was not just
about a phone call.

At the State Department, the revelations destroyed what remained of
Mike Pompeo's goodwill among the diplomatic corps. Pompeo, it turned
out, had known all about what had transpired, although he refused to go
to bat publicly for Yovanovitch when she was fired, or even to allow the
State Department to put out a statement defending her. When a group
of former ambassadors, including Bill Taylor, privately appealed to the
State Department not to let a courageous diplomat be publicly smeared
after decades of service, he did not reply. After initial reports of the Trump
call with Zelensky came out, Pompeo feigned ignorance, only to have it
revealed that he had in fact listened in on the whole conversation.

    Like Rex Tillerson, but for very different reasons, Pompeo was re-
moved on a day-to-day basis from most State Department officials, surrounded by a Praetorian guard of two of his closest friends from West
Point, Ulrich Brechbuhl and Brian Bulatao, whom he had brought in to
help run the State Department. His wife, Susan Pompeo, was also one of
his closest advisers, traveling with him on trips and coordinating so closely
with official government employees on Pompeo's staff that she would ultimately be the subject of multiple ethics complaints to the State Department inspector general. Politics, it had become increasingly clear, were
still very much Pompeo's focus. Regular "Madison Dinners" in the State
Department's antiques-filled Benjamin Franklin diplomatic reception
rooms, with a guest list closely supervised by Susan, brought the secretary
together with important business leaders and Republican Party funders,
along with more traditional guests like foreign ambassadors.[21] Many
thought he was laying the groundwork for a future presidential campaign.

    The actual business of the State Department was conducted among
a tight group of Pompeo confidants and a small handful of career Foreign Service officials he trusted. A wider orbit might expose his secret disagreements with Trump—always a risk, because there were many of them,
from North Korea to Russia. The other reason was less about Trump and
more about Pompeo and his explosive temper. Pompeo would curse and
yell even at early-morning staff meetings with his top advisers. He often
vented about leaks. Women were a particular target, especially Lisa Kenna,
the career diplomat who served as his executive secretary. His tirades at

her, described by three senior officials who observed them directly, were blistering. "I don't know if I've ever seen such sustained abuse in my life," one senior official said about Pompeo's treatment of Kenna.

Mike McKinley, Pompeo's senior adviser and in effect his envoy to the professional diplomatic corps, had been one of the few career Foreign Service officers in the secretary's inner circle since Pompeo called him back as ambassador to Brazil at the start of his tenure. But by Monday, October 7, he had become increasingly concerned about the secretary's failure to stick up for Yovanovitch and apparent willingness to let Trump hijack American foreign policy for improper ends. Three times, he asked Pompeo to issue a statement defending Yovanovitch and three times it did not happen. Now he was considering quitting in protest.

With unrest about the Ukraine affair growing among the diplomats, Pompeo was to meet that morning with the department's senior staff. In an email beforehand, Dave Hale, Pompeo's political director, made clear what was, and was not, appropriate to discuss: the officials should not speak unless spoken to, the Hale email said, and should not, in any case, raise the matter of Ukraine. "They had a party line," McKinley later related to an associate, and their position was "dammit, you stick to the party line." On exiting the meeting, one official turned to McKinley. "It's like a North Korean Politburo meeting," she said.

Soon after, McKinley met alone with Pompeo. The secretary was in his office on the State Department's seventh floor, sitting as was his custom behind a table. Pompeo raised his voice. He was explosively angry that McKinley was considering leaving. "What is it, Mike? What the fuck?" the secretary said. He accused McKinley of disloyalty. "This is why we can never trust anybody in this building," Pompeo told him, vowing to rely exclusively on political appointees in the future, since it was clear that the career diplomats could not be trusted. "This is why everybody thinks you're the Deep State."

Over the previous four decades, McKinley had worked for every president since Ronald Reagan and served as American ambassador to Afghanistan, Colombia, and Peru, in addition to Brazil. Later that week, he handed in his resignation and agreed to testify before Congress.

Pompeo would continue to fulminate about the Ukraine scandal. He refused to hand over documents and claimed Congress was trying to "intimidate, bully, & treat improperly" his officials.[22] His temper spilled into public view. A couple months later, Pompeo was asked about Ukraine by Mary Louise Kelly, a host of NPR's *All Things Considered.* He abruptly cut their interview short and walked out, then sent an aide to demand that

Kelly join him in his private sitting room. There, he erupted in fury and insisted that his staff bring him a map. "Could you even find Ukraine on a fucking map?" he demanded of Kelly, a veteran correspondent who had reported from Ukraine and Russia many times. When she readily pointed to it, this caused Pompeo to get even angrier. "Do you think Americans care about fucking Ukraine?" he yelled.[23]

As investigators closed in on Trump's plan to hijack American foreign policy for his personal political ends, the president called congressional leaders to the White House for an emergency meeting on another brewing crisis. After one more telephone call with Turkey's Recep Tayyip Erdoğan, Trump had again ordered the withdrawal of remaining U.S. forces from Syria, imperiling America's Kurdish allies and effectively handing control over the territory to the Syrian government and the Russians. This time, there was no Jim Mattis to quit over it, but Congress, already in an uproar over the Ukraine scandal, quickly passed a nonbinding resolution rebuking Trump for the pullout. Even two thirds of House Republicans voted for it. Washington, for once, appeared to be united—against Trump.

At the meeting, Nancy Pelosi pointed out the bipartisan resolution to the president. "Congratulations," he snapped in response.[24] Trump got even angrier when Chuck Schumer read out a warning to the president from Mattis that leaving Syria could result in the resurgence of the Islamic State. Nothing could have more predictably set the president off, and he derided his former defense secretary as "the world's most overrated general." On and on Trump went about Mattis. "You know why I fired him?" he said. "I fired him because he wasn't tough enough."

Eventually, Pelosi grew frustrated. She stood and pointed at the president sitting directly across the table from her. "All roads with you lead to Putin," she said. "You gave Russia Ukraine and Syria."

"You're just a politician, a third-rate politician!" Trump shot back.

Finally, House Majority Leader Steny Hoyer, the courtly Maryland Democrat who was Pelosi's number two, cut off the meeting. "This is not useful," he said, standing up to leave with Pelosi.

"We'll see you at the polls," Trump shouted after them as they walked out. It was day 1,000 of his presidency.

In front of the cameras outside the White House, Pelosi told reporters she had left because Trump was having a "meltdown."[25] A few hours later, Trump tweeted out a photograph taken by his White House photographer of Pelosi standing over him, apparently thinking it would prove that she was the one having a meltdown. Instead, the image went viral as an example of Pelosi's confronting Trump, when all the big men at the table could not or would not.

The next day, Pelosi revealed that she had been challenging the president at the time the photo was taken on his bizarre history of supporting Vladimir Putin. "All roads with you lead to Putin" might have been not only Pelosi's sharpest one-liner yet aimed at Trump, but the Democrats' most succinct summary of their case against the president. Although there were fifteen months remaining in Trump's term, Pelosi never spoke with him again.

Sitting to Trump's right throughout the meeting had been General Mark Milley, the new chairman of the Joint Chiefs of Staff. Ten months after Trump had selected him to spite Mattis, Milley had finally taken office just two weeks earlier, and this was his first session with the president and the nation's elected leaders. In the White House photograph, Milley, his hands clenched and head bowed low, looked as though he wanted to sink into the floor. To Pelosi, it was a sign of inexplicable weakness, and she would later say she never understood why Milley had not been more willing to stand up to Trump at that meeting; after all, she would point out, he was the nonpartisan leader of the military, not one of Trump's subservient toadies. "You would have thought that Milley would have had more independence," she said, "but he just had his head down."

That night, Milley called Representative Adam Smith, a Washington Democrat and the chairman of the House Armed Services Committee, who had also been present. "Is that the way these things normally go?" Milley asked, a rhetorical question hardly demanding an answer. To Smith, "that was the moment when Milley realized that the boss might have a screw or two loose." There had been no honeymoon, no grace period. The alarm bells were already blaring. "From pretty much his first day on the job as chairman of the Joint Chiefs," Smith said later, "he was very much aware of the fact that there was a challenge here that was not your normal challenge with a commander in chief."

The closest Trump came to actually being removed from office on the Ukraine matter was almost certainly just hours later on the afternoon of October 17 when Mick Mulvaney gave a solo news conference in the White House briefing room—the first and only time he would do so as acting White House chief of staff.

Mulvaney, looking uncomfortable and combative and wearing one of his trademark loud patterned ties, began by announcing that Trump would host the next G7 annual summit at the Trump National Doral near Miami. Despite the obvious conflict of interest, Mulvaney claimed to reporters that Trump's property had emerged as the best venue after an elaborate selection process scoured sites all around the country. When reporters barraged him with questions, Mulvaney doubled down. Yes, he insisted, in the entire United States of America, the president's own property just happened to be "by far and away the best choice."

Mulvaney then pivoted to his own role in blocking the security aid to Ukraine. This, Mulvaney claimed, just moments after announcing the president's decision to award the contract for an international summit worth millions of dollars to himself, was because he and Trump were big opponents of "corruption" and Ukraine was a corrupt country:

> President Trump is not a big fan of foreign aid. Never has been. Still isn't. Doesn't like spending money overseas, especially when it's poorly spent. And that is exactly what drove this decision. . . . I've been in the office a couple times with him talking about this and he said, "Look Mick, this is a corrupt place." Everybody knows it's a corrupt place.

At the end of this remarkable statement claiming that Trump could simply override Congress's will because he did not like an entire country, Mulvaney let slip that something more than concern about corruption had prompted Trump. "Did he also mention to me in the past, the corruption related to the DNC server? Absolutely. No question about that," he said.

Reporters gasped audibly. Then ABC's Jonathan Karl jumped in, with an exchange that would become a briefing room classic.

> KARL: So the demand for an investigation into the Democrats was part of the reason that he ordered to withhold funding to Ukraine?
>
> MULVANEY: The look back to what happened in 2016 certainly was part of the thing that he was worried about in corruption with that nation. And that is absolutely appropriate.
>
> KARL: But to be clear, what you just described is a quid pro quo. It is: "funding will not flow unless the investigation into the Democratic server happened as well."
>
> MULVANEY: We do that all the time with foreign policy. And I have news for everybody. Get over it. There's going to be political influence in foreign policy. . . . That is going to happen. Elections

have consequences and foreign policy is going to change from the Obama administration to the Trump administration. And what you're seeing now I believe is a group of mostly career bureaucrats who are saying, "You know what? I don't like President Trump's politics, so I'm going to participate in this witch hunt that they're undertaking on the Hill." Elections do have consequences and they should. And your foreign policy is going to change. Obama did it in one way. We're doing it a different way and there is no problem with that.[26]

Mick Mulvaney had just admitted out loud exactly what the president's legal team had been denying, that the aid suspension had in fact been tied to the demand for damaging investigations into Democrats. He could not have been clearer that Trump's White House viewed foreign policy as a weapon to damage political opponents—even if it required blackmail of a country defending itself against Russian aggression.

Until that moment, Mulvaney had rarely made news as Trump's third and least powerful chief of staff. That was just the way Trump wanted it. Trump had learned a lot about getting what he wanted in the White House since firing Reince Priebus and John Kelly, and one thing he had learned was to make sure the chief had no confidence day to day that he would remain in the post. With Mulvaney, Trump accomplished this by never actually giving him the formal title and insisting on keeping the asterisk of "acting" next to his name.

A self-described "right-wing nut job," from the exurbs of Charlotte with triplets, an eight handicap at golf, and a wry sense of humor, Mulvaney had an agenda that was quite different than Trump's.[27] Like Bolton's crusade against arms control treaties, Mulvaney saw the post as an opportunity to accomplish at least some of his true passion in politics: cutting government programs. At the Office of Management and Budget, he set in motion a government-wide effort to roll back the regulatory state, which ultimately blocked hundreds of Obama-era rules. In the White House, he spent much less time with Trump than his predecessors and concentrated on "building an empire for the right wing" inside the administration, as an official told *The Washington Post*, including hiring like-minded aides, reviving the dormant White House Domestic Policy Council, and weekly demands to cabinet secretaries for updates on progress stripping regulations from the books.[28]

Most significantly, Mulvaney took personal control of key policy and spending decisions, centralizing them in the White House. He installed an ally, Russell Vought of the Heritage Foundation, as acting budget director and continued to exercise power over the budget office throughout his time in the White House. "OMB never ran separately from Mick," a cabinet secretary from this time recalled. "He would tell people, 'I'm acting chief of staff and anytime I can go back and run OMB.'"

Both Mulvaney and Vought would privately relate versions of what Mulvaney shocked the media with that day in October: that they believed Trump had every right to use Pentagon security assistance as leverage to get what he wanted from a foreign country. Trump had already done it before, holding up funds for Pakistan, for the Palestinian Authority, and for Central American countries.

When Trump in the spring of 2019 demanded that aid be cut off to Central American countries in retaliation for what Trump considered lax immigration policies, Kirstjen Nielsen several times in Oval Office meetings told him he could not do so, pointing out the money had been appropriated by Congress and that the United States had signed international agreements obligating it. But Trump overrode her. "I don't want them to get that money," he would say. Mulvaney would invariably take Trump's side, promising the president, "Okay, we'll turn it off." Eventually, they did, and Congress had hardly made an impeachable offense of it.

There was another factor, never to be discounted in Trump's backstabbing White House: Mulvaney's feud with John Bolton, the full bitterness of which was only now revealed in the impeachment investigation. As witnesses had explained, it was Mulvaney who had gone around Bolton to become the conduit between Trump and the outside-the-proper-channels officials such as Gordon Sondland on Ukraine; Mulvaney who had transmitted Trump's demand for a hold on the aid and aggressively followed up on it; and Mulvaney who had, over Bolton's objections, scheduled the now infamous July 25 phone call with President Zelensky.

Mulvaney and his camp laid the blame for that on Bolton himself. "John Bolton didn't have a good relationship with anyone in the White House. He thought he was the president of the United States," said one Mulvaney ally. Mulvaney told other White House officials that he was just doing the job that Bolton refused to do, which was to make sure that Trump got what he wanted on Ukraine. It was Bolton's fault, not his, the Mulvaney camp argued, "when Mick has to go and constantly check to see whether the president's getting what he wants from the policy process, and Bolton is treating it as something he won't touch with a ten-foot pole."

That same week as Mulvaney's news conference, Fiona Hill, the former Russia adviser who had worked closely with Bolton and shared his concerns about Ukraine, revealed in her testimony the extent of their mutual qualms about Mulvaney. In her closed-door deposition that Monday, quickly leaked to the press, Hill disclosed that Sondland had told her that he and Mulvaney had specifically agreed that a White House meeting for Zelensky would be contingent on the investigations Trump sought. Bolton had been so alarmed by this that he told Hill to report it to the White House counsel's office. "I am not part of this drug deal that Sondland and Mulvaney are cooking up," Bolton told her to say.[29]

It was this disclosure, in part, that Mulvaney was responding to in his disastrous session with the media. One man's drug deal, he insisted, was another man's foreign policy disagreement. And as far as Mulvaney was concerned, the foreign policy of the United States was whatever Trump wanted it to be. "There is no problem with that," he had declared before walking away from the podium in the White House briefing room.

The damage control began within hours, when Mulvaney released a bellicose statement blaming the media for having "decided to misconstrue" his remarks. "There was absolutely no quid pro quo between Ukrainian military aid and any investigation into the 2016 election," he insisted.[30] (The statement was notably silent about the demands for an investigation into Joe Biden in advance of the upcoming 2020 election.)

Late Saturday night, Trump, who had watched Mulvaney's briefing from Air Force One and grown increasingly angered with him as days of recriminations followed, issued his own walk-back. "We will no longer consider Trump National Doral, Miami, as the Host Site for the G-7 in 2020," he tweeted. He blamed "Irrational Hostility," but the real culprit was congressional Republicans, enough of whom were angry at the White House over the obvious impropriety of the government leasing Trump's own property for an international summit that it would undercut the support he needed in the impeachment fight.

By Sunday, the process of revising reality was well along. "I never said there was a quid pro quo," Mulvaney told Chris Wallace on Fox News, "because there isn't."[31]

The week after Mulvaney's gaffe, testimony by Bill Taylor, the former ambassador who reluctantly returned to Ukraine when Trump fired Marie Yovanovitch, set off the president. Taylor's big reveal, made in his opening statement of a lengthy closed-door deposition and then publicly released, was that Gordon Sondland had told him that "everything" for Ukraine's President Zelensky—meaning the aid and the White House meeting—was contingent on him announcing the opening of the investigation into Joe Biden that Trump demanded.[32] News reports called it "explosive," "damning," and the biggest news yet in the impeachment probe. Trump's response was to call Taylor, and the other Never Trumpers who now threatened his presidency, "human scum."

This was fully in keeping with Trump's strategy, working with fervent supporters Mark Meadows and Jim Jordan to ensure the process was as much of a partisan circus as they could make it. Others willingly embraced the role of ringleaders, most notably Matt Gaetz, a young Florida congressman who appeared regularly on Fox News and had emerged as perhaps Trump's most persistently sycophantic cheerleader in the House. Gaetz had even stormed into the secure basement conference room where the Intelligence Committee was taking testimony, seeking to dramatize what he claimed was the Star Chamber–like approach to impeachment and disrupting Fiona Hill's deposition for nearly two hours as Schiff pleaded with him, "Mr. Gaetz, why don't you take your spectacle outside?"[33] Even Meadows thought that was too much and quietly advised Schiff to have the leadership call floor votes in order to get Gaetz out of the room. Eventually, it took a parliamentarian's ruling to dislodge him

The public hearings that started in November in the Ways and Means Committee room were a tale of two Congresses—and two almost entirely different impeachments. Democrats and Republicans were so far apart as to be almost mutually incomprehensible. Devin Nunes, the panel's top Republican, opened the hearings with a long conspiracy-laden rant that was impossible to decipher without hours of previous Fox News watching, as he rambled on about an alleged Democratic scheme to obtain nude photos of Trump from Russia and the "cult-like atmosphere" they had created during the closed-door depositions. Eventually, he landed on his point, which was that impeachment was part of a nefarious plot against the president whose details did not matter, whether it be "the Russia hoax" or "its low-rent Ukrainian sequel."[34]

Democrats, meantime, embraced the damning details. Over five days and thirty hours of testimony by twelve witnesses, Schiff introduced the country to figures like Marie Yovanovitch, the wronged ambassador who spoke of what it was like to be smeared by the president of the United States, and Bill Taylor, her straight-out-of-central-casting successor with a Walter Cronkite baritone, who had kept notes as he discovered aspects of the plot by the "irregular channel" of rogue figures like Rudy Giuliani bypassing the officials responsible for Ukraine to try to get Trump what he wanted.[35] Lieutenant Colonel Alexander Vindman, in full dress uniform, recounted listening, appalled, to Trump's "perfect" phone call, and conjured in his testimony an immigrant's faith in America, invoking a scene with his Soviet-born father who feared the consequences of confronting the most powerful man in the world for his son. Trump's Washington was not Putin's Russia, Vindman reassured his father. "Here," said Vindman, "right matters."[36]

Several characters emerged as more ambivalent figures. Gordon Sondland, confronted with contradictions between his initial deposition and the testimony of other witnesses, turned on Trump and claimed that "everybody was in the loop" about the president's quid pro quo, including Mike Pence, Mick Mulvaney, and Mike Pompeo, all of whom had refused to cooperate with the investigation.[37] John Bolton and his former deputy, Charles Kupperman, had tried for months to stop Trump and release the money for Ukraine but they let lower-ranking subordinates such as Vindman absorb the risk of testifying while refusing to appear themselves and threatening Democrats with the prospect of lengthy litigation that would have delayed the impeachment timetable well into 2020.

A few days into the hearings, Kurt Volker, the former special envoy whose text messages had been a key early break in the investigation, tried to explain what it was like to carry out the nearly impossible task of wrangling American policy toward Ukraine during the Trump presidency. When he took the job, Volker said, "I believed I could steer U.S. policy in the right direction," an ambitious statement given Trump's obvious pro-Russia tilt. In May, returning from Zelensky's inauguration, he had learned firsthand in the Oval Office that there was, in fact, a "significant problem": the attitude of the president toward Ukraine. Volker believed that Trump was fed misinformation about Ukraine by Giuliani. "I found myself faced with a choice: to be aware of a problem and to ignore it or to accept that it was my responsibility to try to fix it," Volker testified. "I tried to fix it."[38]

Despite being warned by Bolton and Hill, Volker went to meet the former mayor at Trump International Hotel in Washington for breakfast in July. There, he learned from Giuliani that the demand that Zelensky investigate not only 2016 but the Bidens as well was nonnegotiable. There was no fixing it.

The hearings culminated on November 22 with Fiona Hill's appearance. Hill, an immigrant like Vindman, in her case from the coal country of northern England, methodically debunked the big lie at the heart of Trump's demand that Ukraine investigate its own alleged role in the 2016

American election, a "fictional narrative" and a "hoax" that was "perpetrated and propagated by the Russian security services themselves." She begged Republicans to stop spreading this falsehood in defense of the president, insisting the facts were "beyond dispute."[39]

It was too late, though, for facts. Confronted later that day with Hill's testimony that Ukraine had nothing to do with 2016, House Minority Leader Kevin McCarthy simply refused to accept it. "I think they did," he told reporters.[40] In the hearing room, many of his Republican members would not even ask questions of Hill. Some yelled at her. Others defended Russia with strange detours into whataboutism.

As the hearing ended, Will Hurd, a Texas Republican, used his time to announce that he had found "no evidence" of impeachable offenses in the investigation so far. Hurd, a moderate who had served in the CIA before going into politics and often publicly criticized Trump, had been seen as the last remaining potential GOP vote on the committee for impeachment. His announcement showed there was no one left to persuade in the House. It was a surprisingly definitive moment.

By late fall, Democrats knew they were not going to have any Republican votes. They just did not know what they were going to vote on. As Adam Schiff's public hearings wrapped up, Jerry Nadler's Judiciary Committee was to take the lead in drafting articles of impeachment that the House was rushing to vote on before year's end.

Even more than Schiff, Nadler had a fair claim to be the most dedicated and obsessive enemy of the president in the House. A liberal Democrat with a law degree and a debater's tongue, Nadler had battled Trump for more than two decades, first as a state assemblyman and later as a congressman, to try to stop him from rerouting part of the West Side Highway for one of his real estate projects, earning him the title of Trump's "archenemy" from a New York newspaper back in the 1990s. In 2018, Nadler had won an internal House Democratic election to become the top Democrat on the Judiciary panel by making the case that he "would be the strongest member to lead a potential impeachment."[41]

Once the Mueller report came out, Nadler pushed back against Pelosi, Schiff, and others who refused to proceed with impeachment. He lost out and that fall he had the same political problem as the speaker, his previously stated opposition to any impeachment that was purely partisan. Like Schiff and Lindsey Graham and so many others in Washington, Nadler's views of impeachment were shaped by the Clinton imbroglio. An obscure backbencher at the time, Nadler achieved his only previous moment of national fame when he gave an impassioned floor speech against Clinton's impeachment, calling it "a partisan coup d'état." He had repeated that view often in the months leading up to the Ukraine proceedings. "I said this on the floor of the House in 1998, and I meant it: impeachment must not be partisan," Nadler said after winning the House Judiciary election in 2018.[42] But of course that is exactly where the Democrats had ended up.

Democrats were by no means sure how to proceed given this political reality, and behind the scenes there was, a senior member of the impeachment team recalled, "constant vicious infighting." There was the obvious fault line between Schiff and Nadler, two rivals who had taken different positions on impeachment from the beginning and did not get on well personally. There was Pelosi, who was closely involved in most details. There was Douglas Letter, the House counsel, who had a seat at the table and, often, a different point of view. "Everybody was fighting with everybody," recalled the senior impeachment adviser, who described "a constant four-way power struggle," complete with secret communications, siloed information, and enough duplicity to rival the Trump White House.

All fall, there remained big unresolved questions: What were Democrats trying to accomplish with impeachment, given the near-impossibility of securing a Senate conviction? What audience were they aiming at—the senators who would sit in judgment? The public who would be voting on whether to re-elect Trump in less than a year? And what story did they want to tell? Democrats were split between progressives who wanted to throw the book at Trump for all his misdeeds going back to the start of his tenure and the centrists in the Bad-Ass Caucus who did not want to expand the investigation beyond the Ukraine scheme.

An early clash had come on the day of Alexander Vindman's deposition, during a meeting in Pelosi's office to finalize the House resolution setting procedures for the rest of the impeachment process. Schiff approached the matter like a prosecutor seeking to gain as much advantage as possible over the target of his investigation; Nadler wanted a resolution that looked more like previous congressional impeachments, with extensive due process afforded the White House, including the right to call fact witnesses before his committee.

Schiff later recounted their resulting fight. "I resent you dictating what the procedures should be in my committee," Nadler told him, finally expressing months of grievance. "I resent you forcing this issue with the speaker at the last minute," ticking off another finger. "I resent being forced to accept a provision that may be unconstitutional."

Schiff considered this an ambush on Nadler's part. "Well, I resent reaching an agreement with you and the speaker and then having to renegotiate it every time," he said, going on to accuse Nadler of pushing "to throw away any leverage we might have to get them to comply" with their investigation. Schiff was not above getting sanctimonious when challenged. "I've been fighting these people for three years," he lectured Nadler, who had first done public battle with Trump decades earlier, "and you're unilaterally surrendering to Trump."[43]

But however cathartic Schiff considered the fight, it did not resolve the bigger differences. By December, the argument was over just what to include in the articles of impeachment against Trump. On December 7, Judiciary Democrats had a brainstorming session with Laurence Tribe, the famed Harvard Law School professor serving Nadler as a consultant; Schiff, who had studied under Tribe at Harvard, also spoke with him frequently as the proceedings unfolded. Pelosi would sit as the ultimate arbiter. A number of Judiciary Committee members argued for a separate article that would cover Trump's business dealings with foreign powers while in office, considering it a violation of the Constitution's emoluments clause barring presidents from receiving things of value from foreign states, but it was quickly dropped, as various lawsuits related to the issue were still making their way through the courts.

Nadler insisted on an obstruction count against Trump based on Mueller's evidence, even though that had not been the subject of the fall's proceedings. Schiff pushed to stick to Ukraine. He argued that while Trump had in fact committed impeachable conduct documented in the special counsel's investigation, it would prove "complicated and difficult to explain" in a Senate trial—and to the public.[44] His political argument was that vulnerable House Democrats wanted a narrow impeachment centered on the Ukraine scandal. His practical argument was about prosecuting the Senate trial. Rather than rely on bad actors such as Mike Flynn, Paul Manafort, and Roger Stone and other characters from the Mueller report as witnesses in a Senate trial, he said, better to rely on compelling nonpartisan professionals such as Marie Yovanovitch, Fiona Hill, and Bill Taylor.

Schiff won that round and the group ultimately agreed on two articles, one on Trump's Ukraine blackmail scheme and one on obstruction of Congress for refusing to cooperate with the House investigation, written in a way that incorporated a reference to Mueller. Defeated but not deterred, Nadler then argued against the use of the term "bribery" to explain what Trump had done in Ukraine, although Schiff and Pelosi thought it important, given that the Constitution specifically mentioned bribery as an example of "high crimes and misdemeanors." The problem was the Supreme Court had recently thrown out a bribery case involving Bob McDonnell, the former governor of Virginia, suggesting that the threshold for proving the offense was significantly higher than Schiff might be able to demonstrate in the Senate. Nadler insisted that "abuse of power" was a safer bet, while Schiff, correctly anticipating the Republican attacks to come, warned it was a broad and legally meaningless phrase that was not specifically mentioned in the Constitution.

This time, Nadler won, but not before Schiff and the lawyers figured out how to at least insert the word "bribery" into the text of the first article. Exhausted by all the rounds of fighting that went into producing that outcome, a senior member of the legal team said the semantic war among the Democratic leaders of impeachment was exactly "why I would never again want to work for Congress."

On December 10, the two articles were publicly released. Article I, "Abuse of Power," outlined Trump's Ukraine scheme, characterizing the investigations the president demanded of Zelensky as an effort to influence the 2020 election on his behalf and his withholding of the military aid to Ukraine in furtherance of those investigations as a misuse of official resources. Article II, "Obstruction of Congress," charged the president with directing "unprecedented, categorical, and indiscriminate defiance of subpoenas" and undermining the principles of "constitutional governance."[45]

The vote was set to happen a week later, and no one doubted the outcome.

On December 18, 2019, Donald Trump became only the third president impeached by the House of Representatives—and the first to live-tweet his own impeachment. A few days earlier, on a Sunday with nothing much else to do, he had broken his single-day record for tweeting during his presidency, sending out 105 tweets, many of them concerning the "witch hunt" that would permanently mark history's account of his tenure. Four days later, as the Judiciary Committee marked up the articles to send them to the floor, he easily surpassed the record he had just set, hitting ninety tweets before noon and 123 by the end of the day. It was all "very sad," he complained. On the day itself, Trump sent out four dozen tweets and retweets that made it clear he was furious about the permanent blot on his record. Impeachment, he said, was "AN ASSAULT ON AMERICA, AND AN ASSAULT ON THE REPUBLICAN PARTY!!!!"

"He feels like he's been treated unfairly," Lindsey Graham complained on Trump's behalf, after having spoken with him on the phone. "It's been a never-ending effort to undermine his presidency."[46] But Trump had in many ways succeeded where it mattered most, following Graham's counsel and sticking close to Bill Clinton's playbook—at least in part. Unlike Clinton, Trump had no intention of apologizing, and no ability even to pretend he was focusing on work while enemies persecuted him. But he and his allies had kept it partisan just as Clinton had done, and in doing so persuaded even many Republicans concerned about Trump's blackmail of a beleaguered ally to disregard their qualms and stick to their camp. Partisanship was a powerful drug; in Trump's Washington, it was the intoxicant of choice.

No one better illustrated this than Adam Kinzinger, a congressman from Illinois who refused to endorse Trump in 2016 and selectively condemned Trump's various outrages during his first couple years in office when others would not. A national security hawk who had served in Afghanistan and Iraq, Kinzinger was always at the top of the list of Republicans who might consider voting for Trump's impeachment. If he did not go for it, none would.

And when the time came that December, he did not go for it. "I had an openness to vote for it," Kinzinger acknowledged much later. But the easier course was to follow the rest of the Republican Conference. "I wanted a reason to vote against it," he recalled. Trump's lawyers and the Republicans on the House Intelligence Committee had worked all fall to provide one, attacking the process as partisan, rushed, and incomplete. Kinzinger accepted the exit ramp that had been prepared for him and others like him. Where were key witnesses? Fuller hearings? The Democrats were not playing fair. "It became a rush job," Kinzinger said, which was an excuse, "*the* excuse," Kinzinger admitted, that he had been looking for.

On the day itself, Kinzinger made no speeches about impeachment. He just went to the floor and voted no, then released a statement that had not a single critical word of Trump. In it, he decried the "highly partisan, political driven process," and the "weak" impeachment articles.[47] Another statement on Facebook was more pointed, suggesting his vote was not about Trump at all but about the Democrats and their endless crusade to take down the president. "Since the day President Trump was elected, many Democrats in Congress have been searching for any means by which to delegitimize and remove him from office," Kinzinger said. "And since then, we've seen them jump head first from one investigation to another hoping something so treacherous would be uncovered that we'd have no choice but to throw him out. And at that they've failed miserably."[48]

Anti-Anti-Trumpism was a brilliant strategy. It was aimed directly at those Republicans like Kinzinger who could not—would not—justify Trump's actions but felt perfectly comfortable bashing Democrats for taking him on. Trump's defenders had been right: do everything possible to turn impeachment into a partisan circus, knowing that would help convince members not to vote in support of such a partisan circus. "This is the issue that burns me up more than anything," recalled Daniel Goldman, Schiff's lead impeachment counsel. "It is such a circular argument to say that it was a partisan investigation, and therefore we're voting against it." It burned Goldman up so much because it worked.

Long afterward, Kinzinger reflected about his impeachment vote. He had come to consider it a mistake, one of many that he and other Republican members of Congress had made when trying to navigate the impossible situations that Trump had put them in. "Bad on me," he said. Eventually, he would call it "my biggest regret."[49]

The final vote that day was 230 to 197 with one abstention from Tulsi Gabbard, a Putin-admiring, Fox News regular from Hawaii who was nominally a Democrat.[50] The only Republican who voted in favor of impeachment was Justin Amash, a libertarian from Michigan who had quit the party the previous summer over his concerns about Trump and announced he was not running for re-election.

Trump, meanwhile, spent the evening in Amash's district in Battle Creek, Michigan, being cheered at a rally by tens of thousands of his red-hatted fans. When the vote came, around 8:30 that night, an aide carried a sign to the stage so Trump could see the final tally and he exulted that Republicans had stuck with him. "The Republican Party has never been so affronted," Trump said, "but they have never been so united as they are right now."[51] He was right. Trump had sought to extort Ukraine for a personal political favor, and there was not a single Republican congressman willing to call him on it. Not one.

CHAPTER 20

The Age of Impeachment

The day before the House vote, Trump hosted a photo opportunity in the Oval Office to put his name on bipartisan legislation locking in permanent federal funding for historically Black colleges and universities. It was supposed to be a bill-signing ceremony, but the physical document had not yet arrived from the House, which was, of course, busy impeaching him, so Trump decided to proceed with a signing ceremony without the signing. Trump never let details get in the way. For once, he was not looking for a public show. The event was not announced on his public schedule. He invited just a couple of Republican lawmakers and no Democrats, even though they helped pass the measure. He would not brag about it publicly or send a single tweet touting it.

He was in a foul mood, stewing over the impeachment and "mad as hell," as Lindsey Graham put it.[1] He was not going to waste his time with fake displays of bipartisanship as he was about to go on trial in the Senate for high crimes and misdemeanors. While Trump had every reason to assume he would prevail given that Republicans controlled the Senate and conviction required a two-thirds vote, he was livid not only at Adam Schiff and the Democrats, but also at Republicans he deemed weak and unwilling to get out there to aggressively defend him. Every time he turned on the television, "Shifty Schiff" was condemning him, but where were the Republicans? Mark Meadows and Jim Jordan spoke out, sure, but what about the rest? What about the senators?

As it happened, a pair of Republican senators, Lamar Alexander of Tennessee and Tim Scott of South Carolina, were in the Oval Office for the Black college nonsigning signing ceremony, Alexander grinning on his right as Trump sat at the Resolute Desk and Scott standing to his left, with Ivanka Trump just behind him. Soon, they would both serve as jurors in the trial, and Trump seized the chance to do what no ordinary defendant could: lobby those who would sit in judgment on him. "This is a hoax," he told them, as he handed them copies of a six-page letter assailing his enemies and the whole impeachment investigation. Trump did not just want their votes; he wanted to enlist Alexander and Scott to make his case for him.

The senators politely took the letter, but neither of them was going to race to the cameras to wage political war for Trump. Scott, the only Black Republican in the Senate, was a reliable party man and his vote in the trial was not in doubt. But he was no Trumpist either and had done his best to stay out of the line of fire. Alexander, meanwhile, was an actual swing vote, closely watched by leaders of both parties as one of the only Republicans who might break ranks. Since he was not running for re-election, Democrats hoped that he might be open to persuasion, if not on the final guilt-or-innocence vote then at least on the question of calling witnesses during the trial, which was rapidly becoming the main drama.

After eighteen years in the Senate, Alexander was one of Mitch McConnell's closest allies, an exemplar of the old Republican establishment supplanted by Trump. Genteel, bespectacled, and professorial, the seventy-nine-year-old Alexander looked like the university president he once was. He had served as governor and secretary of education and ran for president himself twice, although his campaigns were better remembered for his trademark red plaid flannel shirts and much lampooned "Lamar!" logo than for any votes he collected.

Institutionalists like Alexander privately considered the president distasteful at best, repugnant at worst. "By noon every day, he violates almost every rule I learned about how a president is supposed to act," Alexander observed later, "or every rule my mother taught me about how I was supposed to act." Even so, Alexander had long ago concluded that "my job was not to catalogue all the ways" that Trump transgressed decorum and decency, but instead to work with him "as best I can."

But if Trump was now about to be put on trial, so was Alexander—and his fellow Senate Republicans. For three years, they had largely run away from reporters in the halls of the Capitol asking them to weigh in on the latest Trump outrage, neither willing to defend the indefensible nor eager to risk angering him. Now they had no choice but to cast judgment. There was no way to avoid an up-or-down verdict on Trump's presidency. They would either stand by him or not. Trump was at last forcing them to choose.

Alexander was, in that sense, a fitting man in the middle. He and

McConnell had been friends for fifty years and they commiserated about the toxic Trumpian turn in their party at their regular weeknight dinners. But where McConnell had come to an uneasy truce with the president, Alexander had kept his distance. He had declined to endorse Trump in 2016 and since then had gone against the president at key junctures on trade, health care, and his border wall. He still tried to reach across the ever-widening aisle. The day after the president handed him the six-page screed, Alexander met Senator Dianne Feinstein, the venerable California Democrat, for a convivial dinner at the Prime Rib restaurant in downtown Washington, where they sat at his favorite corner table and talked about everything but impeachment. On the way out, he stopped at the piano to playfully serenade her with "I Left My Heart in San Francisco," prompting the rest of the patrons to burst out in applause. In the car on the way home, he heard the news that the House had just impeached Trump.

At the White House, Trump's advisers were most concerned about Alexander and a handful of other moderates, including Susan Collins, Lisa Murkowski, and the president's old nemesis, Mitt Romney. Even if he was assured of acquittal, Trump was determined not to lose a single Republican. But he wavered on how to proceed. One moment, he demanded that McConnell simply hold a vote to dismiss the case outright without bothering with a trial, an idea that Alexander and the other moderates rejected. Then Trump changed his mind and insisted on a full-scale proceeding complete with witnesses—and suggested that he would make a dramatic appearance in the Senate himself. It was all fanciful and McConnell told him so. Let me handle it, the majority leader implored. He knew how to bring along his members. "Better to be unified than divided," McConnell told Trump.[2]

More than two years after the uneasy rapprochement that John Kelly brokered between the president and the Senate Republican leader, McConnell had made the most of the Trump administration without ever completely joining the team. He had gotten two Supreme Court justices and scores of other federal judges out of the devil's bargain, but privately loathed Trump and bristled at how his party caucus had increasingly been driven by the rabid pro-Trump faction represented by senators such as Rand Paul, the iconoclastic libertarian from his own Kentucky, and Josh Hawley, the Yale-educated lawyer from Missouri who had transformed himself into a born-again populist. The trial would force the rest of them to swallow any reservations, not to mention their own vociferous support for Ukraine in its fight against Russia, to stand with a president who sided with Moscow against Kyiv.

Although the Senate was to serve as Trump's jury, it would be a decidedly partisan proceeding, rather than a legal one. Few even bothered to pretend they were open to making a decision based on the facts of the case. "I'm not an impartial juror," McConnell told reporters on the same day Alexander met with Trump in the Oval Office. "This is a political process. There is not anything judicial about it. Impeachment is a political decision."[3] Indeed, just a few days earlier, McConnell had promised "total coordination" with the White House on the trial.[4] Lindsey Graham around the same time said he did not need a trial to decide Trump's innocence. "I have made up my mind," he said. "I'm not trying to pretend to be a fair juror here."[5] Never mind the oath that he and McConnell were about to take to "do impartial justice according to the Constitution and laws."

Trump and Graham, the defendant and the juror, were on the golf course in Florida enjoying the holidays a few days later when the president made a startling disclosure. He was about to order an airstrike to kill Major General Qassim Suleimani, commander of the Quds Force of the Islamic Revolutionary Guards Corps of Iran.

Even Graham, a staunch hawk, found the idea unnerving. Iran was an enemy and Suleimani a threat. But he was also one of the most powerful figures in the Middle East, who oversaw radical groups across the region. Tehran or one of those terrorist factions might feel compelled to respond forcefully, Graham warned.

"What do you do if they hit you back?" Graham asked. "Then you're in total war. Are you for this?"

Trump insisted he was.

This would not be the first time a beleaguered president ordered military action in the throes of an impeachment battle. Bill Clinton had approved a missile strike aimed at Osama bin Laden in 1998 just two days after admitting to the nation that he had not told the truth about his relationship with Monica Lewinsky and authorized a four-day air barrage against Saddam Hussein's Iraq just as the House was debating whether he had committed high crimes and misdemeanors. Clinton insisted those operations were unrelated to his political battles and had his Republican defense secretary back him up. But Trump did not bother to hide his political motivation and confided in associates that he saw the strike against Suleimani as a way to bolster Republican support in the upcoming Senate trial, even if it brought him closer to full-scale war with another nation than at any point in his presidency.

The attack on Suleimani followed days of rising tension in the region. Two days after Christmas, rockets smashed into a military base near Kirkuk in Iraq, killing an American civilian contractor. While Kataib Hezbollah, the Iranian-backed militia group held responsible for the attack, had previously fired rockets at bases with Americans, this was the first American fatality. Trump was told by intelligence officials that Tehran had probably misinterpreted his restraint in June when he called off the retaliatory strike for the drone downing with just minutes to go as a sign of weakness. So now he decided he needed to act, ordering airstrikes at five targets in Iraq and Syria that killed at least twenty-five members of Kataib Hezbollah.

That in turn provoked pro-Iranian protesters to break into the American embassy in Baghdad on New Year's Eve and set fires, triggering haunting memories of the embassy hostage crisis in Tehran that crippled Jimmy Carter's presidency. Trump sent more Marines, who broke up the protests without bloodshed. But then advisers handed the president a list of further options, including strikes against an Iranian energy facility or a command-and-control ship used by the Revolutionary Guards to direct harassment of foreign oil tankers. The memo also listed a more provocative alternative—targeting specific Iranian officials for death. On the list was Suleimani, whose Quds Force had been responsible for hundreds of attacks against American troops in Iraq during the height of the war there years before.

Shortly after midnight on January 3, Suleimani's plane landed in Baghdad, where he and his entourage were met on the tarmac by Iraqi officials. Two cars carrying the group then headed out into the night—shadowed by American MQ-9 Reaper drones. Minutes later, several missiles ripped into the vehicles, engulfing them in flames and leaving ten charred bodies inside.

Trump was pumped up by the result. He had taken out one of the world's most dangerous men, a "monster," as he put it.[6] Republican lawmakers cheered him. But everyone was nervous about what would come next. "It may be ugly, so buckle up," Gina Haspel, the CIA director, warned Trump.[7]

While he had tipped off Lindsey Graham on the golf course, Trump had given no advance notice to congressional leaders or European allies. Saudi Arabia's Mohammed bin Salman was so worried about escalation that he sent his brother to the United States to meet with Trump. It did not help that Trump and his team gave shifting explanations for why he authorized the operation, with the president at one point claiming that

Suleimani was on the verge of launching terrorist attacks on four American embassies, an assertion that neither military officials nor intelligence agencies backed up in briefings with congressional leaders.

As the president watched television over the weekend, he grew angry that critics were accusing him of recklessness. Mingling with guests at Mar-a-Lago and his nearby golf club, he sought validation that he had done the right thing, recounting for them details of the Baghdad embassy protests. But even some of his most loyal supporters were not convinced. Representative Matt Gaetz, normally the most vocal of Trump backers, urged the president not to get drawn into a wider conflict in the Middle East. Annoyed, Trump had him call Tucker Carlson, another skeptic of action against Iran, and put him on speakerphone.

"Sixteen Republican senators were calling me, demanding I do this," Trump told Carlson, as reported by the journalist Michael Bender. "They want me to do this, and they're running impeachment. And you know it's really not the time to ignore Republican senators. I had to listen to them."

Carlson was having none of it. "Maybe that's why they impeached you in the first place," he said, "to neuter your instincts."[8]

While Trump was contending with missiles from Iran, his estranged former national security adviser fired a different kind of rocket into his impeachment defense. John Bolton, who had refused to testify before the House without a court order, now declared that he would appear before the Senate if subpoenaed. His statement caught everyone off guard. Bolton had called Mitch McConnell to give him a heads-up but never heard back.

Bolton's shift came just a couple weeks after he turned in the manuscript for his $2 million memoir to the White House for a required pre-publication review to make sure it did not reveal classified information. In the book was an indication of what he would testify to if called—that Trump had in fact directly tied the $391 million in Ukraine security aid to his demands for investigations of Democrats, contrary to his later denials. Bolton would have been a bombshell witness, the president's own national security adviser accusing him under oath of the wrongdoing at the heart of the Democrats' case. And Bolton was no Democrat; his account would have been impossible to dismiss as that of a liberal partisan.

Bolton's newfound willingness to talk complicated McConnell's desire to get through the trial with no testimony and no surprises. The day after Bolton's statement, McConnell met with fellow Senate Republicans and emphasized his opposition to calling witnesses. Two days after that,

McConnell met with Trump in the Oval Office, again trying to calm the president's instincts for an all-out firefight with the Democrats. Instead, McConnell produced a set of rules for the trial modeled largely on the ones used at Clinton's trial, delaying any decision on calling witnesses until after both sides made their opening arguments.

After intensive lobbying by Democrats eager for a high-profile assignment, Nancy Pelosi assembled a team of seven House Democrats to prosecute the case in the Senate led by Adam Schiff, once more putting him ahead of Jerry Nadler, to the lasting resentment of the New Yorker. Joining them as managers, as the House prosecutors were called, was a team with carefully calibrated geographic, demographic, age, and experience diversity. Zoe Lofgren of California had been involved in both previous impeachment efforts in modern times, first as a congressional aide during Watergate and then as a member of the House Judiciary Committee during Clinton's impeachment. Hakeem Jeffries of New York, who held the fifth-ranking position in the House Democratic leadership, was a rising star widely seen as a potential successor to Pelosi. Val Demings of Florida was a former Orlando police chief whose questioning of witnesses had impressed party elders. Pelosi rounded out the team with two newly elected members, Sylvia Garcia of Texas, a former trial judge from Houston, and Jason Crow of Colorado, a former Army Ranger who served in Iraq and Afghanistan.

To make their case, Schiff hoped to present Trump's Ukraine scandal as a gripping political narrative of corruption and graft. "I want this to be like a Ken Burns documentary or an HBO miniseries," Schiff told his staff, and he asked them to pull together lots of video, and not just from the witnesses who testified during House proceedings, but of Trump himself. Schiff also told them to feature Mick Mulvaney's "quid pro quo" acknowledgment as many times as possible. "I want them to see that so often they can recite his words in their sleep," he instructed.[9] And he wanted images from the front lines of Ukraine's war with Russia too, hoping to call attention to the real-world consequences of Trump's actions.

Schiff knew that the House managers who prosecuted Clinton had been criticized for droning on too long and repeating their arguments too much, but he concluded that there was a reason to do more or less the same this time. If there was no meaningful chance of securing the two-thirds vote for conviction, he reasoned, then the real goal was to lay out the case for the public, which remained split roughly down the middle on the matter. "We were going to build in redundancy to reach those people even if it annoyed those senators," he decided, "because the public was more important."

To defend him before the Senate, Trump opted for Pat Cipollone, his White House counsel. Unlike Don McGahn, Cipollone was far more in tune with Trump and did not trash-talk him behind his back. A straitlaced fifty-three-year-old son of Italian immigrants and a devout Catholic with ten children of his own, Cipollone had willingly taken on a job most top Washington lawyers considered poisonous, after being recommended to Trump by his old friend, the Fox host Laura Ingraham. Like Bill Barr, for whom he once worked as a speechwriter, Cipollone was a by-the-book lawyer with an expansive view of executive power and eager to push back hard on what he saw as congressional intrusions on Trump's authority.

Cipollone was joined by two deputy counsels, Patrick Philbin and Mike Purpura. Several outside lawyers were brought in as well, including Jay Sekulow and Pam Bondi, a former state attorney general in Florida. Rudy Giuliani wanted to be part of the team, but that was so ludicrous given that he was at the heart of the whole Ukraine scheme that even Trump understood it was a bad idea.

In the buffet line at Mar-a-Lago on Christmas Eve, Trump had bumped into Alan Dershowitz, the eighty-one-year-old retired Harvard Law School professor who gained fame defending celebrity clients such as O. J. Simpson, Claus von Bülow, Patty Hearst, Mike Tyson, and Jeffrey Epstein. Although he already had a long roster of lawyers, Trump asked Dershowitz to represent him in the Senate trial too. "Everybody wants to do this thing, but I want you," he said.[10] Dershowitz, a nominal Democrat who had publicly embraced Trump in the past three years, tried to beg off, explaining that his wife, Carolyn Cohen, would not like it. But that only prompted Trump to hunt down Cohen across the room and convince her.

Trump also enlisted two other high-profile lawyers who knew something about investigating presidents: Ken Starr, the independent counsel whose inquiry led to Clinton's impeachment, and Robert Ray, who succeeded Starr and wrapped up the investigation by negotiating a deal in which Clinton acknowledged not telling the truth under oath, paid a $25,000 fine, and surrendered his law license for five years. The choices were curious if only because they invited unhelpful comparisons to the Clinton case and forced Trump's team to reconcile whatever Starr and Ray said now with the positions they had taken two decades earlier. But Trump was always attracted to television lawyers and collectively Starr, Ray, Dershowitz, and Bondi had made at least 365 weekday appearances on Fox News largely defending the president over the previous year, or basically one a day, according to a count by the liberal tracking group Media Matters.[11]

Lamar Alexander woke up at five in the morning on Tuesday, January 21, 2020, at his home in Nashville, fixed a little breakfast, and headed to the airport to catch the 7:40 a.m. flight to Washington so that he could be in place as the impeachment trial of Donald Trump opened in earnest at 1 p.m. It was a cold, dry winter's day, and Alexander wore a sweater with his coat and tie. "God is watching you," read one protester's sign as he entered the Capitol. Alexander had not paid much attention to the developing Ukraine scandal. The senator was distracted by health issues, falling ill enough after Christmas that he landed in the intensive care unit for six days. Then his wife wound up in the emergency room with pneumonia. But he knew the "perfect call" was in no way perfect. "You can't call up a foreign leader and ask him to investigate your political opponent," he said. "You can't do that, or you shouldn't do that."

Alexander also had more than a passing interest in the history of impeachment. He hailed from Tennessee like Andrew Johnson, the first impeached president, and he held the Senate seat once occupied by Howard Baker, the Republican who made a name for himself during the Watergate investigation asking what did the president know and when did he know it. Alexander even considered himself a bit of an impeachment history buff. At an auction in Knoxville a few years earlier, he had bought an antique book on Johnson signed by every senator who voted at his trial as well as a book published by Senator Edmund Ross twenty-eight years after casting the decisive vote for Johnson's acquittal. Now charged with sitting in judgment himself, he picked up the Ross book again, and a stack of other volumes on impeachment that he brought with him to the trial.

As partisan as Washington had become, it was still a solemn moment. All one hundred senators gathered in the same chamber in the Capitol where Johnson and Clinton had been put on trial. There was none of the usual hustle on the floor. Senators sat at small wooden desks arranged in a semicircle facing a marble rostrum as onlookers and reporters stared down from the galleries. The House managers and the president's lawyers were seated at curved tables custom-built for Clinton's trial and dusted off after sitting in storage unused for two decades.

At 1:10 p.m., Chief Justice John Roberts arrived in the chamber to preside over the trial as mandated by the Constitution, ready to do his duty but not happy being drawn into the messy partisan warfare that was the Trump presidency. The sergeant at arms announced soberly that the senators were "commanded to keep silent on pain of imprisonment." Silence was not the natural state for any senator, much less for hours at a time when they were deprived of their smartphones, newspapers, and retinues of staff. It was particularly poor timing for the four senators then running for the Democratic nomination to challenge Trump—Cory Booker, Amy Klobuchar, Bernie Sanders, and Elizabeth Warren. All of them would have preferred to be in Iowa campaigning for the first-in-the-nation caucuses.

"The president has done absolutely nothing wrong," Pat Cipollone asserted as he opened Trump's defense.[12] Alexander, sitting in the front row just feet away, thought that was certainly not true unless one believed it was all right for a president to ask the leader of another country to investigate his leading political opponent. Adam Schiff then got up and laid out the main elements of the scheme—Rudy Giuliani's machinations, the demonization of Marie Yovanovitch, the holdup of security aid, the not-so-perfect phone call, the pressure on Ukrainians to investigate Trump's opponents, and of course Mick Mulvaney's quid pro quo admission. Alexander thought Schiff was eloquent, direct, and precise but long.

By the first break, Alexander had heard something that he had not thought about before. Trump's lawyers emphasized that conviction would not just remove him from office but bar him from running again later that year. Alexander went over to McConnell and noted that he had not thought about that. McConnell had not focused much on it either.

It did not take long, though, for the acrimony of the House debate to find its way to the Senate floor. When the president's lawyers complained that Trump had not been allowed to call witnesses during the House hearings, Jerry Nadler bristled.

"Adam, that's a lie," he told Schiff. "You need to stand up and tell them it's a lie."[13]

Schiff thought that would be a mistake. They should not call the Trump lawyers liars, they should not make senators into enemies, and they should not lump them together with the president's team and call them treacherous.

Nadler was unpersuaded. "Jerry on the rampage," one of the team's legal advisers wrote in notes. So Nadler took it upon himself when he got up later that evening, ripping into the president's lawyers.

"They will not permit the American people to hear from the witnesses, and they lie and lie and lie and lie," he said. Then Nadler accused Senate Republicans of being complicit. "Unfortunately, so far, I have seen every

Republican senator has shown that they want to be part of the cover-up by voting against every document and witness proposed."[14]

Schiff grimaced. Too hot. Pat Cipollone seized on Nadler's eruption to fire back. "The only one who should be embarrassed, Mr. Nadler, is you," he charged. "For the way you addressed this body. This is the United States Senate. You're not in charge here."[15]

Finally, John Roberts intervened. "I think it is appropriate for me to admonish both the House managers and the president's counsel in equal terms to remember that they are addressing the world's greatest deliberative body," the chief justice said. He noted that a House manager was chided for using the word "pettifogging" during the 1905 impeachment trial of a judge. "I don't think we need to aspire to that high a standard, but I do think those addressing the Senate should remember where they are."[16]

Unbowed, Nadler leaned over to his colleagues at the managers' table. "It *is* treacherous and they *are* lying," he whispered angrily.[17]

Over the next several days, the managers hammered home their charges again and again. Barred from taking live testimony, Schiff and his team in effect called Trump himself as a witness for the prosecution by repeatedly showing or quoting his public remarks. From television screens set up in the chamber, Trump's voice echoed throughout the room. There he was on the South Lawn openly calling on Ukraine to investigate Biden. There he was calling on China to go after Biden too. There he was declaring that he would willingly take foreign help to win an election. And there he was back in 2016 imploring Russia, "if you're listening," to hack Hillary Clinton's email. The House strategy sought to capitalize on Trump's astonishingly unfiltered approach to politics in which he said what other presidents would never say on camera.

As they watched, some of the quasi-jurors took their duties more seriously than others. Susan Collins, a diligent student, scribbled notes. Alexander read one of his impeachment books. The Arkansas Republican Tom Cotton generated a lot of attention when he managed to get a glass of skim milk brought to him, successfully testing the Senate legend that milk was the only exception to the rule limiting senators to water on the floor. Rand Paul doodled. At one point, he scrawled out "S.O.S." on his notepad, followed by "THESE R NOT MY PARENTS!" and "PLEASE HELP ME!"[18]

The days strained the lawyers on both sides. The House managers retreated to the ceremonial office of the Senate Rules Committee, an ornate room that Chuck Schumer's staff called "Santa's workshop."[19] The president's legal team retired after each day's session to the White House to regroup and receive feedback from their opinionated client, who was constantly pushing for more aggressive defense. The lawyers' throats grew so hoarse that Jay Sekulow was treating his with lidocaine. John Roberts was suffering from a cold. Schiff was afflicted by a killer toothache that had him popping prodigious amounts of both Advil and Tylenol. It would not be until the weekend that he would be able to escape long enough to get a root canal. Much worse, Jerry Nadler was splitting his time between the trial and home in New York, where his wife had just been diagnosed with pancreatic cancer.

Toothache or no, Schiff reserved the most speaking time for himself, determined to leave no argument unanswered. He adopted an intentionally more partisan tone than a prosecutor trying to win over skeptical jurors might have, figuring that most senators were not open to persuasion. At most he had in mind the four Republicans considered potentially on the fence—Alexander, Collins, Lisa Murkowski, and Mitt Romney. During breaks, he would go back to the managers' hideaway and remind his team of their audience. "We're speaking to the four and the 40 million," he said. "The four senators we might win and the 40 million who were undecided."

At one point, though, he aggravated at least some of the four. Looking for fresh material, Schiff cited a news report about Trump's efforts to maintain party loyalty. "CBS News reported last night that a Trump confidant said that key senators were warned, 'Vote against the president and your head will be on a pike,'" Schiff said. "I don't know if that's true."

Some of the Republicans in the chamber gasped and took offense. Collins stared directly at Schiff, shaking her head. "Not true," she said.

Schiff, noticing Collins, sought to backpedal a bit. "I hope it's not true," he said.[20]

Afterward, Republicans expressed great indignation about Schiff's remark. But it was hardly surprising to think that Trump would hold it against any Republican who broke with him during the trial. This was a man who considered Republicans who betrayed him "human scum."

Still, Schiff's remarks cut at the senators' self-image as independent actors. As Lamar Alexander watched, he could not help but remember the famous line from the legendary senator Everett Dirksen about occasionally enjoying an unexpressed thought. "Schiff I think," Alexander said after the trial was over, "would have benefited if he had a good editor."

In the speaker's conference room on Sunday night, phones started buzzing. The House managers and their staff collectively glanced down at their screens to discover that *The New York Times* had just posted a blockbuster story that could upend the proceedings.

The paper's Maggie Haberman and Michael Schmidt had gotten hold of the part of John Bolton's unpublished manuscript that directly contradicted Trump's defense and described him conditioning the Ukraine security aid on President Zelensky agreeing to investigate Biden. How could the Senate refuse to hear from Bolton now?

The room buzzed with nervous energy. Bolton apparently had the killer evidence that Republicans had been insisting the case against Trump lacked: the president himself personally demanding the quid pro quo. "Oh my God, he's throwing everyone under the bus," Adam Schiff said. Others thought it completely changed the political odds of getting witnesses. "They're going to have to let him testify now," said Daniel Goldman, Schiff's lawyer.

In another time, in another Washington, that might have been the moment that changed the trajectory of the presidency. It brought to mind the smoking gun tape proving that Richard Nixon had ordered the Watergate cover-up that ultimately brought him down. But this was Trump's Washington. The president who could survive the *Access Hollywood* tape, hush money payments to a porn actress, and a special counsel investigation documenting obstruction of justice had already shown an uncanny ability to deflect revelations that would have ended anyone else's political career.

While Romney, Collins, and Murkowski thought they should call Bolton as a witness, Lindsey Graham worked to head that off, suggesting instead they obtain a copy of Bolton's book manuscript so senators could read it in a special room sealed for classified briefings. That was a nonstarter, but at least it bought some time on Monday, when things could have quickly gone in the other direction. Time was what Mitch McConnell needed. Like other Republican senators, the majority leader was furious at being blindsided and knew the Bolton revelation was problematic. But he had seen too many Trump-velocity news cycles play out. This time, too, he would seek to wait it out and hope, like many Trump scandals, it faded with a few more days. So he urged Republicans to "take a deep breath."[21]

The Trump legal team's response to the revelation was simply to ignore it. The president's lawyers returned to the Senate on Monday and began their detailed defense as if nothing had happened. "Not a single witness testified the president himself said that there was any connection between any investigation and security assistance, a presidential meeting or anything else," Jay Sekulow told the senators, never mind that there was just such a witness ready to testify if summoned.[22]

As if that were not surreal enough, Trump's team then handed the lectern to Ken Starr so that the man who helped impeach one president could argue against conviction of another. More than twenty years earlier, Starr said quite soberly that the rule of law was so important that a president should be held accountable for defying the judicial system even if the underlying issue was just about sex. Now he contended that a president's subversion of foreign policy for the purpose of tearing down a domestic opponent did not rise to the level of high crimes and misdemeanors. "The Senate is being called to sit as the high court of impeachment all too frequently," Starr told the senators. "Indeed, we are living in what I think can aptly be described as the Age of Impeachment." It was, of course, an age he played a role in ushering in. "Like war, impeachment is hell," he allowed. "Or at least presidential impeachment is hell."[23]

Only in the evening did any Trump lawyer finally acknowledge the latest development. "Nothing in the Bolton revelations, even if true, would rise to the level of an abuse of power or an impeachable offense," Alan Dershowitz told the senators. Like Starr, Dershowitz made an argument that conflicted with his position from two decades earlier. He maintained that impeachment required a statutory crime, not something abstract and undefined like "abuse of power"—the opposite of what he contended during the Clinton impeachment, when he said a "technical crime" was not required.

Dershowitz went even further into the constitutional netherworld by arguing that even if Trump's action with Ukraine was self-interested, it could not be impeachable so long as it was not technically criminal and he was at least partially motivated by the public interest. "If a president does something which he believes will help him get elected in the public interest, that cannot be the kind of quid pro quo that results in impeachment," Dershowitz declared.[24]

Was Dershowitz seriously saying that a president could abuse the powers of his office for political gain so long as he believed his own re-election was good for the country? Pat Philbin drew cleanup duty the next day. "The suggestion has been made because of Professor Dershowitz's comments that the theory that the president's counsel is advancing is the president can do anything he wants if he thinks it will advance his re-election, any quid pro quo, anything he wants, anything goes," Philbin said. "And that is not true."[25] Even if it was what he said. Dershowitz never appeared again at the trial.

The more Lamar Alexander listened to the arguments, the more convinced he was that the House managers had made their factual case. Trump had done what the Democrats had accused him of doing. "There obviously was" a quid pro quo, he concluded. It was unseemly and wrong. The call summary alone made that clear. But Alexander reasoned that it was not so wrong that it was worth dislodging an elected president months before the voters could cast their own judgment on the matter. To test his thinking, Alexander wrote out two statements on whether to call witnesses, one announcing he would vote for new testimony from the likes of John Bolton and the other opposing it.

On the morning of January 30, he paced in the cold for forty minutes around the National Mall, and came to his decision. He wandered into the Mansfield Room of the Capitol, where Republican senators were having lunch before the trial was to resume. Mitt Romney and Susan Collins had already decided to support witnesses and Mitch McConnell was urging undecided senators—meaning just Alexander and Lisa Murkowski—not to let the decision on witnesses come to a 50 to 50 vote because it would put the chief justice in the awkward position of either breaking the tie or refusing to intervene. Alexander pulled McConnell aside. "I'll tell you tonight how I'm going to vote during supper break," he said. He then told Murkowski the same thing.

In the cloakroom a few minutes later, Lindsey Graham asked Alexander whether it would help him vote against witnesses if Trump acknowledged that he had, in fact, blocked the security aid in order to pressure Ukraine to open investigations. There would be no need to call John Bolton if Trump admitted the quid pro quo his former adviser would testify to. Graham thought it was a deal Trump could accept, since his lawyers could then argue that even so it did not matter—that the conduct was still not impeachable. Alexander was noncommittal, but Graham spent much of the day trying to cajole Trump into agreeing to such a concession, reaching him by telephone back at the White House repeatedly through the afternoon. Trump resisted, saying he had done nothing wrong. Graham retorted that almost everyone believed he had.

The trial had all come down to this question of whether Alexander would permit witnesses, the only chance of scrambling the political equation—or go straight to the presumed inevitable acquittal for Trump.

No other way out seemed possible, especially after Joe Manchin, the Democratic centrist from West Virginia, tried and failed to forge a bipartisan consensus by floating a censure resolution that would not remove Trump from office but condemn him for crossing a line. That way, as Manchin saw it, Trump could not boast of an acquittal even while finishing his term. Manchin prepared two versions, "an ass-kissing and an ass-kicking" alternative, as he put it.[26] But no Republican would go along with either.

Around 6 p.m., the trial broke for dinner. Alexander approached McConnell and suggested they meet back in his office, each taking a different route to avoid reporters. When they sat down a few minutes later, Alexander revealed his hand. "I don't need more evidence to prove something that is already proven," he told McConnell, then handed him a copy of his statement opposing witnesses. He did not worry that McConnell would leak it; as one of the leader's aides once said, "Telling Mitch McConnell a secret is like speaking into a tomb."

McConnell told Alexander that he agreed that the president had clearly done what he was accused of doing but he still did not think it was impeachable. Alexander slipped out of the office and headed down a back hall to the Mansfield Room, where Mexican food was being served to Republican senators.

Lisa Murkowski was munching on guacamole and chips.

"Why don't we go up to my hideaway?" Alexander suggested.

In his private third-floor office away from the cameras and the crowds, Alexander handed her his statement opposing witnesses, which she read without revealing her own choice.

After dinner, Graham and Ted Cruz, still trying to get around witnesses by having Trump admit the quid pro quo, fashioned a question to the president's lawyers to that effect and asked Alexander and Murkowski to join them, which they did. "Isn't it true," they asked, that even if Bolton testified and everything he said was accurate, it "still would not rise to the level of an impeachable offense, and that therefore his testimony would add nothing to the case?"[27]

When the chief justice read the question out loud at 10 p.m., the fact that Alexander and Murkowski were listed as sponsors resounded around the chamber. Everyone knew what that meant. Pat Philbin, the Trump lawyer, refused to stipulate that there had been a quid quo pro but hastened to agree that it would not matter if there were. "It's over," a Bloomberg reporter in the gallery saw a Democratic senator tell a colleague.[28]

A few minutes later, Jerry Nadler gave a truncated closing statement. He was clearly aware what was about to happen. "They are afraid of the witnesses," Nadler said. "They know Mr. Bolton and others will only strengthen the case."[29] As the Senate adjourned for the night, Senator Debbie Stabenow, Democrat of Michigan, whispered to Norm Eisen, Nadler's impeachment lawyer, that Alexander would vote no on witnesses, delivering the news in a tone suggesting she were assigned to "tell me my parents were getting a divorce," as Eisen would remember it.[30]

Alexander headed out into the cold night and climbed into a car, which delivered him back to his apartment at 10:50 p.m. Ten minutes later, he had his staff release the statement.

"There is no need for more evidence to prove something that has already been proven and that does not meet the United States Constitution's high bar for an impeachable offense," he wrote. "It was," he went on, "inappropriate for the president to ask a foreign leader to investigate his political opponent and to withhold United States aid to encourage that investigation." But, he added, "the Constitution does not give the Senate the power to remove the president from office and ban him from this year's ballot simply for actions that are inappropriate."[31]

Alexander had hit upon the formula that many of the remaining wavering Republicans would seize as their way out of the bind the president had placed them in: Yes, Trump was guilty of sticking up Ukraine's president in furtherance of his own political interests, but no, he should not be convicted. The Constitution was vague about what constituted high crimes and misdemeanors, leaving each senator to define it each time a president was put on trial. In effect, Alexander had fashioned an elegant escape for the establishment Republicans who did not want to declare Trump innocent of conduct they knew he was guilty of but did not want to remove him from office either.

Over the next twenty-four hours, other Republican senators adopted his argument. "Strong statement that I may borrow from!" Rob Portman of Ohio emailed him. Portman, who headed the congressional Ukraine caucus and had been the final voice in Trump's ear begging him to reverse his hold on the Ukraine aid in September when he finally did so, had once seemed like a potential vote to convict.[32] But, like others, he embraced the Alexander formula. Marco Rubio, whose failed 2016 campaign against Trump had been premised on his credentials as an anti-Russia national security hawk, did the same in a statement the next day: "Just because actions meet a standard of impeachment does not mean it is in the best interest of the country to remove a President from office."[33] Ben Sasse, another sometime Trump critic, told reporters, "Lamar speaks for lots and lots of us."[34]

Despite wanting to hear from Bolton, Murkowski was now the last to decide on witnesses and concerned about putting the chief justice on the spot with a tie vote. McConnell, ever attuned to what moved members of his caucus, pressed that point by showing her a Democratic video depicting John Roberts with a MAGA baseball cap photoshopped on his head. This kind of politicization of the chief justice was what would happen if he was forced to take sides. Murkowski got the point and decided to vote against witnesses, but not before bitterly explaining that the whole process had become so partisan "there will be no fair trial in the Senate."[35]

On a 51 to 49 vote, the Senate rejected hearing Bolton or any other testimony, ending what little uncertainty there had been. All fifteen previous impeachment trials in the Senate had witnesses, including the two previous presidential impeachments. But Lamar Alexander had spoken and the trial of Donald Trump that was not really a trial would end without them.

At that point, there was little more to say, but it being the Senate it took days to say it anyway. Facing certain defeat, Adam Schiff delivered final arguments that nonetheless riveted the chamber, Republicans included. Schiff had given numerous speeches by that point. He was by far the most eloquent of the managers, although he had begun to grate on some of the Republicans with his stemwinding. Yet most who heard his closing argument that night considered it his most powerful elocution of the trial.

"It is midnight in Washington," Schiff began. "The lights are finally going out in the Capitol after a long day in the impeachment trial of Donald J. Trump." Over the course of the next twenty-five minutes, he said it was not enough to let voters decide because if the Senate were to let Trump off, he would be free to use his power to advantage himself with impunity in the election. "He has done it before, he will do it again," Schiff warned. "What are the odds if left in office that he will continue trying to cheat? I will tell you: 100 percent. Not five, not 10, or even 50 but 100 percent. If you have found him guilty and you do not remove him from office, he will continue trying to cheat in the election until he succeeds." He also chided Republicans who adopted the Alexander formula, warning that "your name will be tied to his with a cord of steel and for all of history."

Finally, he appealed to Republicans who knew that Trump was dangerous but were leery of standing up to him.

He has betrayed our national security and he will do so again. He has compromised our elections and he will do so again. You will not change him, you cannot constrain him. He is who he is. Truth matters little to him. What's right matters even less, and decency matters not at all. I do not ask you to convict him because truth or right or decency matters nothing to him, but because we have proven our case and it matters to you. Truth matters to you. Right matters to you. You are decent. He is not who you are.[36]

He will do it again. You cannot constrain him. So many had told themselves that they could manage the unmanageable president, that they could keep him from going too far, that they could steer him in the direction of responsible governance. Cabinet secretaries, White House chiefs of staff, national security advisers, political advisers, senators, congressmen, family members—they had all at one point or another adopted this reasoning. They had justified their service to him or their alliances with him or their deference to him on the grounds that they could ultimately control him. And what Schiff was saying is that three years had shown that was not possible.

On the evening of February 4, Trump arrived in the same House chamber where he had been impeached weeks earlier to deliver his State of the Union address. It had a surreal quality, a president on trial for high crimes and misdemeanors addressing the lawmakers who were sitting in judgment of him. He never uttered the I-word during his seventy-eight-minute speech but used the platform to make a case for re-election, boasting of a "great American comeback" three years after diagnosing "American carnage."[37]

Breaking protocol, he refused to shake Nancy Pelosi's hand as he took his place on the rostrum. Trump had no interest in seeking unity, instead pulling off a surprise by awarding the Presidential Medal of Freedom in the middle of the speech to the conservative radio host Rush Limbaugh, one of the most divisive figures in American society, known for juvenile, racist stunts like playing a song called "Barack, the Magic Negro" and dismissing women's activists as "feminazis."[38] Pelosi defied custom too, refusing to introduce Trump with the traditional words saying that she had "the high privilege and the distinct honor" of presenting the president. Once Trump finished speaking, Pelosi made a show of taking her copy of his speech and ripping it up on live television.

Trump could afford to be provocative because he knew he had the votes for acquittal. And he was feeling pumped up because it looked like he was winning not just inside the Senate chamber but outside as well. Senator Bernie Sanders, the self-proclaimed democratic socialist from Vermont, had just won the most first-place votes in the Iowa caucuses and was riding a wave of momentum that would take him to victory in New Hampshire as well and maybe all the way to the Democratic nomination. Joe Biden, who worried Trump so much that he had sought to pressure a foreign leader into investigating him, setting in motion the actions leading to impeachment, finished a miserable fourth place in Iowa and was on his way to an even worse fifth place in New Hampshire. Trump's team was eager to run against Sanders.

But trouble loomed that Trump refused to recognize. The morning after his State of the Union address, just hours before the Senate was poised to vote to acquit him on February 5, Lamar Alexander presided over a closed-door briefing with federal health officials about a mysterious new virus in China that was spreading fast and could be the opening wave of a major deadly outbreak around the world.

During the briefing, Senator Brian Schatz, a Democrat from Hawaii, got into a tense exchange with Alex Azar, Trump's secretary of health and human services, complaining that the federal government's handling of the crisis was "chaotic in the extreme." Azar took offense, saying he was entitled to defend his honor. "Hey man, it's not about you and me and your honor," Schatz snapped back. "I'm telling you what's happening on the ground."

Alexander stepped in to calm the situation. "Why don't you guys talk when the briefing is over?" he suggested.

Many senators emerged from the session disturbed. "Just left the Administration briefing on Coronavirus," Senator Chris Murphy, a Connecticut Democrat, wrote on Twitter. "Bottom line: they aren't taking this seriously enough."[39]

All eyes turned to Mitt Romney. With the senators headed toward the final vote in the trial, the only suspense left was whether the Utah Republican would break party lines to pronounce Trump guilty. Ever since John McCain had died in 2018 and Romney had been elected to the Senate a couple months later, he had been what passed for a Republican opposition to Trump. But even more so than McCain, Romney was not leader of a faction so much as a party of one.

When Romney stood on the floor to announce his decision, it was such an overwhelming moment that he choked up, pausing for twelve long seconds to compose himself, before declaring that he would vote to convict on Article 1, the abuse of power charge, although he would not back Article 2 on obstruction of Congress. His lone vote meant nothing to the outcome, but it would be the first time in American history that a senator voted to convict a president of his own party in an impeachment trial. As a practical matter, it would prevent Trump from bragging that every Republican had stood by him and would give modest consolation to the managers.

"What he did was not perfect," Romney said, rejecting the president's defense. "No, it was a flagrant assault of our electoral rights, our national security and our fundamental values. Corrupting an election to keep oneself in office is perhaps the most abusive and destructive violation of one's oath of office that I can imagine."[40]

With that, Romney made a bid for a place in history along with the Senate's great dissenters, like Margaret Chase Smith denouncing Joseph McCarthy years before other Republicans would join her. While Romney's words reverberated, however, few of his colleagues heard them in person. Senator David Perdue, Republican of Georgia, was presiding but never made eye contact with Romney. The only other Republican present, Senator Roger Wicker of Mississippi, entered a few minutes into the speech and stood silently at his desk before walking out without saying a word. Three Democrats who happened to be on the floor were deeply moved. Chris Murphy choked up as he listened. Brian Schatz wiped tears from his eyes. In the cloakroom, watching on television, Adam Schiff was stunned. "It really took my breath away," he recalled later.

At the White House, there was anger. The president posted a video attacking Romney as a "Democrat secret asset" who "tried to infiltrate Trump's administration as secretary of state" while "posing as a Republican."[41] Don Jr. demanded that the Republican Party banish its 2012 presidential nominee. "He's now officially a member of the resistance & should be expelled from the @GOP," the president's son wrote.

At 4 p.m., the senators, House managers, and presidential lawyers filed in and took their seats in the Senate chamber. John Roberts entered and within a few minutes called the vote on the first article of impeachment.

"Senators, how say you?" he asked. "Is the respondent, Donald John Trump, guilty or not guilty?"

The clerk then began calling the roll in alphabetical order. Lamar Alexander came first.

"Mr. Alexander?" the clerk asked.

"Not guilty," he called out in a firm voice.[42] Mitch McConnell's best friend had done his duty.

In a few minutes, it was over. All Democrats, including the occasionally party-defying centrists Joe Manchin and Kyrsten Sinema, voted to convict. All Republicans aside from Romney voted not guilty. Trump was acquitted, 48 to 52, in a trial that seemed to prove that it might never be possible to remove a president through impeachment and conviction. American politics had grown so polarized that a bipartisan two-thirds majority in the Senate seemed almost inconceivable.

Alexander had no regrets. During a closed-door lunch with Senate Republicans on the day of the vote, he blamed the Democrats. "Don't send us a half-baked, due-process-deficient, wholly partisan impeachment that seeks to make a weapon of perpetual impeachment," he said. In the end, the divisions that Trump stoked had helped save him.

As the trial adjourned, Alexander stepped out of the chamber and took the elevator up to his third-floor hideaway office. After two weeks, his own trial was over too. He knew that critics were calling him a coward and an enabler. He knew he would have been called a profile in courage had he gone the other way. Sitting down in his hideaway minutes after the verdict, he tapped out an email to Romney.

"Mitt," he wrote. "As you already well know, you never make a mistake doing what you believe is right. See you next week. Lamar."[43]

IV

DIVIDED WE FALL

"This is not going to end well."

—DONALD TRUMP

CHAPTER 21

Love Your Enemies

The evening of his acquittal in the Senate trial, Trump hosted a small private dinner in the White House for about a dozen religious leaders in town for the next day's National Prayer Breakfast. He called it his "Un-impeachment Celebration." The annual prayer breakfast was a bipartisan tradition since the Eisenhower era, and it seemed particularly well timed for a nation in need of post-impeachment reconciliation. The president, however, was not thinking about forgiveness, much less atonement.

One of his dinner guests reminded the president of Jesus's injunction to "love your enemies."

Trump turned to Robert Jeffress, the pastor of a Dallas megachurch, for his thoughts on that advice. Trump was not a religious man, but if he had been, Jeffress would have been his kind of cleric. He was a paid contributor to Fox News who often appeared on the president's favorite shows defending this or that Trumpian outrage. Trump's evangelical voters "knew they weren't voting for an altar boy," Jeffress had once said of the thrice-married, hush-money-paying president.[1] He had told Lou Dobbs that "even heaven itself is going to have a wall around it," called Islam "a false religion based on the teachings of a false prophet," and later in 2020 would tell his congregation that only those who "sold their soul to the Devil" would vote against Trump for a second term.[2] In the fall, at the start of the House's impeachment proceedings, Jeffress had even warned that removing Trump from office would "cause a Civil War like fracture in this Nation from which our country will never heal," as Trump's approving tweet about it had quoted him.

This was not a preacher who was going to lecture Trump about turning the other cheek and all that.

"Mr. President," Jeffress replied, "to love your enemies means to want the best for them. But it doesn't mean you're going to be unified with them. Truth divides people."

Truth divides people. Trump took that as dispensation; even God, or at least his favorite televangelist, thought it was all right to embrace division. He had no intention of forgiving or forgetting anyway. When it came to moving on after an impeachment battle, he would not follow the playbook left by Bill Clinton, who, after his own trial and acquittal in 1999, offered an apology, a plea for absolution, and a vow to try to bring Americans together.

The next morning, while in the presidential limousine on the way to the prayer breakfast, Trump ordered aides to rewrite his speech—there were a few more things he wanted to say. But when he arrived, he first had to listen to another love-your-enemies lecture. Glowering on the dais as he waited his turn, Trump frowned and shrugged his way through the keynote address by Arthur Brooks, a prominent conservative thinker who asked the audience, "How many of you love somebody with whom you disagree politically?" Hands shot up around the room. "I'm going to round that off to 100 percent," he said.

Not quite. Among those who had not raised their hands was the president, who smoldered at being forced to share a stage with Nancy Pelosi, the speaker who had just impeached him and ripped up his State of the Union address. "Ask God to take political contempt from your heart," Brooks added. "And sometimes when it's too hard, ask God to help you fake it."

One thing Trump could not fake was love for his enemies, even at a prayer breakfast. For the president, this was a moment for retaliation, not reconciliation. As he followed Brooks to the podium that morning, he chided the scholar for suggesting otherwise. "Arthur, I don't know if I agree with you," he said. Instead, Trump gloated to the audience about his victory, holding up newspapers with banner headlines that said, "Acquitted" and "Trump Acquitted," and then laid out his grievances. "As everybody knows, my family, our great country and your president have been put through a terrible ordeal by some very dishonest and corrupt people," he said. Then he read the lines he had added in the car ride over. First, he lashed out at Mitt Romney, who had cited his religious beliefs in voting to convict. "I don't like people who use their faith as justification for doing what they know is wrong," Trump said. He did not mention Romney by name. He did not need to. Then, in a clear reference to Pelosi, a practicing Catholic who had said that she prayed for the president, he added, "Nor do I like people who say, 'I pray for you,' when they know that's not so."[3]

A few hours later, Trump staged a victory rally in the White House, where he gathered allies, aides, and even the attorney general to hear him unleash a vituperative barrage against his enemies. He assailed "crooked" lawmakers and the "top scum" at the FBI for trying to take him down. No longer avoiding naming his targets, he denounced Pelosi as "a horrible person," Romney as "a failed presidential candidate," James Comey as "that sleazebag," the former FBI officials Peter Strzok and Lisa Page as "two lowlifes," and Adam Schiff as a "corrupt politician."

"It was evil," Trump said of the investigations that led to his Senate trial. "It was corrupt. It was dirty cops. It was leakers and liars, and this should never ever happen to another president, ever. I don't know that other presidents would have been able to take it." Referring to the allegations against him, he said, "It was all bullshit," surely the first time any president had used such profanity on live television from the East Room of the White House.[4] The audience laughed.

Susan Collins, the Maine Republican, had justified her vote to acquit Trump that week by saying she was sure he had learned "a pretty big lesson." She even ventured to predict that "he will be much more cautious in the future."[5] But whatever lesson Collins imagined him taking from impeachment was not the one he began applying.

In the aftermath of his acquittal, Trump felt emboldened, free to use his power as he saw fit to punish enemies and benefit friends. His approval rating had climbed to the highest level of his presidency and now stood at 49 percent in the Gallup poll, which, even though it meant he still had not earned the support of a majority of Americans, was enough to convince him that the public stood with him.[6] With the trial over, he no longer had to worry about alienating squishy Republican senators. He felt no fear of accountability. What were they going to do? Impeach him again?

For those who watched the president in his daily monologues in the Oval Office or Situation Room, the change was hard to miss. "When it really started getting unmanageable was right after he beat the charges of impeachment," Mark Esper, the defense secretary, later observed. The president, he told an associate, was "unleashed."

The morning of the prayer breakfast, Stephanie Grisham, the White House press secretary, declared on Fox News that those who hurt the president "should pay for" it and within forty-eight hours of the Senate vote they did.[7] Alexander Vindman, who had already cleared out his desk knowing what was coming, was marched out of the White House for good, as was Eugene Vindman, his twin brother on the National Security Council staff, for the crime of being related to someone who testified against the president. Gordon Sondland was told to resign immediately as ambassador to the European Union but refused, saying he would rather be fired, which he immediately was.

In the weeks to come, others would be targeted, even those who had tangential roles in impeachment. Joseph Maguire, the acting director of national intelligence who brokered the deal to hand over the Ukraine whistleblower's complaint to Congress, was forced out and replaced by Richard Grenell, the combative ambassador to Germany and a Trump favorite ("my beautiful Ric," the president called him). Maguire's successor as head of the National Counterterrorism Center was also forced out and replaced with a National Security Council official, Christopher Miller. At the Pentagon, John Rood, the undersecretary of defense who had certified that Ukraine met the conditions for the aid that Trump nonetheless froze, was pushed aside, while Elaine McCusker, a Defense Department official who questioned the aid suspension, had her nomination to be Pentagon comptroller withdrawn. So did Jessie Liu, the United States attorney who had prosecuted Roger Stone and had been nominated to be undersecretary of the treasury.

Others left on their own rather than wait to be fired or humiliated. Marie Yovanovitch retired from the Foreign Service, ending her thirty-three-year career. Bill Taylor, who had reluctantly agreed to return to Ukraine as acting ambassador after Yovanovitch was fired, found himself shunned by Mike Pompeo, who did not want to show up on an official trip to Kyiv while one of Trump's impeachment accusers was still leading the American embassy there, so Taylor left Ukraine early and returned to his think tank post. Jennifer Williams, a Mike Pence aide who had listened to the "perfect" phone call and testified under subpoena, worried that she would be next, and her colleague Olivia Troye, another vice presidential adviser, urged her to leave the White House before Trump's enforcers targeted her. "They could destroy your next assignment," she told Williams. "You need to get out of here." Williams quietly moved to the Defense Department.

Trump also went after a series of inspectors general who had angered him, firing or replacing five of them in quick succession, including most prominently Michael Atkinson, who had insisted on telling Congress about the CIA whistleblower complaint. Inspectors general were appointed by the president subject to confirmation by the Senate but intended by Congress to serve as independent checks on executive departments. Trump could hardly care less what Congress intended.

To conduct a broader purge, Trump enlisted Johnny McEntee, his onetime personal assistant, newly returned from exile to take over as director of presidential personnel. McEntee, a twenty-nine-year-old former University of Connecticut football quarterback whose main claim to fame was filming a video of trick passes that drew seven million viewers, had talked his way into Trump's 2016 campaign after a fusillade of unsolicited emails, then went along with him to the White House. In the spring of 2018, he had been fired by John Kelly over undisclosed gambling winnings ("I really know how to play blackjack well," he had tried to explain to the chief of staff) and was escorted out of the compound without even being allowed to grab his coat, a move that upset his friends around the building, including the president, who gave him a job at the campaign as a consolation prize. With Kelly long gone, McEntee was back as an unlikely power broker in the White House and opened a sweeping attack not just on career officials who had played roles, however minor, in the impeachment, but on the president's own political appointees.

McEntee began grilling officials to determine who would be pushed out. He asked one senior government official where he got his news. When the official replied Fox, he was deemed acceptable. McEntee asked another official his opinion of Trump's desire to pull troops out of Afghanistan. "I work at the EPA," the confused official responded.[8] He went after an acting assistant defense secretary because she had worked for the Senate Armed Services Committee under John McCain; she was forced to resign even though by that point she had worked for Trump longer than she had for McCain.

Whether motivated by resentment over how he himself had been treated or a sense that Trump was being undermined by internal enemies, McEntee the loyalty enforcer was harder-edged than the eager young body man had been. Some of his colleagues were stunned at his new persona, including Stephanie Grisham, who had lobbied to bring him back. "The John McEntee I knew in the campaign and the beginning was just this great guy who believed in the boss and wanted to do a good job," she said later. "The John McEntee who came back was vindictive, cocky, angry, manipulative."

Trump made no pretense that his purge was anything other than what it was. Loyalty was now the defining job qualification for service in his administration. The Republican senators who had objected during the trial to the suggestion that Trump would put heads on pikes in retribution for impeachment largely remained silent as the skulls piled up.

That February was in many ways the month that changed his presidency. As the president reveled in his victory over Nancy Pelosi and Adam Schiff, he did not recognize the gathering threat from the coronavirus, to the country and to his own future in that fall's election. Looking ahead to the campaign, Trump thought he had it won. Campaign advisers were telling Trump that, regardless of public polls that showed him losing to pretty much any Democrat, he could not only win a second term but win convincingly, even potentially in a landslide. "Internal REAL polls show I am beating all of the Dem candidates," Trump bragged on Twitter after his campaign team showed him a presentation that, implausibly, had him winning as many as four hundred electoral votes and taking even reliably Democratic states such as Colorado and New Mexico.

Even so, some of his lieutenants tried to warn him that the emerging public health crisis could be serious enough to destroy his administration. "The one thing that makes you lose," Brad Parscale, his campaign manager, told Trump on February 12, was this new virus. Trump could not accept that. How could he? He was riding high. He was invincible.

While his focus was elsewhere, his administration was not only unprepared for the scale of the disaster about to overwhelm it but deeply divided over how to handle it. From the start, Trump's advisers alternated between urgently seeking his attention on the coronavirus and arguing among themselves over what to do once they secured it.

The government had gotten its first warning on New Year's Eve, just before the start of the Senate trial, when Robert Redfield, the Trump-appointed director of the Centers for Disease Control and Prevention, read a notice reporting twenty-seven cases of an unknown virus found in Wuhan, a major Chinese industrial city of more than 11 million. Matt Pottinger, the Asia expert who had been promoted to deputy national security adviser, convened the first interagency meeting about the situation on January 14. But the outbreak came at a delicate time in Trump's trade negotiations with China. The day after Pottinger's meeting, the president announced a preliminary deal to ease the trade war he had been waging for two years as Beijing agreed to open its markets to more American companies and committed to buying an additional $200 billion in American exports by the following year. The last thing Trump wanted to do was disrupt the election-year truce.

That Saturday, while Trump was tweeting about "Crazy Bernie" Sanders and "this Impeachment Scam," Alex Azar, the secretary of health and human services, tried to warn the president about the virus. He called Mick Mulvaney, who was with the president at Mar-a-Lago, and asked to speak with Trump. When the president came on the phone, Trump barely let Azar get a word in before chewing him out for screwing up their policy on e-cigarettes. He was hot. "You lost me the election!" Trump snapped.

But as Trump moved to end the call, Azar interrupted. "There's this new virus out of China that could be extremely dangerous," the health secretary said. "It could be the kind of thing we have been preparing for and worried about."

Trump seemed disinterested. "Yeah, okay," he said before hanging up.

A few days later China abruptly ordered a lockdown in Wuhan, essentially walling off one of its largest metropolises. It did not require secret intelligence briefings to comprehend this was no longer some isolated problem but a serious crisis. Still, Trump seemed more worried about jeopardizing his new trade deal than pressing China on the virus. Hours after the Wuhan lockdown, he told advisers he wanted to publicly praise Xi Jinping for his handling of the outbreak.

Several of his advisers were aghast. "For the love of God, don't do that," Azar said.

Mike Pompeo shook his head. "I'd be really, really careful, Mr. President," he said.[9]

Azar then rushed out of the Oval Office to find Robert O'Brien in hopes that the national security adviser could talk Trump out of it, but was too late. "China has been working very hard to contain the Coronavirus," Trump tweeted. "The United States greatly appreciates their efforts and transparency. It will all work out well. In particular, on behalf of the American people, I want to thank President Xi!"

One adviser who knew better was Pottinger, who had worked as a reporter in China for Reuters and *The Wall Street Journal,* covering the SARS outbreak in Asia in the early 2000s. After leaving journalism, he joined the Marines and served three tours in Afghanistan and Iraq. His time in China left him deeply suspicious of the Beijing regime. Now he was getting information from friends back in China that was not coming through official channels.

Pottinger thought the United States should close its borders to China but ran into uniform resistance from the president's economic advisers, who feared the impact on business, as well as from the public health experts, who relied on the traditional scientific consensus that travel bans did not stop the spread of disease. On January 28, Pottinger heard from a doctor in China that about half the cases there were asymptomatic, making the virus almost impossible to isolate without aggressive testing and lockdowns.

Robert O'Brien brought Pottinger with him to the president's intelligence briefing that day even as Trump's lawyers were wrapping up his defense in the Senate trial. The two tried to impress on Trump the full scale of what a pandemic would look like.

"This will be the largest national security crisis of your presidency," O'Brien warned Trump.

Jumping up from the couch, Pottinger repeated that this could be the worst global health crisis since the influenza pandemic a century earlier and he noted that China was already limiting travel.

"Holy fuck," Trump responded.[10]

With developments growing more ominous, Mick Mulvaney took over the crisis meetings first convened by Pottinger and by late January decided to designate an official White House coronavirus task force headed by Azar. But the group became consumed quickly by the familiar story of Trump White House dysfunction as they fought over a China travel ban. Both Pottinger and Peter Navarro aggressively pushed for it, even getting in the face of an outsider to the Trump White House, Anthony Fauci, the longtime director of the National Institute of Allergy and Infectious Diseases, who argued that experience showed travel limits did not work.

After one heated Situation Room meeting, Mulvaney found Navarro so shrill that he banned him from future meetings. He was also unnerved by Pottinger's persistence. "You've got to get Pottinger under control," Mulvaney told O'Brien.[11]

Undeterred, Navarro retreated to his office and drew up a memo pressing his case. "The lack of immune protection or an existing cure or vaccine would leave Americans defenseless in the case of a full-blown coronavirus outbreak on U.S. soil," he wrote in the memo, dated January 29. "This lack of protection elevates the risk of the coronavirus evolving into a full-blown pandemic, imperiling the lives of millions of Americans." He argued that an unchecked contagion would inflict $3.8 trillion to $5.7 trillion in economic costs and kill up to 543,000 people.[12]

Navarro was no medical expert. His hyperbolic personality and over-the-top hostility toward China made it easy to write off his alarm. He played rough, and he often inserted himself in White House fights far outside his official lane, which in theory was trade and manufacturing. Like Trump, he fancied himself an expert on many things or at least so smart that he could become one overnight. Some of his colleagues therefore had a hard time reconciling their view of Navarro as a rogue actor with the reality that he could still be right about the emerging threat.

As it was, the health advisers were beginning to come around on their own, including Fauci, Azar, and Redfield. The extent of asymptomatic cases meant that screening at airports would not keep the virus out. And new evidence suggested the virus was already being transmitted from human to human within the United States. The CDC did a reversal overnight and on January 30 recommended shutting down as much travel as possible. Azar groaned, knowing that he now had to go back to the White House and advocate for exactly what his team had been opposing.

The next morning, on January 31, Azar and others met with Trump in the Oval Office to present the recommendation to impose travel restrictions on China. While Trump would later falsely claim that he was the only one who wanted to shut down travel in the face of unanimous opposition among his advisers, in fact he was initially wary, cognizant of his trade pact and the economic consequences. "Do we really have to do that?" the president asked. Fauci said yes and walked him through why. Trump agreed.

But rather than announce it himself, he instructed Azar to disclose the decision. If anyone would take a hit for it, Trump wanted it to be his health secretary. Azar went to the Roosevelt Room and signed an order declaring a public health emergency, an action recorded only with a cell phone picture snapped by his chief of staff after Trump's aides refused even to send the official White House photographer.

By then, however, it was already too late to keep the virus out. About 381,000 passengers had entered the United States from China in January, including thousands from Wuhan, and cases were already showing up around the United States. Moreover, Trump's ban did not bar Americans from returning home, meaning that another forty thousand people would arrive on direct flights from China in the two months after the restrictions were put in place.[13]

At most, the travel limits bought time to slow the spread of the virus to the United States, time for the government to get ready for its eventual impact—to make sure hospitals were prepared and personal protection equipment was stockpiled, to develop a robust testing system, and to undertake measures to limit transmission within the United States.

But February came and went without any of that.

Trump was still consumed with punishing his adversaries. Having prevailed over Robert Mueller and defeated congressional Democrats, his goal now was reversing the investigations that had tormented him. One night less than a week after his Senate acquittal, Trump learned that career prosecutors had asked a judge to sentence Roger Stone to seven to nine years in prison. Stone, a political consultant and self-described dirty trickster who proudly showed off the Richard Nixon tattoo on his back and favored swingers' clubs in Miami, had been a friend and adviser to Trump for decades. His political credo matched Trump's: "Admit nothing, deny everything, launch counterattack."[14] Even Trump thought he was a little wacky and from time to time cut him off only to bring him back into his orbit again as Stone whispered wild notions in his ear, like urging him to run for president.

Robert Mueller's investigators looking at how Stone seemed to know about WikiLeaks' plans to expose Democratic emails in advance secured his conviction for lying to Congress and intimidating a witness against him. Now Stone was facing prison and while the sentencing recommendation was within federal guidelines, Trump had no hesitation about intervening. "This is a horrible and very unfair situation," Trump tweeted. "The real crimes were on the other side, as nothing happens to them. Cannot allow this miscarriage of justice!"

If Trump had sent this tweet as a secret memo to Barr, it would have been a huge scandal, a president directing his attorney general to go soft on one of his friends who had been convicted of covering for him. But Trump did not bother to hide actions that other presidents would have considered beyond the bounds of propriety. All the usual critics complained that it was inappropriate, but Trump's fellow Republicans remained quiet.

Barr, it turned out, did not need to be ordered. He shared the president's belief that the sentencing recommendation was excessive. The attorney general later claimed that he was in his office already discussing with aides the extraordinary step of ordering the recommendation withdrawn when his deputy, Jeffrey Rosen, arrived and asked if he had seen Trump's tweet.

Jonathan Kravis, the lead career prosecutor on the case, had been in a dentist's chair when he received a text from his mother about the president's tweet. He was struck but not surprised—as inappropriate as it might be, the president had commented on the case before. Within hours, though, Barr's team filed the papers rescinding Kravis's sentencing recommendation and this time Kravis was caught off guard. He was getting on an elevator in the courthouse when he bumped into Spencer Hsu, a reporter from *The Washington Post*, who held up his phone to show Kravis an alert reporting that the Justice Department was filing a new sentencing memo in the Stone case. The elevator door shut just as a stunned Kravis absorbed the news. Every time friends had asked him about political interference in his high-profile cases, he had told them, "The Justice Department doesn't work like that." Except now it seemed that it did.

Barr's intervention to spare a politically connected friend of the president was a remarkable break from tradition and reeked of favoritism. Barr had never even called Kravis to ask why he and his team of career prosecutors made their recommendation, which was in keeping with federal guidelines. He simply overturned it. To Kravis, the hypocrisy rankled all the more coming right after Trump's Ukraine scandal, when Barr had invoked the credibility of career prosecutors in ruling out a criminal investigation of the whistleblower's allegations.

After a series of phone calls, the four Stone prosecutors decided not to take it without protest. Kravis resigned from the Justice Department altogether, while the other three stepped down from the case in the biggest mass resignation of the Trump era. The judge would ultimately defer to Barr's judgment, sentencing Stone to three years and four months in prison. Trump thought even that was unfair.

The episode seemed to confirm the impression that Barr was a willing instrument of Trump's political wishes, a reputation forged by the way he framed the Mueller report before it was released and reinforced by his decision to sit in the front row clapping at Trump's vindication rally in the White House. Looking uncomfortably compromised, Barr now found the need to reassert some measure of independence. He summoned Pierre Thomas of ABC News for an interview, knowing he would be asked about the president's tweets. When he was, he issued a rare rebuke to his boss.

All the public comments "make it impossible for me to do my job," Barr told Thomas. "I cannot do my job here at the department with a constant background commentary that undercuts me."

He insisted he had not talked with Trump about the Stone sentencing but the tweet, he complained, created the inaccurate impression that the attorney general was taking orders on cases in which the president had an interest. "The fact that the tweets are out there and correspond to things we're doing at the department sort of give grist to the mill and that's why I think it's time to stop the tweeting about the Department of Justice criminal cases."[15]

It was, in effect, a disagreement on tactics. The fact was that Barr tended to share Trump's view of the Russia investigation and was already inclined to dismantle its legacy piece by piece; he just did not want Trump to make it harder. Trump was making him and the Justice Department look bad.

But nothing was going to stop Trump. Just a month after the flareup over Stone, the president publicly intervened in the prosecution of Mike Flynn, the national security adviser who had pleaded guilty to lying to federal investigators. Once again, Barr stepped in—not, he insisted, because Trump wanted him to but because he happened to agree that the prosecution was bogus. The attorney general took the extraordinary action of asking a court to drop the case even though Flynn had pleaded guilty not once but twice. Barr did not argue that Flynn was innocent of lying to the FBI, only that the FBI should never have asked him the questions about his conversations with Russia's ambassador that led him to lie in the first place. The questions, Barr maintained, were "unjustified" by the bureau's counterintelligence investigation into Russian interference and Flynn's lies were not "materially" relevant to the inquiry.[16] Dropping a case where the defendant has already pleaded guilty without new evidence was all but unheard of, especially in such a politically sensitive situation—so much so that a judge refused to rubber-stamp the decision and ordered Barr to explain it, leading to a long set of hearings and appeals.

As with Roger Stone, the president publicly celebrated the decision, heedless of the fact that he himself had fired Flynn. Trump made no effort to disguise his motivations. He wanted revenge. "I hope a lot of people are going to pay a big price because they're dishonest, crooked people," he told reporters. "They're scum—and I say it a lot, they're scum, they're human scum."[17]

Trump was not content to leave to Bill Barr his mission of reversing prosecutions of his friends. The president spent much of February 18, a day when the global coronavirus death toll topped two thousand, issuing formal forgiveness to those he saw as fellow victims of official persecution, a rogues' gallery of celebrity felons and rich Republican insiders with connections to the president who jumped the line ahead of fourteen thousand other petitioners whose requests for clemency were languishing at the Justice Department's Office of the Pardon Attorney.

Trump had come to love his pardon power, which was virtually unfettered under the Constitution. It embodied his idea of being president—he could just sign a decree and not have to persuade Congress or worry that the courts might overrule him. Trump relished the kingly sensation of dispensing mercy so much that he would personally call some of the recipients or their spouses to deliver the good news himself.

His beneficiaries that day included a former football team owner who hosted a pre-inauguration party for Trump, a onetime contestant on *Celebrity Apprentice*, and a former construction company owner whose family contributed more than $200,000 to Trump's re-election campaign in the previous six months and whose son weekended in the Hamptons with Don Jr. Others granted clemency included Michael Milken, the junk bond king and longtime Trump associate who had spent time at Mar-a-Lago; Rod Blagojevich, the flamboyant former governor of Illinois whose case resonated with Trump because he was prosecuted by Barack Obama's Justice Department for trying to sell Obama's Senate seat; and Bernie Kerik, the disgraced former police commissioner of New York who had spent three years in prison for tax fraud and other felonies. Many of these pardons would have constituted a full-blown scandal in any other administration, but Trump did not care.

Kerik was a case study in how executive forgiveness was doled out in the Trump White House. A bald, tough-talking ex-cop whose career had been entwined with Rudy Giuliani's since he started out as his bodyguard and driver decades earlier, Kerik had effectively campaigned for a pardon by appearing more than fifty times on Fox News as a stalwart defender of the president. He knew his intended audience well, telling Fox that the Ukraine impeachment investigation unleashed by Giuliani's intriguing was nothing less than "an attempted coup of the president of the United States."[18] Kerik's crimes had nothing to do with Trump, but the timing of the pardon days after the end of impeachment did.

It came together with remarkable speed over a matter of hours, Trump's adhocracy in action. Kerik got a call that morning from David Safavian, a former government official who had served prison time for covering up ties to the corrupt lobbyist Jack Abramoff. Safavian, who had reinvented himself as a criminal justice reformer, had ties to the White House through his work as general counsel for the American Conservative Union, whose head, Matt Schlapp, was a prominent Trump supporter and husband of Mercedes Schlapp, a Trump campaign adviser. Safavian told Kerik that he was putting together a letter asking Trump to pardon the former police commissioner and needed names of supporters to sign it—by noon. Kerik hit the phones. Shortly after 10 a.m., he reached Geraldo Rivera, the Fox News correspondent and friend of Trump's. Rivera instantly agreed to sign. Kerik also reached out to Representative Peter King of New York, who said yes as well. At 11:57 a.m., Trump called. "As we speak," Trump told him, "I am signing a full presidential pardon on your behalf."[19] Kerik was overcome with emotion.

That was justice, Trump style—not dispassionate and neutral but driven by friendship, fame, and politics. Nor did he limit himself to the civilian legal system. Kerik had been among those who pressed Trump to get involved the year before in the court-martial of Chief Petty Officer Eddie Gallagher, a Navy SEAL who according to colleagues stabbed a secure and sedated prisoner in the neck in Iraq, then posed for a photograph holding the dead captive up by the hair. Gallagher became a cause célèbre on Fox News, prompting Trump to repeatedly intervene in the case, both publicly and privately. At one point, he called Richard Spencer, the Navy secretary, to order him to release Gallagher from solitary confinement, even though he was not actually in solitary confinement.

"Have you been following Fox?" Trump asked Spencer. "They're raking us over the coals for this. These are my voters. Just get him out."

After Gallagher's family appeared on *Fox & Friends* the next morning, Trump called again and had no patience when Spencer said he was working on it.

"I don't give a shit, get him out of there," Trump said. "Do I have to give you a direct order?"

Spencer said he would take care of it. "Okay, I want you to call over to Pete Hegseth at Fox and tell him what you're doing," Trump said.[20]

Moments after Trump hung up, a White House operator phoned Spencer and said she was connecting him to Hegseth, a Fox host and Army veteran who had along with Kerik championed Gallagher's cause. Annoyed, Spencer refused to take the call. Trump would intervene several more times in the months to come, eventually ordering Gallagher's punishment reversed and rank restored—and firing Spencer.

While Trump was seeking to spring an American war criminal, he was determined to make peace with foreign adversaries, including the Taliban. On February 29, despite the qualms of his generals and national security adviser, Trump agreed to a deal with America's enemies in Afghanistan that would lead to a full pullout of the remaining five thousand or so U.S. troops still there by early 2021. He claimed that it was "conditions-based" but his advisers knew that the deal put all the conditions on the Americans, not the Taliban. Trump was so eager to come to terms that he cut the Afghan government itself out of the negotiations altogether, although its troops had been fighting alongside America for two decades. Trump had come to office having campaigned on a promise to end America's longest war and after impeachment he had no more patience for the careful PowerPoint presentations or patronizing lectures from the Pentagon about why doing so would be a disaster.

As for the coronavirus, Trump remained in denial mode. The president repeatedly told the public that the outbreak was "totally under control," that it would "miraculously" disappear on its own with warmer weather, that it "will go away," that it was comparable to the ordinary flu, that the number of cases would go "down close to zero," that a vaccine would be available soon, and that anyone who wanted to be tested could get a test.[21] None of it was true.

On the day after his impeachment trial, while Trump was vowing revenge against his "evil" adversaries in the East Room, an American traveling in Wuhan, China, died from the virus. Despite his public comments, Trump at times seemed to understand it was serious. "This is deadly stuff," he confided to the journalist Bob Woodward the next day for a book that came out later in the year.[22] Five days later, while Trump was withdrawing the nomination of the United States attorney who had prosecuted Roger Stone, the overall death toll in China was about to hit 1,500 and the World Health Organization formally designated the virus SARS-CoV-2 and the disease stemming from it Covid-19. A week after that, while Trump was installing a new intelligence director and Stone was being sentenced, the World Health Organization announced that there were already 75,000 cases around the globe.

In the month following his acquittal, as the health crisis accelerated, Trump took time to publicly attack Supreme Court justices Ruth Bader Ginsburg and Sonia Sotomayor, "crazy" Nancy Pelosi, "failed" Mitt Romney, the "puppet" Senator Joe Manchin, the "lightweight" Senator Doug Jones, Jay Powell, John Kelly, and Jeff Sessions, not to mention various "wacko" and talentless reporters.[23] Much of his attention was focused on the Democratic race to challenge him, and he repeatedly cheered on "Crazy Bernie" Sanders from the sidelines, watching as the socialist senator's boom panicked many Democrats, who then rallied behind Joe Biden. Boosted by the endorsement of the state's powerful congressman Jim Clyburn, Biden in late February finally secured a win in South Carolina that put him on the road to the nomination, a remarkable comeback that spoke to his party's desire to put up the strongest candidate against Trump.

Over five weeks after his trial, Trump posted 1,049 tweets, of which just forty-eight mentioned the coronavirus. Among those, twenty-one bragged about his administration's response and many others were attacks on critics or the media for not giving him more credit for the "GREAT job" he was doing with it. On February 24, he all but declared victory. "The Coronavirus is very much under control in the USA," he announced.

Trump was not dwelling on the coronavirus, but he was not above using it as an excuse to get out of other duties. He toyed with canceling a trip to India in late February that he dreaded, until Jared Kushner talked him into going by telling him that Prime Minister Narendra Modi had promised to produce a stadium with 100,000 people to greet him. Trump exaggerated even that, boasting before he left that "I hear they're going to have 10 million people."[24] Even as the president was preparing to leave, Peter Navarro sent around a second memo warning of the dire potential of the virus. There was, he wrote, an "increasing probability of a full-blown COVID-19 pandemic that could infect as many as 100 million Americans, with a loss of life of as many as 1-2 million souls."[25]

The memo made little evident impression on Trump. But he was abruptly confronted with the reality of what was happening during the return flight from India on February 25 when he heard that a federal health official had said out loud in public what no one had before—that this was a catastrophe in the making and that life in America was about to change drastically. "It's not so much a question of *if* this will happen, but rather more a question of exactly *when* this will happen, and how many people in this country will have severe illnesses," Nancy Messonnier, director of the National Center for Immunization and Respiratory Diseases at the Centers for Disease Control and Prevention, told reporters. "Disruption to everyday life may be severe, but these are things that people need to start thinking about now."[26]

Her assessment sent stock markets into a tailspin and the president into a fury. Twice during the flight home on Air Force One and then a third time once on the ground, he called Alex Azar, the health secretary, who was in charge of the government's coronavirus response. Each time, Trump railed about Messonnier. "She's scaring people!" he fumed.

Azar tried to calm him down. "Listen, Mr. President, she shouldn't have gotten out there yet," he said, "but what she said is true and we were planning to meet with you when you got back to walk you through this."

It did not help that Messonnier was the sister of Rod Rosenstein, the deputy attorney general who had appointed Robert Mueller. Conservative media figures like Rush Limbaugh quickly linked the matters, suggesting that she was trying to undermine the president just like conservatives believed her brother had. This made perfect sense to the conspiracy-theory-driven Trump.

Whatever his suspicions, Trump came to understand after landing back in Washington that he needed at least to appear to be more on top of the growing crisis. But Azar was not the one he wanted as the administration's public face handling the outbreak. Behind the scenes, the health secretary had alienated fellow administration officials by not including in task force meetings officials such as Stephen Hahn, the Food and Drug Administration commissioner, or Seema Verma, who ran Medicaid and Medicare for the government. Azar was also criticized for marginalizing the CDC, resisting bringing in agencies like the Federal Emergency Management Agency that would tread on his turf, and brushing off entreaties to mobilize the private sector to step up production of medical equipment.

So the evening after Trump's return from India, the president marched into the White House briefing room to announce that Mike Pence would head the White House coronavirus task force. "We're very, very ready for this," Trump insisted.[27]

No one bothered to tell Azar he was about to be supplanted until just a few hours before it was announced. As for Pence's team, they could not help wondering if the vice president was put in charge just to have someone to blame when everything went bad. "This is a no win," realized Marc Short, the vice president's chief of staff.

Pence's elevation put him in the public spotlight in a sustained way for the first time since he took office as the nation's forty-eighth vice president. For the preceding three years, he had been the invisible man with the frozen smile, noticed only when he stood silently behind the president, "mustering a devotional gaze rarely seen since the days of Nancy Reagan," as Jane Mayer wrote in *The New Yorker*.[28] Republicans on Capitol Hill nicknamed him "the Bobblehead" for his ritual nodding whenever Trump spoke.[29] Pence was no more revealing in private. Senior administration officials could not recall him saying anything of consequence on virtually any subject at virtually any meeting.

One Republican governor fed up with Trump recalled how determined Pence was never to betray even a hint of criticism of the president. "I say, 'But Mike, this is just crazy,' and sometimes there will be a little pause and I'm waiting for him to say, 'Yes, I know,'" the governor recalled. But "he never, ever takes the bait," the governor added. "He says, 'I understand, thank you for the input.' He won't say, 'I agree.'" To another person who worked with him, the most Pence would say of Trump was, "He's like an untamed lion who came into the city." When this person expressed pointed criticism, the vice president would simply reply, "Well, we're praying for him." It was a ferocious discipline beyond that of any other person who served Trump, and a remarkable exercise in self-preservation.

In taking on the role of Trump's understudy, Pence had resolved to emulate George H. W. Bush, who demonstrated unwavering loyalty as Ronald Reagan's vice president despite differences over policy. Pence concluded that the best way to influence decisions was to spend as much time as possible around the president, whether invited or not. Everyone understood that Trump often sided with the last person he heard from. So Pence would drop by the Oval Office in the morning and, if Trump was not there yet, stride over to the residence to wait at the elevator for him to come down. He was in the Oval Office so often that Trump's executive assistant, Madeleine Westerhout, finally devised a way to pry him out. She would slip him a note from a vice presidential aide that said: "Mr. Vice President, the second lady is wondering when you're going to be home for dinner." Trump would then join in. "Mike, go, have a good night," he would say.[30]

One adviser compared Pence to a stonecutter—it was not the one-hundredth hit that broke the rock but the ninety-nine that came before. Pence would persistently nudge the president over time toward where he wanted him to go, particularly on issues such as abortion, where the vice president's staff declared victory by getting a president who had once called himself "very pro-choice" to address the annual March for Life demonstration. This, at least, was their theory.

But to others in Trump's orbit, Pence was not much of a presence even when he was in the room. To say Pence was vanilla was to underestimate the blandness he projected. "Mike Pence is vanilla ice cream," explained a prominent adviser to Trump, "but he's not Breyers vanilla ice cream or Häagen-Dazs. He's like Stop & Shop vanilla ice cream"—generic, boring, predictable, and not necessarily worth opening the freezer to get.

For Trump, though, loyalty was something to be received, not given. As 2020 approached, the president regularly asked aides, advisers, even visitors to the White House what they thought of Pence and broached the idea of dumping him from the re-election ticket in favor of Nikki Haley, his former U.N. ambassador. Trump raised the possibility during a long Christmas night flight to Iraq in 2018, asking John Bolton whether he thought it was a good idea. He brought it up in an Oval Office meeting, where Jared Kushner, Ivanka Trump, and his campaign manager Brad Parscale all made the case for why such a switch would make sense. He even asked Westerhout, his twentysomething executive assistant, whether

Trump faced constant storms during his presidency, firing dozens of top officials and publicly feuding with others. Nothing obsessed him more than the Mueller investigation into ties with Russia and obstruction of justice, which he called a "hoax" and a "witch hunt" (above, *Doug Mills/New York Times*). In times of trouble, Trump hugged the flag, one time literally so at a conservative conference (below).

As attorney general, William Barr (above) helped clear the president in the Russia investigation, but he believed Trump had "a long history of acting like an asshole." John Bolton, Trump's third national security adviser considered the president a danger to the country and at times organized resistance from within before resigning.
Tom Brenner/New York Times

No one was happier that Bolton was gone than Secretary of State Mike Pompeo (left) and Treasury Secretary Steven Mnuchin (right).

Trump's "do us a favor" phone call with President Volodymyr Zelensky of Ukraine (above) triggered his impeachment by House Democrats, led by Speaker Nancy Pelosi, who in a finger-pointing confrontation told the president "all roads with you lead to Putin" (left) and then ripped up his 2020 State of the Union address (below).
Erin Schaff/New York Times.

But Trump was acquitted by the Republican-controlled Senate and embarked on a campaign of retribution.

While Covid spread in early March 2020, Trump and his family partied at Mar-a-Lago with guests such as Brazil's president, Jair Bolsonaro, whose delegation included people infected with the virus.

Mark Meadows (above left), who took over as chief of staff from Mick Mulvaney (above right, *Jacquelyn Martin/Associated Press*), privately disparaged the doctors on Trump's coronavirus task force, including Anthony Fauci (right). Mike Pence led the task force in a prayer as he was named to head it (below). An aide advised newcomers to bow their head "or you're going to announce to the world that you're the Deep State."

Trump's June 1, 2020, march across Lafayette Square moments after Black Lives Matter protesters were forcibly cleared out (top) in advance of a Bible-wielding photo op outside a damaged church (above) prompted military officials to consider resigning. Trump doubled down on his nationalist message with a July 3 speech at Mount Rushmore (left).

Trump originally passed over Amy Coney Barrett for the Supreme Court, holding her in reserve in case the liberal icon Ruth Bader Ginsburg's seat came open. In a break with tradition, the staunchly anti-abortion judge was confirmed just days before the presidential election.

So many people who attended Trump's Supreme Court nomination ceremony for Barrett became infected with Covid that Ivanka Trump privately joked the only place that had achieved herd immunity was the White House.

After Trump was hospitalized with Covid, he insisted on making a limousine drive to greet supporters. Jared Kushner ordered aides to draft a speech for Trump to use his own sickness to pivot and present a more empathetic face, but the president refused.

Trump relied on Rudy Giuliani to overturn Joe Biden's victory but was disgusted by how the former New York mayor looked when hair dye apparently dripped down his face at a conspiracy-filled news conference (above). *Mandel Ngan/AFP/Getty Images*

Trump's children diverged after the election. Donald Trump Jr. cheered his father's lies about stolen victory while Ivanka Trump and Jared Kushner largely opted out of the fight and made plans to move to Miami.

As Trump told a rally on the Ellipse on January 6, 2021, "if you don't fight, you're not going to have a country anymore," some supporters shouted, "Storm the Capitol," which they soon did (above, *Pete Marovich/New York Times*). Mike Pence finally defied Trump by refusing to try to unilaterally block Joe Biden's victory, but had to be rushed to safety by the Secret Service (below, *Senate Television*).

he should dump his vice president. Trump was breathtakingly indiscreet and naturally word leaked out. In the end, though, Trump decided not to do it—replacing Pence with Haley probably would not gain Trump significant votes and could alienate evangelicals. But the point was made. The vice president, like all those around Trump, served purely at the pleasure of the president.

Through it all, Pence kept his stone face. Even with personal friends, the mask stayed on. "Mike never let his guard down for a second with me or with anybody I know," recalled Jeff Flake, the former senator who had once been one of Pence's closest friends in Congress before he publicly broke with the president.

Flake was not the only one baffled by Pence's transformation. At a ceremony once, Pence ran into an evangelical pastor he had met before. The pastor took the opportunity to implore Pence to look past the politics of his current job.

"You know, Mr. Vice President, more than anything, we need you to find your conscience," the pastor said. "The country desperately needs you to find your conscience."

"It's always easier said than done," Pence replied cryptically and then walked away.[31]

Pence's turn in charge of the greatest crisis yet of the Trump presidency began, perhaps not surprisingly, with an appeal to God. Shortly after the announcement, Pence gathered the coronavirus team in his office to get up to speed. Alex Azar, in the awkward position of just having been replaced, showed up in Pence's suite to brief the vice president and his advisers.

"Alex," Pence said to Azar, "why don't you kick us off with a prayer?"

Azar was deeply religious but not a pray-in-the-office kind of guy and felt uncomfortable. What he may not have known is that every staff meeting in Pence's office started off with a prayer, a highly unusual practice in the federal government. Even at the State Department run by Mike Pompeo, an evangelical Christian who kept an open Bible on his desk, aides said they had never seen him mix official business and prayer. But in the vice president's office, it was a daily practice, and Olivia Troye, the Pence aide who advised him on homeland security and was now staffing the coronavirus task force, used to tell newcomers who came to brief him, "I would recommend bowing your head or you're going to announce to the world that you're the Deep State."

Azar dutifully offered a prayer only to become even more uncomfortable as the Covid meeting progressed. When he outlined what the task force had been doing, he was interrupted by Marc Short, a skilled bureaucratic infighter as Pence's chief of staff.

"The problem here is communications discipline," Short said. "This thing is off the rails because you've got too many people out talking and saying different things. We've got to get control on communications. That's the most important thing to do."

Azar and some of the others thought the most important priorities would be to expand testing, limit large-scale gatherings, and stock up on medical equipment like masks and ventilators, among other things—all actions they should have been taking already.

After the meeting, Azar went up to Mulvaney's office. "This is starting to feel like a hostile takeover," Azar said.

"If Marc Short's involved," Mulvaney replied, "it's a hostile takeover."

Indeed, by the time Azar got back to his office, he was told that all his scheduled media appearances had been canceled, as had Tony Fauci's, albeit temporarily. No one was to go on television or give an interview without permission from the vice president's office. Pence's people quickly made clear they wanted a different tone too, playing down the threat from the virus. The day after Pence was put in charge, Health and Human Services officials submitted their planned communication message to his office. "While the situation could change rapidly, at this time, Americans don't need to change their day-to-day lives, but should stay informed and practice good hygiene," the understated message said. Still, Pence's communications director, Katie Miller, objected. "Even for HHS this is a bit alarmist," she wrote department officials in an email on February 27. "Couldn't we just start with Americans don't need to change their day-to-day lives and leave out the rapid change?"[32]

Where Pence's staff saw a communications problem, Trump saw a political threat. The virus was not a looming public health disaster but an extension of the post-impeachment partisan war he was fighting with Democrats and the Deep State. "The Democrats are politicizing the coronavirus," he told a rally of supporters two days after putting the vice president in charge of the task force. "This is their new hoax." After all, he said, "so far we have lost nobody to the coronavirus in the United States. Nobody." But "the press is in hysteria mode."[33]

Mick Mulvaney expressed Trump's view even more explicitly at a forum that same day. Democrats, he told a conservative audience, "think this will bring down the president; that's what this is all about."[34]

But Trump, still focused on punishment, had one more scalp to take—Mulvaney's. The acting chief of staff had sealed his fate in the fall when he acknowledged the quid pro quo in the Ukraine scheme. Trump seethed about the admission but held off acting so long as the impeachment proceedings were continuing lest he give ammunition to the Democrats and incentivize Mulvaney to come forward and testify.

With the trial over, Trump was ready to get rid of Mulvaney. His choice for his fourth chief of staff was Mark Meadows, the North Carolina congressman and Trump's vocal defender during the House impeachment. In December, Meadows had announced that he would leave the House to work more "closely" with Trump, a move that seemed all but certain to result in him displacing Mulvaney. Now Jared Kushner called to see if Meadows would make it official and replace Mulvaney as chief of staff. Meadows said yes. Assured of a positive response, Trump later pulled Meadows aside following a meeting on foreign surveillance legislation to discuss timing. "Soon," Trump said. "It's going to have to be soon."[35]

The next day, the first American was officially confirmed to have died of Covid on American soil.

CHAPTER 22

Game Changer

The lights were low, the dance floor was crowded, and the disco balls were spinning when the cake with white icing, a ring of strawberries, and a fiery sparkler shooting flames into the air was brought out to a robust rendition of "Happy Birthday." Kimberly Guilfoyle, wearing a thigh-hugging gold leaf dress that disappeared well above the knees, beamed with delight. The president stood beside the birthday girl and clapped.

"Four more years!" Guilfoyle shouted, pumping her arm in the air.

Trump responded with his own toast for Guilfoyle, the former Fox News host now dating his oldest son.

"This is a special deal with Kimberly," he said. "So Kimberly," he teased, "how old are you?" He then let her off the hook. "No, I'm not going to ask you that."

"Twenty-nine!" someone in the crowd called out.

Guilfoyle liked that. "Twenty-nine!" she agreed.

"She looks young to me," Trump offered.[1]

In fact, it was her fifty-first birthday, as Trump probably knew since his own wife, Melania, was just about to turn fifty. It was a lavish, festive, even carefree Saturday evening at Mar-a-Lago, with scores of guests on hand to celebrate at Guilfoyle's $50,000 bash, which would end with her, shoeless, dancing in a conga line dubbed the "Trump train" as Gloria Estefan blared. In addition to the family, the partygoers constituted a who's who of Trumpworld: There was Mike Pence, as stoic and stiff as ever, and Rudy Giuliani with a drink in hand, and Bernie Kerik, his recently pardoned buddy, the convicted former New York police commissioner. In a sports coat with no tie was Lindsey Graham, who took the microphone at one point to praise Guilfoyle. "You represent everything Bernie Sanders hates," he said, and promised to get her a tax cut. Nearby were political donors, some of whom had been hit up to foot the bill. Matt Gaetz, the brash young Republican congressman from Florida, looked right at home at a booze-soaked dance party. Less comfortable perhaps were Robert O'Brien, the national security adviser, and Ric Grenell, the new acting director of national intelligence.

And then there was Jair Bolsonaro, the president of Brazil, because, well, it was Mar-a-Lago and you never knew who would show up.

The first family's awkward dynamics were on full display. First, Ivanka and Jared, dressed for the official business dinner with Bolsonaro they had been included in while the other family members had not, offered toasts to Guilfoyle, who sat next to Don Jr., bathed in the purple and pink lighting that suffused the ballroom for her party. "It's been amazing to get to know you," Kushner told her. "You work so, so hard for the president," Ivanka added.

When it was his turn, Eric Trump pushed sibling boundaries as he wrapped his arm around Guilfoyle. "You're so freaking beautiful I might take you home tonight," he said. "Would Don be upset?" Turning to his wife, Lara, Eric asked, "Honey, would you be upset?"

The president, meanwhile, happily introduced the visiting South American leader—a self-styled populist like himself, often called the Trump of the Tropics—to guests including Tucker Carlson, boasting that he "gave him a good gift" by not imposing tariffs on Brazil and "that made him much more popular." Bolsonaro laughed and agreed.

But it was to be the last tango at Mar-a-Lago, at least for a while. As Trump escorted Bolsonaro into his Palm Beach club that night, a reporter told him that the first coronavirus case had been reported in the Washington area and asked if it worried him that it was getting closer to the White House. "No," Trump said, "I'm not concerned at all."[2]

In fact, it was even closer than that. Several members of Bolsonaro's delegation who mingled with Trump that evening had already been infected. As it turned out, Guilfoyle's birthday bash would incubate a Covid hot zone, offering dramatic proof that no one was safe, not even the president of the United States.

On his way down to Florida the day before the party, Trump had stopped in Atlanta to visit the headquarters of the Centers for Disease Control and Prevention with a clutch of journalists to demonstrate that he had the situation under control. Wearing a red "Keep America Great" baseball cap, he acted as if it were just another campaign event, trashing the Democratic governor of Washington as a "snake," bragging about his "natural ability" to understand science, and claiming that "anybody that wants a test can get a test," which was not even close to true, although none of the officials standing next to him dared correct him.

Trump also said out loud what he had made abundantly clear in private, that his main concern was not the health of Americans at risk but what their illnesses would mean for him politically. Asked whether he would allow people to disembark from a cruise ship idling off the coast of San Francisco where nineteen crew members and two passengers had tested positive for the virus, Trump said he would rather not, since their cases would be added to the total number of infections in the United States. And that would make him look bad. "I like the numbers being where they are," he said. "I don't need to have the numbers double because of one ship that wasn't our fault."[3]

It was hardly the performance of a leader who had the crisis firmly in hand. Neither was Trump's decision, after arriving in Florida later that evening, to take a few minutes out from dinner to fire Mick Mulvaney via tweet, adding yet another White House management shuffle to the concerns of a nation increasingly fearful about what the coronavirus would bring to the United States. "I want to thank Acting Chief Mick Mulvaney," the president wrote at 8:08 p.m., a reminder that, for all fourteen contentious months of his tenure, Trump had never even respected him enough to bestow the full title without the asterisk.

The pretext Trump now seized on was Mulvaney's decision to go ahead with an annual getaway with his brother for the NCAA college basketball tournament in Las Vegas. "How could you leave at a time like this?" Trump had yelled at him over the phone the day before his flight to Mar-a-Lago.[4] It was all a show, though: Mulvaney had previously told him about the trip and Trump had offered the job to Mark Meadows a week earlier.

Trump was changing chiefs yet again with an eye focused on his own re-election and he was sure that in Meadows he had finally found a fighter. But the coronavirus intruded on their plan when Meadows found out that he would have to quarantine following exposure to someone with the virus and would have to delay his official start—meaning the White House would be without a chief of staff entirely for a key stretch as it faced the biggest test of Trump's presidency. Still, Meadows was no more alarmed about the pandemic than Mulvaney was, believing that the public health experts were exaggerating the danger.

There was one person at Mar-a-Lago that weekend who was worried about Covid. Tucker Carlson, who had a home in Florida not far away, had driven to Trump's Palm Beach club that night specifically to try to convince the president to take it more seriously. Carlson did not think he got through. So he was left to try to communicate with the president the way so many had, through his Fox show. Two days later, Carlson warned viewers: "People you trust, people you probably voted for, have spent weeks minimizing what is clearly a very serious problem."[5] No one had any doubt who he had in mind.

By the time Trump left Florida, the virus was chasing him. Matt Gaetz, who had spent much of the weekend at Mar-a-Lago and boarded Air Force One just steps behind the president in Orlando after a fundraising stop en route back to Washington, got a call during the flight informing him that he had been exposed to someone with coronavirus.

Gaetz was so over-the-top in his cheerleading for the president that White House officials would call him when they needed someone to tell Trump how awesome he was. His website promoted him as "Trump's Best Buddy" and "Trump's Ultimate Defender."[6] Gaetz loved nothing more than mocking Trump's liberal enemies. If they were worried about this new virus, then it must be leftist overreaction; he had shown up on the House floor earlier that week in a comically bulky gas mask, pointedly mocking concern about the outbreak.

Now, only a few days later, he might have gotten it himself—and could infect the president. He isolated himself midflight, sitting alone in a compartment of the plane. Aboard the jet racing toward Washington, the television screens were tuned to Fox News as it showed the slow-motion progress of the cruise ship with twenty-one infected people heading to port despite Trump's reluctance. "Virus Ship Watch," said the chyron, while a red box in the lower-left-hand corner showed the sinking Dow Jones Industrial Average, which fell 7 percent and finished the day down more than 2,000 points.

As the plane was landing, Trump summoned Gaetz to his airborne office. Gaetz stood at the door, refusing to step inside for fear of getting Trump sick.

"Do you need to be wrapped in cellophane?" Trump asked.

"I'm willing to jump out of the plane without a parachute if necessary," Gaetz answered.[7] He later tested negative without having to jump.

As Trump arrived back at the White House, where he would now be all but locked in for two months, it had become clear that Gaetz was the least of the president's troubles. Infections were spreading through the United States at a rapid pace. Italy was already locked down, and the rest of Europe was soon to follow. The debate in the White House turned ugly as Trump's officials contemplated shutting down travel with Europe the way they had with China.

The economic team led by Steven Mnuchin objected strenuously. Closing America to Europe could further disrupt supply chains, cripple American businesses, and strangle the economy. "If you shut down air travel from Europe, you will cause a Great Depression," Mnuchin warned. Tomas Philipson, the acting chairman of the President's Council of Economic Advisers, agreed, calling the proposal an overreaction. "This is just like the flu," he insisted.

But then a new player stepped in: Deborah Birx, the State Department's global AIDS chief who had just been abruptly called home from a meeting in South Africa to serve as the White House coronavirus coordinator at Matt Pottinger's urging; she was given the ground-floor office recently vacated by Trump's impeachment lawyers. Birx got in the treasury secretary's face about his Great Depression claim. "Where's your evidence?" she demanded, pointing out that she had charts and graphics demonstrating her point and he had none.

Robert O'Brien also pushed back against Mnuchin. "You are going to be the reason this pandemic never goes away," he declared.

Ivanka Trump seemed most concerned that her father speak to the nation at a time of uncertainty. "There should be an address from the Oval," she said. She turned to her husband for backup: "Jared, don't you agree?" He did.[8]

Trump grudgingly acceded to a partial travel ban on Europe, while exempting Britain in what seemed like some sort of odd reward for its Brexit from the European Union, since its infection rates were as bad as anyone's. And he agreed to give a national address from the Oval Office that very night, leaving his staff only a few hours to notify the television networks, figure out what he should say, and cobble together a speech. Kushner took the lead crafting the address in the Cabinet Room. For the first time, the president would be elevating the crisis to the stage that it demanded after weeks of deflection and delay.

But if the prime-time speech on the night of March 11 was an opportunity to reset, to claim the mantle of national leadership in a time of crisis, it fell short. Trump's delivery was flat and his words hardly reassuring. If anything, they were militaristic and nationalistic. He declared war on the "foreign virus," blaming first China and then the European Union for spreading it while insisting that the coronavirus carried "very, very low risk" for Americans. In the course of just ten minutes, he mischaracterized his own policies repeatedly, even though he was reading from a teleprompter. He said he was "suspending all travel from Europe to the United States," when in fact his order impacted only foreigners, not Americans, and he said it would "apply to the tremendous amount of trade and cargo" crossing the ocean, when in fact it affected only people.[9] He had to correct the second of those misstatements later on Twitter.

Coming on the same day that the World Health Organization declared the coronavirus a global pandemic, at a time when his own country was being radically upended, with travel halting, workplaces and schools closing down, and hospitals bracing for the impact, the address struck even a number of Trump's advisers as unequal to the moment.

The truth was that the crisis generated by the pandemic far exceeded anything in Trump's experience. Not since the Great Depression and World War II had Americans been so universally hit by a major catastrophe. While other events in recent times broadly affected the fabric of the country, such as the September 11 attacks and the 2008 financial crash, none reached into essentially every home and every workplace.

Trump had no idea how to handle it. The virus did not respond to his favorite instruments of power. It could not be cowed by Twitter posts, overpowered by campaign rally chants, or silenced by playground insults. For so long, Trump had believed he could overcome nearly any obstacle through sheer force of will, and in many cases he had been astonishingly successful. Over the course of his seven decades, Trump had managed to bluster and bully his way past bankruptcies, failed business ventures, lenders demanding repayment, fraud and discrimination lawsuits, and, once he reached the White House, a special counsel and even congressional impeachment. But he could not will away a plague. So he tried denial, another favorite Trump tactic. That did not work either.

The emerging pandemic would expose all the weaknesses of his divisive presidency—his distrust of his own staff and the rest of the government, his intense focus on loyalty and purges, his penchant for encouraging conflict between factions within his own circle, his personal isolation, his obsessive war with the media, his refusal, or inability, to take in new information, and his indecisiveness when forced to make tough decisions.

Trump had always been indifferent to most substantive policy matters and skeptical of anything that experts, scientific or otherwise, told him. He turned everything into a political question whose answer was whatever would benefit him politically. And that is how he would approach this crisis too. "From the time this thing hit," said an adviser who spoke frequently with the president, "his only calculus was how does it affect my re-election."

Trump was not the only one ill-equipped for a global pandemic. So, it turned out, was his administration. George W. Bush and Barack Obama had taken steps to ready the federal government for the prospect of a once-in-a-century outbreak, and a study by Johns Hopkins University just a few months earlier had rated the United States the best prepared country in the world for a pandemic. The Obama administration had put together a sixty-nine-page playbook for just such an emergency.

But the pandemic playbook was never taken off the shelf and Trump officials deemed it useless anyway. It did not help that John Bolton had disbanded the stand-alone global health security office in the National Security Council when he came to the White House in 2018, folding it into a larger nonproliferation and biodefense directorate. He had also fired the White House homeland security adviser, Tom Bossert, who supervised the office. Bossert, now in the private sector, had spent days in early March trying to reach Trump and Mike Pence to warn them of the urgent steps that had yet to be taken in the crisis but could not get through and was reduced to tweeting his frustration. After Trump's speech, Bossert complained that its focus on travel bans was a "Poor use of time & energy."[10]

The CDC, the premier public health agency of its kind anywhere, had bungled an important early step in pandemic prevention when the coronavirus first appeared over the winter, failing to establish a widespread testing scheme that would help track the virus and potentially contain it. The agency's original test had been botched, with many kits faulty and producing inconclusive results, even as the CDC barred other labs from creating and deploying their own tests. As a result, tests were hard to come by for critical weeks when it might have been possible to limit the spread.

Because of the wasted time in February and early March when the Trump administration failed to amass medical supplies needed to handle the surge of cases that was coming, the country was also woefully understocked in personal protective equipment, or PPE, such as gloves, medical masks, goggles, face shields, and gowns, as well as lifesaving respirators. As the first wave of the illness hit in force in March, doctors and nurses were told to keep wearing disposable masks meant for a single use, sometimes for days or a week at a time, and those who could not find the real thing resorted to scarves or other improvised facial coverings. In some hospitals, medical personnel wrapped themselves in garbage bags. Ventilators for patients no longer able to breathe on their own were also in short supply.

Trump liked to blame Obama, saying "the cupboard was bare" when he took over, and it was true that the national stockpile was not as full as many thought it should be.[11] Masks used during the 2009 swine flu crisis, for instance, had never been replenished. But Trump did not explain why he had done nothing about it in his first three years in office. "I have a lot of things going on," he eventually said when asked, then blamed the fact that he was investigated over Russian interference and impeached by the House.[12]

On March 12, as the White House finally acknowledged the reality of the pandemic the day after Trump's speech, the president responded to the shortage of tests and medical equipment by assigning Jared Kushner to take charge, and Kushner quickly began to assemble a shadow Covid task force of his own outside the chain of command of Pence's official task force, made up of Silicon Valley contacts, some friendly management consultants, and friends from the private sector, to figure out how to increase supplies.

But when his new advisers pleaded with him to get Trump to invoke the Defense Production Act, a Korean War–era law empowering the president to order private industry to produce needed material in a national emergency, Kushner refused. "The federal government is not going to lead this response," Kushner told them. "It's up to the states to figure out what they want to do."[13] The next week, he and Trump repeated this in a public briefing. "We're not a shipping clerk," the president said.[14] Days into the crisis, the Trump administration had seemingly abandoned a federal leadership role.

Trump was also reluctant to embrace the new guidelines that the official Pence task force recommended he approve, as they would amount to an unprecedented shutdown of much of the country. For days, Fauci, Birx, and the other experts made the impassioned case that such a radical step was the only way to keep Americans away from each other to "stop the spread" and "flatten the curve" of infections. It was already beginning to happen anyway—state and local governments and private sector institutions were closing on their own. Finally, on March 16, Trump bowed to the inevitable and issued the guidance, though it stopped short of a federal mandate and other more stringent measures like those that many European countries were taking. "We will defeat the virus," Trump promised.[15]

Just like that, the United States of America was closed.

One of the worst-hit spots in the country was Queens, the borough where Trump grew up. He was shocked by televised images of a hospital he knew with a refrigerated truck outside to handle the overflow of bodies. But Trump only ever mentioned the personal toll of the pandemic when a major New York real estate developer he knew, Stanley Chera, died of the coronavirus, and even then, he did not dwell on it. To Trump, public displays of grief were a sign of weakness, and he was all about strength. He was "powerful," the government was hitting the virus "strongly." Dying was weak. To the extent that he discussed the coming wave of deaths, he did so in clinical and even prideful terms. "The only thing we haven't done well," he boasted the day after announcing the shutdown, "is get good press."[16]

Ever sensitive to his press, it had taken Trump about a minute to recognize that handing over the coronavirus task force to Pence was one thing but handing the vice president the limelight was quite another. So Trump made a surprise appearance at a 5 p.m. briefing one day to address reporters himself, pushing Pence into the background. Then he came back the next day and the day after that.

For the next two months, Trump commanded the airwaves every night, conducting marathon sessions about the pandemic and anything else that came to mind. At first, he would go on for an hour a day, seven days a week; by the end, he was appearing in the White House briefing room for as long as two and a half hours at a time. The Covid briefings were the twenty-first-century equivalent of the Five O'Clock Follies during the Vietnam War when generals misled reporters each evening about the victory that was perennially just around the corner.

In the modern sequel, the disconnect between Trumpian narrative and actual reality was never on starker display than when the president patted himself on the back while emergency rooms and morgues filled up with sick and dying Americans. "I don't take responsibility at all," he declared at one briefing in March.[17] Asked to assess his own performance, he said, "I'd rate it a ten."[18] He and his team had "done one hell of a job" and "it's lucky that you have this group here right now for this problem or you wouldn't even have a country left."[19] Any problems were the fault of the governors or the media or China or Obama.

The daily follies not only showcased Trump at his Trumpiest but modeled the exact behavior the federal government was discouraging among other Americans. In announcing the shutdown, Trump had in theory endorsed social distancing guidelines urging Americans to stay at home, avoid gatherings of more than ten people, refrain from unnecessary travel, and stop going out to restaurants and bars. When out in public, they were to remain at least six feet apart from anyone outside their families. But there was Trump standing at the podium flanked by a half dozen or more advisers standing inches apart.

Only a handful of reporters were physically in the briefing room every day for Trump's performances, not because the White House, which still resisted precautions, had imposed social distancing rules but because the correspondents themselves insisted upon it. Trump relished combat with the ones who were there, finding it easier to do battle with them than with the elusive virus.

"What do you say to Americans who are watching you right now and are scared?" Peter Alexander of NBC News asked one day.

Trump snapped: "I say that you're a terrible reporter, that's what I say."[20]

The president made clear that governors desperate for help needed to genuflect to get it. When Andrew Cuomo of New York or Gavin Newsom of California, the Democratic governors of two of the biggest and most affected states, publicly thanked Trump for federal help, he lavished praise on them. When they complained they were not getting what they needed, he harshly attacked them. Other Democratic governors were frequent targets at the briefings or on his Twitter feed, including Michigan's Gretchen Whitmer and Washington state's Jay Inslee. At one point, Trump openly admitted that he had told Mike Pence not to help governors who were insufficiently obsequious. "Don't call the woman in Michigan," he said. Asked what he wanted from the governors, he said bluntly, "I want them to be appreciative."[21] (Whitmer scored points of her own a couple weeks later by going on the Trevor Noah comedy show wearing a T-shirt that said, "That Woman From Michigan.")[22]

Throughout, Trump equivocated on just who was really in charge of the response to the disaster, claiming unfettered federal power when he wanted to call the shots and disclaiming responsibility when he wanted to pass the buck. One Sunday in April, he tweeted that governors had to get their act together on testing and medical equipment. "No excuses!" he declared. At his briefing the next day, Trump declared that he would be the one deciding when to reopen the country, not the governors. "They can't do anything without the approval of the president of the United States." Asked what gave him that power, he said, "When somebody's the president of the United States, the authority is total."[23] But then three days later, he told the governors it was up to them after all. "You're going to call your own shots," he told them on a conference call.[24]

There was no script for any of it, of course. This was a president who still preferred to wing it. Trump rarely attended the coronavirus task force meetings themselves, but afterward its members would head up to the Oval Office to brief him just before he would go out on camera. He would try out lines, some of them provocative and unconstructive, some of them flat wrong. The advisers would tell him, *No, you can't say that because it's not true,* and he would nod and use his Sharpie and cross it out on the piece of paper he was holding. But it would stick in his head and often he would blurt out exactly what they had told him not to say.

The briefings also introduced the country to an unlikely new star, the diminutive, grandfatherly Anthony Fauci, an elfin-faced foil to the president. At seventy-nine, Fauci had the reassuring bedside manner and scientific credibility that Trump did not. He was a legend in medical circles, having served as the federal government's top infectious disease specialist under seven presidents going back to Ronald Reagan in the 1980s, when he was at the forefront of the fight against AIDS. Back then, Fauci was initially the subject of enormous anger by the gay community that felt he was not doing enough, but over time he became one of their leading allies in the struggle to defeat the scourge. He was also a prime architect of George W. Bush's program to combat AIDS in Africa, a program credited with saving millions of lives.

Trump was the first president Fauci had served whom he had not even met his first year in office. Their first encounter occurred in late 2019 when the White House asked him to come over for a photo op— and instructed him to make sure to bring his white coat so he looked the part. The first time Fauci had ever been summoned to the White House, way back during the Reagan presidency, a friend who had worked in the Nixon White House advised him to always treat such a visit as if it would be the last and just tell the president the truth rather than shade his views in hopes of a repeat invitation. He leaned heavily on that advice now with Trump, an outlook that made him almost unique for being willing to stand next to the president and correct him in real time. Whenever Trump minimized the seriousness of the disease, Fauci would politely, but unmistakably, make clear that was not so. Where others who had worked for Trump for years kept silent even when confronted with his flamboyant and flagrantly untrue statements, Fauci neither flattered the boss nor outright flouted him either.

In the process, Fauci, near the end of his eighth decade in life, became something of an overnight sensation with the public. Magazines and television shows lavished him with attention. Media savvy after so many years in Washington and not at all averse to the limelight, Fauci made himself available to nearly any producer who asked. Soon there were Fauci dolls,

Fauci mugs, Fauci candles, Fauci doughnuts, Fauci murals, Fauci hoodies, Fauci pillows, and even a Fauci bobblehead. He was a celebrity.

Trump, of course, noticed. He always noticed when someone else was standing in his spotlight.

Trump had agreed to do what Fauci and the others had urged him to do, but he did not really support it. He wanted a solution, not a shutdown. No one seemed to have one for him, and nothing frustrated him more than the people who worked for him not delivering the answers he wanted. On March 18, he was in a ferocious mood when he called Alex Azar, the health and human services secretary, who was in a government car heading to the White House for a meeting.

"Who the hell thought it was a good idea to have the federal government do testing?" Trump demanded.

Azar was perplexed since in fact Jared Kushner just had organized a Rose Garden event about expanding drive-through testing. "Jared's the one," Azar said.

"No, no," Trump stopped him. "Jared's the one solving the problems. What idiot decided CDC should have a test? That was gross incompetence to have a test."

"We had to have something," Azar said.

"No, no, we should never have had a test," Trump said. "Who did that?"

"CDC."

"Well, who does CDC work for?"

"Me," Azar said.

"Well, then I have my answer." Of all the absurd ideas that Trump would entertain about the coronavirus, perhaps the most nonsensical was that the pandemic would not be so bad if the government simply stopped testing so much—as if the testing was causing the virus to spread. It was like a teenager hoping that as long as she did not take a pregnancy test, she would not actually be pregnant.

Azar was a convenient scapegoat. A Yale-trained lawyer who clerked for Justice Antonin Scalia and worked for Ken Starr's Whitewater investigation, Azar had thrived as part of the Republican establishment for more than two decades in Washington. He served as deputy health secretary under George W. Bush and then went into the pharmaceutical industry where he became chief lobbyist and then president of the American division of Eli Lilly. While his $2-million-a-year industry job might have been a disqualifying conflict in other administrations, Trump was not at all bothered with Azar's history in picking a successor for Tom Price, his initial health secretary, who was forced out after less than a year over his use of costly charter jets.

After determining who was at fault for the tests, Trump turned to another of his favorite topics—magic cures for Covid. "Larry Ellison says approve remdesivir today," the president said.

Ellison, the billionaire cofounder of Oracle who had hosted Trump in February for a campaign fundraiser at his Palm Springs estate, had been calling Trump recommending both remdesivir, an antiviral drug that some doctors had been trying on coronavirus patients, and hydroxychloroquine, an antimalarial drug that was being touted on Fox News as a miracle medicine. Neither had been rigorously tested yet to determine effectiveness against Covid but Trump invariably trusted what he was hearing from his rich peers and conservative media, even if they contradicted the experts.

"Mr. President, that's not how it works," Azar tried to explain. "We started trials, but you have to actually test it."

"No, Larry Ellison says it works. Approve it today. And Laura says hydroxychloroquine works. It's perfectly safe, so just approve it."

"Mr. President, we don't have data," Azar protested.

"Laura takes it," Trump said. "It's safe."

"Laura may take it, but hydroxychloroquine with people with heart disease can suffer fatal reactions so we have to be—"

"No," Trump demanded. "I want it approved today. That's an order."

Laura Ingraham had been pushing hydroxychloroquine on her Fox News show for a couple days, hosting a Long Island lawyer, Gregory Rigano, who falsely passed himself off as an adviser to Stanford Medical School. When her guest asserted that hydroxychloroquine would "just get rid of it completely," Ingraham exulted, "That's a game changer." Trump loved it. *Game changer.* That's what he wanted. Why was Azar resisting?

When Azar arrived at the White House a few minutes later, he found Mark Meadows and filled him in. The new chief of staff was not even on the job yet officially, but had started showing up at the White House anyway. He was not technically in charge—no one was, since Mick Mulvaney had been dumped via the Mar-a-Lago tweet—which seemed a perfect metaphor for a country immobilized by crisis.

Azar pressed Meadows: Was he also about to be fired?

"Well, he hasn't *told* me he wants to fire you," Meadows said, in a tone that was hardly reassuring. "I'll let you know. There's no discussion I know about."

Azar wanted Meadows to know he was not prepared to become the president's Covid whipping boy. "I'm no Jeff Sessions," he told the incoming chief of staff. "The minute he says something negative about me publicly, on Twitter or otherwise, you will have my resignation letter on your desk faster than you can whistle. Just know if he criticizes me publicly, then you're finding a health secretary that day."

That night, Fox News continued its drumbeat for hydroxychloroquine as Tucker Carlson brought the same lawyer from Ingraham's show onto his program. The next day, Trump took matters into his own hands. The doctors might not be willing to tell Americans to take hydroxychloroquine, but the president was.

"We are very excited about, specifically, what we talked about with the chloroquine," Trump said at his televised briefing. "I think it could be something really incredible." Adopting Ingraham's term, he said, "it could be a game changer."[25]

Asked by a reporter the next day if there was evidence that the drug would be effective against Covid, Tony Fauci, with Trump standing right next to him, said flatly, "The answer is no."[26]

CHAPTER 23

You're Blowing This

Two days after pandemic fatalities hit triple digits in the United States, Trump picked up the phone and called Chris Christie. The coronavirus that the president had blithely promised would go away was instead spreading rapidly. He had ordered most travel banned with Europe, much as he had done with China, decisions that would do powerful damage to America's economy, and he had just reluctantly agreed to the doctors' demands to shut down most everything inside the United States as well.

"I need you to come down here right now," Trump told Christie.

"Why?"

"Because you're the only person around me who's ever handled a big crisis," Trump said, "and I need to talk to you."

This was classic Trump. He had some of the world's smartest scientists, the most experienced disaster relief managers, and highly educated economists whose job was to prepare for moments like this working for the government, but he did not trust them. He was looking for someone to tell him how to get out of this situation without having to do what they were telling him to do. He was less than eight months from an election, and he just wanted the virus to go away.

Christie had no background with pandemics. He was a lawyer and a Trump confidant who had somehow managed to remain in the president's inner circle despite being dumped as transition director and turning down Trump's invitation to be White House chief of staff. The reason Trump was calling now was Christie's experience as New Jersey governor, when he had overseen the response to a major natural disaster, Hurricane Sandy, and come out ahead politically. No government virologist could tell Trump how to do that. Christie agreed to come to Washington right away and drove south on Interstate 95, eerily emptied of its perpetual traffic.

During the drive, his phone rang again. This time it was Melania Trump. The first lady was generally indifferent to politics and detached from policy fights. But she was rattled by the coronavirus and convinced that Trump was screwing up. Christie was a trusted figure for her as well as her husband; unlike many of Trump's more recent political allies, he had a friendship with the couple that long predated the White House. And he was on the right side of the White House's internal divide as far as the first lady was concerned, a rival of Jared Kushner and Ivanka Trump for the president's ear.

"Listen, he's not taking this seriously," she told Christie. "You have to change his mind about how serious this is."

During their trip to India a few weeks back, she told Christie, she had tried to get Trump to wake up to the danger. "You're blowing this," she recalled telling her husband. "This is serious. It's going to be really bad, and you need to take it more seriously than you're taking it." He had just dismissed her. "You worry too much," she remembered him saying. "Forget it." The president had hardly internalized her concern in the weeks since.

Christie knew from his own interactions with Trump how he was misjudging the virus. In February, the president had called Christie to ask him if he would head the White House coronavirus task force. But then Trump called back later and said never mind, he would have Mike Pence do it. "This thing is too small and too temporary for you," Trump told Christie. That may have been a throwaway line to ease the sting of offering a big job and then taking it away—Christie heard later that Jared Kushner had objected, once again, to having him in such a prominent role and went to Pence to urge him to volunteer for the assignment. But either way, Christie was alarmed by Trump's attitude. "Mr. President," he told Trump, "please don't ever repeat to anybody else that it's too small or too temporary because it is neither small nor temporary."

They had talked by phone again after Trump gave his Oval Office address that nearly everyone considered a disaster. Christie said on ABC News, where he was a paid commentator, that it was terrible and that whoever put Trump in the Oval Office for a speech did not know what they were doing. Soon after, the president had called.

"Why'd you say that?" Trump demanded.

"Tell me the truth," Christie replied. "Do you think you did well tonight?"

Trump said no.

Did he feel comfortable giving speeches from the Oval Office?

No.

"Then why the fuck did you do it?" Christie asked.

Christie blamed the debacle on Kushner, who, along with Ivanka, had lobbied Trump to make the address and then hastily pulled it together in just a few hours. "I don't care what Jared tells you. What the fuck does Jared know about politics?" Christie had said. Trump took the conversation in stride; he was used to advisers who hated each other.

So now as Christie drove down to Washington, he did not have high expectations. He decided to be blunt and put it into terms that the president would care about, his own political prospects: Trump, he would say, would not win in the fall unless he got serious about the pandemic.

Escorted into the Oval Office for what would be a nearly two-hour discussion, Christie tried to channel the first lady's warning. "This is a national and international crisis," he told Trump. "You don't only need to be doing things that help to solve it. You also need to *look* like you're doing things. Because in the end, Mr. President, this is the only thing that's going to matter for re-election."

Christie's lecture was not welcomed. A long and loud argument followed.

"I don't want to overreact," Trump said. "I don't want to scare people."

Trump was convinced that the public health measures he had approved would tank the good economy that he saw as crucial to his campaign; this is what half of his advisers had been telling him, in shouting matches in Trump's gladiatorial Oval Office over the past two months with the other half of his advisers, who thought refusing to take the necessary steps to safeguard public safety in the name of keeping the stock market humming was madness.

"The things you're talking about would destroy the economy," he told Christie.

"They're only temporary," Christie said.

At one point, Christie told him that Governor Ron DeSantis of Florida, a Trump disciple who was largely ignoring Washington's public health guidance, was making the president look bad. To Christie's chagrin, Trump abruptly called out to his assistant and had her get DeSantis on the line right away, then told the governor on speakerphone that he was sitting with Christie. "He thinks you're fucking this thing up," Trump said. DeSantis, predictably, got defensive and pushed back.

It was Trump who had set up the cage match, but Christie took the bait and told DeSantis that he was making Trump look bad because the president was finally beginning to take the virus seriously.

"Let's face it, Ron, he got you elected down there, and you would think you would be loyal to what the president wants you to do," Christie said, knowing that would push one of Trump's buttons.

Sure enough, Trump chimed in. "Yeah, why aren't you being loyal to what I want you to do?" he asked the Florida governor.

When the call was over, Trump turned to Christie and said, "See what I'm dealing with?" as if the real issue were DeSantis.

The governors were not the main problem, Christie said. "Part of this is just you being in charge," he said.[2] Trump was the president of the United States. It was time to lead.

* MARCH 25: DEATH TOLL REACHES 1,000 *

Trump was not convinced, at least not for long. Even as the death toll approached four digits, he began running out of patience for the lockdown. "WE CANNOT LET THE CURE BE WORSE THAN THE PROBLEM ITSELF," he practically shouted on Twitter a few minutes before midnight on Sunday, March 22, adopting the line of reasoning voiced a couple hours earlier by the conservative host Steve Hilton on Fox News.

The next day, Trump declared that he wanted to end the lockdown even though the virus was still gaining momentum. "I would love to have the country opened up and raring to go by Easter," he said in an interview on Fox. He wanted to see "churches packed full of people" for the holiday less than three weeks away, on April 12. It was, he admitted later, a date he picked not based on any scientific evaluation but only because he "just thought it was a beautiful time."[3]

The doctors kept a straight face, but behind the scenes they were panicked. An Easter reopening was inconceivable. New York and other cities were being hammered; deaths would be rising alarmingly by then. Advisers scrambled to change Trump's mind and showed him two sets of numbers. The first indicated that the peak of the coronavirus wave was still weeks away and that anywhere between 100,000 and 240,000 people could die in the United States even with the social distancing measures

Trump wanted to lift, overwhelming hospitals like the one Trump knew in Queens.[4]

"Do you mean that there will be body bags there?" he asked. "Refrigerated trucks? Just like at Elmhurst?"

"Yes, Mr. President," Deborah Birx replied. "Hundreds of hospitals."[5]

The second set of numbers provided to the president came from his campaign pollsters John and Jim McLaughlin. Fully 52 percent of Americans preferred a complete national shutdown requiring everyone other than essential workers to stay at home compared with 38 percent who favored universal testing and isolating only those infected with the virus.[6] Support for a shutdown prevailed in every region and even among those who could not afford to be out of work for a month. Reluctantly, Trump reversed himself and agreed to extend the restrictions. "I want every American to be prepared for the hard days that lie ahead," he told the nation.[7]

But he would only resist his instincts for so long. The economy that he had taken such pride in and that he was counting on to deliver him a second term was reeling. More than 20 million Americans had been thrown out of work in the initial stages of the pandemic, wiping out all the gains from the 113-month economic expansion that had begun under Barack Obama and continued under Trump. Unemployment shot up to nearly 15 percent, higher than any time since the Great Depression.[8] The size of the American economy shrank by 9 percent in a single quarter, three times the next largest such collapse since record-keeping began after World War II.[9] Marquee companies such as Disney, Macy's, Marriott, and various airlines and automakers would soon lay off or furlough tens of thousands of workers each. Name-brand retailers such as Brooks Brothers, JCPenney, J.Crew, Lord & Taylor, Neiman Marcus, Pier 1, and Hertz would go bankrupt and some closed for good. The Dow Jones Industrial Average fell by a mind-blowing 37 percent in less than six weeks.[10]

The dire news temporarily broke the political gridlock in Washington. In a rare bipartisan move, Trump quickly agreed with Democrats on a massive $2.2 trillion package of relief for individuals and businesses hurt by the pandemic. But it had to be negotiated by Steven Mnuchin since the president was still not on speaking terms with Nancy Pelosi following the impeachment. And once it was passed, instead of using the moment to promote national unity as other presidents would have, Trump invited only Republicans to the March 27 signing ceremony in the Oval Office, stiffing the Democrats who helped make it happen. He then made sure that the $1,200 paper checks sent to 35 million American households that did not receive payments electronically bore his own name on them, as if it were his personal largesse, something no president had ever done.

Searching for an escape from disaster, Trump was still pinning his hopes on hydroxychloroquine. For the president, the unproven drug had become a cause, a magic elixir that would somehow make the virus go away even if the experts trusted by the government did not think so.

Having failed to get Alex Azar to circumvent the official approval process, the president got better news the day after the Covid bill signing, on March 28, when Stephen Hahn, the commissioner of the Food and Drug Administration, issued an emergency use authorization endorsing the use of the drug for Covid patients while further tests were conducted. Hahn agreed with Tony Fauci that there did not seem to be any evidence that it would help against the virus, but since the drug had been safely used for other ailments, he figured there was less risk in letting it be tried even as scientists examined it further.

A cancer doctor and chief medical executive at the MD Anderson Cancer Center in Houston before taking over the FDA only weeks ahead of the Covid outbreak, Hahn had never served in government and often remarked on his own naïveté about Washington. It had not occurred to him how quickly his emergency use powers could become politicized. He had based his decision in part on a legal memo from Azar's lawyer at the Health and Human Services Department outlining the agency's authority in the matter. At the time, the memo seemed persuasive; only months later would Hahn begin to suspect it was driven by political will more than legal analysis.

A week after his decision, an international medical organization renounced a study it had published reporting benefits of hydroxychloroquine, saying that the study did not meet its standards. That night, Laura Ingraham showed up in person at the White House with two doctors from her television "medicine cabinet," Ramin Oskoui, a cardiologist, and Stephen Smith, an infectious disease specialist.[11] "I've been watching you," Trump told them.[12] With Hahn also present, they showed Trump spreadsheets purporting to make the case for the drug. Hahn was not impressed, but Trump was. Fox News doctors always seemed smarter to him than the ones in the government.

Soon, he began savagely attacking anyone who raised doubts about hydroxychloroquine, making support for Trump's drug a new test of support for Trump himself. When Neil Cavuto warned on Fox that taking the drug could be harmful, Trump retweeted, "CAVUTO IS AN IDIOT," among other insults. It was as if the entire network had betrayed him. "You have more anti-Trump people, by far, than ever before," he complained in a tweet addressed directly to Fox. "Looking for a new outlet!" Trump even started taking hydroxychloroquine himself as a preventive measure. "What do you have to lose?" he asked.[13]

Quite a lot, it turned out. Studies soon showed that not only was hydroxychloroquine not the wonder drug Trump asserted, but it could cause serious heart trouble, as Azar had warned at the outset. Seven weeks after signing off on experimental use of the drug, Hahn's FDA revoked its emergency authorization, saying the potential benefits "no longer outweigh the known and potential risks."[14] But Trump was undeterred. "I'm taking it. I feel great. It's a miracle," he told Mark Esper, the defense secretary.[15] He even called Esper at home that weekend to push him to preemptively administer the drug to the military—another idea the Pentagon hoped Trump would just forget.

* APRIL 2: DEATH TOLL REACHES 5,000 *

In early April, the CDC decided to recommend that Americans wear masks to guard against infection. Some officials had been advocating masks for weeks, most notably Matt Pottinger, the deputy national security adviser who while living in Asia had seen face coverings help fight infectious disease there. He had been the first in the White House to show up for work wearing a mask in mid-March. Trump was stunned when he saw him.

"Are you okay?" the president asked.

"I don't want to be the guy in the footnote of history books who knocked off the president of the United States by giving him Covid," Pottinger explained.

The doctors, paradoxically, were not as quick to tout the benefit. In the early days of the pandemic, they had urged Americans not to wear masks, in part because shortages meant that they wanted to reserve them for health care professionals and in part because they did not yet know how easily the virus spread by air. "Seriously people—STOP BUYING MASKS!" Jerome Adams, the surgeon general, tweeted early in the pandemic. "They are NOT effective in preventing general public from catching #Coronavirus, but if healthcare providers can't get them to care for sick patients, it puts them and our communities at risk!"[16] Tony Fauci thought at first they would not be effective because people would touch the masks and therefore still infect themselves. Deborah Birx thought Americans would not adjust to masks as Asians had. Pottinger insisted they were wrong, only to be widely mocked and eventually marginalized.

But as the pandemic escalated, the scientists decided that masks were in fact effective at stopping infections, perhaps even the most effective way. Robert Kadlec, a career physician who was assistant secretary of health and human services for preparedness and response, even came up with a plan working with a consortium of a dozen firms led by the Hanes underwear company to manufacture 650 million three-ply cloth masks and send a box of five first to each home in highly infected areas and eventually to every household in America. The initial models looked a bit silly—"like you're wearing little tighty-whities on your face," as Olivia Troye, the Mike Pence aide working for the coronavirus task force, put it—but they were well constructed, had antimicrobial fibers, and could be laundered up to twenty times without degrading their effectiveness.

Kadlec was scheduled to present the plan to the White House coronavirus task force on April 2. Minutes before the meeting was to start, however, Marc Short, the vice president's chief of staff, abruptly ordered the initiative removed from the agenda. The slides were already in the projector. "Take it down!" Troye yelled at Pottinger because she was being yelled at by Short. Pottinger was furious. So was Troye. It seemed like a no-brainer. "I've been told no way in hell should this be discussed today in the meeting," Troye apologized to Kadlec.

Short later explained that key questions about funding and delivery had not been answered, but the idea was never revived, and boxes of the masks initially produced sat around the White House unused. Troye ended up sending some to her family in Texas; her husband brought packs to colleagues at the Defense Department.

A day later, Trump grudgingly agreed to formally announce the new CDC guideline urging mask use at his daily briefing—and then immediately disavowed it. "You can do it," he told Americans, before adding, "You don't have to do it. I am choosing not to do it. But some people may want to do it, and that's okay. It may be good. Probably will—they're making a recommendation. It's only a recommendation, it's voluntary."

Why would he refuse to follow the recommendation? "Wearing a face mask as I greet presidents, prime ministers, dictators, kings, queens—don't know," he said, although of course he had not greeted any foreign leaders recently, nor was he likely to anytime soon. The whole world was closed for Covid. "Somehow, I don't see it for myself."[17]

Whatever mix of vanity or political concern played into Trump's decision to reject masks, it would have a profound effect. Rather than bring the country together behind a simple, modest preventive measure, he helped make mask wearing a political statement and one more battleground in the country's perpetual culture war.

* APRIL 5: DEATH TOLL REACHES 10,000 *

Among those most opposed to masks was Mark Meadows. He ridiculed those who wore them—"That's not going to do you any good"—making it uncomfortable for White House aides to comply with the government's own health guidance without being seen as crossing the president. The mask had quickly become another loyalty test.

Meadows was a confounding figure to many in the White House. A sixty-year-old onetime real estate developer from North Carolina, he was beefy and tall, with a winning smile and seemingly easygoing manner. But his affable demeanor disguised a ruthless ambition and his new colleagues at the White House found him to be a cutthroat bureaucratic infighter determined to consolidate power.

Born on an Army base in France to a soldier and a civilian nurse, Meadows grew up mainly in Florida, a self-described "fat nerd" and aspiring weatherman in a family without much money.[18] He lost weight, married his high school girlfriend, and moved to North Carolina, where he owned a sandwich shop, Aunt D's, for twenty years, homeschooled his children, and eventually got his real estate license. He sold the restaurant, invested the proceeds in some property deals, and soon was a developer. In 2012, he entered politics and won a House seat in western North Carolina. He was one of the original nine conservatives to form the House Freedom Caucus.

While Mick Mulvaney, another cofounder, had jokingly proposed calling them "the Reasonable Nutjob Caucus," to distinguish the group from even more radical lawmakers, Meadows and his allies relished their roles as bomb-throwers. Meadows helped blow up bipartisan deals over the budget, health care, and immigration that he argued had sold out conservative principles.[19] Unlike grating allies such as Jim Jordan, however, Meadows was genial, offering a friendly public face for the Freedom Caucus, and got along with some on the other side of the aisle. Representative Elijah Cummings, the Maryland Democrat often targeted by Trump's racist blasts, called Meadows "one of my best friends" and Meadows gave a moving eulogy when Cummings later died.[20]

But Meadows earned a reputation for playing both sides. Soon after arriving in the House, he cast a vote against Speaker John Boehner's re-election. Not long after, Meadows requested a meeting with Boehner in his Capitol office where, within seconds, the new congressman suddenly slid off the couch onto his knees and put his hands in front of his chest in confessional prostration. "Mr. Speaker, please forgive me," Meadows said. Boehner was flabbergasted, taking an extra-long drag on his Camel cigarette before saying, "For what?"

"I knew he was carrying a backpack full of knives—and sooner or later he'd try to cut me again with them," Boehner later wrote. "Which, of course, he did."[21] By the fall of 2015, Meadows filed a motion to depose Boehner, who soon after stepped down, a major victory for the Freedom Caucus. Paul Ryan, Boehner's reluctant successor, had an equally jaundiced view of Meadows, who at one point blew up at the new speaker on the floor during a contentious vote. A former Republican leadership aide once told the journalists Anna Palmer and Jake Sherman that Meadows was the most dishonest person he had ever met at the Capitol, "convicted criminals included."[22]

Meadows was not a supporter of Donald Trump—until he was. Like Trump, Meadows encouraged the birther lies about Barack Obama, at one point declaring that "2012 is the time we are going to send Mr. Obama home to Kenya or wherever it is." (He later called it "probably a poor choice of words on my part" and acknowledged that Obama was an American citizen.)[23] Still, Meadows was initially suspicious of Trump and privately expressed reluctance to attend the Republican National Convention in 2016 for fear of being associated with a former Democrat who had supported abortion rights and gun control. But he wound up campaigning for the nominee even after the *Access Hollywood* tape was released, an act of loyalty Trump never forgot.

With Trump in office, Meadows reinvented himself as one of his most outspoken defenders. Like Lindsey Graham, another convert, he was entranced by access to the Oval Office and enjoyed showing off the call log on his iPhone to a reporter to prove he was speaking with "VIP POTUS."[24] He telephoned Trump so often, in fact, that he later claimed to have discovered he was number fourteen on a White House switchboard list of approved callers to be put through to the president. By late 2018, he made it up to number seven. He called four times in a single night to urge Trump to veto the spending bill that led to the 2019 partial government shutdown. He spoke with the president probably more than any other congressman—so much so that some White House aides tried to block his calls, prompting Meadows to dial the president's mobile phone in the evening to get around the staff.

Now tapped as Trump's fourth chief of staff in as many years, Meadows planned to avoid what he saw as the mistakes of the previous three. While Reince Priebus and John Kelly tried to manage and control Trump and Mick Mulvaney settled for enabling him, Meadows would channel the president. In some ways, he may have understood Trump the best of all the chiefs, connecting with Trump's disruptive approach as his predecessors did not. No Third Time Rule kind of guy, he eagerly sought to carry out Trump's instructions and was perfectly willing to do the president's political wet work. Soon after settling into the White House, he berated the defense secretary and secretary of the Army for even thinking about promoting Alexander Vindman and insisted they investigate the impeachment witness until they found something to justify denying him a full colonel's eagle. The conversation between Meadows and Mark Esper got so heated that they both hung up on each other.

To many of his new colleagues, Meadows quickly came across as duplicitous and untrustworthy. "He would lie to people's faces," said a fellow White House official. Stephanie Grisham, who was deposed as White House press secretary by Meadows, called him "one of the worst people ever to enter the Trump White House" and said that on a scale of awfulness, with a five being the worst, "I'd give Mark Meadows a twelve."[25] Joe Grogan, the president's domestic policy adviser, also was no fan. Meadows was "an absolute disaster" who played to "all the president's worst instincts," Grogan would tell others. Meadows did not think much of Grisham or Grogan either, or many other staffers he inherited and in some cases would push out.

As for the pandemic, Meadows considered it overblown from the start. He believed that those over sixty with certain preexisting health conditions such as obesity, diabetes, or cancer were vulnerable, but that most everyone else faced little real danger, and it was ridiculous to close down the country. He had no hesitation about confronting Deborah Birx and Tony Fauci, indifferent to their collective decades of experience with infectious disease. A skeptic of the science behind climate change who had even dabbled in the field of "creationist paleontology," Meadows thought the doctors were self-interested, tunnel-visioned, and contradictory, failing to account for the economic reality of a complicated society on the edge of an abyss.[26] He talked about them with scorn. "They're inept, they're idiotic, they're a bunch of scientists," Meadows told people in the

White House at one point, referring to the specialists at the CDC. "Even the most loved Dr. Fauci still has no clue on a whole lot of stuff."

At meeting after meeting that spring, Meadows challenged the doctors, producing his own theories and his own math. "I'm a numbers guy," he would repeat. Like the president, who believed himself smarter than experts on just about every subject, Meadows decided he knew better on many of the most pressing issues raised by the virus. He questioned why people exposed to Covid had to quarantine for fourteen days, insisting that he had crunched the data himself and that ten days would be perfectly sufficient. He dismissed death projections presented to the White House, reasoning that they were based on the experience in other countries such as Italy, which had different demographics than the United States. When Birx told him shortly after he arrived in the White House that 600,000 could die in the United States even with mitigation measures, Meadows thought that was crazy. And he zealously took it upon himself to chastise the doctors when he thought they veered out of their lane. Angry at some comments by Fauci printed in *The Washington Post*, Meadows called to harangue him.

"What the hell do you think you're doing?" he yelled. "You shouldn't be out there editorializing. You should just be giving the facts."

Fauci pushed back. "It's not editorial," he said. "It's a medical opinion."

Meadows considered the existence of the White House coronavirus task force a monumental miscalculation, especially the decision to put it under Mike Pence. You can fire your secretary of HHS; you can't fire your VP, as he explained his reasoning to others. "When you put a VP in charge of something, it becomes problematic. If they don't do a good job, there's no way to express disapproval in concrete terms."

After only a couple weeks as chief of staff, Meadows deemed Pence's task force meetings so laborious that he stopped attending and soon began to wind them down. In part, that was to keep Fauci and Birx from scaring the public. In his view, the doctors were making unfounded public statements about contingencies that might or might not happen and he had diminishing interest in what they had to say. Instead, he formed a small group of advisers to meet in his office every day at 8 a.m. without the doctors to make decisions that were often at odds with the task force.

But Meadows did not believe there was much the government could do to halt the spread of the virus. He was an early convert to the theory of "herd immunity," which held that a pandemic only waned after a large enough share of a society became infected. In the end, everyone was going to get it, he privately confided to people in the White House, even though that was far from the official messaging of the moment. Most Americans were going to get exposed or a vaccine would have to be developed before Covid would go away. While it was important to flatten the curve to avoid overrunning hospitals, he argued, there was no stopping the virus. At least 65 percent or 70 percent of the public would have to be exposed to it. That was the thing Trump and his team could not talk about—everybody was going to get it. Yet by giving up on trying to stop the virus, Meadows was making it a self-fulfilling prophecy—and reinforcing Trump's own instincts.

* APRIL 13: DEATH TOLL REACHES 25,000 *

The turning point in Trump's handling of the pandemic came on the morning of April 17, when the president fired off three tweets in quick succession.

"LIBERATE MINNESOTA!"

"LIBERATE MICHIGAN!"

"LIBERATE VIRGINIA, AND SAVE YOUR GREAT 2ND AMENDMENT. IT IS UNDER SIEGE!"

With that, Trump stopped equivocating and fully threw in his lot with the denialists, opening a campaign against a more cautious, phased reopening policy that he had unveiled at the recommendation of the medical advisers less than twenty-four hours earlier. The tweets came just two minutes after a report on Fox News about anti-lockdown protests like those in Michigan proliferating around the country.

At the start of the lockdown, Trump had styled himself a wartime president, but the pandemic had proved an elusive foe. His tweets that day targeted an enemy he could attack—the scientists and the governors, or at least the Democratic governors who were opposing him. The war from then on would be not with an invisible disease but with oppressive liberals and the Deep State. "I knew after that we were in serious trouble," Fauci recalled later. "He had turned the corner."

Trump was obsessed with his strong economy slipping away and kept asking Dan Scavino for the latest on the stock market ("Are we up or down?") just before heading out to the daily briefing. But more so, Trump worried about his re-election slipping away. If the choice was listening to the smug guys in the white lab coats who rolled their eyes about him or siding with the bearded men in camouflage vests and red MAGA baseball caps waving assault rifles outside the state capitol in Lansing, he would pick the gun toters.

From the day of the LIBERATE tweets, Trump resisted not only masks and lockdowns but even the idea that doctors should be heeded. Less than a week later, on April 23, he made what would come to be one of the most mocked comments of his presidency after scientists at the daily briefing reported that the virus was vulnerable to bleach, alcohol, and ultraviolet light. Trump began musing out loud on camera. "Supposing you brought the light inside the body, which you can do either through the skin or in some other way, and I think you said you're going to test that too," Trump told the scientists. "Sounds interesting." Then he continued. "And then I see the disinfectant, where it knocks it out in one minute. And is there a way we can do something like that? By injection inside or almost a cleaning? Because you see it gets in the lungs and it does a tremendous number on the lungs. So it would be interesting to check that."[27]

Inject bleach? Was he serious? Deborah Birx, who was sitting to the side, did her best not to react, staring at the floor and wishing it would just open up and swallow her, but her face still betrayed a sense of horror and video clips of her reaction to Trump's comments soon went viral. Birx would later say she was haunted by the moment and thought about it every single day afterward. Brad Parscale, Trump's campaign manager, saw it and was increasingly convinced the president was dooming his own re-election bid. "We're fucked," he told colleagues.

The flap all but ended Trump's daily Covid show. Angry at the backlash, he pronounced the briefings "not worth the time & effort" and refused to appear before cameras for days. For nearly two months amid a national crisis of historic proportions, Trump had managed to make it all about himself, holding forth with a torrent of lies, misinformation, and simple foolishness. A *New York Times* analysis of Trump's Covid briefings catalogued a total of 260,000 words spoken from the podium and determined that he made 130 false or misleading statements and 600 self-congratulatory comments, four times as many as his statements expressing empathy or national unity.[28] But Trump had relished the captive audience he commanded. When the *Times* reported that the briefings were "a ratings hit" with an average audience of 8.5 million on cable television, he crowed about it, never mind the people who died that day.[29] Even after officially quitting the briefings, he would periodically return, because he could not help himself, but the pace he had maintained for weeks was over—to the relief of many allies and aides.

His patience with his medical advisers was almost gone too. He had let it pass when Tony Fauci contradicted him at the White House podium on hydroxychloroquine and the timetable for a vaccine. But one day the president saw Fauci on television saying that Trump was wrong to say the virus would eventually disappear. Trump called Fauci at home late that night.

"What the hell are you doing?" Trump exclaimed. "You've got to be more positive."

"Mr. President, I can't be more positive when there's not a reason to be more positive," Fauci replied.

"I know, I know," Trump said, softening. "I don't want to tell you what to do. But you've got to spin it more positively."

* APRIL 24: DEATH TOLL REACHES 50,000 *

Beyond the president's own eruptions, his White House was riven with rivalries that complicated the fight against the pandemic. Everyone seemed to have it out for everyone else. At the center of many of these fights was Alex Azar, the health secretary who in theory should have been the government's field marshal against the disease. Instead, he was busy fending off criticism from both sides—one day he was portrayed as alarmist, the next as complacent.

As much as any of Trump's cabinet officers, Azar struck colleagues as determined not to offend the fickle president and lose his job. When Azar gave television interviews, his press aide even sat on the floor underneath the television camera and crossed her arms to make a T to remind him to credit Trump on air. Azar understood what Trump valued. One time he visited the president shortly after appearing on a cable news show. "That was a great hit," Trump said, evidently having just seen it. The president pointed to the television. "Here, let's watch," Trump said as he hit rewind to play the interview again and give Azar tips to improve his performance.

Azar's focus on not becoming another Jeff Sessions left him isolated among other administration officials. Even before the coronavirus, he had famously competed over turf and Trump's favor with Seema Verma, the administrator of the Medicare and Medicaid agency who was close to Mike Pence, to the point that the president had to call them both in and tell them to knock it off. Now the same kinds of friction arose with the heads of the public health agencies that reported to him. The differences were not really philosophical or even on policy matters. "This was all about pleasing the president," said one of his internal rivals.

Stephen Hahn felt pressured to speed up timetables to satisfy the president. "You're going to be in trouble with the White House," Azar would tell him if he resisted. Robert Redfield, the CDC director, bristled when Azar's staff tried to alter the agency's weekly morbidity reports for what seemed like political reasons. And Rick Bright, head of drug and vaccine development in Azar's department, eventually went public after he was removed from his post, saying he had resisted political pressure to endorse hydroxychloroquine. It did not help Azar that he told colleagues in the Situation Room that Bright had been promoted just moments before the doctor's statement revealing he had in fact been demoted.

The medical advisers did not think they could count on Azar to defend them against Trump. Hahn, Redfield, Tony Fauci, and Deborah Birx formed what they called the Doctors Group and began meeting separately, sometimes in Birx's White House office, otherwise by video. One day that spring, they agreed on a mutual suicide pact, deciding that an attack on one would constitute an attack on all of them. If any of them were attacked, they would come to each other's defense; if any of them were fired, the others would resign in protest. Birx marched into Mark Meadows's office to inform him. "If you fire one of us, you fire all of us," she told him, according to an account she gave colleagues.[30]

Even so, there were stresses within the Doctors Group. Unlike Fauci, who had somehow managed the art of contradicting Trump without outright criticizing him, Birx had publicly embarrassed herself with a few examples of the audience-of-one management technique practiced by other Trump appointees, praising the fact-challenged president early on, for example, for being "so attentive to the scientific literature and the details and the data" in an interview with the Christian Broadcasting Network and performing linguistic acrobatics to avoid overtly refuting his more peculiar claims on hydroxychloroquine and bleach. She justified it as a way to avoid having Trump dump her altogether in favor of a less responsible alternative. Fauci, who had worked with Birx for decades fighting AIDS, never publicly chided her but privately told colleagues that she was too willing to defer to the president, considering it a betrayal of the scientific community for political ambition. At key early junctures, "Debbie was totally into gaming the system in order to make the administration look like it was doing something," a close associate of Fauci's said. For her part, there were times when Birx felt that Fauci and the others did not back her up against the denialists; the other doctors did not have to put up with what she did because they could return to their offices while she worked all day inside the White House just one floor removed from the president.

Perhaps Azar's most toxic relationship was with Joe Grogan, the president's domestic policy adviser. A onetime lobbyist for a drugmaker, Grogan had been one of Mick Mulvaney's closest allies in the White House. He had crossed swords with Azar even before the pandemic, when Grogan resisted the secretary's proposal to bring down drug prices by limiting rebates to middlemen, which Grogan argued could raise costs for seniors. Azar thought Grogan was sabotaging him by leaking negative stories to the media and resented the White House adviser going around him to work with his staff.

Grogan told colleagues that Azar was lazy, uncooperative, arrogant, and not in command of the facts. Grogan even speculated to others that Azar was medicated because how else could his performance be explained. When Mark Meadows took over, both Azar and Grogan lobbied the new chief of staff to get rid of the other. Asked who should take over the health department, Grogan suggested Birx. "Listen, dude," he told Meadows. "She's a Republican and she's more conservative than a lot of people around here."

The conflict came to a head the last weekend in April after a *New York Times* story included inside information that Azar's enemies considered a self-serving effort by the health secretary to blame the administration's failings on others. Soon rumors were racing around that Azar was about to be fired. Azar tried to ignore the talk by going on a five-mile hike but by the time he got back, CNN had reported the speculation. After what seemed like no more than twenty minutes, Jared Kushner broke sabbath to call Azar and deny it. "Mr. Secretary, this is not true," he said. Kushner arranged for Azar to meet the next day with two of his lieutenants, Adam Boehler and Brad Smith, at Boehler's house off Foxhall Road in an exclusive woodsy area of Washington. Hoping to salvage his job, Azar showed up with Brian Harrison, his chief of staff, and laid out an agenda for how they could be successful going forward. Number one on Azar's list: Fire Joe Grogan.

Later that afternoon, Trump called to reassure Azar he would not be sacked. "This is bullshit," he said. "It's totally untrue." The president added, "Even if it were true—and it's not, you're great—but if you were mediocre, why would I get rid of you when I have six months left?" Trump's calculations were evident: he *had* thought about it but concluded that it would be too politically costly to get rid of his health secretary in the middle of a pandemic right before an election.

Still, Trump chided Azar for leaking the story to the *Times*. Azar pushed back, saying it was the president's aides who were the leakers, and unloaded months of grievance. "Grogan is a cancer on your presidency," Azar told him.

Three days after Azar complained about him to Trump, Grogan publicly announced his departure, accelerating his previous plans to leave by Memorial Day.

The feuds within the Trump team over personality and policy were problematic enough, but the schism over a simple piece of cloth was rapidly widening into a larger rift that would divide the broader country and undermine resolve to defeat the virus. Now that Meadows and Trump had rejected mask wearing, other administration officials had to pick a side. That included Mike Pence, whose uncomfortable efforts to straddle the line between science and politics collapsed in an embarrassing spectacle during a visit to the Mayo Clinic on April 28 that normally would have generated little attention.

The advance team's memo the night before the trip noted the clinic's policy that everyone entering the building wear a mask. But when a staffer on Air Force Two en route to Minnesota began handing out masks, cute homemade ones that someone's mother had sewn, Pence's political aides refused to put them on. Stephen Hahn, who was accompanying the vice president, and Olivia Troye, the task force staff member, were horrified and challenged Marc Short.

"He's not going to wear a mask," Short told them.

"But it's a medical facility," Troye protested.

Hahn agreed. "He should wear a mask," Hahn said. "It's the Mayo Clinic."

But Short said if Pence wore a mask, there would be pictures. "We don't want this being in the campaign later, the vice president wearing a mask," he said. And while he did not say so, they knew Trump did not want to see his number two covering his face.

Hahn and Troye were mystified. No reasonable person would give Pence grief for that. "I feel like if you're criticizing the vice president for wearing a mask during a potential pandemic that's about to explode, then you're the asshole," Troye told Short. He was unmoved.

Neither Hahn nor Troye was able to appeal the decision directly to the vice president and soon enough pictures of the bare-faced vice president surrounded by masked doctors flashed across the internet, triggering the predictable social media uproar even before Pence finished his tour. In response, with the vice president still in the building, clinic officials posted a message on Twitter: "Mayo Clinic had informed @VP of the masking policy prior to his arrival today." Short found and berated the Mayo Clinic's public affairs official and soon the tweet was deleted, which of course only made matters worse.

After Air Force Two arrived back in Washington, the normally unflappable Pence seemed to be stewing and approached Hahn and Troye on the tarmac. "Thanks for what *was* and *should* have been an amazing visit," the vice president said, an uncharacteristically bitter tone in his voice, "and I'm sorry it got derailed and didn't work out that way."

He started to walk away, then turned back. "Nobody told me that they had a policy on masks," he said reproachfully. "It would have been nice to know."

Troye was livid. It had been in the briefing. Hadn't anyone told him?

Hahn was confused too. "Didn't we have this discussion?" he asked Troye.

They did. It did not matter. Barely a week later, the vice president's mask-less staff confronted Covid in a personal if completely predictable way. Katie Miller, his press secretary, who was married to Stephen Miller, tested positive, forcing a delay in Pence's departure for a trip to Iowa so six other staff members who had worked closely with her could be taken off Air Force Two to be tested. A military valet who served Trump also tested positive. The virus was now inside the White House.

* MAY 7: DEATH TOLL REACHES 75,000 *

Trump needed someone to blame and settled on China. On May 18, he announced that he planned to withdraw the United States from the World Health Organization because of its "China centric" Covid response and "alarming lack of independence" from Beijing.[31] The move capped two months of escalating hostility, a sharp change from Trump's initial praise for Xi Jinping's leadership on the pandemic.

The president had increasingly taken to calling Covid "the Chinese virus" or "China virus" or even more overtly racist variations like "kung flu." Following his lead, Mike Pompeo had insisted in March that fellow foreign ministers refer to it as "the Wuhan virus" in an official G7 communiqué and refused to sign when they declined.[32] The president's use of such charged language was blamed for fueling a surge of harassment and violence against Asian Americans. By the time the year ended, hate crimes against people of Asian descent would rise by 76 percent.[33]

There was no question that China had initially obscured the threat from the virus, delaying public notice for six crucial days and punishing eight doctors who dared to raise alarms. Beijing blocked American and other international experts from entering the country and many critics agreed that the WHO had been too willing to accept reassurances from China, one of its major funders. There were suspicions that the virus was not a natural occurrence, but the result of experimentation gone wrong in a Wuhan lab, although there was no definitive evidence proving it. China even tried to spread disinformation that the virus originated at an American military research facility in Maryland.

Still, the idea of pulling the United States, the WHO's largest funder, out of the planet's main international health agency in the middle of a global pandemic struck many as putting politics ahead of saving lives. Flawed as even its defenders considered the WHO to be, there was no other equivalent mechanism to coordinate a unified response to a disease that respected no boundaries. Trump's advisers tried to talk him out of withdrawing when he asked them about it in the Situation Room. "Well, they're the only thing we got," Tony Fauci said.

For China hawks like Pompeo, Peter Navarro, and Matt Pottinger, Trump's pandemic-fueled shift on China marked a final end to three years of presidential flip-flopping between accommodation and confrontation toward Beijing. Outreach to China was over. Washington would now take a harsher view of Beijing. For the first time, Trump announced sanctions on senior Chinese officials and revoked preferential economic treatment for Hong Kong. The trade talks with Beijing were dead. "That was the beginning of the full-on political war on China," a White House official observed.

For Trump, focusing on China's misconduct was not so much a foreign policy pivot as a political one, allowing him to avoid scrutiny of his own administration's failings. He had a narrative he could sell—it was not his fault, it was Beijing's.

* MAY 27: DEATH TOLL REACHES 100,000 *

As the cemeteries filled up, Trump took no time publicly to lead a nation in grief. Not once since the start of the pandemic had he gone to a church to mourn the victims. He refused to order the nation's flags lowered until Democratic congressional leaders pleaded with him to do so. He did not call for a moment of silence. At various points, he had invited to the White House health company executives, governors, cruise boat company heads, religious leaders, and others affected by the crisis—but never Americans who had actually lost someone to the virus.

When the official number of Covid fatalities in the United States hit the macabre milestone of 100,000, roughly equivalent to all the American troops killed during wars in Korea, Vietnam, Iraq, and Afghanistan combined, *The New York Times* marked the moment with a stark and powerful front page with no stories or photographs, just six columns, top to bottom, listing the names of 1,000 dead Americans, who together represented only 1 percent of the nation's grim total.[34] In the capital, Washington National Cathedral rang its largest bell 100 times over the space of ten minutes, with each strike of the clapper against the bourdon representing 1,000 lives in a haunting reminder to grieve. Mike Pence got a personalized reminder as well, as the owners of a home along his motorcade route hung a giant banner that said "Hey Pence" along with the latest casualty count in blood red.

But at the White House, the president who had talked and talked and talked his way through the pandemic had nothing to say on that grim day, leaving it to a spokesman to issue an emailed statement offering "prayers for comfort and strength" to those mourning.[35] Instead, Trump marked the passing of 100,000 Americans from a disease no one had heard of just a few months earlier by retweeting a post from a Fox Business host who called him "arguably the greatest president in history."

CHAPTER 24

The Battle of Lafayette Square

For a week, Mark Milley had been going through drafts of the letter he wanted to send to Trump—in his head, when he was on the phone, with his staff. There were short versions, there were long versions. His favorite, the one he would keep in his desk drawer in his big office at the Pentagon and sometimes pull out and look at just to remember what it said, was the one he wrote himself. In its entirety, it read:

> I regret to inform you that I intend to resign as your Chairman of the Joint Chiefs of Staff. Thank you for the honor of appointing me as senior ranking officer. The events of the last couple weeks have caused me to do deep soul-searching, and I can no longer faithfully support and execute your orders as Chairman of the Joint Chiefs of Staff. It is my belief that you were doing great and irreparable harm to my country. I believe that you have made a concerted effort over time to politicize the United States military. I thought that I could change that. I've come to the realization that I cannot, and I need to step aside and let someone else try to do that.
>
> Second, you are using the military to create fear in the minds of the people—and we are trying to protect the American people. I cannot stand by idly and participate in that attack, verbally or otherwise, on the American people. The American people trust their military and they trust us to protect them against all enemies, foreign and domestic, and our military will do just that. We will not turn our back on the American people.
>
> Third, I swore an oath to the Constitution of the United States and embodied within that Constitution is the idea that says that all men and women are created equal. All men and women are created equal,

no matter who you are, whether you are white or Black, Asian, Indian, no matter the color of your skin, no matter if you're gay, straight or something in between. It doesn't matter if you're Catholic, Protestant, Muslim, Jew, or choose not to believe. None of that matters. It doesn't matter what country you came from, what your last name is—what matters is we're Americans. We're all Americans. That under these colors of red, white, and blue—the colors that my parents fought for in World War II—means something around the world. It's obvious to me that you don't think of those colors the same way I do. It's obvious to me that you don't hold those values dear and the cause that I serve.

And lastly it is my deeply held belief that you're ruining the international order, and causing significant damage to our country overseas, that was fought for so hard by the Greatest Generation that they instituted in 1945. Between 1914 and 1945, 150 million people were slaughtered in the conduct of war. They were slaughtered because of tyrannies and dictatorships. That generation, like every generation, has fought against that, has fought against fascism, has fought against Nazism, has fought against extremism. It's now obvious to me that you don't understand that world order. You don't understand what the war was all about. In fact, you subscribe to many of the principles that we fought against. And I cannot be a party to that. It is with deep regret that I hereby submit my resignation.

But Milley did not send the letter. He had spent days apologizing and agonizing. He had called old friends, longtime mentors, his predecessors, his rivals. The voluble general had talked all around the problem. And then he decided. "Fuck that shit," he told his staff. "I'll just fight him."

Milley had listened to all the advice and decided that there was no benefit to himself or the country in stepping down now. The challenge was to stop Trump from doing any more damage and somehow pulling it off in a way that was consistent with the Constitution and his obligation to carry out the orders of his commander in chief. Yet the Constitution offered no practical guide for a general faced with a rogue president. Never before since the position had been created in 1949, or at least since Richard Nixon's final days in 1974, had a chairman of the Joint Chiefs encountered such a situation. "If they want to court-martial me, or put me in prison, have at it," Milley told his staff. "But I will fight from the inside." And he did.

The letter was dated June 8. One week earlier, on June 1, Trump had staged what would become the most infamous photo op of his presidency, marching across Lafayette Square minutes after it had been violently cleared of Black Lives Matter protesters, with a phalanx of his advisers behind him, to historic St. John's Church, which had suffered a small fire in its basement during the protests the night before. Milley and Defense Secretary Mark Esper had fallen in line right behind Trump, and the image of the burly general dressed in Army combat fatigues seemed to signal to the country that the United States under Trump was, finally, a nation at war with itself.

Milley knew right away that he had made a terrible mistake. "I think we've been duped," Esper said to him as they realized what was happening.[1] The president had been trying for three years to politicize and co-opt the military on his behalf and now he had done so. As Milley crossed the square, with the scent of tear gas in the air, he understood that he should not be there and had made his exit, quietly peeling away to his waiting black Chevy Suburban. But the damage was done. No one would care or remember that he was not in the final photo with Trump in front of the church; they had already seen him striding with the president on live television. Milley, a faithful Irish Catholic from outside Boston, realized this was his "road to Damascus moment," a few minutes of misjudgment that would haunt him forever.[2]

As always with Trump, however, there was an intense element of farce mixed with the fury, which made it hard for Milley or anyone else to discern what was really happening. Was this an actual authoritarian crackdown or just another politicized show in a presidency full of them? It certainly was a cringe-inducing spectacle when Trump strode across the emptied park where minutes earlier police had used tear gas and rubber bullets on peaceful protesters. At the church, Ivanka Trump, in heels and a sparkly face mask, extracted a Bible from her oversize white purse, a $1,500 number from Max Mara, and handed it to her father. Trump then brandished it for the cameras. Was it his family Bible? a reporter shouted at him. It was "*a* Bible," he replied.[3]

Bill Barr later described the entire Lafayette Square experience as a deeply uncomfortable one. As they began walking, Barr was near Milley and Esper, looking at Trump ahead of them, scowling, "and it just felt like: What the fuck is going on here?" Once the group made it to the church and Milley had peeled off, Barr tried to hide behind someone else, but Trump kept calling for him and Esper to be in the pictures. The attorney general was hardly opposed to a muscular display of force. Although he had not known about the photo op, he had approved a plan to clear the square earlier in the day to expand the security perimeter around the

White House and was surprised to learn it had not already taken place. But Barr regarded the president's handling of the situation as absurd theatrics, taking what should have been a more or less routine matter of crowd control and turning it into "the Battle of Midway." Besides, Barr knew that Trump's photo op was not just isolated folly for the cameras.

For days, in fact, the president had been arguing with advisers over how to respond to protests that had erupted outside his front door and in cities across the country since a Black man named George Floyd was killed by a white police officer in Minneapolis. The nation had been shocked by the deadly incident on the evening of May 25 when Officer Derek Chauvin pressed his knee on Floyd's neck for nine minutes as the handcuffed and subdued man cried for mercy and struggled to breathe. An onlooker filmed the scene on her phone and the video soon went viral, setting off a moment of racial reckoning. Most of the demonstrations were peaceful as tens of thousands of people in cities, including Washington, came out of their homes en masse for the first time during the pandemic and protested police brutality and racial injustice. But there were also eruptions of looting, street violence, and arson, including the burning of a police precinct in Minneapolis and an attack on the CNN Center in Atlanta.

Trump, long a believer in flooding the streets with law enforcement to put down civic unrest, immediately called for a forceful response. In the Oval Office the Friday after Floyd's death, Milley got into an argument with Stephen Miller, who was pushing Trump to invoke the Insurrection Act of 1807 to quell the protests using active-duty military.

"Mr. President," Miller said, "they are burning America down. Antifa, Black Lives Matter, they're burning it down. You have an insurrection on your hands. Barbarians are at the gate."

"Shut the fuck up, Stephen," Milley told others he had replied. "Shut the fuck up."

In another clash with Miller in the Oval Office, Milley had resorted to pointing at a painting of Abraham Lincoln on the wall. "That guy up there, Lincoln had an insurrection," Milley said. This was not the same thing.

Barr also pushed back. Harkening back to his first stint as attorney general, he explained to Trump that he had been in office the last two times the Insurrection Act was invoked, after Hurricane Hugo hit South Carolina in 1989 and during the Los Angeles riots that followed the Rodney King verdict in 1992. "I would be the last one to hesitate to use whatever force is necessary if it's really necessary," Barr recalled telling Trump, "but here it's clear we don't need it. It should be a break-glass option. It's a last resort. We can have some in the vicinity if we need them, but we're not going to need them."

On June 1, however, when Trump convened his top advisers that morning, he insisted on action. "We look weak," he told them. "We don't look strong." He demanded ten thousand troops. He wanted the Eighty-second Airborne Division called up. He wanted them outside the White House by nightfall. This time, Esper joined Barr and Milley in resisting. There was no need for the active-duty military, they told him. The National Guard was sufficient. Red-faced and agitated, Trump disagreed. "You're all losers!" he yelled. "Fucking losers!"[4] Trump insisted that Milley would have to take personal command of the operation. "Whoa, whoa, whoa, whoa, the military is not in charge of this, Mr. President," Milley responded. He added, "This is not a military responsibility—we will provide support as appropriate to a civilian agency. But we are not going to take the lead and be in charge of this." Only then did Trump reluctantly agree that Barr, as a civilian, would have the lead. But he made it clear that he wanted uniformed troops in the streets. He wanted thousands of them. He wanted *strength*. He even turned to Milley and asked, "Can't you just shoot them? Just shoot them in the legs or something?"[5]

Eventually, Trump was pulled out to go to the Situation Room for an 11 a.m. video call with the nation's governors. Trump opened the call by announcing that he was there with Milley—a true "fighter" and "war hero"—and that he was placing the chairman "in charge" of the government's response. Milley blanched. It was a what-the-fuck moment. Hadn't they just had this fight? "You have to dominate," Trump told the governors. "If you don't dominate, you're wasting your time. They're going to run all over you, you'll look like a bunch of jerks. You have to dominate, and you have to arrest people, and you have to try people and they have to go to jail for long periods of time."

Although they had been arguing with him before the call, Barr and Esper joined Trump in the macho posturing when Trump asked them to speak to the governors.

"Law enforcement response is not going to work unless we dominate the streets as the president said," Barr told them.

"I agree, we need to dominate the battlespace," Esper added.[6]

Esper and Milley would always swear they knew nothing in advance of the Lafayette Square photo op, which took place a few hours after the call with the governors. They had a different plan in mind, to tour the city reinforcing a message of calm with National Guard troops flooding into Washington. But the call and Esper's unfortunate "battlespace" comment quickly leaked to the media, provoking outrage all over again. Television cameras captured the Pentagon pair that night gladhanding with troops even as a National Guard helicopter buzzed a quiet Washington street.

It was another show of militarized force that gave every appearance of being part of a coordinated assault on behalf of a president who was pivoting his floundering re-election campaign to "LAW & ORDER!" Within hours, the White House reinforced the point, releasing a triumphal video of Trump's march through Lafayette Square, complete with stirring soundtrack.

The whole affair had been precipitated at least in part by the president's fury at being mocked on Twitter and television as "#BunkerBoy," following a report by Maggie Haberman in *The New York Times* that he had been taken to the White House's underground bunker the previous Friday.[7] Trump disputed the report, claiming falsely that his visit to the bunker was "more for an inspection" that had lasted only a "tiny, little, short period of time," a face-saving fiction later debunked by Bill Barr himself, who admitted that the president had to be sheltered underground for his safety.[8] A few days later, Kayleigh McEnany, the latest White House press secretary, announced to reporters with a straight face that Trump's walk to St. John's was just like Winston Churchill touring London during the Blitz.

Esper offered perhaps the lamest initial spin to justify his participation in the walk, telling NBC News the day after the photo op that he thought he was there to accompany the president as he met with troops and "inspected" a looted toilet in the park. "I didn't know where I was going," Esper said. "I wanted to see how much damage actually happened."[9]

His statement inflamed an already disastrous situation for the two top leaders of the nation's armed services. Esper appeared to be earning the unflattering nickname that had shadowed him since the beginning of his tenure, "Yesper," for what was seen as his habit of acceding to Trump's demands. Yet the president, according to other advisers, had little regard for Esper—in a tweet he once called him "Mark Esperanto" by mistake— and often bypassed him to deal directly with Milley.

Milley's dominance came with the price of being seen as Trump's handpicked general, however. When Trump chose Milley for the position in late 2018, it was meant as an explicit snub of Jim Mattis. Trump's advisers expected Milley to be more willing to do and say what the president wanted than his predecessor. His participation in the walk across Lafayette Square seemed to prove the point.

In fact, both Esper and Milley had harbored serious doubts about Trump long before the incident. Now, both were seriously considering resigning. But first they went into frantic damage control mode. The same night as Esper's disastrous interview with NBC, he stayed up until 2 a.m. writing a statement he planned to give the next morning in the Pentagon press room seeking to clarify, after two days of agonizing missteps, what he actually thought. And Milley worked on a letter to the troops he would send out reminding them of their duty to protect freedom of speech and of their oath to the Constitution. "We will stay true to that oath and the American people," Milley handwrote in the margins of the letter.[10]

The next morning, Esper convened his top aides, as well as Milley and Air Force General John Hyten, the vice chair of the Joint Chiefs, on a call to go over his statement, line by line, then went to the podium and read his remarks to reporters. He spoke of the horror of racism and the First Amendment right to protest. He also apologized for the unfortunate "battlespace" language. And he did something that few expected, which was to explicitly rebut Trump. He opposed the use of active-duty troops to deal with the unrest in the streets and the use of the Insurrection Act, which was only for "the most urgent and dire of situations," Esper said. This, he added pointedly, was not one of them.

Esper closed on a note sure to infuriate Trump. "Most importantly, I want to assure all of you and all Americans that the Department of Defense, the Armed Services, our uniformed leaders, our civilian leaders and I take seriously our oath to support and defend the Constitution of the United States and to safeguard those very rights contained in that document we cherish so dearly," Esper said. In the choice between founding document and Trump, he seemed to be saying, he would choose the Constitution.[11] Milley greeted Esper in his office afterward. "Great job," he said. The president, he warned, "is going to rip your face off."

In one of those unlucky accidents of scheduling, Esper and Milley were due at the White House for a meeting on Afghanistan with Trump. Esper now said that he did not want to go.

"It's going to be ugly," he told Milley, and asked the chairman and General Frank McKenzie, the Central Command chief, to go without him. "Tell the president I have a dentist appointment," he joked.

Milley urged him to reconsider. "What's he going to do? Yell at you?" Milley said.

Eventually, the defense chief decided to face Trump's wrath sooner rather than later. "If we're going to have a showdown, let's have a showdown," he said.

Arriving in the Oval Office, Milley had not even sat down before Trump started screaming at Esper. It was, Milley later recalled, "the worst reaming out" he had ever heard. Other advisers in the room remained silent. "You betrayed me!" Trump yelled. "I'm the president, not you." He had no right, Trump said, to disagree on the Insurrection Act. "You took away my authority."[12] When Esper defended himself, pointing out that he had simply explained in public the position he had already taken in private with Trump, the president roared louder. Esper pulled out a copy of the transcript of his remarks. Trump appeared even angrier. "I don't care a fuck about your fucking transcript!" he shouted. Eventually, he turned to Milley and said, "You're fucked up too!" Then he turned to the others in the room. "You're all fucked up!" he added.

From that point forward, there was little doubt among White House officials—or Esper himself—what would happen to the defense secretary. They were convinced that Trump would fire him as soon as he felt he could. Trump, Mark Meadows, and Robert O'Brien, the national security adviser, told others they had been blindsided by the Esper statement to the press that morning. "Mark Meadows and the president had made a judgment at that point that he was not trustworthy, that he was not sufficiently loyal," a senior White House adviser recalled. "That's what sealed his fate."

Eventually, Trump's tirade was interrupted by a reminder that they had people waiting for them in the Situation Room. The entire group then went downstairs. Mike Pompeo caught Esper's eye as he walked in. "Courage never quits," the secretary of state said quietly to the beleaguered secretary of defense—the motto of their West Point class.[13] Trump hardly seemed in a decisive, or even rational, frame of mind. But he was still the commander in chief, and the subject on the agenda that day was his demand, once again, to withdraw from Afghanistan.

"Make them fire you," Bob Gates told Mark Milley when he called in the days after Lafayette Square. "Don't resign." The former defense secretary told Mark Esper the same thing when he called too.

Milley had been making phone calls, sending up flares. He reached out to Joe Dunford, the predecessor whose tenure had ended awkwardly when Trump shoved him aside early to announce Milley's appointment, as well as to mentors such as retired General James Dubik, now a thoughtful expert on military ethics. He called political contacts as well, including members of Congress and former Bush and Obama administration officials. Milley asked Colin Powell, the former chairman of the Joint Chiefs and secretary of state, if he should quit. "Fuck no!" Powell said, although he could not resist reminding Milley, "I told you never to take the job. You never should have taken the job. Trump's a fucking maniac."[14]

Most of his counselors offered Milley variations of what he heard from Gates, who had served both Bush and Obama, perhaps the last example of a senior cabinet official willing to cross party lines. Milley, who as a colonel had been Gates's military adviser, had long sought his advice about Trump. "My sense is Mark had a pretty accurate measure of the man pretty quickly," Gates would recall. "He would tell me over time, well before June 1, some of the absolutely crazy notions that were put forward in the Oval Office, crazy ideas from the president, things about using or not using military force, the immediate withdrawal from Afghanistan, pulling out of South Korea. It just went on and on."

Milley was not the only senior official to seek Gates's counsel. Many members of Trump's national security team had made the pilgrimage out to his home in Washington state over the past two years. Jim Mattis had been appointed to two different commands by Gates. John Kelly had been his senior military assistant when Gates was defense secretary. Gates would pour them a drink, grill them some salmon, and help them wrestle with the latest Trump conundrum. "The problem with resignation is you can only fire that gun once," he told them. All the conversations were variations on a theme: "How do I walk us back from the ledge? How do I keep this from happening because it would be a terrible thing for the country?"

This time, Gates told both Milley and Esper that they needed to stay in the Pentagon as long as they could given Trump's increasingly erratic and dangerous behavior. His reasoning was that "if you resign, you make it easy for them—for him." Most likely, Gates told them, "if you resign, it's a one-day story. If you're fired, it makes it clear you were standing up for the right thing." Gates, a savvy student of Washington power politics, advised Milley that he had another important card and urged him to play it. "The other piece of advice I gave to him was to keep the chiefs on board with you and make it clear to the White House that if you go, they all go, so that the White House knows this isn't just about firing Mark Milley, this is about the entire Joint Chiefs of Staff quitting in response."

Publicly, Lafayette Square looked like a debacle for Milley. Admiral Mike Mullen, a former Joint Chiefs chairman, said he was "sickened" by the thuggish display of armed force.[15] Several retired generals publicly called on Milley to resign, pointing out that the leader of the racially diverse military with more than 200,000 Black troops could not be seen opposing a movement for racial justice. Even Mattis, who had refrained from publicly criticizing Trump and published a memoir citing a "duty of silence" to the current commander in chief, issued a critical statement about the "bizarre photo op." Mattis said he was "angry" and "appalled" by the week's events, warned against "militarizing our response" to protests, and blamed Trump for three years of "deliberate effort" to divide the country.[16] People close to Mattis told *The Washington Post* at the time that he had been motivated to write his scathing broadside in part because of the image of Milley parading through the streets of Washington in combat fatigues.

Whatever their personal differences, Mattis and Milley both knew that there was a tragic inevitability to the moment. Throughout his presidency, Trump had sought to redefine the role of the military in American public life. He never recognized the boundaries that other presidents had. He had campaigned in 2016 as a supporter of torture and other methods that the military considered war crimes. He had ordered thousands of troops to the southern border to combat a fake "invasion" by a caravan of illegal immigrants just before the 2018 midterms. In 2019, he had intervened to spare a Navy SEAL accused of murdering a captive ISIS fighter and attempted murder of civilians in Iraq, undermining military justice and the chain of command. The photo-op-loving president had used the uniformed generals as props in his political stagecraft going back to the first days of his presidency when he signed his executive order barring immigrants from a number of Muslim-majority countries at the Pentagon with an uncomfortable Mattis standing behind him.

Many considered Trump's consequence-free 2018 decision to use the military in his pre-election border stunt as "the predicate—or the harbinger—of 2020," as Peter Feaver, a Duke University expert on civil-military relations who taught the subject to generals at command school, put it. When Milley, who had been among Feaver's students, called for advice after Lafayette Square, Feaver told him to apologize but to resist the calls for resignation. "It would have been a mistake," Feaver said. "We have no tradition of resignation in protest amongst the military." One argument Feaver made is that resigning over a controversial but legal decision by the president is "very, very subversive of civilian control." Another argument was practical. Trump and his White House would inevitably seek to politicize the military even more in response, ensuring that whoever succeeded Milley would be a loyalist who blindly followed orders. "You can be damn sure that the person that they replace you with is going to be as MAGA as they can find, so they will never ever put Trump in that bind again," Feaver told Milley. "So it's a cure worse than the disease."

Whether or not he resigned, Milley understood that he would have to speak out. He decided to use a commencement address at the National Defense University already on his schedule the following week for an apology. As with the resignation letter he continued to write and rewrite, Milley sought comment on the speech from many quarters. Feaver's counsel was to own up to the error but make it clear that the mistake was his and not Trump's. Presidents, after all, "are allowed to do political stunts. That's part of being president."

In the end, Milley's apology, like the man, was blunt and unequivocal. "I should not have been there," Milley said in the prerecorded address, wearing his dress uniform and looking straight at the camera, a backdrop of service flags behind him. He did not mention Trump. "My presence in that moment, and in that environment, created a perception of the military involved in domestic politics." It was, he added, "a mistake that I have learned from."[17]

Milley's apology tour was private as well as public. With the presidential election fueling Trump's urgency, the general sought to get the message to Democrats that he was not going along with any further efforts by Trump to subvert the machinery of war toward domestic political ends. He called both Nancy Pelosi and Chuck Schumer. "After the Lafayette Square episode, Milley was extremely contrite and communicated to any number of people that he had no intention of playing Trump's game any longer," as Robert Bauer, the former Obama White House counsel who was then advising the Biden campaign, recalled. "He was really burned by that experience. He was appalled. He apologized for it and it was pretty clear he was digging his heels in."

This message was received, so much so that it may have caused Democrats to underestimate the threat that Trump would ultimately pose to the peaceful transfer of power. As decisions were made that summer about preparations for the election and its potentially messy legal aftermath, Bauer said, "I just didn't think on any legal, institutional, leadership level that there was any chance that Trump could just say, 'I really like it here and I don't feel like leaving.'"

On Capitol Hill, however, some Democrats were skeptical of Milley. To them, Lafayette Square proved that he had been a Trumpist all along. "There was a huge misunderstanding about Milley," recalled Adam Smith, the House Armed Services Committee chairman who was close to the general. "A lot of my Democratic colleagues after June 1 were concerned about him." Smith had worked closely with Milley throughout the Trump years, first when Milley was Army chief of staff and then when he was chairman. The congressman assured other Democrats they were wrong, that "there was never a single solitary moment where Milley was going to do anything to help Trump do anything that shouldn't be done."

Among the skeptics was Pelosi, who felt burned by how Milley had dealt with Congress earlier that year when Trump ordered the killing of Iranian commander Qassim Suleimani without briefing congressional leaders in advance. Milley had been given the lead in the operation and Smith said Pelosi believed the chairman was "evasive" and disrespectful of Congress's role as a coequal branch. Milley, for his part, felt he could not disregard Trump's insistence that lawmakers not be notified—a breach due to the president's pique over the impeachment proceedings against him. "The navigation of Trumpworld was more difficult for Milley than Nancy gives him credit for," Smith said. He vouched for the chairman as a "total straight shooter," but he never convinced the speaker.

Afghanistan was not the only pressing national security issue on which Milley and Esper found themselves at odds with Trump after Lafayette Square. Even as he was ordering an intimidating show of force at home, Trump was deciding to withdraw tens of thousands of troops from Germany because he was furious with Angela Merkel. The Germany problem would now become another huge irritant in the troubled dealings between the Pentagon's leadership and the president.

A few days earlier, Merkel had informed Trump in a phone call that, because of the ongoing Covid lockdowns, she would not attend the G7 summit he was insisting on holding in Washington in late June. "No, I'm not going to come," Merkel told him. "We have rules in Germany, we have rules in Europe. I'm not going to be a leader who's going to ignore rules." Trump tried to change her mind. When that did not work, the president called Emmanuel Macron in France "to get Macron to convince her," a senior European diplomat said. The next day, Robert O'Brien called Merkel's ambassador in Washington, Emily Haber, and urged her to get Merkel to come. But that was impossible.

In part, the decision reflected Merkel's conclusion that there was nothing to be gained anymore from dealing with Trump in person. She was sick and tired of him. Once, when an adviser urged her to go to Washington to talk with the president, she replied: "I see him a lot. I see him at the

G7 meetings. I see him at the G20 meetings. I see him at NATO meetings and every time we meet, he promises something and then goes to the press and he bashes me. Why should I give him the opportunity?"

After a couple days of unsuccessfully lobbying Merkel, Trump announced the cancellation of the G7 summit altogether. The pandemic made it impossible to have the meeting in person, as Merkel's decision made clear. "It wasn't going to work anyway, frankly," a senior State Department official recalled. "But she was the one who first gave voice to it."

Trump was peeved in the extreme, calling the collection of close allies "very outdated" and inviting Russia to rejoin the group for a September gathering.[18] Europeans quickly rejected the idea of welcoming Russia back to the G7 it had been kicked out of after the 2014 invasion of Ukraine, but Trump was undaunted, and called Vladimir Putin to formally propose the plan on the morning of June 1, hours before marching through Lafayette Square.

Trump's retaliation against Merkel was swift. On June 2, Esper was stunned to receive an official written directive from Trump, essentially giving the Pentagon until the end of September to withdraw ten thousand of the thirty-five thousand American troops stationed in Germany. It was the only such direct order from the president that Esper would receive in his time as defense secretary, and despite its enormous national security implications, it had gone through no normal decision-making process. "This is reckless," Esper immediately protested to Robert O'Brien. "We can't do this in ninety days."

Ric Grenell, the ambassador to Germany who had clashed with Merkel's government before being brought back to Washington to take over as acting director of national intelligence, had been pushing for months for such punitive troop cuts, backed by O'Brien. But Trump had only approved them now, in the heat of his anger. "Do you know why the withdrawal of the troops happened?" asked a senior German official. "Because she said 'no' when he called her." A few days later, the decision leaked to *The Wall Street Journal* before Germany, NATO, or even the State Department was formally notified. Eventually, the White House even sent a formal tasking to the Pentagon to produce a plan for withdrawing all troops from Germany or Europe or both—just like the one that the White House had sent over two years earlier when Trump blew up the NATO summit by threatening to pull out of the alliance.

At the Pentagon, Esper and Milley were looking at a costly logistical mess. Most of the troops were not there to protect Germany, but because the country was a significant base of operations for the United

States throughout the world. It served as headquarters for military commands for Europe and Africa, as well as the main medical evacuation facility for American personnel outside the United States. Trump wanted to bring them all back to the United States, an idea he raised repeatedly with Pentagon leaders. "Mr. President, we can't do that," Esper told him at a June 29 meeting. Even after Trump acceded, Meadows continued to press the point. "Why can't we bring them home?" he demanded. Esper decided to take Trump's word as final and ignored the chief of staff. Ultimately, they got the president to agree that of 11,900 troops to be removed from Germany, 6,400 would be sent home and more than 5,500 would be repositioned elsewhere in Europe. Both the European and Africa command headquarters would be relocated.

There was also the matter of what message this sent the Russians. Milley and Esper negotiated with the Germans over the delicate language of the official announcement. Their concern, shared by the allies, was that Trump had just made a destabilizing decision that would embolden Putin by demonstrating America's lack of commitment to Europe. "We wouldn't want the Russians to see the U.S. and NATO like this," a senior German official said. "It's a dangerous thing if you send a message out there that between two major allies there's a significant rift."

The statement, released in late July, tried to reframe the move as an effort to "strengthen NATO, enhance the deterrence of Russia," and increase the flexibility of the American military.[19] Minutes after its release, however, Trump told reporters at the White House that those were not the real reasons at all. American troops "are there to protect Germany, right? And Germany is supposed to pay for it," Trump said. "Germany's not paying for it. We don't want to be the suckers anymore. The United States has been taken advantage of for twenty-five years, both on trade and security. So we're reducing the force because they're not paying their bills."[20] But Trump had been complaining about "suckers" and unpaid bills for years without actually ordering troops withdrawn. The simple truth was that this was happening now because Merkel had refused to come to Washington in the middle of a public health crisis, thus ruining Trump's plans to use the G7 summit as a stage set for his "Pandemic? What pandemic?" re-election campaign.

Trump was not done picking fights with the Pentagon either. If anything, Lafayette Square inspired him to make the military another front in the culture wars that he believed would help win the election. With many Americans after the George Floyd killing repulsed by white supremacist symbols in prominent places around the country, including Confederate flags and bases named in honor of Confederate generals at numerous military installations, Trump renewed his stand in favor of them.

Esper and Milley pushed back on that too. Soon after Lafayette Square, Trump overruled Milley in an Oval Office conversation when the general urged him to support renaming bases bearing the names of Confederate generals, such as Fort Bragg in North Carolina and Fort Benning in Georgia. Milley called Bragg and Benning and the rest "traitors." Trump the native New Yorker claimed he did not want to insult the nation's "heritage." His Southern chief of staff, Mark Meadows, enthusiastically supported him. So did Keith Kellogg, the NATO-bashing retired general formally on Mike Pence's staff. To make sure his defense chiefs got the point, Trump then tweeted it out. "These Monumental and very Powerful Bases have become part of a Great American Heritage," he wrote. "Our history as the Greatest Nation in the World will not be tampered with. Respect our Military!"

Esper and Milley later infuriated Trump by publicly supporting a congressional measure to proceed with the renaming, a bill that eventually passed the Republican-controlled Senate as well as the Democratic House. In July, following the lead of the Marines, Esper also issued a new Pentagon policy that effectively barred the display of the Confederate flag on military installations, despite Trump's support of such displays as "freedom of speech."

How long could this standoff between the Pentagon and the president go on? Many mornings for the next few months, Milley woke up not knowing whether he would be fired before the day was over. His wife told him she was shocked he had not been cashiered outright when he made his apology. Esper, in his office one floor directly above Milley's, was also on notice. The day after Trump's explosive tirade, Mark Meadows called Esper at home—three times—to get him to recant his opposition to invoking the Insurrection Act. When he refused, Meadows took "the Tony Soprano approach," as Esper later wrote, threatening him before eventually backing off.[21] Esper resolved to stay as long as he could, "to endure all the shit and run out the clock," as he put it, and tried to follow the advice from Alex Azar, another cabinet officer often on Trump's target list during this pandemic. Make yourself scarce, Azar counseled. Avoid the White House and stay out of Trump's line of fire. Esper felt he had a particular responsibility to hold on. By law, the only person authorized to deploy troops other than the president is the secretary of defense. He was determined not to hand that power off to the likes of Robert O'Brien or Ric Grenell.

Both Esper and Milley found new purpose in waiting out the president. "They both expected, literally on a daily basis, to be fired," Gates recalled. Milley "would call me and essentially say, 'I may not last until tomorrow night.' And he was comfortable with that. He felt like he knew he was going to support the Constitution and there were no two ways about it."

After his remorseful commencement address, Milley had had his own confrontation with Trump. It was not the expletive-filled rant that Esper experienced. But Trump made clear his unhappiness. He was seated at the Resolute Desk in the Oval Office as Milley stood—the president's preferred position for showing visitors who was in charge. "Why did you apologize?" he demanded. "It's a sign of weakness."

"Mr. President, not where I come from," Milley replied. "When you make a mistake, you go to confession, you say ten Hail Marys and five Our Fathers, and you move on. You ask for forgiveness, but you move on."

Trump had not moved on. "Aren't you proud to have walked with the president?" he asked.

Milley said it was not about Trump. "What I was apologizing for was me. My actions. I was in uniform and I was getting the uniform involved in political action." Milley insisted that he had a responsibility to own up to his mistake and to clarify how wrong it was for a uniformed officer to take part in such an explicitly political event. "I don't expect you to understand that, Mr. President," he said. "It's an ethic for us, a duty."

Trump would later confirm that this was a turning point for him too. "I saw at that moment he had no courage or skill," the president said after leaving office.[22] Whatever he had hoped to find in Milley when he was using him to get back at Jim Mattis, Trump had been disappointed by yet another general. Their fight over calling out the military, as with most involving Trump, never really ended. For the rest of the summer, the president would demand troops in the streets, would threaten, once again, to invoke the Insurrection Act. Whenever he saw something on Fox News, it seemed to Milley, he would be ordering up "ten thousand troops." And he was never sorry about Lafayette Square. Quite the opposite, in fact. Trump loved the scowling photograph of himself brandishing the Bible in front of the church so much that he signed a copy for Doug Mills, the legendary White House photographer for *The New York Times*.

Back in his office at the Pentagon, Milley put the resignation letter away in his desk and drew up a plan. It was a guide for how to get through the next few months. For how to fight from the inside. It had four goals:

First, make sure Trump did not start an unnecessary war overseas. Second, make sure that the military was not used in the streets against the American people for the purpose of keeping Trump in power. Third, maintain the military's integrity. And fourth, maintain his own integrity. He would refer back to them often.

Even in June, Milley understood it was not just a matter of making it until the presidential election on November 3. He knew that Election Day might be the beginning, not the end, of the challenges Trump would pose. The portents were worrisome. Barely one week before Lafayette Square, Trump had sent out a tweet that would soon become a refrain. The 2020 presidential race, he warned for the first time, would end up as "the greatest Rigged Election in history." The date that Milley was now aiming for, the focus of all his fears and anxieties, was January 20.

CHAPTER 25

The Divider

Trump was stewing in the Oval Office. He hated being criticized on Fox News. The continuing street unrest around the country in the wake of the George Floyd killing had provoked a predictable backlash in conservative media, which was now turning on the president for not doing more to reestablish order. Trump was aggravated at Tucker Carlson for questioning his toughness.

Trump turned to Alyssa Farah, a former aide to Mark Meadows on Capitol Hill who had worked for the administration for years and had been tapped by the chief of staff as the president's strategic communications director. "Call Tucker and let him know we're going to do more," he instructed. "We're going to crack down. We're deploying federal law enforcement." Farah said she would. But after she left the Oval Office and before she could even dial the Fox host's number, her own phone rang. It was Meadows doubling down. "You need to do it immediately," he insisted. Trump was agitated.

The president was leaving for a trip and on the ride out to Joint Base Andrews, Farah tracked down Carlson. The host began shouting at her. One line in particular stuck in her memory. "These animals," he screamed, "these thugs looted Hermès!" For several minutes, Carlson railed at her about the riots and what he saw as the president's failure to respond more vigorously. It seemed abusive, even unhinged. After Air Force One took off, she entered the president's cabin. "I talked with Tucker," she reported, then left it at that without saying how he had responded.

Even in the context of the president's symbiotic relationship with Fox, Carlson occupied a singular place in the Trump universe. The other hosts sometimes prodded or pushed Trump, but ultimately were on his side. Sean Hannity was a regular confidant off air and willing collaborator on air. Jeanine Pirro was a reliable cheerleader. Sometimes Lou Dobbs or Laura Ingraham would take shots at the president, but they never bothered him as much as Carlson, who was willing to go after Trump head-on, as he had at the beginning of the pandemic. The wavy-haired evening host had once fashioned himself as a bow-tie-wearing reincarnation of William F. Buckley, the very personification of the conservative establishment. But in recent years he had rebranded himself as a race-baiting populist, whipping up his audience with nightly fulminations in support of America First isolationism. Often, he was more Trumpy than Trump. He was, in short, a potential threat who appealed directly to Trump's most fervent supporters. To some of his advisers, Trump seemed almost afraid of Carlson. "I think he thought that Tucker's more popular than I am and could potentially run and beat me with my base," one adviser said.

Highlighting images of looting and cars burning in the streets as some of the racial justice protests turned violent, Carlson had been sharply critical of Trump on his show. "You can regularly say embarrassing things on television," Carlson said one night at the beginning of June even as the president was promising to dominate the streets. "You can hire Omarosa to work at the White House. All of that will be forgiven if you protect your people. But if you don't protect them—or worse, if you seem like you can't be bothered to protect them—then you're done. It's over. People will not forgive weakness."[1]

Nothing bothered Trump more than a suggestion that he might be weak. Which, of course, Carlson knew well when he said it. "I'm getting killed," Trump railed at aides at one point. "Tucker is talking to millions of people."[2]

It was all about the base. For Trump, the only Americans who really counted were the ones who supported him. His entire approach as a politician was about feeding them the red meat that would keep them energized and angry at whoever was the enemy of the day. Often and not at all coincidentally, Trump seized on adversaries who were people of color or their white allies among the coastal elites of Blue America.

In the White House, Trump advisers often explained the president's single-minded attention to the base as a response to the constant investigations targeting him, a reaction to feeling besieged that drove him to stick with those he perceived to be most loyal. How could he reach out to people like Nancy Pelosi bent on his destruction? Yet Trump's penchant for pugilism long predated the Mueller probe. He was genetically an in-your-face figure who needed enemies real or imagined. As a politician, that made him inordinately dependent on his base, perhaps even fearful of it at times. Television hosts like Tucker Carlson were his barometer for the state of his relationship with his own voters.

Heading into the 2020 election, Trump seemed to believe that he could win again by replicating the polarizing strategy that worked in 2016, however much of a fluke its success had been. He made no effort to expand his predominantly white, rural-and-rich coalition. In his first couple years in office, he traveled nearly five times as often to states that backed him as to those that had supported Hillary Clinton. He gave nearly four times as many interviews to Fox News as to all the other major networks combined. His social media advertising was aimed disproportionately at older Americans who were the superstructure of his original campaign. He acted as though he was the president of Trump's America, not the president of all Americans.

The twin crises of 2020 would only amplify that. Rather than try to bring the country together to combat the deadliest pandemic in a century, he eagerly turned it into a culture war over masks and lockdowns. And rather than try to heal the racial wounds ripped open by the grotesque police killing of a Black man in their custody, he declared himself a "law and order president" fighting the "racist" Black Lives Matter movement.

Trump's obsession with the base worried some of his team. He had pulled off an improbable win in 2016 by cobbling together a victory in the Electoral College despite losing the national popular vote by three million, but plenty of seasoned advisers thought it was folly to expect lightning to strike twice in the same way.

Among them was Bill Barr, who had watched George H. W. Bush go down in 1992 and thought Trump was heading in the same direction. The attorney general had approached Jared Kushner in the spring to warn him. "People are tired of the fucking drama and chaos," Barr told him, and voters would blame Trump if he did not change course. Kushner agreed and said he had been trying to enlist others to make the same point to the president, an intervention of sorts. At Kushner's urging, Trump invited Barr to meet in April and listened as the attorney general told him that his strategy would not work.

"You're going to lose the election because you're focusing only on your base," Barr told him. "Your base is with you and they are going to turn out. But the election, I think, is going to be over a very small segment of voters, independents and Republicans in the suburbs, who think you're an asshole."

Trump did not think much of that. "I *need* my base," he told Barr. "I need to fight. My opponents are vicious."[3]

Chris Christie also saw defeat on the horizon. He drafted a three-page memo arguing that 2020 was not 2016. "Your team is taking the same approach as four years ago and expecting the same result," Christie wrote, pointedly placing blame on advisers in hopes of not making Trump defensive. "It will not happen. By taking the same approach, we are making this race a referendum on you rather than a binary choice between you and Vice President Biden. You will lose a referendum that looks backwards under the current circumstances."[4] To get Trump's attention, Christie underlined the last sentence. But his recommendation that the president run a positive, forward-looking, optimistic campaign under the rubric of leading a "Great American Comeback" belied Trump's essential nature.

Other advisers were urging the president to be more aggressive against Joe Biden, who had consolidated the Democratic Party after a slow start and convinced voters he was the best-positioned candidate to take on Trump in the fall. Tony Fabrizio, one of Trump's pollsters, drafted a memo reporting that the president was trailing in key states. "We have seen the enemy and the enemy is us," Fabrizio wrote.[5] It would be hard to increase Trump's positive numbers, he added, so what they needed was to bring down Biden.

Trump was not resisting because he did not want to attack Biden. He loved to attack. Instead, he worried that he could demolish Biden too early with a sustained political assault, leading Democrats to dump him for another nominee at their convention. "I know that there is some concern (which I strenuously disagree with) that if we go after Biden too soon, we can collapse him, and the Dems will replace him at their convention," Fabrizio wrote. "I know POTUS tends to share this opinion. But whether or not they can steal it from Biden is quickly becoming a moot point."[6]

Trump was so disconnected from reality that he became gripped by fear that the Democrats would throw over Biden and name a stronger ticket with Governor Andrew Cuomo of New York as their presidential candidate and Michelle Obama as his vice presidential running mate, an absurdity to anyone who understood politics generally or how much the former first lady hated politics specifically. At the time, Cuomo was a darling of Democrats and the media because of his empathetic daily briefings during the coronavirus crisis that contrasted so much with Trump's own blustery, bleach-endorsing spectacles. No one realized that Cuomo's mishandling of nursing homes and, later, allegations of sexual misconduct would soon sink his career. But the notion that Democrats would overturn the will of their own primary voters was ludicrous, suggesting how out of touch the president had become.

Unable to persuade Trump, Brad Parscale, his campaign manager, summoned reinforcements, convincing the president to invite Karl Rove, the veteran Republican strategist and a longtime Trump skeptic who, like many in the GOP establishment, had stopped short of fully disavowing him, to hear his assessment. Rove was flabbergasted that the president believed this far-fetched Andrew Cuomo–Michelle Obama scenario but agreed to come.

He arrived at the White House on May 13 and was screened for Covid before being ushered into the Oval Office. There were about fifteen others there, which freaked Rove out because it had been months since he had been in a room with so many people, but the mask-less president and his team seemed oblivious to social distancing.

Trump opened up with his theory. "Biden is so weak, so weak, I'm hearing the Obama people are going to replace him with Andrew Cuomo," Trump said. "I can beat him, I can beat him, but it's going to be tougher."

"With all due respect, that's idiotic," Rove said. "If he died tomorrow, they would nominate Bernie Sanders."

Trump was unconvinced. "Michelle, Michelle, she might be the running mate," he insisted.

"No way, no way," Rove said. What he was thinking, but did not say out loud, was, *Goddamn it, you're the village idiot if you think this.*

Rove argued that Trump had already waited too long to define his opponent. By this point in the 2004 cycle, when Rove was running his re-election campaign, George W. Bush had already painted John Kerry as a flip-flopping elitist, and by spring of 2012, Obama had already defined Mitt Romney as a heartless, job-killing plutocrat. "You have to disqualify your opponent," Rove said. "You're late."

The task was admittedly harder for Trump than for his predecessors. As long as the nation's consuming focus was the coronavirus, the campaign was effectively a referendum on Trump and that was a dynamic his team feared he could not win. If the choice for Americans was do you want four more years of Trump or not, he would lose. "We basically were one foot in the grave, one foot on a banana peel," as a senior campaign adviser put it. They had to find a way to change the equation.

So when George Floyd was killed, Trump was pulled between the imperatives of calming the nation, as a president was expected to do, and stirring his voters up even more, as both his personality and his own sense of politics dictated. There was never any question which Trump would choose.

Jared Kushner was the first senior official in the West Wing to recognize the power of the Floyd case. "The biggest story in the world is about to be what's happening in Minneapolis," he said soon after the killing. It took days for others in the White House to catch up.

But Kushner's instinct for pacification ran counter to his father-in-law's inclination for provocation. Kushner tried to reach out to African American leaders and celebrities, while pushing for "listening sessions." At one point, he wanted to get Kanye West to come to the White House for a religious service and even convinced Kim Kardashian West, but Trump rejected the idea. Kushner did manage to persuade his father-in-law to sign an order meant to leverage federal grant money to encourage police departments to adopt better practices and bolster training but it stopped short of an outright ban on chokeholds or other measures sought by protesters.

The blowup in the streets—and Trump's swift effort to exploit it—undercut what Kushner thought of as one of the president's most important achievements, and his own. However improbable, given his father-in-law's penchant for race-baiting, Kushner had spent significant time in the White House trying to build new bridges to the Black community. He had steered Trump into signing the criminal justice reform bill, ultimately one of Trump's few bipartisan legislative accomplishments. Now he was watching any goodwill among Black leaders that he had hoped to generate in time for the election evaporate.

Instead, Trump seemed to be channeling Richard Nixon circa 1968, the height of Vietnam and civil rights protests, filling his Twitter feed with phrases famous from the Nixon lexicon like "LAW & ORDER" and "SILENT MAJORITY." With his talk of "shooting" looters and turning "vicious dogs" and "ominous weapons" on "thugs" in the street, Trump arguably went beyond Nixon to emulate the segregationist George Wallace's even more bellicose campaign that year.

Trump had never cared much about criminal justice reform. That was Kushner's deal. To the extent he saw it as his administration's success, Trump had grown increasingly resentful that Black Americans were not more grateful to him for it, lashing out at Kushner for making him sign the legislation in the first place. When he was first shown the video of

Floyd's killing while on Air Force One heading to Florida, aides said later that the president was genuinely horrified and sickened. But his revulsion was quickly overcome by anger at the resulting protests, and his instinct was more Richard Daley than Martin Luther King Jr.

Staying up late watching images of Minneapolis in flames, Trump even echoed the late Chicago mayor who ordered police to "shoot to kill arsonists" and "shoot to maim looters" after the riots that followed King's assassination. "Any difficulty and we will assume control but, when the looting starts, the shooting starts," Trump typed out on Twitter late one night, hitting send at 12:53 a.m. By morning, Trump's chagrined staff tried to save him from himself, proposing they tell the media that all he meant was that more rioting would inevitably escalate and that the president condemned all violence.

"Oh, no, no," he said. That was not what he meant. "What I meant is if they loot, we will shoot them." So much for pleading misunderstanding.

Alyssa Farah, the communications adviser, urged him to walk it back with a new tweet anyway and drafted multiple versions. He finally agreed to a statement declaring that his middle-of-the-night message was simply stating "a fact" and that he was not encouraging further violence. "I don't want this to happen, and that's what the expression put out last night means," it said, which, as with most walk-backs issued in Trump's name, was hardly sincere.

A few days after Floyd's death, aides convinced him to add some lines at the top of a speech at the Kennedy Space Center in Florida marking the launch of the first manned SpaceX rocket to the International Space Station. "The death of George Floyd on the streets of Minneapolis was a grave tragedy," Trump said, reading from the script they gave him. "It should never have happened. It has filled Americans all over the country with horror, anger and grief." But his remarks on a Saturday afternoon, typically a media dead zone, attracted little attention, which simply made him bitter that he had gone along with aides in the first place. The more revealing part of his statement came when he condemned not the killing, but the violent response to it. "The memory of George Floyd is being dishonored by rioters, looters and anarchists," Trump said, a line he would repeat versions of many times that summer.[7]

Where other leaders saw an overdue moment of racial reckoning, Trump saw an opportunity. Without much of a campaign theme and with the country still hobbled by the coronavirus, suddenly Trump had a law-and-order message. He would channel the backlash among white Americans and position himself as the defender of American heritage against the forces of political correctness. This was the best chance he had of changing the subject from the pandemic at a time when he was trailing Joe Biden by 10 percentage points in public polls.[8] His base would love it.

He quickly browbeat Democratic governors and mayors for being weak in responding to rioting and looting, denounced Black Lives Matter as a "symbol of hate," and lambasted NASCAR for kowtowing to the left by banning Confederate flags at its races. He mocked Democrats for embracing activists' call to "defund the police." He denied the existence of systemic racism. Police brutality, he opined, was just the work of a few "bad apples."[9] He seized on the excesses of the other side. When leftist protesters blocked off a six-block section of Seattle and declared it a police-free "Capitol Hill Autonomous Zone," after the name of a local neighborhood, Trump repeatedly assailed Democratic leaders.

"Take back your city NOW," he tweeted. "If you don't do it, I will."

"Make us all safe," Mayor Jenny Durkan retorted. "Go back to your bunker."[10]

Trump, in fact, was determined not to remain in the White House anymore, in the bunker or otherwise. After months largely caged at the executive mansion, he wanted to resume campaign rallies and bring his new "Law & Order" campaign theme directly to his voters. Brad Parscale suggested a car rally at the Florida State Fairgrounds in Tampa where supporters could remain in their vehicles, safe from Covid. But Trump rejected that. He wanted a real rally with a real crowd in a real arena, just like the pre-pandemic days.

Parscale then approached Mike Pence in a White House hallway. "What's one state we could pull it off in?" he asked. Oklahoma, Pence obligingly answered. It had a low infection rate and would be safer than many other places. It was also a staunchly pro-Trump state with a Republican leadership that would not balk at a crowded indoor rally. The vice president who was supposed to be leading efforts to curb the virus was increasingly conforming himself to Trump's wishes to pretend it was no longer a threat. Pence had even published an op-ed in *The Wall Street Journal* declaring that there was no "second wave" of the pandemic, weeks before the second wave would crest.[11]

The Trump team set the rally for June 19, with the president's predominantly white campaign staff oblivious to the fact that it was a holiday known as Juneteenth, marking the day in 1865 when the last state was notified of the Emancipation Proclamation. Nor did Trump's advisers realize that Tulsa was the historic site of one of America's worst race riots. Had the president wanted to send an explicit message of disdain for the

Black community, he could hardly have designed a more perfect blunder. When it all blew up, Parscale tried to convince the president to go through with the rally anyway, enlisting Sean Hannity to call Trump to tell him it was all right to proceed. Just find twenty Black supporters to put onstage behind you, he wanted Hannity to advise Trump, so they would appear on camera. But a week before the event, at 11:23 p.m., Trump, without telling Parscale, tweeted that he would move the rally from the following Friday to Saturday.

The campaign turned out to have problems with Tulsa beyond poor timing and racial insensitivity. Buoyed by a big online response, Parscale claimed on Twitter that there had been "over 1M ticket requests for the @realDonaldTrump #MAGA Rally in Tulsa on Saturday," and hurriedly arranged for an outdoor stage to handle the expected overflow from the nineteen-thousand-seat BOK Center.[12] When the day arrived, however, there were nowhere near that many people. Teenagers using TikTok had organized a campaign to register for hundreds of thousands of tickets they never intended to use to fool the Trump team into expecting a huge turnout.

As Trump flew in on Air Force One, a sick realization came over aides that disaster was looming. The president called Parscale from the plane to ask how it was looking.

"Sorry, sir, I couldn't get it done," Parscale said, describing security measures around the arena. "It's like Beirut outside. It's like the bombing of the '80s. No one can get here, sir. I'm sorry, and people are too scared."

Trump hung up on him.

Parscale ordered the second stage removed. In the end, only six thousand people filed into the arena, less than a third of its capacity, and the building had an empty feeling that Trump had never seen at one of his rallies.

The reckless event led to multiple Secret Service agents and advance staff members coming down with Covid. So did Herman Cain, the former pizza mogul and onetime Republican presidential candidate who was among Trump's highest-profile Black supporters. Cain, who like others in the crowd went without a mask, tested positive nine days after the rally, and died a month later.

Trump had long approached America's racial, ethnic, and religious divisions opportunistically, not as wounds to be healed but as openings to achieve his goals, whether ratings, fame, money, or power. It was perfectly consistent with his life story for Trump to turn to race-baiting once again, now that his presidency was at stake.

Trump was a product of his place and time, born and raised in the Queens of another era when race was a regular flashpoint forcing New Yorkers to choose sides. As he was making his mark in Manhattan real estate in the 1980s and 1990s, the city struggled with racial episodes like the Bernie Goetz subway shooting, the Howard Beach racial killing, the Tawana Brawley rape hoax, and the Crown Heights riots.

Trump thrust himself into the middle of raucous racial controversies even when he did not need to. Most memorably, he injected himself into the 1989 case of the Central Park Five, a group of Black and Hispanic teenagers accused of the brutal rape of a twenty-eight-year-old white woman jogging at night. Trump inflamed the situation by spending $85,000 to place ads in four newspapers with the screaming headline: "BRING BACK THE DEATH PENALTY. BRING BACK OUR POLICE!"[13] The teenagers were convicted, but years later they were exonerated, and the city paid $41 million in a legal settlement, while another man eventually admitted to being the attacker, a confession confirmed by DNA evidence. Trump never accepted that outcome, insisting that the five really were guilty.

Trump not only embraced racial animosity, he sought to instigate it. While hosting *The Apprentice*, he even toyed with setting up a race conflict as the main theme for its fourth season.

"It would be nine blacks against nine whites, all highly educated, very smart, strong, beautiful people, right?" Trump said, previewing the idea on Howard Stern's radio show.

"Yes," Stern said.

"Do you like it?"

"Yes," Stern said.

Trump asked Robin Quivers, the Black cohost. "Do you like it, Robin?"

"Well," she said, "I think you're going to have a riot."

"It would be the highest-rated show on television," Trump exulted.[14]

NBC executives rejected Trump's vision of a Black-versus-white theme. But at the end of that same season, Trump again drew accusations of bias when he undercut Randal Pinkett, the Black contestant who won. During the finale, Trump suggested Pinkett share the honor with the white woman he had just beaten. Shocked, Pinkett declared it "racist."[15]

At the time, Trump was a registered Democrat in a diverse city, and he could show a different side of himself depending on the audience. Charles Rangel, the powerful Black congressman from Harlem, collected fundraising checks from Trump and vouched for him. The Reverend Al Sharpton, the civil rights leader, said he had "never heard him say anything racial," although "I always sensed he was not comfortable being around us."[16] Over the years, Trump had befriended Black celebrities such as Muhammad Ali, Mike Tyson, and the promoter Don King. When he briefly owned the USFL team, he grew close to running back Herschel Walker. Trump loved that rappers often used his name in their lyrics as a symbol of wealth and flash—*"Get money like Donald Trump,"* sang Lil Wayne, *"double barrel on that pump"*—and he got to know Sean Combs, Snoop Dogg, and Russell Simmons.[17] "The Blacks love me," he once boasted.[18]

But it was hardly mutual. Jack O'Donnell, former president of the Trump Plaza Hotel and Casino, said Trump would be upset if he noticed too many Black Americans on the gambling floor. "It's a little dark tonight," he would tell O'Donnell, who also claimed that Trump asserted that "laziness is a trait in Blacks" and complained about an African American accountant. "Black guys counting my money! I hate it. The only kind of people I want counting my money are short guys that wear yarmulkes every day." Once on a construction site, Trump noticed a Black worker. "What is that Black guy doing over there?" he demanded, according to Barbara Res, one of his executives. "Get him off there right now and don't ever let that happen again. I don't want people to think that Trump Tower is being built by Black people."[19]

The foundation of Trump's original presidential campaign was built on questioning the birth of the first Black American president. Behind closed doors, he denigrated Barack Obama in crude terms. "Obama is a fucking phony," he screamed, according to Michael Cohen, his onetime personal attorney. "He's a Manchurian candidate. He's not even fucking American. The only reason he got into fucking Harvard Law School and Columbia was fucking affirmative action." Trump expanded his indictment to include every Black head of state. "Tell me one country run by a Black person that isn't a shithole. They are complete fucking toilets."[20]

Campaigning in 2016, Trump vilified illegal immigrants as rapists, vowed to ban Muslims from entering the country, suggested a return to racial profiling by police, and insisted that an American-born judge could not rule fairly in a case involving Trump because of his Mexican heritage. He did little to disavow the support of prominent racists such as Richard Spencer or David Duke. When his children worried that his rhetoric would hurt the family business, Trump brushed it off. "I will never get the Hispanic vote," he said. "Like the Blacks, they're too stupid to vote for Trump. They're not my people."[21]

In fact, Trump, who won 28 percent of the Hispanic vote in 2016 and 6 percent of the Black vote, used the supporters of color that he did have as heat shields to deflect allegations of racism.[22] When a man carrying a "Blacks for Trump" sign showed up at rallies, campaign aides crudely nick-named him Michael the Black Man and positioned him behind the candi-date in camera angle—not realizing that Michael the Black Man had once belonged to a violent religious cult and was charged, although acquitted, of two murders. Trump himself noticed a pair of sisters named Lynnette Hardaway and Rochelle Richardson who called themselves Diamond and Silk and had become internet sensations supporting him in 2016; he was so excited when they attacked Megyn Kelly of Fox News for being tough on him that he began using them as a regular opening act.

Trump ritually denied being a bigot. "I am the least racist person you have ever met," he said over and over.[23] But he did not seem to mind that he left the opposite impression. Once he became president, his "very fine people" remarks in the aftermath of the white supremacist march in Charlottesville were followed by plenty of others—the Haitian immi-grants who "all have AIDS," the African visitors who would never "go back to their huts," the "shithole" countries sending too many people to the United States.[24] He declared that four liberal Democratic congresswomen of color who called themselves the Squad should "go back" to their home countries, even though three of them were born in the United States and all were citizens.[25] He attacked Elijah Cummings, the Black congress-man from Baltimore who was Mark Meadows's friend, for representing a "disgusting, rat and rodent infested mess" where "no human being would want to live." In meetings, he deployed racial and ethnic stereotypes that shocked even senior military types accustomed to rough language. "He would say stuff like, 'Who gives a shit about Korea? You can't sell a god-damn Ford in Korea, who cares? Why the fuck are we there? Why do I give a shit about these rathole countries in Africa? What the fuck are we doing in Niger?'" recalled a senior national security official who spent a lot of time with him.

Trump was hardly the only president to embrace racism, but he did so more overtly than any in generations. He had few Blacks working for him. When he took office, his was the first cabinet in nearly three decades without a single Hispanic, and overall it was the least diverse since Ronald Reagan's three decades earlier.[26] He typically deflected accusations of rac-ism by noting that unemployment for Black and Hispanic Americans had fallen to all-time lows. Those trends, however, began under Obama and simply continued after Trump took over, and were not clearly related to any specific policy the new president advanced.[27] He had signed Lamar Alexander's bill making federal funding for historically Black colleges permanent, but it was a bipartisan measure that Trump expended little energy to pass and his own budgets requested less such financing than Congress provided each year. Still, Trump regularly claimed that he had done more for Black Americans than any president with the possible exception of Abraham Lincoln.

By the latter half of his presidency, some friends who had defended Trump against charges of racism finally gave up. "As much as I have denied it and averted my eyes from it, this latest incident made it impossible," Geraldo Rivera told *The New York Times* after the president's attacks on the Squad. "The critics," he added, "were much more right than I."[28]

When Anthony Scaramucci publicly criticized the assault on the Squad as "racist and unacceptable," Trump called to complain.[29] Scaramucci told him it was counterproductive to attack people of color and immigrants. If nothing else, he could turn off white suburbanites who recoiled at racist tactics.

"'Aren't you trying to attract the independents and moderates?'" Scaramucci asked.

"No," Trump replied flatly. "I'm worried about the base. If I take care of the base, everything else will take care of itself."[30]

To appeal to the base, Trump flew to South Dakota to deliver a campaign speech in front of Mount Rushmore on the day before the Fourth of July, defending American history against what he called a "new far-left fascism." Even as medical authorities warned against the sort of large gathering he insisted upon, Trump declared that America's real enemy was not disease or discrimination but radical progressivism. "Our nation is witnessing a merciless campaign to wipe out our history, defame our heroes, erase our values and indoctrinate our children," he thundered.[31]

The trip was a pick-me-up for Trump after months of isolation in the White House and the debacle in Tulsa. Aides had noticed "a certain slackness in his shoulders," as Mark Meadows put it, indicating that the president was growing "disheartened."[32] The trip boosted his spirits and his ego as he told other Republicans that he thought he should be added to Mount Rushmore alongside Washington, Jefferson, Lincoln, and Roosevelt.

But he was losing, no matter how much he denied it. Trump needed someone to blame and Brad Parscale was an obvious target. At six-foot-eight with a scraggly beard, the campaign manager was hard to miss in any room, usually towering above the crowd, a giant "who dressed like a lumberjack and spoke like a young tech billionaire," as Meadows put it.[33] Parscale had originally signed on to work with Trump as a web designer, creating internet sites for the boss's winery, real estate business, and other ventures, and he had little national political experience when he was tapped as digital director of the 2016 campaign. A favorite of Jared Kushner's, Parscale was tapped to run the re-election campaign more than two years before the vote.

But Parscale courted trouble with Trump by assuming an unusually public role, addressing campaign rallies, appearing in advertising, and putting his name on fundraising events. He loved the celebrity, loved signing autographs. Parscale had fooled himself into thinking he was practically family. He told anyone who would listen that he was born in the same eleven-day part of the calendar as Don Jr., Eric, and Jared, albeit in different years, as if that made them brothers. He advertised his close ties with Kushner, with whom he spoke several times a day. "I don't think I'm here without him, I don't think he thinks he's here without me," Parscale told Michael Bender of *The Wall Street Journal* heading into 2020. "Are two people any closer than me and Jared? We're tied at the hip. Who else has that? Nobody, right? I'm surprised no one has gone far enough to call me a Trump kid."[34]

But as Trump's fortunes fell, Parscale was reminded that his relationship was neither blood nor marriage. After a bad poll, Trump screamed at him on the phone. "I'll fucking sue you," the president threatened.[35] Trump did not like reports that Parscale had taken in millions from his campaign work and made a series of splashy purchases, including a $2.4 million waterfront home in Fort Lauderdale, two $1 million Florida condominiums, a $400,000 yacht, and a Ferrari. Trump, always resentful of people he believed were getting wealthy off him, called Parscale to yell again. Parscale yelled back. "Fuck you, I was already rich before I met you," he said. Kushner defended the manager, explaining to Trump that in fact Parscale was not pulling that much money from the campaign.

But Parscale never recovered from Tulsa or his decision to work remotely during the pandemic, which annoyed the president, who wanted him around in person. So in mid-July, Kushner called to tell Parscale he was out as campaign manager. He could stay in a lower position or leave altogether. Parscale, feeling betrayed yet unwilling to be cast out, agreed to the humiliation of a demotion.

Parscale was deeply wounded, telling himself that Trump and Kushner wanted him gone to prove that they did not need him to win. In conversations with associates, he blamed Trump for his own problems, deeming the president sloppy in his messaging, increasingly narcissistic, and basically just a jerk. Parscale believed his enemies were investigating him, looking for dirt. To colleagues, he seemed increasingly unstable. He was already in a dark place, his marriage troubled after he and his wife endured the death of premature twins. But his disgrace accelerated a spiral that would lead a couple months later to an hour-long standoff with police officers who confronted a half-naked, beer-drinking Parscale outside his Florida home after a 911 call from his wife expressing fear that he might use one of the ten guns later found inside. Parscale was tackled by police and involuntarily committed for psychiatric examination.

Taking Parscale's place was Bill Stepien, a former Chris Christie adviser who had served as Trump's White House political director and deputy campaign manager. Stepien and his deputy, Justin Clark, discovered that the campaign was in dire financial trouble and would run out of money by early October. The two scaled back television spending and did what they could to right the ship. But in the end, it would be up to Trump.

Trump's plan—it was always his plan, for everything—was to fight. He had decided to wage a culture war to win a second term and Black Lives Matter protesters were not the only ones on the other side. Even officials inside his own administration working day and night to stop the pandemic were now declared the enemy.

Trump had begun stoking public anger at Tony Fauci as early as April when he reposted a Twitter message from a Republican declaring that it was "time to #FireFauci."[36] By July, it was no longer even that subtle. Appearing on Sean Hannity's show, the president dismissed Fauci as "a nice man" who had made "a lot of mistakes."[37]

A few days later, the White House produced campaign-style opposition research on Fauci, drawing up a list of when he was "wrong on things" and distributing it to *The Washington Post*.[38] The next day, Peter Navarro published an op-ed in *USA Today* headlined, "Anthony Fauci Has Been Wrong About Everything I Have Interacted with Him On."[39] Such open assaults by White House officials on a sitting adviser to the president would have been a firing offense in any other administration, but the drumbeat of attacks was clearly authorized or at least tolerated by Trump. At bottom, Trump was jealous of Fauci's poll numbers. One survey in July found that 65 percent of Americans trusted the doctor on the virus versus just 30 percent who had faith in the president's information.[40]

Navarro had been the bane of the doctors for months. At one meeting, he showed up with a stack of documents and slammed them down on the table. "That's more than fifty scientific studies in support of hydroxy," he shouted, pushing the president's favorite drug. "Fifty!"[41] Fauci pushed back. "Peter, I'm sorry, but you're really dead wrong." Navarro got so worked up that Mike Pence had to intervene.

Whenever Navarro was asked what qualified him to make medical pronouncements, he would say, "I have a Ph.D.," although it was in economics, not science.[42] Nonetheless, he treated the doctors as if they were not only idiots but disingenuous liars and enablers of the Deep State. "He tried to make our lives a living hell," one of the doctors said. Navarro sought to get some of them fired and separately told both Fauci and the FDA's Stephen Hahn that "you have blood on your hands," a line that did not go over well with people who had devoted their careers to saving lives.[43]

It was not that Fauci and the other doctors had not made mistakes—they would concede that they had. They initially opposed masks and travel restrictions and Fauci said in a television interview in January, before the first American death, that the virus "is not a major threat to the people of the United States and this is not something that the citizens of the United States right now should be worried about."[44] But he caveated it by saying *right now*. Unlike Trump, who continued to publicly downplay the pandemic long after it was clear how serious it was and to push quack therapies, the doctors shifted their views as more information became available. And after early misjudgments, they consistently pushed for serious measures.

By summer, the president had all but stopped speaking with Fauci, or "Dr. Doom" as the Trump team called him, and was looking for someone to reinforce his own preconceptions. At one point, Trump promoted on Twitter a "very impressive" doctor who shared his faith in hydroxychloroquine and skepticism about masks—without realizing that she also blamed various ailments on demon sperm, believed medical treatments were being developed from alien DNA, and preached about the dangers of having sex with witches in your dreams.[45]

In late July, Trump enlisted Scott Atlas, a Stanford University radiologist and public health scholar who, while not an epidemiologist, was on Fox News frequently saying what Trump wanted to hear. Arriving in the Situation Room, Atlas essentially argued against everything the coronavirus task force had been doing. Masks were largely ineffective and unnecessary except in limited circumstances, lockdowns did more harm than good, testing should be limited to those who had already come down with symptoms. The government, he argued, should focus on protecting those most at risk, like seniors. The "Birx-Fauci lockdowns," he believed, were "reprehensible, totally unforgivable, a crime against humanity." Since most people did not die from Covid, he explained in meetings, the threat would eventually fade once enough Americans were infected and recovered, essentially the "herd immunity" concept embraced by Mark Meadows and others in the White House. While Atlas insisted that he was not advocating herd immunity as a policy, he left the impression that he was.

Atlas denigrated the doctors, accusing them of "glaring incompetence." Scornful, brash, and combative, he maintained that Fauci was taking an "alarmist interpretation," that Birx was ignorant, and that the CDC's Robert Redfield "was consistent in his uncanny ability to be completely wrong." Fauci and the others repeatedly rejected Atlas's theories—"you are at the fringe," Birx told him—but found themselves sidelined by the president.[46] As the one with a White House office, Birx found her increasing isolation during Atlas's rise all the more debilitating. "Tony, I'm not going to play this game," she told Fauci. No longer welcome in the Oval Office, she hit the road, heading by car from state capital to state capital to stress the importance of public health measures to governors one at a time. She hit twenty-six states in July and August alone.

This was in keeping with the pattern Trump had established throughout his presidency, setting his advisers against each other while turning away from those who delivered unwelcome information to favor sycophants who played to his wishes. The ascendance of Atlas also underscored how marginalized Pence had become on the issue he was supposedly managing. While the vice president could not be fired, Trump simply layered over him. And he was not listening to contrary news anymore.

The day after Birx said on CNN in early August that the virus was "extraordinarily widespread," Trump called her up to berate her. "What do you think you're doing?" he demanded. "Don't you ever do that again." He said the media would feast on her statement. "These people live for fake news, and all you've done is feed them."

"Mr. President, the virus *is* widespread—" she tried to interject.

"That's it! Do you understand me? Never again! The virus is under control!"[47]

With his campaign struggling to find traction, Trump intensified his law-and-order theme. Dick Morris, a Republican strategist who had been a close adviser to Bill Clinton until being forced out of the 1996 campaign in a toe-sucking scandal involving a prostitute he allowed to eavesdrop on his calls with the president, reached out to Trump to urge him to play the police card. Morris was a cousin of Roy Cohn and shared his us-versus-them approach to politics, which appealed to Trump.

At Morris's urging, Trump's campaign soon released an ad showing a woman watching news of Democrats "defunding the police" on television as an intruder broke into her house. Her call to the police went to voice-mail: "Hello, you've reached 911. I'm sorry that there is no one here to answer your emergency call. But leave a message and we'll get back to you as soon as we can." As the intruder confronted her, the phone dropped to the floor and the words "You won't be safe in Joe Biden's America" came onto the screen.[48] It was a gross distortion of Biden's position—in fact, he had a long record of supporting law enforcement and had frustrated liberal activists by opposing "defund the police"—but it encapsulated Trump's primal message of fear and racial backlash.

As summer turned to fall, Trump became especially fixated on Port-land, where demonstrations had morphed into bedlam. Night after night, police struggled to keep control as troublemakers hurled firebombs, rocks, mortars, and other objects at them. Some men showed up in helmets, gas masks, and body armor. Hundreds were arrested. Long a liberal bastion in a liberal state, Portland was an easy target for Trump's crackdown rhetoric and he berated the mayor and governor for not doing more to suppress the unrest.

While Mark Esper and Mark Milley resisted sending troops, Trump ordered Bill Barr to deploy law enforcement officers from various federal agencies into the streets of Portland. After some federal officers in camou-flage used unmarked minivans to snatch people off the streets and other officers covered their names for fear of exposure, the furor over federal tactics grew.

The focus on racial justice had upended Biden's campaign as well. On matters of race, the Democratic base was in effect the opposite of Trump's, pushing the nominee to do more and faster to advance the cause of diver-sity and equity. Biden had already committed to picking a woman as his vice presidential running mate but in the wake of the George Floyd killing, there was little doubt Biden would choose a woman of color. In selecting Senator Kamala Harris of California, the daughter of immigrants from Jamaica and India, he opted for the barrier-breaking possibility of Harris becoming the first Black woman and first Asian American to win national office.

At the White House, Trump sought to turn that to his advantage as part of his election message aimed at stoking white grievance. Trump quickly began to demonize Harris, calling her "nasty," "the meanest," and "a mad woman," while reminding voters that she herself had suggested during the Democratic primaries that Biden had a "racist" past.[49] Another possible weapon presented itself in the form of a guest column in *Newsweek* by John Eastman, a conservative law professor from Chapman University, who argued that Harris might not really be a natural-born American eligible to serve as vice president because her parents were immigrants when she was born in California, essentially a Harris-specific version of the Obama birther lie.[50] When reporters asked Trump about it, he said that he had heard about the issue without disavowing it, leaving it to hang out there as if it were a reasonable question.

But when he asked aides in an Oval Office meeting whether they should pursue the matter more aggressively, a debate broke out. Stephen Miller and Jenna Ellis, a campaign lawyer, pushed him to adopt Eastman's attack on Harris. Alyssa Farah, the communications chief, objected. "Sir, this is a trap," she said. "The media would love nothing more than to revive this issue and say you're a racist." Trump for once opted to take a pass on a racial conspiracy theory, although that would not stop his supporters.

On August 24, the Republican National Convention opened to formally nominate Trump and launch him into the general election. Over the next four days, the gathering would showcase all the fissures of the Trump era, highlighting a country at war with itself over culture, economics, ideology, race, and even disease. "Always remember," the president told his supporters, "they are coming after me because I am fighting for you."[51]

It turned out to be the most unconventional of conventions, forced out of North Carolina and then Florida by Covid crowd limits and relocated at the last minute to Washington. The fireworks-punctuated finale on the South Lawn of the White House featured at least a thousand supporters without masks. While other presidents had made political speeches at the White House, none had ever used the majesty of the executive mansion so brazenly as the backdrop for their party's electioneering. Nor was the setting the only breach of tradition. Trump pardoned a reformed bank robber and presided over the naturalization of five immigrants as part of the convention, transforming official acts into campaign advertisements. To top it off, Mike Pompeo beamed in an endorsement speech to the convention from Jerusalem, the only time a secretary of state had ever used the backdrop of a diplomatic mission to participate in a partisan event.

The convention highlighted just how much the Republican Party had become an adjunct of the Trump family. The roster of speakers included seven people named Trump and an eighth who aspired to the name. In addition to the president and the first lady, those addressing the conclave included Donald Trump Jr., Ivanka Trump, Eric Trump, Lara Trump, and Tiffany Trump. Even Kimberly Guilfoyle, the girlfriend of the president's oldest son, had a turn at the podium, where she concluded her speech with a widely mocked cheer, shouting as if addressing a crowd of thousands rather than a camera in a mostly empty room: "The Best! Is Yet! To Come!"[52]

The Trumpification of the party was so complete that the convention produced no platform, the document traditionally adopted by a party every four years to outline its agenda and positions on major issues of the day, an abdication unheard of in modern times. Instead, the Republican National Committee simply released a resolution declaring that it "enthusiastically supports President Trump," rendering it a party that stood for nothing other than its leader.[53]

Small wonder, perhaps, since that leader could articulate no strong idea of what he wanted to do with a second term anyway. Asked just before the convention about his agenda for the next four years, he rattled off a few accomplishments from his first term, then added, meanderingly, "But so, I think, I think it would be, I think it would be very, very, I think we'd have a very, very solid, we would continue what we're doing, we'd solidify what we've done and we have other things on our plate that we want to get done."[54]

After a summer of fanning racial flames, Trump and other speakers made little mention of George Floyd or the issues raised by his killing. Instead, Trump painted a frightening picture of "Democrat-run cities" afflicted by "rioting, looting, arson and violence." Pinning blame on his opponent, Trump warned ominously, "No one will be safe in Biden's America."[55] It was a convention as if produced by Fox News.

That at least was a message that Trump and Tucker Carlson could agree on. The week after the convention, on the night of September 1, the president sat in his private dining room watching Fox as Carlson interviewed Christopher Rufo, a conservative scholar who had been waging a personal campaign against "critical race theory" and its supposed infiltration into government programs, which he asserted were "being weaponized against the American people."[56]

Trump was not going to let himself get on Carlson's wrong side again. The next morning, he had Mark Meadows call Rufo for more information. Two days after that, the president directed his budget director to issue a memo intended to purge the federal government of racial sensitivity training, adopting much of the language that Rufo had been using.

"This is a sickness that cannot be allowed to continue," Trump tweeted. "Please report any sightings so we can quickly extinguish!" He retweeted a post hailing his order: "Sorry liberals! How to be Anti-White 101 is permanently canceled!" This time, Carlson approved. His program on race, he noted on air, "apparently got the attention of the president and he acted."[57]

The Divider thought he had found a way to avoid having his presidency canceled.

CHAPTER 26

Secretary of Everything

Before he could close the biggest Middle East deal of the Trump presidency, Jared Kushner had one final negotiation to conduct—with Melania Trump.

For nearly four years, he had pursued the elusive dream of reconciliation between Israelis and Palestinians only to see it evaporate in a cloud of overconfidence. Yet in the final months of his father-in-law's term, a different kind of diplomatic breakthrough had presented itself as Israel agreed to suspend annexation of occupied territory in exchange for diplomatic relations with several of its Arab neighbors.

It was not the landmark agreement ending generations of conflict over the West Bank that he and Trump had promised, but in an unspeakably grim year of disease and domestic unrest it was by far the most tangible good news for the administration before the election. Trailing Joe Biden in the polls, the president wanted a splashy signing ceremony that September on the South Lawn, mimicking historic peace accords of the past to present himself as a transformational figure and maybe even revive his quixotic quest for a Nobel Peace Prize.

That is, if only they could convince the first lady. She was worried about the grass.

Or at least her staff was. The first lady's office controlled use of the White House grounds, and the South Lawn had just been resodded after a thousand energized supporters tromped all over it during the Republican National Convention. The last thing Melania's office wanted was to ruin the expensive repair work with another large crowd tearing up the backyard. So it rejected the request.

Kushner and his team were dumbfounded. They were making history and could not use the lawn? After all the delicate bargaining to bring

Israelis and Arabs together, resolving part of the world's greatest geopolitical turf battle, the final obstacle to their day of celebration would be the actual turf?

Kushner's staff scrambled for alternatives. The Rose Garden was also out because it too had just been resodded. His team brought a Secret Service scouting party to scope out the North Lawn, but it was too close to the outside gates and therefore too noisy and not secure enough. The indoor rooms of the State Floor were ruled out amid the threat of Covid. Finally, Kushner appealed directly to the president, who immediately agreed that they should use the South Lawn.

Still, the first lady's office refused to bend. It would cost too much to redo the South Lawn all over again if the crowds tore it up.

How much? Kushner asked.

About $80,000.

"No problem," he said. "It's on me."

Kushner, whose personal fortune was estimated in the many hundreds of millions, said he would personally write a check to cover any expense if the grass was damaged. That finally broke the deadlock. But the first lady's office rejected his team's request to use the same desk on which the Camp David Accords in 1978 and the Oslo Accords in 1993 were signed. It was too fragile, they were told. Kushner took what he could get.

That navigating the divisions inside Trump's White House would prove more vexing than finalizing a complicated Middle East agreement seemed like a metaphor for an administration that had spent the better part of four years fighting with itself as much as with its adversaries. But at last, the ceremony was on.

On September 15, a band struck up "Ruffles and Flourishes" and then "Hail to the Chief" before an announcer introduced Trump, Benjamin Netanyahu, and the foreign ministers of Bahrain and the United Arab Emirates, Abdullah bin Zayed al-Nahyan and Abdullatif bin Rashid al-Zayani. Standing on the deck overlooking the crowd on the South Lawn on a sunny morning, Trump hailed the agreement his team had grandly named the Abraham Accords, in honor of the biblical father common to Christianity, Judaism, and Islam. "Today's signing sets history on a new course," Trump declared, heralding nothing less than "the dawn of a new Middle East." Even more countries, he promised, would join, "very, very soon."[1]

The accords were, in fact, a genuine breakthrough in the region. They were not truly peace agreements since, unlike Egypt or Jordan, neither the UAE nor Bahrain had ever been at war with Israel, and the Arab nations now welcoming Israeli embassies to their capitals had long ago established ties with the Jewish state behind the scenes. The agreements made official what had been previously unacknowledged. But that was important. For Israel, it mattered that, for the first time in a quarter century, more Arab countries were willing to openly and unreservedly acknowledge its right to exist, recognition that had been withheld since it became a state more than seventy years earlier. The accords also broke the diplomatic knot holding Israel's future hostage to the Palestinian conflict. After years of refusing to openly accept Israel until it gave in to the Palestinians, several important Arab nations were now saying that the dispute over territory occupied by Israel since the 1967 war would no longer be an insuperable barrier to better relations. Two more Muslim countries, Morocco and Sudan, would soon follow suit, and others, even if not ready to go quite as far, were increasingly willing to deal with Israel; even Saudi Arabia opened its airspace to Israeli flights and hinted that it might eventually join the Abraham Accords.

At the same time, the diplomatic normalizations were far less significant than the peace agreement Trump had promised to forge between Israel and the Palestinians, who were not invited and mentioned only in passing at the ceremony. For all his boasting, Trump made no more progress on that than any of his recent predecessors, and the Israeli-Palestinian rapprochement that he once boasted would be "not as difficult as people have thought" turned out to be every bit as difficult as people thought.[2] In fact, Trump arguably set the process back by giving away multiple bargaining chips to Israel without getting anything in return. As for the Palestinians, Trump was not on speaking terms with their leader, Mahmoud Abbas, and had cut off aid to the Palestinian Authority for refusing to participate in talks. After the Abraham Accords, peace between the two appeared even more distant than when the administration started.

So, having failed to make the deal he had promised, Trump settled for the one that he could make, or at least that his son-in-law could. And when the trumpets stopped playing and the documents were all signed, the grass turned out to be just fine. Kushner could keep his check.

For nearly four years, Jared Kushner had been the force to be reckoned with in Trump's West Wing, the Secretary of Everything who assembled an expansive portfolio both domestic and international, from the pandemic to electoral politics, crossing every line on whatever org chart ruled the moment in the ever-shifting White House. Unfailingly composed, with a whispery voice, Kushner, all of thirty-six when he arrived in Washington, had supplanted chiefs of staff, overshadowed cabinet secretaries, and negotiated with congressional leaders and foreign potentates with the mandate of a virtual prime minister.

While other presidents enlisted their children to help out, no presidential progeny had ever wielded quite the authority that Kushner had. Trump entrusted him to do everything from renegotiate the North American Free Trade Agreement to pass criminal justice reform to find medical equipment to cope with the pandemic. A conventionally centrist New York Democrat until his father-in-law entered the 2016 presidential race, Kushner never became a Twitter-trolling MAGA warrior in keeping with the rest of the clan's reinvention, and Trump maintained a certain skepticism of the younger man. Kushner did not win every fight, and he opted out of many. It was true, however, that crossing Kushner was almost always fatal to a career in the Trump administration, a reality that some recognized only too late.

Cool and collected where Trump was hot and combustible, Kushner had become as polarizing a figure within the West Wing as his father-in-law was in the country at large. To some, he was a low-key, nuts-and-bolts pragmatist who could navigate the complicated politics of his family and actually get things done in Trump's sclerotic and factionalized White House—the Mechanic, to use his Secret Service codename. To others, he was a self-serving and self-interested dilettante—the Slim Reaper, as the first lady's chief of staff, Stephanie Grisham, dubbed him, a killer in a European-cut suit. Every news story that did not trash Kushner was seen as an example of his personal sub rosa public relations campaign to puff himself up while every story that trashed someone else on the staff was assumed to be an orchestrated leak kneecapping a rival. "If the building burned to the ground and one man was standing, all he would care about was that it was him," complained one White House official.

For all his influence with Trump, Kushner understood its limits. While many expected him to restrain the rash president, Kushner had learned the hard way that it was impossible to change or reliably manage Trump, concluding that it was foolish and even counterproductive to try. But he believed it was possible to steer him in strategic moments, at least if his argument was framed in a way that appealed to Trump's particular vanities or reinforced his preconceived notions.

One key to handling Trump, Kushner told others, was feeding him good news, even if it was in short supply. In fact, Kushner came up with a specific mathematical formula for his own peculiar brand of Trump management: 2 to 1. Any phone call, any meeting should include this good-news-to-bad-news ratio. He would give twice as much upbeat information as grim updates. He similarly made a habit of telling Trump to add five points to any bad poll, recognizing how much the president craved positive numbers and rationalizing that traditional surveys missed many Trump voters anyway.

Even for his son-in-law, though, the president was a demanding boss, not given to showing appreciation. Kushner understood that Trump was never going to call him and say, "You're doing a great job, I just want to thank you for this." Instead, Kushner once explained to an associate, his dealings with Trump invariably began with the president saying, "What the fuck is going on with this?" Often, that was in a phone call at one or two in the morning. Having watched dozens of senior officials come and go through Trump's perpetually troubled White House, Kushner had realized the essential element of surviving in it: never forgetting it was Trump's show, Trump's party, Trump's way. People like John Kelly were planners, but Trump would never go along with the plan. He always needed people to know that he was in control, not his team. "You have to realize *you* don't make the waves," Kushner regularly advised other officials. "*He* makes the waves. And then you have to do your best to kind of stay on the surfboard."

Kushner the surf-rider suffered no shortage of self-confidence. In Kushner's telling, he was the wunderkind who had really run the 2016 campaign, the one who built the digital operation, assembled the speechwriting team, ran the finances, bought the media, and made the ads. When he arrived in Washington, he assumed that he could handle governance and statecraft too. The lesson he learned from his father-in-law's unlikely election was that the political establishment was overrated, that all these people advertised as experts had no clue what happened outside their echo chamber.

But it was Kushner who at first did not have much of a clue about how Washington really worked. Like everyone else in that White House during its chaotic start, he was whipsawed by one controversy after another, preoccupied by insider knife fights, forced to hire lawyers and testify before hostile questioners. The first couple of years, he confided to friends, were brutal and humiliating.

Trump, for his part, refused to help. Essentially, he told his son-in-law that it was his own problem to fix. For a while, Jared and Ivanka had mulled moving back to New York, which the president might have preferred. But while the Mueller investigation was still under way and questions still swirled about his involvement in questionable episodes like the firing of James Comey and the Trump Tower meeting with Russian proxies, Kushner resolved not to leave until he had cleared his name. And he felt he was getting things done. On his own scorecard, he took credit for renegotiating NAFTA, creating a diplomatic channel to China, opening the original negotiating line to North Korea, and passing criminal justice reform.

One lesson he learned through painful experience was to use his capital sparingly and only when it suited him, not every time someone rushed into his office crying out, *You've got to stop him*. Trump did not appreciate the appearance of the kids in the residence carrying someone else's water; it diluted their credibility with him if they were constantly making arguments that would not sway him anyway.

Kushner concluded that the administration's biggest failing was its personnel—the president kept putting people into positions for which they were not suited and, despite his reputation for an itchy Twitter finger, was too slow to fire people who were not working out. If anything, the former *Apprentice* host did not say "you're fired" enough.

Which was an ironic conclusion perhaps for one whose remarkable power in Trump's Washington derived in large measure from the singular fact that he could not be fired himself.

When they arrived in the capital, it was Ivanka Trump who was the star, the first daughter and former model who spoke at rallies. She was the child who could do no wrong in her father's eyes, the one who had known him longer than anyone else in the White House, including his wife. But fame only goes so far in Washington. Ivanka chose to use her sway far more tactically than her husband, focusing on a constellation of targeted projects that she framed as pro-family, pro-woman, and pro-child.

Ivanka had not intended to join her father's White House. Perhaps because Trump seemed so unlikely to win, she had given little thought during the campaign to what victory would mean for her. She lived a cosseted life of privilege in New York, running her own fashion line, hanging out with friends like Chelsea Clinton, and updating followers on her adventures through Instagram. Her media mentions were of the cotton candy variety, rarely including a negative word. So when she formally joined the White House staff, she had no idea what she was in for.

The dinner parties at their swank Kalorama mansion three times a week were, at first, bipartisan affairs, but as feelings hardened they became one-party gatherings. Ivanka found herself on an island of her own, hated by the left and distrusted by the right. Every presidential deviation from what the Steve Bannon crowd considered Trump orthodoxy was blamed on her, but she got no credit from Democrats who considered her a poseur and enabler. She was wounded by Scarlett Johansson's *Saturday Night Live* portrayal of her in 2017 as a smoky-eyed perfume model selling a fragrance called "Complicit."[3] She was shocked in 2018 when the comedian Samantha Bee lashed out at her on her late-night show, saying, "Do something about your dad's immigration practices, you feckless cunt."[4]

Her father left little doubt that she was his favorite child and clearly aimed to advance her as his political heir. Even after being talked out of his nonsensical notion of making her his vice presidential running mate in 2016, he routinely floated her name for high-profile jobs, including United Nations ambassador and president of the World Bank. He was more serious about the U.N. idea and considered appointing her to the post after Nikki Haley resigned in late 2018, which would have the side benefit of getting her and Jared back up to New York. But Ivanka thought her father was "messing with me," as she told associates, and she eventually shot down his trial balloons.

Hers was not exactly a Trumpian agenda. She prided herself on fighting for policies like the child tax credit increase she got into the tax cut legislation and paid family leave for federal workers. She focused on women's economic empowerment, forcing the issue onto the agenda of G20 meetings. She pushed for vocational education, science and technology schooling, and the Farmers to Families Food Box Program providing meals to those in need. She could be relentless when needed and did not let her father's staff get in the way. After John Kelly excised a line touting family leave from the draft State of the Union address in 2018, she went around him and told Rob Porter to slip it back in.

The years of attacks, though, had pushed her further into her father's camp. There was no place for a moderate in Washington with the last name Trump. She was mocked when she once tried to awkwardly interject herself into a conversation with the leaders of Britain, France, and Canada as a camera caught the moment. Her efforts to influence her father sometimes backfired, as when she urged him to deliver that Oval Office address about the coronavirus that flopped or when she suggested visiting the church across Lafayette Square for that infamous photo op. She and Jared often wore masks while her father refused to, but not often enough to satisfy the private Jewish day school where they sent their children; after administrators raised concerns about the family's adherence to health guidelines, the couple would withdraw the kids.

By the time she stood up at the Republican convention on that summer day in 2020, still only thirty-eight years old, she had shed her past Democratic affiliation and formally registered as a Republican. In her address that night she still avoided taking a lot of direct shots at her father's opponents, but it was a more partisan speech than any she had ever given, a strikingly full-throated defense of her father.

"I recognize that my dad's communication style is not to everyone's taste," she told the national television audience. "And I know his tweets can feel a bit—unfiltered. But the results speak for themselves." She tried to humanize him, saying she had "seen the pain in his eyes" over those killed by the pandemic and "the emotion on his face" when Alice Johnson, a great-grandmother he pardoned at the urging of Kim Kardashian West, was released from prison. She portrayed him as authentic in a town of artifice. "For the first time in a long time, we have a president who has called out Washington's hypocrisy and they hate him for it," she said. "Dad, people attack you for being unconventional, but I love you for being real, and I respect you for being effective."[5]

Of all the Trump children, however, the one who had turned out to be the natural heir to the MAGA flag was Don Jr. Despite the deep tension in their history, or perhaps because of it, the eldest son, now forty-two, had made himself into a Trump mini-me, emulating his father's combative style in social media posts, fundraising appeals, and campaign rallies. He relished going after the president's enemies. He put his name on vanity books with titles like *Triggered: How the Left Thrives on Hate and Wants to Silence Us* and positioned himself as a bearded, gun-toting, camo-wearing culture warrior. He tweeted or retweeted posts calling George Soros "a nazi" and suggesting that Joe Biden was a pedophile.[6] Like his father, his appeal to the evangelical right did not apply to his own private life; his marriage to the former model Vanessa Haydon broke up in the middle of Trump's presidency, leaving five children as he took up with the twice-divorced Kimberly Guilfoyle, who nicknamed him "Junior Mint" because, she insisted, he was so sweet.[7] "They are like the prom king and queen of MAGA land," a senior Trump adviser told a reporter.[8]

Don Jr. was the most popular surrogate for Trump with the base. The crowds roared for him with a gusto they did not exhibit for Mike Pence or Lindsey Graham. While Pence led polls among Republicans to succeed Trump in 2024, Don Jr. came in a stunningly strong second place, with 29 percent.⁹ In fact, his appeal to Trump voters often seemed greater than his appeal to Trump himself. Despite all his son's appearances on the trail, the president never gave him any real responsibility in the campaign or administration. Don Jr. remained an unguided missile that his father tried to keep pointed in the other direction.

But in the end, it was the son-in-law, not the son, who turned out to be the heaviest hitter in the Trump White House.

Kushner's adventures in high-stakes diplomacy began in typical Trump fashion. Weeks after the 2016 election, the newly elected president announced during a visit to *The New York Times* editorial board that Kushner would lead a fresh effort to finally resolve the intractable Israeli-Palestinian conflict. It was news to Kushner, who only learned about his new assignment when a *Times* reporter called his public relations representative.

The grandson of Holocaust survivors, Kushner was raised in an Orthodox Jewish home in New Jersey and graduated from a Jewish day school before attending Harvard. Kushner's parents, Charlie and Seryl, were generous donors in Israel, committing $20 million to the Shaare Zedek Medical Center, which named a new 11.5-acre campus after them. Charlie Kushner was also part of an Israeli-American real estate investment firm. Jared got to know Benjamin Netanyahu during his early rise to power in the 1990s when he visited New Jersey to give paid speeches at Charlie's invitation and even stayed at the Kushner house, sleeping in Jared's bedroom.

But Jared had no experience in diplomacy or Middle East politics and knew few other players—and none on the Palestinian side. During Trump's campaign, he became friendly with Ron Dermer, the American-born Israeli ambassador to the United States, a former political consultant wired into the GOP who helped fashion the campaign's positions on the region. And after the election, of course, Kushner had met and became close with Mohammed bin Salman of Saudi Arabia and other Gulf Arabs.

With Israel and its Arab neighbors increasingly seeing the region through a similar geopolitical lens dominated by the threat of Iran, the Palestinian conflict had receded in urgency in recent years, all but dismissed as an essentially ignorable stalemate. Trump, however, was always attracted to the idea of doing what no one else could. "Over the course of my lifetime, I've always heard that perhaps the toughest deal to make is the deal between the Israelis and the Palestinians," he said when he met early in his tenure with Mahmoud Abbas, the Palestinian Authority president.[10] Undaunted, Trump said it was "frankly maybe not as difficult as people have thought," and declared, "We will get this done." After all, it was basically a real estate disagreement, right? Who knew real estate better?

To make it happen, Kushner was teamed with two lawyers who had worked for Trump's businesses, Jason Greenblatt and David Friedman. Greenblatt, the top attorney for the Trump Organization, was tapped to serve as a special representative, despite no experience in the Middle East. Friedman, Trump's bankruptcy lawyer, had personally implored his client to name him ambassador to Israel, where he had been an active fundraiser for a Jewish settlement deep in the Israeli-occupied West Bank. He had polarizing, even extreme, views, once declaring that Jewish Americans belonging to the liberal organization J Street were "worse than kapos," the Jews who cooperated with the Nazis.[11]

Kushner set about educating himself by reading books and consulting with the likes of Henry Kissinger. He tried to immerse himself in the nuances, at one point looking up the definition of "sovereignty" and discovering something like two dozen different variations on Wikipedia. But he approached the mission with more hubris than humility, openly expressing disdain for those who had come before him and suggesting they had no idea what they were doing while he, with no diplomatic experience, knew how to get things done.

"If we are going to fail, we don't want to fail doing it the same way it's been done in the past," he said in a rare public appearance at a forum hosted by the Washington Institute for Near East Policy.

"You want to be *original* in your failure," joked Rob Satloff, his interviewer and the institute's director.[12]

Kushner did not think it was very funny, but Satloff's joke turned out to be prescient.

At the urging of mega-donors like the billionaire Sheldon Adelson and an evangelical Republican political base that considered support for Israel a defining issue, Trump had come into office resolved to do what his predecessors promised but did not—move the American embassy from Tel Aviv to Jerusalem, the city claimed by both sides as their capital. Trump had initially wanted to do it on the stroke of noon on his Inauguration Day, only to be talked out of it by his original foreign policy team, but by the end of his first year in office, he returned to it, despite Palestinian protests.

"If you do this, you will have disqualified yourself from any role in the peace process," Saeb Erekat, the longtime Palestinian negotiator, told

Kushner at the White House. "Don't threaten me," Kushner snapped back.[13] Trump tried explaining his decision to Mahmoud Abbas over the phone, but when the Palestinian leader went on a long rant, the phone line suddenly dropped. The White House operator asked Trump if he wanted to be reconnected, but he shrugged it off, deciding not to bother. It would be the last time he would speak with Abbas. The next day, December 6, 2017, Trump announced the embassy move.

While Abbas denounced "the slap of the century," the decision did not trigger major riots in the Arab street as its opponents had long warned, a development that encouraged Trump's view that challenging conventional wisdom was not as dangerous as everyone said.[14] But in every past formulation, an eventual peace deal was expected to have the two sides share Jerusalem, and now Trump had effectively given one side its reward without requiring anything in return. "The challenge the Americans have with the Israelis is that if this is to make any sense, it's got to give something pretty good to the Palestinians," Jordan's King Abdullah II said of the embassy move at the World Economic Forum in Davos, Switzerland, a month later.[15]

But that was not Trump's plan. Instead, he called Steven Mnuchin in the middle of a meeting with the king in Davos and had his treasury secretary pass the phone to Abdullah. Trump had something to give *him*.

As the king later related the story, their call went like this: "Abdullah," Trump said, "we've got a great deal for you! We're going to give you the West Bank!" And then he hung up.

To Abdullah, this was hardly a great deal. The last thing a Jordanian king wanted was control of the West Bank. As it was, Jordan already played host to more than two million Palestinian refugees in addition to its own Palestinian population. Radical Palestinians had assassinated Abdullah's great-grandfather and sought to overthrow his father. Taking possession of the West Bank could topple the Hashemite monarchy. With Trump's words still ringing in his ears, Abdullah panicked. "I thought I was having a heart attack," he told an American friend. "I couldn't breathe. I was bent doubled over." Fortunately for Abdullah, Trump's crazy idea never went anywhere, nor did it leak. The secret overture might have been far more disruptive than the embassy move had it become public.

Trump punished the Palestinians for their defiance by cutting off humanitarian aid, closing the Palestinian Authority office in Washington, and shutting down the American consulate in Jerusalem devoted to dealing with the Palestinians. At the same time, Trump kept offering one gift after another to Netanyahu, pulling out of the nuclear agreement with

Iran that the Israeli prime minister hated and even recognizing Israeli sovereignty over the Golan Heights seized from Syria in 1967, the action that prompted Netanyahu's decision to name a settlement Trump Heights.

At Kushner's urging, Trump was approaching the Palestinians the same way he had handled New York condominium owners he wanted to force out so he could redevelop their property—turning off the heat, refusing to make repairs, ordering the doorman not to accept packages. If he made their life miserable, they would be ready to take any lowball deal that Trump offered, or so the theory went. Same with the Palestinians. "I'm going to drive their price down as much as possible," Kushner confided to one Middle East expert.

But the Palestinians were not recalcitrant tenants who would simply move elsewhere, and the conflict was about far more than just property.

Kushner had grand visions for transforming the region beyond the Palestinian dispute. He aspired to knit together the Sunni Arab states in a new security coalition against the Shiite regime in Iran. Building on a line inserted into Trump's speech during his early visit to Saudi Arabia, Kushner had the National Security Council develop a proposal for an Arab equivalent of NATO, called the Middle East Strategic Alliance, or MESA.

The alliance he envisioned would link the United States to Egypt, Jordan, Saudi Arabia, Oman, Qatar, Bahrain, Kuwait, and the United Arab Emirates under a single security umbrella, much like the Atlantic Alliance. The idea morphed over time, with different sides pushing for a pact that would include trade or energy or conflict resolution elements. "It was like a Chinese restaurant menu," said a senior State Department official. The fact that the president was busy trying to undermine or even withdraw from the original NATO did not deter Kushner from seeking to bind the United States to a new web of security commitments in the Middle East.

The proposal freaked out national security veterans at the Pentagon and State Department, who deemed it "half-baked," as the State Department official put it. An ironclad commitment to mutual defense, à la NATO, could oblige the American military to come to the aid of an Arab potentate who embarked on some reckless adventure, which was hardly a theoretical problem, given the ill-considered Saudi war then being fought in Yemen. "It landed like a lead balloon," the official recalled. But that did not curb the enthusiasm coming from the White House, which went so far as to order up MESA stickers and even limited-edition MESA challenge coins as memorabilia.

The brutal assassination of Jamal Khashoggi in 2018, though, soured Saudi relations despite Kushner's refusal to break ties with his fellow princeling MBS, and the idea of a sweeping alliance was watered down to the point that it became little more than an energy cooperative before finally dying amid bureaucratic resistance in Washington and waning interest in the region. Instead, some on the Trump team suggested brokering nonbelligerence agreements between Israel and its Arab neighbors—not quite full diplomatic relations but at least a commitment not to attack each other. But that notion faded as well, as Netanyahu faced political trouble at home.

Kushner's long-awaited plan for Israeli-Palestinian peace proved no more successful. It was predicated on the idea of buying off the Palestinians with $50 billion in international investment on the assumption that what they really wanted was prosperity, not conflict. Israel would keep all its West Bank settlements while freezing new construction for four years and the Palestinians would have a state of their own but with limited sovereignty and only the outskirts of East Jerusalem and its suburbs for a capital. Trump unveiled the plan at the White House on January 28, 2020, with Netanyahu at his side. Back in his West Bank headquarters in Ramallah, Mahmoud Abbas remained defiant. "A thousand times over: no, no, no," he declared.[16]

What the Palestinians were not able to do, however, Netanyahu did himself—drive a wedge between himself and his benefactor in the Oval Office. The announcement of the Kushner plan came amid Israel's biggest political crisis in years. The country had just held back-to-back stalemated elections without forming a new government and was heading toward a third and, eventually, a fourth. With his premiership at stake, Netanyahu essentially turned the White House ceremony presenting Kushner's plan into a campaign event, speaking from the podium for a full twenty minutes and even declaring that Israel would now "apply its laws" to disputed territory in the West Bank, code for annexation.

Although Netanyahu lavished all the usual praise on Trump ("the greatest friend that Israel has ever had in the White House"), the president grew more impatient the longer the speech went on.[17] Trump did not like anyone stealing his thunder, especially in his own house.

"What the hell was that?" he demanded of aides afterward.[18] Trump was doing him a favor, the latest of a whole slew of favors, the president told others, and Netanyahu had upstaged him.

Netanyahu compounded the problem afterward. In an interview with reporters at Blair House, the American government residence across from the White House where foreign leaders stayed, Netanyahu announced that he would ask his cabinet to approve unilateral annexation of the strategically important Jordan Valley and all Jewish settlements in the West Bank. Such a preemptive move would upend Kushner's laboriously crafted plan and potentially destabilize the region. Trump, already angry at Netanyahu, thought that was "really going too far" and vented his anger at Kushner.[19]

The president's son-in-law, in turn, called David Friedman, who was in the middle of a presentation describing Kushner's plan. As his phone kept vibrating repeatedly, Friedman finally excused himself to take the call. Kushner "jumped down my throat," as the ambassador later recalled.

"Did you know that Bibi is annexing the freaking Jordan Valley today?" Kushner demanded, using Netanyahu's nickname.

"No," Friedman said.[20]

Kushner accused Friedman of encouraging Netanyahu to freelance. After what was described as "a rough conversation," Kushner ordered Friedman to march over to Blair House and tell the Israeli prime minister to back down.

Friedman dutifully complied. After initially resisting, Netanyahu walked back his comments with reporters on the plane ride home to Tel Aviv, suggesting there had been a misunderstanding. But he was furious at Trump and his son-in-law, and the Israeli leader's allies lashed out in the press, with one settler leader even declaring that "Kushner took a knife and put it in Netanyahu's back."[21]

Netanyahu sent his ambassador, Ron Dermer, to complain but Trump would not see him. "The president doesn't like you guys now," Avi Berkowitz, Kushner's deputy, told the envoy. Dermer went to see Kushner instead. In a heated meeting, the Israeli envoy blamed Kushner for betraying Netanyahu and damaging his credibility. "We had a deal and you changed the terms of the deal," Dermer said.

After everything he and his father-in-law had done for Netanyahu, Kushner erupted in anger. "Get the hell out of here!" the usually even-keeled Kushner snapped, kicking the Israeli ambassador out of his office.

Berkowitz diverted Dermer to his own office to try to smooth things over. But Netanyahu was no longer willing to take direction from Washington. Soon, he was moving toward annexation again, setting a July 1 deadline to take sovereignty over 30 percent of the West Bank, a maneuver he hoped would finally break the election deadlock. Trump and Netanyahu, who had forged such a close alliance over Trump's first three years in office that the Israeli prime minister had hung giant campaign posters of the two of them together on buildings in Jerusalem and Tel Aviv, were now so estranged they would not speak for months.

Netanyahu's annexation plan upset the careful balance that had emerged in recent years between Israel and its Arab neighbors. Arab leaders had grown weary of the Palestinians; they had poured billions of dollars into the territories only to see much of it disappear into a corrupt establishment that resisted efforts to resolve the dispute. The United Arab Emirates, Bahrain, and even Saudi Arabia were more interested in linking up with Israel's technologically advanced economy and military, particularly against their common adversary in Tehran. Behind the scenes, the Saudis and others had forged robust intelligence cooperation with Israel, while publicly, the Emiratis invited Israel to stage a pavilion at the Expo 2020 Dubai and hosted Israeli sports teams.

During a discussion with Kushner in mid-2019, Yousef al-Otaiba, the politically connected ambassador to the United States from the UAE, had even raised the idea of officially normalizing ties with Israel, complete with embassies and an exchange of ambassadors, although the idea went nowhere as Israel headed into its string of elections.

But annexation would make normalization politically impossible. Arab leaders were stunned that Netanyahu would throw away all the progress for what seemed like a domestic political move.

Mohammed bin Zayed, the Emirati leader known as MBZ, decided to intervene and directed Otaiba to write an op-ed arguing that Israel had to choose between annexing territory and improving relations with its neighbors. After drafting the piece, Otaiba called Haim Saban, the politically connected Israeli-American billionaire and major Democratic donor, for help placing it. Saban agreed, advising that the op-ed should be written in Hebrew, published in *Yedioth Ahronoth*, Israel's largest paid-circulation newspaper, and appear on Friday, the best-read day of the week.

No Gulf diplomat had ever written a column in Hebrew in an Israeli newspaper so its publication on June 12 made a huge splash. Much of the Arab world "would like to believe Israel is an opportunity, not an enemy," Otaiba wrote, outlining the ways normalized relations could benefit both sides. But annexation "will certainly and immediately upend Israeli aspirations for improved security, economic and cultural ties with the Arab world and with UAE."[22] In other words, Israel could have annexation or it could have better relations with its Arab neighbors, but it could not have both.

———

Nobody had a plan for what came next. Netanyahu, who after a third straight election had barely put together a fragile governing coalition which would not last long, was irate about the op-ed, realizing that the message from the Arab world would undermine his plan to claim West Bank territory. In Washington, Ron Dermer, his ambassador, called Otaiba and ripped his head off for a half hour. But no matter how mad Netanyahu was, the column changed the geopolitical equation.

David Friedman pushed for a meeting with Trump to lobby for Netanyahu's annexation, but the president would not hear of it. "Why are we talking about this?" he demanded. He was increasingly convinced that Netanyahu never really wanted peace but only used Trump's friendship to advance his electoral interests.

In late June, Kushner sent his aide Avi Berkowitz back to Jerusalem along with Friedman to talk Netanyahu down. A thirty-one-year-old Harvard Law School graduate who first met Kushner playing pickup basketball at a Passover celebration, the baby-faced Berkowitz was an unlikely peace negotiator. Smart, friendly, and congenial, he had little of the scar tissue that marked the veterans of the conflict, but had a way of ingratiating himself with the older men he found across the table.

Israel was in lockdown during the pandemic, so Berkowitz stayed at a hotel that was otherwise largely closed, barred from leaving the premises except to meet the prime minister. The meetings with Netanyahu were equally surreal. The hard-nosed prime minister refused to budge, and the Americans had in effect two different positions: that of Berkowitz, representing the skeptical Kushner, and that of Friedman, an outright cheerleader for annexation.

Berkowitz warned Netanyahu that if he proceeded with claiming sovereignty over the West Bank, Trump would very likely tweet against him. Netanyahu asked if the president would really criticize a pro-Israel move shortly before his own election, essentially counting on his allies in the evangelical Christian community to influence Trump.

But Berkowitz insisted that Trump meant it. "The president doesn't really like you these days," he told Netanyahu, repeating the line he had used with Dermer earlier. "You will take your best friend and turn him into an enemy."

Netanyahu was unmoved. "We are nowhere here," Berkowitz told Kushner by phone afterward. "We could not be further from a resolution."

Finally, after a second meeting with Netanyahu yielded no more progress, Berkowitz and Kushner discussed the Otaiba op-ed and whether they should float the possibility of trading normalization for annexation—the

UAE would recognize Israel if it gave up the sovereignty plan. During a third meeting with Netanyahu, Berkowitz raised the idea. The testy prime minister was not enthusiastic, but did not rule it out either, which Berkowitz took as a green light to proceed.

After a long commercial flight back to Washington, Berkowitz climbed into a military car waiting at Reagan National Airport and then got on the phone with Otaiba during the ride into the city. Berkowitz explained the grim results from his talks. To get around the stalemate, Otaiba suggested reviving the nonbelligerency agreements that had been discussed two years earlier: Would Israel forgo annexation in exchange for such pacts? No, Berkowitz said, that was not enough. But what about full normalization in exchange for stopping annexation? Berkowitz asked. That was essentially the implicit tradeoff in the op-ed. Otaiba said he had been thinking the same thing and would check with his capital.

MBZ, the Emirati leader, was reluctant, not trusting Netanyahu to live up to a deal. What if the Emiratis extended diplomatic recognition only to have Israel embark on annexation a few months later anyway? Otaiba suggested a conditional deal to make that harder. They would ask for a permanent halt to annexation with the understanding that Israel would never agree to that; the Emiratis could then, as a fallback, accept a five-year freeze. In five years, it was very likely the world would have changed anyway—Trump would be out of office and Netanyahu probably would be too. MBZ consented.

Otaiba took the proposed deal to Kushner and Berkowitz. In a negotiation faux pas, he made the mistake of telling the Americans that the official Emirati position was a permanent halt to annexation, but they would settle for a five-year freeze, trading away the backup plan from the start. Kushner pocketed the concession and countered by suggesting a three-year pause instead. Otaiba said he could make that work. As he got up to leave, Kushner suggested Otaiba finalize the details directly with Dermer, but after their fractious phone call following his op-ed, the Emirati envoy wanted nothing to do with his Israeli counterpart.

Kushner and Berkowitz began meeting separately with Otaiba and Dermer, sometimes at their embassies, sometimes at their private homes, but never together. For six weeks, during the long Covid summer, when Trump's re-election was slipping away and Kushner was also nominally in charge of running the campaign, the two sides sent messages through the Americans.

Berkowitz talked by phone with Otaiba or Dermer five or seven times a day. It did not always go smoothly. At one point, Dermer called Berkowitz to say that Netanyahu would only go along if three Arab nations agreed to normal diplomatic relations, not just one, making it easier to sell to his right-wing allies. But getting a single nation was hard enough. An exasperated Kushner erupted. "Tell Ron that one country is all he's going to get and if he doesn't want it, he can go fuck himself," Kushner told Berkowitz.[23] Dermer privately agreed it was too much to ask and persuaded Netanyahu to back down.

The draft agreement went through 117 edited versions, each word fraught with meaning. The term "annexation," for instance, was unacceptable to the Israelis because, in their view, it would imply a violation of international law, so they used the phrase "declaring sovereignty" instead.[24] The two sides also quarreled over how to describe Israel's commitment not to declare sovereignty; would Israel "suspend" or "postpone"? Berkowitz eventually searched Google to see whether one word implied more of a temporary stoppage than the other. In the end, the Israelis decided that "suspend" seemed less permanent, so agreed to that. The formal document did not specify that the suspension would last three years, but that was included in a separate, secret letter that Trump gave to the Emiratis, who locked it in a safe in their Washington embassy.

After the arduous back-and-forth, the deal was finally set. But as often happened in Middle East negotiations, it was never final until the pen hit the paper. Just days before the agreement was to be formally sealed, Dermer met with Kushner and Berkowitz and unloaded his grievances. "This is nuts," he said. "I have not spoken to an Emirati official."

Kushner turned to Berkowitz. "Have you told him?" Kushner asked.

Berkowitz shook his head no.

"Can I tell him?" Kushner asked.

Berkowitz nodded yes.

Turning to Dermer, Kushner said, "They don't like you."

They were teasing, but it was also true.

Kushner arranged to have the agreement finalized in a telephone call involving the three leaders set for August 13—Trump, Netanyahu, and MBZ. But the night before the call, Netanyahu got nervous about a domestic backlash and proposed postponing for a few days to see if other Arab countries could be enlisted to join. Dermer told him that would be a huge mistake but dutifully conveyed the message. Sure enough, an angry Berkowitz told Dermer that the call was happening the next day with or without the prime minister. David Friedman, who was in Berkowitz's office, forcefully pushed back over the speakerphone as well. "Let me work on it," Dermer said, making clear he agreed with them. Within an hour, Dermer got his prime minister to back down. Netanyahu would get on the call. Only later did Dermer hear that Kushner's initial reaction was to say, "Fuck Bibi."

Unlike presidents who had been intensively hands-on during Middle East negotiations, Trump had left the details to Kushner and his team, no more involved in this foreign policy achievement than he had been in his big domestic policy initiative, the first-year tax cuts. But he was happy to swoop in now to take credit. Soon, he would be touting it on the campaign trail as his shot at a Nobel Peace Prize.

As they gathered for the call the next day, however, Trump's team realized they did not have a name for the agreement to present the branding-focused president. Major General Miguel Correa, a National Security Council official involved in the negotiations, suggested the Abraham Accord. Trump predictably joked that it should be named the Trump Accord but went along with the idea. Even then, the call almost did not happen due to a last-minute technical glitch. The White House switchboard got MBZ and Netanyahu on the line but when Trump tried to join, the connection to Abu Dhabi suddenly went dead. For several long, awkward minutes, the operator could not get MBZ back while Netanyahu in Israel and Trump in the Oval Office waited. Berkowitz, sitting near the president, was on edge. Yousef al-Otaiba, listening in from his embassy, felt his hands sweating. Finally, the connection was reestablished, and everything proceeded as planned. MBZ was enthusiastic about the agreement. "Mr. President," he said, "this is the only good news we've had out of 2020."

For the Emiratis, the agreement was also a chance to resolve their problems in Congress, where their long-standing desire to buy sophisticated F-35 fighter jets from the United States had run into resistance due to fears that it would diminish Israel's military advantage. While the Trump team insisted it was not directly a part of the deal, the fact that the Emiratis now had diplomatic relations with Israel suddenly made it easier to sell them high-technology weaponry. The White House eventually went to bat for a $23 billion package of F-35 jets, Reaper drones, and other precision weapons, overcoming Senate resistance by two votes shortly before Trump left office.

Hours after the phone call between Trump, Netanyahu, and MBZ, Bahrain's finance minister was on the phone with Berkowitz saying his small Gulf state wanted to go next, eventually making the deal in time to be included in the South Lawn ceremony, at which point the Abraham

Accords became plural. Now that it was clear that the Trump administration was willing to pay to play, others came to the table too.

Sudan wanted to be taken off the State Department's list of state sponsors of terrorism. Trump agreed. As for Morocco, which had long had friendly relations with Israel, it offered to formalize ties in exchange for American recognition of its sovereignty over the Western Sahara, a territory that had been in dispute for many years. Old hands like James Baker, the former secretary of state who had served as a U.N. special envoy on the Western Sahara, objected when Kushner called, telling him he was trading away a long-standing point of principle for not much in return given that Morocco was already on good terms with Israel.

Trump's decision to give Morocco what it wanted was a case study in how policy was made in his White House. Until then, Trump had resisted making any concession on the Western Sahara out of deference to Senator Jim Inhofe, a Republican ally from Oklahoma and Washington's most outspoken champion of the Polisario Front, the rebel movement fighting Moroccan occupation. But Trump was mad at Inhofe for unrelated reasons—as chairman of the Armed Services Committee, Inhofe was steering passage of the annual defense bill through the Senate but refused to put in a provision Trump wanted punishing social media companies or to take out a provision Trump opposed renaming military bases honoring Confederate generals.

So in buying off Morocco on behalf of Israel, Trump could also take revenge against Inhofe. For Trump, even making peace involved some element of making war. And for all of the fanfare on the resodded grass of the South Lawn as the Abraham Accords were signed, Trump's goal that fall was not so much making peace as it was keeping control of the White House.

In theory, that was Kushner's mission too. The Secretary of Everything was supposed to be riding herd on the campaign even as he was also dealing with the pandemic and police reform. He was the one who had to remove Brad Parscale as campaign manager and he was the one on the phone with Bill Stepien and Justin Clark, going over the budget and data in his cool analytical way.

But it was Trump who was deciding the message, not his son-in-law. Kushner's attention was divided between the political battleground states of the Midwest and the geopolitical battlegrounds of the Middle East. After nearly four years in Washington, he found his passion in a diplomatic opportunity he could seize, not in a campaign whose fate was out of his control.

CHAPTER 27

The Altar of Trump

Heading into the final weeks of the campaign, Trump was fixated on one thing he was sure could guarantee his re-election and save his presidency: getting a vaccine against the coronavirus before November 3.

No matter his efforts to deny, dismiss, and generally make light of the virus, Trump knew he could not persuade enough Americans outside his hard-core fan base to simply pretend Covid was not a threat, not when nearly 200,000 people had already died, and there was no cure. So while he campaigned at mask-less rallies all but ignoring the pandemic, he pressured his public health officials to deliver rapid, pre-election approval for the shots.

The vaccine was to be the miracle solution that hydroxychloroquine had not been. Even after his relentless promotion of the drug blew up in his face, Trump had continued to take it himself that fall, according to a senior government official, despite telling the public that he had "finished" in May. But hydroxychloroquine would not make the pandemic go away nor would it rescue his campaign. For that, he was counting on Operation Warp Speed, an $18 billion initiative to speed development and eventual distribution of a vaccine. Trump enthusiastically supported it, although the idea had originated with one of the Deep State officials he disparaged, Peter Marks, director of the FDA's Center for Biologics Evaluation and Research, who originally called it Project Warp Speed, in a nod to *Star Trek*.

By September, Trump had become increasingly explicit in demanding that the vaccine be released before the election, insisting that science meet his political timetable. On Labor Day, he touted progress of vaccine trials and promised approval would soon be forthcoming. The vaccine was "incredible," he said, and "it's going to be done in a very short period of time," maybe as soon as October.[1] He continued to express optimism for the next couple weeks. "Vaccines are moving along fast and safely!" he tweeted in mid-September. A day later, he was so sure the vaccine would benefit him, he made it an attack line against the opposition. "The Democrats are just ANGRY that the vaccine and delivery are so far ahead of schedule. They hate what they are seeing. Saving lives should make them happy, not sad!"

Trump's FDA commissioner, however, had a different plan. After months of what he considered inappropriate pressure from the president and his political team at the White House, Stephen Hahn had reached his breaking point with Trump. The president, in his quest to find another miracle drug when hydroxychloroquine did not work out, had fixated over the summer on a treatment for those who were already sick called convalescent plasma therapy. The idea was to use plasma drawn from blood donated by patients who had recovered from Covid to introduce antibodies into the system of those currently ailing. It was a well-established medical approach and the FDA had been testing it, but not quickly enough for Trump, who pressed at the last minute for it to be approved before the Republican National Convention opened.

Both Mark Meadows and Brad Smith, an adviser to Jared Kushner, called Hahn to lobby for immediate approval, and Trump personally called Francis Collins, head of the National Institutes of Health, to make clear he wanted it done by the Friday before the convention. None of them was subtle about the political motivation behind the timing.

When action was not forthcoming, Trump took his grievance public on Saturday, August 22, two days before the convention. "The deep state, or whoever, over at the FDA is making it very difficult for drug companies to get people in order to test the vaccines and therapeutics," he tweeted. "Obviously, they are hoping to delay the answer until after November 3rd. Must focus on speed, and saving lives!"

In fact, as Trump learned later that day from Alex Azar, approval for plasma therapy was about to happen. The president insisted on making the announcement himself at the White House the following afternoon, just twenty-four hours before the convention would open. But even as Trump hailed the news with Azar and Hahn at his side, they overstated the treatment's effectiveness and claimed the plasma had reduced deaths by 35 percent. A "tremendous" number, Trump declared. Hahn said that thirty-five out of 100 patients "would have been saved because of the administration of plasma."[2] Except it was not true. The figure seemed to be calculated based on a small subgroup of patients under age eighty who were not on ventilators and received plasma within three days of diagnosis.

Hahn, who had earned his professional reputation as a rigorous research scientist, should have known better and was devastated by the resulting furor. It was a rookie mistake, he felt, made after enormous political pressure from the president. Hahn claimed that he had not even looked at the political calendar to understand why the president was so anxious, an omission for which he later declared himself "dumb as a doornail." With his own credibility on the line and scientists within his agency furious about the repeated blows to their scientific integrity, Hahn decided to post a correction. "The criticism is entirely justified," he wrote on Twitter on the first night of the convention. "What I should have said better is that the data show a relative risk reduction not an absolute risk reduction."[3]

His tweet did not satisfy critics who thought it still misstated the data and it predictably infuriated Trump. But it was a turning point for Hahn. After months of battering, he was done with the president. He had bowed to the White House before, generating consternation by many within the FDA, but he now told others he understood that Trump was a bully, surrounded by other bullies like Meadows. He was determined not to cave in anymore—especially with the trustworthiness of a lifesaving vaccine on the line.

If you're going to play this way, I've got to play a different way, he thought. *We just do what we want. I'm going to go rogue.*

Trump's tweet accusing "the deep state, or whoever" of trying to delay a vaccine until after the election set off alarms not just at the FDA but at the pharmaceutical companies developing the shots. Albert Bourla, the chief executive of Pfizer, was outraged. He had launched his own company's Project Lightspeed nearly two months before Operation Warp Speed got underway and he was not about to allow his vaccine to be politicized. Trump's tweet, he said later, was "the straw that broke the camel's back."[4] Bourla rallied his counterparts at eight other drug companies to issue a joint public pledge in fourteen newspapers on September 8 vowing to "only submit for approval" any new vaccines "after demonstrating safety and efficacy."[5] They would not be rushed by a president seeking to salvage his flailing election hopes.

The industry declaration bolstered Hahn and his FDA to resist Trump's escalating pressure. Over the summer, the agency had been finalizing its rules for emergency approval of the vaccines. Hahn and Peter Marks, whose center was in charge of evaluating the vaccines, had been particularly concerned about the risk-benefit ratio, given that the vaccines would be used for presumably healthy people, and determined that a minimum of sixty days of follow-up would be required after conclusion of Stage 3 trials to ensure there were no dangerous side effects. It was already September, which meant that sixty days would make it impossible for vaccine approval before the election.

But Trump and his political officials seemed oblivious to what was coming. When the draft guidelines leaked to *The Washington Post* on September 22 with a headline pointing out the timetable for vaccine approval made it "unlikely one will be cleared by Election Day," Trump erupted.[6] He accused Hahn and the rest of the agency of "colluding to prevent his re-election," as the FDA commissioner later told associates.

In public, Trump was alternately incredulous and defiant. "I don't see any reason why it should be delayed further," he tweeted. He later hinted that he would personally block the FDA from adopting the sixty-day standard. "That has to be approved by the White House," he said, adding, "We may or we may not approve it"—comments that further shook confidence at a time when the public was increasingly worried that Trump would rush the shots heedless of the risks.[7] Polls showed the number of Americans saying they were ready to take a vaccine had fallen from 72 percent in the spring to 51 percent in September.[8]

The subsequent bombardment of the FDA chief, now referred to by Trump as "that fucking Hahn," was relentless, including multiple phone calls from Trump, Meadows, and Kushner's adviser, as well as face-to-face meetings—all focused on getting Hahn to change the sixty-day timetable so the vaccine could be approved before the election.[9] Once again, the White House officials did not bother to hide their political motivation and accused Hahn of "sabotaging the election effort." Had the intense pressure campaign become public at the time, it almost certainly would have further reduced public faith in the shots. But Hahn, finally, refused to relent. "I was adamant about the fact that we weren't going to change one word of that document," he would later tell associates. "I absolutely refused because I knew that the minute we changed one word in that guidance people would not trust our process."

The hectoring phone calls would continue as would Trump's public claims that the vaccine was imminent, but as a practical matter the fight was over. Legally, it appeared unlikely that the president could overrule the FDA on an emergency use decision that required "scientific evidence" and certification that it was in the public health interest. And while Trump could fire Hahn, that would be a disaster in the heat of the fall campaign. And so, by the end of September, Trump's best hope to revive his rapidly shrinking chances to win a second term was effectively dashed. Hahn had gone rogue and won.

With no magic end to the pandemic in sight and only weeks until the election, even the Trump campaign's internal surveys of seventeen battleground states showed a win was unlikely. Brad Parscale, the former campaign manager demoted to running campaign data before being iced out altogether, told others that more than 90 percent of voters had made up their minds by August.

But if Trump could not win, he had no intention of losing either. He preemptively declared the election the most crooked in history—unless he won. For months, he had been laying the groundwork to dispute any result other than his own victory. He began calling the contest "rigged" in May, months before any votes were cast.

This was an old playbook for Trump. Anytime he was beaten in any kind of contest he cried foul. When *The Apprentice* lost an Emmy to *The Amazing Race* in 2004, he complained that the awards were a con game. "We were robbed!" he fumed as he stormed out of the auditorium. "They cheated us!"[10] When Republicans lost the 2012 presidential race, he called the election "a total sham." When Ted Cruz beat him in the Iowa caucuses in 2016, he cried "fraud," and claimed that "Cruz didn't win Iowa, he stole it." In the fall of that year, fearing he would lose to Hillary Clinton, he said the outcome was "absolutely being rigged"—until he actually won. Even then, while victorious in the Electoral College, he claimed that Clinton's three-million-vote margin in the popular vote was fraudulent, an assertion for which his own handpicked commission found no evidence. A search of Trump's public statements on the Factbase website going back to 2012 found that he had questioned voting or suggested that an election would be rigged, unfair, or otherwise compromised 713 times.[11] And that was before Labor Day.

Over the summer, as it became increasingly clear that the pandemic was going to lead to a historic increase in voting by mail and states were working to make it easier, Trump had even proposed postponing the fall election, saying it would be the most "INACCURATE & FRAUDULENT Election in history." Why should the United States not "Delay the Election," he asked, "until people can properly, securely and safely vote???" While Republican leaders including Mitch McConnell and Liz Cheney forcefully shot down that proposal and made clear the election would take place as it had even during times of war, Trump continued to inveigh against mail-in ballots and new state laws facilitating them, never mind that he himself had voted by mail during Florida's primary earlier in the year. His newly installed postmaster general, Louis DeJoy, a major Trump donor, imposed sharp cutbacks at the Postal Service and warned states of slower than normal turnaround time for absentee ballots. The election results, Trump insisted in September, "MAY NEVER BE ACCU-RATELY DETERMINED" because of more voting by mail.

On September 23, just a day after Trump's hopes for a pre-election reprieve from the pandemic with a vaccine were dashed, he went even further.

"Win, lose, or draw in this election, will you commit here today to making sure for a peaceful transferral of power after the election?" Brian Karem, a correspondent for *Playboy*, asked at a news conference.

"Well, we're going to have to see what happens," he responded non-committally. "You know that I've been complaining very strongly about the ballots. And the ballots are a disaster." Pressed, he added, "Get rid of the ballots and you'll have a very—we'll have a very peaceful—there won't be a transfer, frankly. There'll be a continuation."[12]

The closer the election came, the more Trump embraced extreme positions. Rather than toning down his divisive rhetoric, he amped it up. At every turn, Trump now spoke of Red America, the true America, versus the "badly managed, high crime, Blue States," as he put it in a September tweet. At one point in mid-September, he argued that the Covid death toll was not so bad—as long as states that voted for Democrats were not counted. "If you take the blue states out, we're at a level that I don't think anybody in the world would be at," he said.[13] He even personally ordered a review of federal aid with the goal of withholding funds from "anarchist" Democratic-run cities that allowed "themselves to deteriorate into lawless zones."[14]

He broadcast so much misinformation that fall that Twitter for the first time regularly warned readers that some of his posts were misleading. He lied so much that *The New York Times* found 131 of his statements during a single rally false or misleading.[15] He also issued orders threatening to politicize the government even after he was gone, including an executive order to remove key protections from the professional civil service; the potential consequences of this move were so significant that the Republican Trump appointee charged with overseeing it resigned in protest, warning that the decision would "replace apolitical expertise with political obeisance."[16]

No matter how besieged he felt, Trump remained a believer in his own destiny. He could not be counted out and even many political pros thought Biden at the end of September was just a bad debate, a campaign stumble or two, and an October surprise away from a repeat of Trump's 2016 shocker. On September 18, fate seemed to intervene again on Trump's behalf when Justice Ruth Bader Ginsburg died at the age of eighty-seven after a long battle with cancer.

Ginsburg, a liberal icon, had famously and, as it turned out, unwisely refused to retire during Barack Obama's second term. Now Trump insisted he would name a replacement and work with Mitch McConnell to get a new justice confirmed regardless of how close it was to the election. The opening gave Trump a rare shot to name three members of the court in a single term and decisively shift it to a six-to-three conservative majority for a generation.

On Saturday, September 26, Trump held a ceremony to announce his nomination of Amy Coney Barrett, a Notre Dame law professor and appeals court judge from Indiana, packing the Rose Garden with unmasked supporters seated closely together. Barrett's selection was no real surprise, coming two years after Trump had privately told the Federalist Society's Leonard Leo that he was holding her in reserve in case he got to fill Ginsburg's seat. She was a favorite of anti-abortion conservatives, a former clerk of the late Justice Antonin Scalia and just forty-eight years old, meaning she could serve for decades.

But the timing was unprecedented, another busted norm in a presidency full of them. Trump wanted Barrett confirmed just days before the election, after millions of Americans would have already cast early ballots. There would barely be time for hearings or even the pretense of a process in the Senate, where McConnell obligingly arranged a lightning-fast confirmation only four years after denying Obama's final Supreme Court nominee, Merrick Garland, a hearing because the nomination came eight months before the 2016 presidential election. Trump would eventually be extraordinarily blunt in admitting that he wanted to push Barrett's nomination through so close to November 3 to ensure his own victory. "I think this will end up in the Supreme Court," Trump said of the election, "and I think it's very important that we have nine justices," rather than risk a four-to-four tie. Trump appeared to believe that, with three of his appointees on the bench, they would surely swing the outcome his way if necessary.[17]

The White House ceremony for Barrett ended with an impromptu indoor reception where Trump and guests mingled in the Diplomatic Room without observing any social distancing guidelines. Within days, at least a dozen people who attended, from Republican senators to senior White House officials to the president of Notre Dame, tested positive for the coronavirus, causing Tony Fauci to refer on air to the gathering as a reckless "superspreader event." Ivanka Trump, who along with her husband were two of the few not to get infected, joked privately that the only place that had achieved herd immunity was the White House.

Among those attending the Barrett reception were members of the debate team that Trump had, reluctantly, assembled to prepare for his first in-person confrontation with Joe Biden, scheduled just a few days later in Cleveland. Trump never liked preparation, whether for international summits or campaign debates, and at his insistence the sessions at a long conference table in the White House Map Room felt more like free-form kibitzing than a formal mock debate.

Chris Christie played Biden while Kellyanne Conway acted the part of Chris Wallace, the *Fox News Sunday* anchor who would moderate the debate. In four sessions over two days, they punched hard at Trump, seeking to rattle him. Christie was especially scathing about the pandemic. "You messed up Covid—you killed people!" he said at one point, channeling an expected Biden attack line. "All you think about is politics!"[18]

Trump bristled at the barbed attacks coming from Christie and turned to Hope Hicks, who had returned to the White House in March to help him through the election. "How lucky are we that we are not debating Chris," Trump said. As for Biden, though, the president seemed to believe his own caricature of the Democratic nominee as a doddering old man. "Joe Biden will never be able to do that," he told Christie after a particularly tough line.

Some advisers counseled Trump to hit Biden hard. Rudy Giuliani, who despite having gotten Trump impeached scored an invite to two prep sessions, lobbied Trump to bring up Hunter Biden. But others said Trump took their advice too far. Christie would later claim that he was not advocating that the president swing punches at the Democrat so much as stand his ground if Biden tried to cut him off as he had with opponents in past debates. "The plan was: If he interrupts you, don't let him," Christie would explain. "The rest of the plan was: Let him talk. The more he talked the better chance he was going to lose his train of thought." Conway was especially insistent on that last point. "I was pushing to be aggressive," another adviser ruefully acknowledged later, but "I meant more surgical-strike rifle shot than shotgun blast."

After their last session, Christie had a moment alone with the president in the Oval Office. His final advice: "If you let him talk, he'll hang himself. Remember what my old political science professor used to say to me: If your adversary is in the midst of committing suicide, there's no reason to commit murder. The result is the same."

"Got it," Trump replied.

But he did not. When the debate began on the evening of Tuesday, September 29, it took only minutes for that to become clear as Trump shouted, bullied, hectored, lied, and interrupted, over and over again. Losing in the polls and still trying to distract from the pandemic, the president offered incoherent bluster, inflammatory racism, and personal attacks on his opponent's son. He talked over Biden. He talked over Chris Wallace. He talked over Biden some more. How bad was it? Biden's most memorable line was his lament, at the end of the debate's first segment: "Will you shut up, man? This is so unpresidential."

To the extent there was a substantive headline, it was Trump's refusal to disavow white supremacy. Asked by Wallace if he would tell extremist groups like the Proud Boys to "stand down" and not stir violence in the streets, Trump said, "Proud Boys, stand back and stand by"—a twist of Wallace's words that the radical group took as validation and a call to be ready. And the president foreshadowed what could come as he continued to undermine public confidence in the election. "This is not going to end well," he said. He then repeated it, as if for emphasis. "This is not going to end well."[19] It sure sounded like a threat.

Afterward, even Lindsey Graham privately admitted the debate had been a "disaster" and warned other Republicans it might well have been Trump's "downfall." On CNN, Jake Tapper called it a "hot mess inside a dumpster fire inside a train wreck." Dana Bash called it a "shitshow."[20] On ABC, Chris Christie was skewered by other guests. "Was that the debate you prepared for?" host George Stephanopoulos asked. "No," Christie said. "On the Trump side, it was too hot."[21]

But Trump did not get it. His own advisers by that point rarely confronted him with unpleasant realities. The day after the debate, he was sure he had crushed Biden when Christie called to check in.

"Chris, everybody I speak to tells me I did great, I won," the president said. "What do you think?"

"All those people are lying to you," Christie replied. "You lost."

"No, I didn't," Trump said.

"Mr. President, you interrupted him seventy-one times in ninety minutes," he pointed out. "I didn't think that was physically possible. You can argue with me all you want but you watch—your poll numbers are going to go down and this race is going to get tougher to win."

Trump was not buying it. "You're wrong, I won," he said.

For Trump and some around him, Christie's public apostasy of admitting on television that the debate had not gone according to plan was an exercise in self-preservation for a man who had been involved in the debate prep and it soured relations. "Everyone saw that as a real Judas moment," one of Christie's rivals in Trump's circle recalled. It was a turning point for Christie as well. Within days, he would come down with Covid himself, as would some of the others who had participated in the debate prep. Christie became seriously ill and spent seven days in an intensive care unit in the hospital, coming closer to death than many realized. By the time he came out, he knew who was to blame and his years-long friendship with Trump was all but over.

Two days after the debate, the president announced that he and the first lady had contracted the coronavirus, sending out the news in a tweet at 12:54 a.m. For months, Trump had made Covid denialism his signature at great cost to millions of Americans. He had courted personal as well as political disaster by refusing to wear a mask and encouraging others not to do so either. His positive test had the feel of an inevitable plot twist.

The White House defaulted to deception, a long tradition when it came to presidents and their health, notably including the failure even to admit that Woodrow Wilson had contracted the flu during the twentieth century's deadliest pandemic, although it almost killed him. The morning of Trump's tweet, Mark Meadows appeared, mask-less, in the White House driveway and announced to reporters that Trump was in "good spirits" and "very energetic." He acknowledged that, well, yes, actually, Trump was experiencing "mild symptoms." But, he insisted, "The American people can rest assured that we have a president that is not only on the job, will remain on the job, and I'm optimistic that he'll have a very quick and speedy recovery."[22]

By late afternoon, the "mild symptoms" included a fever, and Trump was being given an experimental antibody treatment. By day's end Friday, the White House announced that, "out of an abundance of caution," he would be flown to Walter Reed National Military Medical Center.[23]

In a memoir released after his time in office, Meadows revealed the extent of the cover-up in hiding both the timeline of the illness and its severity. Meadows, to Trump's fury, acknowledged that the president had received his first positive test result on September 26, the same day as the Amy Coney Barrett "superspreader" event, but had nonetheless continued to travel around the country without quarantining or taking any real precautions to avoid infecting others. Meadows learned of the positive test result while the president was already on Marine One headed for Joint Base Andrews and an out-of-town rally in Pennsylvania. After Trump boarded his plane at Andrews, he called the chief of staff.

"Mr. President," Meadows said, "I've got some bad news. You've tested positive for Covid-19."

"Oh shit, you've got to be fucking kidding me," Trump replied.

But after Trump took a second rapid test and it came out negative, the president considered the new result "full permission to press on as if nothing had happened," Meadows later wrote, and off to Pennsylvania he went.[24] On Air Force One, Trump mingled with aides and reporters, some of whom later fell sick, and over the next few days attended the rally, a news conference in the White House, a private session with families who lost loved ones in Afghanistan, another debate prep session with advisers, and two public events in the White House including one on a new coronavirus testing plan. On September 29, he flew to Cleveland for the debate with Biden, where he mocked the Democratic nominee for wearing a mask even as Trump's family members sat in the audience defying the rules by refusing to wear theirs. "I don't wear masks like him," Trump said during the debate. "Every time you see him, he's got a mask."[25]

Over the next two days, exhibiting what Meadows later admitted was "an uncharacteristic level of fatigue," Trump traveled to a rally in Duluth, Minnesota, and a fundraiser at his club at Bedminster before returning to the White House on October 1. Melania Trump had already tested positive for the virus that afternoon, as had Hope Hicks, who had been with him at the debate and throughout the week.

While waiting for Trump to land in Washington, Meadows called the chief executive officer of the drug company that made the experimental monoclonal antibody therapy Regeneron and asked for four doses to be sent by plane to the White House immediately. "I impressed upon him once more that secrecy was of the utmost importance, and he agreed," Meadows wrote.

But the medicine had not yet been approved even for emergency use by the FDA. Meadows treated his effort to circumvent the process for Trump as a clandestine operation, gathering Pat Cipollone and his deputy counsel in a secure room to call Stephen Hahn, the same FDA chief he had been screaming at with some regularity. Meadows demanded that Hahn personally authorize emergency "compassionate" use of the drug, immediately that night, but told him only that "someone close" to Trump had come down with Covid and it was a matter of "national importance."

Several hours later, by which point Trump had already returned to the White House and tested positive on a rapid test, Meadows called back Hahn when he heard the FDA was balking at approving the drugs. "Stephen," Meadows told him. "This is of national importance. You are going to issue the emergency use authorization *now.*" Then he revealed what he had not yet told the public. "It's for the president of the United States."

At the White House, Trump had in fact taken a marked turn for the worse that Friday. While Kayleigh McEnany's press shop issued upbeat bulletins, the president's oxygen levels dropped—Meadows later said they reached 86 percent, well in the danger zone below 90 percent—and he only agreed to go to the six-room presidential suite at Walter Reed's Ward 71 when aides stressed that it would be better to do so while he could still walk to the helicopter rather than waiting until he became so ill he had to be taken in a stretcher or wheelchair.[26] His condition was uncertain enough that Meadows caused a furor the next day when he approached reporters after an overly upbeat briefing by doctors to admit on background, without his name being used, that it was not true. In fact, Trump's condition was "very concerning," Meadows acknowledged without realizing that a camera was catching his comments. "We're still not on a clear path to a full recovery."[27]

But doctors pumped Trump full of drugs, a mix that eventually included not only Regeneron but also remdesivir, an existing drug which had been found to be effective against Covid, and even steroids, which were thought to lower the risk of death in coronavirus patients receiving oxygen. Trump soon got an energy burst, and by Saturday evening was eating McDonald's burgers and fries fetched for him by the Secret Service along with Meadows, Jared Kushner, and Dan Scavino, his omnipresent social media aide. By the next day, he was so antsy he insisted on being taken on a ride in the presidential limousine outside the hospital so he could wave at his fans;

the Secret Service made sure his driver and agents had all previously had Covid so he would not infect them.

At the White House and the campaign, some Trump advisers hoped the rash defiance of even basic safety protocols during the pandemic would finally come to an end, now that the president and first lady were stricken and others were testing positive too, including McEnany and Stephen Miller. Maybe, some imagined, there might even be a reckoning, and a political reset. Could Trump use his own life-threatening battle with Covid to present a more empathetic face to Americans as he closed out the campaign? Kushner had Alyssa Farah, the strategic communications director, and other aides draft a speech for a recovering Trump to give, expressing compassion for the suffering of others with Covid and a new-found understanding of the hardships afflicting the country.

But of course it was not to be. By Monday evening, Trump was back at the White House, a return punctuated with a dramatic, made-for-television-commercials helicopter arrival in the fading early-evening light followed by an appearance on the Truman Balcony where he stripped off his mask with a flourish. He did not rip open his shirt to reveal a Super-man costume underneath, as he had joked about doing with Mark Meadows before they left the hospital. But he had thought about it. He had survived the virus and the country could too.

There would be no remorse, no second-guessing, no new approach to the crisis.

"Don't let it dominate your lives," he exhorted in an address to the nation. "Get out there."[28]

Trump emerged from the hospital more desperate than when he went in, and his obsession with finding dirt on Joe Biden took a darker, almost frantic turn. Undaunted by his impeachment for trying to strongarm Ukraine into opening a politically charged investigation of the Bidens, Trump now tried to do the same with his own attorney general. He wanted Bill Barr not just to investigate Biden but to put him in prison. And while he was at it, Barack Obama and Hillary Clinton too. All in time to win him the election.

"Where are all the arrests?" Trump demanded on Twitter on the morning of October 7, twisting the FBI investigation into Russian election interference into a Democrat-led conspiracy against him. By the afternoon, he had grown even more strident. "BIDEN, OBAMA AND

CROOKED HILLARY LED THIS TREASONOUS PLOT!!! BIDEN
SHOULDN'T BE ALLOWED TO RUN—GOT CAUGHT!!!"

At the Justice Department, Barr was exasperated. Never in American
history had a sitting president sought to use the power of the state to
imprison his main political challenger a month before the election. Barr
agreed with Trump that the Russia investigation had been politicized and
had appointed John Durham to investigate the origins of the inquiry. But
he knew of no evidence that Biden or Obama had done anything illegal, and he was not going to rush Durham just to suit Trump's political
needs. For months, the relationship between the president and attorney
general had soured over Trump's desire to prosecute his opponents. Now,
it seemed to Barr that Trump had crossed a line. "That pissed me off," he
recalled later.

Barr had been privately drawing lines with Trump for months. As
far back as the spring, he thwarted a move to fire Chris Wray, the FBI
director. He knew nothing about the plot until showing up one day at
the White House for a meeting with Mark Meadows, only to be told
he was wanted in another meeting in the Roosevelt Room. While Barr
waited there confused, in walked Johnny McEntee, Kash Patel, and William Evanina, a career FBI agent and counterintelligence director. Barr
immediately suspected what was up—this was about pushing out Wray
and replacing him with Evanina while installing Patel as his deputy. Barr
bolted down the hall to Meadows's office and confronted the chief of staff.
"What the fuck?" he exclaimed. "I know what's going on." Meadows dis-
claimed knowledge. "I didn't know they were going to do that," he said.
But Barr's adamant opposition quashed the attempted coup.

For all of that, Barr had not broken with the president entirely. Just a
few months later, he intervened in a case that went undisclosed at the time
when Trump demanded that the Justice Department sue John Bolton to
stop him from publishing his critical book. Bolton's book, the one confirming that Trump had linked his suspension of Ukraine security aid to
investigations of the Democrats, had been cleared by a career professional
who after some edits judged there was no classified information in it, only
to have Robert O'Brien, the president's national security adviser, insist on
another review in an effort to stop publication before the election.

The matter fell to Jody Hunt, the assistant attorney general in charge
of the civil division. Hunt had been involved in many prepublication
reviews of books by former officials and never in his experience had the
department gone to court to try to stop a book before it was published,
not even one by Edward Snowden, the NSA leaker. The Supreme Court

had ruled against such prior restraint in the Pentagon Papers case and typically the Justice Department only went to court against government officials who disclosed classified information after their books were published. Hunt thought there was no way they could win such a prior restraint case against Bolton. But before he could send his memo recommending against a lawsuit, Barr preemptively sent him a letter on June 15 authorizing him to take Bolton to court and "pursue all available remedies against him" without even being asked—what seemed clearly like an effort to avoid any contrary advice being put in writing. The next day, a message was forwarded to Hunt from Meadows at the White House ordering that the suit be filed by 4 p.m. "or heads will roll."

Hunt was stunned. This was not the way the Justice Department was supposed to work. There was a process for a reason yet this was the culmination of so many times when it seemed like the department's work was being subjected to political influence. He told his staff to go ahead and file the suit according to Barr's orders but decided it would be the last time he would go along. "Guys, when we get out of this meeting," Hunt told his aides, "I'm going to go over and send my resignation letter." After nearly four years in the administration, he stepped down without publicly disclosing why.

But now, with the election just weeks away, Barr had had enough. He was fed up with Trump's effort to politicize justice. Shortly after his "where are all the arrests" temper tantrum, Trump called the attorney general to increase the pressure in an episode that was not revealed until Barr published his own memoir more than a year later.

"You know this stuff from Hunter Biden's laptop?" Trump asked, referring to a computer that Biden's son had abandoned at a repair shop that, according to the latest story line advanced by conservative media, contained incriminating emails.

Barr said he cut him off. "Mr. President, I can't talk about that." What Trump did not know, and Barr was not about to reveal, was that federal prosecutors were in fact investigating Hunter Biden's financial and foreign activities.

Trump persisted and Barr interjected again, this time raising his voice. "Dammit, Mr. President, I am not going to talk to you about Hunter Biden. Period!"[29]

A couple weeks later, a reinvigorated Trump showed up in Nashville for his final debate with Joe Biden. This time, the debate commission insisted on changing the rules so he could not talk over the moderator or interrupt Biden's answers. They even installed kill buttons on the microphones.

The president still hoped for a sudden reversal of fortunes. Four years earlier, struggling against Hillary Clinton, he had sought to distract from the *Access Hollywood* tape by inviting several women who had accused Clinton's husband of sexual misconduct to one of their debates. This time, Biden's son Hunter was the target, but the strategy was essentially the same.

Trump's guest was Tony Bobulinski, Hunter Biden's estranged former business partner, who had accused the younger Biden son of dirty dealings abroad, allegations that the president was determined to elevate to a last-minute scandal. Hunter Biden had evidently profited handsomely from his family name, not unlike some members of the Trump clan, but that same evening, *The Wall Street Journal* published a major article debunking the allegation that the former vice president had anything to do with his son's overseas business.[30] Not that Trump was exactly scrupulous about facts. Over the course of the campaign, he would accuse Hunter Biden forty-two times of taking $3.5 million from a Russian oligarch, an allegation that would later be discredited by *The Washington Post*.[31]

Bobulinski was at the debate in Nashville to take the attention off everything else: the pandemic, the economic crisis, a new report just that week in *The New York Times* that Trump had paid only $750 in federal income taxes in 2016 while running for president and again in 2017 while serving as president.[32] But inviting Bobulinski did not work out the way that Trump intended. For one thing, the president had a hard time explaining the allegations. There was something about a "laptop from hell" and how Biden was hardly an "innocent baby." Anyone who did not watch Fox News intensively would have been hard-pressed to decipher Trump's claims. The former vice president, clearly prepared for the attack, mostly avoided descending into complicated arguments about his son's murky business dealings, instead hitting Trump for his own questionable foreign business ties and less-than-transparent finances.

None of Trump's allegations seemed to stick, especially on a day when more than 75,000 new cases were recorded in the United States, one of the highest single-day totals since the pandemic began, and the death toll was topping 1,000 a day. Yet Trump insisted again that it was no big deal. "We're rounding the corner," he said. "It's going away." But Biden's opening salvo about the pandemic may have been the only one-liner that mattered at the debate. "Anyone who is responsible for that many deaths should not remain as president of the United States of America," he said.[33]

Trump, more obsessed with Hunter Biden's emails than with the plague stalking Americans, hardly bothered to rebut him.

Two days later, Trump showed up at a public library in West Palm Beach, Florida, making a rare appearance in a mask, to cast his ballot during in-person early voting. He was one of an estimated 56 million Americans—roughly 35 percent of what would end up being the total electorate—who had already voted. "I voted for a guy named Trump," he said.[34]

Two days after that, the Senate confirmed Amy Coney Barrett to the Supreme Court, voting almost entirely along party lines just a week before the November 3 presidential contest. No justice had ever been sped through confirmation so quickly to be installed so close to an election. For Trump, it was one last attempt to tilt the odds in his favor if the voting did not go his way.

In the early hours of Monday morning, November 2, Trump finished his fifth and final rally of the day, at Miami's Opa-Locka airport. At every stop, he had complained about the virus that he feared had doomed his campaign. "Covid, Covid, Covid" was his closing lament of 2020, a new hoax to replace Russia, Russia, Russia. He promised the crowd that, come November 4, the media would not even be talking about the pandemic anymore, as if the disease that would kill 231,000 Americans by Election Day was just a conspiracy to deny him a second term in office.[35]

The country was already headed into another fall and winter surge of the virus. Tony Fauci and the other doctors had warned of this, but Trump no longer even met with them. The White House task force had all but ceased to exist. Fauci, Stephen Hahn, and Robert Redfield, the CDC director, avoided going to the White House whenever possible, considering it a Covid hot zone filled with liars and leakers out to sabotage them. "There were weeks and weeks at a time we didn't talk with him," Fauci recalled of this period.

Trump would not have listened anyway. The coming spike, the president said in a tweet to begin his final few days as a candidate, was simply another "fake news media conspiracy." The country, he repeated, was "rounding the turn," and besides, even if you got it, he told the crowd at another Florida rally, "You're going to get better." His own recovery was proof. "If I can get better, anybody can get better," he said. "And I got better fast."[36]

One of the last times Fauci had spoken with Trump, in fact, came when the president was in the hospital with Covid being treated with an array of drugs not available to the average American. "You've got this monoclonal antibody. It's a miracle," Trump told him. "You know what you need to do, Tony? That needs to get pushed out—it's a miracle."

Once again, Fauci had tried to explain. "N=1," he told Trump, meaning that the president was just a one-person sample size, hardly enough to draw larger conclusions. "We really need a study."

"We don't need a study," Trump insisted. "It works."

To Trump, Fauci's transformation was complete. No longer an adviser he would listen to, he was now an adversary to target—and a useful political foil. At Trump's final Florida rally, the crowd took up a new chant, one Trump had not heard before. "Fire Fauci! Fire Fauci! Fire Fauci!" they roared.

Trump cocked his ear to listen and took it in. He had dabbled in Fauci-bashing before, but always pulled back, well aware that the television-friendly doctor had far higher approval ratings than his own. But not this time. The months of attacks on Fauci—and the painstaking scientific approach to the pandemic that he represented—had turned him into yet another partisan lightning rod. Democrats in Blue America put up yard signs that said, "Thank you, Dr. Fauci," so now Republicans, and Trump, were against him. As the crowd called for Fauci to be fired, the president hesitated for a minute, then made his choice. "Don't tell anybody but let me wait until a little bit after the election," he told his supporters, all but promising to oust the doctor who was leading America's response to Covid. "I appreciate the advice. He's been wrong on a lot."[37]

Since his recovery from the virus, Trump had demanded a swift return to the trail and had appeared at forty-five rallies, crisscrossing a locked-down country in Air Force One, encouraging supporters to forget about local curfews and mask mandates and crowd-size restrictions. "He wanted to get right back on the road," Justin Clark, his campaign adviser, recalled. It did not matter that it was irresponsible amid a public health crisis. His staff had given up trying to tell Trump what to do. It did not matter that he had just recovered from a life-threatening illness, or that his campaign's actions might spread it to others. "There wasn't any talk of scaling back," Clark said.

In one memorable appearance, Laura Ingraham joined Trump at a rally only to have him react in dismay when he saw she was wearing a mask. "I've never seen her in a mask," he said.[38] Just the night before, Ingraham had hosted Don Jr. while he claimed falsely on her show that Covid deaths in the United States were down to "almost nothing."[39] But here she was, refusing to go along with the fictional premise of the rally—and the entire

Trump campaign. Had even one of his favorite Fox anchors, Trump wondered out loud to the crowd, turned "politically correct"?[40] Later that day, in Wisconsin, when Trump bragged once again about his swift recovery from the virus, the crowd shouted, "Superman! Superman!"

By the time it was over, Trump would travel repeatedly to Michigan, Pennsylvania, and Wisconsin—the three once-blue states that had flipped to decide the race in 2016—and to shore up his Southern base in Florida, Georgia, and North Carolina. He would fly to Arizona and Ohio, Iowa and New Hampshire, and even make a couple stops in the red parts of reliably blue Minnesota and Nevada. He campaigned as he had governed, heedless of the center, seeking to inflame his own voters against an array of enemies real and imagined. Trump was always a minority president, a leader for part of the country in opposition to the rest of it.

He ended up on November 2 back near Scranton, Pennsylvania; Grand Rapids, Michigan; and Kenosha, Wisconsin, superstitiously booking a couple of the same locations for his final rallies as he had four years earlier, on the night of what he called "the beautiful victory." Forever after, his 2016 election upset had been the template for his campaign. Why do something different when he had defied everyone and won the first time? Indeed, he opened his final rally with a riff about "Crooked Hillary" and "Barack Hussein Obama" and all the old reliable enemies he had targeted for so many years. "Lock her up! Lock her up! Lock her up!" the crowd chanted in response, this time aimed at the state's Democratic governor. On Trump's aging-rocker tour, the old hits were always the most popular ones.

He then launched into the history of his presidency as he saw it, a narrative of "fake investigations, fake scandals, fake impeachments," of "fake news" and the treasonous "Deep State." He talked about the "Russian hoax," and the "Mueller investigation scam," about "eighteen angry Democrats" and James Comey, "who choked like a dog." He talked about the "perfect" phone call and Ukraine and Hunter Biden.

He also laid out a program for conquering the coronavirus, the fantasy of Covid, Covid, Covid as a hoax briefly displaced by the fantasy of an imminent end to the pandemic. "We will mass distribute the vaccine in just a few short weeks," he promised, although officials in his administration knew that was an impossible logistical feat even if his Republican supporters had been willing to take a vaccine. "It will quickly eradicate the virus and wipe out the China plague once and for all," he vowed.[41]

On the brink of losing to Biden, Trump could hardly bear the thought of it. Public polls had shown him behind from the beginning—and indeed, the final pre-election projections on the political website *FiveThirtyEight* gave Trump only a 10 percent chance of winning—but after 2016, he never trusted them.[42] His campaign also had plenty of indications of what was coming, although some of Trump's advisers could not resist puffing him up with inflated predictions. Brad Parscale told others that Covid may not have killed Trump, but it had destroyed his chances for re-election. Despite what Trump and some advisers would later claim, the campaign's final surveys tracked closely with the final results.

Even if his aides had been blunter with Trump, he might not have believed them. He had spent months attacking Biden in the starkest personal terms. He had hit Biden's age, his mental competence, his family. Trump did not want to run against Democratic policies. He wanted to run against a person, to rip him down, to insult, belittle, and degrade him. By the end, Trump seemed to believe his own pitch—making losing to Biden all the more unacceptable, impossible even. "I am running against the worst candidate in the history of presidential politics," Trump said as he closed out the campaign. "Can you even imagine losing to a guy like this?"[43]

In his final days as a candidate, Trump kept up the barrage questioning any election result that did not have him as the winner. Before any votes were counted, he called it a "Rigged Election!" Not once or twice, but nearly two hundred times since August and the closer to the election, the more he said it. "It's the only way we can lose, in my opinion, is massive fraud," he said.[44]

The contours of his post-election strategy were clear: to disrupt the counting, to ensure as few votes as possible in Democratic areas were cast, to claim there was widespread fraud. The goal was to get into court and sue. Trump, saying the quiet part out loud, as was his habit, admitted it a few days before the election, declaring that as soon as the campaign ended, "we're going in with our lawyers."[45]

On the Sunday before the election, Benjamin Ginsberg, for a generation the leading Republican election attorney, whose former law firm had worked for Trump's campaign four years earlier, took the extraordinary step of denouncing that strategy in an op-ed for *The Washington Post*. By Ginsberg's count, the Trump campaign and the Republican Party had already filed more than forty lawsuits around the country in advance of the balloting, challenging various local and state-level voting and ballot measures, every single suit aiming to limit the vote in some way. Ginsberg

said Trump's claims of widespread fraud were being enabled by a compliant Republican Party pursuing a mythical "Loch Ness Monster" of a story.
He did not make it public, but Ginsberg had even decided to retire from
his law firm, Jones Day, earlier that year, in order to avoid advising the
Trump campaign, which remained the firm's client. "My party is destroying itself on the Altar of Trump," he warned.[46]

At precisely 11:20 p.m. on election night, whatever illusion Trump still
harbored of a miraculous 2016 do-over was dashed. Fox News, the network that Trump began and ended his day with, the one whose hosts
shaped his White House agenda and took his nightly phone calls, had
betrayed him. Alone among the networks, Fox called Arizona for Biden,
a remarkable turnaround for a historically Republican state that had only
voted for a Democrat for president once since 1952. Other swing states,
including all three of 2016's decisive ones, remained in play, but the early
call on Arizona strongly suggested which way the momentum was headed.

At the White House, Trump sulked upstairs in the residence. Close
family and aides were with him. Trump barked out commands. Jared
Kushner was deputized to call Rupert Murdoch. Stephen Miller called
the Fox election desk. Mark Meadows telephoned Bill Sammon, the Fox
News Washington managing editor who had made the Arizona call. On
what basis, Meadows demanded, had Fox decided? "Math," Sammon
answered. After Meadows yelled some more, the Fox staffers nearby could
hear Sammon's response: "I'm not going through the arithmetic with
you." He also made a point to Meadows that he had made when the chief
of staff had called him a couple weeks earlier to complain that Fox was airing a Biden rally instead of a Trump rally: "The Trump campaign doesn't
tell Fox News what to do."

In fact, Fox had already been sitting on the decision for close to an
hour at that point. The network, in partnership with the Associated Press,
had invested heavily in a large-scale national survey and new methodology to call elections after 2016, jettisoning the old exit polls still relied on
by other networks. According to their model, a computerized statistical
tool called T-stat, a rating of 2.4 or higher was enough to make a call, and
at that point on election night, Arizona was showing as a 3.77. Sammon
had held on to the call for a while to make sure it held up, then sent an
email and checked the box on his computer screen—Arizona for Biden—
startling the anchors as they read it on air.

At the White House, it was like a bomb had gone off. Downstairs,

Rudy Giuliani roamed through the party, agitated and visibly drunk. For a while, he held court in the State Dining Room, then went to the Map Room, which the campaign had taken over for the evening as a command center. "They got it wrong," he insisted to Trump's campaign team. "The president's going to win this thing—he won." The political advisers tried to brush him off, but Giuliani kept going. "He had his own set of facts and figures," one senior campaign aide recalled. "Was it worrisome? Yeah, sure. But it's Trumpworld, you get a lot of that. It wasn't crazy that he was there."

By 12:44 a.m., Trump had chosen his course, the course he had spent months if not years preparing for. All fall, he had said quite clearly and openly that there was only one outcome for the election he would accept: his own victory. Any other result would be fake, false, and rigged. Trump could not lose, therefore Trump would not lose.

"They are trying to STEAL the Election," he tweeted. "We will never let them do it. Votes cannot be cast after the Poles are closed!"

Soon after 2:20 a.m., Trump spoke to supporters in the White House, where he was even more explicit. He declared that he had won and that he would go to the Supreme Court to stop the millions of votes that were still being counted. "This is a fraud on the American public," Trump claimed.[47] What fraud? He did not say. There would be plenty of time to decide—first came the indictment, only later the evidence. He would declare victory, then find a way to secure it. "Frankly," he said, "we did win this election."

The worst-case scenarios were coming true. Trump had warned of a crisis of confidence in the political system. He was his own self-fulfilling prophecy.

V

TRUMPERDÄMMERUNG

"We've lost the line! We've lost the line! All MPD pull back."

—POLICE RADIO DISPATCH, JANUARY 6, 2021, 2:28 P.M.

CHAPTER 28

Art of the Steal

On Thursday, November 5, barely twenty-four hours after Trump's late-night claim that "frankly, we did win this election," Jared Kushner woke up in his Kalorama mansion and, as he later told the story to aides and associates, announced to his wife that it was time to leave Washington. "We're moving to Miami," he said.

The election had not even been called for Joe Biden, but the White House's young power couple felt no need to wait for the official results. They saw which way the votes were going and understood that barring some sort of unforeseen surprise the president had lost his bid for a second term. Even if he refused to accept it himself. Whatever Trump said, neither Jared nor Ivanka believed then or later that the election had been stolen. While Trump had spent the hours since the polls closed complaining about imagined fraud in battleground states and plotting a strategy to hold on to power, his daughter and son-in-law were washing their hands of the Trump presidency.

They realized that Trump was not willing to concede defeat yet and would ask for recounts and file lawsuits, but believed it was all just a way of soothing a wounded ego and excusing defeat. Trump would lash out, he would make outlandish claims, and then he would accept reality and move out of the White House in eleven weeks. Jared and Ivanka had no interest in being part of the show. They had their own future to think about, one that would no longer involve the White House. And so they began making plans. They quickly ruled out returning to New York. Like Trump, who had officially become a Florida resident earlier in 2019, they had soured on their former home just as it had soured on them. For them, the city was now a liberal bastion of anger toward their family, not to mention a jurisdiction filled with state and local authorities with subpoena power, eager to investigate. Their travels in the predominantly Democratic social circles of Manhattan were over. They would not return to their Park Avenue penthouse. But they did not want to live in Palm Beach either. That was the president's turf, where, as Kushner put it, old people went to spend their money. Miami on the other hand seemed exciting.

While Kushner attended strategy meetings in the days to come discussing how to challenge the results in swing states, he and Ivanka began thinking about where they would live and what schools they could send their three children to and what business ventures they would pursue. They had to be discreet about it. The last thing they wanted to do was make it look like they were moving on. Indeed, Ivanka would text her father's top advisers that same day Kushner proposed moving to Miami and prod them to "Keep the faith and the fight!"[1] But the pair were, in fact, beginning to move on. Soon they were scouting properties in Florida, and within weeks were buying a $32 million lot formerly owned by Julio Iglesias on the private island of Indian Creek near Miami, an exclusive haven for a couple dozen wealthy families called the "Billionaire's Bunker" by the tabloids.[2]

In what remaining time they had in the White House, Kushner wanted to focus on expanding the Abraham Accords, which he felt validated his whole time in Washington—and would also help him cement contacts in the wealthy Gulf states that would prove lucrative in the private equity fund he would open after leaving Washington. As his father-in-law refused to authorize transition cooperation with the new team, Kushner quietly began working with Biden aides Jake Sullivan and Jeffrey Zients to prepare for their takeover. And although Trump may not have been thinking about his legacy yet, Kushner was. While still in the White House, he began writing a memoir focused on Middle East peacemaking. In the weeks to come, as Trump continued to insist that he would remain for a second term, Kushner set about chronicling the first. He even took an online MasterClass on how to write a book, taught by the prolific bestselling novelist James Patterson, and in the course of a two-week stretch following the election secretly batted out the first forty thousand words of an initial draft.

Trump's favorite daughter and the son-in-law who had been the most powerful family member in his White House, the keeper of his campaign and the fireman called in to deal with his most complicated crises, were opting out of the fight of Trump's life.

———

On the same day, with the election still not yet officially called, Don Jr. was pushing his father's team to fight to stay in power. Which was exactly what Trump wanted to hear. For once, he was the child who had his father's ear.

"STOP THE COUNT!" the president tweeted just after nine that morning, right around the time the Kushners were discussing Florida real estate.

At 12:21 p.m., he tweeted again. "STOP THE FRAUD!"

What fraud, it still was not clear, but a half hour later, at 12:51 p.m. that Thursday, Don Jr. sent a text to Mark Meadows previewing a strategy that a number of the president's hardline favorites on Capitol Hill were already converging on, a plan to subvert the verdict of the voters to keep Trump in the White House. It did not matter that the results were still being tabulated or that the rest of the world was still obsessively focused on absentee ballots in Pennsylvania after the battleground states of Michigan and Wisconsin had been called for Joe Biden the day before. Anticipating that Trump would lose the count, they were figuring out how to overturn it. "It's very simple," Don Jr. texted. "We have multiple paths," he added later. "We control them all." He suggested that Republican-led legislatures in states won by Biden—places such as Michigan and Wisconsin—set aside the election results and substitute their own Trump slates for the Electoral College.

He was already looking ahead to January 6, the day by law when Congress was supposed to count the Electoral College votes and formally ratify the results. If they could not swing enough states their way, then at the least, he suggested, they could prevent a majority in the Electoral College so the decision would go to the House. Under the Constitution, in such a circumstance, the House would vote by state delegation and while Republicans did not have the most members overall, they controlled twenty-six of the fifty state delegations. "We either have a vote WE control and WE win OR it gets kicked to Congress 6 January 2021," Don Jr. wrote.

At the same time, the president's son suggested that the White House purge those seen as internal enemies. "Fire Wray; Fire Fauci," he wrote, echoing the chant that the MAGA faithful had started in the final days of Trump's campaign. In place of Christopher Wray at the FBI, he proposed that Ric Grenell, the short-lived acting intelligence director and a fervent partisan, be named acting FBI director, guaranteeing someone loyal to Trump at the nation's premier law enforcement agency. Trump's son even suggested that Trump should have Bill Barr "select Special prosecutor" to investigate the "Biden crime family."[3] In public, Don Jr.'s message was similar, if not quite so explicit. In a tweet that night, he urged his father to pursue "total war over this election," and claimed the vote fraud was so bad it was making the United States look "like a banana republic."[4] Twitter flagged the post for spreading election misinformation.

Don Jr. was not the only one proposing ways to annul the will of the voters. The White House chief of staff had received a similar proposal a day earlier from Rick Perry, the former Texas governor who once called Trump a "cancer on conservatism" only to then serve as his energy secretary.[5] Much like Don Jr., Perry advocated having Republican legislatures declare Trump the winner regardless of the election results. "HERE's an AGRESSIVE STRATEGY," the text said, complete with misspellings. "Why can t the states of GA NC PENN and other R controlled state houses declare this is BS (where conflicts and election not called that night) and just send their own electors to vote and have it go to the SCOTUS."[6] In other words, before the votes had even been counted in those states and without any evidence of fraud, Republicans should ignore the decision of the voters, award electoral votes to the president, and fight all the way to the Supreme Court, with its newly installed, presumably pro-Trump majority.

Meadows was being inundated with messages like that from Republicans unwilling to accept defeat and primed by Trump's months of rhetoric undermining the legitimacy of the vote. Virginia "Ginni" Thomas, a far-right political activist and wife of Justice Clarence Thomas, who would be one of those to decide the matter if it got to the high court, sent Meadows a passage circulating on right-wing websites talking about having the "Biden crime family" and "ballot fraud co-conspirators (elected officials, bureaucrats, social media censorship mongers, fake stream media reporters, etc)" arrested and thrown in prison and even sent to "barges off GITMO to face military tribunals for sedition."[7]

Andy Biggs, who succeeded Meadows as chairman of the House Freedom Caucus, also proposed what he called a "highly controversial" strategy of getting Republican legislatures to appoint alternate electors for Trump in states he lost.

"I love it," Meadows wrote back, echoing the language that Don Jr. used in 2016 when offered dirt on Hillary Clinton from an intermediary said to represent the Russian government.[8]

And this was all before Trump had actually lost.

From the start, Trump and his allies were focused on an elaborate scheme to hold on to power that would go way beyond lawsuits and recounts, the standard options in an election lawyer's arsenal. Long before most people in Washington, they had identified not just December 14, the date the Electoral College by law was to vote, but January 6 as the critical day of confrontation. Even as Jared Kushner and Ivanka Trump were assuming the whole election protest would be mainly for show and fizzle out in a few weeks, Don Jr., Meadows, and the rest of the president's more zealous allies were pursuing serious plans to upend the democratic system as it had been practiced for generations. Kushner had spent years by Trump's side as he trampled one norm after another, but he had badly underestimated just how far his father-in-law was willing to go to keep power.

The first thing Trump needed were Republicans to stand by him. In the early hours after the election, a number of Republicans who had previously supported Trump abandoned him. Chris Christie rejected claims of a stolen election, saying "there's just no basis to make that argument," and even Rupert Murdoch's *New York Post*, which had trumpeted stories about Hunter Biden before the election, referred to Trump's assertions as "baseless election fraud claims" while Fox News said there was no "hard evidence" of widespread wrongdoing.[9]

To stem the tide, Don Jr. and his brother Eric took up the role of enforcers. "The total lack of action from virtually all of the '2024 GOP hopefuls' is pretty amazing," Don Jr. wrote on Twitter that same Thursday night.[10] "Where are Republicans!" Eric added, complete with distinctive punctuation and spelling. "Have some backbone. Fight against this fraud. Our voters will never forget you if your sheep!"[11] The threats seemed to work. After Don Jr. singled out Lindsey Graham, the senator went on Sean Hannity's show later that evening, asserting without evidence that "Philadelphia elections are crooked as a snake" and that the "allegations of wrongdoing are earth shattering."[12]

Now the Trump team just needed to find some actual earth-shattering allegations to justify their unprecedented plan. Just as he had done during the Ukraine episode, Trump turned to Rudy Giuliani, who eagerly reinforced the president's conspiratorial instincts and vowed to wage an all-out battle to discredit the election results. For those who had lived through the Ukraine scandal and resulting impeachment, it was mind-boggling. "The irregular channel reemerges," one Trump adviser recalled later. "It's history repeating itself only one year later."

Just as with the Ukraine scheme, Giuliani quickly overwhelmed the regular channel, consisting in this case of Trump's campaign staff and lawyers, and began orchestrating one legal challenge after another based on little more than rumor, conjecture, assumption, and shoddy research. On the Friday after the election, with the outcome still not called by the news media as the pandemic flood of mail-in votes was laboriously counted but clear to anyone watching the tallies coming in, Giuliani swept into Trump election headquarters in Rosslyn, Virginia, just over the bridge from Washington, and planted himself in a conference room, where he began making extravagant claims about voter fraud.

"I have eight affidavits," he announced, which impressed some members of the campaign team. If he really did have eight witnesses to election misconduct, they thought, then maybe they had something.

But Giuliani was blowing smoke. Later that day, he and some of the campaign advisers went to the White House to meet with Trump. While waiting in the Roosevelt Room, Giuliani restated his claim, only this time he declared, "I have twenty-seven affidavits."

Matt Morgan, who had served as Mike Pence's lawyer and was now general counsel to the Trump campaign, was stunned. He had been with Giuliani the entire time. Where did he suddenly get nineteen more affidavits?

By the time they sat down in the Oval Office with Trump a few minutes later, Giuliani had nearly tripled his alleged pile of evidence. "I have eighty affidavits," he claimed.

Dumbfounded, Morgan later called lawyers at a private firm working on the election challenges and asked them to call Giuliani to request copies of the supposed affidavits. Don't use my name, Morgan instructed. Not long afterward, one of Giuliani's assistants popped into Morgan's office. "Hey, Rudy needs all the affidavits you have," the assistant said. All the affidavits *he* had? Wasn't Giuliani the one who said he had affidavits?

Trump had spent months predicting there would be a "rigged election," but when it came down to it, neither he nor Giuliani appeared to have an actual plan for how to prove it. As far as Trump advisers like Morgan were concerned, Giuliani's whole venture was a flim-flam scam. There was no there there. But none of that would stop Trump.

The White House and Trump campaign were not the only organizations reeling after the vote. The election had thrown Fox News into turmoil. Ever since its election night call on Arizona, the network's executives and leading anchors had come under tremendous pressure from Trump and his allies.

As far as the journalists manning the Decision Desk were concerned, there was no serious question about Arizona, even though the other networks still had not put it in Biden's column. But Fox executives were freaking out. At 8:30 the morning after the election, Suzanne Scott, the chief executive officer, even suggested that Fox should not call any more states until they were officially certified by election authorities, heedless of the fact that official state certifications typically took days or even weeks and no network had ever waited until then before telling their viewers who had won.

"We better think it through," said Bill Sammon, the Washington managing editor who oversaw the Decision Desk. "Our enemies—and there are many—will portray this as follows: For the first time in its history, Fox News refuses to project the next president, who just happens to be the Democrat who defeated Donald Trump."

But a couple other top executives backed up Scott, reflecting how nervous the Fox hierarchy was. With the president now attacking rather than promoting their network, the executives saw ratings fall as many of their Trump-supporting viewers turned to Newsmax, the far smaller conservative outlet run by the president's friend Chris Ruddy, which had not called Arizona for Biden. Ron Mitchell, the Fox ratings guru, would later warn at an internal meeting that the network risked heading down to second or even third place in some hours, "maybe permanently."

By Thursday, Bret Baier, the lead Fox evening news anchor, who had long insisted that he was different than the Trump-cheerleading opinion hosts whose programs aired on Fox's prime time, was ready to give in to the White House pressure to rescind the Arizona call. "The Trump campaign was really pissed," he wrote in an email to Jay Wallace, the president and executive editor at Fox. "This situation is getting uncomfortable. Really uncomfortable. I keep having to defend this on air." He accused the Decision Desk of "holding on for pride" and added: "It's hurting us. The sooner we pull it—even if it gives us major egg—and we put it back in his column the better we are in my opinion."

That was stunning. Arizona never was in Trump's column. While the margin of his defeat in the state had narrowed since election night, he still trailed by more than ten thousand votes. The T-stat on the Fox Decision Desk's scale still showed it at 3.2, lower than when they had called it, but well above the system's 2.4 threshold for calling a state. Yet the leading news anchor for Fox was pushing not just to say Arizona was too close to call but to pretend that the president had won it.

Jay Wallace was not ready to do that. But on Friday he overruled the Decision Desk team including Bill Sammon, Arnon Mishkin, and Chris Stirewalt, refusing to let them call Nevada for Biden even after other networks did, a level of interference that had been unheard of in past elections. The reason had little to do with Nevada. Because of the Arizona projection, calling Nevada would give Biden enough electoral votes for victory. Wallace did not want Fox to be the first to call the election and declare Biden president-elect.

The message about Fox's course was clear. Sammon, who over twelve years at Fox had called every election correctly and had just been offered a three-year contract extension, was summarily fired. So was Stirewalt, the political editor, who had been with the network for a decade. The executives did not want the embarrassment of publicly owning their decision to push out journalists for making the right call, so they delayed the announcements by two months. They would force Sammon to call his dismissal a "retirement" and negotiate a severance package with a nondisclosure agreement, while Stirewalt's firing would be characterized as part of a "restructuring." Whatever they called it, Fox had decided that deference to Trump was more important than getting the story right. "I respect the hell out of you," Wallace told Sammon, "but it's turned into a war."

By the morning of Saturday, November 7, the other networks finally calculated that Biden had won enough states to secure an Electoral College majority. CNN reported at 11:24 a.m. that Biden had defeated Trump. Within minutes, the Associated Press, ABC, CBS, and NBC all followed. At Fox, where Neil Cavuto was anchoring, the executives held back until they could rush Bret Baier, his Arizona qualms notwithstanding, into the chair to make the call along with Martha MacCallum at 11:40 a.m. Now all the major news outlets in America had read the results the same way. Joe Biden would be the next president. Voters had rejected Donald Trump.

In a victory speech a few hours later, as Washington erupted in a spontaneous street party in front of Trump's White House, Biden promised the nation that, after his "clear" and "convincing" win, he would govern as the un-Trump. "I pledge to be a president who seeks not to divide but unify," he said, "who doesn't see red states and blue states, only sees the United States."[13]

At the end of the day, it was both a close election and not at all close. Trump collected 74 million votes, far more than four years earlier, but Biden drew even more, an all-time record of 81 million. Biden's popular vote margin of 4.5 percentage points was larger than the winner had in eight of nineteen presidential elections since World War II, and turnout of 66.8 percent, despite the pandemic, was the highest it had been since 1992. Biden's Electoral College victory with states totaling 306 votes to

232 was identical to Trump's total over Hillary Clinton four years earlier, an outcome that Trump had labeled a "landslide."[14] Despite Trump's loss, Republicans down the ballot still did well, an outcome that might, with a different president, have deterred the party from claiming that the results were a consequence of massive fraud. The party even picked up more than a dozen seats in the House. Two Senate contests in Georgia were so close that they would go to a January 5 runoff that would determine which party won control of that chamber. But broadly speaking, voters made clear they were willing to elect Republicans—just not Trump.

In the Electoral College, however, Trump came much closer to prevailing despite his decisive repudiation in the popular vote. Had he won a cumulative 76,515 more votes distributed precisely in Arizona, Georgia, Nevada, and Wisconsin or 102,792 more votes in Pennsylvania, Arizona, and Georgia, he would have flipped enough electoral votes to win a second term.[15] Still, it was far more than the number Clinton would have needed in 2016 to beat Trump in Michigan, Pennsylvania, and Wisconsin and nowhere even close to the deadlocked 2000 election, which came down to a Florida recount that Al Gore ultimately lost by just 537 votes.

But Trump would not accept the verdict. As he left the White House that Saturday morning in a white MAGA hat to spend the day on his Trump-branded golf course in Virginia, he claimed defiantly, "I WON THIS ELECTION BY A LOT!" Instead of conceding defeat, as all America's other presidents had done when faced with the overwhelming evidence of their loss, he announced that his team would be holding an important event. "Lawyers Press Conference at Four Seasons, Philadelphia. 11:00 A.M.," he tweeted at 9:35 a.m. Just ten minutes later, he tweeted out a correction: "Big press conference today in Philadelphia at Four Seasons Total Landscaping—11:30am!"

While the president thought his legal representatives planned to hold forth at a prestigious five-star hotel, for reasons no one could explain even months later, Giuliani's team had booked a lawn care company with the same name in an industrial section of northeast Philadelphia, across the street from a crematorium and just down the block from the Fantasy Island Adult Bookstore.

If ever there were a metaphor for a flailing, amateur campaign refusing to accept reality, this would be it. Even as Bret Baier and the others were announcing that Biden was America's next president, Giuliani appeared in the parking lot of the landscaping firm with his pardoned friend Bernie Kerik, the 2016 Trump campaign manager Corey Lewandowski, and a group of Republican poll watchers. Giuliani had no evidence of actual fraud. He simply argued that, because Trump's lead vanished as votes were counted, something untoward must have happened. "You just don't lose leads like that without corruption," he said. In fact, there was no surprise that Trump did better among votes cast on Election Day while Biden rolled up larger numbers in mailed ballots that took longer to count.

When it was Lewandowski's turn at the microphone, he dramatically presented proof that the election was stolen. A woman named Denise Ondick had requested an absentee ballot but died, according to her obituary, nine days before her ballot arrived at her local election office. "This is hard evidence!" Lewandowski thundered, challenging reporters to "do your jobs" and find more examples.[16]

Reporters did do their jobs. Ondick's daughter, it turned out, had helped her fill out her ballot for her favorite candidate—Donald Trump. So the only actual example of an illegitimate vote cited by Trump's team that day was cast for Trump.

In the days to come, Jared Kushner and others close to the White House sent word to Mitch McConnell and other key Republican congressional leaders that Trump would eventually accept the reality that he lost. It was all just a matter of time. Trump would huff and puff and claim he really won until his options ran out.

"We'll get through it, bear with us," Kushner told Josh Holmes, a former chief of staff and campaign manager for McConnell who would pass along the message to the majority leader. "We've got a couple of challenges that have some merit, we'll see how they go, but there's a pretty good chance we come up short." And once the results were certified, he suggested, that would be the end of it. Trump just needed time to come to terms with his defeat.

This view had taken hold around Washington, where even many Republicans close to the White House assumed that surely the electoral math was too daunting even for a determined fantasist like Trump. Trump's former chief of staff Mick Mulvaney, who had privately confided to a fellow Republican before the election that "if Trump loses I'm not sure he'll leave office willingly," published a column in *The Wall Street Journal* on the day the election was called headlined "If He Loses Trump Will Concede Gracefully," which was more a plea to the audience of one than a prediction."[17] Another Republican official, hiding behind the cloak of anonymity, said, "What is the downside for humoring him for this little bit of time? No one seriously thinks the results will change." Noting that Trump had golfed over the weekend, the official told *The Washington Post*, "It's not like he's plotting how to prevent Joe Biden from taking power on Jan. 20. He's tweeting about filing some lawsuits, those lawsuits will fail, then he'll tweet some more about how the election was stolen, and then he'll leave."[18]

Fearing the consequences for the Senate majority in the two Georgia Senate runoff races if they defied Trump, McConnell and other Republican senators decided to bow to Kushner's interpretation and hold off recognizing Biden's victory and issuing the traditional congratulations. Mitt Romney and Lisa Murkowski had each called Biden and congratulatory letters, calls, and tweets were coming from world leaders—even, to Trump's fury, from Israel's Benjamin Netanyahu—but that was pretty much it as far as Republican members of Congress. They would humor Trump just a bit longer.

On Monday, November 9, the first workday after the election was called, some advisers sat with Trump in his private dining room next to the Oval Office and urged him to declare that he would run for president again in 2024, signaling that he would transfer power peacefully even as he asserted his determination to be a force on the political scene. But Peter Navarro, the trade adviser, freelance Covid counselor, and self-appointed Trump firebrand, overheard and interjected that doing so would be tantamount to admitting defeat. "What you damn well need to do right now is fight," Navarro told the president.[19]

To some of his advisers, it seemed that Trump wavered in those first few days after his loss. There was a brief window when they thought that Trump understood he had genuinely fallen short. Sitting in his dining room at one point, he saw Biden on the television screen. "Can you believe I lost to this fucking guy?" he groused. When someone raised an issue during a national security meeting, Trump replied with something to the effect of, "We're going to leave it to the next guy." But the kind of advisers who might have steered him toward acceptance were no longer around the brooding president, who remained cloistered for days after the election and talked of little else.

Even long-awaited good news about the pandemic did not really engage him. On that same Monday after the election was called, Pfizer announced that its vaccine had proven more than 90 percent effective in trials, the breakthrough the country had been awaiting in its struggle with the disease. It was just a matter of time now before Americans would get shots and a chance to return safely to some version of their pre-pandemic lives.

But Trump saw it only through his own personal lens, viewing the timing as a betrayal. "As I have long said," he wrote on Twitter, "@Pfizer and the others would only announce a Vaccine after the Election, because they didn't have the courage to do it before." When Britain then moved quickly to approve the vaccine, Mark Meadows lashed out at Stephen Hahn, demanding to know why the FDA had not acted. How can a social-ist medicine country make an approval within 24 hours with basically a hundredth of the people you have or less and you can't make a decision, he texted. Hahn, who knew that the FDA had a more elaborate process than the British, took it as a rhetorical question and did not reply.

Trump was largely checked out anyway, as were many of the aides who might have counseled him to give up on the election. Jared and Ivanka had decided not only to move to Florida but to explicitly step aside from the fight in the time that remained to them in Washington. Once they saw that the president was empowering Rudy Giuliani, the man they believed had gotten Trump impeached with his out-of-bounds adventurism, they surrendered the field. They had no appetite for waging what would prob-ably be a losing battle to persuade a president who did not want to be persuaded on the folly of his chosen course.

"Obviously, I support you, but I can't help you on that," Kushner told Trump, as he related the story to another Republican at the time.

And it was not just Jared and Ivanka. Hope Hicks, who remained one of the West Wing's most skilled Trump-whisperers, was now preparing to leave and stayed away from the election challenges. Hicks told the presi-dent what he did not want to hear, that he had lost and it was time to move on. Trump responded bitterly. "Well, Hope doesn't believe in me," he would say in meetings. "No, I don't," she would reply. "Nobody's con-vinced me otherwise." She concluded any further efforts to try to steer Trump would simply be, as she told an associate, "a waste of time." Others concurred. Alyssa Farah, the strategic communications director who had sometimes been a voice of restraint on the president, would soon resign out of disgust, unwilling to go along with what she considered a massive deception.

Mark Meadows, the chief of staff who was supposed to serve as a gate-keeper for the president although he only occasionally did so, was missing for a crucial few days after the election was called. Although he tried to keep it secret, he had tested positive for Covid on November 6 and was at home quarantining. The void was filled by the likes of Giuliani and other conspiracy theorists like Sidney Powell, the lawyer who represented Mike Flynn and had her own wild ideas about how the election had supposedly been rigged.

The more Trump listened to them, the more he hardened around the notion that he had been robbed, and in the days following the election he would resolve to do what no other sitting president has done in the history of the United States—hold on to power despite the indisputable will of the voters. The next ten weeks would prove to be the most elaborate and extensive campaign to overturn a presidential election since the ratification of the Constitution, all orchestrated from the Oval Office.

By the time it was over, Trump and his allies would file more than sixty lawsuits in more than half a dozen states, going all the way to the Supreme Court twice, only to lose nearly across the board. They sought recounts and audits and forensic investigations and, when those still did not change the results, pushed for extraordinary interventions by Republican state officials. The president would personally summon legislative leaders from Michigan to the White House to lean on them to reverse the results. He would call the governors of Arizona and Georgia, state lawmakers in Pennsylvania, Georgia's secretary of state, and even an election investigator, members of the Maricopa County Board of Supervisors in Arizona, members of the Wayne County canvassing board in Michigan, and attorneys general in multiple states, desperately searching for anyone who would help him switch the results. When none of that succeeded, he would pressure his own Justice Department, his allies in Congress, and ultimately his vice president. And perhaps most pernicious of all, he would continue to tell the American people over and over again that the election was stolen by the other side even though he was the one trying to steal it.

None of this should have been a surprise, yet somehow it was. After years of experience, Trump knew how to sell a big lie. He had done it many times before. As a real estate developer, he had claimed his buildings were taller than they were. As a reality television star, he had made up conflicts between contestants to juice his ratings. As a political provocateur, he had claimed without a lick of proof that the nation's first Black president was secretly born in Africa. The trick with conspiracy theories, he had demonstrated, was repetition and conviction. "You say something enough times," he once told Chris Christie's wife, "and it becomes true."

To lead his election challenges, Trump had initially chosen David Bossie, his campaign adviser, but when Bossie arrived at the White House over the weekend, he tested positive for Covid, sidelining him. That left Rudy Giuliani. The die was cast in a meeting in the Oval Office on November 12. Even as Chris Krebs, head of a Department of Homeland Security cyber agency, declared that day that the election had been "the most secure in American history," Trump was talking with Giuliani on a speak-erphone about how he could prove otherwise.[20] (Trump would fire Krebs a few days later.)

With a room full of campaign advisers listening, Giuliani talked about taking legal action in Georgia, where Trump was trailing by about four-teen thousand votes. He wanted to claim that Dominion Voting Systems machines had somehow converted thousands of Trump votes to Biden. "We've got to file a lawsuit in federal court tomorrow," Giuliani insisted.

Justin Clark, the deputy campaign manager and a lawyer himself, was fed up. Floating a conspiracy theory in a federal lawsuit would go nowhere and just embarrass the president. "Rudy, we're going to lose," he said. "We're going to get bounced out of court."

Giuliani snapped. "Oh, they're lying to you, sir," he told Trump.

Clark lost his patience. "Rudy, you're a fucking asshole!" he said.

Trump, typically, let them fight. But it was clear where he was headed. That night, he called Clark and his political adviser Jason Miller to com-plain they were not doing enough. Miller had doubts about the elabo-rate conspiracies Giuliani was peddling, but he texted Mark Meadows the next day that he was not sure whether even to present them to Trump. "POTUS clearly hyped up on them," Miller wrote.

Trump effectively settled the debate that same day by formally putting Giuliani in charge of the effort to overturn the election. In some ways, it was one of the most consequential decisions of his presidency. He would pick the guy who wanted to fight over the guy who said there was no way to win. It did not matter if it was farcical or if it corroded public faith in the system.

Many of the campaign advisers thought Trump was being fed a line of nonsense and, like Clark and Bill Stepien, one by one they would pull back or leave altogether. Team Normal, as Stepien dubbed them, was losing out to Team Rudy. But even among the more radical outsiders who were now taking over, there were rifts. Sidney Powell and some of the other con-spiracy theorists scorned Giuliani as an old man who drank too much and was in over his head. Giuliani, as much as he had drifted away from reality, thought Powell was way too far out there. The same day Giuliani received Trump's imprimatur, Powell told Trump favorite Lou Dobbs on Fox Busi-ness that she had proof of a diabolical secret plot to steal the election and, borrowing a catchphrase from the movie *Clash of the Titans* referring to a giant sea monster, vowed to "release the Kraken."[21]

There was no Kraken. The claims that Giuliani, Powell, and the oth-ers kept throwing out there were far-fetched, ever shifting, and sometimes contradictory. In the days that would follow, Giuliani claimed that more absentee ballots were cast in Pennsylvania than were requested by voters. But he was flat wrong, having apparently contrasted the number of absentee ballots sent out to voters during the lower-turnout spring primary election to the number of absentee ballots returned in the fall election, an apples-to-oranges comparison. The real numbers showed nothing suspicious: 3.1 million absentee ballots were sent out in the fall and 2.6 million were returned. One of Giuliani's favorite claims was the charge that anywhere between 8,000 and 30,000 dead people voted in Philadelphia. In fact, investigations would show that it was exactly two. Similarly in Georgia, he variously claimed that 800 or 6,000 or 10,515 dead people voted. There, as well, it would eventually be determined that at most it was just four. But that did not deter Giuliani. He also asserted that 65,000 or 165,000 underage people voted in Georgia, when, in fact, the number was zero. In Arizona, he said at different points that "way more than 10,000" or "32,000" or "probably about 250,000" or "a few hundred thousand" undocumented immigrants had voted illegally in the state, but investigators found no evidence that any had.[22] Not hundreds of thousands, not tens of thousands, not any.

As November went on, no judge was buying it and, increasingly, establishment lawyers were dropping out of cases rather than represent the rapidly tarnishing Trump brand. On November 18, Giuliani had to go to court in Pennsylvania himself to argue a motion, his first time in a federal courtroom in twenty-eight years—and it showed. He seemed befuddled. He admitted that for all his public cries of fraud, none was actually alleged in the legal filings. "This is not a fraud case," he said. When the judge asked what legal standard of scrutiny should be applied to the government's action, Giuliani had no clue and tried to get out of it by saying "the normal one."[23]

Back at Trump headquarters, where campaign lawyers were listening through a telephone hookup, there were groans. "Oh man, we're sunk," Matt Morgan thought. That was the moment, he told associates later, that he knew that "any competent legal strategy went out the window."

The whole effort became even more of a carnival show the next day, November 19, when Giuliani, Powell, and other lawyers staged a news conference at Republican National Committee headquarters. Giuliani did an impression of the lawyer played by Joe Pesci in *My Cousin Vinny* and made repeated false statements while Powell suggested that the election was skewed by "communist money through Venezuela, Cuba and likely China" and alleged that machines made by Dominion Voting Systems, a

Denver-based firm, were created "at the direction of Hugo Chávez," the late Venezuelan socialist dictator, who had been dead for more than seven years.

"This is real! It's not made up! There's nobody here who engages in fantasies," Giuliani shouted at the news media at one point.[24]

In fact, Trump campaign aides had already prepared an internal memo debunking the wild allegations about Dominion. The crazy claims, though, would ultimately not be what the event would be remembered for. Under the glare of the hot lights, a dark liquid seeped down the sides of Giuliani's face. Oblivious, he kept ranting. Social media exploded with speculation: Was it hair dye? Or perhaps makeup? Trump, watching on television, erupted. It was the first time Stephanie Grisham had ever seen him irritated at Giuliani—not because of the bizarre assertions but because he looked so "sloppy" and "disgusting," as she put it.

Still, Powell was even worse in the view of many around the president. Her ramblings about the Kraken and foreign ties discredited the whole effort. Giuliani used the blowback to push Powell out, convincing Trump to let him issue a statement on November 22 declaring that "she is not a member of the Trump legal team."[25] Ginni Thomas asked Meadows over text why Powell was sidelined. "She doesn't have anything or at least she won't share it if she does," he texted back.[26]

None of which diminished Trump's fervor for the fight. If Powell did not have a Kraken, then he would trust Giuliani to find some other way. And if that did not work, he would push allies in state after state. And if that did not work, then he would take the battle all the way to January 6. This was not just about feeding his ego for a few weeks as his son-in-law had thought. As Trump sat upstairs in the White House residence that Sunday night, he picked up his phone shortly before midnight and tweeted out his battle cry: "We will win!"

CHAPTER 29

Can Anyone Land This Plane?

With the possible exception of Mike Pence, no one had been more slav-ishly loyal in public to Trump or more privately obsequious than Mike Pompeo. But on the evening of November 9, he could not take it any-more. He called up Mark Milley, who lived just a few houses away from him at Fort Myer on a tree-lined street known as "Generals Row" on a hilltop looking to the capital across the Potomac.

"We've got to talk," the secretary of state told the general, who was at home in Quarters Six, the stately red-brick house that has been the official residence of chairmen of the Joint Chiefs since the early 1960s. "Can I come over?"

Milley invited him over. "The crazies have taken over," Pompeo told him when they sat down at his kitchen table around 9 p.m.[1] He was vis-ibly upset. Not only was Trump surrounded by the crazies, they were in fact ascendant in the White House and, as of that afternoon, inside the Pentagon itself.

Just a few hours earlier, on the first workday after the election was called for Joe Biden, Trump had fired Mark Esper, the secretary of defense whose defiance of Trump after the disastrous Lafayette Square photo op in June had sealed his fate. For months, Esper had come into work each day and joked with his staff at their morning meeting. "What do we need to do today," he would ask, "in case I get fired tomorrow?"

Tomorrow had finally come and both Milley and Pompeo feared it was a sign of a dark turn in Trump after the election he was still refusing to concede. Mark Meadows had delivered the news to Esper shortly before 1 p.m. "The president is going to fire you this afternoon," Meadows told the defense secretary. The reason, he added, was "you haven't been suf-ficiently loyal."

"That's his prerogative," Esper responded. But he offered a final jab at Trump. "My oath is to the Constitution," he reminded Meadows, "not to him."

Minutes later, like so many Trump officials before him, the defense secretary got The Tweet. "Mark Esper has been terminated," it said.

But dumping a defense secretary was not like getting rid of just another member of the cabinet. In fact, no president had outright fired a Pentagon chief in decades. Pompeo and Esper had worked together closely and in the moment of crisis, the secretary of state now turned to Milley. "They were already converging as fellow travelers," a senior State Department official said. Both were alarmed that Esper was being replaced by a virtual unknown, a former midlevel official at Trump's National Security Council named Christopher Miller, who arrived at the Pentagon that afternoon flanked by a team of what appeared to be Trump political minders.

To a general already vigilant for signs of Trump preparing to go rogue, it seemed downright ominous. From the beginning, Milley understood that "if the idea was to seize power," as he told his staff, "you are not going to do this without the military." Milley had studied the history of coups. They invariably required the takeover of what he referred to as the "power ministries"—the military, national police, or interior forces. The guys with guns.

As soon as he heard about Esper's ouster, Milley had rushed upstairs to the secretary's office one flight directly above his. "This is complete bullshit," he told Esper. Not for the first time and not for the last, Milley wondered: Was this an attempted coup or just another episode of the Trump clown show?

Flush with anger, Milley said he would resign in protest.

"You can't," Esper insisted. "You're the only one left."

Once he cooled off, the chairman knew Esper was right; it was what he had decided after the Lafayette Square debacle, to stay and to fight from the inside. For months, he and Esper had hoped to make it through the election while safeguarding the military from political interference. But now it was clear the crisis was not over just because the election was. Milley met with Miller soon after he arrived. "First things first here, you are one of two people in the United States now with the capability to launch nuclear weapons," the chairman told him before briefing the new secretary on his role overseeing the world's most powerful force.

In the coming days, Milley would convene the Joint Chiefs to bolster their resolve to resist any political schemes from the White House now that Esper was out. He quoted Benjamin Franklin to them on the virtues of hanging together rather than hanging separately, and told his staff that, if need be, he and all the chiefs were determined to "put on their uniforms and go across the river together"—to threaten to quit en masse—to stop Trump from any effort to use the military for his personal campaign to stay in power. Milley was every bit as riled up as Pompeo.

Trump was not the only one who had been looking to take out Esper. Milley later told associates that the firing of the defense secretary was a "hit job" by Robert O'Brien. Esper told the same thing to at least one colleague the next day. Unlike his two immediate predecessors as national security adviser, O'Brien had fashioned himself as a Trump loyalist, a partisan who in private conversations referred to the "Russia hoax." He was even said to harbor aspirations to run for president himself, despite his lack of public name recognition or elective experience. "He was actively trying to do everything he could do to curry favor with the president," Esper would tell associates.

Despite Trump's defeat, O'Brien and other senior Trump officials were still jockeying for appointments in a Trump second term. Indeed, Johnny McEntee, the young and empowered White House personnel chief, had already put out word that none of Trump's political appointees should even think about looking for work outside the administration in the post-election period, lest it be taken as betrayal. O'Brien was said to want to be defense secretary in a second term. Chris Miller would be a convenient placeholder.

Within hours, the *Military Times* released an interview conducted in advance with Esper to be used, the publication said, in case of his firing. The ousted Pentagon chief seemed most concerned with debunking the rap on him as "Yesper" kowtowing to the president. "My frustration is I sit here and say, 'Hmm, eighteen Cabinet members. Who's pushed back more than anybody?' Name another Cabinet secretary that's pushed back," Esper told *Military Times.* "Have you seen me on stage saying, 'Under the exceptional leadership of blah-blah-blah, we have blah-blah-blah-blah'?"[2]

In fact, Esper had privately pushed back against Trump far more than was publicly known, well before Lafayette Square. He had lobbied Trump to restore the suspended aid to Ukraine that would lead to impeachment. He had resisted White House efforts to install various Fox News military pundits at the Pentagon and tried, not entirely successfully, to protect several of his own aides from being fired. And he beat back a proposal by Stephen Miller when Covid first emerged to deploy more than 250,000 active-duty troops to the border with Mexico to stop a supposed influx of foreigners hoping to ride out the pandemic in the United States. Esper first heard about the plan in the Oval Office while waiting for Trump when Miller offhandedly mentioned it. Esper thought he was joking. "For what?" he asked Miller. "Are more caravans coming?" But when Esper returned to the Pentagon, he learned that Miller was not joking and had set his plan in motion working with the Department of Homeland Security and the military's Northern Command. Esper ordered Pentagon officials to stand down.

His resistance had not gone unnoticed. Johnny McEntee had listed Esper's supposed sins in a bullet-pointed memo in October recommending he be fired the day after the election and replaced with Chris Miller—the exact plan now being carried out. The memo from the Presidential Personnel Office, later given to ABC's Jonathan Karl, cited not just Esper's refusal "to utilize American forces to put down riots," as Trump wanted that summer, but his support for "diversity and inclusion" in the military. It also faulted Esper for focusing on "competition with Moscow"—in other words, being too tough on Vladimir Putin. It was, of course, official United States policy to compete with Russia, but the memo put in writing what many Republicans still denied, that America's Russia policy was not Trump's Russia policy.[3]

Still, it was true that Esper was never the most forceful official to resist Trump. "He pushed back in a way that the captain of an aircraft carrier steers his ship two degrees to the port side," said a senior administration official. "Not everyone's going to see it; it's a gargantuan ship. It wasn't donnybrooks with the president. That was much more Milley."

Pompeo was not the only Trump ally upset at the way Esper had been thrown overboard. "That's it," Dave Urban, the lobbyist who had pushed for Esper's appointment, told a top Trump aide. "I'm out. Good luck."

Now, with Esper gone, Milley was headed into what he considered the most dangerous period for the republic of his lifetime. And he could no longer trust even the Pentagon's own civilian leadership.

Chris Miller showed up at the Pentagon little more than an hour after Esper's firing and only a few minutes after his predecessor had left the building. Almost a complete unknown in high-level politics, Miller had helped command a storied team of Special Forces that covertly entered Afghanistan, partially on horseback, soon after September 11 to begin the war there. The former colonel's rise in the Trump administration was meteoric. While working as the senior director for counterterrorism and transnational threats at the National Security Council, he was plucked from obscurity to run the National Counterterrorism Center as part of a previous White House loyalty purge earlier in 2020. Now he was acting secretary of defense.

A Pentagon colleague who had worked closely with Miller for years had heard a rumor about him potentially replacing Esper more than a week before the election. "My first instinct was this is the most preposterous thing I've ever heard," the colleague recalled. But then he remembered how Miller had changed the closer he got to power in the Trump White House. "He's inclined to be a bit of a sail, and as the wind blows, he will flap in that direction," the colleague said. "He's not an ideologue. He's just a guy willing to do their bidding."

By coincidence, the colleague happened to be walking into the Pentagon that afternoon just as Miller, having rushed home to put on a suit before taking up his new post, was entering—a video of Miller tripping as he walked up the stairs soon made the rounds. Accompanying the new acting secretary were three men who would, for a few weeks at least, have influence over the most powerful military in the world: Kash Patel, Miller's new chief of staff; Ezra Cohen, who would ascend to acting undersecretary of defense for intelligence; and Anthony Tata, a retired general and talking head on Fox News who would become the Pentagon's acting head of policy.

It was an extraordinary trio. Tata's claims to fame were calling Barack Obama a "terrorist leader" and asserting that the CIA had tried to assassinate Trump.[4] Patel, the former Devin Nunes aide and conspiracy theorist, was so polarizing that John Bolton and his deputy threatened to quit rather than put him on their staff, only backing down when told it was the personal order of the president. Patel found his way around them to deal with Trump directly, feeding him packets of information on Ukraine, and eventually was sent to help Ric Grenell carry out a White House–ordered purge of the intelligence community. And Cohen, one of the original "Flynnstones" under Mike Flynn pushed out of the National Security Council by H. R. McMaster, floated between a series of administration jobs before landing in the spring of 2020 at the Pentagon, where he now assumed the military's top intelligence post. Suddenly, this thirty-four-year-old Trumpist was overseeing American Special Forces and organizations like the Defense Intelligence Agency and National Security Agency.

In the chairman's office, Milley watched with apprehension. In a notebook, he kept writing down worrisome details, data points, leads. He called McMaster. "H.R.," Milley said, "help me to understand what the fuck I'm dealing with here." McMaster described the enemies "inside the wire" during his time at the National Security Council. Now, it seemed, some of the same figures were inside the wire at the Pentagon.

Milley had firsthand reason to be wary. Just before the election, he and Mike Pompeo had become infuriated when a top secret Navy SEAL Team 6 rescue mission to free an American hostage held in Nigeria almost had to be canceled at the last minute because, it turned out, the Nigerians had not been formally notified in advance as required, despite Patel's assurances. "Planes were already in the air and we didn't have the approvals," a senior State Department official recalled. The rescue team was kept circling while diplomats tried to find Nigerian counterparts, which they did only minutes before the planes would have had to turn back. As a result, the official said, both Pompeo and Milley, who believed he had been personally lied to, "assigned ill will to that whole cabal." The CIA had refused to have anything to do with Patel, Pompeo recalled to his State Department staff, and they should be wary as well. "The secretary thought these people were just nuts, wackadoodles, and dangerous," a second senior State Department official said.

After Esper's firing, Milley called Patel and Cohen separately to his office to deliver stern lectures. Whatever machinations they were up to, he told each of them, "life looks really shitty from behind bars. And whether you want to realize it or not, there's going to be a president at exactly 1200 hours on the twentieth and his name is Joe Biden. And if you guys do anything that's illegal, I don't mind having you in prison."

He ended with a warning: They were being watched. "Don't do it, don't even try to do it. I can smell it. I can see it. And so can a lot of other people," Milley told them. "And by the way, the military will have no part of this shit."

Part of the new team's agenda soon became clear: making sure Trump fulfilled his 2016 campaign promise to withdraw American troops from the "endless wars" overseas. Two days after Esper was fired, Patel slid a piece of paper across the desk to Milley during a meeting with him and Chris Miller. It was an order with Trump's trademark signature in black Sharpie ink decreeing that all 4,500 remaining troops in Afghanistan be withdrawn by January 15 and a smaller contingent of under a thousand troops on a counterterrorism mission in Somalia be pulled out by December 31.

Milley was stunned. "Where'd you get this?" he demanded.

Patel said it had just come from the White House.

"Did you advise the president to do this?" he asked Patel, who said no.

"Did you advise the president to do this?" he asked Miller, who said no.

"Well, then who advised the president to do it?" Milley asked. "By law, I'm the president's adviser on military action. How does this happen without me rendering my military opinion and advice?"

With that, he announced that he was putting on his dress uniform and going to the White House. Miller and Patel jumped in their cars and went too. They all ended up in Robert O'Brien's office.

"Where did this come from?" Milley demanded, putting the withdrawal order on the national security adviser's desk.

"I don't know. I've never seen that before," O'Brien replied. The format was unlike any typically used for a presidential order. "It doesn't look like a White House memo."

Keith Kellogg, the retired general serving as Pence's national security adviser and a backdoor conduit to Trump, asked to see the document. "This is not the president," he said, skeptically examining it. "The format's not right. This is not done right."

At that point, Milley was even more flabbergasted. "Keith, you've got to be kidding me," he said. "You're telling me that someone's forging the president of the United States' signature?"

O'Brien took the order—Patel told him it was the only copy—and asked the others to sit tight in his office. "Let me get to the bottom of it." He headed upstairs to see Pat Cipollone, but the White House counsel knew nothing about the order either. Then he went to see Trump in the Oval Office.

The order, it turned out, was not fake. But the real story was even more revealing. It was the work of a rogue operation inside Trump's own White House supported by the president himself. The order had been drafted by a junior personnel aide working with Douglas Macgregor, a retired colonel and Trump favorite from his Fox News appearances. Johnny McEntee then took it into the president, bypassing the national security apparatus and Trump's own senior officials, to get him to sign it on the spot. Thus had Trump attempted to end the twenty-year American war in Afghanistan.

Macgregor had often been on Fox demanding an exit from Afghanistan and blaming Trump's advisers for blocking the president from doing what he wanted. "He needs to send everyone out of the Oval Office who keeps telling him, 'If you do that and something bad happens, it's going to be blamed on you, Mr. President,'" Macgregor had told Tucker Carlson that January. "He needs to say, 'I don't give a damn.'"[5]

That interview and others like it had gotten Macgregor into the Oval Office to meet Trump that spring—exactly the kind of meeting John Kelly would have blocked. The president had immediately hit it off with Macgregor and offered to bring him into the administration. But Mark Esper resisted pressure to hire him and Macgregor's subsequent nomination as Trump's ambassador to Germany foundered that summer over his comments calling for martial law at the Mexican border and terming Middle East immigrants to Europe "unwanted Muslim invaders."[6]

On the day that Esper was fired, McEntee had invited Macgregor to his office, offered him a Pentagon job as the new acting defense secretary's senior adviser, and handed Macgregor a piece of paper with a handwritten list of priorities that he claimed had come directly from Trump. The memo, later revealed by the journalist Jonathan Swan, had four items:

1. Get us out of Afghanistan.
2. Get us out of Iraq and Syria.
3. Complete the withdrawal from Germany.
4. Get us out of Africa.[7]

Once the Afghanistan order was discovered, Trump's advisers persuaded the president to back off by reminding him that he already had approved a plan for leaving over the following few months. "Why do we need a new plan?" Pompeo asked. Trump agreed, and O'Brien then told the rest of the rattled national security leadership that the order was "null and void."

The compromise, however, was a new order that now codified the drawdown to 2,500 troops in Afghanistan by mid-January, which Milley and Esper had been resisting, and a reduction in the remaining 3,000 troops in Iraq as well. The State Department was given one hour to notify leaders of those countries before it became public.

Milley had two nightmare scenarios in his head. One was an external crisis, such as a war overseas with Iran, to divert attention or create the pretext for a power grab at home. The other was a manufactured internal crisis to justify ordering the military into the streets of America to prevent the transfer of power. And the more he thought about it and worried about it and watched what was happening, the more real it became.

Milley's study of history took him to a disturbing parallel. He feared that what he considered Trump's "Hitler-like" embrace of the big lie about the election would prompt the president to seek out a "Reichstag moment," in which, like Adolf Hitler and the burning of the German parliament in 1933, he would manufacture a crisis in order to swoop in and save the nation. He envisioned Trumpian brownshirts in the streets, renewed orders from Trump to invoke the Insurrection Act, even martial law.

His concern increased in mid-November when a weekend "Stop the Steal" rally in Washington drew several thousand angry Trump supporters including members of the far-right extremist Proud Boys organization—and an approving drive-by from Trump himself in the presidential limousine—before ending up in hours of running street fights with counter-protesters. Was this a rehearsal for what would come next?

The maneuverings at the Pentagon only deepened Milley's worries. A White House liaison installed by Johnny McEntee ordered more personnel moves that raised hackles. The liaison, a twenty-five-year-old college dropout from New Hampshire aptly named Joshua Whitehouse, had hand-delivered the official letter terminating Esper and he now set about forcing out other holdovers deemed insufficiently loyal. The day before Thanksgiving, Whitehouse removed all but a handful of the members of the Defense Policy Board, including eminences such as Henry Kissinger and Madeleine Albright. They were replaced with Trump loyalists such as Newt Gingrich and Michael Pillsbury, a China hawk who had become a Trump favorite. Pillsbury, tapped to chair the board, told an interviewer that Trump had personally demanded the house-cleaning after being told that Albright had called him "the first anti-democratic president" in American history.[8]

The Defense Business Board, another advisory group, was also purged of nine members. "If you are receiving this e-mail, your membership on the Defense Business Board has expired or is coming to an end," they were told in a terse missive from Whitehouse.[9] Among those named to replace the board members were the Trump campaign advisers Corey Lewandowski and David Bossie. Whitehouse would eventually secure an appointment for himself as well to a new commission established by Congress to rename military bases honoring Confederate generals—a commission Trump opposed.

Right after Thanksgiving, Whitehouse summoned Christopher Maier, who headed the Pentagon task force dedicated to combating the Islamic State.

"The president long ago declared the ISIS campaign defeated," Whitehouse told Maier to explain that he was being pushed out.

"You mean, *ISIS* defeated?" Maier said. It was hard to imagine Trump proclaiming victory otherwise.

"Yes," Whitehouse corrected himself awkwardly, before resuming his scripted firing. "The acting secretary has therefore decided to disband the task force—and you're hereby terminated, immediately."

The same day Kissinger and Albright were purged, Trump rewarded the one general he considered most loyal by pardoning Mike Flynn. Bill Barr's effort to reverse Flynn's guilty plea had gotten tied up in appeals so Trump, out of patience and in a mood to do what he wanted, decided to effectively override the courts.

Like his lawyer, Sidney Powell of release-the-Kraken fame, Flynn had become a proponent of the allegation that a massive number of votes had been stolen from Trump using Dominion voting machines. Since the election, Flynn had even privately advocated calling out the military to cancel the results—exactly the nightmare scenario Milley feared. At some point in November, Flynn called Ezra Cohen, who had gotten his start under him at the Defense Intelligence Agency. Cohen was in Saudi Arabia on a work trip.

"You need to come home right now," Flynn told him. "We need to declare martial law."

Cohen was a Trump partisan but told associates later that he was deeply alarmed and brushed Flynn off. Soon after returning home, however, while driving to a friend's house around Thanksgiving, he got another call from the retired general.

"We need to seize the voting machines," Flynn said.

"This is crazy," Cohen told him, in the account he provided associates. "The election is over. Done. Trump lost. It's done. You need to stop. This is crazy."

Flynn erupted in anger. "Are you kidding me?" he barked. "I'm disgusted by you. You're a quitter."

"The election is done," Cohen tried again. "Stop. You're making a fool of yourself."

Undaunted, a week after his pardon, Flynn endorsed an ad calling on Trump to invoke martial law, "temporarily suspend the Constitution," and authorize the military to conduct a national "re-vote" of the presidential election.[10]

Milley's fears of a coup no longer seemed far-fetched.

Like Milley and Pompeo, Bill Barr was trying to keep the situation from getting even further out of hand. In the immediate aftermath of the vote, Barr had authorized U.S. attorneys to investigate any serious allegations of fraud, prompting the department's election crime chief to resign in protest on the assumption that the policy shift was one more favor to the president. But the attorney general told confidants that his motive was the opposite: he needed ammunition in case Trump tried to force him to undercut the election. Barr figured that if his investigators found the allegations to be as flimsy as they appeared, then he would be in a stronger position to stand up to Trump.

At Pat Cipollone's suggestion, Barr came to the White House just before Thanksgiving to meet with Trump, their first conversation since their blowup over the phone in October and their first in person since September. Barr had been talking with Mark Milley, Mitch McConnell, and others who were worried about what the endgame was. Now was his chance to find out. Even in private, Barr found Trump was unbalanced. He railed about supposed election fraud, claiming that he won by "a lot" and criticizing the Justice Department for not investigating.

"The claims just aren't panning out," Barr told him. He urged Trump to focus on the upcoming Senate races in Georgia instead.

Trump looked sullen and did not reply at first. "Well," he finally said bitterly, "our Republican senators haven't done much for me."

Barr finished the meeting convinced that Trump would not help the party win those Senate seats. All that mattered to Trump was himself, not his party or country. On the way out, Barr ran into Jared Kushner and Dan Scavino. "I am worried about how far the president is taking this stolen election thing," Barr said.

Mark Meadows, joining them, told Barr not to worry. "I think he is becoming more realistic and knows there is a limit on how far he can take things," Meadows said.

"We are working on it," Kushner added, even though he was largely absenting himself from the fight.[11]

Barr left somewhat reassured and called McConnell to report there was "encouraging news." Sure enough, whether coincidence or not, that night, the General Services Administration, which for two weeks had held up resources and access for the transition, issued the formal "ascertainment" of Biden as the apparent winner. At least the official gears of the bureaucracy could begin preparing for a Biden presidency.

But that did not mean that Trump was giving up; rather than becoming more realistic, as Meadows had asserted, the president was becoming even more detached from reality. The more avenues that closed off to him—courts, election bureaus, the Justice Department—the more desperate he became to find another way to hold on to power. And Meadows was playing both sides, assuring establishment Republicans that he was trying to calm Trump down while encouraging the fervent Trumpists calling on him to burn down the system to preserve power.

The day after telling Barr that Trump was becoming more realistic about the hopeless fight, Meadows exchanged more texts with Ginni Thomas, who for nearly three weeks had been pelting Meadows with messages urging him to resist "the greatest Heist of our History," as she put it at one point. In this latest exchange, he framed the battle in messianic terms.

"This is a fight of good versus evil," he wrote. "Evil always looks like the victor until the King of Kings triumphs. Do not grow weary in well doing. The fight continues. I have staked my career on it."[12]

Barr's refutations did nothing to deter Trump from his election fraud claims. Instead, the president began pressing the matter with state legislators, trying to get them to ignore their own voters and choose electors to support the president. Worried, McConnell called Barr again. The Senate leader had stayed publicly silent through all of Trump's histrionics for fear that an open break with Trump would endanger Republican chances in the Georgia runoff elections. But if he could not speak out, he said, someone should.

"You're the best positioned to say something," McConnell said.

"Yeah," Barr agreed. "I think so, too, and I will."

Before he could, the president decided to air his complaints with the Justice Department. "Missing in action," he huffed during a call-in to Maria Bartiromo's show on Fox News over Thanksgiving weekend, his first interview since the election. "Can't tell you where they are."[13]

Irritated, Barr decided to push back. He invited Michael Balsamo, a reporter from the Associated Press, to lunch on December 1 and then planted a line that he knew would generate headlines. "To date, we have not seen fraud on a scale that could have effected a different outcome in the election," Barr told Balsamo.[14] Boom. The president's own attorney general was calling Trump's claim bogus.

Barr knew exactly what he was doing. So when he headed to the White House shortly after lunch for a 3 p.m. meeting with Mark Meadows and

Pat Cipollone, he understood that he might be called on the carpet by the president—and conceivably put out of a job.

Sure enough, Trump learned that Barr was in the building and summoned him. Barr found the president in his private dining room with the large-screen television tuned to One America News Network showing a Michigan hearing into election allegations. Meadows joined them along with Cipollone and two other lawyers, Pat Philbin and Eric Herschmann.

Barr approached the dining room table but did not sit down. Instead, he stood and put his hands on the back of one of the chairs. Trump held up a printout of the AP story.

"Did you say this?" he demanded.

"Yes."

"Why?"

"Because it's the truth," Barr said.

"You didn't have to say that," Trump said. "You could have just said no comment."

"We've been looking at these things and they're bullshit," Barr said. "Your team is still shoveling this shit out."

"You must hate Trump," the president shot back, referring to himself in the third person. "You would only have said that if you hate Trump."

"No, Mr. President, I don't hate you," Barr said.

In Trump's world, if someone challenged his false assertions, it was a sign of disloyalty, period.

Barr addressed some of the claims, pointing out in granular detail how the Giuliani team had distorted perfectly normal counting processes to make them seem sinister. He told Trump that he was being ill advised by his "clown car of lawyers" and noted that "no respectable lawyers" would touch the effort to overturn the election.

"I understand you are very frustrated with me, Mr. President," Barr said, "and I am willing to submit my resignation. But I have—"

Before he said another word, he heard a bang that sounded like a gunshot.

"Accepted!" Trump yelled, his hand slamming down on the table. "Leave and don't go back to your office. You are done right now. Go home!"

Cipollone and Herschmann both yelled "No!" but Barr simply turned and left. He strode out of the building and climbed into his government car, which began to pull away. Suddenly, in an echo of the day Jeff Sessions almost resigned more than three years earlier, Cipollone and Herschmann caught up with the car before it left the White House grounds and banged on the windows until it stopped. They climbed into the vehicle and implored Barr to return, telling him Trump had changed his mind.

"He is not firing you," Cipollone said. "Come on back in."

"I hear you, Pat, but I am not going back in tonight," Barr said.

Still, he agreed not to resign. Yet.

As it happened, Barr was scheduled to have dinner that night with Mike Pompeo. When he arrived at the restaurant, an obscure Italian place in an out-of-the-way strip mall in Virginia, Pompeo joked about what kind of day Barr must have had. Then the two commiserated about how out of control Trump had become since the election. Pompeo was worried about what was happening at the Pentagon. Barr thought Trump had taken "a dangerous turn" and was "beyond restraint," listening only to "a few sycophants who told him what he wanted to hear."[15] Pompeo agreed.

At the dinner, the secretary of state revealed to Barr that he had taken a striking step with Mark Milley. Pompeo had proposed, and Milley readily agreed, that they convene regular morning phone calls with Mark Meadows to make sure the country was in steady hands until the inauguration. The two soon took to calling them the "land the plane" phone calls.

"Our job is to land this plane safely and to do a peaceful transfer of power the twentieth of January," Milley told his staff. "This is our obligation to this nation." There was a problem, however. "Both engines are out, the landing gear are stuck," Milley would say. "We're in an emergency situation."

In public, Pompeo had remained his usual staunchly pro-Trump self. The day after he had secretly gone to Milley's house to express concern about the "crazies" taking over, in fact, the secretary of state had created a furor by not only refusing to acknowledge Trump's defeat but snidely telling a news conference, "There will be a smooth transition—to a second Trump administration."[16]

Behind the scenes, though, he knew the election was over and his concerns had only escalated in the weeks since his kitchen-table confessional with Milley. Despite his public comment, Pompeo was no supporter of the effort to overturn the will of the voters. "He was totally against it," a senior State Department official recalled. To the remaining Pompeo supporters inside Foggy Bottom, the jarring contrast between what he said in public and private reflected Pompeo's way of sticking around—as a final constraint, they hoped. "It was important for him to not get fired at the end too, to be there to the bitter end," the senior official said.

Both Milley and Pompeo were angered by the bumbling team of ideologues Trump had sent to the Pentagon and saw clearly that his attacks on the election were escalating rather than dialing down. As the crisis accelerated, their partnership deepened, although Milley was under no illusions about the secretary of state. He believed that Pompeo, a longtime enabler of Trump, wanted "a second political life," but the president's final descent into denialism was the line that, finally, he would not cross. "At the end, he wouldn't be a party to that craziness," the chairman told his staff. By late November, he and Pompeo were holding their land-the-plane calls at 8 a.m. most days along with Meadows. Milley was confident that Pompeo was genuinely on board in trying to achieve a peaceful handover of power to Biden. But he was never sure what to make of Meadows. Was the chief of staff actually trying to land the plane, or one of the hijackers trying to crash it?

Most days, Milley would also get on the phone with Pat Cipollone, hardly the normal interlocutor for a chairman of the Joint Chiefs. He had been connected to the White House counsel through Adam Smith, the Democratic House Armed Services Committee chairman, who had been close college friends with Cipollone at Fordham University. Cipollone, a true believer in Trump's conservative agenda, was also a staunch rule-of-law guy and emerged in the final weeks of the administration as a principal actor in the near-daily drama over Trump's various ideas for trying to overturn his election defeat. After getting off one call with Cipollone, Milley told a visitor that he was "constructive," "not crazy," and a force for "trying to keep guardrails around the president." Milley was also regularly on the phone with Robert O'Brien, who, like Pompeo, appeared to be no supporter of election denialism but proved otherwise unhelpful.

At the same time, Milley reached out to Democrats close to Biden to assure them that he would not allow the military to be misused to keep Trump in power. One regular contact was Susan Rice, the former Obama national security adviser, in what Democrats came to call "the Rice channel."

He also spoke several times with Senator Angus King, an old-school independent from Maine who caucused with the Democrats. "My conversations with him were about the danger of some attempt to use the military to declare martial law," King said, and he took it upon himself to reassure fellow senators. "I can't tell you how I know this," he would tell them, "but the military will absolutely do the right thing."

The loyalty purge extended into December. While Trump had considered getting rid of the FBI's Christopher Wray as Don Jr. and others had urged him to do, he knew that would cause an open rupture with Bill Barr and a public outcry. Instead, he focused on one of Pompeo's chief allies, Gina Haspel, the CIA director who in Trump's view had failed to produce the evidence he wanted to show that he had been unfairly targeted in the Russia investigation.

Kash Patel, the mysterious new power at the Pentagon, had a particular animus toward Haspel, whom he blamed for personally blocking his effort to declassify a 2018 report he wrote for Devin Nunes on the origins of the Russia investigation. After Patel was abruptly called back from a trip to Asia on which he was accompanying Chris Miller, rumors flew that he was about to get the nod to run either the FBI or the CIA. Haspel, aware that her job was in peril, decided to find out what was happening by showing up at the White House for the president's intelligence briefing on December 11.

The briefing was contentious, as Trump and his advisers berated Haspel and accused her of not being truthful with them about an incident in Syria, as if that might be the pretext for her ouster. Meadows asked her to come to his office after the briefing, where he proceeded to deliver the news: her deputy Vaughn Bishop, a career agency analyst, would be pushed out to make room for Patel. Implicit was the understanding that Patel would effectively be her political overseer for the remainder of the term. And if she were later fired, he could slide into her office as acting director.

Haspel dug in. If Patel were installed at the CIA, she told Meadows, she would resign in protest.

Meadows realized that could be politically damaging at a time when the president needed Republican support to challenge the election, so he asked Haspel to wait in his office while he rushed down the hall to tell Trump they had a problem.

By the time he got there, Trump had changed his mind. "Making those changes in the CIA—let's hold off on those," he told Meadows.

"Sir," he replied, "I've already told this to the director." What's more, he added, "She has indicated she'll quit if we do that."

Call it off, Trump reiterated. Meadows returned to his office to tell Haspel: Never mind.

Mark Milley heard about the firing-that-wasn't and caused a stir about it the next day at West Point, where he and other top officials were watching the annual Army-Navy Game in a private box with Trump. He noticed the president and Meadows whispering in a corner. As Meadows walked away, Milley approached him. "Hey, Chief," he said. "What's up? Why'd you bring Kash home?"

"Nothing, nothing," Meadows responded.

"So what's the president talking about with personnel moves?" Milley asked. "Are you guys really going to fire Wray or Gina?"

Meadows did not reply, but after he walked away Milley heard Trump tell his chief of staff that he wanted him to take care of "that personnel thing" by Monday. Milley then called out to Patel in his booming voice. "Hey, Kash," he asked loudly. "Which one? Which one are you going to take? CIA or FBI? Kash? Which one is it?" Once again, the chairman thought he was at least putting the plotters on notice.

Two days later, Monday, December 14, was supposed to be the day Trump's fantasies came crashing up against the hard reality of electoral math once and for all. He had run out the clock and gotten nowhere. The legal team led by Rudy Giuliani, who was still recovering after having been hospitalized with Covid, had been rebuffed by one court after another. When the Supreme Court unanimously rejected two petitions to intervene, even the three justices Trump appointed blew him off, despite his expectation of loyalty. Mitch McConnell, Jared Kushner, Bill Barr, and many others assumed it was almost over. Kushner took off for a trip to the Middle East.

December 14 was the date prescribed by federal law for members of the Electoral College to meet in all fifty states and the District of Columbia to cast their presidential votes. Every state except Wisconsin had already certified its popular vote counts by the deadline six days earlier, and when the electors met that day none of the outcomes changed. Biden had won the presidency with 306 electoral votes, far more than the 270 he needed.

It was not for lack of trying. Trump and Giuliani had been working the phones in seven key states that gave Biden his victory—Arizona, Georgia, Michigan, Nevada, New Mexico, Pennsylvania, and Wisconsin—promoting a scheme to appoint "alternate electors" who would disregard the will of the voters and hold rump electoral meetings that day to give their fake votes to Trump to be used to contest the results when Congress later met to ratify them. The plot, actively coordinated by Giuliani and Trump campaign officials, even resulted in fake electoral certificates being sent by plotters in those states to the National Archives. But despite Trump's hype, no state legislature agreed to seat the renegade Trump electors. At the time, it seemed like just another farce.

The one remaining step was for Mike Pence and Congress to count the actual electoral votes at the Capitol on January 6. But that was seen as a formality. No presidential election had ever been seriously contested after an Electoral College majority anointed the next president.

The window for legitimate challenges had shut. McConnell decided to put the charade behind them. The next day, he notified Mark Meadows that he was about to acknowledge Biden's victory.

"The Electoral College has spoken," McConnell said on the Senate floor. "So today, I want to congratulate President-elect Joe Biden."[17]

It was a simple, commonsense statement, but one most Republicans had avoided until then. By finally making it, McConnell signaled that it was time to move on, that Trump had played his hand and lost and Republicans needed to face the future. He had been so afraid of further angering Trump and jeopardizing the Georgia Senate elections that he had refused even to speak privately with Biden since the election. But now he sent word to Biden's close friend Senator Chris Coons of Delaware that he would welcome a call with the next president. He was done trying to manage this one.

Trump was irate and called McConnell to chew him out. "It's over," McConnell told him. That would be the last time they would ever talk.

But McConnell knew there could still be mischief on January 6. Some of Trump's fervent allies in the House were planning to object to electors from battleground states. The rules required at least one senator to participate in any objection as well for it to even reach a debate; if no senator went along, Trump's plot would fizzle quickly. During a conference call after his statement, McConnell implored fellow Senate Republicans not to join the rogue effort to disrupt the counting. But at least a couple of them were not listening.

With the Electoral College count complete, Bill Barr figured the matter was all but settled and took the moment to announce that he would resign before Christmas. To avoid a public feud with Trump, he drafted a resignation letter heaping praise on the insecure president for his "many successes and unprecedented achievements," while keeping his disgruntlement to himself.[18] In his place would now step Jeffrey Rosen, the deputy attorney general. Barr had faith in him. But no matter what Bill Barr and the others thought, the plane had not landed yet.

CHAPTER 30

All Hell Is Going to Break Loose

On the day that Mitch McConnell congratulated Joe Biden on his victory, Trump fairly shouted his rage over Twitter: "This Fake Election can no longer stand," "ridiculous," "DO NOT TAMPER, a crime," "Tremendous evidence," "Can't let this happen." By this point, when he did have meetings with other officials, no matter what the ostensible subject, they routinely began with a presidential outburst:

"YOU KNOW WE WON THE ELECTION."
"YOU KNOW WE GOT SCREWED."
"YOU KNOW THEY STOLE IT FROM US."

Trump and the country were in uncharted territory. No other sitting president had persisted in challenging an election after it was decided by the Electoral College. Chris Liddell, his deputy White House chief of staff, had mapped out multiple scenarios for the transition between the election and the inauguration—clear victory, clear defeat, disputed win, disputed loss that would be contested for a few weeks, disputed loss that would be contested for a long time. None of his scenarios lasted past December 14. Any resistance now was constitutionally pointless as far as most lawyers and political experts were concerned. But while Trump was at a dead end, he was nowhere near ready to give up.

One of those who found himself increasingly shut out was the vice president, the other person on the ticket and therefore the one with almost as much at stake as Trump. Mike Pence had not explicitly told the president to abandon his pointless quest. That was not how Pence worked. Even now, he and others were still humoring Trump. But he had been, in his own way, trying to gently steer Trump away from the scorched-earth approach to the post-election period, encouraging him instead to use the time they had left to travel the country and talk about their accomplishments. They had a story to tell—tax cuts, economic growth, a tougher policy toward China, a renegotiated NAFTA. Why not focus on that, he suggested, without directly adding the rest of the thought—instead of a hopeless and fundamentally dishonest campaign to upend democracy. But that was not what Trump wanted to hear.

And so the president did not object when Mark Meadows, intent on making himself Trump's indispensable man, increasingly kept Pence out of the Oval Office, not including the vice president in meetings that he used to attend as a matter of course, much less the sessions being held to plot ways to overturn the election.

Meadows by this point was actively helping the conspiracy theorists who were filling Trump's head with all sorts of fantasies, acting less as a gatekeeper than a door-opener. "Meadows was basically a matador," said one Republican involved in discussions with the White House at the time. "He sort of just let in anybody and everybody who wanted to come in." Moreover, he was still playing both sides. "Meadows admitted to people privately . . . 'Trust me, I'm going to get the president there, he's going to drop this issue. Just kind of give him time to mourn and grieve and then he's going to come around,'" said a White House colleague who heard him say variations of this repeatedly. But then "he was bringing the crazies into the West Wing."

At this point, Trump was only interested in those who could help him keep power. With Bill Barr on his way out, the president wanted to find out whether his replacement would assist in carrying out his scheme. A half hour before he tweeted news of Barr's departure, Trump had his assistant email Jeffrey Rosen, the soon-to-be acting attorney general, two documents "From POTUS": a set of talking points on presumed voter fraud in Antrim County, Michigan, and a supposed "forensic report" on the voting machines there.[1] The next day, Trump summoned Rosen and his deputy Richard Donoghue to the Oval Office, where they were joined by Meadows, Pat Cipollone, and Ken Cuccinelli from the Department of Homeland Security.

Tall with gray hair, a receding chin, and a perennially dark suit, Rosen was a veteran of Republican legal circles in Washington, a Harvard Law graduate who served as a senior lawyer in the administration of George W. Bush and was then tapped for a judgeship, only to have the nomination die without a vote in an election year. When Trump took office, Rosen returned to government as Elaine Chao's deputy transportation secretary, then moved to the Justice Department to succeed Rod Rosenstein when he stepped down following the release of the Mueller report. Among some in the department, Rosen quickly earned a reputation as a true Trumpist, eager to curry favor with the White House in hopes of becoming attorney general in a second term.

But as he sat down in the Oval Office, any ambitions foundered on the reality that he was no more willing than Barr to join in Trump's plan to wrest an election away from the victor. To Trump's disappointment, Rosen rebuffed the pressure to find corruption where there was none. The Antrim County case was a classic example. A Republican clerk on election night had mistakenly credited Biden with thousands of votes that were really cast for Trump, but the error had been quickly fixed. Trump's team was not willing to accept the explanation. The "audit" he was given claimed a 68 percent error rate in Dominion voting machines in the county, a completely bogus conclusion. In fact, a hand recount completed two days later found a net change of just twelve votes out of 15,962 cast, or 0.075 percent.[2]

But as he pressed his incoming attorney general, Trump simply spouted one rumor and conspiracy after another. With the integrity of American democracy at stake, all he had to offer was "people are telling me this" and "people are telling me that."

Rosen pushed back. "Well, people are telling you things that are not right," he said. "This is not accurate."

"Well, what about this?" Trump said, citing a claim that Georgia election workers pulled thousands of fake votes for Biden out of a suitcase. "I saw it on the videotape, somebody delivering a suitcase of ballots."

Rosen knew the allegation. "It wasn't a suitcase," he explained. "It was a bin. That's what they use when they're counting ballots. It's benign."[3] He was not the only one to push back on it. Jared Kushner, who had mostly kept his promise to stay out of the post-election mess, had even texted Mark Meadows an article debunking the false Georgia story.[4]

But it did not matter to Trump. No matter how many times he was told the conspiracies he saw were not true, he refused to give up.

Trump was eager to hear from anyone telling him he really won. When Peter Navarro, his trade adviser turned self-appointed Covid authority, refashioned himself a voting expert, Trump touted his report, "The Immaculate Deception," a thirty-six-page greatest-hits compilation of stolen election conspiracies Navarro released on December 17 "in his private capacity."[5]

The next night, Friday, December 18, Trump agreed to meet another set of supporters feeding his fantasy in the Oval Office at 7:30 p.m. For all of the wild meetings he had presided over there in the last four years, ranting about his enemies, lashing out at "shithole" countries, berating congressional leaders and cabinet officers, none of them would compare with the discussion he was about to have. For the first time in American history, a president would seriously entertain using the military to over-turn an election he lost.

It was an entourage that would never have made it past the gate of any other White House. Among them were Mike Flynn, the convicted liar who had just been pardoned by Trump; his lawyer, Sidney Powell, the Kraken promiser who had been publicly shunned by the campaign but never truly pushed out; and Patrick Byrne, the eccentric millionaire founder of Overstock.com, a Trump supporter who had an affair with the Russian agent Maria Butina and later claimed to be the target of Russian mobsters. They were secretly cleared into the building that evening by an aide to Navarro, a move approved not even by Mark Meadows the mata-dor, underscoring how a White House rarely known for its discipline was breaking down even further in its final weeks.

Flynn, Powell, and the others had come to present Trump with a plan straight out of an over-the-top movie script. With the election results now certified, the best chance to hang on to power, they told the president, was to use the armed forces. Trump, they said, should send the National Guard, federal marshals, or some combination to six swing counties to seize paper ballots, recount them on live television, and, assuming impro-prieties were found, hold new elections in those states before January 20. Flynn did not use the phrase "martial law," which he had uttered the day before on Newsmax, but what he was proposing was an unprecedented military intervention in American democracy.[6]

In this scenario, Flynn would serve as Trump's "field marshal" over the effort to reverse the results while Powell would be appointed special counsel to lead a government investigation aimed at proving her imagi-nary far-flung plot. Powell insisted to Trump that the election was stolen by Dominion voting machines rigged as part of that wild international conspiracy she had publicly claimed involving Venezuela, Iran, China, and other foreign adversaries. It was no coincidence that Giuliani was not invited. As outrageous as his own theories had been, Powell and the rest considered him too timid.

They handed Trump a three-page draft executive order dated December 16 for him to sign citing the bogus "audit" of Antrim County and unspecified "evidence of international and foreign interference" in the election. The order called for appointment of a special counsel, presumably Powell, to institute criminal actions; while not named, it referred to "her duties." It also would authorize the secretary of defense—the acting Chris Miller, who had been chosen for his loyalty—to "seize, collect, retain and analyze" voting machines and provide a final assessment of any findings in sixty days, well after the inauguration was to take place.[7] Another version of the order substituted the Department of Homeland Security for the Defense Department, an avenue Trump had in fact already pursued, directing both Meadows and Giuliani to call Chad Wolf, the acting secretary, and ask him to seize voting machines. Wolf told them, "time and time again," that he had "zero authority" to do so, he later told associates, and even had the department general counsel prepare a three-page memo explaining why, but Trump's advisers persisted.

By this point, Trump's official lawyers were in the room, and they began to robustly object. One of them, Eric Herschmann, had spotted the conspiracy theorists entering the Oval Office and summoned Pat Cipollone, who rushed over. So did Derek Lyons, the staff secretary. Matt Morgan, the campaign lawyer, was patched in by telephone.

Their arrival prompted an angry clash over who was truly representing Trump's interests. Herschmann poked holes in Powell's assertions, accusing her of nonsensical claims. Flynn, just days from his sixty-second birthday, was still in fighting trim and jumped to his feet to confront the lawyer.

"You're a quitter!" Flynn erupted at Herschmann. "You're not fighting!"

Herschmann continued pressing Powell. "All you do is promise but never deliver," he said.

Flynn yelled at him some more.

"Why the fuck do you keep standing up and screaming at me?" Herschmann finally addressed the retired general. "If you want to come over here, come over here. If not, sit your ass down."

Flynn backed down, an Oval Office fistfight averted. But Patrick Byrne, who was financing an effort to find election fraud, reinforced the notion that Trump's staff was betraying him. "This guy is lying to you through his teeth," Byrne recalled telling Trump in a lengthy account of the meeting he later published online. "They want you to lose."

Rather than throwing plotters pushing for martial law out of the Oval Office, Trump let the conversation drag on for hours, with others patched in over time by speakerphone, including, eventually, Giuliani as well as

Meadows and Robert O'Brien. Even Giuliani, who had advanced some of the most implausible election theories, objected to calling in the military. Cipollone made clear to Trump that it was unthinkable.

"Never in American history has there been this kind of a challenge to an election," Cipollone said.

"Never in American history has there been a situation like this," Flynn retorted, "with counting being shut down for hours, foreigners connecting to our equipment—"

Cipollone could hardly believe what he was hearing. The president "does not have the authority to do this," he said.

"Of course he does," Powell argued, citing an executive order meant to counter foreign interference in American elections.

"You know, Pat," Trump said, "at least they want to fight for me. You don't even fight for me. You just tell me everything I can't do."

The conversation grew more heated, and it was a mark of how out of control the discussion had become that Giuliani would be the one to urge everyone to calm down.

Aggravated, Cipollone turned to go.

"Let him leave," Powell said to Trump. "I'll take the job and you'll win."

"Go ahead, Pat," Trump taunted Cipollone as he withdrew. "Leave. Don't come back as far as I'm concerned."

Cipollone did, however, come back to rejoin the group and try to talk Trump out of the reckless course he was seriously considering. At one point, the president declared that he would go ahead and appoint Powell as special counsel. But the fight persisted. Eventually, as the evening wore on, the president invited his guests up to the Yellow Oval Room in the family quarters, where the residential staff brought meatballs. The conversation did not break up until around 12:15 in the morning, nearly five hours after it started.

No one was entirely sure what Trump would do. Even he seemed to understand just how far from American norms he was straying. "You know," Trump said as they left the Oval Office before relocating to the residence, "in 200 years there probably has not been a meeting in this room like what just happened."[8]

After his guests left, Trump could not sleep. The meeting had reminded him how little time was left: January 6 loomed large. It was his last real chance to keep power. Already, a rally was being planned for that day to pressure Congress to reject Joe Biden's election and keep Trump in the White House.

At 1:42 a.m., Trump sent a Twitter message beckoning his followers to descend on the capital to help him hold on to office. "Big protest in D.C. on January 6th," he wrote. "Be there, will be wild!"

The middle-of-the-night tweet from a president who earlier that fall had called on extremist groups to "stand back and stand by" resonated loudly in the darker corners of Trump's America. Members of far-right extremist groups like the Proud Boys, the Oath Keepers, the 1st Amendment Praetorian, and the Three Percenters saw the message as a call to arms and began mobilizing to flood Washington on January 6. "He called us all to the Capitol and wants us to make it wild!!!" Kelly Meggs, an Oath Keepers leader from Florida, wrote on Facebook. Stewart Rhodes, the founder of the group, declared that if Biden were inaugurated there would be "a massively bloody revolution."[9]

Trump had increasingly flirted with such radical groups. QAnon, the internet conspiracy movement, had made him the hero of its fantasy version of reality, a savior recruited by military generals to run for president in 2016 in order to destroy a cabal of Satan-worshipping pedophiles who had taken over the world. In the weeks before the 2020 election, Trump endorsed Marjorie Taylor Greene, a onetime QAnon follower with a history of racist and anti-Semitic comments running for Congress from Georgia, calling her a "future Republican Star." Asked whether he subscribed to QAnon's beliefs, Trump did not disavow the group. "I don't know much about the movement, other than I understand they like me very much," he told reporters.[10]

On December 21, two days after his "will be wild" tweet, Trump invited Greene, who won her election and was soon to be sworn in, to an Oval Office strategy session along with Matt Gaetz, the congressman who advertised himself as "Trump's Best Buddy," and Mark Meadows's other longtime colleagues from the Freedom Caucus including Jim Jordan, Louie Gohmert, Mo Brooks of Alabama, Paul Gosar of Arizona, and Scott Perry of Pennsylvania. With Rudy Giuliani joining them, the group discussed plans for House members to object on January 6 to electoral votes from swing states that went for Biden. They could push to accept alternate pro-Trump electoral slates or perhaps simply negate enough states that the election would be thrown to the House to decide. "This sedition will be stopped," Gosar tweeted afterward.[11]

Key to this would be the vice president, who under the Constitution was to preside over the counting of the Electoral College votes. This time,

Pence was in the White House and met with the lawmakers in the Cabinet Room after they saw Trump. For weeks, the vice president's staff had picked up talk among Trump's more extreme allies that he might pressure Pence to intervene on January 6 and throw the election to him. Greg Jacob, the vice president's counsel, had already researched the question for a memo explaining the process to Pence. But now that the Electoral College had voted, it was becoming clear that Trump really seemed to be pursuing this absurd scheme.

The Constitution was maddeningly vague on the process. Article II said simply, "The President of the Senate shall, in the Presence of the Senate and House of Representatives, open all the Certificates, and the Votes shall then be counted." The vice president serves as president of the Senate, but by switching to the passive voice for the second half of the sentence the provision left open who should do the counting and therefore might theoretically have power to decide if votes were improper. After the hotly contested election of 1876, in which Rutherford B. Hayes was awarded Electoral College votes from three disputed states to give him the presidency, Congress passed the Electoral Count Act of 1887 to clarify procedures, although it had not entirely succeeded.

Past vice presidents had always treated the Electoral College count as ceremonial, even those in the awkward position of presiding over their own ticket's defeat, like Richard Nixon in 1961, Walter Mondale in 1981, Dan Quayle in 1993, and Al Gore in 2001. None of them had sought to use the role to change the outcome.

Privately, Pence understood there was no evidence of fraud widespread enough to undercut Biden's victory. But he had straddled a quintessentially Pence-ian line since November 3. "As our election contest continues, I'll make you a promise," he told a conservative gathering in West Palm Beach, Florida, the day after meeting with the lawmakers at the White House. "We're going to keep fighting until every legal vote is counted. We're going to keep fighting until every illegal vote is thrown out."[12] Which sounded like he was backing Trump without actually saying that he believed there were enough illegal votes to change the outcome.

But the pressure was rising on Pence. He had grown uncharacteristically testy in recent weeks, even snapping at Deborah Birx during a Covid meeting. Birx was struck that the vice president "looked gaunt and exhausted" and that "stress had sunken his eyes and hollowed his cheeks."[13] As Pence headed off to Vail, Colorado, for the holidays, he found himself on a tightrope that was becoming less steady with each passing day.

While Trump was being urged by "the crazies" to order troops to intervene at home, the leadership of America's uniformed military was also worried that he would order action abroad. Mark Milley and his fellow generals were concerned the president would authorize a strike against Iran, generating a foreign crisis at a time when the country was in a spiraling domestic political crisis of Trump's making.

For much of his presidency, Trump's foreign policy hawks had agitated for a showdown with Iran, accelerating their efforts with the possibility that Trump might lose the election. In early 2020, when Mike Pence advocated a strike, Milley asked why. "Because they are evil," Pence said. Milley recalled replying, "Mr. Vice President, there's a lot of evil in the world, but we don't go to war against all of it." Milley grew even more nervous when an administration official before the election explicitly told Trump that if he lost, he should strike Iran's nuclear program. Milley at the time told his staff it was a "What the fuck are these guys talking about?" moment. Now, it seemed frighteningly possible.

Robert O'Brien was another consistent cheerleader for going after Iran, as the Pentagon leaders saw it. "Mr. President, we should hit 'em hard, hit 'em hard, with everything we have," the national security adviser would say when the subject came up, what Mark Esper would later call his "tedious signature phrase."[14] Esper considered O'Brien a dangerous influence on Trump, "very unhelpful and unhinged," as he told associates. Mike Pompeo, who had supported O'Brien's appointment, told Esper he now regretted it.

In the week after Esper's firing, Milley was called to the White House to present various military options for going after Iran and found himself fending off a disturbing performance by Chris Miller, the new acting defense secretary. By his own account later to ABC's Jonathan Karl, Miller had intentionally acted like a "fucking madman" at the meeting, just three days into his tenure, pushing to surface various escalatory scenarios for responding to Iran's breakout nuclear capacities.[15]

Trump kept asking for alternatives, including even an attack inside Iran on its ballistic weapons sites. Milley explained that would be illegal. "If you attack the mainland of Iran, you will be starting a war," the chairman cautioned him. During another clash with Trump's more militant advisers without the president, Milley was even more explicit. "If we do what you're saying," the general warned, "we are all going to be tried as war criminals in the Hague."

Trump often seemed more bluster than bite. "This was a guy who spoke loudly and didn't really want to get in a fight," as one of the generals put it. The Pentagon brass still believed that Trump did not want an all-out war, but he kept pushing for a missile strike on Iran even after that November meeting. If Trump said it once, Milley told his staff, he said it a thousand times. "The thing he was most worried about was Iran," a senior Biden adviser who spoke with Milley in this period recalled. "Milley had had the experience more than once of having to walk the president off the ledge when it came to retaliating."

The biggest fear was that Iran would provoke Trump, and, using an array of diplomatic and military channels, officials in Trump's own government now warned the Iranians not to exploit the volatile domestic situation in the United States. "There was a distinct concern that Iran would take advantage of this to strike at us in some way," recalled Adam Smith, the House Armed Services chairman who spoke regularly to Milley. "They were really concerned that with all of this other nonsense going on, they wanted to make sure we were doing our job and protecting ourselves, whatever Iran might do."

Among those pushing the president to hit Iran, Milley believed, was Israel's Benjamin Netanyahu, who was anxious for Trump to take action before he turned the office over to Biden. On December 18, the same day that Trump was meeting with Mike Flynn to discuss martial law at home, Milley met with Netanyahu at his home in Jerusalem to personally urge him to back off. "If you do this, you're gonna have a fucking war," Milley told him.

Just two days later, on December 20, Iranian-backed militias in Iraq fired nearly two dozen rockets at the American embassy in Baghdad. Trump responded by publicly blaming Iran and threatening major retaliation if so much as a single American were killed. It was the largest attack on the Green Zone in more than a decade, and exactly the sort of provocation Milley had been dreading.

Trump's fury over the election was splitting his administration and his party apart. The Divider now saw the world in a new binary: those who were helping him to battle on and those who were not. He lashed out at anyone and anything in the latter category, even threatening to veto a bipartisan $900 billion Covid relief bill that he denounced as a "disgrace" even though it was negotiated by his own administration.[16] While at Mar-a-Lago for the holidays, Trump withheld his signature, abruptly demanding that the bill be rewritten to provide Americans $2,000 apiece to help deal with the pandemic instead of the $600 payments that Steven Mnuchin and the Republican leaders had agreed to with the Democrats.

The veto threat was a jab at Mitch McConnell, who had drawn the president's ire for declaring the election over. By demanding $2,000 payments, Trump was embracing a proposal long resisted by McConnell's Republicans. McConnell saw Trump's last-minute tantrum undercutting his two Republican senators in the upcoming Georgia runoff elections, who would be pressed by their Democratic opponents to embrace an idea they had rejected. For days, Trump held the package hostage until David Perdue, one of the two Georgia senators, came to see him on Christmas Day at Mar-a-Lago to personally plead with him. "If you don't sign this bill, I'm going to lose," Perdue told him, as he recounted to a colleague. Trump finally backed down two days after Christmas and signed the measure after all.

On the same day, one of Trump's more extreme congressional allies took the vice president to court. The Texas congressman Louie Gohmert, who had attended the White House strategy session with Trump on December 21, filed a lawsuit asking a court to overrule the rules limiting the vice president's role on January 6, in effect seeking to force Pence to take action to reject Biden electoral votes. It was a spurious claim and Trump's Justice Department went to court to argue against it before a judge promptly tossed it out. But it indicated the rising pressure on Pence to claim powers he did not have to reverse the election. Trump was going to force his vice president to make a choice.

Marc Short, Pence's chief of staff, saw the collision coming. Over the holidays, he called Jared Kushner asking him to get his father-in-law to stand down. "Look, can you help us with this?" Short asked.

But Kushner brushed him off. He had not changed his mind about the election, but he remained resolute about not having anything to do with it, no matter how far Trump now seemed intent on pushing. "Look, when Rudy got involved, I stopped being involved," he told Short. The vice president "is a big boy" and if he disagreed with the president on a legal issue, he should bring in his lawyers. "I'm too busy working on Middle East peace right now, Marc."

The closer to a final decision he came, the more Trump increased the pressure on all those he thought might still swing things his way. On the Sunday after Christmas, he twice called Jeff Rosen at home. On the second call, after a half hour, they patched in Rich Donoghue, Rosen's deputy, then talked for another hour as the president declared that "people are really very mad" at the Justice Department for not intervening.

"You guys are not following the internet the way I do," Trump complained. He pushed Rosen at least to make a public statement saying there were serious allegations of wrongdoing, regardless of what any investigation was finding. "Just have a press conference," he said.

"No, we can't have a press conference because there isn't a factual foundation to justify that," Rosen said.

Trump insisted that it was "statistically impossible for me to lose" and claimed there were more votes cast in Pennsylvania than there were voters, which was not true.

"You can't just go and just flip a switch and change the election," Rosen responded.

"I don't expect you to do that," Trump said. "Just say the election was corrupt and leave the rest to me and the Republican congressmen."[17] *Just say it was corrupt.* Even though Rosen had told him there was no evidence that it was. Much as with his campaign to get Ukraine to undermine Joe Biden, Trump was not looking for corruption, just someone to *say* there was so he could weaponize it.

Over the next few days, Trump called Rosen and Donoghue repeatedly, pushing. But he also went behind their backs, reaching into their department for an ally without telling them. Scott Perry, the Freedom Caucus congressman from Pennsylvania who had also been at the December 21 meeting, tipped the president off to Jeffrey Bossert Clark, the acting assistant attorney general for the civil division. Clark had told Perry, who now told Trump, that he was willing to help overturn the election. A Philadelphia native and Harvard graduate, Clark had worked in the Bush administration and private practice before heading the Justice Department's environmental section under Trump. After being promoted to lead the civil division, he showed a willingness to use the department for the president's personal ends by seeking to defend him against a lawsuit by a woman who accused Trump of raping her and by suing Melania Trump's estranged friend Stephanie Winston Wolkoff for publishing an unflattering book about the first lady.

Clark now prepared a five-page letter for Rosen to sign declaring that the department had found "significant concerns that may have impacted the outcome of the election in multiple States, including the State of Georgia."[18] The letter urged Georgia authorities to call their legislature into session to reconsider their results and potentially choose electors for Trump instead of the ones chosen by the voters. Clark saw it as a template for other swing states that went for Biden.

When Clark sent it for signature on December 28, Rosen and Donoghue were aghast. Not only did the letter falsely claim there were significant problems with the election, but it invoked authority the Justice Department did not have to lean on a state to take political action in favor of a candidate who had not won. It was an outrageous power grab. "I am not prepared to sign such a letter," Rosen told Clark.[19]

Where was Trump's Roy Cohn? Who would step up to deliver for him? Increasingly, it was clear that it would not be Jeff Rosen. Nor had Rudy Giuliani, Sidney Powell, or any of the others come through. With just a week left until Congress was to finalize the election results, Trump needed help on Capitol Hill—and he would not get it from Mitch McConnell, who at long last was in open opposition to his plans.

But Senator Josh Hawley, the young Ivy League–trained lawyer turned populist firebrand from Missouri, eagerly raised his hand. On December 30 he announced he would defy McConnell and object to Biden electoral votes from swing states on January 6. During a New Year's Eve call among Senate Republicans the next day, an angry McConnell challenged Hawley to explain himself, only to get no response because the senator had not bothered to dial into the call.

McConnell made clear that trying to overturn a democratic election was beyond the pale. "I'm finishing thirty-six years in the Senate and I've cast a lot of big votes," McConnell told his colleagues, citing war and impeachment. "And in my view, just my view, this will be the most consequential I have ever cast."[20]

Undeterred by McConnell and eager not to be outflanked as the Senate's biggest Trump ally, Ted Cruz quickly announced that he and ten other senators would object to Biden electoral votes too, promoting an unorthodox scheme to "remand" the challenged votes back to the states for ten days while an extralegal commission investigated.

As McConnell struggled to keep his Republicans in line, his House counterpart, Kevin McCarthy, was making no effort at all to rein in his. During a New Year's Day conference call, Liz Cheney, the number three Republican, argued against challenging the election, but McCarthy undercut her by saying that was just her opinion. Far more than the Senate, most Republicans in the House were ready to object to Biden votes from key states even if it would not succeed just to show fealty to Trump—including McCarthy himself.

At Mar-a-Lago, Trump decided to head back to Washington early without waiting until after New Year's. Amid the tension in the Middle

East leading up to the first anniversary of the killing of Qassim Suleimani, the Iranian commander, threats had been emanating from Tehran, both public and private, including a warning by Ayatollah Ali Khamenei that "those who ordered the murder of General Soleimani" would "be punished."[21] At a cocktail party, Trump told several of his Florida friends that he was afraid Iran would try to assassinate him, so he had to go back to Washington where he would be safer.

Returning to the capital, Trump turned up the heat on Mike Pence. Even some of Trump's closest allies were worried about how far he seemed willing to take things. Pat Cipollone had objected to a number of schemes by now and repeatedly suggested he might resign along with his staff. "We can't lose the entire WH counsels office," Sean Hannity texted Meadows that day. "I do NOT see January 6 happening the way he is being told."[22] Jared Kushner seemed less concerned, dismissing the resignation threats as just so much "whining."[23]

Trump's advisers believed he would be furious about Pence fighting Gohmert's lawsuit—and by extension, defying him. "He's going to blow his stack on this if he isn't already aware," Trump's political aide Jason Miller texted Meadows on that New Year's Eve. "Oh boy I don't understand what the VP was thinking here." Neither seemed concerned that what they wanted Pence to do was a blatantly illegal power grab.

On New Year's Day, Johnny McEntee sent Short a document advancing an argument that would also be used in Gohmert's lawsuit against Pence, citing an instance when Thomas Jefferson, in the election of 1800, had to decide whether to accept a flawed electoral certificate from Georgia; that surely meant a vice president did have discretion to intervene. That same day, Lin Wood, a far-right Georgia lawyer who had been waging his own battles on Trump's behalf, sometimes with Sidney Powell, lashed out at Pence for resisting Gohmert's suit, accusing the vice president of "treason" and predicting that he could "face execution by firing squad."[24]

After leaving Vail to return to Washington, Pence reached out to one of the few people on the planet who would understand his position, former vice president Dan Quayle. The two Indiana Republicans had known each other for three decades. Quayle had called him shortly after November 3 to urge Pence and the president to move on rather than wage a pointless fight against the results. Now, Pence explained to Quayle that some lawyers working for Trump were telling him that the vice president could unilaterally reject some of Biden's electoral votes.

Quayle was appalled. "I don't know who these lawyers are, but forget it," he said. "It's ridiculous."

Pence seemed to agree, but the ever-discreet vice president hinted at the pressure he was under within the White House. "I'm having a hard time convincing Trump," he said.

That afternoon, Meadows sent Jeff Rosen and Rich Donoghue over at the Justice Department an email about the latest conspiracy theory to look into, this one a QAnon fantasy passed along to Trump by a guest at Mar-a-Lago on Christmas Eve. Two men who had been arrested in Italy had supposedly been involved in an elaborate plot to hack into military satellites from Rome to rig the balloting in the United States.

"Pure insanity," Donoghue emailed Rosen after receiving the message with attached YouTube video from Meadows.

But Meadows followed up with a phone call. As he had repeatedly, the White House chief of staff also pushed Rosen to at least meet with Rudy Giuliani. Rosen refused. "If he has evidence, he can do what any American can do," Rosen said. "He can walk into an FBI field office and present his evidence. But I'm not meeting with him, no."

Meadows called back a little while later. "Mr. Giuliani is insulted that you think he should have to walk into an FBI office," he said.[25]

Of all the battleground states where defeat rankled the president, Georgia stood out. No way it should have gone for Biden, he believed. Mark Meadows encouraged him, and the day after the election asked Cleta Mitchell, a conservative election attorney, to go to Georgia and lead their legal fight there. Meadows even flew to Georgia himself to quiz officials conducting the absentee ballot audit, hardly a typical role for a White House chief of staff. Flipping Georgia by itself would not keep Trump in the White House, but he hoped it would encourage legislators in states like Michigan, Pennsylvania, and Wisconsin to decertify their elections and switch their electors to him.

The White House had tried for weeks to get hold of Brad Raffensperger, the Republican secretary of state overseeing the election in Georgia, calling eighteen times before Meadows finally set up a phone call with him and Trump on Saturday, January 2. In the hour-long conversation that followed, the president repeatedly asserted that he had won Georgia and it was up to Raffensperger to prove it.

"There's nothing wrong with saying that, you know, um, that you've recalculated," Trump told him as Meadows, Cleta Mitchell, and other law-yers listened.

"Well, Mr. President," Raffensperger said, "the challenge that you have is the data you have is wrong."

Raffensperger and his lawyer, Ryan Germany, refuted every rumor, claim, and wild theory that Trump advanced. While Trump's allies insisted that five thousand dead people voted, Raffensperger noted, "The actual number were two. Two." When Trump alleged that Dominion had ille-gally removed voting machines from Fulton County and that ballots were shredded, Germany told him flatly that he was wrong.

It did not matter. Trump seemed to threaten the Georgia officials with prosecution for not going along. "It is more illegal for you than it is for them because you know what they did and you're not reporting it," he said. "That's a criminal—that's a criminal offense. And you can't let that happen. That's a big risk to you and to Ryan, your lawyer." Then Trump laid out his demand. "All I want to do is this: I just want to find 11,780 votes, which is one more than we have, because we won the state," he said, by which he meant one more than he needed to change the outcome.[26]

Listening to all this while sitting on a barstool in his kitchen at home, Raffensperger was astonished at the blend of fiction, conspiracy, and men-ace coming from the president, but he held firm. While his staff recorded the call, he did not want it made public unless Trump misrepresented their conversation. When the president predictably did just that, the recording was leaked to *The Washington Post*.

State Republican officials were not the only ones resisting Trump's last stand. Liz Cheney that same day sent House Republicans a twenty-one-page memo decrying the plan to reject Biden electoral votes. "Such objections set an exceptionally dangerous precedent, threatening to steal states' explicit constitutional responsibility for choosing the President and bestowing it instead on Congress," her memo stated. "This is directly at odds with the Constitution's clear text and our core beliefs as Republicans."[27]

Cheney had always had reservations about Trump but, coming from Wyoming, one of the most pro-Trump states in the country, she had gen-erally avoided voicing them publicly and even endorsed him for re-election in 2020. But his attack on the legitimacy of the vote outraged her and now she feared, much like Mark Milley, an outright effort by Trump to remain in power. She was so concerned that she secretly enlisted her father, for-mer Vice President Dick Cheney, who led the Pentagon under George H. W. Bush, to recruit all ten living former defense secretaries from both parties, including both of Trump's Pentagon chiefs, Jim Mattis and Mark

Esper, to sign a public letter warning against using the military to overturn the election. "Efforts to involve the U.S. armed forces in resolving election disputes would take us into dangerous, unlawful and unconstitutional territory," read the letter, published that Sunday in *The Washington Post*.[28]

Late that afternoon, around 5 p.m., Trump met with his military and national security advisers to discuss the escalating tensions with Iran. In addition to Milley, Robert O'Brien, Chris Miller, Kash Patel, and Mike Pompeo joined the meeting. With new threats that weekend, Trump overruled Miller and ordered the USS *Nimitz* aircraft carrier to remain in the Persian Gulf.

Pompeo and Milley also presented the latest from a worrisome new report from the International Atomic Energy Agency on Iran's nuclear program. But by the end, even Pompeo the Iran hawk had opposed a strike on Iran at this late hour in Trump's presidency. "He realized that the clock ran out," Milley told his staff. Trump was convinced. He would not order the strike.

At the end of the meeting, in a pull-aside that Milley later reckoned had lasted no more than ninety seconds, the president asked the acting defense secretary if he was ready for the upcoming January 6 protest that Trump had promised would "be wild."

"It's going to be a big deal," Milley heard Trump tell Miller. "You've got enough people to make sure it's safe for my people, right?" Miller assured him he did.

Even as Trump held off pulling the trigger against Iran, he was on the verge of pulling it against his acting attorney general. At a meeting that Sunday, Jeff Clark, the assistant attorney general who had been surreptitiously working with Trump, told Jeff Rosen that he had decided to accept an offer from the president to take over as acting attorney general—in other words, to take Rosen's job and assume command of the Justice Department.

Rosen stiffened at the affront. "Well, I don't get to be fired by someone who works for me," he said.

Rosen called Mark Meadows and demanded to see the president. A meeting was set for 6:15 p.m.

Over the next two hours, the Justice Department's leadership prepared for an all-out showdown with Trump. If he was going to fire Rosen, then they would all leave. Rich Donoghue began cleaning out his office and reached out to the department's other senior officials, ten of whom agreed to quit in protest. If Trump went through with it, it would be a bigger scandal than the Saturday Night Massacre under Richard Nixon. As the clock ticked toward the hour of confrontation in the Oval Office, they drafted and signed letters of resignation, ready to be released as soon as the meeting was over.

Rosen and Donoghue arrived at the White House shortly before the assigned time and saw Mark Milley as he was heading out. "Good luck," Mark Meadows told the lawyers but then left, absenting himself at one of the key moments of his tenure. Donoghue, caught off guard by an unexpected visit to the White House on a Sunday, was dressed in jeans, an Army T-shirt, and mud-covered boots and, embarrassed, waited outside the Oval Office until the president insisted he come in. In addition to Rosen and Donoghue, sitting in chairs in a semicircle across from the president at his desk were Clark, Pat Cipollone, Pat Philbin, Eric Herschmann, and Steve Engel, the head of the Justice Department's Office of Legal Counsel. Once again, Mike Pence was left out.

Trump did not beat around the bush. Rosen in his view had failed him as attorney general. Clark was offering to fight for him by calling the election corrupt and pressuring Republican legislatures in battleground states that went for Biden to send alternate slates for Trump.

"Well, what do I have to lose?" Trump asked. "What would I lose at this point if I put Jeff Clark in?"

"Sir, you have a great deal to lose," Donoghue said.

"So, suppose I do this, suppose I take him out and I put him in," Trump said, gesturing at Rosen and then Clark. "What do you do?"

"Sir, I'd resign immediately," Donoghue said.

Trump turned to Steve Engel. "Steve, you wouldn't resign, would you?"

"Absolutely, I would, Mr. President. You would leave me no choice."

"Well, and Steve is not the only one, sir," Donoghue said. All his assistant attorneys general would step down and many United States attorneys as well. These were not career bureaucrats, he reminded Trump. "This is the team you sent to the Senate, you got confirmed, and they are all going to walk away on you at once. What does that say about you as a leader?"

"Jeff Clark will be leading a graveyard," Engel added. "And what are you going to get done with a graveyard?"

Donoghue then went after Clark directly, saying he was hardly qualified to be attorney general since he had never conducted a criminal case in his life.

Clark bridled. "Well, I've done a lot of very complicated appeals and civil litigation, environmental litigation and things like that," he said.

"That's right," Donoghue replied scornfully. "You're an environmental lawyer. How about you go back to your office and we'll call you when there's an oil spill?"

Neither Trump nor Clark found any backup in the room. Cipollone made clear that he stood with the Justice team and would resign if they did. "I'm not going to stay around here for this," the White House counsel said. Pointing to the letter that Clark wanted to send to Georgia, Cipollone said, "That letter is a murder-suicide pact. And it will damage anyone and anything that it touches."

Eventually, Trump realized there was no practical way forward. He shook his head with great frustration. "All right," he said, surrendering, "we're not going to do this."

Turning to Clark, Trump said, "I appreciate you being willing to step up and take all the abuse, but the reality is it's not worth the breakage. We're going to have mass resignations. It's going to be a disaster. You're not going to be able to get this stuff done anyway and the bureaucracy will eat you alive."

Clark was not ready to give up. "Mr. President, we can do this. We can get it done. History is calling."

"No, no, we're not going to do it."

But as the meeting broke up after nearly three hours, Trump took one last shot at pressuring Rosen and Donoghue. "I know that these two here, they're not going to do anything," he said. "They're not going to fix this. But that's the way it is and I'm going to let it go anyway."[29]

There was only one way left. Trump's last chance, as he saw it, was Mike Pence. If he could somehow convince the vice president to reject Biden's electoral votes or even to delay by sending enough votes back to the states, he could still win.

Pence thought he had made clear that a vice president had no such power. "Never once did I see him budge from that view," Greg Jacob, his counsel, recalled later.[30] The president had already solicited a two-page memo from John Eastman, the conservative California professor who had advanced wild theories about birthright citizenship and Kamala Harris's eligibility to run for vice president and represented Trump in a couple election challenges. Now he asked Eastman to fly to Washington to personally lobby the vice president.

Eastman expanded his original memo into a six-page version marked "PRIVILEGED AND CONFIDENTIAL," asserting that Pence could reverse the outcome of the American presidential election without having to prove any actual fraudulent votes. Eastman argued that Trump's objections to various voting policies in key states would be enough to invalidate the results—not stolen votes, in other words, just practices that Trump's team opposed or deemed illegal, like the use of drop boxes in response to the pandemic. Under a section titled "War Gaming the Alternatives," Eastman outlined how the vice president could reject the certified results put forward by states and either accept the fake Trump electoral certificates orchestrated by his allies or simply negate votes from those states altogether.

In one scenario, Pence would determine that without the disputed states there was no majority and therefore the election would be thrown to the House with Republicans holding a majority of delegations. "BOLD, Certainly," Eastman wrote. "But this Election was Stolen by a strategic Democrat plan to systematically flout existing election laws for partisan advantage; we're no longer playing by Queensbury Rules, therefore."[31]

During a ninety-minute meeting in the Oval Office late on the afternoon of Monday, January 4, Trump forced Pence to hear out Eastman as he pressed his theory on an unconvinced vice president. Eastman said that of the two routes he was suggesting, it would be wiser to send the issue back to the disputed states rather than ruling out their electoral votes entirely. Pence pushed back, rejecting specious historical precedents and questioning the legal conclusions.

"Do you think I have that authority to count that alternate slate of electors and declare him president?" Pence challenged Eastman.

"Mr. Vice President, I think it's an open question," Eastman said. "I frankly think it's the weaker argument. But even if you have that authority, because the Republican legislatures have not certified alternative slates, it would be foolish to exercise that authority."

The vice president considered that validation and turned to Trump, sitting behind the Resolute Desk. "Did you hear that, Mr. President?" Pence asked. *It would be foolish.*

Trump remained undeterred. Eventually the meeting ended so the president could leave for a last-minute campaign rally in Georgia on the eve of the next day's runoff election. But on the flight down, all he could talk about was his own election—and Mike Pence. Accompanying him was Lindsey Graham, who had publicly encouraged Trump's bogus election claims but was now telling him that the vice president could not single-handedly reverse the results.

"That's just complete bullshit," Graham remembered telling Trump. The president refused to back down. Even so, Graham chose not to blame Trump but the "complete nuts" who were misinforming him. "He would have believed Martians fixed the election if we had told him because he wanted to believe it," Graham later said.

As for Eastman, he went back to the Willard InterContinental Hotel, where he joined a "war room" that had been set up with Rudy Giuliani, Bernie Kerik, Steve Bannon, and others organizing efforts to pressure Pence and Congress to block Biden's victory. The Trump campaign was footing the cost of the command center, a bill that would eventually run to tens of thousands of dollars. Roger Stone wandered in and out with members of the Oath Keepers militia serving as bodyguards. Giuliani asked Eastman how his meeting went. Eastman told him he did not think Pence was going to do it.

The next morning, Eastman met again with the Pence team of Greg Jacob and Marc Short. At that point, Jacob recalled later, Eastman was now advocating an outright power grab by the vice president, not just sending the issue back to the states. "I'm here asking you to reject the electors," Eastman began.

Jacob pointed out how easily such a power could be abused by any vice president unhappy with the results of an election they had just lost.

"Are you really saying, John, that Al Gore could have just declared himself the winner of Florida and moved along?" Jacob asked.

"Well, no, no, there wasn't enough evidence for that," Eastman said, a remarkable assertion from someone telling the president that he did not need to cite any evidence at all of fraud to overturn the 2020 election.

Jacob suggested there would be no way judges would agree with Eastman's interpretation. "If this case got to the Supreme Court, we'd lose 9–0, wouldn't we?" he said.

Eastman conceded they would probably lose but said he thought it would be more like 7–2.

"Who are the two?" Jacob demanded.

"Well, I think maybe Clarence Thomas," said Eastman, who had served as a clerk for the conservative justice.

"Really? Clarence Thomas?"

Perhaps not knowing about Ginni Thomas's text messages to Mark Meadows pushing for Trump to challenge the election, Jacob went through a few of Justice Thomas's rulings until Eastman backed down and conceded that maybe even he would not rule in their favor on this. "Yeah, all right, it would be 9–0," he said.

"Can't we just acknowledge that this is a really bad idea?" Jacob said.

"Well, all right, I get everything you're saying," Eastman said. "They're going to be really disappointed that I wasn't able to persuade you."[32]

Mike Pence had one more meeting with Trump on the afternoon of January 5, this time just the two of them. What exactly was said would remain a mystery to aides of both men. Two people close to Pence said they heard that during the conversation the president even dangled the possibility that if Pence gave him a second term, Trump might not serve the entire four years, stepping down early and allowing Pence to become president. But neither heard that directly from Pence. The vice president remained mum.

Either way, he was not convinced. For nearly four years, Pence had navigated Trump more carefully than anyone else—never challenging him directly, never drawing even a single nasty tweet. Now, after all this time, he would finally have to defy Trump. There was no getting around it.

After their meeting, Trump was in a reckless frame of mind. "Im very worried about the next 48 hours," Sean Hannity texted Mark Meadows.[33] At some point, the president called Giuliani, Eastman, and the others at the Willard command center to discuss the next day's rally. Bannon had big plans for January 6, what he called the "Green Bay Sweep," according to Peter Navarro.[34] "All hell is going to break loose tomorrow," Bannon said on his *War Room* podcast on the eve of the day of reckoning. "So many people said, 'Man if I was in a revolution, I would be in Washington.' Well, this is your time in history."[35]

CHAPTER 31

Trial by Combat

On the morning of January 6, Mitch McConnell was fuming. It was not final yet but returns from the two Georgia special elections overnight looked bad for Republicans. McConnell, for whom being the Senate majority leader was the highest end of his Washington aspirations, was about to lose his majority. "That infuriated him," recalled a senator who spoke with McConnell. "It was intensely personal. In another two years he would have been the longest majority leader in Senate history," beating the legendary Mike Mansfield, "and Mitch cares about things like that." McConnell blamed Trump, and his sustained attack on the integrity of the voting: How could anyone expect their voters to show up when the president was telling them it was all a crooked scam?

Trump could not have cared less about that. He had not spoken with the Republican leader since their bitter phone call in December after McConnell congratulated Joe Biden on his election. But now Congress was preparing to meet in a few hours to confirm that victory, in a quadrennial and, until 2021, purely ceremonial ritual of counting the electoral votes. Trump was desperate to stop it, and at 9:16 that morning ordered the White House switchboard to place a call to McConnell. He would not take it. Trump checked in again with the White House switchboard at 10:40 a.m. McConnell still would not speak with the president. The senator was furious about Trump's last-ditch effort to disrupt one of the most important rituals of American democracy—a reckless folly that more than a dozen of his own Republican senators were enabling.

McConnell had always been critical of Trump in private, at least with trusted colleagues. Now he was excoriating. Trump, he told others, had been "spiraling downward to the point of derangement" since the election. For years, McConnell had swallowed his distaste for Trump and gotten what he could out of the White House. His own wife served in Trump's cabinet as secretary of transportation. But he might have been the one person in Washington even more transactional than Trump and he was done humoring a president he now saw as "crazy" and "delusional."

In his ornate offices in the Capitol, McConnell was going over for a final time the speech he planned to give when Congress met that afternoon, a speech he had been laboring over with his staff for a week. McConnell was more a backstage machinator than an orator, but he believed this was a historic speech at a historic moment, when thirteen of his Republican colleagues led by Ted Cruz and Josh Hawley were planning to object to the electoral count in furtherance of Trump's preposterous scheme. He wanted to look them in the eye, to shame them, and, if he could not stop them, at least to tell them, as a longtime McConnell adviser put it, "Some of you are about to make a decision you know is wrong. You know it's not worth doing what you're about to do, and I'm going to make sure you know you should be throwing up in the trash can when you do it."

McConnell had an unwavering eye for how to get to his colleagues. "It's a primal skill of McConnell," his adviser said. "He knows when people are inherently uncomfortable." He wanted to make them squirm.

At the White House, Trump had not yet given up his relentless lobbying of Mike Pence. He refused to take no for an answer. In a tweet early that morning, Trump once again promoted the unconstitutional plan he had settled on to get the vice president to refuse to accept the electoral certificates from states that Cruz and his allies were challenging. "All Mike Pence has to do is send them back to the States, AND WE WIN," Trump wrote. "Do it Mike this is a time for extreme courage!"

The president was scheduled to speak at noon to supporters on the Ellipse, the "wild" rally he had been promoting for weeks. Before leaving for what would turn out to be the most consequential speech of his presidency, Trump called the vice president's residence just after 11 a.m. to push one last time. Pence was meeting with his staff to finalize a three-page letter declaring that he would not do what Trump wanted. Told that the president was on the phone, Pence excused himself and headed upstairs to take the call privately. As was his habit, Trump in the Oval Office made even this most crucial call while the room was crowded with aides and family members.

If Pence did not do as he now demanded and block Biden's victory, Trump said, "then I picked the wrong man four years ago."

"You can either go down in history as a patriot," Trump told him, "or you can go down in history as a pussy."[1]

Ivanka Trump was there listening, as was Keith Kellogg. "Mike Pence is a good man," she said to Kellogg after hearing her father berate the vice president.[2] Her siblings were already gathering in the Oval Office as well, preparing to go to the rally with their father—Don Jr. with Kimberly Guilfoyle, Eric with his wife, Lara. They were all on board with Trump's attack on the election results. But Ivanka had declined to attend, and her husband, Jared Kushner, was not even in town. He was on a plane back from the Middle East, after brokering a rapprochement between Saudi Arabia and Qatar to end a three-year blockade of the small Gulf state. Given what she had heard, though, Ivanka changed her mind and decided to accompany her father to the rally after all—not to speak onstage but in hopes of keeping his fury at Pence in check. To the end, she had not entirely given up the fantasy of managing Trump.

Pretty much everyone else who could do so had already walked or been pushed away. Bill Barr had quit, leaving Jeffrey Rosen and Pat Cipollone as the last legal lines of defense. Hope Hicks, marginalized after she told Trump that his election challenge was wrong, did not even bother to go into the office that day. The first lady was so checked out she was staying home from the rally for a valedictory photo shoot in the White House. Mark Meadows, it was now clear, was not only an enabler but just as much an active participant in the rigged-election charade as the conspiracists he allowed in to see the president.

As the first family was about to leave for the rally, Rudy Giuliani clambered up to the microphone onstage at the Ellipse, a perfect view of the White House framed behind him, accompanied by John Eastman. Giuliani assured the crowd that it was both "perfectly legal" and "perfectly appropriate" for the vice president to go ahead and "cast it aside."

For the next few minutes, the man introduced as "America's mayor" offered a tour of the dark corners of the conspiracy, inflaming the crowd with tales of "crooked Dominion machines" and "votes deliberately changed" by a sinister "algorithm" whose malice was so well established "it is a matter of scientific proof." The election, Giuliani added, had been stolen in seven battleground states that had a combination of Democrat-run big cities and sufficient electoral votes. "This was the worst election in American history," he said. All could be proven, he insisted, if only the Democrats and Pence would let them keep investigating.

"So let's have trial by combat," Giuliani concluded with a flourish. "I'm willing to stake my reputation, the president is willing to stake his reputation on the fact that we're going to find criminality there."[3]

Shortly before Trump's speech was to begin, the president and his family arrived in a VIP tent set up near the stage. Don Jr. held up his cell phone and shot a video he posted to social media that gave off a sort of rigged-election dance party vibe. It showed his girlfriend, wearing a black cape against the January chill, shimmying to the 1980s Laura Branigan hit "Gloria." Guilfoyle, who later bragged that she had helped the rally organizers raise $3 million, without mentioning that she was paid $60,000 herself for a two-and-a-half-minute speech, mugged for the camera. "Have the courage to do the right thing," she exhorted. "Fight!" Mark Meadows, grinning broadly, gave a thumbs-up as Don Jr. praised him. "An actual fighter," he said of his father's chief of staff. "One of the few."[4] His brother Eric, who was celebrating his thirty-seventh birthday that day, smiled excitedly. The only person who did not seem to be happy was Ivanka, standing near Trump a few feet away from her brothers as he stared at a large television monitor.

Don Jr. had already made his speech by then, a rambling, expletive-filled rant threatening Republican members of Congress to go along with the election challenge or face revenge in primary campaigns. "This gathering should send a message to them," he shouted. "This isn't their Republican Party anymore! This is Donald Trump's Republican Party!"

Trump's own speech started at noon and lasted for a full hour and eleven minutes, as if he were purposefully refusing to relinquish the stage at the appointed hour of 1 p.m. when Congress would finally meet to end the weeks of uncertainty caused by his refusal to concede defeat. He started and finished with his specific demand of the day, for Pence to "do the right thing" and overturn the election: "Because if Mike does the right thing, we win." Of course, Pence had already told Trump that he would follow the Constitution by affirming Joe Biden's victory; in fact, Pence's chief of staff estimated he had done so as many as two dozen times already.

Trump, however, was deep in his alternate reality. Harkening back to one of his first lies of the presidency, the one about the inauguration and his vast supposed crowd size of 1.5 million people, Trump claimed the crowd that had gathered to help him stop Congress from confirming his loss was an "all-time record" of more than 250,000; in later months, he would inflate the number to more than a million.

Where Giuliani called the election the worst in American history, Trump upped the ante, insisting, "This is the most corrupt election maybe in the history of the world." He talked of illegal migrants voting, incarcerated felons voting, dead people voting, illegal ballot-harvesting operations, mysterious duffel bags full of votes—all part of the "explosions of bullshit" orchestrated by the Democrats to stop him from a second term. "Bullshit! Bullshit! Bullshit!" the crowd cried in response. Trump said he would never concede. He urged the audience to fight for him. "You will never take back our country with weakness," he said, a personal credo as well as his political rallying cry. "You have to show strength, and you have to be strong."

In the end, Trump did not bother to hide his decision to simply flout the Constitution. "When you catch somebody in a fraud, you're allowed to go by very different rules," he said, which was both a revealing comment about the thinking of a president who believed that the rules did not apply to him and also his pitch to Pence for why it was necessary to join him. "So I hope Mike has the courage to do what he has to do," Trump then said. He promised to punish those who did not go along, "the ones that aren't any good, the Liz Cheneys of the world." Watching at home, Dick Cheney immediately called his daughter to warn her that Trump was riling up the crowd against her.

Trump was entirely unconcerned with the effect his rabble-rousing words had on an already seething mass of protesters. At one point, he referred to supporters "peacefully" marching to the Capitol, a word his defenders would later make much of. But the speech was in no other way peaceful, nor did the crowd take that message from him. "We fight," he declared. "We fight like hell. And if you don't fight, you're not going to have a country anymore." In the back of the crowd, some shouted, "Storm the Capitol." As he concluded, Trump urged them to "take back our country," even suggesting he would go with them to confront Congress, before finally, at 1:10 p.m., walking offstage to return to the White House.[5] The part about him marching with them to the Capitol was no spontaneous ad lib. The idea had been planted by his congressional allies in the days before the rally, according to later testimony. But he had no intention of doing it—that was pure bluster.

The whole speech was, really. Pence could not be swayed by Trump or anyone else at that point, and the president knew it. In the middle of his speech, the vice president had arrived at the Capitol to preside over the electoral count. As he pulled up to the East Front, his aides released the three-page letter debunking Trump's crackpot legal theories, citing Michael Luttig, a widely respected conservative former appeals court judge for whom John Eastman once clerked. The idea that a vice president could singlehandedly decide the outcome of a presidential election was simply "antithetical" to the Constitution, Pence wrote, and a violation of the oath he had sworn to uphold and defend. "I will do my duty," the vice president said.[6]

Accompanying Pence was his lawyer, Greg Jacob, who had helped write the letter and navigate the days of wrangling over constitutional law that Trump's demands had set off. As they were about to leave in the motorcade from Pence's residence at the Naval Observatory and head to the Capitol, Jacob had sent John Eastman a final email objecting to the illegality of the "essentially made up" course of action he proposed. At the end, Jacob dropped his civil, lawyerly tone. "And thanks to your bullshit," he wrote, "we are now under siege."[7]

By the time Mitch McConnell stood in the well of the Senate to give his speech, the one he had labored over for days, it was just a few minutes after Trump had finished his inflammatory rant. Pence was sitting on the dais, presiding. The mob Trump had exhorted to march on the Capitol was now doing so by the thousands, but Pence and McConnell did not yet know it. Nor had Pence seen the wooden gallows for him that someone had erected on the lawn of the Capitol. He did not yet know they were chanting, "Hang Mike Pence! Hang Mike Pence!" He and McConnell and the rest of the senators still thought that January 6 was a Washington set piece, one of those long, exhausting days in Congress when there would be lots of shouting and many angry words exchanged but no suspense in the ultimate outcome. Whether Trump accepted it or not, they were sure this was to be the day of his reckoning.

Still, McConnell's speech was an unsparing condemnation of the reckless course Trump had set the Republican Party on, words that, on any other day, would have been a headline-grabbing break with the president he had enabled for so long. "If this election were overturned by mere allegations from the losing side," he said, "our democracy would enter a death spiral."

Politically, the most important part of McConnell's speech was its finale, in which he chided his own Republican senators who were careening down a path of opportunism so cynical that he would not follow them there. He had warned what would happen if they pursued this course, and they had done it anyway. "I will not pretend such a vote would be a harmless protest gesture," McConnell now thundered, "while relying on others to do the right thing."[8]

But it was already too late. By the time McConnell was finished, the mob was attacking the Capitol. Within minutes, he and Pence were taken off the floor by security details and McConnell was on his way to the safety of Fort McNair with other members of the congressional leadership, their constitutional duty to finalize the election having been successfully stopped by Trump's insurrectionists. As Eugene Goodman, a Capitol Police officer, singlehandedly lured the mob away from the Senate chamber, the rest of the senators fled down the hallways of the Capitol, coming as close as fifty-eight steps away from the attackers.

At 2:24 p.m., Trump was still stewing over Pence's betrayal. He already knew what was happening to Congress, he was watching it on television. But instead of condemning the mob, he condemned its target. "Mike Pence didn't have the courage to do what should have been done to protect our Country and our Constitution, giving States a chance to certify a corrected set of facts, not the fraudulent or inaccurate ones which they were asked to previously certify," Trump tweeted. "USA demands the truth!"

As investigators later established, at that same moment, the vice president and his entourage were being rushed out of the ceremonial office just off the Senate floor where they had originally been taken. Twice, the Secret Service had come to Pence demanding that he be evacuated from the Capitol entirely and twice he had refused. No, he insisted, the last thing the marauders should see was a long VIP motorcade fleeing. This time, Tim Giebels, his lead agent, came in and said it was no longer optional. "We're moving," Giebels said. "I can't protect you here." Security footage showed that Pence was steps away from a group of rioters as he, his family, and his military aide carrying the briefcase with America's nuclear codes raced down a set of stairs. But Pence still refused to leave the complex entirely, and he was taken to a loading dock underneath the Capitol where his motorcade was parked. Giebels tried to persuade Pence to just sit in the parked armored car where he would be safer, but the vice president refused, assuming that if he did, his agents would drive him out of there despite his determination to stay.

Outside, the situation had dramatically deteriorated. Police battling the rioters were outnumbered and could not prevent the mob from storming inside to do what Trump had wanted and stop the electoral count. At 2:28 p.m., only four minutes after Trump's tweet denouncing Pence, a chilling message came over the police radio, from the Metropolitan Police Department commander on the scene.

"We've lost the line!" he screamed. "We've lost the line! All MPD pull back!"[9]

The Capitol was breached.

At the White House, the man who had spent months campaigning on "LAW & ORDER" did nothing but watch television. Some of his staff, horrified by Trump's tweet, had in the intervening few minutes pleaded with him to release a message urging his followers to stand down. The resulting tweet at 2:38 p.m. was hardly that.

It read in its entirety: "Please support our Capitol Police and Law Enforcement. They are truly on the side of our Country. Stay peaceful!"

Trump would not call off his mob.

Mark Meadows and other White House officials were being bombarded with text messages and calls begging for something more from the president. Even Don Jr., who had just a couple hours earlier whipped up the crowd, now frantically urged Meadows to get his father to turn down the temperature. "He's got to condem this shit Asap," he texted the chief of staff. "The Capitol Police tweet is not enough."

"I'm pushing it hard," Meadows responded. "I agree."[10]

How hard was not clear, however. Alyssa Farah, the strategic communications adviser who had quit in disgust over the post-election campaign to overturn the results, texted Meadows, who had been her boss for years on Capitol Hill and at the White House: "You guys have to say something. Even if the president's not willing to put out a statement, you should go to the sticks and say, 'We condemn this. Please stand down.' If you don't, people are going to die."

When she received no reply, she texted Ben Williamson, Meadows's senior adviser. Trump's tweet was terrible, she said; couldn't they get him to do more? "Is someone getting to POTUS?" she asked. "He has to tell the protestors to dissipate. Someone is going to get killed."

Williamson responded in a way that suggested neither Trump nor Meadows was reacting with any urgency: "I've been trying for the last 30 minutes. Literally stormed in outer oval to get him to put out the first one. It's completely insane."[11] As it turned out, Trump had not even wanted to include the "stay peaceful" in the original tweet and had to be convinced to do so.

The barrage of messages to Meadows included several from Trump's favorite Fox News hosts, who had cheered the president for months as he attacked the election's integrity but now privately wavered when they saw the violent culmination of his campaign. "Hey Mark, the president needs to tell people in the Capitol to go home," Laura Ingraham texted, "he is destroying his legacy." Brian Kilmeade was even more succinct. "Destroying everything you have accomplished."

Meadows's former colleagues in the House were now trapped, sending him desperate pleas to do something. "This is a shitshow," texted Chip Roy, the Texas congressman who had urged Meadows just a few days earlier to call the whole charade off. "Fix this now."[12] Lindsey Graham called Pat Cipollone and told him if Trump did not speak out more forcefully to stop the attack, "we'll be asking you for the Twenty-fifth Amendment" removing the president from office.[13]

On the House floor, at the same time as Trump's 2:38 p.m. tweet, the locked doors of the chamber were barricaded with furniture and guarded by Capitol Police with guns drawn. Preparing to use tear gas to repel the attackers, police instructed the members to take out gas masks stored under the seats and put them on. When they did so, the whole room echoed with an unforgettable buzzing sound. Adam Schiff, a certain target of the rioters just outside, remembered it as "the surreal hum of the motors on these hoods, like there's a swarm of bees in the chamber." As the members were rushed out the rear doors, Schiff found himself next to a newly elected Republican from Texas, who had grabbed a wooden post that had been affixed to a hand sanitizer dispenser to defend himself. "It's not always like this," Schiff deadpanned. "Someone really should have impeached that son of a bitch."

Schiff was on the floor because Nancy Pelosi had asked him, along with Representatives Zoe Lofgren, Joe Neguse, and Jamie Raskin, to manage the debate on the electoral count. The group had been preparing since December once it became clear that Trump's Senate allies were willing to join House Republicans in objecting, triggering what everyone expected to be an hours-long process that might even drag into the next day.

But now both houses of Congress had now been hastily gaveled into recess as their members fled. It was unclear if or when they would resume. Adam Kinzinger barricaded himself in his office with a Ruger 380 pistol. Two minutes after the last of the members were rushed off the floor, Ashli Babbitt, a military veteran and QAnon adherent swathed in a Trump flag, was shot to death as she tried to climb through a smashed window close to the House chamber by an undercover police officer guarding the members' retreat.

Kevin McCarthy, the House minority leader, heard the shot fired. He did not know yet what it was, but he was at that moment speaking with Trump on the telephone. McCarthy had taken a very different approach to January 6 than Mitch McConnell, announcing in December that he would support the challenge to the election, a green light to his caucus to follow. Initially a Trump skeptic, McCarthy had seen there was no place for Trump-skeptical leaders in the House GOP after Paul Ryan left his speakership. He had become such a loyalist that Trump called him "my Kevin." But, with his office under attack, McCarthy's tone shifted again.

Trump seemed to have no clue what was happening as McCarthy described the bedlam. "Well, Kevin, I guess these people are more upset about the election than you are," the president said.

This infuriated McCarthy. "Who the fuck do you think you are talking to?" he screamed at Trump. His office windows were being smashed in. Someone had just been shot. Trump needed to do something to stop it. These were his people.

"I'll put a tweet out," Trump responded.[14] At 3:13 p.m., he did. "I am asking for everyone at the U.S. Capitol to remain peaceful. No violence! Remember, WE are the Party of Law & Order—respect the Law and our great men and women in Blue. Thank you!" he tweeted.

He was not repudiating the mob. They were fighting for him. Informed of the threats to hang Mike Pence, Trump told aides, "Maybe our supporters have the right idea." Pence, he said, "deserves" it.

At the Pentagon, Mark Milley was in his office when the Capitol was stormed, meeting with Christine Wormuth, the lead Biden transition official for the Defense Department. In the weeks since the election, he had started putting up four networks on the large-screen monitor directly across from the round table where they were sitting: CNN and Fox News, as well as the small pro-Trump outlets Newsmax and One America News Network, which for weeks had been airing rigged-election disinformation that even Fox would not broadcast. Wormuth was surprised to see what the chairman of the Joint Chiefs was watching. "You've got to know what the enemy is up to," he said wryly.

They were supposed to be discussing the Pentagon's plans to draw down troops in Afghanistan, as well as the incoming Biden team's hopes to mobilize large-scale vaccination sites around the country.

But as they realized in horror what was transpiring on the screens in front of them, Milley was summoned to an urgent meeting with Chris Miller and Ryan McCarthy, the secretary of the Army. They had not landed the plane, after all. It was crashing and burning.

Milley roared into the defense secretary's office one flight up from his at 2:30 p.m. and began rattling off actions to be taken. He urged Miller to immediately deploy the D.C. National Guard—pleas had been coming in already begging for them, from Mayor Muriel Bowser, the Capitol Police, and others—and to make sure all available federal agents under the umbrella of the Justice Department were also mobilized. He also suggested mobilizing National Guard units from nearby states. Miller agreed and at 3:04 p.m. issued an order to send in the D.C. Guard.

Both Milley and Miller were combat veterans—as Miller would later testify, he had personally been in "riots, fist fights and brawls, gunfights, aircraft mishaps, mortared, rocketed, attacked with improvised explosive devices"—and they knew that they were watching a battle unfold without sufficient troops in place to hold the Capitol.[15] They would send the Guard to the Hill now to retake the building along with the hundreds of police officers from neighboring Virginia and Maryland who were already arriving, but it was too late to prevent the humiliation of Congress being overwhelmed by a ragtag assembly of election deniers. The decisions that had made that outcome inevitable were not happening that afternoon; they had already been made.

Miller would later testify that "concerns and hysteria" about the prospect of a repeat of the Lafayette Square incident had influenced his reluctance to deploy the military in Washington in advance of the January 6 rally. He viewed any use of American combat forces as a "last resort." Milley's fears were even more acute. He worried that this truly was Trump's "Reichstag moment," the one he had been warning about since the election, the crisis that would cause the president to invoke martial law and try to hold on to power. But even he had never anticipated that Trump would unleash the mob on the Capitol itself.

From the secure facility at Fort McNair where they had been whisked by their security, congressional leaders called the Pentagon demanding troops. They wanted active-duty forces at the Capitol right away. Nancy Pelosi and Chuck Schumer were suspicious of Miller; whose side, exactly, was this unknown Trump appointee on? Milley jumped in. He wanted to reassure the Democrats that the uniformed military was on the case, and not there to do Trump's bidding. The Guard, he told them, was coming.

But it was already after 3:30 by then, and the leaders were furious that it was taking so long. They also spoke with Mike Pence, who offered to call the Pentagon as well. He reached Miller around 4 p.m. "Clear the Capitol," he ordered.[16]

———

Trump had not been on any of the calls with the Pentagon. He never called anyone seeking help for the besieged Capitol. Nor did he speak with Pence or with congressional leaders. But Mark Meadows wanted to pretend Trump was taking action when he was not. He called Milley. "We have to kill the narrative that the vice president is making all the decisions," Meadows said. "We need to establish the narrative that the president is still in charge." Milley later dismissed it as "politics, politics, politics."

Hoping to goad the strangely passive president into really taking action, Meadows called up to Ivanka Trump's office, imploring her to come down to speak with her father. When she got there, Ivanka found her dad sitting in his private dining room gawking at the insurrection on television. She was surprised to see that the events on his screen were not actually live, eventually realizing that Trump must have walked away for a time and never caught back up once he hit play again.

None of his tweets had produced any result other than to enrage those who were actually appalled by the riot. Ivanka had also enraged them with a tweet of her own, urging the "American patriots" who were not so patriotically storming their seat of government to stand down and go home, a message she later deleted when she saw it being interpreted as praise for the rioters. The first daughter, who later told others she felt she spent the entire afternoon "running up and down stairs" trying to convince her father to act more responsibly, eventually joined those suggesting Trump make a short video statement to his supporters urging them to leave the Capitol. But when they got Trump outside to shoot the video, he balked and balked. It took three takes to get footage that was usable.

It was midafternoon by then and Jared Kushner had just arrived home after his long flight from the Middle East. He was in the bathroom with the shower already running and about to jump in when his phone rang. Kevin McCarthy was trying one more Trump family member in hopes of persuading the president to do something. "We need help!" McCarthy insisted. Kushner turned off the shower and rushed to the White House.

The video Ivanka had urged Trump to make had been posted before Kushner made it there. "I know your pain. I know your hurt," Trump said to the camera. "We had an election that was stolen from us. It was a landslide election and everyone knows it, especially the other side." He repeated his lies about the "fraudulent election" and complained about enemies who were "so bad and so evil" and would use the riot against Trump and their cause. Only then did he add, "We have to have peace. We have to have law and order." And finally, he said, "So go home. We love you, you're very special."[17]

We love you? That was hardly what Ivanka and the others had been asking for. And the video had been Trump's third attempt. Kushner quickly decided there was little that he could do.

The congressional leaders sequestered at Fort McNair soon focused on a singular goal: returning to the Capitol as quickly as possible to vote. They could not let Trump's mob stop their constitutional obligation, which was to get him out of office as expeditiously as possible. McConnell was especially insistent. As he had feared, those Georgia Senate elections had gone against the Republicans, costing him the majority and his chance to make Senate history as its longest-serving leader; he had thought that January 5 was the worst day of his life. But now it turned out that actually January 6 was. "We're going back into that building," he told one caller. "I don't care if there are no windows left. We're going back and voting."

In the Ways and Means Committee room, the cavernous space in the Longworth House Office Building across from the Capitol where lawmakers had been brought to shelter, this was also top of mind. Tom Malinowski, a New Jersey Democrat, saw Liz Cheney and went over to the Republican Conference chair. He was angry.

"I hope you'll agree with me that the minute they give the all-clear, once they get all these fuckers out of here, we march right back into the chamber—"

"—and impeach the son of a bitch," Cheney said, finishing the sentence.

Actually, that was not what Malinowski was going to say. He meant that they should march back in to finish the vote count. But he certainly agreed with Cheney's sentiment and found Steny Hoyer, the House majority leader, to tell him that one of the top Republicans in the House not only blamed Trump for their predicament but was in favor of immediately charging him with high crimes and misdemeanors.

Cheney certainly was furious. At one point, trapped in that room, she called into Fox News. "There is no question that the president formed the mob. The president incited the mob. The president addressed the mob. He lit the flames," she told the network that had so often over the last four years given Trump a match and explained exactly where to strike it.[18]

By late in the afternoon, much of the talk, at least among the Democrats in the room where Adam Schiff had led the impeachment hearings into Trump's Ukraine blackmail scheme barely a year earlier, was about impeaching him again. Even though there were only two weeks until Biden's inauguration, they believed it was dangerous for Trump to remain in the White House. But no one really knew if it was possible to remove him with so little time left. Others wondered if Trump had finally gone far enough that Mike Pence and the cabinet might act themselves to remove Trump from office by invoking the Twenty-fifth Amendment. No one was sure how to proceed, but the sentiment was clear: they had to do something.

Soon, two different groups of Democrats were huddling in the Ways and Means room working on draft impeachment language, one that included Ilhan Omar of Minnesota and other members of the progressive Squad, and another led by a trio of Judiciary Committee members—Jamie Raskin, David Cicilline, and Ted Lieu—who began batting out proposed language and sending drafts to committee lawyers on their iPhones. By 10 p.m. the Judiciary Committee staff had a full working draft and *Politico* was reporting that more than three dozen Democrats had already indicated support.

The National Guard finally arrived on Capitol Hill at 5:40 p.m., "sprint speed" for the military, as Mark Milley would later put it, but not nearly fast enough for the members of Congress who would spend many months investigating why it took so long.[19] By 7 p.m. a secure perimeter was set up outside the Capitol and FBI agents were going door-to-door in the Capitol's many hideaways and narrow corridors, searching for remaining rioters.

That night, waiting like the rest of Washington for Congress to return and finally get the election over with, Milley called back one of his contacts in the incoming Biden administration. He explained that he had spoken with Mark Meadows and Pat Cipollone at the White House, and that he had been on the phone with Pence and the congressional leaders as well. But the chairman of the Joint Chiefs had never heard from the commander in chief on a day when the Capitol was overrun by a hostile force for the first time since the War of 1812. Trump, he said, was both "shameful" and "complicit."

When Mike Pence reconvened the Senate soon after 8 p.m., the Capitol was filled with piles of broken glass and shattered reputations. Five people were dead and more would die in the days to come. Nearly 140 police officers were injured. Thousands of Trumpists had invaded the building, and hundreds of them would soon face arrest and prison. Among them were active-duty military and police officers, assorted Republican state legislators, and organized battalions of white supremacist militia members from the Oath Keepers and the Proud Boys. The vice president lectured the rioters. "You did not win. Violence never wins," he said. "Let's get back to work."[20] There was applause.

"Our job is to convene, to open the ballots, and to count them. That's it," Mike Lee of Utah, a staunch Trump supporter and self-described legal nerd, said when debate resumed on the floor.[21] For two months, Lee had been secretly working with Mark Meadows and others advising Trump on how to contest the election results, even, at one point in November, plugging the services of Sidney Powell to Trump and sending along her contact information. Lee had, by his own account, spent hours and hours working the phones trying to convince state legislators in battleground states to disregard the will of voters and switch their electors to Trump.

But after Trump's plan came down to demanding that Mike Pence singlehandedly overturn the election without officially sanctioned competing slates from the contested states, Lee had bowed out of the plot. He had even texted Meadows two days earlier a warning about his cynical colleagues, "Ted and Josh"—Cruz and Hawley—and how they were pushing the president to go through with a blatantly unconstitutional plan that would only backfire to Trump's "detriment."[22]

Support for their scheme in the Senate had collapsed quickly. Cruz and Hawley began the day with perhaps thirteen votes. But there were only six left by the time the Senate considered objections to Arizona's electoral votes, including their own. The senators whose chamber had been invaded were spooked. "There were fingerprints all over our desks, which was eerie," remembered Susan Collins, who would end the night sleeping over at her colleague Lisa Murkowski's Capitol Hill townhouse, drinking wine in front of the fireplace just before dawn and wondering how it had come to this. Kelly Loeffler, one of the Georgia senators whose defeat the previous day had cost Mitch McConnell the majority, changed her mind. "I cannot now in good conscience object to the certification of these electors," she said. "The violence, the lawlessness and siege of the halls of Congress are abhorrent and stand as a direct attack on the very institution my objection was intended to protect: the sanctity of the American democratic process."[23] Ninety-three senators voted down the objection, and it was very hard to get ninety-three senators to agree on anything by that point.

Even Lindsey Graham, whose reinvention from Trump-basher to Trump-lover had been one of Washington's running dramas, finally broke with the president. Or at least he seemed to. Sounding oddly jovial, or, perhaps, liberated, Graham said, "Count me out. Enough is enough. I've tried to be helpful." Graham mocked the hollow pretensions of his colleagues, who claimed to be making a principled objection that would somehow grant Pence the power to unilaterally "disenfranchise 155 million people." Graham concluded with words that might have mattered, had he uttered them two months earlier: "Joe Biden and Kamala Harris are lawfully elected and will become the president and the vice president of the United States on January the 20th."[24]

But Trump's defeat was not the repudiation it might have been. As Don Jr. had shouted at that morning's rally, "This is Donald Trump's Republican Party!" In the House, unlike in the Senate, the vast majority of Republican members who had started out the day planning to object to the electoral results ended the day still doing so. More than 120 House Republicans supported the objections to the lawfully certified results from Arizona and nearly 140 of them—roughly two thirds of the House GOP—objected hours later when Pennsylvania's electoral certificate was challenged. Kevin McCarthy, despite his screaming phone call with Trump and his plea to Jared Kushner to help stop the mob, was one of them.

Just after 3:40 a.m., Pence stood on the rostrum of the House, as inscrutable and unruffled as always. The pointless votes to object had all failed, as everyone had known all along they would. In his deep baritone, he read out the electoral results that ended Trump's presidency—and his own vice presidency. "Joseph R. Biden, Jr., of the state of Delaware, has received three hundred and six votes," Pence said.[25] He had finally gotten a chance to do his duty, as he promised in that letter he had released nearly fifteen hours earlier. Trump had not stopped him. The rampaging mob chanting his name had not stopped him. In his motorcade on the way home ten minutes later, Pence received a text from Marc Short, his chief of staff who had been with him through the whole endless day and night. It said simply, "2 Timothy 47." Pence knew the words to the biblical verse by heart, and he would quote them to his staff a few days later at a farewell party. *I have fought the good fight, I have finished the race, I have kept the faith.*

A grudging statement from Trump, negotiated over the previous few hours by his political adviser Jason Miller, Ivanka Trump, and others, soon followed, tweeted out by Trump's aide Dan Scavino at 3:49 a.m. because Twitter, after four years of Trump's false and incendiary posts, had finally locked him out of his account. "Even though I totally disagree with the outcome of the election, and the facts bear me out, nevertheless there will be an orderly transition on January 20th," the statement said. It was no concession. Nor, for the first time in American history, would it be a peaceful transfer of power, not after the deadly events of January 6, 2021. But it was done.

This Uncivil War

On the morning after, with combat troops bivouacked in the Capitol for the first time since the Civil War and the rest of Washington locked up under a curfew befitting a country at war with itself, Trump met his national security adviser in the Oval Office. Robert O'Brien brought with him papers to be signed, and Trump duly pulled out his black Sharpie to inscribe his name. Neither one of them said a word about the storming of Congress the day before.

But pretending would only go so far. With thirteen days to go, Trump's presidency had imploded. In his reckless, failed effort to overturn the election, Trump had destroyed his administration, marred his place in history, and had very likely guaranteed that he would be impeached for a second time. His staff may not have wanted to tell him so to his face. But that was what they thought. "His presidency is yesterday. Period. End of story," a dejected former White House official, one of the few who had left Trump's perennially dysfunctional staff on good terms, texted privately that day.

On Capitol Hill, Democrats and, for a time, many Republicans focused on what could be done to restrain Trump and get the country through his final days. There was talk of pressuring him to resign, of getting Mike Pence and the cabinet to invoke the Twenty-fifth Amendment. A second impeachment seemed a near-certainty, and there was even the possibility that Mitch McConnell and his Senate Republicans might go along with it and actually remove the president. Nothing like that had ever happened before. Never had anyone felt the need to worry that a defeated president was such a danger to the country that he could not be trusted to finish his last days in office—or trusted to leave office at all. In his overnight statement following the congressional votes, Trump had finally acknowledged that Joe Biden would take office on January 20, committing in effect to surrendering the White House. But many were not ready to take that at face value. A lot could still happen in thirteen days.

When O'Brien returned to his office on the other side of the West Wing, his deputy Matt Pottinger was gone, having resigned the night before. He was not the only one out the door. Before day's end, he would be joined by two cabinet members, Elaine Chao, the transportation secretary who was married to McConnell (the attack "has deeply troubled me in a way that I simply cannot set aside"), and Betsy DeVos, the wealthy education secretary who had been one of Trump's earliest and most generous political benefactors ("there is no mistaking the impact your rhetoric had on the situation").[1] Also quitting were Stephanie Grisham, the first lady's chief of staff and former White House press secretary; Tyler Goodspeed, the acting chairman of the President's Council of Economic Advisers; Sarah Matthews, a deputy White House press secretary; and Rickie Niceta, the White House social secretary. Mick Mulvaney, the ousted acting chief of staff who had been given a consolation post as special envoy to Northern Ireland, quit as well.

More significantly, given the potential consequences, some of those who had tried to act as restraining influences on Trump in the weeks since the election were thinking of resigning too, including Pat Cipollone and Chris Liddell, the deputy chief of staff, both of whom were seen as steadying figures in a White House increasingly devoid of them. It got so bad that Republican senators and Bush administration veterans such as Condoleezza Rice, Josh Bolten, and Steve Hadley were calling around trying to convince at least someone to stay. Several of them called O'Brien and Cipollone that day. The next two weeks could be incredibly dangerous and more than ever, they argued, Trump should be surrounded by reliable hands lest he do something even more dangerous. "We can't have an empty West Wing completely empty of anyone of good sense and good judgment," Bolten told them. "You've got a patriotic duty to stay."

Several officials, including chief economic adviser Larry Kudlow, huddled in a meeting upstairs to discuss whether they should resign en masse, but ultimately decided someone needed to land the plane. Besides, they would get no credit from Trump's critics while alienating the president and his supporters. Kudlow was close to signing a contract with Fox News and figured resigning early would only mess that up.

The pressure rose by the hour. Republican elected officials including Governors Charlie Baker of Massachusetts, Larry Hogan of Maryland, and Phil Scott of Vermont, and Representatives Adam Kinzinger and

Steve Stivers of Ohio said Trump should be removed from office. Kinzinger said Trump was "unmoored not just from his duty or even his oath but from reality itself."[2] Many more thought so privately. The *Wall Street Journal* editorial page declared that Trump's behavior was "impeachable" and called on him to resign.[3] More of Trump's former advisers broke their silence and spoke out. Jim Mattis denounced the president for fomenting "mob rule."[4] Bill Barr accused him of a "betrayal of his office."[5] John Kelly announced that he would vote to invoke the Twenty-fifth Amendment if he were still in the cabinet. The National Association of Manufacturers became the first major business organization to urge Pence to consider the Twenty-fifth Amendment "to preserve democracy."[6] It was as if after all this time it was finally okay to say what they really thought.

Consequences, it seemed, were finally piling up for Trump, who had evaded them for so long. Perhaps the cruelest blow of all came the following day, when Twitter announced that it was permanently suspending Trump's account, citing the "risk of further incitement of violence." After more than 25,000 tweets during his presidency, Trump's final tweet was a fittingly petulant announcement, at 10:44 a.m. on January 8, of one more norm he intended to shatter: "To all of those who have asked, I will not be going to the Inauguration on January 20th."

Ivanka Trump took it upon herself to try to salvage what could be salvaged by persuading her father to tape another video, this one more forcefully denouncing the rioters he had encouraged. He was reluctant. Only when Pat Cipollone warned him that he could face criminal exposure for unleashing the mob on January 6 did Trump finally agree. But once again, his heart was not in it. He shot multiple takes that were unusable because he kept caveating his statement, just as he had in the midst of the riot itself.

In the final version, Trump called the storming of the Capitol a "heinous attack" and said he was "outraged by the violence, lawlessness and mayhem." But he sounded flat, exhibiting none of the passion that he normally did when he was genuinely outraged. "The demonstrators who infiltrated the Capitol have defiled the seat of American democracy," he said in a monotone. "To those who engaged in the acts of violence and destruction, you do not represent our country and to those who broke the law you will pay." He called for "healing and reconciliation" and acknowledged that a new president would now take office, without naming Joe Biden.

But Trump admitted no wrongdoing and retreated not an inch from his false claims that the election was stolen, insisting that he was just trying to get the real result. "My only goal was to ensure the integrity of the vote," he said. "In so doing, I was fighting to defend American democracy."[7]

Ivanka Trump texted Susan Collins with a link to the video at 7:31 p.m. Collins watched it and thought it struck a better tone. "How I wish the president had posted it yesterday," she wrote back at 10:58 p.m. What Collins did not say was that she was still nervous about what Trump would do. "What I worried about," she said later, was "whether he would literally refuse to leave the White House and, if so, what would happen?"

For the first time in American history, this remained an open question. Collins was not the only one to fear the once unthinkable. In post–January 6 Washington, this was not just the fever dream of Trump's opposition, but the nightmare scenario of some of those who surrounded and promoted him too. "Right up until the last night," one top aide recalled later, "I was concerned something would happen."

So was Nancy Pelosi. The speaker of the House called Mark Milley at the Pentagon looking for reassurance. "What precautions are available to prevent an unstable president from initiating military hostilities or from accessing the launch codes and ordering a nuclear strike?" she asked the chairman.

"I can tell you we have a lot of checks in the system," Milley replied. "And I can guarantee you, you can take it to the bank, that there'll be, that the nuclear triggers are secure and we're not going to do—we're not going to allow anything crazy, illegal, immoral or unethical to happen."

Pelosi pointed out that something crazy, illegal, immoral, and unethical had just happened and no one had stopped it. She pressed Milley about how the military would respond to an out-of-control president and complained that Republicans were not stepping up to push Trump out when they knew how dangerous he had become.

"He's crazy," she said. "You know he's crazy. He's been crazy for a long time."

Milley offered no rebuttal. "Madam Speaker, I agree with you on everything."[8]

Within hours, Pelosi sent a letter to fellow House Democrats informing them about her call with Milley, which made many wonder if that was the real point, just to make a public show of it, and the transcript of the call was later given to the journalists Bob Woodward and Robert Costa.

Milley was no less concerned himself. That morning he called his Chinese counterpart to reassure him the United States would not launch an unprovoked attack, then held his regular land-the-plane call—now even more urgent—with Pompeo and Meadows. He also called senior officers including at the Pentagon's round-the-clock command center, this time to reaffirm the importance of making sure no one in the armed forces bypassed the regular chain of command to carry out some rash order by a commander in chief anxious to hold on to power. Milley reminded the officers to share with him any decree that came from the president. He could not countermand it, but it was crucial that they take no action without informing him. To the historically minded chairman, the echo of Richard Nixon's volatile final days, when Defense Secretary James Schlesinger warned his generals against executing any nuclear launch order from Nixon without checking with him or Secretary of State Henry Kissinger, must have been palpable.

The most pressing fear was over how to secure Joe Biden's inauguration at the Capitol in less than two weeks. "The immediate worry was, 'Oh, holy shit, this could derail the whole inauguration,'" recalled a senior official on the incoming Biden team. Determined that no more disasters should happen on his watch, Milley immediately began to review the security plans for January 20, and first thing the morning after the riot, he convened a meeting in his office with the two-star general in charge of the capital area task force to go over the details. Eventually, with his prodding, a five-hour military-style "ROC drill" rehearsal for the inauguration was convened at Fort Myer, with the chairman personally presiding. "None of that would have happened without Milley," the senior Biden official said.

Those two weeks seemed, in the immediate aftermath of the Capitol attack, like far too long to wait and Pelosi and Chuck Schumer called Mike Pence the morning after the insurrection to urge him to invoke the Twenty-fifth Amendment. Marc Short, his chief of staff, believed it was just a stunt by the Democratic leaders and refused to put the call through.

In fact, Mike Pompeo, Steven Mnuchin, and other cabinet officers quietly discussed invoking the amendment to remove Trump. But once it became clear that Pence would not consider it even after being abandoned to the mob by the president, they dropped the issue or, like Betsy DeVos, resigned.

Whatever reluctance Pelosi felt about the first impeachment, she felt none about a second one. There was never any question in almost anyone's mind that the House would once again charge Trump with high crimes and misdemeanors if Pence did not act to remove him first. Even if time was too short to get him out of the White House before he was due to leave on

January 20 anyway, the threat could deter him from taking further action to hang on to power. Or so the theory went.

The draft article of impeachment that Jamie Raskin and the others had begun scratching out while still locked down in the House Ways and Means Committee room had started out accusing Trump of incitement of insurrection. Over the next few days, it evolved into an abuse of power charge and then was changed back to incitement. Some thought there should be a second article on dereliction of duty but that was dropped. The final version of the article outlined Trump's actions before and on January 6, then concluded:

> In all this, President Trump gravely endangered the security of the United States and its institutions of Government. He threatened the integrity of the democratic system, interfered with the peaceful transition of power, and imperiled a coequal branch of Government. He thereby betrayed his trust as President, to the manifest injury of the people of the United States.[9]

Trump was angry about the repeat impeachment—and about everything really—and even those who had once been confident in their ability to manage the president were now unsure what to do. The president was still stuck on the election, even if the rest of Washington was desperate to move on. "Guys we have a clear path to land the plane in 9 days," Sean Hannity texted Mark Meadows and another close ally, Jim Jordan, on January 10. "He can't mention the election again. Ever. I did not have a good call with him today. And worse I'm not sure what is left to do or say, and I don't like knowing if it's truly understood."[10]

On Capitol Hill, Republican leaders were similarly despairing of Trump and believed impeachment was sure to pass in the House and possibly even lead to a Senate conviction. That same day, January 10, Kevin McCarthy told his GOP leadership team on a call he was thinking of calling up and asking Trump to resign given where impeachment was headed. "I've had it with this guy," McCarthy said. "What he did is unacceptable. Nobody can defend that, and nobody should defend it."[11] But McCarthy's bluster was just that. He never made the call.

In the White House, one focus was trying to get Trump over his fury at Pence. On January 11, Jared Kushner asked Marc Short to come to his office to broker an internal peace deal. Would the vice president be willing to get together with the president? Kushner asked.

"He's always willing," Short replied. "But that's not his responsibility to reconcile this relationship. That invitation should come from the other end of the hall."

"That's what I'm doing, Marc," Kushner said.

At Kushner's arrangement, Trump and Pence sat down that afternoon with no staff for an hour and a half. Pence reported back to aides that it was somewhat warm. But it was only a bandage over a gaping wound.

If Pence was trying to move on, other Republicans began falling back in line too. Among the first to repent was Lindsey Graham. Two days after the riot, Graham had been accosted at Reagan National Airport by Trump supporters angry at him for breaking with the president over the electoral certification on January 6.

"You are a traitor, Lindsey Graham!" a man shouted at him.

Others started chanting, "Traitor! Traitor!"

Police officers escorted Graham away as Trump supporters shouted profanities, called Graham a "garbage human being," and vowed to haunt him for "the rest of your life."[12]

Graham soon reached out to the president to explain that when he said "I'm done" in that dramatic late-night floor speech after the attack on the Capitol, he only meant that the election was over. "It wasn't I'm done with *you*," Graham told Trump. "It was I'm done with *this*."

Within days, he was back at the White House, hanging out for half a day with the president as well as Jared and Ivanka, talking about how the president could use his remaining time in office to trumpet his accomplishments. He found a president on edge, "defiant" and "nervous." Graham also carried a message from fellow Senate Republicans like Roy Blunt warning Trump not to pardon the January 6 rioters as some of the "crazies" were urging him to do. "Mr. President, that's insane," Graham said.

On January 12, Graham accompanied the president to the border as Trump finally agreed to take the legacy trip his staff had been advocating, although what legacy remained after the previous week's events was hard to imagine. Yet Trump still seemed to think he was the aggrieved one, and he barely spoke with Graham on the flight down. The hastily arranged trip, to tout his signature though incomplete promise to build a big, beautiful wall at the southern border, was to the town of Alamo, Texas, named for the mission more than two hundred miles away where a small group of Texas independence fighters made their famous last stand. Few doubted that Trump had chosen it to signal his defiance to the end.

Certainly, he was unrepentant. In his first public appearance since the insurrection at the Capitol, Trump said in Texas that not only did he bear no blame for the attack, but Democrats were the ones ripping the country apart by seeking to punish him. That afternoon, a House committee met to approve the article of impeachment against him. "It is causing tremendous anger and division and pain—far greater than most people will ever understand," Trump said, warning ominously that impeachment was "very dangerous for the USA, especially at this very tender time."[13]

The next day, exactly one week since the attack, the full House reconvened to impeach Trump again, this time for trying to topple American democracy itself. The Capitol bristled with heavily armed soldiers and newly installed metal detectors even for members of the House, and there remained a sense that anything was possible.

Especially because Trump was still ensconced in the White House, refusing to move on. Even with impeachment, the president raged at his advisers that he would not give up his rigged-election talk. His political adviser Jason Miller had new polling data showing "⅔ of the MAGA base wants us to move on," he told other aides in a text. "I tried to walk the President through this earlier but he won't have any of it."[14]

But this time Trump was ahead of his political team. He seemed to get instinctively that the Republicans on the Hill would still stick with him, even after everything. The impeachment debate that day showed that he was right: for all the outrage over what had happened, partisan lines were re-forming and however mad Republicans were at Trump, the vast majority were not willing to break with him.

"The president bears responsibility for Wednesday's attack on Congress by mob rioters," Kevin McCarthy declared on the floor where just a week earlier his members cowered in fear for their lives just as much as their Democratic colleagues had. "He should have immediately denounced the mob when he saw what was unfolding."[15] But McCarthy then went on to reject impeachment and nearly all of his caucus joined him. As for what consequences Trump should suffer, they were, as always, vague.

Perhaps no one was more forceful in condemning Trump than Liz Cheney, who released a statement in advance of the debate echoing the comment she made on the day of the attack:

> The President of the United States summoned this mob, assembled the mob, and lit the flame of this attack. Everything that followed was his doing. None of this would have happened without the President. The President could have immediately and forcefully intervened to stop the violence. He did not. There has never been a greater betrayal

by a President of the United States of his office and his oath to the Constitution.[16]

At 4:33 p.m., after six and a half hours of debate, the House voted 232 to 197 to make Trump the only president impeached twice in American history. Ten Republicans joined every Democrat in supporting impeachment, including Cheney and Kinzinger, the highest number of lawmakers ever to vote to impeach a president of their own party. But ten was not the thirty or forty or fifty members that seemed possible in the immediate aftermath of the attack. Other Republicans who had been ready to impeach grew nervous and retreated back to the security of partisanship. Anti-anti-Trumpism had survived the insurrection at the Capitol as the party's most powerful ideological force.

This was true in the Senate too, where any chance of removing Trump early was quickly scuttled when Mitch McConnell decided not to call the chamber back from recess to hold a quick trial. Procedurally it would have been complicated and McConnell judged that even if he were to get senators back to town, there was no way to hold a trial with even a veneer of due process in the six days left before the inauguration. The trial would have to be held after he left office. So in the end the president who had repeatedly skirted accountability—in the Mueller investigation and the Ukraine scheme and his tax returns and every other scandal—would avoid a final reckoning during his presidency.

Impeached again and just days from the end of his term, Trump was still entertaining allies urging him to find a way to stay in power. On January 15, he received Mike Lindell, the founder of MyPillow and an outspoken public defender of the president, in the Oval Office. Lindell, a mile-a-minute talker who marketed his crack-cocaine-addict-finds-God life story into a multimillion-dollar bedding business, arrived with what he called proof that the election had been rigged by China through corrupted computers. He also brought with him a two-page paper that he said a lawyer he refused to identify had asked him to pass along to Trump, prodding him once more to call in the military to seize voting machines. "Martial law if necessary," said the paper, which was photographed by a *Washington Post* photographer as Lindell entered the White House, provoking an uproar when it was revealed late that Friday.

The actual meeting had been brief, no more than a few minutes before Trump instructed Robert O'Brien, "Bring Mike upstairs and see what we've got here." Lindell was then escorted up to the counsel's office, where lawyers looked at his papers and promptly ushered him out of the White House with a don't-call-us-we'll-call-you farewell.

By now, Trump was no more ready to accept his defeat but his options had narrowed and he was resigned to leaving office. On January 19, his last full day in the White House, Trump turned once again to his authority to grant clemency. It was something in his control, a final act to lash out at a system that had fought him from the start. He granted 143 pardons or commutations to a breathtaking array of crooked politicians and businessmen, including Elliott Broidy, one of his top fundraisers in 2016, who pleaded guilty to conspiracy to illegally lobby the administration on behalf of Chinese and Malaysian interests; the rappers Lil Wayne and Kodak Black, who faced gun-related charges; Ken Kurson, a friend of Jared Kushner's arrested for cyberstalking; and three Republican congressmen convicted of corruption. Trump knew many of the recipients personally and many had been represented by Trump-connected lawyers, like his own attorney in the Mueller probe, John Dowd, who had engaged in a virtual lottery sweepstakes representing clients seeking clemency in Trump's final days.

Prominent on the pardon list was Steve Bannon, who had started out the presidency at Trump's side, his most powerful adviser and coauthor with Stephen Miller of his combative Inaugural Address, celebrated on the cover of *Time* magazine as Trump's "Great Manipulator." Bannon had been handcuffed by federal agents while aboard a fugitive Chinese billionaire's $28 million yacht the previous August and charged with bilking Trump's own supporters who were told donations would go to build the border wall when instead much of the money went into Bannon's pocket. He had yet to go to trial even and a pardon hardly seemed like a politically wise move for a president seeking public rehabilitation. Some advisers tried to talk him out of it, especially Kellyanne Conway, who sent the president articles quoting Bannon trashing him.

But Bannon enlisted allies like Rudy Giuliani to call the president and lobby for him. Trump called Jared Kushner to ask what he thought and the onetime Bannon rival acquiesced, saying, "I'm for second chances." Ultimately, a final phone call with Bannon himself convinced Trump, who added the former adviser to the final list at 9 p.m. Their fallout and eventual reconciliation followed a pattern with Trump, who could never resist those he saw fighting for him, as Bannon had from his war room on January 6.

Notably not on the list were Trump himself, his family members, Giuliani, or other organizers of January 6. Trump became convinced that pardoning himself or those so close to him would be an admission that he did something wrong.

Trump woke up the next morning, January 20, two weeks to the day after the attack on the Capitol, and for the last time as president put on his uniform of dark suit, white shirt, and red tie. His belongings had been hurriedly packed in the last few days and most of his staff had moved on, even the ones who had not resigned in protest. His mind was on the forthcoming impeachment trial in the Senate. He picked up the phone around 6:30 a.m. to call Mark Meadows at home.

"How do we look in Congress?" Trump asked. "I've heard that there are some Republicans who might be turning against us. That would be a very unwise thing for them to do."

Meadows reassured Trump that his Senate allies were still with him.

"This was nothing," Trump then said, dismissing the significance of January 6. "They are impeaching me over—"

Before the president could finish the thought, Meadows interrupted what he knew would be a long soliloquy. "I hate to cut you off, but it's almost seven o'clock," Meadows said. He had to get to Joint Base Andrews in Maryland in a little over an hour to attend the president's farewell ceremony, he noted, and "I haven't even showered yet."[17]

As he had so many times, Trump was flouting tradition, leaving early in the morning on Marine One for a last time and flying off to Florida after a ceremony at Andrews rather than hosting the incoming president for the usual coffee before heading together to the Capitol for the inauguration. Trump was the first president since Andrew Johnson to refuse to attend his successor's swearing in. Still, he was not missed. "One of the few things he and I have ever agreed on," Joe Biden had said when Trump first announced his decision to skip the ceremony.[18]

When Trump landed at Joint Base Andrews, a sparse crowd attended. He was finally down, as his late adversary John McCain might have remarked, to family members and paid staff. Conspicuously absent was Mike Pence; he was at the Capitol to watch Biden take the oath, once again doing his duty, which in this case consisted of merely showing up, as outgoing vice presidents typically did.

At Andrews, Trump took the stage to "Hail to the Chief" and a twenty-one-gun salute. In a ten-minute farewell, Trump dispensed with the prepared text. Speechwriters had written the sentence, "We wish President Biden and Vice President Harris great success in keeping America strong, prosperous and free," but put it in brackets since they did not know if he would say it. He would not. He could not bring himself to utter the words

"President Biden." Without naming him, Trump said simply, "I wish the new administration great luck and great success."

Trump boasted of his accomplishments, including the Covid vaccine he and Melania had secretly taken before leaving the White House that month—a fact he did not mention. Nor did he take note that the death toll from the coronavirus in the United States had just passed 400,000. While he had been waging a war for power, Covid had been ravaging the country worse than ever, with daily deaths shooting up to four or five times what they were on Election Day, the equivalent of another September 11 attack every twenty-four hours.

Before throwing a perfunctory thank-you to the absent Pence, Trump hinted that he was not done. "We will be back in some form," he said.[19] With that, he left the stage to his campaign rally staple, "YMCA" by the Village People. He and Melania marched up the staircase to Air Force One, which took off at 9 a.m. as Frank Sinatra's "My Way" played over loudspeakers on the tarmac. After landing in Florida, Trump announced his last official act less than forty-five minutes before his term expired, adding one more pardon to his list, this one for the ex-husband of his unwavering Fox News cheerleader Jeanine Pirro.

As Joe Biden took the oath back in Washington, he did not name Trump either, but his predecessor hung over the ceremony. "We've learned again that democracy is precious," Biden said in his Inaugural Address. "Democracy is fragile. And at this hour, my friends, democracy has prevailed." Taking over a country ravaged by disease, dislocation, and division, Biden sought to bring Americans together, using the word "unity" or some variation eleven times. "We must end this uncivil war that pits red against blue, rural versus urban, conservative versus liberal," he said.[20]

Trump was gone but not forgotten. While he simmered at Mar-a-Lago, his presidency had gone into overtime back in Washington as the Senate prepared to put him on trial for a second time. No president had ever faced an impeachment proceeding after leaving office, putting Trump once again on new and untested constitutional ground. But although he could no longer be removed from the presidency, his pursuers argued that it was important to put him on trial anyway as a measure of accountability. With Trump's "we will be back" still echoing, they also sought to bar him from seeking office again, one of the consequences of impeachment conviction envisioned by the Constitution.

This would be a different trial than the first, not just because of the constitutional novelty. Unlike the Ukraine scheme to blackmail little-known players in a far-off land, the events at issue in this impeachment were raw, visceral, and deeply personal to the senators, who had all experienced the insurrection firsthand. Certainly the two were connected: the Ukraine case, after all, had been an effort by Trump to use his power to tilt the 2020 election in his favor and the January 6 attack was the violent result when he was not able to. But this time there would be no argument about whether the offense met the constitutional threshold for "high crimes and misdemeanors," only whether Trump should be held responsible for it.

To prosecute Trump, Nancy Pelosi named a different team of House managers, choosing to put Jamie Raskin in charge, only days after his twenty-five-year-old son committed suicide. A fifty-eight-year-old former constitutional law professor who had long pursued Trump over issues like emoluments, Raskin was a liberal Maryland Democrat who supported Elizabeth Warren for president. But he had drawn sympathy on both sides of the aisle in those days of personal trauma and Pelosi believed he could bring a moral clarity to the cause. Raskin's grief for his son had blended with fury over the insurrection. A bereft father was harder to dismiss as a calculating partisan. But he knew his family tragedy would not inoculate him against attacks. As he began preparing for trial, his family cheekily debated the nicknames they imagined Trump might bestow, like "Ratskin" or "Pointy Head."[21]

In addition to Ted Lieu and David Cicilline, the congressmen who started drafting an article of impeachment with Raskin while hiding from the mob, the team included Joe Neguse of Colorado, Joaquin Castro of Texas, Madeleine Dean of Pennsylvania, Diana DeGette of Colorado, Eric Swalwell of California, and Stacey Plaskett, a delegate representing the Virgin Islands. They brought none of the caustic rivalries that afflicted that earlier group of Democrats. But once again, Pelosi opted not to make the impeachment effort bipartisan, leaving off the team Republicans like Liz Cheney or Adam Kinzinger, reflecting her own partisan instincts to save coveted assignments for members of her own caucus.

The managers figured they had a better shot at winning over Republican senators than in the first impeachment. But their optimism took a bruising on January 26 when Senator Rand Paul, the quirky libertarian from Kentucky, surprised even his own colleagues by offering a motion to dismiss the case, arguing that a former president could not constitutionally be put on trial since he could no longer be removed from office. Mitch McConnell predicted to an aide that Paul would get about thirty votes. But he got forty-five—not enough to pass the motion but more than the thirty-four ultimately required to block conviction. Only five Republicans voted with the fifty Democrats to proceed to trial. "We needed to show we were fighting for Trump because the base was agitated," a senior Republican leadership aide explained later. Instead, what they showed was that any suspense in the trial was over before the trial had even begun. The case was now "dead on arrival," Paul crowed.[22] Despite the raw feelings of a few weeks earlier, Republicans had not yet broken with Trump.

Still, Raskin and his team told themselves that it was still possible to win sixty-seven votes for conviction. Since the Senate had just ruled that a trial was in order, Republicans would now, in theory, have to consider the case on the merits. To get the seventeen Republicans they needed, the managers focused on convincing McConnell, knowing that his rift with Trump was as real as his outrage at the January 6 mob. They figured if they won the leader's vote, he would bring with him other establishment Republicans. They found a seating chart of the Senate and used a yellow highlighter to mark the desks of the Republicans they most wanted to target, including Senators Richard Burr of North Carolina, Rob Portman of Ohio, Jerry Moran of Kansas, and James Lankford and Jim Inhofe of Oklahoma.

As Raskin and his team prepared their case, they resolved to avoid what they saw as the mistakes of Adam Schiff and his managers in the first impeachment trial. In their view, that case had been too long, too abstract, too repetitive, too partisan, too condescending, and the managers far too wordy. With no chance of conviction, Schiff and company had lectured senators rather than wooed them. This time, the managers sought to appeal to the opposition. "Our goal was to learn to speak Republican," said one of their advisers. Counseled by several former Republican officials they dubbed their "jury consultants," the managers excised words like "equality" and "dignity" from their speeches and instead embraced more GOP-friendly buzzwords like "honor" and "oath" and "patriotism." They played down the relevance of race in the Capitol attack and avoided arguments implying that Senate Republicans had been complicit by enabling Trump. Reasoning that Republican senators were fonder of Mike Pence than Nancy Pelosi, they emphasized the danger to the vice president rather than the speaker.

Barry Berke, once again serving as the chief impeachment counsel for the managers, planned America's first video-driven impeachment trial. His goal was to show how violent the rioters really were, how close the mob came to Pence, how much they were hanging on Trump's words and claiming his authority in staging their assault on the Capitol. The House team even insisted on larger televisions on the Senate floor than during the first trial—two massive, seventy-seven-inch screens this time instead of fifty-five-inch ones. "We should be prosecuting this as a violent crime, not a constitutional convention," Berke kept telling the team. No florid speeches on American democracy. And absolutely no using the Benjamin Franklin quote that had become one of the most tiresome clichés of the Trump era, the one about America being "a republic, if you can keep it." Berke threatened to bench any manager who quoted it; as it was, the staff discovered the phrase in a couple drafts and had to delete it.

At every turn, the managers aimed for maximum emotional appeal to the senators. Raskin even scrapped his planned opening speech focusing on the constitutional argument about putting a former president on trial, to speak more bluntly about his tragic personal story and to show a thirteen-minute video of the riot. It was full of footage never seen in public before, gathered from security cameras, police body cameras, and videos taken by the rioters themselves. "Part of the goal was how do we traumatize these people?"—meaning the senators, said a lawyer working for the managers.

As for Trump, the former president was struggling to find someone to defend him. He had burned through much of the conservative legal community during the post-election scheming and lost his few remaining lawyers on January 6. None of the attorneys who represented him at his first impeachment trial would defend him a second time. Pat Cipollone, Jay Sekulow, Pat Philbin—they were done. They would not break with Trump publicly, but they did not want to speak on his behalf again. Alan Dershowitz, who rarely met a camera he did not like, was the only one willing, but he was ruled out given his efforts to use his influence to secure last-minute pardons.

Lindsey Graham referred Trump to Butch Bowers, a prominent South Carolina attorney, but that quickly fell apart over money and strategy. Then Roger Stone recommended David Schoen, one of his defense attorneys during the Mueller prosecution, who agreed to represent the former president. Trump also hired Bruce Castor, a former district attorney in Pennsylvania best known for having once declined to prosecute Bill Cosby for sexual assault, and Michael van der Veen, an attorney whose website boasted that his was "Philadelphia's foremost personal injury and dog-bite law firm."

The second impeachment trial of Donald Trump opened on Tuesday, February 9, and unlike any in history it unfolded in the scene of the crime itself with all one hundred jurors having themselves been witnesses. John Roberts was not in the chair this time, on the theory that the Constitution called for the chief justice to preside only in the case of a sitting president, so Senator Patrick Leahy, the veteran Democrat from Vermont and president pro tempore of the Senate, presided instead.

Shortly after 1 p.m., Jamie Raskin took the podium on the floor but quickly turned to the thirteen-minute video. Riveting, ghastly, and relentless, it showed Trump delivering his "you have to fight" speech even as the surging mob of his supporters burst through security barriers, beat police officers with hockey sticks, smashed windows, and poured into the building hunting the vice president and members of Congress.

Never had such gut-churning video footage been shown on the floor of the Senate. Many senators had not spent that much time viewing pictures of what transpired that day. A few had tears in their eyes. Raskin jotted down notes on his pad about their reactions. Lisa Murkowski looked "shell-shocked," he wrote, Mitt Romney "shaken" and "disapproving." Richard Burr "ashen-faced, pissed," Mitch McConnell "pained, confused—crying?" When the video showed a police officer crushed by the mob in a door and screaming in agony, Raskin wrote that McConnell "was tearing up, could lose it."[23]

"If that's not an impeachable offense," Raskin told the senators when the screens went dark, "then there is no such thing."[24]

The presentation caught Trump's pickup team of lawyers off guard. Worried that the managers had produced a powerful case, they suddenly scrambled their plans and Bruce Castor took it upon himself to give a largely off-the-cuff peroration. Castor's speech was a rambling forty-seven-minute word salad of non sequiturs and head-scratchers, leaving senators in the chamber rolling their eyes and Trump down at Mar-a-Lago screaming at his television set. Castor called himself "the lead prosecutor" instead of defense counsel, talked about the violation of the "very subtle of democracy," noted that he had gotten lost walking around the Capitol, and explained that a record album was "the thing you put the needle down on and you play it." He won no favor from his client by telling the senators there were other forms of accountability than impeachment. "After he's out of office," he ventured, "you go and arrest him."[25]

Andrew Ferguson, Mitch McConnell's chief counsel, told colleagues it was "the most uncomfortable thirty minutes I've ever experienced in my professional life." Susan Collins remarked, "I think I could have done a better job than that." To which another senator replied, "Don't say that too loud, they'll hire you." Castor realized that he had bombed. The next day, he asked Ferguson, "How badly am I in the doghouse with your boss?" Ferguson glared at him, then left the room without replying.

Among those cheering on the prosecution was Liz Cheney. The managers had not emphasized Cheney's condemnation of the president for fear of further exposing her to conservative backlash after such a tough vote. But she did not want to be protected. She called the Democrats during the trial, expressing surprise that they had not cited her line about Trump summoning the mob and lighting the flame. "I gave you the best quote," she said. "Why didn't you use it?"

Finally taking the floor on Friday, Trump's attorneys rambled through a presentation that was less defense of the president than counterattack against his enemies. They played a rat-a-tat montage of video clips showing nearly every Democratic senator sitting in the room before them, as well as Joe Biden and Kamala Harris, using words like "fight" or "fight like hell" in speeches or interviews. "Spare us the hypocrisy and false indignation," Michael van der Veen said.[26] Then, after using just three of their allotted sixteen hours, they sat down.

Even Trump's most loyal allies thought it was a nightmare. But it was a particularly Trumpian sort of show: they had the votes, so what did it matter how dysfunctional and incompetent they were. "Are we still under seventeen?" the Trump lawyers kept asking McConnell's staff. As long as they kept the Republican senators in line, that was all that counted.

Democrats were not always all that organized either, as a last-minute scramble over whether to call witnesses the next day showed. Neither side had been planning to do so, but the calculus changed Friday night after CNN reported on Trump's conversation on January 6 with Kevin McCarthy in which the president seemed indifferent to the threat of the attackers, citing Representative Jaime Herrera Beutler of Washington state, who heard the leader describe it. By Saturday morning, sometime after 6 a.m., Eric Swalwell began sending messages to other managers and aides over a text chain on Signal, the encrypted messaging system, arguing that they would be screwed if they did not call Herrera Beutler to testify. When managers and their staff members arrived at the Capitol, Barry Berke agreed they should call the congresswoman, but Joshua Matz and Aaron Hiller, two other lawyers working for the managers, resisted, noting it was too late and could sap their momentum. Soon, Trump's lawyer Michael van der Veen was threatening retaliation, saying they would demand "over one hundred depositions" in response.[27]

As the trial seemed in danger of spiraling out of control, Senator Chris Coons, Joe Biden's friend from Delaware, visited the managers in their back room twice to talk them out of witnesses. Although he insisted he was "speaking for myself," everyone assumed he was reflecting Biden's desire to move on with his presidency.

"I know when a jury is ready to vote and that jury is ready to vote," Coons told the managers. "You only have fifty-four, fifty-six votes and you're losing a vote an hour as long as this continues, so you should make a deal and end this."

Berke said they could conduct a quick Zoom deposition of Herrera Beutler that day and Trump's team could interview McCarthy by Sunday. "We'll wrap up on Monday," he said.

"Are you kidding me?" Coons said. "You can't be serious. You think you're going to be able to depose the minority leader of the House of Representatives in three hours? You don't think he's going to insist on a two-week pause so he can consult with his lawyers?"

Finally, Andrew Ferguson, McConnell's lawyer, suggested a way out. The two sides could insert Herrera Beutler's written statement into the trial record and stipulate that she would testify the same way had she been interviewed. Then no witnesses need be called. Both sides agreed.

In the end, the trial would all come down to Mitch McConnell. The Senate Republican leader was the key. If he voted to convict, it would make it politically safer for Republicans. McConnell had made perfectly clear in conversations with allies and advisers that he was through with Trump. Unlike the first trial, when he served as Trump's de facto defense chief, McConnell this time was not on the president's side. "You need to vote your conscience," he told fellow Republicans.

Joe Neguse made it his mission to win McConnell's vote. A thirty-six-year-old Black Democrat from Colorado and the first Eritrean American ever elected to Congress, Neguse had little in common with McConnell, a white Southern conservative descended from slaveholders just days from his seventy-ninth birthday. But he was convinced he could reach him. At 2 a.m. one night, Neguse googled his way to a speech the senator delivered earlier in his career against South African apartheid, then learned that McConnell voted to override Ronald Reagan's veto of sanctions against South Africa in 1986. Neguse thought he had an opening.

But before closing arguments got underway, McConnell sent a note to his fellow Senate Republicans informing them that he would vote not guilty after all—not because Trump was blameless but because impeachment was supposed to be about removing an outlaw president, not dealing with one after he left office. Neguse plowed forward anyway, delivering a closing argument aimed right at McConnell. He threw in references to Senator John Sherman Cooper, McConnell's mentor, and Henry Clay, the famed senator from Kentucky, while also mentioning that there were just two senators left in the chamber who had voted against Reagan's apartheid sanctions veto, without directly naming him. McConnell got the message and was impressed. "He had done his homework," he told aides. But the senator was not to be swayed by even the most personal of arguments.

Finally, just after 3 p.m., on February 13, twenty-four days after Trump left office, the clerk called the roll. Early in the alphabetical list, she called out Richard Burr, the North Carolina Republican who had led the Senate Intelligence Committee's investigation into Russian election interference.

"Guilty," he said.

Suddenly, there were cheers in the back room where most of the managers were watching on television. Burr had voted against proceeding with the trial just days ago but now was declaring Trump guilty. For Burr, the "straw that broke the camel's back" had been hearing about the president still pushing allies to stop the count of the Electoral College votes even as the Capitol was under siege, and doing nothing to rescue his own vice president. "That was the killer for me," Burr said later.

A few moments later, the clerk came to Bill Cassidy of Louisiana.

"Guilty," he said.[28]

So did Susan Collins, Lisa Murkowski, Mitt Romney, Ben Sasse, and Pat Toomey of Pennsylvania. In the end, seven Republicans abandoned Trump for the final 57 to 43 vote, the most senators ever to vote to convict a president of their own party. Trump had been acquitted, again, but this time the vote against him was bipartisan.

Yet the managers who had convinced themselves they had a real chance to win took little solace in that at first. After the vote was over, a wave of despondency came over Jamie Raskin. "I feel like I've let you down," he told the other managers, tearing up and burying his head in his hands. "That's when it all hit him—his son, he couldn't save democracy single-handedly," one person in the room recalled.

As they were still processing the vote, though, the managers looked up at the television to notice McConnell taking the floor. To their astonishment, he proceeded to denounce Trump in a speech every bit as lacerating as any of theirs:

There is no question that President Trump is practically and morally responsible for provoking the events of that day. The people who stormed this building believed they were acting on the wishes and instructions of their president. And their having that belief was a foreseeable consequence of the growing crescendo of false statements, conspiracy theories, and reckless hyperbole which the defeated president kept shouting into the largest megaphone on planet Earth. . . . This was an intensifying crescendo of conspiracy theories, orchestrated by an outgoing president who seemed determined to either overturn the voters' decision or else torch our institutions on the way out.[29]

McConnell then went on to explain why, despite his disgust at Trump, he voted to acquit, relying on the constitutional argument that the Senate had no power to try a president once he left office. But he hinted that had it not been for that, he would have supported removing Trump from office. And he all but called for a criminal investigation of the president now that he was no longer immune from indictment. "President Trump is still liable for everything he did while he was in office, as an ordinary citizen, unless the statute of limitations has run, still liable for everything he did while he's in office. Didn't get away with anything yet. Yet."

Democrats were not entirely sure whether to emphasize McConnell's speech as a moral victory or condemn it as a shameful betrayal.

"So he's saying Trump's factually guilty, but he lets him off on this phony technicality," Raskin observed in the managers' back room.

"Profile in courage," Eric Swalwell said sarcastically.

"Profile in politics," Raskin replied.[30]

But McConnell's speech rippled through Republican circles, with some cheering him on for finally saying what they had felt while others worried about an open war within the party between its former president and its Senate leader. Sean Hannity called Lindsey Graham even as McConnell was still on the floor delivering his broadside.

"Are you watching Mitch?" Hannity asked.

"No," Graham said. "I'm walking home."

"On a scale of one to ten," Hannity told him, "this is a hundred."

Once again, Trump had beat the rap. And once again he wasted no time claiming victory. He released a statement one minute before the presiding officer in the Senate even officially declared that he had been acquitted, denouncing his impeachment as "yet another phase of the greatest witch hunt in the history of our country."[31]

But this time *was* different. Trump was an ex-president now, whether he accepted the title or not, only the fifth president in a century to be evicted from the White House by the voters. He was, in the end, a twice-impeached loser, and more senators from his party had just voted to convict him than had ever happened before. Even those who stuck by Trump on the vote had hardly defended him.

For Trump, in his Mar-a-Lago exile, stripped of his Twitter megaphone, of his White House stage set and the fawning staff he had assembled to surround him at the Resolute Desk with praise, this was an escape, not an exoneration. Still, it was an escape.

Kevin McCarthy had already come to Florida seeking his favor even before the trial started. In the heat of the moment, McCarthy had said Trump bore responsibility for the insurrection at the Capitol. Now, after a grinning photo op with Trump in the Mar-a-Lago lobby, he said it was ridiculous to say Trump had "provoked" it. Others made similarly swift amends. Polls showed that millions of Republicans—a huge majority of them—believed Trump's manifestly false claims that the election had been stolen.

Even Mitch McConnell, who hated Trump so much he had vowed never to speak to him again, who had called him crazy to the point of derangement, could never fully disavow him. Less than two weeks after the trial, which concluded with him denouncing Trump's "disgraceful dereliction of duty," McConnell was asked if he would support Trump for president again if he were the party's nominee in 2024. McConnell did not hesitate for a second. "Absolutely," he said.[32]

With Donald Trump, it was never over.

A Close-Run Thing

When we sat down with Donald Trump a year after his defeat, the first thing he told us was a lie.

We were in his upstairs office at his Mar-a-Lago estate, which was filled with artifacts of his time as president—a rack of challenge coins, a plaque commemorating his border wall, odd gifts from admirers. Among them was a portrait of Trump fashioned out of bullet casings, a present from Jair Bolsonaro, the so-called Trump of Brazil.

On the wall hung six of Trump's favorite photographs from the White House. Four were of Trump by himself or with his family. One showed Trump, the son of a Scottish immigrant mother who had been a diehard royalist, with Queen Elizabeth II. Another caught the scene of him shaking hands at the DMZ with Kim Jong-un, the homicidal dictator he had courted in the failed effort to strike a nuclear accord.

Trump held forth from behind a bulky wooden desk. He was wearing a white golf shirt, khakis, and red "SAVE AMERICA" ballcap rather than his usual suit and tie, and crowing about the millions of dollars he had made that evening by renting out the rest of his club for a lavish Iranian wedding. "The money is just like unbelievable," he gushed.

As we began our second interview for this book on a humid Florida afternoon in November 2021, we asked Trump about something he had told us during our first session seven months earlier. He had mentioned back then that he had been asked to tape a public service announcement urging Americans to get their Covid vaccine shots. "They want me to do a commercial because it seems that a lot of people that are inclined to be with me don't like the concept of—you know, they're antivax," he said at the time, adding that he was considering doing it. People in the government had asked? "Yes," he said.

But months had passed and no Trump commercial materialized even as tens of millions of his people refused to get vaccinated, putting themselves at increased risk of death from the virus. So we asked why he had not spoken out after he had been asked to.

"Nope, they have not asked me," he told us.

But Trump was the one who had told us about it in the first place. We pointed that out. Was he sure?

"Not that I know of, no," Trump blithely responded.

Was he telling the truth the first time? The second? Neither? With Trump, one could never really tell.

Regardless, the bottom line was clear: the development of the Covid vaccine in record time constituted one of the most important achievements that occurred during Trump's presidency. He claimed to be "very proud" of it. But Trump would not advertise the vaccine to his millions of followers. He would not even tell the truth about his refusal to do so. Having fueled the schism in society over the pandemic, making masks and lockdowns and even belief that the virus existed into litmus tests in the tribal war between Red and Blue America, he now found that extraordinary scientific achievement defined by the same polarization. More than a million Americans would ultimately die in the pandemic, hundreds of thousands of them after a safe, effective vaccine was available. Yet Trump, who had been booed by his own fans at an Alabama rally that spring when he urged them to get the vaccine, had turned mostly quiet, reluctant to challenge his own base.

Of his many falsehoods, this lie to us was hardly one of the most egregious. Trump, after all, finished his presidency with a total of 30,573 false and misleading claims, according to the *Washington Post* fact-checking project. It was not even the biggest fabrication in our three and a half hours of conversation over two interviews with him, which featured his usual cocktail of misinformation and falsehood about matters large and small. But it underscored an important reality about the forty-fifth president and the movement he continued to lead even in his gilded Florida exile: Trump today is both the avatar of Trumpism and its hostage.

As he plotted his next move at Mar-a-Lago, Trump seemed like a surreal cross between Napoleon at Elba and banquet hall greeter. "Can I get you a drink?" he asked the first time we sat down in the lobby of the club he had styled the Winter White House, an open area where he now conducted most of his interviews as a form of post-presidential performance art. "Hello, folks, how are you?" he would greet guests, interrupting a long rant about "thousands and thousands of dead folks voting." Kimberly Guilfoyle in a sleeveless Kelly green cocktail dress wandered through at one point during our April 2021 interview, heading to a party on the terrace sponsored by Eric and Lara Trump to benefit pediatric cancer research.

"Are you going to stop by for a few minutes?" she asked.

"Yeah, I'll see you outside," Trump said.

What was the event? we asked after she left.

"I don't know," he confessed. Nonetheless, he would end the evening entertaining the crowd down by the pool, taking the microphone to welcome them after a hula dance show by young women in grass skirts.

A conversation with the former president was like a live-action reenactment of the Twitter feed he no longer had access to—rambling, bizarre, untruthful, and strikingly vituperative. Trump rarely answered a question directly, instead wandering off into some digressive riff, usually bringing the discussion back to the "rigged" election. He was jarringly incoherent, impossibly contradictory. There was rarely a noun, a verb, and a specific ending to a sentence.

He had a hard time keeping his story straight even in the same interview. One minute he said he did not march with protesters to the Capitol on January 6, as he told them he would, because "Secret Service wouldn't let me do it." Then less than thirty seconds later he said, "Well, I never told Secret Service." Then less than thirty seconds after that, he said again that the "Secret Service wouldn't let me go."

He likewise denied ever pressing for Joe Biden or his son to be prosecuted despite tweets doing exactly that. "I specifically didn't want them to go into Biden and I didn't want him to go after the son either because frankly I viewed that as a tragedy," he said, an assertion that would have surprised Bill Barr, who had been harangued by Trump demanding to know "where are all the arrests?"

The former president, strangely, dissembled even about his own well-documented family history. When we noted that his grandfather Frederick Trump died of influenza during the pandemic of 1918–19 (an outbreak that for some reason he always incorrectly identified as happening in 1917), he denied it. "Nope, he didn't die of that," Trump insisted. "He died of pneumonia. He went to Alaska and he died of pneumonia." In fact, he died seventeen years after leaving Alaska. The future president's father, Fred Trump, told the family biographer Gwenda Blair a dramatic story about how Frederick had succumbed to the Spanish flu, falling ill in the midst of a parade and dying within hours. "I never heard that," Trump insisted.

As he sat in Mar-a-Lago, Trump had little interest in hashing over the results of his presidency, positive or negative. When we asked about his accomplishments, Trump could barely think of what to mention, eventually settling awkwardly on the establishment of the Space Force for the American military and the defeat of the Islamic State in Syria. He waxed nostalgic about his "excellent" Helsinki summit with Vladimir Putin—and indeed, months later, on the eve of Putin's invasion of Ukraine he would praise the Russian's strategic "genius," and go on to oppose a major $40 billion American assistance package for Kyiv. The only regrets Trump expressed to us were that he was not able to push through all the tough policies he hoped to against America's allies, whether imposing tariffs on German cars or sticking up South Korea for $5 billion in payment for American troops stationed there—both preoccupations of his he told us he planned to pursue in a second term.

He had other achievements he could have boasted about, including renegotiating the North American Free Trade Agreement, signing a large package of tax cuts, increasing military spending, and curbing regulations, even if none of these actions was quite as sweeping as he liked to claim. He left a major impact on the federal judiciary, appointing 226 judges, including three conservative justices who would dramatically transform the Supreme Court and ultimately push for the reversal of *Roe v. Wade*. But policy was never what animated him, and his post-presidency, as his presidency, was more about personal grievance than what he did or didn't manage to get done in the job.

Some of Trump's misstatements when we spoke were repetitions of his greatest-hits whoppers from the 2020 campaign trail, and repeating them did not make them any more true. Trump, no matter how much he talked about it, never built the wall he promised. At the end of the day, 453 miles of steel bollards anchored in concrete went up, but most of it just replaced older barriers; only forty-seven miles of new primary wall were added along the two-thousand-mile border. And none of it was paid for by Mexico.

As always with Trump, he never stopped overstating even legitimately good news. The "best economy in history" was not really that. Even putting aside the pandemic, Trump's economy was roughly similar to what he inherited from Barack Obama, growing 7.7 percent and adding 6.2 million jobs during his first three years compared with 7.5 percent and 7.6 million new jobs in the previous three years. The stock market did significantly better; the S&P index grew 44 percent in Trump's first three years compared with 25 percent in Obama's final three years. But Trump failed to fulfill pledges to reduce the trade deficit (it went up instead) or revive the coal industry (it went down instead). The national debt, which Trump boasted he could wipe out in its entirety in eight years, instead increased by $7.8 trillion.

More broadly, America grew even more polarized in the Trump years. It was already a divided country when he took over; the schisms of society did not start with him. But he profited from the divisions and widened them. After four years of Trump's war on the truth—and on the independent media that challenged him—three quarters of Americans said that Republican and Democratic voters could no longer agree even on basic facts, much less plans and policies.

Trump took no responsibility for any of that, nor for any of the setbacks of his time—not for the rising tide of racist violence, not for the peace deal with the Taliban that when implemented by his successor would lead to the takeover of Afghanistan, not for the crushing toll of the pandemic. When Deborah Birx, his White House coronavirus coordinator, said after leaving office that the first 100,000 deaths from the virus were unavoidable but the rest were due to Trump's handling of the pandemic, the former president accepted no fault. "I did a great job with the pandemic," he insisted. Trump dismissed Birx, saying he never had any respect for her. "The only thing she did well was scarves," he said of her fashion sensibility.

In the course of our two sessions, Trump freely dispensed insults about many of those who worked with and for him, disparaging John Bolton ("a degenerate"), Chris Christie ("sloppy Chris"), Mark Esper ("just wasn't meant for the job"), John Kelly ("wasn't mentally fit for the job"), Jim Mattis ("the world's most overrated general"), H. R. McMaster ("a total lightweight"), Mark Milley ("one of the dumbest people in the world"), Jeff Sessions ("not up to the job"), and Marc Short ("Marc Long"). And those were just the people he had picked to advise him. He also did not think much of Joe Biden, Liz Cheney, James Comey, Ashraf Ghani, Andrew McCabe, John McCain, Angela Merkel, Lisa Page, Mitt Romney, Ben Sasse, Adam Schiff, Peter Strzok, Alexander Vindman, or Marie Yovanovitch.

Of all his many targets, Trump reserved special fury in both our interviews for Mitch McConnell, the "disloyal son of a bitch," a "schmuck," "stupid person," and "stiff" with "no personality" who was "like a dead fish." People he had no words of criticism for? Putin, Xi Jinping, Kim Jong-un, the January 6 rioters, or white supremacists.

For all that, Trump never explained why he hired so many stupid and mentally unfit people in the first place, much less what that would say about his judgment if they really were so incompetent. Jared Kushner left the White House concluding that poor personnel decisions represented the biggest problem of their administration. But Trump constructed ever-evolving explanations for why his own people turned on him. He explained Barr's apostasy on the election fraud claims as a response to being criticized. "When you start calling somebody a puppet," he said, the reaction was to say, "I'll do the exact opposite." Similarly, Trump decided that Brett Kavanaugh had ruled against his election lawsuits at the end because the justice's enemies "changed him" during the confirmation process. "Kavanaugh is petrified of still being impeached," he claimed.

As for his own vice president, Trump said he would not pick Mike Pence as his running mate if he ran again in 2024. January 6 was now the admissions test for being a Trump Republican, and the vice president who had risked his life to stand by his oath to the Constitution had, in Trump's view, failed. "It would be totally inappropriate," Trump said. "Mike committed political suicide by not taking votes that he knew were wrong."

Donald Trump was, by many measures, the most politically unsuccessful occupant of the White House in generations. He was the first president since Benjamin Harrison to lose the popular vote twice. He was the only president in the history of Gallup polling never to have the support of a majority of Americans for a single day of his tenure. Instead, surveys showed that he was the most polarizing president in the history of surveys. And he was the first president since Herbert Hoover to lose the White House, the House, and the Senate in just four years. As Trump himself might put it, he was not just a loser, but a big loser.

Yet Trump still emerged from a seven-million-vote defeat, two impeachments, and the January 6 insurrection as the dominant force in the Republican Party. He remains the undisputed frontrunner for its nomination in 2024 should he mount a comeback. In the months after his reluctant exit from the White House, he cowed Republicans like Kevin McCarthy, purged the party of those who stood against him, and set about stacking primaries for the upcoming 2022 midterm elections with his supporters.

Rather than disgrace and banishment, the normal fate for a president with such a record, Trump turned his big lie about the election into a post-presidential business model—and an unlikely formula for his own continued relevance. Practically no day went by in his new life when he did not bomb his followers' email inboxes with frenetic fundraising appeals and they responded by filling a war chest with $250 million in the weeks after the election, including for a fund that investigators found did not even exist, with much more to follow in the months to come. Many of the missives were signed by Trump's new favorite child, Don Jr., still a zealous promoter of his father's fantastic claims.

Trump's old favorite Ivanka and her husband, Jared Kushner, had taken up their far more tasteful exile in a Miami waterfront rental, waiting out the years of construction it would take to make their $32.2 million empty lot on an exclusive private island nearby ready for them. Indeed, construction was taking so long the couple purchased a second, $24 million mansion on the island to move into in the meantime. Kushner, no longer Trump's consigliere, turned away from American politics to monetize the network of relationships he built in the Middle East, including raising more than $2 billion for his private equity venture from a Saudi government investment fund which appeared to be acting on the direct order of his fellow princeling, Mohammed bin Salman. The former first lady, in theory in residence at Mar-a-Lago, was nowhere to be seen during our visits, although she too was pursuing her own moneymaking venture, in her case selling digital art and mementos of the Trump presidency on a Melania Trump–branded NFT platform, essentially a trendy effort to capitalize on the cryptocurrency boom. She even auctioned off the hat she wore during the French president's 2018 state visit, though the sale, poorly timed during a cryptocurrency bust, netted far less than the $250,000 she had asked for it.

If his family was fractured by the strains of the presidency, Trump's involuntary exit from office made him an object of almost religious faith to followers who continued to believe in his outlandish claims about the "stolen" 2020 election. A month after his second Senate impeachment trial, 65 percent of Republicans told pollsters they believed Joe Biden's victory resulted solely from voter fraud; by the one-year anniversary of the January 6 attack one poll found that 71 percent of Republicans thought Biden's victory was probably or definitely illegitimate. Trump may have even convinced himself; at some point he started telling allies that he expected to have the election annulled and to be reinstated as president, no matter that nothing in the Constitution permitted such a scenario.

His insistence on his alternate reality was relentless. "They cheated, they stole this election," he would say again and again, as if sheer repetition would make it true. "It's a fraud. Don't forget." Trump, as ever, was road-testing lines, test-marketing his next outrage, rewriting history.

"The insurrection took place on November 3," he insisted in our second interview. "What took place on January 6 was literally a protest." Trump must have thought the line worked; he was soon using it in the public statements he now sent by email since Twitter had banned him, and in the occasional interviews he granted to his cheering squad on Fox News.

It did not matter, to Trump or his followers, that not one independent authority, not one judge, not one prosecutor, not one election agency, not one official who was not a Trump partisan ever found widespread fraud. None. Even an audit in Arizona sponsored by Trump allies only confirmed the result. A federal judge described the effort to overturn the election as a "coup in search of a legal theory" and opined that Trump most likely committed conspiracy to defraud the United States and obstruct the work of Congress. A bipartisan House investigating committee concluded that Trump had committed a crime.

Those rejecting Trump's assertions included many of his own allies and advisers—two attorneys general, his election security chief, his campaign manager, lawyers, and advisers, Republican governors and secretaries of state, loyalists like Lindsey Graham, and even his oldest daughter and son-in-law.

Indeed, most of the people still circling in Trump's orbit knew he was promoting a fantasy yet went along with it, humoring the volatile deposed president. "None of us are willing to say to him, 'It wasn't stolen from you,'" one Trump campaign adviser confided to a Republican friend. Because if they did, the friend said, "he just goes into complete meltdown."

Mike Pompeo, who privately worried about the "crazies," said nothing of the sort publicly in hopes of running for president himself. Sarah Huckabee Sanders won the Republican nomination for governor of Arkansas with Trump's endorsement and refused to disavow his 2020 election lies. The Republican National Committee called the January 6 protest "legitimate public discourse." Even Mike Pence sought to avoid a running debate with Trump, before finally declaring more than a year after leaving office that "President Trump is wrong. I had no right to overturn the election."

Democrats, meanwhile, continued to chase after the fantasy of a knockout punch, a transformative moment when a federal prosecutor's indictment or an eviscerating judge's decision or an embarrassing defeat of one of his protégés would finally shatter Trump's armor and deliver the accountability he had managed to evade for so long. But a long-running criminal investigation of Trump's business by the Southern District of New York yielded no charges against him. His Trump-branded hotel in Washington's Old Post Office Building closed down, with no more Gulf princes seeking to hold events, but Trump did not go bankrupt. With crushing loans hanging over him, he simply found new lenders.

Some faced consequences even if Trump did not. Steve Bannon, granted a last-minute pardon by Trump for bilking Trump supporters, was indicted for contempt of Congress after defying a subpoena from the January 6 investigating committee. Giuliani's law license was suspended and he and Sidney Powell were sued for defamation stemming from their false claims; Powell defended herself by saying that "no reasonable person" would have believed her Kraken assertions "were truly statements of fact." Mark Meadows, who facilitated Trump's allegations of vote fraud, came under investigation for vote fraud himself after casting an absentee ballot from a mobile home in North Carolina where he did not live and had never even visited. Even that embarrassing disclosure did not cause Meadows to forswear his lies about the election—or the former president who told them.

On January 6, and in the days immediately afterward, it was still possible to envision a post-Trump world in America, one where Trump was expelled from the realm of active politics after having been the first defeated president in American history to refuse to accept his loss and the peaceful transfer of power that should have come with it. But it did not happen.

Trump, the Napoleon of Mar-a-Lago, knew little about history. But like the French emperor banished to Elba, his aspirations for a comeback could not be ruled out. History is full of similarly improbable might-have-beens. Just because no American president before or since Grover Cleveland has managed the feat of returning to office once cast out of it does not mean it cannot happen.

After Napoleon reclaimed the throne and was finally defeated once and for all at the Battle of Waterloo in 1815, the victorious British general, the Duke of Wellington, summed up the twelve-hour fight. It was, he wrote a friend, "the nearest-run thing you ever saw." John Kelly thought of Waterloo when he would tell the story about the time Trump almost blew up the NATO alliance at a Brussels summit less than twenty miles away from where the famous battle took place. "That was a very close-run thing," Kelly would say. Mark Milley thought of the famous quote about Waterloo when he considered how nearly the country came to losing its democracy altogether. "It was a very close-run thing," he told an associate. After it was all done and over, Milley believed that Trump had tried something never tried before in the 230 years of the republic—to illegitimately hold on to power.

And yet Trump today might very well regain the office he lost. In a second term, many of the restraints that inhibited Trump in the first would be gone. He would have no worry about a future election, assuming he respected the two-term limit in the Constitution. The threat of a third impeachment would hardly serve as a check either, given his survival the first two times. Trump would not make the same mistake of hiring advisers who stood up to him—he would choose matadors like Mark Meadows, not obstacles like John Kelly. He would pursue vengeance against his enemies. He would politicize the courts, the Justice Department, and the military. He would challenge allies and seek common cause with autocrats. We know he would do these things because those are exactly the things that he did and said for all four years of his first term in the presidency.

Even if he were not to run again, he would leave behind a Republican Party reborn in his image. Trump is already seventy-six years old, but there is a whole new generation of would-be Trumps waiting to succeed him—whether Ron DeSantis or Josh Hawley or Tucker Carlson. And while Trump failed in his effort to exact revenge on some of his Republican targets in party primaries in 2022, most notably Georgia's governor Brian Kemp and secretary of state Brad Raffensperger, his influence remained powerful and intoxicating. Even many Republicans who did not believe in him took the lesson that it was better not to overtly challenge his lies but to channel the forces he mastered for their own benefit. There will be no return to the pre-Trump era of American politics.

In the meantime, there was Trump himself, biding his time in Mar-a-Lago, still basking in the adulation of a crowd, no matter how diminished. Each evening that he was at his club, he would stage a grand entrance to his own patio for dinner. His table, theatrically cordoned off behind red velvet rope, sat empty waiting for him. He would stride in and the guests at the other tables would give him a standing ovation. On the spring night when we visited, Trump grinned and waved as if to acknowledge the applause of thousands, then sat down to eat with no company other than two young aides he had brought with him from the White House. When we left, Trump was talking on the phone as he finished dessert, one of Mar-a-Lago's signature vanilla ice cream sundaes. He smiled and flashed his trademark thumbs-up at us, happy—at least for the moment—in his forced retirement in his rococo palace by the sea.

Acknowledgments

Covering the presidency of Donald Trump was not what we thought we would be doing these last few years. Like the rest of Washington, we had a very different plan in mind on the night of November 8, 2016—to become foreign correspondents again, at least for a while. Peter planned to take a break from the White House, where he had long served as the chief correspondent for *The New York Times*, and with our son, Theo, had already taken up his new posting in Jerusalem. Susan was in Washington, in the newsroom of *Politico*, where she was the editor, overseeing the website's election coverage before heading overseas to join them that weekend.

At 1:03 a.m. East Coast time, Donald Trump had not claimed victory yet in the biggest upset in American history. But he was about to do so. Susan sent an email to Peter in Jerusalem. He had covered every president since Bill Clinton: How could he miss the epic story of disruption that a President Trump promised to usher in? The email read in its entirety: "Do you want to come back to DC for Trump?" A few weeks later, we did.

On January 20, 2017, as Trump was taking the oath of office and talking darkly of "American carnage," we were moving into a new house little more than a mile, and a whole alternate reality, away from the one we had left so recently. For the next few years, we would be foreign correspondents not in the Middle East but in Trump's Washington.

The idea for this book took shape two and a half years later, when we ran into Lindsey Graham on the street on a muggy September evening in 2019 at the start of Trump's first impeachment. Graham, who met Peter when Peter wrote his first book, *The Breach*, on Bill Clinton's impeachment, wondered if we now planned to write the story of Trump's. Graham's question got us started on a project that, with all the crises of 2020, eventually turned into this four-year history of Trump in the White House. So our thanks to the senator for that, all blame for the book that resulted of course being wholly our own.

We interviewed hundreds of people for *The Divider* and many of them were strikingly candid with us and generous with their time in explaining events that, to this day, are still hard to imagine. Many of them cannot be named, but you know who you are, and we thank you.

We have had the great fortune to work for many of the country's best independent news organizations, organizations that have been under attack in the last few years in ways that would have been unthinkable when we began our working life in Washington. We salute all our colleagues in the press corps who worked to cover the Trump administration while being denigrated as "enemies of the people"; you are true patriots and every page in this book is informed by your work and made better by the courage, diligence, critical thinking, and fortitude with which you did it. There have been so many important chroniclers of Trump and his presidency, too many to thank but in addition to our colleagues at the *Times* and *The New Yorker*, we would like to acknowledge the indispensable work of our friends at *The Washington Post*, *The Wall Street Journal*, *Politico*, *Axios*, the wire services, broadcast networks, cable news outlets, and magazines; and especially Tim Alberta, Michael Bender, Alexander Burns, Robert Costa, Josh Dawsey, Steve Holland, Carl Hulse, Jennifer Jacobs, Jonathan Karl, Jonathan Lemire, Carol Leonnig, Jonathan Martin, Jeff Mason, Anna Palmer, Ashley Parker, Jeremy Peters, Philip Rucker, Michael Schmidt, Jake Sherman, Jonathan Swan, and Bob Woodward. Glenn Kessler and his team of fact-checkers at the *Post* and Linda Qiu at the *Times* were invaluable. This book is built on the back of their unparalleled journalism.

We have the good fortune to work at two great institutions that have supported us and this work. At *The New York Times*, A. G. Sulzberger, Dean Baquet, and Joe Kahn have blessed us with commitment to journalistic excellence in tumultuous times. They stood strong and defended the role of independent journalism under ferocious assault. We thank them as well as Matt Purdy, Alison Mitchell, Dick Stevenson, Elizabeth Kennedy, and most especially Elisabeth Bumiller, who has run the Washington Bureau through these years of challenge with incredible energy and determination and been a wonderful editor and friend through it all. Michael Shear has been the best partner and best friend for three decades, endlessly supportive and wise. The coauthor of his own scoop-filled book on Trump, he took time out to read this manuscript and offer invaluable feedback. Maggie Haberman set the gold standard on Trump coverage and the rest of our team of Katie Rogers, Annie Karni, Michael Crowley, Julie Hirschfeld Davis, Mark Landler, and Glenn Thrush broke one jaw-dropping story after another; no one ever had better colleagues in a foxhole. And Peter is lucky today to work alongside Zolan Kanno-Youngs, David Sanger, and Jim Tankersley.

At *The New Yorker*, David Remnick remains without peer as the greatest magazine editor of our time; he is also a wonderful human being and ridiculously supportive of his writers and of fierce independent journalism. Susan has been privileged to work with many wonderful colleagues there, including Michael Luo, Dorothy Wickenden, and David Rohde, a true friend, advocate, and partner. Susan works beside some of the best writers in America in the magazine's Washington office, especially the great Jane Mayer, Adam Entous, Evan Osnos, and Margaret Talbot.

Both of us have found second television homes in the last few years—at MSNBC for Peter and CNN for Susan. We're deeply grateful to the hosts, producers, and bookers at both places, too many to name here, who put us on live television and, even when we were beaming in over Skype or Cisco from our living room, made it look easy. Even when Ellie barked, they never missed a beat. We are both grateful too to Jeff Bieber, Sandy Petrykowski, and the crew at PBS's *Washington Week*, where we have appeared going back more than two decades.

This is the third book now that Kris Puopolo at Doubleday has edited from one or both of us and we could not have a better, smarter, more supportive partner in this important project. She was endlessly patient with a generous it-ain't-over-till-it's-over approach to deadlines. Bill Thomas, the editor in chief at Doubleday, has offered unwavering support. The rest of the team at Doubleday has been remarkable to work with, including Carolyn Williams, Michael Goldsmith, Ana Espinoza, Anne Jaconette, Daniel Novack, Fred Chase, Milena Brown, Kristen Bearse, Zachary Lutz, Kathy Hourigan, and Michael Windsor. For nearly two dozen years now, Rafe Sagalyn has been our unfailing guide and unstinting advocate in the world of publishing. Doug Mills, who is as much a presidential historian as he is White House photographer, took the author picture for the book jacket.

Aidan Ryan contributed early research and a fantastic team of fact-checkers helped make the final version so much better, especially Shera Avi-Yonah, Christopher Cameron, Genevieve Glatsky, Hilary McClellen, and Jordan Virtue, who looked over so many chapters, as well as Delano Franklin and Lakshmi Varanasi. Needless to say, any remaining errors are our own.

Our friends have sustained us through long days and nights devoted to this project, which largely unfolded during the extended Covid lockdowns, making getting together in person both rarer and far more cherished. A special shout-out to our village of Martina Vandenberg and Alan, Marshall, and Max Cooperman, and our friends Heidi Crebo-Rediker and Doug and Charlotte Rediker. We are so lucky to live near Jane Mayer and Bill Hamilton, to have worked with each of them over the years, and to have benefited from their counsel and friendship for the entirety of our married life. In fact, even our marriage was very likely the result of Bill's good works; we are eternally in their debt.

So many others have supported us as well, including John Smith and Jan Eckendorf, whose fairy-tale wedding in a German castle was the high point of the pandemic; Heather McLeod Grant, a great friend since college and a dreamer of big plans for us ever since, and her wonderful family of Elliott and Somerset Grant; Susan Ascher and Paul and Audrey Kalb; Cristina Dominguez and Michael Grunwald; Julia Ioffe; Sarabeth Berman; Steven Weisman; Indira Lakshmanan and Dermot, Devan, and Rohan Tatlow; Valerie Mann and Tim Webster; Nicole Rabner and Andie Kanarek; and Sabrina Tavernise and Rory MacFarquhar. Susan's book club has been a source of support and delight for more than a decade, so thank you Nicole, Evan, Diana, Juleanna, Erin, Rachel, Autumn, Veronica, and Jen. And thanks as well to the wonderful class of '90 ladies and our special trips to Arizona that bookended the pandemic: Heather, Leslie, Becca, Robbie, and Amy.

The last few years have made us value friendship and times together more than ever. We also want to thank Deb Futter and Bill Cohan for a special summer and fall of seaside dinners when we were lucky enough to take a break from the daily news grind to work on this book.

Our family has once again been loving and supportive in every way possible and we are so grateful that our fathers, Ted and Steve, have been here with us, even through the pandemic and the trials of aging, cheering us on as we dug into yet another all-consuming project. We have learned so much from them and dedicate this book in part to them. We cherish the rest of our wonderful two families as well: Lynn Glasser; Linda and Keith Sinrod; Martha Baker; Karin Baker and Kait Nolan; Laura Glasser, Emily Allen, and Will and Ben Allen-Glasser; Jeff, Diana, Caroline, and Elizabeth Glasser; Jennifer Glasser and Matthieu, Alex, and Oliver Fulchiron; and Tiffany Hudson. Rosamaria Brizuela has been the key to our family's success and happiness for nearly eighteen years. And Ellie is the very definition of a good girl.

Finally, and most importantly, there is Theo Baker. Many of the milestones of his life have coincided with our sideline in book-writing; he was born on the day we finished our first book together and will move into his college dorm on the day this one is published. He has been endlessly patient with and supportive of our constant work, reading drafts and helping to find the photographs for this book even while finishing high school, cooking us delicious meals when he is at home, faithfully calling us every day as promised from school—even if often past our bedtime. We thank him for bringing us inspiration and joy every minute since he came into our life, and for always wanting the world to be a better place.

Notes

This book is primarily based on more than three hundred original interviews with White House officials, cabinet officers, members of Congress, generals, diplomats, business executives, and others, including two interviews with former President Trump. We also obtained contemporaneous notes, diaries, memos, and other documents provided by participants in the events, as well as relying on reporting we originally did as events unfolded for *The New York Times*, *The New Yorker*, and *Politico*. Most of the interviews were on background.

We have benefited from the enormous range of excellent books and real-time journalism about the Trump presidency, as well as the flood of memoirs that have emerged from key players, and wherever possible we have checked accounts against each other and sought to confirm them with the original sources. Below are notes of sources other than our own reporting. While President Trump's Twitter account has been suspended, his tweets are available through the Trump Twitter Archive online. For Trump's speeches and public comments, we relied heavily on the Trump White House website maintained by the National Archives and the American Presidency Project at the University of California at Santa Barbara.

CHAPTER 1. Ready, Set, Tweet

1. Michael Cohen, *Disloyal*, p. 177.
2. Ibid.
3. Corey R. Lewandowski and David N. Bossie, *Let Trump Be Trump*, p. 23.
4. Donald J. Trump, speech, June 30, 2015.
5. Donald J. Trump, campaign rally, Hilton Head, S.C., December 30, 2015.
6. The letter was released in December 2015. Dr. Harold Bornstein admitted to CNN in May 2017 that Trump dictated it. See Alex Marquardt and Lawrence Crook II, "Exclusive: Bornstein Claims Trump Dictated the Glowing Health Letter," CNN, May 2, 2018.
7. Madeleine Westerhout, *Off the Record*, pp. 165–67.
8. David E. Sanger and Maggie Haberman, "In Donald Trump's Worldview, America Comes First, and Everybody Else Must Pay," *The New York Times*, March 26, 2016.
9. Rick Gates, *Wicked Game*, p. 131.

10. Donald J. Trump with Tony Schwartz, *The Art of the Deal*, p. 364.

11. Donald J. Trump, interview with Chuck Todd, *Meet the Press*, NBC News, August 16, 2015.

12. John L. Helgerson, *Getting to Know the President*, p. 243.

13. Ibid., p. 268.

14. Trump attributed "the convincing argument" that narcissism is useful to Michael Maccoby, a psychoanalyst and consultant, but clearly is applying it to himself. See Donald J. Trump with Meredith McIver, *Trump: Think Like a Billionaire*, p. xvi.

15. Wayne Barrett, *Trump*, p. 130.

16. Jeremy W. Peters, *Insurgency*, p. 130.

17. Ibid., pp. 187–88.

18. Francis X. Clines, "Trump Quits Grand Old Party for New," *The New York Times*, October 25, 1999; and Steve Kornacki, "When Trump Ran Against Trump-ism: The 1990s and the Birth of Political Tribalism in America," NBC News, October 2, 2018.

19. Donald J. Trump, *Meet the Press*, NBC News, 1999.

20. "Trump Says He's a 'Very Big Second Amendment Person,'" Associated Press, October 4, 2015.

21. Mary L. Trump, *Too Much and Never Enough*, p. 103.

22. Trump also criticized the house, saying its rooms were too small and staircases too narrow and asserting that he would have done a better job. Eliana Johnson and Daniel Lippman, "Trump's 'Truly Bizarre' Visit to Mt. Vernon," *Politico*, April 10, 2019.

23. David Shulkin, *It Shouldn't Be This Hard to Serve Your Country*, p. 137.

24. Julie Hirschfeld Davis, "Obama's Moments of Freedom Send His Aides Scrambling," *The New York Times*, June 10, 2014.

25. The District of Columbia has voted in presidential elections since 1964 after passage of the Twenty-third Amendment. "Federal Elections 2016: Election Results for the U.S. President, the U.S. Senate and the U.S. House of Representatives," p. 28.

26. Michael S. Rosenwald, "Mar-a-Lago 3, Camp David 0. With Trump as President, Is the Rustic Md. Retreat Doomed?," *The Washington Post*, February 20, 2017.

27. Michael Scherer and Zeke J. Miller, "Trump After Hours," *Time*, May 11, 2017.

28. Westerhout, *Off the Record*, pp. 151–52.

29. Alexi McCammond and Jonathan Swan, "Scoop: Insider Leaks Trump's 'Executive Time'–Filled Private Schedules," *Axios*, February 3, 2019.

30. Maggie Haberman, Glenn Thrush, and Peter Baker, "Inside Trump's Hour-by-Hour Battle for Self-Preservation," *The New York Times*, December 9, 2017.

31. Michael M. Grynbaum, "Trump's Attack on Mika Brzezinski Draws Rebukes Across a Fractious Media," *The New York Times*, June 29, 2017. See also Cristina Caron, "Trump Mocks LeBron James's Intelligence and Calls Don Lemon 'Dumbest Man' on TV," *The New York Times*, August 4, 2018.

32. Michael D. Shear, Maggie Haberman, Nicholas Confessore, Karen Yourish, Larry Buchanan, and Keith Collins, "How Trump Reshaped the Presidency in Over 11,000 Tweets," *The New York Times*, November 2, 2019.

33. Ibid.

34. Westerhout, *Off the Record*, p. 213.

35. Donald J. Trump, Remarks at the Central Intelligence Agency in Langley, Virginia, January 21, 2017.

36. Scherer and Miller, "Trump After Hours."

37. Kevin Quealy, "The Complete List of Trump's Twitter Insults (2015–2021)," *The New York Times*, January 19, 2021.

38. Cliff Sims, *Team of Vipers*, p. xvii.

39. Aaron Blake, "President Trump Wants to Know Why He's Not Considered 'Elite,'" *The Washington Post*, June 21, 2018.

40. Peter Baker, "Instead of Evolving as President, Trump Has Bent the Job to His Will," *The New York Times*, August 27, 2020.

41. Jennifer Wang, "Donald Trump's Fortune Falls $800 Million to $3.7 Billion," *Forbes*, September 28, 2016.

42. Barbara Res, *Tower of Lies*, p. 12.

43. Jon Meacham, *Destiny and Power*, p. 326.

44. Cohen, *Disloyal*, p. 111.

45. Michael D'Antonio, interview with Don Lemon, CNN, August 15, 2019.

46. Donald J. Trump, Inaugural Address, January 20, 2017.

47. After *New York* magazine reported the comment citing three unnamed sources, Hillary Clinton included it in her campaign memoir, *What Happened*, but wrote "George W. Bush reportedly said," as if she were just conveying the media account. In later years, she freely acknowledged that he said it, as during an interview with Howard Stern on December 4, 2019. When asked by the authors, Bush said coyly that it had never been confirmed but allowed "it sounds like me." Clinton told the authors that it was "absolutely" accurate. See Yashar Ali, "What George W. Bush Really Thought of Trump's Inauguration," *New York*, March 2017; and Hillary Clinton, *What Happened*, p. 11.

48. Steve Bannon, interview, *Frontline*, PBS, March 17, 2019.

49. Ibid.

CHAPTER 2. Team of Amateurs

1. Steve Bannon, interview, *Frontline*, PBS, excerpted from interviews on March 17 and September 19, 2019.

2. "Trump: Paranoia Good for Business," *USA Today*, March 12, 2004.

3. Sally Bradshaw, a longtime adviser to Jeb Bush, was one of the project's co-chairs. See Shushannah Walshe, "RNC Completes 'Autopsy' on 2012 Loss, Calls for Inclusion Not Policy Change," ABC News, March 18, 2013.

4. Tim Alberta, *American Carnage*, p. 244.

5. Jeremy W. Peters, "Stephen Bannon Reassures Conservatives Uneasy About Trump," *The New York Times*, February 23, 2017.

6. Joshua Green, *Devil's Bargain*, p. 5.

7. Bannon *Frontline* interview.

8. Ibid.

9. Michael D. Shear, Maggie Haberman, and Alan Rappeport, "Donald Trump Picks Reince Priebus as Chief of Staff and Stephen Bannon as Strategist," *The New York Times*, November 13, 2016.

10. Kellyanne Conway, *Here's the Deal*, pp. 185 and 226.

11. Mary Jordan, *The Art of Her Deal*, pp. 234–35.

12. Stephanie Winston Wolkoff, *Melania and Me*, p. 157.

13. Ibid., p. 141.

14. Ibid., pp. 186–88.

15. Wayne Barrett, *Trump*, pp. 12–13.

16. Donald J. Trump, appearance with Ivanka Trump, on *The View*, March 6, 2006.

17. Rick Gates, *Wicked Game*, pp. 64–66.

18. Ibid.

19. Ibid.

20. Ibid.

21. Jennifer Senior, "Having Trouble Having It All? Ivanka Alone Can Fix It," *The New York Times*, May 2, 2017.

22. Sharon LaFraniere, Maggie Haberman, and Peter Baker, "Jared Kushner's Vast Duties, and Visibility in White House, Shrink," *The New York Times*, November 25, 2017.

23. Mark Salter, *The Luckiest Man*, p. 514.

24. Alberta, *American Carnage*, p. 375.

25. Rudy Giuliani transition dossier, obtained by *Axios* and posted online on June 25, 2019.

26. Robert M. Gates, "Sizing Up the Next Commander-in-Chief," *The Wall Street Journal*, September 16, 2016.
27. Dexter Filkins, "Rex Tillerson at the Breaking Point," *The New Yorker*, October 6, 2017.
28. Tillerson said this in an interview with the *Independent Journal Review*. See Louis Nelson, "'I Didn't Want This Job. I Didn't Seek This Job,'" *Politico*, March 22, 2017.
29. Gates, *Wicked Game*, pp. 74–78.
30. David Shulkin, *It Shouldn't Be This Hard to Serve Your Country*, p. 21.
31. Kim Darroch, *Collateral Damage*, p. 139.
32. Chris Cillizza, "This 34-Second Clip of President Trump Today Is Remarkably Eye-Opening," *The Washington Post*, January 20, 2017.
33. Alan Rappeport, "Who Is Mike Pence?," *The New York Times*, July 15, 2016.
34. Mike Pence, campaign website.
35. Michael Barbaro and Monica Davey, "Mike Pence: A Conservative Proudly Out of Sync with His Times," *The New York Times*, July 15, 2016.
36. Gates, *Wicked Game*, p. 37.
37. Author interview. See also Tom LoBianco, *Piety & Power*, p. 273.
38. Bannon *Frontline* interview.
39. Patrick Healy and Michael Barbaro, "Donald Trump Calls for Barring Muslims from Entering U.S.," *The New York Times*, December 7, 2015.
40. Michael Hastings, *The Operators*, p. 27.
41. Chris Christie, *Let Me Finish*, p. 258.
42. Ken Bensinger, Miriam Elder, and Mark Schoofs, "These Reports Allege Trump Has Deep Ties to Russia," *BuzzFeed News*, January 20, 2017.
43. David Ignatius, "Why Did Obama Dawdle on Russia's Hacking?," *The Washington Post*, January 12, 2017.
44. Greg Miller, Adam Entous, and Ellen Nakashima, "National Security Adviser Flynn Discussed Sanctions with Russian Ambassador, Despite Denials, Officials Say," *The Washington Post*, February 9, 2017.
45. Andrew McCabe, *The Threat*, p. 203.

CHAPTER 3. Never Put Rupert Murdoch on Hold!

1. Full Transcript and Video: Trump News Conference, *The New York Times*, February 17, 2017.
2. Craig Silverman, "How Teens in the Balkans Are Duping Trump Supporters with Fake News," *BuzzFeed News*, November 3, 2016.
3. Hillary Clinton remarks at Harry Reid portrait unveiling ceremony, December 8, 2016.
4. Susan B. Glasser, "Forced to Choose Between Trump's 'Big Lie' and Liz Cheney, the House G.O.P. Chooses the Lie," *The New Yorker*, May 6, 2021.
5. "Khrushchev's Secret Speech, 'On the Cult of Personality and Its Consequences,' Delivered at the Twentieth Party Congress of the Communist Party of the Soviet Union," February 26, 1956, Digital Archive, Woodrow Wilson International Center for Scholars.
6. Michael M. Grynbaum, "Trump Strategist Stephen Bannon Says Media Should 'Keep Its Mouth Shut,'" *The New York Times*, January 26, 2017.
7. Julie Hirschfeld Davis and Matthew Rosenberg, "With False Claims, Trump Attacks Media on Turnout and Intelligence Rift," *The New York Times*, January 21, 2017.
8. Alexandra Jaffe, "Kellyanne Conway: WH Spokesman Gave 'Alternative Facts' on Inauguration Crowd," NBC News, January 22, 2017.
9. Paul Bond, "Leslie Moonves on Donald Trump: 'It May Not Be Good for America, but It's Damn Good for CBS,'" *The Hollywood Reporter*, February 29, 2016.
10. Trump News Conference transcript, February 17, 2017.

11. Martin Baron, Recode's Code Media Conference, February 15, 2017.
12. "Lesley Stahl: Trump Admitted Mission to 'Discredit' Press," CBS News, May 23, 2018.
13. Madeleine Westerhout, *Off the Record*, p. 139.
14. "Is Donald Trump a Serious Candidate for President?," *The Five*, Fox News, June 16, 2015.
15. Rupert Murdoch, Twitter message, July 18, 2015.
16. Megyn Kelly, *Settle for More*, p. 244.
17. Transcript of the 2015 GOP Debate (9 p.m.), CBS News, August 7, 2015.
18. John Koblin, "Republican Debate Draws 24 Million Viewers," *The New York Times*, August 7, 2015.
19. Brian Stelter, *Hoax*, p. 56.
20. Holly Yan, "Donald Trump's 'Blood' Comment About Megyn Kelly Draws Outrage," CNN, August 8, 2015.
21. Jane Mayer, "The Making of the Fox News White House," *The New Yorker*, March 4, 2019.
22. Rick Gates, *Wicked Game*, p. 96.
23. Gabriel Sherman, Twitter message, April 12, 2017.
24. Data from Mark Knoller, the longtime CBS News correspondent and unofficial archivist of White House activities.
25. Peter Baker, "From an Anchor's Lips to Trump's Ears to Sweden's Disbelief," *The New York Times*, February 21, 2017.
26. Ibid.
27. Matt Gertz, "STUDY: Trump Sent 657 Live Tweets of Fox Programming in 2019," Media Matters for America, January 19, 2020.
28. Stelter, *Hoax*, p. 254.
29. Jim Jordan, *Do What You Said You Would Do*, p. 138.
30. Matthew Shaer, "How Far Will Sean Hannity Go?," *The New York Times Magazine*, November 28, 2017.
31. Fox News press releases, December 12, 2017, and December 16, 2020.
32. Kelly, *Settle for More*, p. 241.
33. L. Brent Bozell, interview on Fox News, January 22, 2016; and L. Brent Bozell III, contribution to a symposium titled "Conservatives Against Trump," *National Review*, January 22, 2016.
34. Tim Alberta, *American Carnage*, pp. 363–64.
35. Ibid., pp. 267–69.
36. Larry O'Connor, "Mediaite Deep Dive: Hugh Hewitt Tells Never Trumpers to 'Find the Good and Praise It,'" *Mediaite*, August 9, 2017.
37. Brian Stelter, "Donald Trump Rips into Possible AT&T–Time Warner Deal," CNN, October 22, 2016.
38. Ben Smith, "Jeff Zucker Helped Create Donald Trump. That Show May Be Ending," *The New York Times*, September 20, 2020.
39. Cecilia Kang and Kenneth P. Vogel, "AT&T Chief Says It Made a 'Big Mistake' Hiring Michael Cohen," *The New York Times*, May 11, 2018.
40. "No Big Worries in AT&T Deal for Time Warner," BNN Bloomberg, October 24, 2016.
41. Hamza Shaban, "Trump's New Attorney General Had Charged Justice Department's Antitrust Chief with Giving an 'Inaccurate' Account of Meeting with Time Warner," *The Washington Post*, December 7, 2018.
42. Sarah Huckabee Sanders, Press Briefing, December 14, 2017.
43. Jill Brooke, "The Real Story Behind Donald Trump's Infamous 'Best Sex I've Ever Had' Headline," *The Hollywood Reporter*, April 12, 2018.
44. "Excerpts: The Times Publisher Asks Trump About Anti-Press Rhetoric," *The New York Times*, February 1, 2019.

45. Glenn Kessler and Michelle Ye Hee Lee, "Fact-Checking President Trump's News Conference," *The Washington Post*, February 16, 2017.
46. Trump News Conference transcript, February 17, 2017.

CHAPTER 4. Allies and Adversaries

1. Glenn Plaskin, "The Playboy Interview with Donald Trump," *Playboy*, March 1, 1990.
2. Susan B. Glasser, "How Trump Made War on Angela Merkel and Europe," *The New Yorker*, December 17, 2018.
3. Ibid.
4. Ibid. See also Ben Rhodes, *The World As It Is*, p. xiii.
5. Brian Mulroney, *Memoirs*, p. 534.
6. David Von Drehle, "Is Steve Bannon the Second Most Powerful Man in the World?," *Time*, February 2, 2017.
7. Glasser, "How Trump Made War on Angela Merkel and Europe."
8. Greg Miller, Julie Vitkovskaya, and Reuben Fischer-Baum, "'This Deal Will Make Me Look Terrible': Full Transcripts of Trump's Calls with Mexico and Australia," *The Washington Post*, August 3, 2017.
9. Strobe Talbott, interview with Susan B. Glasser, *Politico*, June 5, 2017.
10. Kevin Liptak, "At Mar-a-Lago, Trump Tackles Crisis Diplomacy at Close Range," CNN, February 13, 2017.
11. Patrick Radden Keefe, "McMaster and Commander," *The New Yorker*, April 23, 2018.
12. H. R. McMaster, *Dereliction of Duty*.
13. Versions of this quote appeared in Michael Wolff, *Fire and Fury*; Peter Bergen, *Trump and His Generals*; Bob Woodward, *Fear*; and Keefe, "McMaster and Commander."
14. Colin Kahl, now-deleted Twitter messages. See Samantha Power Twitter message, March 16, 2017.
15. Jacob M. Schlesinger and Bojan Pancevski, "Summit Looms for a Strained NATO Alliance," *The Wall Street Journal*, July 9, 2018.
16. David D. Kirkpatrick, "Who Is Behind Trump's Links to Arab Princes? A Billionaire Friend," *The New York Times*, June 13, 2018.
17. David D. Kirkpatrick, Ben Hubbard, Mark Landler, and Mark Mazzetti, "The Wooing of Jared Kushner: How the Saudis Got a Friend in the White House," *The New York Times*, December 8, 2018.
18. Ibid.
19. This section from author interviews as well as Susan B. Glasser, "Can a 'Wrecking Ball' of a President Evolve?," *Politico*, February 13, 2017.
20. "Transcript and Video: Trump Speaks About Strikes in Syria," *The New York Times*, April 6, 2017.
21. Donald J. Trump, interview with Maria Bartiromo, Fox Business, posted online, April 12, 2017.
22. Lauren Gambino, "Trump's Attack on Syria Was 'After-Dinner Entertainment' Says US Commerce Secretary," *The Guardian*, May 2, 2017.
23. "Zakaria: Trump Just Became President," CNN, April 7, 2017.
24. Elliott Abrams, "The Strike At Syria," *Washington Examiner*, April 7, 2017. *The Weekly Standard* website on which Abrams originally published this is no longer available after its owner shut down the publication and moved its archives to the more Trump-friendly *Examiner* site he also owned.
25. Trump interview with Maria Bartiromo.
26. Stephen J. Adler, Steve Holland, and Jeff Mason, "Exclusive: Trump Says 'Major, Major' Conflict with North Korea Possible, but Seeks Diplomacy," Reuters, April 28, 2017.

27. "Lt. Gen. H. R. McMaster on Foreign Policy; Sen. Schumer on President Trump's First 100 Days," *Fox News Sunday*, April 30, 2017.
28. Maggie Severns, "Trump Pins NAFTA, 'Worst Trade Deal Ever,' on Clinton," *Politico*, September 26, 2016.
29. Binyamin Appelbaum and Glenn Thrush, "Trump's Day of Hardball and Confusion on Nafta," *The New York Times*, April 27, 2017.
30. Ibid.
31. Ashley Parker, Philip Rucker, Damian Paletta, and Karen DeYoung, "'I Was All Set to Terminate': Inside Trump's Sudden Shift on NAFTA," *The Washington Post*, April 27, 2017.
32. Ibid.
33. Peter Baker, "For Tillerson, Diplomatic Breakthrough with Trump Proves Elusive," *The New York Times*, October 5, 2017.
34. Peter Baker and Michael D. Shear, "Trump Softens Tone on Islam but Calls for Purge of 'Foot Soldiers of Evil,'" *The New York Times*, May 21, 2017.
35. Kim Darroch, *Collateral Damage*, p. 201.
36. Susan B. Glasser, "The 27 Words Trump Wouldn't Say," *Politico*, June 6, 2017.
37. H. R. McMaster and Gary D. Cohn, "America First Doesn't Mean America Alone," *The Wall Street Journal*, May 30, 2017.
38. Jon Henley, "Angela Merkel: EU Cannot Completely Rely on US and Britain Any More," *The Guardian*, May 28, 2017.

CHAPTER 5. The Ghost of Roy

1. Report on the Investigation into Russian Interference in the 2016 Presidential Election (Mueller Report), Volume II, p. 65.
2. Senator Bob Casey, Democrat of Pennsylvania, said "Nixonian," while Senator Richard Blumenthal, Democrat of Connecticut, said "not since Watergate." See Peter Baker, "In Trump's Firing of Comey, Echoes of Watergate," *The New York Times*, May 9, 2017.
3. Report of the Select Committee on Intelligence, United States Senate, on Russian Active Measures Campaigns and Interference in the 2016 U.S. Election.
4. Rosalind S. Helderman, "Here's What We Know About Donald Trump and His Ties to Russia," *The Washington Post*, July 29, 2016.
5. Eric Trump reportedly made the comment to James Dodson, a golf writer, who described it in an interview after Donald Trump took office. Eric Trump denied making the comment. Bill Littlefield, "A Day (And a Cheeseburger) with President Trump," WBUR, May 11, 2017.
6. Trump bought the Maison de L'Amitié ("House of Friendship") in a bankruptcy in 2004, had a contestant from *The Apprentice* renovate it, and sold it in 2008 to Dmitry Rybolovlev, a fertilizer tycoon and then number fifty-nine on the *Forbes* list of billionaires. Arlene Satchell, *South Florida Sun-Sentinel*, July 18, 2008. Rybolovlev tore down the mansion and sold the property in three parts for a combined $108 million. See Keith Larsen, "Russian Oligarch Sells Last Piece of Former Trump Estate in Palm Beach for $37M," *The Real Deal*, July 8, 2019.
7. Alexandra Clough, "'Don't Say Russian': Trump Didn't Want to ID Palm Beach Mansion Buyer," *The Palm Beach Post*, September 15, 2020.
8. Anita Kumar, "Buyers Tied to Russia, Former Soviet Republics Paid $109 Million Cash for Trump Properties," McClatchy, June 19, 2018.
9. Donald J. Trump, interview on *Meet the Press*, NBC News, December 20, 2015; and Donald J. Trump, interview with Bill O'Reilly on Fox News. See Reena Flores, "Donald Trump Gives Russia's Putin an 'A' in Leadership," CBS News, September 30, 2015.

10. "Donald Trump Running for President," *The O'Reilly Factor*, Fox News, June 16, 2015.

11. Transcript: Donald Trump's Foreign Policy Speech, *The New York Times*, April 27, 2016.

12. Donald J. Trump, interview with George Stephanopoulos. Transcript, ABC News, July 31, 2016.

13. Ashley Parker and David E. Sanger, "Donald Trump Calls on Russia to Find Hillary Clinton's Missing Emails," *The New York Times*, July 27, 2016.

14. Donald J. Trump, news conference, July 27, 2016.

15. Jo Becker, Adam Goldman, and Matt Apuzzo, "Russian Dirt on Clinton? 'I Love It,' Donald Trump Jr. Said," *The New York Times*, July 11, 2017.

16. Donald J. Trump, interview with MSNBC, November 2013; and Donald J. Trump, interview with David Letterman, October 17, 2013.

17. Donald J. Trump, remarks at National Press Club, May 27, 2014. See Andrew Kaczynski, Chris Massie, and Nathan McDermott, "80 Times Trump Talked About Putin," CNN.

18. Republican Debate, Milwaukee, November 10, 2015.

19. Charlotte Alter, "Here's the Deal with That Putin *60 Minutes* Episode Trump Mentioned," *Time*, November 11, 2015.

20. Kaczynski, Massie, and McDermott, "80 Times Trump Talked About Putin."

21. Donald J. Trump, interview with Bill O'Reilly, Fox News, February 5, 2017.

22. Cohen, *Disloyal*, p. 257.

23. Susan Hennessey and Benjamin Wittes, *Unmaking the Presidency*, pp. 155–56.

24. Jessica Sidman, "Trump Hotel Employees Reveal What It Was Really Like Catering to the Right Wing Elite," *Washingtonian*, February 19, 2021.

25. United States Constitution, Article I, Section 9, Clause 8.

26. Shane Goldmacher, "Trump Foundation Will Dissolve, Accused of 'Shocking Pattern of Illegality,'" *The New York Times*, December 18, 2018.

27. Mueller Report, Volume II, p. 33.

28. James Comey, *A Higher Loyalty*, p. 243.

29. Ibid., p. 238.

30. Mueller Report, Volume II, p. 38.

31. James B. Comey, untitled memorandum, February 14, 2017.

32. James B. Comey, untitled memorandum, April 11, 2017.

33. Bob Woodward, *Fear*, p. 268.

34. Ken Auletta used the word, for example, with Michael Kruse in "He Brutalized for You," *Politico Magazine*, April 8, 2016.

35. Jonathan Mahler and Steve Eder, "'No Vacancies' for Blacks: How Donald Trump Got His Start, and Was First Accused of Bias," *The New York Times*, August 27, 2016.

36. Donald Trump, *Trump: Art of the Deal*, p. 99. With Tony Schwartz.

37. "Realty Outfit Loses Suit for 100-Million," *The New York Times*, January 26, 1974.

38. Michael Kranish and Robert O'Harrow Jr., "Inside the Government's Racial Bias Case Against Donald Trump's Company, and How He Fought It," *The Washington Post*, January 23, 2016.

39. Arthur Villasanta, "Trump's Tax Break Cost New York $410 Million in Revenue," *International Business Times*, January 22, 2020; and Charles V. Bagli, "A Trump Empire Built on Inside Connections and $885 Million in Tax Breaks," *The New York Times*, September 17, 2016.

40. Kruse, "He Brutalized for You."

41. Wayne Barrett, *Trump*, pp. 156, 125.

42. Kruse, "He Brutalized for You."

43. Barrett, *Trump*, p. 81.

44. Mary Trump, *Too Much and Never Enough*, p. 189.

45. Barrett, *Trump*, pp. 278–79.

46. David L. Marcus, "Trump Is a Lot Like His Mentor, My Cousin Roy Cohn. Now He's Leaving Like Him, in Disgrace," *USA Today*, January 20, 2021.
47. Mueller Report, Volume II, p. 117.
48. Don McGahn, interview by House Judiciary Committee, June 4, 2021, p. 161.
49. Adam Goldman, "James Comey 'Mildly Nauseous' over Idea He Swayed the Election," *The New York Times*, May 3, 2017.
50. Mueller Report, Volume II, p. 64.
51. Ibid., p. 65.
52. Rod J. Rosenstein, Memorandum for the Attorney General, May 9, 2017. Posted by *The New York Times*.
53. Jenna Johnson, "After Trump Fired Comey, White House Staff Scrambled to Explain Why," *The Washington Post*, May 10, 2017.
54. Daily Briefing by Principal Deputy Press Secretary Sarah Sanders, May 10, 2017. See also Mueller Report, Volume II, p. 72.
55. Jeff Zeleny and Eugene Scott, "Pence: Comey's Firing Wasn't Due to Russia Probe," CNN, May 10, 2017.
56. Matt Apuzzo, Maggie Haberman, and Matthew Rosenberg, "Trump Told Russians That Firing 'Nut Job' Comey Eased Pressure from Investigation," *The New York Times*, May 19, 2017.
57. Donald J. Trump, interview with Lester Holt, NBC News, May 11, 2017.
58. James Comey, Senate testimony, video posted by the Associated Press, June 8, 2017.
59. Andrew G. McCabe, Untitled Memorandum, May 16, 2017. Posted by Judicial Watch.
60. Author interview. See also Mueller Report, Volume II, p. 78.
61. Ibid. See also Chris Whipple, *The Gatekeepers*, paperback edition.
62. Adam Goldman and Michael S. Schmidt, "Trump's Nominee to Lead F.B.I. Pledges to Resist White House Pressure," *The New York Times*, July 12, 2017.
63. Mueller Report, Volume II, p. 80.
64. Jo Becker, Matt Apuzzo, and Adam Goldman, "Trump Team Met with Lawyer Linked to Kremlin During Campaign," *The New York Times*, July 8, 2017.
65. Omarosa Manigault Newman, *Unhinged*, p. 183.
66. Ivana Trump, *Raising Trump*, p. 63.
67. Marie Brenner, "After the Gold Rush," *Vanity Fair*, September 1990.
68. Cohen, *Disloyal*, pp. 97–98.
69. Aaron Blake, "Donald Trump Jr. Says Media Would Be 'Warming Up the Gas Chamber' if Trump Lied Like Clinton," *The Washington Post*, September 15, 2016.
70. Manigault Newman, *Unhinged*, p. 106.
71. David A. Fahrenthold and Jonathan O'Connell, "From Rebellious to Reliable," *The Washington Post*, November 15, 2018.
72. Peter Baker, Michael Schmidt, and Maggie Haberman, "Citing Recusal, Trump Says He Wouldn't Have Hired Sessions," *The New York Times*, July 19, 2017.

CHAPTER 6. My Generals

1. President Trump's Cabinet Meeting, June 12, 2017.
2. James Mattis, U.S. Military Academy Commencement 2017, May 28, 2017.
3. Susan B. Glasser, "Trump National Security Team Blindsided by NATO Speech," *Politico Magazine*, June 5, 2017.
4. President Donald Trump Speaks at Inaugural Luncheon, January 20, 2017.
5. Dexter Filkins, "James Mattis, a Warrior in Washington," *The New Yorker*, May 22, 2017.
6. Gretel C. Kovach, "Just Don't Call Him Mad Dog," *The San Diego Union-Tribune*, January 19, 2013.

7. Ibid.
8. Phil Stewart and Idrees Ali, "Russia, Iran Likely Focus at Hearing on Trump Pick for Defense Chief," Reuters, January 12, 2017.
9. Filkins, "James Mattis, a Warrior in Washington."
10. David Ignatius, "Joseph Dunford's Steady Hand in the Turmoil of Trump's Washington," *The Washington Post*, September 12, 2019.
11. Susan B. Glasser, "The Trump White House's War Within," *Politico*, July 24, 2017.
12. Ibid.
13. H. R. McMaster and Gary D. Cohn, "America First Doesn't Mean America Alone," *The Wall Street Journal*, May 30, 2017.
14. Bob Woodward, *Fear*, p. 133.
15. Rosie Gray, "Erik Prince's Plan to Privatize the War in Afghanistan," *The Atlantic*, August 18, 2017.
16. See for example Tony Lee, "White House Globalists Form 'Committee to Save America'—From Trump and His Voter Base," *Breitbart News*, August 10, 2017.
17. Fiona Hill, *There Is Nothing for You Here*, p. 245. See also Adam Entous, "What Fiona Hill Learned in the White House," *The New Yorker*, June 22, 2020.
18. Timothy Johnson, "Former NSC Staffer Fiona Hill Testified About Receiving Death Threats After Being Labeled a 'Soros Mole.' It Started with Roger Stone," Media Matters for America, November 8, 2019.
19. Rosie Gray, "An NSC Staffer Is Forced Out over a Controversial Memo," *The Atlantic*, August 2, 2017.
20. See accounts of the Tank meeting by Philip Rucker and Carol Leonnig, *A Very Stable Genius*; Woodward, *Fear*; and Peter Bergen, *Trump's Generals*. Our account is based primarily on original author interviews with participants, including several who have not previously spoken.
21. Ryan Lizza, "Anthony Scaramucci Called Me to Unload About White House Leakers, Reince Priebus, and Steve Bannon," *The New Yorker*, July 27, 2017.
22. Nick Miroff, "In Latin America, John Kelly Trained for a Job Serving Trump," *The Washington Post*, January 7, 2018.
23. Molly O'Toole, "Ex-General to Top Brass: Stay Out of the 'Cesspool of Domestic Politics,'" *Foreign Policy*, July 11, 2016.
24. Ibid.
25. Glenn Thrush and Peter Baker, "Trump's Threat to North Korea Was Improvised," *The New York Times*, August 9, 2017.
26. Peter Baker and Gardiner Harris, "Deep Divisions Emerge in Trump Administration as North Korea Threatens War," *The New York Times*, August 9, 2017.
27. Peter Baker, "Trump Says Military Is 'Locked and Loaded' and North Korea Will 'Regret' Threats," *The New York Times*, August 11, 2017.
28. Glenn Thrush and Maggie Haberman, "Trump Gives White Supremacists an Unequivocal Boost," *The New York Times*, August 15, 2017.
29. Lauren Fox, "Paul Ryan: Trump 'Messed Up' Charlottesville Response," CNN, August 22, 2017.
30. Cliff Sims, *Team of Vipers*, pp. 202–3.
31. Demetri Sevastopulo and Gillian Tett, "Gary Cohn Urges Trump Team to Do More to Condemn Neo-Nazis," *Financial Times*, August 25, 2017.
32. Sims, *Team of Vipers*, p. 198.
33. Fred Barbash, "Bannon: Trump Firing of Comey Was the Biggest Mistake 'Maybe in Modern Political History,'" *The Washington Post*, September 11, 2017.
34. Vicky Ward, *Kushner, Inc.*, p. 138.
35. Robert Kuttner, "Steve Bannon, Unrepentant," *The American Prospect*, August 16, 2017.
36. Donald J. Trump, Address to the Nation on United States Strategy in Afghanistan and South Asia from Joint Base Myer-Henderson Hall, Virginia, August 21, 2017.

37. Stephanie Winston Wolkoff, *Melania and Me*, p. 113.
38. Guy Snodgrass, *Holding the Line*, p. 206.

CHAPTER 7. The Adhocracy

1. Stephanie Grisham, *I'll Take Your Questions Now*, p. 34.
2. Cliff Sims, *Team of Vipers*, p. 152.
3. Roger B. Porter, *Presidential Decision Making*, p. 25.
4. John F. Kelly and Rob Porter, Memorandum for Cabinet Officials and Assistants to the President, "Paper Flow to and from the President," August 21, 2017, obtained by authors.
5. Ron Nixon, "Coast Guard Still Supports Transgender Troops, Commandant Says," *The New York Times*, August 1, 2017.
6. John F. Kelly and Rob Porter, Memorandum for Cabinet Officials and Assistants to the President, "Securing Presidential Decisions," August 21, 2017, obtained by authors.
7. Matt Flegenheimer and Maggie Haberman, "Mitch McConnell's 'Excessive Expectations' Comment Draws Trump's Ire," *The New York Times*, August 9, 2017.
8. Ibid.
9. Matt Flegenheimer, "Deepening Rift, Trump Won't Say if Mitch McConnell Should Step Down," *The New York Times*, August 10, 2017.
10. Peter Baker, Thomas Kaplan, and Michael D. Shear, "Trump Bypasses Republicans to Strike Deal on Debt Limit and Harvey Aid," *The New York Times*, September 6, 2017.
11. Peter Baker and Sheryl Gay Stolberg, "Energized Trump Sees Bipartisan Path, at Least for Now," *The New York Times*, September 7, 2017.
12. Peter Baker, "Instead of Evolving as President, Trump Has Bent the Job to His Will," *The New York Times*, August 27, 2020.
13. Peter Baker, "Bound to No Party, Trump Upends 150 Years of Two-Party Rule," *The New York Times*, September 9, 2017.
14. Miranda Green, "At Values Voter Summit, Bannon Declares 'War' on GOP Establishment," CNN, October 16, 2017.
15. Michael D. Shear and Sheryl Gay Stolberg, "Trump and McConnell Strive for Comity Among Rising Tensions," *The New York Times*, October 17, 2017.
16. Russell Berman, "A Remarriage of Convenience Between Donald Trump and Mitch McConnell," *The Atlantic*, October 16, 2017.
17. Kim Darroch, *Collateral Damage*, p. 176.
18. Peter Baker and Rick Gladstone, "With Combative Style and Epithets, Trump Takes America First to the U.N.," *The New York Times*, September 19, 2017.
19. Michael D. Shear, "Leading Homeland Security Under a President Who Embraces 'Hate-Filled' Talk," *The New York Times*, July 10, 2020.
20. Daniel Dale, "Trump Defends Tossing Paper Towels to Puerto Rico Hurricane Victims: Analysis," *Toronto Star*, October 8, 2017.
21. Peter Baker and David E. Sanger, "Trump Says Tillerson Is 'Wasting His Time' on North Korea," *The New York Times*, October 1, 2017.
22. The first report quoting Tillerson saying "moron" came from Carol E. Lee, Kristen Welker, Stephanie Ruhle, and Dafna Linzer, "Tillerson's Fury at Trump Required an Intervention from Pence," NBC News, October 4, 2017. The adjective "fucking" was added by Dexter Filkins, "Rex Tillerson at the Breaking Point," *The New Yorker*, October 6, 2017.
23. Randall Lane, "Inside Trump's Head: An Exclusive Interview with the President, and the Single Theory That Explains Everything," *Forbes*, October 10, 2017.

24. Devlin Barrett, "DHS Secretary Kelly Says Congressional Critics Should 'Shut Up,' or Change Laws," *The Washington Post*, April 18, 2017.
25. Mark Landler and Yamiche Alcindor, "Trump's Condolence Call to Soldier's Widow Ignites an Imbroglio," *The New York Times*, October 18, 2017.
26. Yamiche Alcindor and Michael D. Shear, "After Video Refutes Kelly's Charges, Congresswoman Raises Issue of Race," *The New York Times*, October 20, 2017.
27. Maggie Astor, "John Kelly Pins Civil War on a 'Lack of Ability to Compromise,'" *The New York Times*, October 31, 2017.
28. Tara Palmeri, "'The Cut Cut Cut Act': Trump, Hill Leaders Differ on Tax Overhaul Bill's Name," ABC News, November 2, 2017.
29. Author interview. See also Sims, *Team of Vipers*, p. 249.
30. Sims, *Team of Vipers*, p. 249.
31. The tax credit increase was also limited in that it would expire in 2025 unless renewed. See "2017 Tax Law's Child Credit: A Token or Less-Than-Full Increase for 26 Million Kids in Working Families," Center on Budget and Policy Priorities, August 27, 2018.
32. Cristina Marcos, "GOP Lawmaker: Donors Are Pushing Me to Get Tax Reform Done," *The Hill*, November 7, 2017. Collins, the first member to endorse Trump for president, would later be convicted and sent to prison for insider trading stemming from frantic phone calls he made to his son from the White House Lawn sharing confidential information about a drug company.
33. Thomas Kaplan and Alan Rappeport, "Republican Tax Bill Passes Senate in 51–48 Vote," *The New York Times*, December 19, 2017; Thomas Kaplan, "House Gives Final Approval to Sweeping Tax Overhaul," *The New York Times*, December 20, 2017.
34. John Wagner, "Republicans Celebrate Their Tax Bill—and Heap Praise on Trump," *The Washington Post*, December 20, 2017.
35. Kathryn Watson, "'You All Just Got a Lot Richer,' Trump Tells Friends, Referencing Tax Overhaul," CBS News, December 24, 2017.
36. Michael Rothfeld and Joe Palazzolo, "Trump Lawyer Arranged $130,000 Payment for Adult-Film Star's Silence," *The Wall Street Journal*, January 12, 2018.
37. Emily Jane Fox, "Michael Cohen Would Take a Bullet for Donald Trump," *Vanity Fair*, September 6, 2017.
38. "Trump Says He Did Not Know About $130,000 Payment to Stormy Daniels," Reuters, April 5, 2018.
39. Grisham, *I'll Take Your Questions Now*, p. 107.
40. Ibid., p. 108.
41. Ibid., p. 60.
42. Sara James, "Memo Pad: Martha Speaks," *Women's Wear Daily*, May 6, 2005.
43. Stephanie Winston Wolkoff, *Melania and Me*, pp. 4–6.
44. Grisham, *I'll Take Your Questions Now*, pp. 114–17.
45. Ibid., p. 119.
46. Jonathan Karl, *Front Row at the Trump Show*, p. 207.
47. Peter Navarro and Greg Autry, *Death by China*, p. 8.
48. Elizabeth Warren, Twitter message, August 7, 2018.
49. "Exclusive: Omarosa Reveals Secret White House Recording with John Kelly," *Meet the Press Daily*, MSNBC, August 12, 2018.
50. Corey R. Lewandowski and David N. Bossie, *Trump: America First*, p. 22.
51. Martin Gould, "EXCLUSIVE: White House Romance! Trump's Comms Director Hope Hicks Is Seen Canoodling with President's High Level Staff Secretary Rob Porter," *Daily Mail*, February 1, 2018.
52. Louise Boyle, "EXCLUSIVE: 'He Pulled Me, Naked and Dripping from the Shower to Yell at Me.' Ex-Wife of Trump Aide Rob Porter Who's Dating Hope Hicks, Tells How He Called Her a 'F***ing B***h' on Their Honeymoon and She Filed a Protective Order Against Him," *Daily Mail*, February 6, 2018.

53. Louise Boyle, "EXCLUSIVE: 'He Can Go from Being the Sweetest Person to a Complete Abusive Monster.' Woman Who Was Living with Trump Aide Rob Porter at the Time He Began Dating Hope Hicks Confided to His Ex-Wives About Living in Fear," *Daily Mail*, February 7, 2018.

54. Ryan Grim and Alleen Brown, "Former Wives of Top White House Aide Rob Porter Both Told FBI He Abused Them," *The Intercept*, February 7, 2018.

55. Andrew Restuccia and Eliana Johnson, "White House Aide Rob Porter Resigns After Allegations from Ex-Wives," *Politico*, February 7, 2018.

56. Maggie Haberman and Katie Rogers, "Rob Porter, White House Aide, Resigns After Accusations of Abuse," *The New York Times*, February 7, 2021; and Katie Rogers, "Rob Porter's Charisma and Ambition Disguised Flare-ups of Anger," *The New York Times*, February 19, 2021.

57. "White House Says It 'Could Have Done Better' Handling Rob Porter Allegations," C-SPAN, February 8, 2018.

CHAPTER 8. I Like Conflict

1. Fiona Hill, *There Is Nothing for You Here*, p. 220.

2. Peter Baker and Matthew Rosenberg, "Michael Flynn Was Paid to Represent Turkey's Interests During Trump Campaign," *The New York Times*, March 10, 2017; and Theodoric Meyer, "The Most Powerful Lobbyist in Trump's Washington," *Politico Magazine*, April 2, 2018.

3. Carol D. Leonnig, David Nakamura, and Josh Dawsey, "Trump's National Security Advisers Warned Him Not to Congratulate Putin. He Did Anyway," *The Washington Post*, March 20, 2018.

4. Peter Baker, "A Whirlwind Envelops the White House, and the Revolving Door Spins," *The New York Times*, February 12, 2018.

5. Donald J. Trump, interview with Laura Ingraham, Fox News, November 2, 2017.

6. Susan B. Glasser, "The Foreign Capital Rex Tillerson Never Understood: Trump's Washington," *Politico Magazine*, March 13, 2018.

7. Hill, *There Is Nothing for You Here*, p. 198.

8. Lena Felton, "Read the State Department's Account of Tillerson's Ousting," *The Atlantic*, March 13, 2018.

9. Lisa Marie Segarra, "'We Disagreed on Things.' Read President Trump's Remarks After Firing Rex Tillerson," *Yahoo News*, March 13, 2018.

10. David E. Sanger, "Trump's National Security Chief Calls Russian Interference 'Incontrovertible,'" *The New York Times*, February 17, 2018.

11. Dexter Filkins, "John Bolton on the Warpath," *The New Yorker*, April 29, 2019.

12. Katie Rogers and Elizabeth Williamson, "'Kiss Up, Kick Down': Those Recalling Bolton's U.N. Confirmation Process Say He Hasn't Changed," *The New York Times*, March 29, 2018.

13. Peter Baker, "The Final Days," *The New York Times Magazine*, August 29, 2008.

14. H. R. McMaster, *This Week*, ABC News, August 13, 2017.

15. Jim Mattis, *Face the Nation*, CBS News, May 28, 2017.

16. Jack Keane, Fox News, January 28, 2018.

17. Peter Bergen, *Trump and His Generals*, p. 217.

18. Mark Esper, *A Sacred Oath*, p. 16.

19. Greg Jaffe, John Hudson, and Philip Rucker, "Trump, a Reluctant Hawk, Has Battled His Top Aides on Russia and Lost," *The Washington Post*, August 15, 2018.

20. Isaac Arnsdorf, "How Donald Trump Turned to a Comics Titan to Shape the VA," *ProPublica*, October 22, 2019.

21. Dan Merica, "Dr. Ronny Jackson's Glowing Bill of Health for Trump," CNN, January 16, 2018.

22. David Shulkin, *It Shouldn't Be This Hard to Serve Your Country*, pp. 312–15.
23. Ashley Parker, Josh Dawsey, and Philip Rucker, "'When You Lose That Power': How John Kelly Faded as White House Disciplinarian," *The Washington Post*, August 7, 2018.
24. Chris Cillizza, "Why Donald Trump Likes It When John Kelly and John Bolton Fight," CNN, October 18, 2018.

CHAPTER 9. Heat-Seeking Missile

1. Jake Sherman and Anna Palmer, *The Hill to Die On*, p. xi.
2. Ibid., p. 23. See also "Breitbart Audio Has Paul Ryan Pledging Not to Defend Trump," CBS News, March 14, 2017; and Tim Alberta, "The Tragedy of Paul Ryan," *Politico Magazine*, April 12, 2018.
3. Susan Ferrechio, "Paul Ryan Defends Trump's 'Darn Good' Cabinet," *Washington Examiner*, April 26, 2018.
4. Paul Ryan, *Face the Nation*, CBS News, October 1, 2017.
5. John Wagner, "Republicans Celebrate Their Tax Bill—and Heap Praise on Trump," *The Washington Post*, December 20, 2017.
6. Mark Leibovich, "This Is the Way Paul Ryan's Speakership Ends," *The New York Times Magazine*, August 7, 2018.
7. Alberta, "The Tragedy of Paul Ryan."
8. Jake Sherman, "Why Ryan Called It Quits," *Politico*, April 11, 2018.
9. Leibovich, "This Is the Way Paul Ryan's Speakership Ends."
10. George Will, "Vote Against the GOP This November," *The Washington Post*, June 22, 2018.
11. John Boehner, *On the House*, p. 149 and title of chapter six.
12. Mike Pompeo, *Meet the Press*, NBC News, October 18, 2015.
13. Tim Alberta, *American Carnage*, p. 347.
14. Susan B. Glasser, "Mike Pompeo, the Secretary of Trump," *The New Yorker*, August 19, 2019.
15. Ibid.
16. Alberta, *American Carnage*, p. 408.
17. Glasser, "Mike Pompeo, the Secretary of Trump."
18. Ibid.
19. Roll Call Vote, 115th Congress—1st Session, Senate Clerk, January 23, 2017.
20. Glasser, "Mike Pompeo, the Secretary of Trump."
21. Ibid.
22. Ibid.
23. Ibid.
24. Ibid.
25. Ibid.
26. Ibid.
27. Ibid.
28. Olivia Nuzzi, "My Private Oval Office Press Conference with Donald Trump," *New York*, October 10, 2018.
29. Glasser, "Mike Pompeo, the Secretary of Trump."
30. Ibid.
31. Ibid.
32. Susan B. Glasser, "How Jim Mattis Became Trump's Last Man Standing," *The New Yorker*, April 20, 2018.
33. Ibid.
34. Bradley Klapper, "Iran Deal Endangered if Trump Seeks to Renegotiate Its Terms," Associated Press, November 11, 2016.

35. Kevin Liptak, "Trump Blasts Iran Deal as 'Insane' and 'Ridiculous' as Macron Looks On," CNN, April 24, 2018.

36. John Bolton, *The Room Where It Happened*, p. 70.

37. Ibid.

38. Ibid., p. 74.

39. Megan Specia, "E.U. Official Takes Donald Trump to Task: 'With Friends Like That' . . . ," *The New York Times*, May 16, 2018. Donald Tusk, Twitter message, May 16, 2018.

40. Glasser, "Mike Pompeo, the Secretary of Trump."

41. Peter Baker, "In John Bolton, Trump Finds a Fellow Political Blowtorch. Will Foreign Policy Burn?," *The New York Times*, April 8, 2018.

42. Author interviews. See also Mark Mazzetti and Mark Landler, "North Korea's Overture to Jared Kushner," *The New York Times*, June 17, 2018, which first reported on Schulze's role.

43. Bolton, *The Room Where It Happened*, p. 78.

44. Ibid., p. 82.

45. Kang Jin-Kyu, "White House Pulls Back from Libya Model for North Korea," *Korea JoongAng Daily*, May 17, 2018.

46. Bolton, *The Room Where It Happened*, p. 87.

47. Ibid., p. 92.

48. Ibid., p. 96.

49. Susan B. Glasser, "Under Trump, 'America First' Really Is Turning Out to Be America Alone," *The New Yorker*, June 8, 2018.

50. Jennifer Hansler, "Trump Again Calls for Readmitting Russia to G7, Blames Obama for Crimea's Annexation," CNN, June 9, 2018.

51. Ibid.

52. Susan B. Glasser, "How Trump Made War on Angela Merkel and Europe," *The New Yorker*, December 18, 2018. The White House later said he threw the candy in jest and that Trump was stressing the importance of burden sharing in NATO.

53. Gregg Re, "There's a 'Special Place in Hell' for Trudeau After His G7 'Stunt,' Top WH Trade Adviser Peter Navarro Says," Fox News, June 10, 2018.

54. Stephanie Grisham, *I'll Take Your Questions Now*, p. 7.

55. Bolton, *The Room Where It Happened*, p. 106.

56. Ibid.

57. Anna Fifield and Philip Rucker, "Trump and Kim Jong Un Arrive in Singapore for Historic Summit," *The Washington Post*, June 10, 2018; and Mark Moore, "Singapore Pays for Kim Jong Un's Hotel During Trump Summit," *New York Post*, June 11, 2018.

58. Bolton, *The Room Where It Happened*, p. 109.

59. Ibid., p. 110.

60. Video produced by Destiny Productions for the National Security Council, posted on YouTube by *The Guardian*, June 12, 2018.

61. Michael Crowley and Louis Nelson, "'Ludicrous': Pompeo Snaps at Reporters Seeking Clarity on North Korea Deal," *Politico*, June 13, 2018.

62. Bolton, *The Room Where It Happened*, p. 119.

63. Donald J. Trump, remarks to reporters, February 15, 2019.

64. Author interview. See also Motoko Rich, "Shinzo Abe Won't Say if He Nominated Trump for a Nobel Prize," *The New York Times*, February 18, 2019. The *Asahi Shimbun* newspaper in Japan reported, correctly if not quite completely, that the nomination had come "after receiving a request from the U.S. government." The report caused a stir and Abe refused to confirm even that he had made the nomination, despite Trump saying publicly that he had. Abe was eventually confronted in parliament about it. "It's shameful for Japan," said Junya Ogawa, an opposition lawmaker.

CHAPTER 10. Russia, Russia, Russia

1. Donald J. Trump, joint news conference with Vladimir Putin, Helsinki, Finland, July 16, 2018.
2. Fiona Hill, *There Is Nothing for You Here*, p. 234.
3. John McCain, Twitter message, July 16, 2018.
4. Shane Harris, Felicia Somnez, and John Wagner, "'That's Going to Be Special': Tensions Rise as Trump Invites Putin to Washington," *The Washington Post*, July 19, 2018.
5. Andrew Weissmann, *Where Law Ends*, p. 223.
6. Hill, *There Is Nothing for You Here*, p. 197.
7. Peter Baker and Sophia Kishkovsky, "Trump Signs Russian Sanctions into Law, with Caveats," *The New York Times*, August 2, 2017.
8. Andrew McCabe, *The Threat*, p. 136.
9. Marie Yovanovitch, *Lessons from the Edge*, p. 237.
10. Susan B. Glasser, "'An Amateur Boxer Up Against Mohammed Ali': Washington Fears Trump Will Be No Match for Putin in Helsinki," *The New Yorker*, July 13, 2018.
11. Ibid.
12. Neil MacFarquhar and David E. Sanger, "Putin's 'Invincible' Missile Is Aimed at U.S. Vulnerabilities," *The New York Times*, March 1, 2018.
13. John Bolton, "Trump's New Start with Russia May Prove Better than Obama's," *The Wall Street Journal*, February 13, 2017.
14. Hill, *There Is Nothing for You Here*, p. 208.
15. The former prime minister was Guy Verhofstadt. See Matt Stevens, "A Trump Photo Goes Viral, and the World Enters a Caption Contest," *The New York Times*, June 10, 2018.
16. Susan B. Glasser, "How Trump Made War on Angela Merkel and Europe," *The New Yorker*, December 17, 2018.
17. "Trump Says Germany Is a 'Captive of Russia,'" posted by Bloomberg, July 11, 2018.
18. Rebecca Tan, "When Trump Attacked Germany in Brussels, His Aides Pursed Their Lips and Glanced Away," *The Washington Post*, July 11, 2018.
19. Glasser, "How Trump Made War on Angela Merkel and Europe."
20. John Bolton, *The Room Where It Happened*, p. 135.
21. Ibid., pp. 142–43.
22. Ibid.
23. Ibid.
24. Glasser, "How Trump Made War on Angela Merkel and Europe."
25. Bolton, *The Room Where It Happened*, p. 145.
26. Glasser, "How Trump Made War on Angela Merkel and Europe."
27. Tim Alberta, *American Carnage*, pp. 511–12.

CHAPTER 11. The Eighty-five Percenter

1. Lindsey Graham, interviews on Fox News, February 17, 2016, and on *New Day*, CNN, December 8, 2015.
2. Emily Heil, "Lindsey Graham Takes Aim at Cruz, Trump: My Party Has Gone 'Batsh**' Crazy," *The Washington Post*, February 28, 2016.
3. Lindsey Graham, Twitter message, December 8, 2015.
4. Lindsey Graham, interview with Kate Bolduan on CNN, November 30, 2017.
5. Meghan McCain, *Bad Republican*.
6. Peter Baker, "In McCain Memorial Service, Two Presidents Offer Tribute, and a Contrast to Trump," *The New York Times*, September 2, 2018.

7. Lindsey Graham, interview with Dana Bash, *Inside Politics*, CNN, August 29, 2018.

8. Lindsey Graham, *My Story*, published online by his presidential campaign, pp. 15–16.

9. Rep. Lindsey Graham on 2 a.m. Phone Calls, C-SPAN, February 6, 1999.

10. Mark Salter, *The Luckiest Man*, p. 317.

11. "Trump on John McCain: 'He's Not a War Hero,'" video posted by CNN, March 30, 2016.

12. Salter, *The Luckiest Man*, p. 506.

13. Lindsey Graham, interview on *CBS This Morning*, July 21, 2015.

14. Nick Gass and Adam B. Lerner, "Donald Trump Gives Out Lindsey Graham's Cellphone Number," *Politico*, July 21, 2015.

15. Nicholas Fandos, "Lindsey Graham Destroys Cellphone After Donald Trump Discloses Number," *The New York Times*, July 22, 2015.

16. Tom Kludt, "McCain: I 'Might Write in Lindsey Graham' for President," CNN, October 11, 2016.

17. "U.S. Senators McCain, Graham: Order May Help Recruit Terrorists," Reuters, January 29, 2016.

18. Lindsey Graham, Twitter message, October 9, 2017.

19. "'He Hit the Ball on the Screws': Sen. Graham Details President Trump's Improbable 73," *Golf.com*, October 11, 2017.

20. Salter, *The Luckiest Man*, pp. 513–14.

21. Donald J. Trump, author interview.

22. Liz Stark, "Sen. Lindsey Graham Vows 'Holy Hell to Pay' if Attorney General Jeff Sessions Is Fired," CNN, July 27, 2017.

23. Stephanie Grisham, *I'll Take Your Questions Now*, p. 71.

24. Jeffrey Goldberg, "Trump: Americans Who Died in War Are 'Losers' and 'Suckers,'" *The Atlantic*, September 3, 2020.

25. Annie Karni, "The White House Tried to Rescind an Order to Lower Flags to Half-Staff After John McCain Died, a Former Official Says," *The New York Times*, September 4, 2020.

26. Katie Rogers, Nicholas Fandos, and Maggie Haberman, "Trump Relents Under Pressure, Offering 'Respect' to McCain," *The New York Times*, August 27, 2018.

27. Emma Brown, "California Professor, Writer of Confidential Brett Kavanaugh Letter, Speaks Out About Her Allegation of Sexual Assault," *The Washington Post*, September 16, 2018.

28. Michael M. Grynbaum, "Supreme Court Fight Goes Prime Time with Kavanaugh's Fox News Interview," *The New York Times*, September 25, 2018.

29. Sheryl Gay Stolberg and Nicholas Fandos, "Brett Kavanaugh and Christine Blasey Ford Duel with Tears and Fury," *The New York Times*, September 28, 2018.

30. Peter Baker, "She Said. Then He Said. Now What Will Senators Say?," *The New York Times*, September 28, 2018.

31. Peter Baker and Nicholas Fandos, "Show How You Feel, Kavanaugh Was Told, and a Nomination Was Saved," *The New York Times*, October 6, 2018.

32. Renae Reints, "Trump Calls Christine Blasey Ford a 'Very Credible Witness,'" *Fortune*, September 28, 2018.

33. Baker and Fandos, "Show How You Feel."

34. Author interviews. See also Carl Hulse, *Confirmation Bias*, p. 253.

35. Stolberg and Fandos, "Brett Kavanaugh and Christine Blasey Ford Duel with Tears and Fury."

36. Author interviews. See also Michael S. Schmidt, *Donald Trump v. the United States*, p. 346.

37. Sarah Huckabee Sanders, *Speaking for Myself*, pp. 156–57.

38. Lindsey Graham, Senate Judiciary Committee hearing, September 27, 2018.

39. Ruth Marcus, *Supreme Ambition*, p. 309.

40. Jackie Calmes, *Dissent*, p. 300.
41. Jamie Lovegrove, "SC Conservatives Say Lindsey Graham Rebuilt Reputation in Kavanaugh Hearing," *The Post and Courier*, September 28, 2020.
42. Ibid.
43. Ronan Farrow and Jane Mayer, "Senate Democrats Investigate a New Allegation of Sexual Misconduct, from Brett Kavanaugh's College Years," *The New Yorker*, September 23, 2018.
44. Video posted on YouTube by *Time* magazine, September 28, 2018.
45. Maggie Haberman and Peter Baker, "Trump Taunts Christine Blasey Ford at Rally," *The New York Times*, October 2, 2018.
46. Kate Kelly, "Details on F.B.I. Inquiry into Kavanaugh Draw Fire from Democrats," *The New York Times*, June 22, 2021.
47. Winthrop University poll, cited in "President Trump's Approval Rating in South Carolina Above National Average, Poll Finds," WLTX, November 1, 2018.
48. Lindsey Graham, interview with Kate Bolduan, CNN, June 15, 2018.

CHAPTER 12. Shut It Down

1. Author interview. See also Michael D. Shear, "Border Officials Weighed Deploying Migrant 'Heat Ray' Ahead of Midterms," *The New York Times*, August 26, 2020.
2. Author interview. See also Craig Mauger, Michigan Campaign Finance Network; and Omarosa Manigault Newman, *Unhinged*, p. 133.
3. Anonymous, "I Am Part of the Resistance Inside the Trump Administration," *The New York Times*, September 5, 2018. Miles Taylor revealed himself as its author and author of a subsequent "Anonymous" book, *A Warning*, published in late 2019, on October 28, 2020.
4. Joseph Guinto, "'That's Not the Kirstjen We Know,'" *Politico Magazine*, July 2, 2018. The comment was made by Arick Wierson, a fellow Georgetown student who went on to become a television producer, columnist, and consultant to Mayor Michael Bloomberg of New York.
5. Border crossings fell from 1.6 million in the 2000 fiscal year to 409,000 in 2016 and then to 304,000 in 2017 before rising again to 397,000 in 2018. Total Encounters by Fiscal Year, Southwest Border Sectors, U.S. Border Patrol.
6. Michael D. Shear, Katie Benner, and Michael S. Schmidt, "'We Need to Take Away Children,' No Matter How Young, Justice Dept. Officials Said," *The New York Times*, October 5, 2020.
7. Peter Baker, "Leading Republicans Join Democrats in Pushing Trump to Halt Family Separations," *The New York Times*, June 17, 2018.
8. Katie Rogers and Sheryl Gay Stolberg, "Trump Resisting a Growing Wrath for Separating Migrant Families," *The New York Times*, June 18, 2018.
9. "Kirstjen Nielsen Addresses Family Separation at Border: Full Transcript," *The New York Times*, June 18, 2018.
10. Guinto, "'That's Not the Kirstjen We Know.'"
11. The exact number of those separated under the policy was a point of dispute. The American Civil Liberties Union put the number at 5,500. A task force formed by the Biden administration concluded in mid-2021 that there were 5,636 separations under Trump but only 3,913 fell under the task force's scope. The others were still being reviewed and most of them were believed to have come across the border unaccompanied. See Myah Ward, "At Least 3,900 Children Separated from Families Under Trump 'Zero Tolerance' Policy, Task Force Finds," *Politico*, June 8, 2021.
12. Katie Rogers, "Melania Trump Wore a Jacket Saying 'I Really Don't Care' on Her Way to Texas Shelters," *The New York Times*, June 21, 2018.
13. Stephanie Grisham, *I'll Take Your Questions Now*, pp. 136–37.

14. Stephanie Winston Wolkoff, *Melania and Me*, p. 322.

15. Donald J. Trump, campaign rally, October 18, 2018.

16. Philip Bump, "The Caravan Has All But Vanished from Cable News," *The Washington Post*, November 9, 2018.

17. Paul Davidson and Zlati Meyer, "If Trump Closes Mexican Border, Avocados Could Cost More and Auto Factories Could Shut," *USA Today*, April 2, 2019.

18. Brad Heath, Matt Wynn, and Jessica Guynn, "How a Lie About George Soros and the Migrant Caravan Multiplied Online," *USA Today*, October 31, 2018.

19. Jeremy W. Peters, "How Trump-Fed Conspiracy Theories About Migrant Caravan Intersect with Deadly Hatred," *The New York Times*, October 29, 2018.

20. Itay Hod, "Shepard Smith Rebuts 'Fox & Friends' Report of 'Unknown Middle Easterners' in Migrant Caravan," *The Wrap*, October 22, 2018.

21. Criminal Complaint, *U.S. v. Robert Bowers*, Western District of Pennsylvania, October 27, 2018.

22. Guy Snodgrass, *Holding the Line*, pp. 302–3.

23. "'Consider It a Rifle': Trump on Migrants Throwing Rocks," video posted by Reuters to YouTube, November 1, 2018.

24. Julie Hirschfeld Davis and Michael D. Shear, *Border Wars*, p. 337.

25. Ibid.

26. Shepard Smith, Fox News, October 29, 2018.

27. Peter Baker, "Fox Rebukes Sean Hannity's and Jeanine Pirro's Participation in a Trump Rally," *The New York Times*, November 6, 2018.

28. Ibid.

29. Brian Stelter, "Fox Canceled Hannity's Attendance at Tea Party's Tax Day Rally in Cincinnati," *The New York Times*, April 16, 2010.

30. Baker, "Fox Rebukes Sean Hannity's and Jeanine Pirro's Participation in a Trump Rally."

31. Jason Schwartz and Michael Calderone, "Fox News Goes Out on a Limb on House Democrats," *Politico*, November 7, 2018.

32. Frank Newport, "Top Issues for Voters: Healthcare, Economy, Immigration," Gallup, November 2, 2018.

33. "Advertising Issue Spotlight (10/1/18–10/31/18)," Wesleyan Media Project, November 5, 2018.

34. "How Republicans Lost 2018 by Being Too Close to Trump," Niskanen Center, June 17, 2020.

35. Brian Kemp, campaign ad, posted to Facebook, July 16, 2018.

36. "Ron DeSantis Has Released an Ad Indoctrinating His Children into Trumpism," video posted by *The Guardian*, September 13, 2018.

37. Susan B. Glasser, "The Trials of a Never Trump Republican," *The New Yorker*, March 23, 2020.

38. Mitt Romney, "The President Shapes the Public Character of the Nation. Trump's Character Falls Short," *The Washington Post*, January 1, 2019.

39. Peter Baker and Michael D. Shear, "Trump Vows 'Warlike Posture' if Democrats Investigate Him," *The New York Times*, November 7, 2018.

40. In the ten midterm elections that followed the election of a new president from 1934 to 2010, the average loss for the incumbent president's party was eighteen seats. The biggest losses came under Barack Obama, whose Democrats lost sixty-three seats in 2010, and under Bill Clinton, whose Democrats lost fifty-two in 1994. The American Presidency Project, "Seats in Congress Gained/Lost by the President's Party in Mid-Term Elections," Santa Barbara: University of California.

41. Baker and Shear, "Trump Vows 'Warlike Posture' if Democrats Investigate Him."

42. Brian Stelter, "White House Pulls CNN Reporter Jim Acosta's Pass After Contentious News Conference," CNN, November 7, 2018.

CHAPTER 13. The Adults Have Left the Building

1. Eileen Sullivan, "Takeaways from Trump's Midterms News Conference: 'People Like Me,'" *The New York Times*, November 7, 2018.
2. Peter Baker, Katie Benner, and Michael D. Shear, "Jeff Sessions Is Forced Out as Attorney General as Trump Installs Loyalist," *The New York Times*, November 7, 2018.
3. Bob Woodward, *Fear*, p. 216. After Woodward's book was published, Trump denied using those words about Sessions. "I don't talk the way I am quoted," he said. But in fact, there were examples of him using exactly those phrases before, including about his own in-laws. See Peter Baker and Maggie Haberman, "'I Don't Talk That Way,' Trump Says. Except When He Does," *The New York Times*, September 7, 2018.
4. Brooke Singman, "Sessions Fires Back at Trump's Latest Slam: DOJ Won't Be 'Improperly Influenced' by Politics," Fox News, August 23, 2018.
5. Ibid.
6. Lauren Fox and Jeremy Herb, "Lindsey Graham Says Trump Could Replace Jeff Sessions After Midterms," CNN, August 23, 2018.
7. Peter Baker and Alissa J. Rubin, "Trump's Nationalism, Rebuked at World War I Ceremony, Is Reshaping Much of Europe," *The New York Times*, November 11, 2018.
8. Jeffrey Goldberg, "Trump: Americans Who Died in War Are 'Losers' and 'Suckers,'" *The Atlantic*, September 3, 2020.
9. Annie Karni and Maggie Haberman, "John Kelly to Step Down as Trump, Facing New Perils, Shakes Up Staff," *The New York Times*, December 8, 2018.
10. William J. Barr, Memorandum to Rod Rosenstein and Steve Engel, "Re: Mueller's 'Obstruction' Theory," June 8, 2018.
11. Peter Baker and Maggie Haberman, "What Do You Learn About Trump in an 85-Minute Interview?," *The New York Times*, February 1, 2019.
12. "I Wouldn't 'Do a Coup' with Milley, Trump Says of Top U.S. General," Reuters, July 15, 2021.
13. Josh Dawsey, Seung Min Kim, and Philip Rucker, "Chief of Staff John Kelly to Leave White House by End of Month, Trump Says," *The Washington Post*, December 9, 2018.
14. Maggie Haberman, "Mulvaney Called Trump a 'Terrible Human Being' in 2016," *The New York Times*, December 15, 2018.
15. This tracks from the 2017 fiscal year, which began on Barack Obama's watch and ended on September 30, 2017, through the 2019 fiscal year, which ended on September 30, 2019. Federal Reserve Bank of St. Louis.
16. Jim N. Mattis, letter to Donald J. Trump, full text published by *The New York Times*, December 20, 2018.
17. "Trump on Prospect of Mattis' Departure: 'At Some Point, Everybody Leaves,'" CBS News, October 14, 2018.

CHAPTER 14. Going Full Napoleon

1. President Trump Meeting with Democratic Leaders, C-SPAN, December 11, 2018.
2. Stephen Miller, interview, *Face the Nation*, CBS News, December 16, 2018.
3. "Modern Immigration Wave Brings 59 Million to U.S., Driving Population Growth and Change Through 2065," Pew Research Center, September 28, 2015.
4. Remarks by the President at INS Naturalization Ceremony, White House, July 10, 2001.
5. Obama won 71 percent of the Hispanic vote to Romney's 27 percent. Mark Hugo Lopez and Paul Taylor, "Latino Votes in the 2012 Election," Pew Research Center, November 7, 2012.

6. Michael D. Shear and Julie Hirschfeld Davis, "Stoking Fears, Trump Defied Bureaucracy to Advance Immigration Agenda," *The New York Times*, December 23, 2017.

7. Mark Esper, *A Sacred Oath*, p. 222.

8. Bess Levin, "In Race for 'World's Biggest Bastard,' Stephen Miller's Star Continues to Rise," *Vanity Fair*, November 19, 2020. See also Jean Guerrero, *Hatemonger*.

9. Rick Gates, *Wicked Game*, p. 40.

10. Kesha Ram, quoted by Laurie Winer, "Trump Advisor Stephen Miller Has Always Been This Way," *Los Angeles Magazine*, October 30, 2018.

11. Winer, "Trump Advisor Stephen Miller Has Always Been This Way."

12. Stephen Miller, "Political Correctness Out of Control," *Santa Monica Lookout*, undated.

13. Jason DeParle, "How Stephen Miller Seized the Moment to Battle Immigration," *The New York Times*, August 17, 2019.

14. Nick Miroff and Josh Dawsey, "The Trump Adviser Who Scripts Trump's Immigration Agenda," *The Washington Post*, August 17, 2019.

15. Julie Hirschfeld Davis and Michael D. Shear, *Border Wars*, p. 282.

16. Stephen Miller, *Face the Nation*, CBS News, February 12, 2017.

17. Stephen Miller, White House news briefing, August 2, 2017. Video posted by *The Washington Post*.

18. The emails were leaked to the Southern Poverty Law Center, a liberal group that opposed Miller's policies and called for him to resign, by the recipient, Katie McHugh, who was fired from *Breitbart News* after posting anti-Muslim tweets and subsequently renounced the far right. See Michael Edison Hayden, "Stephen Miller's Affinity for White Nationalism Revealed in Leaked Emails," Southern Poverty Law Center, November 12, 2019. Writers on VDare.com sometimes used the term "white genocide" to describe what is also called the "great replacement theory," fretting that white Americans are being displaced by people of color.

19. For a description of the book, see Paul Blumenthal and JM Rieger, "This Stunningly Racist French Novel Is How Steve Bannon Explains the World," *HuffPost*, March 4, 2017.

20. Davis and Shear, *Border Wars*, p. 76.

21. Cliff Sims, *Team of Vipers*, p. 191.

22. Ibid., pp. 208–9.

23. Elana Schor, "Graham Tees Off on Stephen Miller over Immigration," *Politico*, January 21, 2018.

24. Susan Page, *Madam Speaker*, pp. 264–65.

25. On the same day, June 19, 2006, that Trump sent $20,000 to the Democratic Congressional Campaign Committee, Ivanka Trump and Donald Trump Jr. also sent $15,000 apiece. Open Secrets.

26. Donald J. Trump, interview on *Morning Joe*, MSNBC, January 26, 2016.

27. Cynthia Littleton, "How Nancy Pelosi Emerged as a Media Star and Trump's Most Formidable Foe," *Variety*, March 3, 2020.

28. Rachael Bade and Burgess Everett, "Congress Averts Shutdown, Postponing Fight over Trump's Wall," *Politico*, December 6, 2018.

29. Sheryl Gay Stolberg and Michael Tackett, "Trump Suggests Government Shutdown Could Last for 'Months or Even Years,'" *The New York Times*, January 4, 2019.

30. Jennifer Agiesta, "CNN Poll: Trump Bears Most Blame for Shutdown," CNN, January 14, 2019.

31. Davis and Shear, *Border Wars*, pp. 369–70.

32. Full Transcripts: Trump's Speech on Immigration and the Democratic Response, *The New York Times*, January 8, 2019.

33. Multiple accounts, including from Democrats and from the White House. See also Sarah Huckabee Sanders, *Speaking for Myself*, p. 210.

34. Emily Flitter and Tara Siegel Bernard, "Another Loan? Furloughed Employees Balk at Wilbur Ross's Suggestion," *The New York Times*, January 24, 2019.

35. Caitlin Oprysko, "White House Economic Adviser Appears to Compare Shutdown to 'Vacation' for Furloughed Workers," *Politico*, January 11, 2019.
36. On Christmas Day, Trump said that "many of those workers have said to me and communicated, 'Stay out until you get the funding for the wall.'" See, however: Kathy Ehrich Dowd, "President Trump Said Federal Workers Support the Shutdown. Not True, Say Unions Representing Hundreds of Thousands," *Time*, December 26, 2018.
37. Sanders, *Speaking for Myself*, p. 216.
38. Jessica Taylor, "Trump Signs Short-Term Bill to End Government Shutdown, but Border Fight Still Looms," NPR, January 25, 2019.
39. Ron Nixon, "Democrats Grill ICE Nominee About Child Detentions and a Derogatory Tweet," *The New York Times*, November 15, 2018.
40. Ron Nixon, "Migrant Detention Centers Are 'Like a Summer Camp,' Official Says at Hearing," *The New York Times*, July 31, 2018.
41. Davis and Shear, *Border Wars*, p. 380.
42. Miriam Jordan, "Is America a 'Nation of Immigrants'? Immigration Agency Says No," *The New York Times*, February 22, 2018.
43. Jonathan Blitzer, "How Stephen Miller Manipulates Donald Trump to Further His Immigration Obsession," *The New Yorker*, February 21, 2020.

CHAPTER 15. Split Screen in Hanoi

1. Maggie Haberman, Sharon LaFraniere, and Danny Hakim, "Michael Cohen Has Said He Would Take a Bullet for Trump. Maybe Not Anymore," *The New York Times*, April 20, 2018.
2. Michael Cohen, interview with Sean Hannity, Fox News, January 11, 2017.
3. Michael Cohen's remarks from his sentencing in late 2018. He was sentenced to three years in prison and ordered to pay $1.3 million in restitution, $500,000 in forfeiture, and $100,000 in fines. He pleaded guilty to a variety of financial crimes; lying to Congress; and illegally concealing Trump's hush money payments to Stormy Daniels. Dan Mangan and Kevin Breuninger, "Trump's Ex-Lawyer and Fixer Michael Cohen Sentenced to 3 Years in Prison After Admitting 'Blind Loyalty' Led Him to Cover Up President's 'Dirty Deeds,'" CNBC, December 12, 2018.
4. Peter Baker and Nicholas Fandos, "Michael Cohen Accuses Trump of Expansive Pattern of Lies and Criminality," *The New York Times*, February 27, 2019.
5. "Michael Cohen's Warning for Trump's Defenders," CNN, posted on YouTube, February 27, 2019.
6. Susan B. Glasser, "Donald Trump Went to Vietnam, and Michael Cohen Made It Hell," *The New Yorker*, February 28, 2019.
7. Donald J. Trump, letter to Kim Jong-un, December 28, 2018, as published in Bob Woodward, *Rage*, p. 174.
8. Glasser, "Donald Trump Went to Vietnam, and Michael Cohen Made It Hell."
9. Susan B. Glasser, "Audience of One: Why Flattery Works in Trump's Foreign Policy," *The New Yorker*, February 22, 2019.
10. Susan B. Glasser, "The International Crisis of Donald Trump," *The New Yorker*, January 11, 2019.
11. Katie Bo Williams, "Outgoing Syria Envoy Admits Hiding U.S. Troop Numbers; Praises Trump Mideast Policy," *Defense One*, November 12, 2020.
12. John Bolton, *The Room Where It Happened*, p. 320.
13. Ibid., p. 321.
14. Ibid., p. 320.
15. Author interview. See also Adam Shaw, "Trump Lands in Vietnam for Kim Jong Un Summit," Fox News, February 26, 2019.

16. "North Korea Says Trump Was Open to Easing Sanctions with 'Snapback' Clause: South Korean Media," Reuters, March 25, 2019.

17. Joby Warrick and Simon Denyer, "As Kim Wooed Trump with 'Love Letters,' He Kept Building His Nuclear Capability, Intelligence Shows," *The Washington Post*, September 30, 2020.

18. Michael Burke, "Rubio Defends Trump on North Korea: 'No Deal Is Better Than a Bad Deal,'" *The Hill*, February 28, 2019.

CHAPTER 16. King Kong Always Wins

1. William P. Barr, *One Damn Thing After Another*, p. 551.

2. Trump said this in a 1997 interview with Howard Stern that was unearthed during his campaign. Ale Russian, "Trump Boasted of Avoiding STDs While Dating: Vaginas Are 'Landmines . . . It Is My Personal Vietnam,'" *People*, October 28, 2016.

3. Andrew Weissmann, *Where Law Ends*, p. 36.

4. Justin Elliott, "Trump Lawyer Marc Kasowitz Threatens Stranger in Emails: 'Watch Your Back, Bitch,'" *ProPublica*, July 13, 2017.

5. Peter Baker and Kenneth P. Vogel, "Trump Lawyers Clash over How Much to Cooperate with Russia Inquiry," *The New York Times*, September 17, 2017.

6. Weissmann, *Where Law Ends*, p. 10.

7. Ibid.

8. Julia Ioffe and Franklin Foer, "Did Manafort Use Trump to Curry Favor with a Putin Ally?," *The Atlantic*, October 2, 2017.

9. Weissmann, *Where Law Ends*, p. 197.

10. Receipts from the House of Bijan, Beverly Hills, California, submitted to court by the Office of Special Counsel.

11. Robert S. Mueller III, Report on the Investigation into Russian Interference in the 2016 Presidential Election (Mueller Report), Volume I, p. 23.

12. Ibid., p. 25.

13. Indictment, *U.S. v. Internet Research Agency et al.*, February 16, 2018.

14. Mueller Report, Volume I, p. 29.

15. Weissmann, *Where Law Ends*, p. 226.

16. Michael S. Schmidt, *Donald Trump v. the United States*, p. 315.

17. Office of the Inspector General, U.S. Department of Justice, A Report of Investigation of Certain Allegations Relating to Former FBI Deputy Director Andrew McCabe, February 2018.

18. Text messages between Paul Manafort and Sean Hannity, filed in court, June 21, 2019.

19. Schmidt, *Donald Trump v. the United States*, p. 5.

20. Mueller Report, Volume II, p. 86.

21. Ibid., p. 115.

22. Weissmann, *Where Law Ends*, pp. 254–55.

23. Ibid., p. 128.

24. Ibid., p. 118.

25. Ibid., pp. 275–76.

26. Peter Baker, "'I Do Not Remember': Trump Gave a Familiar Reply to the Special Counsel's Queries," *The New York Times*, April 20, 2019.

27. Weissmann, *Where Law Ends*, p. 139.

28. Mueller Report, Volume I, p. 129.

29. William P. Barr, letter to Senate and House Judiciary Committees, March 24, 2019.

30. Mark Landler and Maggie Haberman, "Trump Declares Exoneration, and a War on His Enemies," *The New York Times*, March 24, 2019.

31. Weissmann, *Where Law Ends*, pp. xv–xvi.
32. Robert S. Mueller III, letter to William P. Barr, March 27, 2019.
33. Peter Baker, "Barr Defends Handling of Mueller Report Against Withering Rebukes," *The New York Times*, May 1, 2019.
34. "Read Barr's News Conference Remarks Ahead of the Mueller Report Release," *The New York Times*, April 18, 2019.
35. Tim Mak, "Elderly Trump Critics Await Mueller's Report—Sometimes Until Their Last Breath," *Morning Edition*, NPR, March 5, 2019.
36. Adam Schiff, *Midnight in Washington*, p. 195.
37. Laurence Tribe, Twitter message, July 24, 2019.
38. Search on Factba.se database.

CHAPTER 17. John Bolton's War

1. Susan B. Glasser, "Mike Pompeo, the Secretary of Trump," *The New Yorker*, August 19, 2019.
2. Ibid.
3. Ibid.
4. Ibid.
5. Ibid.
6. Peter Baker, "Trump Says Military Is 'Locked and Loaded' and North Korea Will 'Regret' Threats," *The New York Times*, August 11, 2017.
7. Julia Limitone, "Military Action Possible in Venezuela, Pompeo Says," Fox Business, May 1, 2019.
8. Karen DeYoung, Josh Dawsey, and Paul Sonne, "Venezuela's Opposition Put Together a Serious Plan. For Now, It Appears to Have Failed," *The Washington Post*, May 1, 2019.
9. Anne Gearan, Josh Dawsey, John Hudson, and Seung Min Kim, "A Frustrated Trump Questions His Administration's Venezuela Strategy," *The Washington Post*, May 8, 2019.
10. Ibid.
11. Donald J. Trump, Remarks on Surprise Medical Billing and an Exchange with Reporters, May 9, 2019.
12. White House Twitter message, February 11, 2019.
13. John Bolton, *The Room Where It Happened*, p. 388.
14. Mark Esper, *A Sacred Oath*, p. 73.
15. Adam Schiff, *Midnight in Washington*, p. 189.
16. Bolton, *The Room Where It Happened*, pp. 401–2.
17. Ibid., p. 402.
18. Peter Baker, Maggie Haberman, and Thomas Gibbons-Neff, "Urged to Launch an Attack, Trump Listened to the Skeptics Who Said It Would Be a Costly Mistake," *The New York Times*, June 21, 2019.
19. Bolton, *The Room Where It Happened*, p. 403.
20. Andrew Kaczynski and Chris Massie, "Trump Army Secretary Pick Gave a Lecture Arguing Against the Theory of Evolution," CNN, May 2, 2017.
21. Eric Lipton, Maggie Haberman, and Mark Mazzetti, "Behind the Ukraine Aid Freeze: 84 Days of Conflict and Confusion," *The New York Times*, December 29, 2019.
22. Bolton, *The Room Where It Happened*, p. 464.
23. Rudy Giuliani, interview on *Fox & Friends*, April 24, 2019.
24. Donald Trump Jr., Twitter message, March 24, 2019.
25. Bolton, *The Room Where It Happened*, p. 456.
26. Kurt D. Volker, Opening Statement, House Intelligence Committee, November 19, 2019.

27. Fiona Hill, Deposition, House Permanent Select Committee on Intelligence et al., October 14, 2019.
28. Kate Brennan, "Exclusive: Unredacted Ukraine Documents Reveal Extent of Pentagon's Legal Concerns," Just Security, Reiss Center on Law and Security at New York University School of Law, January 2, 2020.
29. William B. Taylor Jr., Excerpts from Joint Deposition, House Permanent Select Committee on Intelligence et al., October 22, 2019.
30. Bolton, *The Room Where It Happened*, p. 458.
31. Ibid.
32. Sarah Huckabee Sanders, *Speaking for Myself*, pp. 226–27.
33. Bolton, *The Room Where It Happened*, p. 463.

CHAPTER 18. The Summer of Crazy

1. Peter Baker and Michael Crowley, "Trump and Putin Share Joke About Election Meddling, Sparking New Furor," *The New York Times*, June 28, 2019.
2. Michael Brice-Saddler, "While Bemoaning Mueller Probe, Trump Falsely Says the Constitution Gives Him 'The Right to Do Whatever I Want,'" *The Washington Post*, July 23, 2019.
3. Glenn Thrush and Michael Tackett, "Trump and Pelosi Trade Barbs, Both Questioning the Other's Fitness," *The New York Times*, May 23, 2019.
4. Kevin Quealy, "The Complete List of Trump's Twitter Insults," *The New York Times*, January 19, 2021.
5. Joe Biden's Campaign Announcement Video, April 25, 2019.
6. Matt Flegenheimer, "Ted Cruz Unburdens Himself: 'What I Really Think of Donald Trump,'" *The New York Times*, May 3, 2016.
7. Rand Paul, interview on *The Nightly Show with Larry Wilmore*, Comedy Central, January 26, 2016.
8. Bandy Lee, ed., *The Dangerous Case of Donald Trump*.
9. Author interview. A version of this episode was first reported by the French newspaper *Le Monde*. See "Trump Confused Baltics with Balkans at a Meeting with Baltic Presidents in April—Newspaper," *The Baltic Times*, November 11, 2018.
10. Jimmy Carter, "Presidential Disability and the Twenty-fifth Amendment," *Journal of the American Medical Association*, December 7, 1994.
11. Katie Rogers, "A Hot Microphone Catches Senate Gossip, but No Duel Transpires," *The New York Times*, July 25, 2017.
12. Bob Corker, Twitter message, October 8, 2017.
13. Daniel W. Drezner went on to write a book titled *The Toddler in Chief*.
14. Nancy Cook, "Trump Is Tiring of Mulvaney," *Politico*, June 25, 2019.
15. Stephanie Grisham, *I'll Take Your Questions Now*, p. 192.
16. Author interview. See also Anna Palmer, Jake Sherman, Daniel Lippman, Eli Okun, and Garrett Ross, "Politico Playbook PM: What George W. Bush's Economist Said About Trump Behind Closed Doors," *Politico*, May 15, 2019.
17. Nikki R. Haley, *With All Due Respect*, p. 126.
18. William P. Barr, *One Damn Thing After Another*, p. 313.
19. President Trump: "I Am An Extremely Stable Genius," C-SPAN, May 23, 2019.
20. Alex Morris, "Trump's Mental Health: Is Pathological Narcissism the Key to Trump's Behavior?," *Rolling Stone*, April 5, 2017.
21. John Wagner, "Kellyanne Conway Dismisses Her Husband's Concerns That Trump's Mental Health Is Deteriorating," *The Washington Post*, March 19, 2019.
22. *Diagnostic and Statistical Manual of Mental Disorders*. See also George Conway, Twitter messages, March 19–21, 2019.

23. George T. Conway III, "Unfit for Office," *The Atlantic*, October 3, 2019.

24. Trump Twitter Archive searches. Cited in Susan B. Glasser, "Trump's Wacky, Angry, and Extreme August," *The New Yorker*, September 3, 2019.

25. Glenn Kessler, Salvador Rizzo, and Meg Kelly, "President Trump Has Made 12,019 False or Misleading Claims over 928 Days," *The Washington Post*, August 12, 2019.

26. Nancy A. Youssef, Vivian Salama, and Michael C. Bender, "Trump, Awaiting Egyptian Counterpart at Summit, Called Out for 'My Favorite Dictator,' " *The Wall Street Journal*, September 13, 2019.

27. Josh Barro, "The World's Best Bureaucrat," *New York*, October 27, 2020.

28. Kevin Granville, "A President at War with His Fed Chief, 5 Decades Before Trump," *The New York Times*, June 13, 2017.

29. Grisham, *I'll Take Your Questions Now*, p. 235.

30. Jerome H. Powell, "Challenges for Monetary Policy," delivered at a symposium sponsored by the Federal Reserve Bank of Kansas City, Jackson Hole, Wyoming, August 23, 2019.

31. See for example Diane Swonk, "The Powell Pivot," Grant Thornton, February 12, 2019.

32. Omarosa Manigault Newman, *Unhinged*, pp. 154–55.

33. Ibid., p. 166.

34. Jonathan Swan and Margaret Talev, "Scoop: Trump Suggested Nuking Hurricanes to Stop Them from Hitting U.S.," *Axios*, August 25, 2019.

35. Ronald S. Lauder, statement, January 8, 2018. Posted by Maggie Haberman.

36. "Ex-DHS Official: Trump Wanted to Trade Puerto Rico for Greenland," MSNBC, August 19, 2020.

37. Vivian Salama, Rebecca Ballhaus, Andrew Restuccia, and Michael C. Bender, "President Trump Eyes a New Real-Estate Purchase: Greenland," *The Wall Street Journal*, August 16, 2019.

38. Peter Baker, "Trump Ousts John Bolton as National Security Adviser," *The New York Times*, September 10, 2019.

39. Robert O'Brien, letter to Prosecution Authority of the Kingdom of Sweden, July 31, 2019.

40. Susan B. Glasser, " 'It Won't End Well': Trump and His Obscure New National-Security Chief," *The New Yorker*, September 19, 2019.

41. Ibid.

CHAPTER 19. Fucking Ukraine

1. Norman Eisen, *A Case for the American People*, pp. 101–2.

2. Joe Heim, "Nancy Pelosi on Impeaching Trump: 'He's Just Not Worth It,' " *The Washington Post Magazine*, March 11, 2019.

3. Adam Schiff, *Midnight in Washington*, p. 214.

4. The piece was signed by seven freshman House Democrats: Gil Cisneros of California; Jason Crow of Colorado; Chrissy Houlahan of Pennsylvania; Elaine Luria of Virginia; Mikie Sherrill of New Jersey; Elissa Slotkin of Michigan; and Abigail Spanberger of Virginia. See "Seven Freshmen Democrats: These Allegations Are a Threat to All We Have Sworn to Protect," *The Washington Post*, September 23, 2019.

5. Nancy Pelosi statement, September 24, 2019.

6. Susan B. Glasser, " 'Do Us a Favor': The Forty-eight Hours That Sealed Trump's Impeachment," *The New Yorker*, September 25, 2019.

7. Donald J. Trump, phone call with Volodymyr Zelensky, White House call summary, released September 24, 2019.

8. Schiff, *Midnight in Washington*, p. 217.

9. Alexander Vindman, *Here, Right Matters*, p. 19.

10. R. Jeffrey Smith, "Trump Administration Officials Worried Ukraine Aid Halt Violated Spending Law," Center for Public Integrity, December 21, 2019.

11. Aaron Blake, "John Bolton's Crusade to Debunk Trump's Revisionist History on Russia and Ukraine," *The Washington Post*, March 15, 2022.

12. Kate Brennan, "Exclusive: Unredacted Ukraine Documents Reveal Extent of Pentagon's Legal Concerns."

13. Caitlin Emma and Connor O'Brien, "Trump Holds Up Ukraine Military Aid Meant to Confront Russia," *Politico*, August 28, 2019.

14. Patrick McGreevy, "'I-Word' in the Air as Rogan Seeks Reelection to House," *Los Angeles Times*, January 9, 2000.

15. Schiff, *Midnight in Washington*, pp. 141–42.

16. Mike DeBonis and Karoun Demirjian, "Trump and GOP Target 'Pencil-Neck' Adam Schiff as Their Post-Mueller Villain," *The Washington Post*, March 29, 2019.

17. Kevin Quealy, "The Complete List of Trump's Twitter Insults (2015–2021)," *The New York Times*, January 19, 2021.

18. Adam Schiff, Statement at House Permanent Select Committee on Intelligence, C-SPAN, September 26, 2019.

19. Pat A. Cipollone, letter to Nancy Pelosi, Adam Schiff, Eliot Engel, and Elijah Cummings, October 8, 2019.

20. Charlie Savage and Josh Williams, "Read the Text Messages Between U.S. and Ukrainian Officials," *The New York Times*, October 4, 2019.

21. Josh Lederman, Laura Strickler, and Dan De Luce, "Pompeo's Elite Taxpayer-Funded Dinners Raise New Concerns," NBC News, May 19, 2020.

22. Mike Pompeo, Twitter message, October 1, 2019.

23. Contemporaneous notes provided by Mary Louise Kelly.

24. Stephanie Grisham, *I'll Take Your Questions Now*, pp. 236–37.

25. Author interview. See also ibid.

26. Press Briefing by Acting Chief of Staff Mick Mulvaney, October 17, 2019.

27. Michael Grunwald, "Mick the Knife," *Politico Magazine*, September/October 2017.

28. Seung Min Kim, Lisa Rein, Josh Dawsey, and Erica Werner, "'His Own Fiefdom': Mulvaney Builds 'an Empire for the Right Wing' as Trump's Chief of Staff," *The Washington Post*, July 15, 2019.

29. Fiona Hill deposition.

30. "Read Mulvaney's Conflicting Statements on Quid Pro Quo," *The New York Times*, October 17, 2019.

31. Ronn Blitzer, "Mulvaney Insists No Quid Pro Quo with Ukraine After WH Comments: 'I Didn't Say That,'" Fox News, October 20, 2019.

32. William B. Taylor Jr., Opening Statement, House Permanent Select Committee on Intelligence et al., November 13, 2019.

33. Fiona Hill deposition.

34. Devin Nunes's Opening Statement in First Public Impeachment Hearing, November 13, 2019. Posted by *U.S. News & World Report*.

35. William B. Taylor Jr. opening statement.

36. Transcript: Alexander Vindman and Jennifer Williams Testify in Front of the House Intelligence Committee, November 19, 2019. Posted by *The Washington Post*.

37. Transcript: Gordon Sondland's November 20 Public Testimony in Front of the House Intelligence Committee, November 20, 2019. Posted by *The Washington Post*.

38. Kurt Volker opening statement.

39. Fiona Hill, Opening Statement, House Intelligence Committee, November 21, 2019.

40. Manu Raju, Jeremy Herb, and Zachary Cohen, "House GOP Disregards Expert Warnings That Debunked Ukraine Theory Helps Russia," CNN, November 22, 2019.

41. Susan B. Glasser, "The New York Congressman Who Could Lead an Impeachment Charge Against Trump," *The New Yorker*, February 26, 2018.

42. Ibid.

43. Schiff, *Midnight in Washington*, pp. 286–87.

44. Ibid., pp. 331–32.

45. Articles of Impeachment Against Donald John Trump, House Resolution 755, One Hundred Sixteenth Congress, First Session.

46. Nancy Cook, Burgess Everett, and Gabby Orr, "Impeachment Day for Trump: A Bruised Ego, a Twitter Eruption and a Winding Rally," *Politico*, December 18, 2019.

47. Adam Kinzinger, statement, December 18, 2019.

48. Derek Barichello, "U.S. Rep. Adam Kinzinger Says He Will Vote 'No' on President's Impeachment," Shaw Local News Network, December 17, 2019.

49. Adam Kinzinger, Twitter message, March 11, 2022.

50. Roll Call 695, Bill Number: H. Res. 755, House Clerk's Office. The vote on Article II passed 229 to 198.

51. Christine Ferretti, "Trump Addresses Impeachment at Rally as House Votes to Impeach Him," *The Detroit News*, December 18, 2019.

CHAPTER 20. The Age of Impeachment

1. Lindsey Graham, interview on Fox News, December 19, 2019.

2. Kevin Sullivan and Mary Jordan, *Trump on Trial*, p. 388.

3. "Mitch McConnell: 'I'm Not an Impartial Juror' in a Senate Impeachment Trial," NBC News, December 17, 2019.

4. Victor Garcia, "Hannity Exclusive: McConnell Says 'Zero Chance' Trump Is Removed, 'One or Two Democrats' Could Vote to Acquit," Fox News, December 12, 2019.

5. Veronica Stracqualursi, "'I'm Not Trying to Pretend to Be a Fair Juror Here': Graham Predicts Trump Impeachment Will 'Die Quickly' in Senate," CNN, December 14, 2019.

6. Annie Karni and Maggie Haberman, "Suleimani's Killing Creates New Uncertainty for Trump Campaign," *The New York Times*, January 7, 2020.

7. Keith Kellogg, *War by Other Means*, p. 155.

8. Michael C. Bender, *"Frankly, We Did Win This Election,"* p. 41.

9. Adam Schiff, *Midnight in Washington*, p. 340.

10. Eric Tucker and Zeke Miller, "Now on Trump's Team, Dershowitz Says, 'I Haven't Changed,'" Associated Press, January 24, 2020.

11. Bobby Lewis, "Trump's New Impeachment Defense Team Has Been on Fox News Over 350 Times in the Past Year," Media Matters for America, January 17, 2020.

12. "Factbox: 'They're Here to Steal Two Elections': Trump's Attorneys Push Back on Impeachment," Reuters, January 21, 2020.

13. Schiff, *Midnight in Washington*, p. 359.

14. Ibid., pp. 365–66.

15. Meg Wagner, Mike Hayes, and Veronica Rocha, "Trump's Lawyers Slam Nadler After He Accuses Senate Republicans of 'Voting for a Coverup,'" CNN, January 22, 2020.

16. Adam Liptak, "Rebuke from Roberts Signals His Limited Role in Trump's Senate Trial," *The New York Times*, January 22, 2020.

17. Norman Eisen, *A Case for the American People*, p. 213.

18. Dana Milbank, "'S.O.S.! PLEASE HELP ME!' The World's Greatest Deliberative Body Falls to Pettifoggery," *The Washington Post*, January 22, 2020.

19. Eisen, *A Case for the American People*, pp. 216–18.

20. "GOP Senators Incensed by Schiff 'Head on a Pike' Remark at Impeachment Trial," NBC News, January 25, 2020.

21. Michael D. Shear and Nicholas Fandos, "Bolton Revelations Anger Republicans, Fueling Push for Impeachment Witnesses," *The New York Times*, January 27, 2020.

22. Christina Wilkie, Kevin Breuninger, and Yelena Dzhanova, "Trump Impeachment

Trial: Defense Ignores Bolton Bombshell About Ukraine Aid for Investigations," CNBC, January 27, 2020.

23. "Ken Starr: 'We Are Living in the Age of Impeachment,'" C-SPAN, January 27, 2020.

24. "Senate Impeachment Trial, Day 7, Defense Opening Arguments from Ray, Dershowitz, and Cipollone," C-SPAN, January 27, 2020.

25. Charlie Savage, "Trump Lawyer's Impeachment Argument Stokes Fears of Unfettered Power," *The New York Times*, January 30, 2020.

26. Eisen, *A Case for the American People*, p. 250.

27. Susan B. Glasser, "The Senate Can Stop Pretending Now," *The New Yorker*, January 31, 2020.

28. Ibid.

29. Ibid.

30. Eisen, *A Case for the American People*, p. 245.

31. Lamar Alexander, Statement on Impeachment Witness Vote, January 30, 2020.

32. Rob Portman, email to Lamar Alexander, January 30, 2020, obtained by authors.

33. Zach Montague, "Despite Evidence, Republicans Rallied Behind Trump. This Was Their Reasoning," *The New York Times*, January 31, 2020.

34. Ibid.

35. Lisa Murkowski, Statement on Senate Impeachment Process Vote, January 31, 2020.

36. "House Managers and Trump Lawyers Wrap Closing Arguments," Transcript, CNN, February 3, 2020.

37. Donald J. Trump, Address Before a Joint Session of the Congress on the State of the Union, February 4, 2020.

38. Christi Parsons, "Parody Stirs Racial Debate," *Chicago Tribune*, May 6, 2007.

39. Chris Murphy, Twitter message, February 5, 2020.

40. "Full Text: Romney's Speech on Why He'll Vote to Convict Trump of Abuse of Power," NBC News, February 5, 2020.

41. J. Edward Moreno, "Trump Tweets Video That Claims Romney Is a 'Democrat Secret Asset,'" *The Hill*, February 5, 2020.

42. Senate Impeachment Trial Vote, C-SPAN, February 5, 2020.

43. Lamar Alexander, email to Mitt Romney, February 5, 2020, obtained by authors.

CHAPTER 21. Love Your Enemies

1. Michael J. Mooney, "Trump's Apostle," *Texas Monthly*, August 2019.

2. Ibid. See also Michael J. Mooney, "How First Baptist's Robert Jeffress Ordained Himself to Lead America," *D Magazine*, December 21, 2011; and Anugrah Kumar, "'Only Evangelicals Who've Sold Their Soul to the Devil' Will Vote for Biden: Robert Jeffress," *Christian Post*, August 3, 2020.

3. Peter Baker, "Trump Lashes Out at Impeachment Foes and Pelosi Hits Back," *The New York Times*, February 6, 2020.

4. Peter Baker, "Trump Hails Acquittal and Lashes Out at His 'Evil' and 'Corrupt' Opponents," *The New York Times*, February 6, 2020.

5. Grace Segers, "Susan Collins Will Vote to Acquit Trump, Saying He's 'Learned' from Impeachment," *CBS Evening News*, February 4, 2020.

6. Jeffrey M. Jones, "Trump Job Approval at Personal Best 49%," Gallup, February 4, 2020.

7. Talia Kaplan, "Stephanie Grisham: Dems Must Be Held Accountable for 'Corrupt' Impeachment," Fox News, February 6, 2020.

8. Josh Dawsey, Juliet Eilperin, John Hudson, and Lisa Rein, "In Trump's Final Days, a 30-Year-Old Aide Purges Officials Seen as Insufficiently Loyal," *The Washington Post*, November 13, 2020.

9. Author interview. See also Yasmeen Abutaleb and Damian Paletta, *Nightmare Scenario*, pp. 13–14.

10. Multiple author interviews. See also Abutaleb and Paletta, *Nightmare Scenario*, pp. 30–32; Lawrence Wright, *The Plague Year*, pp. 44–46; and Josh Rogin, *Chaos Under Heaven*, p. 257.

11. Rogin, *Chaos Under Heaven*, p. 258.

12. Peter Navarro, Memorandum to NSC, Re: Impose Travel Ban on China?, January 29, 2020.

13. Steve Eder, Henry Fountain, Michael H. Keller, Muyi Xiao, and Alexandra Stevenson, "430,000 Have Traveled from China to U.S. Since Coronavirus Surfaced," *The New York Times*, April 4, 2020.

14. Jeffrey Toobin, "The Dirty Trickster," *The New Yorker*, May 23, 2008.

15. Transcript of Attorney General Bill Barr's Exclusive Interview with ABC News, February 13, 2020.

16. Adam Goldman and Katie Benner, "U.S. Drops Michael Flynn Case, in Move Backed by Trump," *The New York Times*, May 7, 2020.

17. Ibid.

18. Nick Givas, "Former NYPD Commissioner Calls Trump Whistleblower a 'Covert Operative' Who Participated in an 'Attempted Coup,'" Fox News, September 30, 2019.

19. Peter Baker, J. David Goodman, Michael Rothfeld, and Elizabeth Williamson, "The 11 Criminals Granted Clemency by Trump Had One Thing in Common: Connections," *The New York Times*, February 19, 2020.

20. David Philipps, *Alpha*, pp. 275–77.

21. Trump interview with Joe Kernan in Davos, Switzerland. Matthew J. Belvedere, "Trump Says He Trusts China's Xi on Coronavirus and the US Has It 'Totally Under Control,'" CNBC, January 22, 2020; President Trump Rally in Manchester, New Hampshire, C-SPAN, February 10, 2020; Michael Crowley, "Some Experts Worry as a Germ-Phobic Trump Confronts a Growing Epidemic," *The New York Times*, February 10, 2020; and President Trump with Coronavirus Task Force Briefing, C-SPAN, February 26, 2020.

22. Bob Woodward, *Rage*, p. xx.

23. Kevin Quealy, "The Complete List of Trump's Twitter Insults," *The New York Times*, January 19, 2021.

24. Peter Baker, "For a President Who Loves Crowd Size, India Aims to Deliver," *The New York Times*, February 23, 2020.

25. Peter Navarro, Memorandum to President, Re: Request for Supplemental Appropriation, February 23, 2020.

26. Transcript for the CDC Telebriefing Update on COVID-19, Centers for Disease Control and Prevention, February 26, 2020.

27. Annie Karni, Michael Crowley, and Maggie Haberman, "Trump Has a Problem as the Coronavirus Threatens the U.S.: His Credibility," *The New York Times*, February 26, 2020.

28. Jane Mayer, "The Danger of President Pence," *The New Yorker*, October 16, 2017.

29. Tim Alberta, *American Carnage*, p. 500.

30. Madeleine Westerhout, *Off the Record*, p. 161.

31. Tom LoBianco, *Piety & Power*, p. 299.

32. Katie Miller, email, February 27, 2020, obtained by authors.

33. Peter Baker and Annie Karni, "Trump Accuses Media and Democrats of Exaggerating Coronavirus Threat," *The New York Times*, February 28, 2020.

34. Ibid.

35. Mark Meadows, *The Chief's Chief*, p. 47.

CHAPTER 22. Game Changer

1. Guests that night posted video on social media of the evening. See also Peter Baker and Katie Rogers, "On a Saturday Night in Florida, a Presidential Party Became a Coronavirus Hot Zone," *The New York Times*, March 14, 2020.
2. Ibid.
3. "Trump: Anyone Who Wants Virus Test Can Get a Test," Associated Press, March 6, 2020.
4. Yasmeen Abutaleb and Damian Paletta, *Nightmare Scenario*, p. 86.
5. Oliver Darcy, "Tucker Carlson Delivers Coronavirus Warning as His Fox Colleagues Attack Media's Coverage," CNN, March 10, 2020.
6. Fred Barbash, "Matt Gaetz, the 'Trumpiest Congressman,' Cites Principles for Bucking President on War Powers. Kevin McCarthy Is 'Very Shocked,'" *The Washington Post*, January 10, 2020.
7. Peter Baker, Maggie Haberman, and Annie Karni, "Trump Floats Economic Stimulus in Response to Coronavirus," *The New York Times*, March 9, 2020.
8. Author interviews. See also Abutaleb and Paletta, *Nightmare Scenario*, pp. 96–97.
9. Peter Baker, "U.S. to Suspend Most Travel from Europe as World Scrambles to Fight Pandemic," *The New York Times*, March 11, 2020.
10. Tom Bossert, Twitter message, March 12, 2020.
11. Remarks by President Trump, Vice President Pence, and Members of the Coronavirus Task Force in Press Briefing, April 6, 2020.
12. Jane C. Timm, "Fact Check: Trump Falsely Claims Obama Left him 'Nothing' in the National Stockpile," NBC News, May 6, 2020.
13. Katherine Eban, "'That's Their Problem': How Jared Kushner Let the Markets Decide America's COVID Fate," *Vanity Fair*, September 17, 2020.
14. Remarks by President Trump, Vice President Pence, and Members of the Coronavirus Task Force in Press Briefing, March 19, 2020.
15. Katie Rogers and Emily Cochrane, "Trump Urges Limits Amid Pandemic, but Stops Short of National Mandates," *The New York Times*, March 16, 2020.
16. Donald J. Trump, briefing with reporters, March 17, 2020.
17. Remarks by President Trump, Vice President Pence, and Members of the Coronavirus Task Force in Press Briefing, March 13, 2020.
18. Ibid.
19. Remarks by President Trump, Vice President Pence, and Members of the Coronavirus Task Force in Press Briefing, March 28, 2020.
20. Remarks by President Trump, Vice President Pence, and Members of the Coronavirus Task Force in Press Briefing, March 20, 2020.
21. Remarks by President Trump et al., March 28, 2020.
22. Justine Lofton, "Gov. Gretchen Whitmer Wears 'That Woman from Michigan' Shirt on Comedy Central," *MLive*, April 2, 2020.
23. Remarks by President Trump, Vice President Pence, and Members of the Coronavirus Task Force in Press Briefing, April 13, 2020.
24. Peter Baker and Michael D. Shear, "Trump Says States Can Start Reopening While Acknowledging the Decision Is Theirs," *The New York Times*, April 16, 2020.
25. Remarks by President Trump et al., March 19, 2020.
26. Remarks by President Trump et al., March 20, 2020.

CHAPTER 23. You're Blowing This

1. The death tolls here and throughout this chapter are taken from "An Incalculable Loss," *The New York Times*, May 27, 2020.

2. Author interview. See also Chris Christie, *Republican Rescue*, pp. 35–38.

3. Remarks by President Trump, Vice President Pence, and Members of the Coronavirus Task Force in a Fox News Virtual Town Hall, March 24, 2020.

4. Michael D. Shear, Michael Crowley, and James Glanz, "Coronavirus May Kill 100,000 to 240,000 in U.S. Despite Actions, Officials Say," *The New York Times*, March 31, 2020.

5. Deborah Birx, *Silent Invasion*, p. 147.

6. John and Jim McLaughlin, "Coronavirus Changes US Voter Opinions—Like 9/11," Newsmax, March 28, 2020.

7. Remarks by President Trump, Vice President Pence, and Members of the Coronavirus Task Force in Press Briefing, April 1, 2020.

8. Nelson D. Schwartz, Ben Casselman, and Ella Koeze, "How Bad Is Unemployment? 'Literally Off the Charts,'" *The New York Times*, May 8, 2020.

9. Ben Casselman, "A Collapse That Wiped Out 5 Years of Growth, with No Bounce in Sight," *The New York Times*, July 30, 2020.

10. Liz Frazier, "The Coronavirus Crash of 2020, and the Investing Lesson It Taught Us," *Forbes*, February 11, 2021.

11. Philip Rucker, Robert Costa, Laurie McGinley, and Josh Dawsey, "'What Do You Have to Lose?': Inside Trump's Embrace of a Risky Drug Against Coronavirus," *The Washington Post*, April 6, 2020.

12. Yasmeen Abutaleb and Damian Paletta, *Nightmare Scenario*, p. 308.

13. Annie Karni and Katie Thomas, "Trump Says He's Taking Hydroxychloroquine, Prompting Warnings from Health Experts," *The New York Times*, May 18, 2020.

14. Food and Drug Administration, Coronavirus (COVID-19) Update: FDA Revokes Emergency Use Authorization for Chloroquine and Hydroxychloroquine, June 15, 2020.

15. Mark Esper, *A Sacred Oath*, pp. 269–70.

16. Maria Cramer and Knvul Sheikh, "Surgeon General Urges the Public to Stop Buying Face Masks," *The New York Times*, February 29, 2020.

17. Michael D. Shear and Sheila Kaplan, "A Debate over Masks Uncovers Deep White House Divisions," *The New York Times*, April 3, 2020.

18. Caitlin Bowling, "Meadows Touts Rise as Self-Made Businessman," *Smoky Mountain News*, October 31, 2012.

19. Tim Alberta, *American Carnage*, p. 222.

20. Annie Karni, "Tlaib Accuses Meadows of Using 'a Black Woman as a Prop,'" *The New York Times*, February 27, 2019.

21. John Boehner, *On the House*, p. 19.

22. Jake Sherman and Anna Palmer, *The Hill to Die On*, p. 18.

23. Jonathan Miller, "North Carolina: Candidate Appears to Flirt with Birtherism," *Roll Call*, June 26, 2012.

24. Tara Golshan, "Meet the Most Powerful Man in the House," *Vox*, August 28, 2017.

25. Stephanie Grisham, *I'll Take Your Questions Now*, pp. 260–61.

26. Charles Bethea, "Mark Meadows and the Undisclosed Dinosaur Property," *The New Yorker*, October 1, 2019.

27. Remarks by President Trump, Vice President Pence, and Members of the Coronavirus Task Force in Press Briefing, April 23, 2020.

28. Jeremy W. Peters, Elaina Plott, and Maggie Haberman, "260,000 Words, Full of Self-Praise, from Trump on the Virus," *The New York Times*, April 26, 2020.

29. Not surprisingly, Trump ignored the main point of the story, which was questioning whether television networks should carry the briefings live given that he was so prone to providing misinformation. Michael M. Grynbaum, "Trump's Briefings Are a Ratings Hit. Should Networks Cover Them Live?," *The New York Times*, March 25, 2020.

30. Author interview. See also Abutaleb and Paletta, *Nightmare Scenario*, pp. 223–24.

31. Donald J. Trump, letter to Tedros Adhanom Ghebreyesus, May 18, 2020.

32. John Hudson and Souad Mekhennet, "G-7 Failed to Agree on Statement After U.S.

Insisted on Calling Coronavirus Outbreak 'Wuhan Virus,'" *The Washington Post*, March 25, 2020.

33. Luke Barr, "Hate Crimes Against Asians Rose 76% in 2020 Amid Pandemic, FBI Says," ABC News, October 25, 2021.
34. "U.S. Deaths Near 100,000, an Incalculable Loss," *The New York Times*, May 24, 2020.
35. Peter Baker, "Trump Tweets and Golfs, but Makes No Mention of Virus's Toll," *The New York Times*, May 24, 2020.

CHAPTER 24. The Battle of Lafayette Square

1. Mark T. Esper, *A Sacred Oath*, p. 352.
2. This account of Lafayette Square and the events surrounding it is drawn primarily from original author interviews, some of which was first reported in Susan B. Glasser, "'You're Gonna Have a Fucking War': Mark Milley's Fight to Stop Trump From Striking Iran," *The New Yorker*, July 15, 2021.
3. Katie Rogers, "Protesters Dispersed with Tear Gas So Trump Could Pose at Church," *The New York Times*, June 1, 2020.
4. William P. Barr, *One Damn Thing After Another*, p. 495. See also Mark Esper, *A Sacred Oath*, p. 338.
5. Esper, *A Sacred Oath*, p. 1.
6. President Trump's Call with U.S. Governors over Protests, CNN, June 1, 2020.
7. Peter Baker and Maggie Haberman, "As Protests and Violence Spill Over, Trump Shrinks Back," *The New York Times*, May 31, 2020.
8. Donald J. Trump, radio interview with Brian Kilmeade of Fox News, June 3, 2020.
9. Eric Schmitt, Helene Cooper, Thomas Gibbons-Neff, and Maggie Haberman, "Esper Breaks with Trump on Using Troops Against Protesters," *The New York Times*, June 3, 2020.
10. Mark A. Milley, Message to the Joint Force, June 2, 2020.
11. Secretary of Defense Esper Addresses Reporters Regarding Civil Unrest, Transcript, June 3, 2020.
12. Esper, *A Sacred Oath*, p. 382.
13. Ibid., p. 384.
14. Bob Woodward and Robert Costa, *Peril*, p. 106.
15. Mike Mullen, "I Cannot Remain Silent," *The Atlantic*, June 2, 2020.
16. Jeffrey Goldberg, "Jim Mattis Denounces President Trump, Describes Him as a Threat to the Constitution," *The Atlantic*, June 3, 2020.
17. Mark Milley, prerecorded graduation speech, National Defense University, June 11, 2020.
18. Maggie Haberman, "Trump Postpones G7 Summit and Calls for Russia to Attend," *The New York Times*, May 30, 2020.
19. Department of Defense Senior Leaders Brief Reporters on European Force Posture, July 29, 2020.
20. Lara Seligman, "U.S. to Pull 12,000 Troops from Germany After Trump Calls Country 'Delinquent,'" *Politico*, July 29, 2020.
21. Esper, *A Sacred Oath*, p. 390.
22. Donald J. Trump, statement, July 15, 2021.

CHAPTER 25. The Divider

1. Tucker Carlson, Fox News, June 2, 2020.
2. Michael Wolff, *Landslide*, pp. 15–16.
3. Author interview. See also William P. Barr, *One Damn Thing After Another*, pp. 514–15.

4. Chris Christie, Memo to the President, "131 Days to Go," obtained by the authors.
5. Bob Woodward, *Peril*, p. 68.
6. Michael C. Bender, *"Frankly, We Did Win This Election,"* pp. 114–15.
7. Remarks by President Trump at Kennedy Space Center, May 30, 2020.
8. Biden held a lead of 53 percent to 43 percent among registered voters and 51 percent to 46 percent among likely voters in late May. ABC News/*Washington Post* Poll, May 31, 2021.
9. Remarks by President Trump During a Roundtable on "Transition to Greatness: Restoring, Rebuilding, and Renewing," Dallas, Texas, June 12, 2020.
10. Jenny Durkan, Twitter message, June 10, 2020.
11. Mike Pence, "There Isn't a Coronavirus 'Second Wave,'" *The Wall Street Journal*, June 16, 2020.
12. Brad Parscale, Twitter message, June 15, 2020.
13. Jan Ransom, "Trump Will Not Apologize for Calling for Death Penalty over Central Park Five," *The New York Times*, June 18, 2019.
14. Peter Baker, Michael M. Grynbaum, Maggie Haberman, Annie Karni, and Russ Buettner, "Trump Employs an Old Tactic: Using Race for Gain," *The New York Times*, July 20, 2019.
15. Ibid.
16. Ibid.
17. Lil Wayne lyrics from "Racks," on his 2011 album, *Sorry 4 the Wait*. A count by CNN found 318 mentions of Trump in hip-hop songs between 1989 and 2016. Deena Zaru, "How Hip-Hop Turned on Trump and Settled for Clinton in 2016," CNN, August 16, 2017.
18. Baker et al., "Trump Employs an Old Tactic: Using Race for Gain."
19. Author interviews. See also John R. O'Donnell, *Trumped!*, p. 115; and Barbara A. Res, *Tower of Lies*, pp. 162–63.
20. Michael Cohen, *Disloyal*, pp. 106–10.
21. Ibid., pp. 224–25.
22. "An Examination of the 2016 Electorate, Based on Validated Voters," Pew Research Center, August 9, 2018.
23. Peter Baker, "Trump Fans the Flames of Racial Fire," *The New York Times*, July 14, 2019.
24. Michael D. Shear and Julie Hirschfeld Davis, "Stoking Fears, Trump Defied Bureaucracy to Advance Immigration Agenda," *The New York Times*, December 23, 2017; and Julie Hirschfeld Davis, Sheryl Gay Stolberg, and Thomas Kaplan, "Trump Alarms Lawmakers with Disparaging Words for Haiti and Africa," *The New York Times*, January 11, 2018.
25. Katie Rogers and Nicholas Fandos, "Trump Tells Congresswomen to 'Go Back' to the Countries They Came From," *The New York Times*, July 14, 2019.
26. John Gramlich, "How Trump Compares with Other Recent Presidents in Appointing Federal Judges," Pew Research Center, January 13, 2021.
27. Starting in 2011, six years before Trump took office, the unemployment rate among Black Americans began dropping steadily, from a high of 16.5 percent in April 2011 to 7.4 percent in January 2017 when Trump took office, and 5.4 percent in September 2019. It began to climb again even before the pandemic sent it shooting up to 16.7 percent. Bureau of Labor Statistics.
28. Baker et al., "Trump Employs an Old Tactic: Using Race for Gain."
29. Anthony Scaramucci, Twitter message, July 16, 2019.
30. Jonathan Allen and Amie Parnes, *Lucky*, pp. 292–93.
31. Remarks by President Trump at South Dakota's 2020 Mount Rushmore Fireworks Celebration, Keystone, South Dakota, July 4, 2020. (The remarks were delivered July 3 but the transcript posted on July 4.)

32. Mark Meadows, *The Chief's Chief*, p. 101.
33. Ibid.
34. Bender, *"Frankly, We Did Win This Election,"* pp. 69–70.
35. Author interview. See also Maggie Haberman and Annie Karni, "Polls Had Trump Stewing, and Lashing Out at His Own Campaign," *The New York Times*, April 29, 2020.
36. Peter Baker, "Trump Lashes Out at Fauci Amid Criticism of Slow Virus Response," *The New York Times*, April 12, 2020.
37. Rebecca Shabad, "Trump Says Fauci 'Made a Lot of Mistakes,'" *NBC News*, July 10, 2020.
38. Yasmeen Abutaleb, Josh Dawsey, and Laurie McGinley, "Fauci Is Sidelined by the White House as He Steps Up Blunt Talk on Pandemic," *The Washington Post*, July 11, 2020.
39. Peter Navarro, "Anthony Fauci Has Been Wrong About Everything I Have Interacted with Him On," *USA Today*, July 14, 2020.
40. See Brian Stelter, "New Poll Reaffirms That Most Americans Don't Trust the President, but They Do Trust Dr. Fauci," CNN, July 16, 2020.
41. Peter Navarro, *In Trump Time*, p. 97.
42. Chandelis Duster, "Peter Navarro on His Qualifications to Disagree with Dr. Anthony Fauci on Coronavirus Treatments: 'I'm a Social Scientist,'" CNN, April 6, 2020.
43. Multiple author interviews. In his White House memoir, *In Trump Time*, Navarro repeated the blood-on-your-hands formulation and added that the FDA's handling of hydroxychloroquine "was tantamount if not to murder, then certainly to negligent homicide." See p. 96.
44. Anthony Fauci, interview with Newsmax, January 21, 2020. See Aaron Blake, "The White House's Maligning of Anthony Fauci, Annotated," *The Washington Post*, July 13, 2020.
45. Will Sommer, "Trump's New Favorite COVID Doctor Believes in Alien DNA, Demon Sperm, and Hydroxychloroquine," *The Daily Beast*, July 28, 2020.
46. Scott W. Atlas, *A Plague Upon Our House*, pp. 240, 201, 182, 212, 200.
47. Deborah Birx, *Silent Invasion*, pp. 277–79.
48. Trump campaign ad, "Break In," July 20, 2020.
49. Ashley Parker, "'Extraordinarily Nasty': Trump Hurls One of His Favorite Insults at a New Target in Kamala Harris," *The Washington Post*, August 12, 2020; and Derrick Clifton, "Trump Deploys the 'Angry Black Woman' Trope Against Kamala Harris," NBC News, August 17, 2020.
50. The magazine's opinion editor, Josh Hammer, was a former aide to Senator Ted Cruz. After the column posted online, it triggered an uproar, including among *Newsweek*'s staff, prompting the editors to apologize and post a note with the piece. "All of us at *Newsweek* are horrified that this op-ed gave rise to a wave of vile Birtherism directed at Senator Harris." John C. Eastman, "Some Questions for Kamala Harris About Eligibility," *Newsweek*, August 12, 2020.
51. Donald Trump's 2020 Republican National Convention Speech, August 28, 2020.
52. Kimberly Guilfoyle, speech at the Republican National Convention, August 24, 2020.
53. In dispensing with a new platform, Republican leaders simply rolled over their 2016 platform, even though it was clearly outdated, including three dozen condemnations of the "current" president, Barack Obama. Resolution Regarding the Republican Party Platform, August 23, 2020.
54. Peter Baker, "Instead of Evolving as President, Trump Has Bent the Job to His Will," *The New York Times*, August 27, 2020.
55. Donald Trump convention speech.
56. Christopher Rufo, interview with Tucker Carlson, Fox News, September 1, 2020.
57. Tucker Carlson, Fox News, September 8, 2020.

CHAPTER 26. Secretary of Everything

1. Remarks by President Trump, Prime Minister Netanyahu, Minister bin Zayed, and Minister Al Zayani at the Abraham Accords Signing Ceremony, September 15, 2020.
2. Peter Baker, "Trump, Bullish on Mideast Peace, Will Need More than Confidence," *The New York Times*, May 3, 2017.
3. *Saturday Night Live*, May 12, 2017. Posted to YouTube.
4. Samantha Bee, *Full Frontal with Samantha Bee*, TBS, May 30, 2018. Bee was contrasting a gauzy photo that Ivanka had posted of her cuddling one of her children with the separation of children from their parents at the border. Bee apologized the next day, saying using the expletive was "inappropriate and inexcusable."
5. Ivanka Trump, "Full Text: Ivanka Trump's 2020 Republican National Convention Speech," August 27, 2020.
6. "Donald Trump Jr. Retweets Roseanne Barr's Discredited George Soros Claims," *Yahoo News*, May 29, 2018.
7. Ian Mohr, "Kimberly Guilfoyle's Nickname for Donald Trump Jr. is Junior Mint," *New York Post*, August 14, 2018.
8. Leah Carroll, "How Kimberly Guilfoyle, the 'Human Venus Flytrap,' Has Groomed Boyfriend Don Jr. into a Political Powerhouse and Turned Herself into a Conservative Star," *Business Insider*, October 31, 2020.
9. Erin Pinkus, "*Axios*/Survey Monkey: 2024 GOP Presidential Vote," *Axios*, December 14–17, 2019. Pence was picked by 40 percent, while Nikki Haley trailed Don Jr. with 26 percent and Ivanka Trump, Marco Rubio, Mike Pompeo, and Governor Greg Abbott of Texas were all in the teens.
10. Baker, "Trump, Bullish on Mideast Peace, Will Need More than Confidence."
11. David Friedman, "Read Peter Beinart and You'll Vote Donald Trump," *Arutz Sheva/Israel National News*, May 6, 2016.
12. 2019 Soref Symposium Dinner with Jared Kushner, C-SPAN, May 2, 2019.
13. Saeb Erekat described the conversation during an appearance at the Doha Forum in Qatar. Tom Gara, "Here's How the Chief Palestinian Negotiator Described His Last Meeting with Jared Kushner," *BuzzFeed News*, December 16, 2018.
14. "Palestinian Leader Rebukes Trump," Associated Press, January 14, 2018.
15. Jacob Magid, "Abdullah: US Must Get a Major Israeli Concession After Jerusalem Recognition," *Times of Israel*, January 25, 2018.
16. Michael Crowley and David M. Halbfinger, "Trump Releases Mideast Peace Plan That Strongly Favors Israel," *The New York Times*, January 28, 2020.
17. Benjamin Netanyahu, "PM Netanyahu's Remarks at the Joint Statements with U.S. President Donald Trump at the White House," Israel Ministry of Foreign Affairs, January 28, 2020.
18. Author interview. See also Barak Ravid, "Trump Says Netanyahu 'Never Wanted Peace' with the Palestinians," *Axios*, December 13, 2021.
19. Donald Trump interview with Barak Ravid for his book, *Trump's Peace*, as excerpted in *Axios*.
20. David Friedman, *Sledgehammer*, pp. 194–95.
21. Steve Hendrix, Ruth Eglash, and Anne Gearan, "Jared Kushner Put a Knife 'In Netanyahu's Back' over Annexation Delay, Says Israeli Settler Leader," *The Washington Post*, February 4, 2020.
22. Yousef al-Otaiba, "Annexation Will Be a Serious Setback for Better Relations with the Arab World," *Yedioth Ahronoth*, June 12, 2020. Translated into English on Ynetnews, the online English-language outlet for *Yedioth Ahronoth*.
23. Barak Ravid, "Netanyahu's Cold Feet Almost Killed the Abraham Accords," *Axios*, December 13, 2021.

24. Joint Statement of the United States, the State of Israel, and the United Arab Emirates, August 13, 2020.

CHAPTER 27. The Altar of Trump

1. Remarks by President Trump in Press Conference, September 7, 2020.
2. Remarks by President Trump in Press Briefing, August 23, 2020.
3. Stephen M. Hahn, Twitter message, August 24, 2020.
4. Albert Bourla, *Moonshot*, pp. 165–67.
5. Letter from chief executive officers of AstraZeneca, BioNTech, GlaxoSmithKline, Johnson & Johnson, Merck, Moderna, Novavax, Pfizer, and Sanofi, September 8, 2020.
6. Laurie McGinley and Carolyn Y. Johnson, "FDA Poised to Announce Tougher Standards for a Covid-19 Vaccine That Make It Unlikely One Will Be Cleared by Election Day," *The Washington Post*, September 22, 2020.
7. Remarks by President Trump in Press Briefing, September 23, 2020.
8. Alec Tyson, Courtney Johnson, and Cary Funk, "U.S. Public Now Divided over Whether to Get COVID-19 Vaccine," Pew Research Center, September 17, 2020.
9. Yasmeen Abutaleb and Damian Paletta, *Nightmare Scenario*, p. 291.
10. Omarosa Manigault Newman, *Unhinged*, pp. 40–41.
11. Susan B. Glasser, "Trump Is the Election Crisis He Is Warning Us About," *The New Yorker*, July 30, 2020.
12. Remarks by President Trump in Press Briefing, September 23, 2020.
13. Peter Baker, "For Trump, It's Not the United States, It's Red and Blue States," *The New York Times*, September 24, 2020.
14. Eric Beech and Jan Wolfe, "Trump Threatens to Cut Federal Funds to 'Lawless' Cities," Reuters, September 2, 2020.
15. Linda Qiu and Michael D. Shear, "Rallies Are the Core of Trump's Campaign, and a Font of Lies and Misinformation," *The New York Times*, October 26, 2020.
16. Eric Yoder, "Trump Appointee Resigns over the President's Order Removing Job Protections for Many Civil Servants," *The Washington Post*, October 26, 2020.
17. Peter Baker, "Trump Says He Wants a Conservative Majority on the Supreme Court in Case of an Election Day Dispute," *The New York Times*, September 23, 2020.
18. Michael C. Bender, *"Frankly, We Did Win This Election,"* p. 260.
19. Presidential Debate at Case Western Reserve University and Cleveland Clinic in Cleveland, Ohio, September 29, 2020. Transcript posted by the Commission on Presidential Debates.
20. Jake Tapper and Dana Bash, CNN, September 29, 2020.
21. Chris Christie, ABC News, September 29, 2020.
22. Mark Meadows, remarks to reporters, October 2, 2020.
23. "Trump to Move to Military Medical Facility for Next Few Days as Precaution—White House," Reuters, October 2, 2020.
24. Mark Meadows, *The Chief's Chief*, p. 47.
25. Presidential debate transcript, September 29, 2020.
26. Meadows, *The Chief's Chief*, pp. 154, 166, 169, 175.
27. Maggie Haberman and Peter Baker, "Trump Says He Feels Better, but His Chief of Staff Says He Is 'Still Not on a Clear Path to a Full Recovery,'" *The New York Times*, October 3, 2020.
28. Donald J. Trump, video, October 5, 2020.
29. William P. Barr, *One Damn Thing After Another*, p. 531.
30. Andrew Duehren and James T. Areddy, "Hunter Biden's Ex-Business Partner Alleges Father Knew About Venture," *The Wall Street Journal*, October 23, 2020.
31. Glenn Kessler, "Unraveling the Tale of Hunter Biden and $3.5 Million from Russia," *The Washington Post*, April 8, 2022.

32. Russ Buettner, Susanne Craig, and Mike McIntire, "Long-Concealed Records Show Trump's Chronic Losses and Years of Tax Avoidance," *The New York Times*, September 27, 2020.

33. Presidential Debate at Belmont University in Nashville, Tennessee, October 22, 2020. Transcript posted by the Commission on Presidential Debates.

34. Christine Stapleton and Antonio Fins, "'I Voted for a Guy Named Trump.' President Casts Historic Ballot in Palm Beach County," *Palm Beach Post*, October 24, 2020.

35. Amanda Watts, "At Least 231,000 People Have Died of Covid-19 in the US," CNN, November 3, 2020.

36. Adam Edelman and Shannon Pettypiece, "In Dueling Florida Rallies, Trump and Biden Paint Different Pictures of Covid—and America," NBC News, October 29, 2020.

37. Matt Stevens, "At Late-Night Rally, Trump Suggests He May Fire Fauci 'After the Election,'" *The New York Times*, November 2, 2020.

38. Maggie Haberman, "Trump, in Michigan, Calls Laura Ingraham 'Politically Correct' for Wearing a Mask," *The New York Times*, October 30, 2020.

39. Glenn Thrush, "Donald Trump Jr. Said Virus Deaths Had Fallen to 'Almost Nothing' as Over 1,000 Died in the U.S.," *The New York Times*, October 30, 2020.

40. Haberman, "Trump, in Michigan, Calls Laura Ingraham 'Politically Correct' for Wearing a Mask."

41. Donald J. Trump rally, November 2, 2020. Posted on YouTube.

42. "Biden Is Favored to Win the Election," *FiveThirtyEight.com*, November 3, 2020.

43. Donald Trump rally, Allentown, Pennsylvania, October 26, 2020.

44. See for example Donald J. Trump, rally in Allentown, Pennsylvania, October 26, 2020. Posted by *The Hill*.

45. Allan Smith, "Trump Says He's Sending in His Lawyers as Soon as the Election Ends to Review Swing State Votes," NBC News, November 1, 2020.

46. Benjamin L. Ginsberg, "My Party Is Destroying Itself on the Altar of Trump," *The Washington Post*, November 1, 2020.

47. President Trump's Remarks on Election Status, C-SPAN, November 3, 2020.

CHAPTER 28. Art of the Steal

1. Ivanka Trump text message, "Text Messages Sean Hannity, Marjorie Taylor Greene, Ivanka Trump and Others Sent to Mark Meadows," CNN, April 25, 2022.

2. Sara Nathan and Emily Smith, "Ivanka and Jared Buy $30M Lot on High-Security Miami Island," *New York Post*, December 7, 2020. The deal was set to close on December 17, just three days after the Electoral College would meet.

3. Donald Trump Jr., text to Mark Meadows, November 5, 2020; Ryan Nobles, Zachary Cohen, and Annie Grayer, "CNN Exclusive: 'We Control Them All': Donald Trump Jr. Texted Meadows Ideas for Overturning 2020 Election Before It Was Called," CNN, April 9, 2022.

4. Donald Trump Jr., Twitter message, November 5, 2020.

5. Ali Dukakis, "Rick Perry Calls Donald Trump a 'Cancer on Conservatism,'" ABC News, July 22, 2015.

6. Text message to Mark Meadows, November 5, 2020; Jeremy Herb and Ryan Nobles, "'Need to End This Call': January 6 Committee Reveals New Text Messages to Meadows on House Floor," CNN, December 14, 2021.

7. Virginia Thomas, text message to Mark Meadows, November 5, 2020; Bob Woodward and Robert Costa, "Virginia Thomas Urged White House Chief to Pursue Unrelenting Efforts to Overturn the 2020 Election, Texts Show," *The Washington Post*, March 24, 2022.

8. Text message to Mark Meadows, November 5, 2020; Luke Broadwater and Alan Feuer,

"Jan. 6 Committee Examines PowerPoint Document Sent to Meadows," *The New York Times*, December 10, 2021.

9. Peter Baker and Maggie Haberman, "In Torrent of Falsehoods, Trump Claims Election Is Being Stolen," *The New York Times*, November 5, 2020.
10. Donald Trump Jr., Twitter message, November 5, 2020.
11. Eric Trump, Twitter message, November 5, 2020.
12. Baker and Haberman, "In Torrent of Falsehoods, Trump Claims Election Is Being Stolen."
13. Joe Biden Victory Speech, November 7, 2020.
14. Official 2020 Presidential General Election Results, Federal Election Commission. Several electors for both Trump and Clinton, called "faithless electors," cast their votes for someone other than the victor of their state as protests; when those are subtracted from the total, Trump won 304 to 227.
15. Ibid.
16. Trump Campaign Pennsylvania News Conference, C-SPAN, November 7, 2020.
17. Mick Mulvaney, "If He Loses, Trump Will Concede Gracefully," *The Wall Street Journal*, November 7, 2020. See also Jonathan Martin and Alexander Burns, *This Will Not Pass*, p. 84.
18. Amy Gardner, Ashley Parker, Josh Dawsey, and Emma Brown, "Top Republicans Back Trump's Efforts to Challenge Election Results," *The Washington Post*, November 9, 2020.
19. Peter Navarro, *In Trump Time*, p. 219.
20. Joint Statement from Elections Infrastructure Government Coordinating Council & the Election Infrastructure Sector Coordinating Executive Committees, November 12, 2020.
21. Sidney Powell, "Release the Kraken," *Lou Dobbs Tonight*, Fox Business, November 13, 2020. Posted on YouTube.
22. The Appellate Division of the New York Supreme Court effectively debunked these claims as part of an order suspending Giuliani's law license on June 24, 2021.
23. Lisa Lerer, "Giuliani in Public: 'It's a Fraud.' Giuliani in Court: 'This Is Not a Fraud Case,'" *The New York Times*, November 18, 2020.
24. Trump Campaign News Conference on Legal Challenges, C-SPAN, November 19, 2020.
25. Maggie Haberman and Alan Feuer, "Trump Team Disavows Lawyer Who Peddled Conspiracy Theories on Voting," *The New York Times*, November 22, 2020.
26. Virginia Thomas, text message to Mark Meadows, November 22, 2020; Woodward and Costa, "Virginia Thomas Urged White House Chief to Pursue Unrelenting Efforts to Overturn the 2020 Election, Texts Show."

CHAPTER 29. Can Anyone Land This Plane?

1. Author interviews. Versions of this have also been reported by Bob Woodward and Robert Costa in *Peril*.
2. Meghann Myers, "Exclusive: Esper, on His Way Out, Says He Was No Yes Man," *Military Times*, November 9, 2020.
3. Jonathan Karl, *Betrayal*, pp. 161–62.
4. Phil Stewart and Idrees Ali, "Senate Cancels Confirmation Hearing for Trump Nominee Who Called Obama 'Terrorist,'" Reuters, July 30, 2020.
5. Victor Garcia, "Douglas Macgregor Calls on Trump to Pull Troops from Afghanistan: 'That's Why We Voted for Him,'" Fox News, January 13, 2020.
6. Em Steck and Andrew Kaczynski, "German Ambassador Pick Disparaged Immigrants and Refugees, Called for Martial Law at US-Mexico Border," CNN, August 4, 2020.

7. Jonathan Swan and Zachary Basu, "Episode 9: Trump's War with His Generals," *Axios*, May 16, 2021.
8. Owen Churchill, "Michael Pillsbury, New Chairman of Pentagon's Policy Board, Aims to Bridge Gap in Understanding China," *South China Morning Post*, December 10, 2020.
9. Lara Seligman, Daniel Lippman, and Jacqueline Feldscher, "White House Fires Pentagon Advisory Board Members, Installs Loyalists," *Politico*, December 4, 2020.
10. The full-page ad in *The Washington Times* was sponsored by a right-wing organization called We The People Convention.
11. Author interview. See also William P. Barr, *One Damn Thing After Another*, pp. 544–46.
12. Bob Woodward and Robert Costa, "Virginia Thomas Urged White House Chief to Pursue Unrelenting Efforts to Overturn the 2020 Election, Texts Show," *The Washington Post*, March 24, 2022.
13. Talia Kaplan, "Trump: DOJ 'Missing in Action' on Alleged Election Fraud," Fox News, November 29, 2020.
14. Michael Balsamo, "Disputing Trump, Barr Says No Widespread Election Fraud," Associated Press, December 1, 2020.
15. Author interview. See also Barr, *One Damn Thing After Another*, pp. 5–10, 549–51.
16. Dan De Luce and Abigail Williams, "'There Will Be a Smooth Transition to a Second Trump Administration,' Pompeo Claims," NBC News, November 10, 2020.
17. Nicholas Fandos, "Defying Trump, McConnell Seeks to Squelch Bid to Overturn the Election," *The New York Times*, December 15, 2020.
18. William P. Barr, letter to Donald J. Trump, December 14, 2020.

CHAPTER 30. All Hell Is Going to Break Loose

1. "Subverting Justice: How the Former President and His Allies Pressured DOJ to Overturn the 2020 Election," Senate Judiciary Committee Majority Staff Report, p. 13.
2. Clara Hendrickson and Paul Egan, "Antrim County Hand Tally Affirms Certified Election Results," *Detroit Free Press*, December 17, 2020.
3. Jeffrey Rosen, staff interview, Senate Judiciary Committee, August 7, 2021.
4. Jared Kushner text December 4, 2020, "Text Messages Sean Hannity, Marjorie Taylor Greene, Ivanka Trump and Others Sent to Mark Meadows," CNN, April 25, 2022.
5. Peter Navarro, "The Immaculate Deception: Six Key Dimensions of Election Irregularities," December 17, 2020.
6. Solange Reyner, "Michael Flynn to Newsmax TV: Trump Has Options to Secure Integrity of 2020 Election," Newsmax.com, December 17, 2020.
7. Presidential Findings to Preserve, Collect and Analyze National Security Information Regarding the 2020 General Election, December 16, 2020.
8. Jonathan Swan and Zachary Basu, "Inside the Craziest Meeting of the Trump Presidency," *Axios*, February 2, 2020. Patrick Byrne also wrote an extensive account of this meeting online. Patrick Byrne, "How DJT Lost the White House, Chapter 3: Crashing the White House," *DeepCapture.com*, February 1, 2021.
9. Alan Feuer, Michael S. Schmidt, and Luke Broadwater, "New Focus on How a Trump Tweet Incited Far-Right Groups Ahead of Jan. 6," *The New York Times*, March 29, 2022.
10. Michael D. Shear, "Trump Speaks Positively About Conspiracy Theorists Who Believe in QAnon," *The New York Times*, August 19, 2020.
11. Paul Gosar, Twitter message, December 22, 2020.
12. Antonio Fins and Christine Stapleton, "Pence Echoes Trump on Election Loss in West Palm Speech to Conservative Youths," *Palm Beach Post*, December 22, 2020.
13. Deborah Birx, *Silent Invasion*, pp. 415–17.

14. Mark Esper, *A Sacred Oath*, p. 121.
15. Jonathan Karl, *Betrayal*, p. 167.
16. Luke Broadwater and Alan Rappeport, "Trump Demands Changes to Coronavirus Relief Bill, Calling It a 'Disgrace,'" *The New York Times*, December 22, 2020.
17. Rosen staff interview, Senate Judiciary Committee.
18. Jeffrey Clark, draft letter to Governor Brian Kemp and Georgia legislative leaders, dated December 28, 2020.
19. Katherine Faulders and Alexander Mallin, "DOJ Officials Rejected Colleague's Request to Intervene in Georgia's Election Certification: Emails," ABC News, August 3, 2021.
20. Jonathan Swan, "McConnell Calls Jan. 6 Certification His 'Most Consequential Vote,'" *Axios*, December 31, 2020.
21. Ayatollah Ali Khamenei, Twitter message, December 16, 2020.
22. Sean Hannity, text to Mark Meadows, December 31, 2020, cited in motion filed in *Mark Meadows v. Nancy Pelosi et al.*, April 22, 2022.
23. Jared Kushner, testimony to House Select Committee to Investigate the January 6th Attack on the United States Capitol.
24. Joshua Zitser, "Pro-Trump Lawyer Lin Wood Insists He Is Not Insane After Tweeting That Mike Pence Should Face Execution by Firing Squad," *Business Insider*, January 2, 2021.
25. Senate Judiciary Committee report.
26. Amy Gardner and Paulina Firozi, "Here's the Full Transcript and Audio of the Call Between Trump and Raffensperger," *The Washington Post*, January 5, 2021.
27. Liz Cheney, Memorandum to House Republican Colleagues, January 3, 2021.
28. Ashton Carter, Dick Cheney, William Cohen, Mark Esper, Robert Gates, Chuck Hagel, James Mattis, Leon Panetta, William Perry, and Donald Rumsfeld, "All 10 Living Former Defense Secretaries: Involving the Military in Election Disputes Would Cross into Dangerous Territory," *The Washington Post*, January 3, 2021. Liz Cheney's role reported in Susan B. Glasser, "Forced to Choose Between Trump's 'Big Lie' and Liz Cheney, the House G.O.P. Chooses Trump," *The New Yorker*, May 6, 2021.
29. Richard Donoghue, deposition by Senate Judiciary Committee, August 6, 2021.
30. Greg Jacob, deposition with January 6 Committee.
31. Unsigned and undated memo by John Eastman.
32. Jacob deposition with January 6 Committee.
33. Sean Hannity, text to Mark Meadows, January 5, 2021, cited in motion filed in *Mark Meadows v. Nancy Pelosi et al.*, April 22, 2022.
34. Peter Navarro, *In Trump Time*, p. 243.
35. Aaron Blake, "Who Could Have Predicted the Capitol Riot? Plenty of People—Including Trump Allies," *The Washington Post*, January 28, 2021.

CHAPTER 31. Trial by Combat

1. Peter Baker, Maggie Haberman, and Annie Karni, "Pence Reached His Limit with Trump. It Wasn't Pretty," *The New York Times*, January 12, 2021. Months later, Jonathan Karl asked Trump about this exchange and the former president said, "I wouldn't dispute it."
2. Keith Kellogg, deposition, January 6 Committee. In his book, *War by Other Means*, Kellogg cites Ivanka's comment without mentioning when she made it or the context. See p. 151.
3. Rudy Giuliani and Professor John Eastman, Rally on January 6, 2021, C-SPAN.
4. Donald Trump Jr. cell phone video, posted by *The Telegraph*, January 8, 2021.
5. Transcript of Trump's Speech at Rally Before U.S. Capitol Riot, Associated Press, January 13, 2021.

6. Michael R. Pence, "Dear Colleague" letter, January 6, 2021.

7. Greg Jacob, email to John Eastman, January 6, 2021, obtained by January 6 Committee.

8. Mitch McConnell, Remarks on the Electoral College Count, January 6, 2021.

9. Police Dispatch Audio, posted by *USA Today*, February 10, 2021.

10. Donald Trump Jr., text message to Mark Meadows, January 6, 2021, obtained by January 6 Committee.

11. Alyssa Farah, text message, January 6, 2021, obtained by authors.

12. Laura Ingraham, Brian Kilmeade, and Chip Roy, text messages, January 6, 2021, obtained by January 6 Committee.

13. Jonathan Martin and Alexander Burns, *This Will Not Pass*, p. 204.

14. Jaime Herrera Beutler, statement, February 12, 2021.

15. Christopher C. Miller, Statement for House Oversight and Reform Committee, May 12, 2021.

16. Lisa Mascaro, Ben Fox, and Lolita C. Baldor, "'Clear the Capitol,' Pence Pleaded, Timeline of Riot Shows," Associated Press, April 10, 2021.

17. President Trump Video Statement on Capitol Protesters, C-SPAN, January 6, 2021.

18. Charles Creitz, "Rep. Liz Cheney Slams Trump for 'Intolerable' Conduct, Says President 'Incited the Mob,'" Fox News, January 6, 2021.

19. Missy Ryan and Dan Lamothe, "Military Reaction Was 'Sprint Speed,' Top Officer Says as Pentagon Takes Heat for Capitol Riot Response," *The Washington Post*, March 2, 2021.

20. Mike Pence's Statement to the Senate on the Storming of the Capitol, January 6, 2021. Posted by *U.S. News & World Report*.

21. Mike Lee, Statement on Counting Electoral Votes, January 6, 2021.

22. Mark Meadows's texts with Mike Lee and Chip Roy, CNN, April 15, 2022.

23. Sen. Kelly Loeffler (R-GA): "I Cannot Now in Good Conscience Object," C-SPAN, January 6, 2021.

24. Sen. Lindsey Graham: "All I Can Say Is Count Me Out, Enough Is Enough," C-SPAN, January 6, 2021.

25. Pence Declares Biden the Winner of the 2020 Presidential Election, January 7, 2021. Posted by *The Washington Post*.

CHAPTER 32. This Uncivil War

1. Elaine L. Chao, statement posted on Twitter, January 7, 2021, and Betsy DeVos, letter to Donald J. Trump, January 7, 2021.

2. Adam Kinzinger, video posted to Twitter, January 7, 2021.

3. The Editorial Board, "Donald Trump's Final Days," *The Wall Street Journal*, January 7, 2021.

4. Eric Schmitt, "Jim Mattis, Trump's Former Defense Secretary, Calls Out President for Fomenting 'Mob Rule,'" *The New York Times*, January 7, 2021.

5. Peter Baker and Maggie Haberman, "Capitol Attack Leads Democrats to Demand That Trump Leave Office," *The New York Times*, January 7, 2021.

6. "Manufacturers Call on Armed Thugs to Cease Violence at the Capitol," National Association of Manufacturers, January 6, 2021.

7. President Trump on Election and Breach of the U.S. Capitol, C-SPAN, January 7, 2021.

8. Bob Woodward and Robert Costa, *Peril*, pp. xix-xxiv.

9. H. Res. 24, Impeaching Donald John Trump, President of the United States, for High Crimes and Misdemeanors, January 13, 2021.

10. Sean Hannity text, January 10, 2021, cited in letter seeking Hannity's testimony from Bennie Thompson, chairman of the House Select Committee to Investigate the January 6th Attack on the United States Capitol, January 4, 2022.

11. Jonathan Martin and Alexander Burns, *This Will Not Pass*, p. 223.
12. Hannah Knowles, "Sen. Lindsey Graham Labeled a 'Traitor' by Pro-Trump Hecklers at Airport," *The Washington Post*, January 8, 2021.
13. Donald J. Trump, Remarks by President Trump at the 45th Mile of New Border Wall, Reynosa-McAllen, Texas, January 12, 2021.
14. Jason Miller text, January 13, 2021, in "Text Messages Sean Hannity, Marjorie Taylor Greene, Ivanka Trump and Others Sent to Mark Meadows," CNN, April 25, 2022.
15. Nicholas Fandos, "Trump Impeached for Inciting Insurrection," *The New York Times*, January 13, 2021.
16. Liz Cheney, "I Will Vote to Impeach the President," January 12, 2021.
17. Mark Meadows, *The Chief's Chief*, pp. 254–56.
18. Eric Bradner, "Biden Says Trump Skipping Inauguration Is 'A Good Thing,'" CNN, January 8, 2021.
19. Matthew Impelli, "Read the Full Text of Donald Trump's Final Farewell Speech at Joint Base Andrews," *Newsweek*, January 20, 2021.
20. Peter Baker, "Biden Inaugurated as the 46th President Amid a Cascade of Crises," *The New York Times*, January 20, 2021.
21. Jamie Raskin, *Unthinkable*, p. 272.
22. Andrew Desiderio, Burgess Everett, and Marianne Levine, "'Dead on Arrival': Trump Conviction Unlikely After GOP Votes to Nix Trial," *Politico*, January 26, 2021.
23. Jamie Raskin, *Unthinkable*, p. 303.
24. Eileen Sullivan, "5 Takeaways from Day One of Trump's Second Impeachment Trial," *The New York Times*, February 9, 2021.
25. Chris Cillizza, "The 21 Most Utterly Bizarre Lines from Trump Impeachment Lawyer Bruce Castor," CNN, February 10, 2021.
26. Peter Baker and Nicholas Fandos, "Trump's Lawyers Deny He Incited Capitol Mob, Saying It's Democrats Who Spur Violence," *The New York Times*, February 12, 2021.
27. Eileen Sullivan, "Takeaways from Day 5 of Trump's Impeachment Trial," *The New York Times*, February 13, 2021.
28. Senate Impeachment Trial, Day 5, Closing Arguments, C-SPAN, February 13, 2021.
29. Senate Minority Leader Mitch McConnell Remarks Following Senate Impeachment Vote, C-SPAN, February 13, 2021.
30. Raskin, *Unthinkable*, p. 295.
31. Peter Baker, "For Trump, an Escape, Not an Exoneration," *The New York Times*, February 13, 2021.
32. Jeff Field, "Mitch McConnell 'Absolutely' Would Support Trump if GOP Nominee in 2024," Fox News, February 25, 2021.

Bibliography

Abutaleb, Yasmeen, and Damian Paletta. *Nightmare Scenario: Inside the Trump Administration's Response to the Pandemic That Changed History*. New York: Harper, 2021.

Alberta, Tim. *American Carnage: On the Front Lines of the Republican Civil War and the Rise of President Trump*. New York: HarperCollins, 2019.

Allen, Jonathan, and Amie Parnes. *Lucky: How Joe Biden Barely Won the Presidency*. New York: Crown, 2021.

Anonymous [Miles Taylor]. *A Warning*. New York: Twelve, 2019.

Atlas, Scott W. *A Plague Upon Our House: My Fight at the Trump White House to Stop COVID from Destroying America*. New York: Bombardier Books, 2021.

Barr, William P. *One Damn Thing After Another: Memoirs of an Attorney General*. New York: William Morrow, 2022.

Barrett, Wayne. *Trump: The Deals and the Downfall*. New York: HarperCollins, 1992. (Rereleased by Regan Arts in 2016 as *Trump: The Greatest Show on Earth: The Deals, the Downfall, the Reinvention*.)

Bender, Michael C. *"Frankly, We Did Win This Election": The Inside Story of How Trump Lost*. New York: Twelve, 2021.

Bennett, Kate. *Free, Melania: The Unauthorized Biography*. New York: Flatiron Books, 2019.

Bergen, Peter. *Trump and His Generals: The Cost of Chaos*. New York: Penguin, 2019.

Birx, Deborah. *Silent Invasion: The Untold Story of the Trump Administration, Covid-19, and Preventing the Next Pandemic Before It's Too Late*. New York: Harper, 2022.

Blair, Gwenda. *The Trumps: Three Generations That Built an Empire*. New York: Simon & Schuster, 2000.

Blaskey, Sarah, Nicholas Nehamas, Caitlin Ostroff, and Jay Weaver. *The Grifter's Club: Trump, Mar-a-Lago, and the Selling of the Presidency*. New York: PublicAffairs, 2020.

Boehner, John. *On the House*. New York: St. Martin's Press, 2021.

Bolton, John. *The Room Where It Happened: A White House Memoir*. New York: Simon & Schuster, 2020.

Bourla, Albert. *Moonshot: Inside Pfizer's Nine-Month Race to Make the Impossible Possible*. New York: Harper Business, 2022.

Bowden, Mark, and Matthew Teague. *The Steal: The Attempt to Overturn the 2000 Election and the People Who Stopped It*. New York: Atlantic Monthly Press, 2022.

Brennan, John O. *Undaunted: My Fight Against America's Enemies at Home and Abroad*. New York: Celadon Books, 2020.

Calmes, Jackie. *Dissent: The Radicalization of the Republican Party and Its Capture of the Court*. New York: Twelve, 2021.

Christie, Chris. *Let Me Finish: Trump, the Kushners, Bannon, New Jersey, and the Power of In-Your-Face Politics.* New York: Hachette, 2019.

———. *Republican Rescue: Saving the Party from Truth Deniers, Conspiracy Theorists, and the Dangerous Policies of Joe Biden.* New York: Threshold Editions, 2021.

Clinton, Hillary. *What Happened.* New York: Simon & Schuster, 2017.

Cohen, Michael. *Disloyal: A Memoir: The True Story of the Former Personal Attorney to President Donald J. Trump.* New York: Skyhorse Publishing, 2020.

Comey, James. *A Higher Loyalty: Truth, Lies, and Leadership.* New York: Flatiron Books, 2018.

Conway, Kellyanne. *Here's the Deal: A Memoir.* New York: Threshold Editions, 2022.

D'Antonio, Michael. *Never Enough: Donald Trump and the Pursuit of Success.* New York: Thomas Dunne Books, 2015.

Darroch, Kim. *Collateral Damage: Britain, America, and Europe in the Age of Trump.* New York: PublicAffairs, 2020.

Davis, Julie Hirschfeld, and Michael D. Shear. *Border Wars: Inside Trump's Assault on Immigration.* New York: Simon & Schuster, 2019.

Drezner, Daniel W. *The Toddler in Chief: What Donald Trump Teaches Us About the Modern Presidency.* Chicago: University of Chicago Press, 2020.

Drucker, David M. *In Trump's Shadow: The Battle for 2024 and the Future of the GOP.* New York: Twelve, 2021.

Eisen, Norman. *A Case for the American People: The United States v. Donald J. Trump.* New York: Crown, 2020.

Esper, Mark T. *A Sacred Oath: Memoirs of a Secretary of Defense During Extraordinary Times.* New York: William Morrow, 2022.

Flake, Jeff. *Conscience of a Conservative: A Rejection of Destructive Politics and a Return to Principle.* New York: Random House, 2017.

Fox, Emily Jane. *Born Trump: Inside America's First Family.* New York: Harper, 2018.

Friedman, David. *Sledgehammer: How Breaking with the Past Brought Peace to the Middle East.* New York: Broadside Books, 2022.

Gates, Rick. *Wicked Game: An Insider's Story on How Trump Won, Mueller Failed, and America Lost.* Brentwood, Tenn.: Post Hill Press, 2020.

Gilsinan, Kathy. *The Helpers: Profiles from the Front Lines of the Pandemic.* New York: W. W. Norton, 2022.

Green, Joshua. *Devil's Bargain: Steve Bannon, Donald Trump, and the Storming of the Presidency.* New York: Penguin, 2017.

Grisham, Stephanie. *I'll Take Your Questions Now: What I Saw at the Trump White House.* New York: Harper, 2021.

Guerrero, Jean. *Hatemonger: Stephen Miller, Donald Trump, and the White Nationalist Agenda.* New York: William Morrow, 2020.

Haley, Nikki R. *With All Due Respect: Defending America with Grit and Grace.* New York: St. Martin's Press, 2019.

Helgerson, John L. *Getting to Know the President: Intelligence Briefings of Presidential Candidates and Presidents-Elect, 1952–2016.* Langley, Va.: Center for the Study of Intelligence, 2021.

Hennessey, Susan, and Benjamin Wittes. *Unmaking the Presidency: Donald Trump's War on the World's Most Powerful Office.* New York: Farrar, Straus & Giroux, 2020.

Hill, Fiona. *There Is Nothing for You Here: Finding Opportunity in the Twenty-first Century.* New York: Mariner Books, 2021.

Hubbard, Ben. *MBS: The Rise to Power of Mohammed bin Salman.* New York: Tim Duggan Books, 2020.

Hulse, Carl. *Confirmation Bias: Inside Washington's War over the Supreme Court, from Scalia's Death to Justice Kavanaugh.* New York: Harper, 2019.

Hurt, Harry, III. *Lost Tycoon: The Many Lives of Donald J. Trump.* New York: W. W. Norton, 1993.

Johnston, David Cay. *It's Even Worse Than You Think: What the Trump Administration Is Doing to America.* New York: Simon & Schuster, 2018.

————. *The Making of Donald Trump.* Brooklyn: Melville House, 2016.

Jordan, Jim. *Do What You Said You Would Do: Fighting for Freedom in the Swamp.* Brentwood, Tenn.: Post Hill Press, 2021.

Jordan, Mary. *The Art of Her Deal: The Untold Story of Melania Trump.* New York: Simon & Schuster, 2016.

Kahl, Colin, and Thomas Wright. *Aftershocks: Pandemic Politics and the End of the Old International Order.* New York: St. Martin's Press, 2021.

Karl, Jonathan. *Betrayal: The Final Act of the Trump Show.* New York: Dutton, 2021.

————. *Front Row at the Trump Show.* New York: Dutton, 2020.

Kellogg, Keith. *War by Other Means: A General in the Trump White House.* New York: Regnery, 2021.

Kelly, Megyn. *Settle for More.* New York: Harper, 2016.

Kessler, Glenn, Salvador Rizzo, and Meg Kelly. *Donald Trump and His Assault on Truth.* New York: Scribner, 2020.

Kranish, Michael, and Marc Fisher. *Trump Revealed: An American Journey of Ambition, Ego, Money, and Power.* New York: Scribner, 2017.

Lee, Bandy, ed. *The Dangerous Case of Donald Trump: 27 Psychiatrists and Mental Health Experts Assess a President.* New York: Thomas Dunne Books, 2017.

Leonnig, Carol. *Zero Fail: The Rise and Fall of the Secret Service.* New York: Random House, 2021.

Leonnig, Carol, and Philip Rucker. *I Alone Can Fix It: Donald J. Trump's Catastrophic Final Year.* New York: Penguin, 2021.

Lewandowski, Corey R., and David N. Bossie. *Let Trump Be Trump: The Inside Story of His Rise to the Presidency.* New York: Center Street, 2017.

————. *Trump: America First: The President Succeeds Against All Odds.* New York: Center Street, 2020.

————. *Trump's Enemies: How the Deep State Is Undermining the Presidency.* New York: Center Street, 2018.

Lewis, Michael. *The Premonition: A Pandemic Story.* New York: W. W. Norton, 2021.

LoBianco, Tom. *Piety & Power: Mike Pence and the Taking of the White House.* New York: Dey Street, 2019.

Lozada, Carlos. *What Were We Thinking: A Brief Intellectual History of the Trump Era.* New York: Simon & Schuster, 2020.

Manigault Newman, Omarosa. *Unhinged: An Insider's Account of the Trump White House.* New York: Gallery Books, 2018.

Marcus, Ruth. *Supreme Ambition: Brett Kavanaugh and the Conservative Takeover.* New York: Simon & Schuster, 2019.

Martin, Jonathan, and Alexander Burns. *This Will Not Pass: Trump, Biden, and the Battle for America's Future.* New York: Simon & Schuster, 2022.

Marton, Kati. *The Chancellor: The Remarkable Odyssey of Angela Merkel.* New York: Simon & Schuster, 2021.

Mattis, Jim, and Bing West. *Call Sign Chaos: Learning to Lead.* New York: Random House, 2019.

McCabe, Andrew. *The Threat: How the FBI Protects America in the Age of Terror and Trump.* New York: St. Martin's Press, 2019.

McCain, Meghan. *Bad Republican.* New York: Audible Originals, 2021.

McEnany, Kayleigh. *For Such a Time as This: My Faith Journey Through the White House and Beyond.* New York: Post Hill Press, 2021.

McMaster, H. R. *Battlegrounds: The Fight to Defend the Free World.* New York: HarperCollins, 2020.

————. *Dereliction of Duty: Lyndon Johnson, Robert McNamara, the Joint Chiefs of Staff, and the Lies That Led to Vietnam.* New York: HarperCollins, 2011.

Meacham, Jon. *Destiny and Power: The American Odyssey of George Herbert Walker Bush.* New York: Random House, 2015.

Meadows, Mark. *The Chief's Chief.* New York: All Seasons Press, 2021.

Mulroney, Brian. *Memoirs.* Toronto: Douglas Gibson Books, 2007.

Navarro, Peter. *In Trump Time: A Journal of America's Plague Year.* New York: All Seasons Press, 2021.

Navarro, Peter, and Greg Autry. *Death by China: Confronting the Dragon—A Global Call to Action.* Upper Saddle River, N.J.: Prentice Hall, 2011.

Obama, Barack. *A Promised Land.* New York: Crown, 2020.

O'Brien, Timothy L. *Trump Nation: The Art of Being the Donald.* New York: Warner Business Books, 2005.

O'Donnell, John R., with James Rutherford. *Trumped! The Inside Story of the* Real *Donald Trump—His Cunning Rise and Spectacular Fall.* Hertford, N.C.: Crossroad Press, 2017.

Page, Susan. *Madam Speaker: Nancy Pelosi and the Lessons of Power.* New York: Twelve, 2021.

Palazzolo, Joe, and Michael Rothfeld. *The Fixers: The Bottom-Feeders, Crooked Lawyers, Gossipmongers, and Porn Stars Who Created the 45th President.* New York: Random House, 2020.

Peters, Jeremy W. *Insurgency: How Republicans Lost Their Party and Got Everything They Ever Wanted.* New York: Crown, 2022.

Philipps, David. *Alpha: Eddie Gallagher and the War for the Soul of the Navy SEALs.* New York: Crown, 2021.

Pogrebin, Robin, and Kate Kelly. *The Education of Brett Kavanaugh: An Investigation.* New York: Portfolio, 2019.

Porter, Roger B. *Presidential Decision Making: The Economic Policy Board.* New York: Cambridge University Press, 1980.

Raffensperger, Brad. *Integrity Counts.* Brentwood, Tenn.: Forefront Books, 2021.

Raskin, Jamie. *Unthinkable: Trauma, Truth, and the Trials of American Democracy.* New York: Harper, 2022.

Ravid, Barak. *Trump's Peace: The Abraham Accords and the Reshaping of the Middle East.* Tel Aviv: Miskal Publishing/Yedioth Books, 2021 (Hebrew).

Res, Barbara A. *Tower of Lies: What My 18 Years of Working with Donald Trump Reveals About Him.* Los Angeles: Graymalkin Media, 2020.

Rhodes, Ben. *The World as It Is: Inside the Obama White House.* New York: Random House, 2018.

Rogin, Josh. *Chaos Under Heaven: Trump, Xi, and the Battle for the Twenty-first Century.* New York: Houghton Mifflin, 2021.

Rohde, David. *In Deep: The FBI, the CIA, and the Truth About America's "Deep State."* New York: W. W. Norton, 2020.

Rucker, Philip, and Carol Leonnig. *A Very Stable Genius: Donald J. Trump's Testing of America.* New York: Penguin, 2020.

Salter, Mark. *The Luckiest Man: Life with John McCain.* New York: Simon & Schuster, 2020.

Sanders, Sarah Huckabee. *Speaking for Myself: Faith, Freedom, and the Fight of Our Lives Inside the Trump White House.* New York: St. Martin's Press, 2020.

Sanford, Mark. *Two Roads Diverged: A Second Chance for the Republican Party, the Conservative Movement, the Nation—and Ourselves.* Charleston, S.C.: Vertel Publishing, 2021.

Scaramucci, Anthony. *Trump: The Blue-Collar President.* New York: Center Street, 2018.

Schiff, Adam. *Midnight in Washington: How We Almost Lost Our Democracy and Still Could.* New York: Random House, 2021.

Schmidt, Michael S. *Donald Trump v. the United States: Inside the Struggle to Stop a President.* New York: Random House, 2020.

Sherman, Jake, and Anna Palmer. *The Hill to Die On: The Battle for Congress and the Future of Trump's America.* New York: Crown, 2019.

Shulkin, David. *It Shouldn't Be This Hard to Serve Your Country: Our Broken Government and the Plight of Veterans.* New York: PublicAffairs, 2019.

Sims, Cliff. *Team of Vipers: My 500 Extraordinary Days in the Trump White House.* New York: Thomas Dunne Books, 2019.

Snodgrass, Guy. *Holding the Line: Inside Trump's Pentagon with Secretary Mattis.* New York: Sentinel, 2019.

Spicer, Sean. *The Briefing: Politics, the Press, and the President.* New York: Regnery, 2018.

Stelter, Brian. *Hoax: Donald Trump, Fox News, and the Dangerous Distortion of Truth.* New York: Atria/One Signal, 2020.

Strzok, Peter. *Compromised: Counterintelligence and the Threat of Donald J. Trump.* New York: Houghton Mifflin Harcourt, 2020.

Sullivan, Kevin, and Mary Jordan. *Trump on Trial: The Investigation, Impeachment, Acquittal and Aftermath.* New York: Scribner, 2020.

Toobin, Jeffrey. *True Crimes and Misdemeanors: The Investigation of Donald Trump.* New York: Doubleday, 2020.

Trump, Donald J., with Tony Schwartz. *The Art of the Deal.* New York: Random House, 1987.

Trump, Donald J., with Meredith McIver. *Trump: Think Like a Billionaire.* New York: Random House, 2004.

Trump, Ivana. *Raising Trump.* New York: Gallery Books, 2017.

Trump, Ivanka. *Women Who Work: Rewriting the Rules for Success.* New York: Portfolio, 2017.

Trump, Mary L. *Too Much and Never Enough: How My Family Created the World's Most Dangerous Man.* New York: Simon & Schuster, 2020.

Tur, Katy. *Unbelievable: My Front-Row Seat to the Craziest Campaign in American History.* New York: Dey Street, 2017.

Vindman, Alexander S. *Here, Right Matters: An American Story.* New York: HarperCollins, 2021.

Von Hoffman, Nicholas. *Citizen Cohn: The Life and Times of Roy Cohn.* New York: Doubleday, 1988.

Ward, Vicky. *Kushner, Inc.: Greed. Ambition. Corruption: The Extraordinary Story of Jared Kushner and Ivanka Trump.* New York: St. Martin's Press, 2019.

Weissmann, Andrew. *Where Law Ends: Inside the Mueller Investigation.* New York: Random House, 2020.

Westerhout, Madeleine. *Off the Record: My Dream Job at the White House, How I Lost It, and What I Learned.* New York: Center Street, 2020.

Whipple, Chris. *The Gatekeepers: How the White House Chiefs of Staff Define Every Presidency.* New York: Crown, 2018 (paperback edition).

Wolff, Michael. *Fire and Fury: Inside the Trump White House.* New York: Henry Holt, 2018.

———. *Landslide: The Final Days of the Trump Presidency.* New York: Henry Holt, 2021.

———. *Siege: Trump Under Fire.* New York: Henry Holt, 2019.

Wolkoff, Stephanie Winston. *Melania and Me: The Rise and Fall of My Friendship with the First Lady.* New York: Gallery Books, 2020.

Woodward, Bob. *Fear.* New York: Simon & Schuster, 2018.

———. *Rage.* New York: Simon & Schuster, 2020.

Woodward, Bob, and Robert Costa. *Peril.* New York: Simon & Schuster, 2021.

Wright, Lawrence. *The Plague Year: America in the Time of Covid.* New York: Alfred A. Knopf, 2021.

Yovanovitch, Marie. *Lessons from the Edge: A Memoir.* Boston: Mariner Books, 2022.

Zion, Sidney. *The Autobiography of Roy Cohn.* Secaucus, N.J.: Lyle Stuart, 1988.

Index

ABOUT THE AUTHORS

PETER BAKER is the chief White House correspondent for *The New York Times*, a political analyst for MSNBC, and the author of *Days of Fire* and *The Breach*.

SUSAN GLASSER is a staff writer for *The New Yorker* and author of its weekly "Letter from Trump's Washington," as well as a CNN global affairs analyst. Their first assignment as a married couple was as Moscow bureau chiefs for *The Washington Post*, after which they wrote *Kremlin Rising*. They also coauthored *The Man Who Ran Washington*, a *New York Times* bestseller. They live in Washington, D.C., with their son.